A First Book of C++

C++

Fourth Edition

Gary Bronson
Fairleigh Dickenson University

COURSE TECHNOLOGY
CENGAGE Learning

Australia • Brazil • Japan • Korea • Mexico • Singapore • Spain • United Kingdom • United States

COURSE TECHNOLOGY
CENGAGE Learning™

A First Book of C++, Fourth Edition
Gary Bronson

Executive Editor: Marie Lee

Acquisitions Editor: Brandi Shailer

Senior Product Manager: Alyssa Pratt

Development Editor: Lisa M. Lord

Copyeditor: Michael Beckett

Proofreader: Camille Kiolbasa

Indexer: Michael Brackney

Editorial Assistant: Jacqueline Lacaire

Content Project Manager: Lisa Weidenfeld

Associate Marketing Manager: Shanna Shelton

Art Director: Faith Brosnan

Print Buyer: Julio Esperas

Cover Photo: ©istockphoto.com/xmanphoto

Compositor: GEX Publishing Services

Some of the product names and company names used in this book have been used for identification purposes only and may be trademarks or registered trademarks of their respective manufacturers and sellers.

Any fictional data related to persons or companies or URLs used throughout this book is intended for instructional purposes only. At the time this book was printed, any such data was fictional and not belonging to any real persons or companies.

Course Technology, a part of Cengage Learning, reserves the right to revise this publication and make changes from time to time in its content without notice.

The programs in this book are for instructional purposes only.

For product information and technology assistance, contact us at
Cengage Learning Customer & Sales Support, 1-800-354-9706
For permission to use material from this text or product, submit all requests online at **www.cengage.com/permissions**
Further permissions questions can be emailed to
permissionrequest@cengage.com

Library of Congress Control Number: 2010939813

ISBN-13: 978-1-111-53100-3

ISBN-10: 1-111-53100-5

Course Technology
20 Channel Center Street
Boston, MA 02210
USA

They have been tested with care, but are not guaranteed for any particular intent beyond educational purposes. The author and the publisher do not offer any warranties or representations, nor do they accept any liabilities with respect to the programs.

Cengage Learning is a leading provider of customized learning solutions with office locations around the globe, including Singapore, the United Kingdom, Australia, Mexico, Brazil, and Japan. Locate your local office at: **international.cengage.com/region**

Cengage Learning products are represented in Canada by Nelson Education, Ltd.

To learn more about Course Technology, visit **www.cengage.com/coursetechnology**

Purchase any of our products at your local college store or at our preferred online store **www.cengagebrain.com**

Printed in the United States of America
1 2 3 4 5 6 7 16 15 14 13 12 11

Part One
Fundamentals of C++ Programming 1

The main goal of this fourth edition of *A First Book of C++* remains the same as in previous editions: to introduce, develop, and reinforce well-organized programming skills using C++. All topics are presented in a clear, unambiguous, and accessible manner to beginning students. Students should be familiar with fundamental algebra, but no other prerequisites are assumed.

Therefore, like the first three editions, this new edition begins by providing a strong foundation in structured programming. This foundation is then expanded to an object-oriented design and programming approach in a pedagogically sound, achievable progression. In addition to a number of minor changes throughout the book, the major changes in this edition are the following:

- Part I has been restructured to include arrays, files, and pointers, so it can be used as the basis for a complete introductory semester course in C++.
- The four chapters covering object-oriented programming have been revised and moved to Part II so that they form a logical continuation from structured programming to object-oriented programming.
- More than 50 new exercises have been added, and all exercises are labeled to indicate their function (Review, Practice, Program, Modify, Debug, Desk check, or For thought).
- Three new Chapter Supplements have been added to introduce the fundamentals of object-oriented design and the Unified Modeling Language (UML).
- A complete set of case studies has been added and is available on the Cengage Web site, *login.cengage.com*, for instructors to distribute.

The following features from the third edition have been retained:

- Fundamentals of software engineering are discussed from both procedural and object-oriented viewpoints.
- Each chapter contains a Common Programming Errors section that describes problems beginning C++ programmers typically encounter.
- The ANSI/ISO C++ `iostream` library and `namespace` mechanism are used in all programs.
- Exception handling is discussed in a separate section, with practical applications of exception handling included throughout the book.
- The C++ `string` class is covered.
- A thorough discussion is included of input data validation and functions to check the numerical data type of input items and allow reentering invalid numerical types.

In practical terms, this book has been written to support both a one- and two-semester technical C++ programming course; the only prerequisite is that students should be familiar with fundamental algebra. This book is constructed to be flexible enough so that instructors can mold the book to their preferences for topic sequence. This flexibility is achieved in the following ways.

Part I includes the basic structured syntax, flow control, and modularity topics needed for a thorough understanding of C++'s structural features. With the topics of arrays (Chapter 7) and files (Chapter 9) moved to Part I, this part now provides a comprehensive one-semester course. As Chapters 7 and 9 have been written to depend only on Chapters 1 through 6, their order of presentation (arrays first and files second, or vice versa) is entirely up to the instructor's discretion. With time permitting, the basics of classes, introduced in Chapter 10, can also be covered to create a one-semester course with an introduction to object-oriented programming. Figure 1 illustrates this one-semester topic dependency, and Figure 2 shows the topic dependency chart for the entire book.

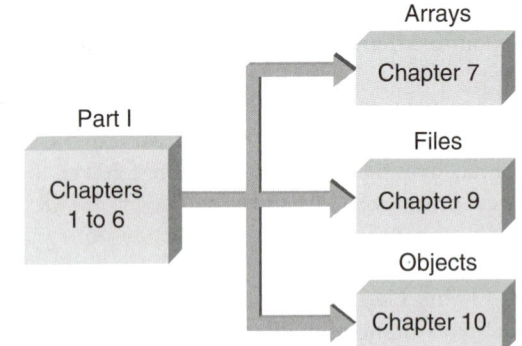

Figure 1   Topic dependency for a one-semester course

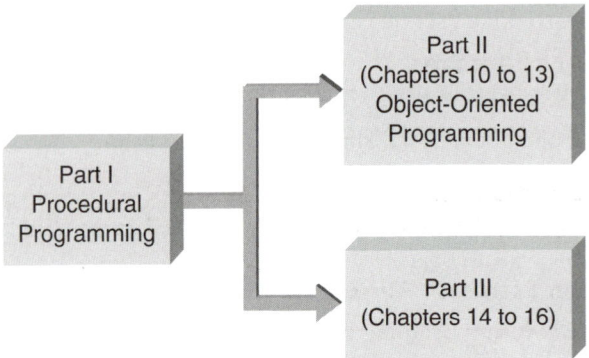

Figure 2   Topic dependency chart

Distinctive Features of This Book

Writing Style   One thing I have found to be essential in my own classes is that after the instructor sets the stage in class, the assigned book must continue to encourage, nurture, and assist students in acquiring and "owning" the material. To do this, the book must be written in a manner that makes sense to students. My primary concern, and one of the distinctive features of this book, is that it has been written for students. Therefore, I believe the writing style used to convey the concepts is one of the most important aspects of this book.

Software Engineering   Rather than simply introduce students to programming in C++, this book introduces students to the fundamentals of software engineering, from both a procedural and object-oriented viewpoint. It begins with a discussion of these two programming approaches in Section 1.1 and is reinforced throughout the book.

Introduction to References and Pointers   A unique feature of my book *A First Book of ANSI C* was introducing pointer concepts early by displaying addresses of variables and then using other variables to store these addresses. This approach always seemed a more logical method of understanding pointers than the indirection description in vogue at the time *A First Book of ANSI C* was released.

I have since been pleased to see that using an output function to display addresses has become a standard way of introducing pointers. Although this approach is no longer a unique feature of this book, I'm proud of its presentation and continue to use it in this book. References are also introduced early, in Chapter 6, before the introduction of pointers in Chapter 8.

Program Testing   Every C++ program in this book has been compiled and run successfully and has been quality-assurance tested with Microsoft Visual C++ 2010. Source code for all programs is available for student download at *www.cengagebrain.com*. Using this source code enables students to experiment with and extend the existing programs and modify them more easily, as required for a number of end-of-section exercises.

Pedagogical Features

To facilitate the goal of making C++ accessible as a first-level course, the following pedagogical features have been incorporated into the book.

Point of Information Boxes   These shaded boxes in each chapter highlight important concepts, useful technical points, programming tips, and tricks used by professional programmers.

End-of-Section Exercises   Almost every section in the book contains numerous and diverse skill-building and programming exercises. In addition, solutions to selected exercises are given in Appendix E.

Pseudocode Descriptions   Pseudocode is used throughout the book. Flowchart symbols are introduced but are used only in illustrating flow-of-control constructs.

Common Programming Errors and Chapter Summary   Each chapter ends with a section on common programming errors and a summary of the main topics covered in the chapter.

Appendixes   This book includes appendixes on operator precedence, ASCII codes, and solutions to selected exercises. Additional appendixes on bit operations and floating-point number storage are available for student download at *www.cengagebrain.com*.

Note to students: Microsoft offers a free C++ compiler and development system called Microsoft Visual C++ Express 2010. To get this development system, go to *www.microsoft.com/express/Downloads/#2010-Visual-CPP* and select English as the language. The vc_web file is downloaded automatically to your Downloads folder. (If you don't have this folder, do a search to see where the file was downloaded.) After this file is downloaded, double-click it to install Visual C++ Express 2010.

All programs in this book can be run as Visual C++ Express 2010 CLR Console Applications or Win32 Console Applications programs, with two additions:

- The code line `#include "stdafx.h"` must be added at the beginning of the program.
- The code line `cin.ignore();` must be included before the `return` statement.

These added code lines hold the window open after the program runs so that you can view it. Pressing Enter terminates the program and closes the window. For example, to compile and run Program 1.1 in this book, you should enter the program in Visual C++ Express 2010 as follows:

```cpp
#include "stdafx.h"   // needed for Visual C++ Express 2010
#include <iostream>
using namespace std;

int main()
{
  cout << "Hello there world!";

  cin.ignore();   // needed for Visual C++ Express 2010

  return 0;
}
```

All the solution files provided for this book (and available to instructors) include these two extra code lines. In programs requiring user input, a second `cin.ignore()` statement is included to prevent the Enter key used when entering data from closing the window.

Supplemental Materials

The following supplemental materials are available to instructors when this book is used in a classroom setting. Most of the materials are also available on the Instructor Resources CD.

Electronic Instructor's Manual. The Instructor's Manual that accompanies this book includes the following:

- Additional instructional material to assist in class preparation, including suggestions for lecture topics
- Solutions to all end-of-section exercises

ExamView. This book is accompanied by ExamView, a powerful testing software package that allows instructors to create and administer printed, computer (LAN-based), and Internet exams. ExamView includes hundreds of questions that correspond to the topics covered in this book, enabling students to generate detailed study guides that include page references for further review. These computer-based and Internet testing components allow students to take exams at their computers and save instructors time because each exam is graded automatically. The Test Bank is also available in WebCT and Blackboard formats.

PowerPoint Presentations. This book comes with Microsoft PowerPoint slides for each chapter. They are included as a teaching aid for classroom presentations, to make available to students on the network for chapter review, or to be printed for classroom distribution. Instructors can add their own slides for additional topics they introduce to the class.

Source Code. The source code for this book is available for students at *www.cengagebrain.com* and is also available on the Instructor Resources CD.

Solution Files. The solution files for all programming exercises are available at *login.cengage.com* and on the Instructor Resources CD.

Case Studies. A complete set of case studies, keyed to Chapters 1 through 10, are available to instructors at *login.cengage.com*.

To Rochelle, David, Matthew, Jeremy, and Winston Bronson

Acknowledgments

The writing of this fourth edition is a direct result of the success (and limitations) of the previous editions. In this regard, my most heartfelt acknowledgment and appreciation is to the instructors and students who found the previous editions to be of service in their quests to teach and learn C++.

Next, I would like to thank Alyssa Pratt, my Senior Product Manager at Course Technology. In addition to her continuous faith and encouragement, her ideas and partnership were instrumental in creating this book. After the writing process was completed, the task of turning the final manuscript into a book depended on many people other than myself. For this, I especially want to thank my developmental editor, Lisa Lord, who provided an outstanding job. Her editing so dovetailed with both the spirit and idiosyncrasies of my own writing style that it was an absolute pleasure working with her. She stayed true to what I was attempting to achieve while patiently going through both the technical and grammatical content. A truly incredible feat! This editing was supplemented by the equally detailed work of my colleague Professor Joan Zucker Hoffman. Finally, I would like to thank Serge Palladino from Course Technology's MQA Department, who was the validation tester for this book, as well as GEX Publishing Services, especially the interior designer. The dedication of this team of people was extremely important to me, and I am very grateful to them.

The following reviewers provided extensive, extremely useful, and detailed information and corrections that made this edition better and more accurate. No matter how careful I was, each reviewer pointed out something that I missed or could be stated better. I am very thankful to them. Naturally, all errors rest squarely on my shoulders, but these reviewers made the load much easier: Lynne Band, Middlesex Community College, and Alexandra Vaschillo, Lake Washington Technical College.

I would also like to acknowledge, with extreme gratitude, the wonderful academic environment for learning and teaching created at Fairleigh Dickinson University—starting with the President, Dr. Michael Adams, followed through in the academic departments by the university and campus provosts, Dr. Joseph Kiernan and Dr. Kenneth Greene, and finally to the encouragement and support provided by my dean, Dr. William Moore, and my chairperson, Dr. Paul Yoon. Without their support, this book could not have been written.

Finally, I deeply appreciate the patience, understanding, and love provided by my friend, wife, and partner, Rochelle.

Gary Bronson

Part

One

Fundamentals of
C++ Programming

Chapter

1

Getting Started

This chapter explains the basic structure of a C++ program and how to develop a working first program. An additional element required for programming a computer successfully is understanding what an algorithm does, how programs can be built with a modular design, and what constitutes a "good" program, and these topics are covered in this chapter. The goal of all professional programmers is to create readable, efficient, reliable, and maintainable programs. One method for helping you develop such programs is explained in Section 1.7.

1.1 Introduction to Programming

A computer is a machine, and like other machines, such as automobiles and lawn mowers, it must be turned on and then controlled to do the task it was meant to do. In an automobile, the driver, who sits inside and directs the car, provides control. In a computer, a computer program provides control. More formally, a **computer program** is a structured combination of data and instructions used to operate a computer to produce a specific result. Another term for a computer program is **software**, and both terms are used interchangeably in this book.

Programming is the process of writing a computer program in a language the computer can respond to and other programmers can understand. The set of instructions, data, and rules used to construct a program is called a **programming language**.

Programming languages are usefully classified by level and orientation. Languages using instructions resembling written languages, such as English, are referred to as **high-level languages**. Visual Basic, C, C++, and Java are examples of high-level languages.[1] The final program written in these languages can be run on a variety of computer types, such as those manufactured by IBM, Apple, and Hewlett-Packard. In contrast, **low-level languages** use instructions that are tied to one type of computer.[2] Although programs written in low-level languages are limited, in that they can run only on the type of computer for which they were written, they do permit direct access to specialized internal hardware features in a manner not possible with high-level languages. They can also be written to run faster than programs written in high-level languages.

In addition to programming languages being classified as high or low level, they're also classified by orientation, as procedural or object oriented. Until the 1990s, high-level programming languages were predominantly procedural. In a **procedural language**, instructions are used to create self-contained units, referred to as **procedures**. The purpose of a procedure is to accept data as input and to transform the data in some manner so as to produce a specific result as an output. Effectively, each procedure moves the data one step closer to the final output, along the path shown in Figure 1.1.

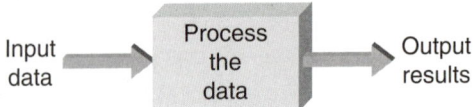

Figure 1.1   Procedure-oriented program operations

The programming process in Figure 1.1 mirrors the input, processing, and output hardware units used to construct a computer. This similarity wasn't accidental because high-level programming languages were designed to match and, as optimally as possible, control corresponding hardware units. In C++, a procedure is referred to as a **function**.

Currently, an object-oriented approach has taken center stage. One motivation for **object-oriented languages** was the development of graphical screens and support for graphical user interfaces (GUIs), capable of displaying windows containing both graphics and text. In a GUI environment, each window is considered a separate object with associated characteristics, such as color, position, and size. With an object-oriented approach, a program must first define the objects it's manipulating. This definition must include descriptions of the objects' general characteristics and specific operations to manipulate them. These operations, for example, could include changing an object's size and position and transferring data between objects. Equally important is that object-oriented languages tend to support reusing existing code more easily, which removes the need to revalidate and retest new or modified code.

---

[1]C++ is sometimes classified as a middle-level language to convey that, although it's written to be a high-level language, it can also take advantage of machine features that historically could be accessed only with low-level languages.

[2]In actuality, a low-level language is defined for the processor around which the computer is constructed.

C++, which is classified as an object-oriented language, contains features of both procedural and object-oriented languages. The reason for C++'s dual nature is that it began as an extension to C, which is a procedural language developed in the 1970s at AT&T Bell Laboratories. In the early 1980s, Bjarne Stroustrup (also at AT&T) used his background in simulation languages to develop C++. A central feature of simulation languages is that they model real-life situations as objects that respond to stimuli in well-defined ways. This object orientation, along with other procedural improvements, was combined with existing C features to form the C++ language.

Algorithms and Procedures

Because algorithms are central to C++'s procedural side, understanding what an algorithm does is essential in learning C++. From a procedural point of view, before writing a program, a programmer must clearly understand the data to be used, the intended result, and the procedure used to produce this result. This procedure is referred to as an algorithm. More precisely, an **algorithm** is a step-by-step sequence of instructions that describe how to perform a computation.

Only after you clearly understand the data you're using and the algorithm (the specific steps to produce the result) can you write the program. Seen in this light, procedure-oriented programming is translating a selected algorithm into a computer program by using a programming language, such as C++.

To understand how an algorithm works, take a look at a simple problem: A program must calculate the sum of all whole numbers from 1 through 100. Figure 1.2 illustrates three methods you could use to find the required sum. Each method constitutes an algorithm.

Most people wouldn't bother to list the possible alternatives in a detailed step-by-step manner, as shown here, and then select one of the algorithms to solve the problem. Most people, however, don't think algorithmically; they tend to think heuristically. For example, if you have to change a flat tire on your car, you don't think of all the steps required—you simply change the tire or call someone else to do the job. This is an example of heuristic thinking.

Unfortunately, computers don't respond to heuristic commands. A general statement such as "Add the numbers from 1 through 100" means nothing to a computer because it can respond only to algorithmic commands written in a language it understands, such as C++. To program a computer successfully, you must understand this difference between algorithmic and heuristic commands. A computer is an "algorithm-responding" machine; it's not an "heuristic-responding" machine. You can't tell a computer to change a tire or to add the numbers from 1 through 100. Instead, you must give it a detailed, step-by-step sequence of instructions that collectively form an algorithm. For example, the following sequence of instructions forms a detailed method, or algorithm, for determining the sum of the numbers from 1 through 100:

> *Set n equal to 100*
> *Set a equal to 1*
> *Set b equal to 100*
> *Calculate sum = n (a + b)/2*
> *Print the sum*

These instructions are not a computer program. Unlike a program, which must be written in a language the computer can respond to, an algorithm can be written or described in various ways. When English-like phrases are used to describe the steps in an algorithm, as in this example, the description is called **pseudocode**. When mathematical equations are used, the description is called a **formula**. When diagrams with the symbols shown in Figure 1.3 are used, the description is called a **flowchart**. Figure 1.4 shows using these symbols to depict an algorithm for determining the average of three numbers.

Method 1 - Columns: Arrange the numbers from 1 to 100 in a column and add them

$$
\begin{array}{r}
1 \\
2 \\
3 \\
4 \\
\cdot \\
\cdot \\
\cdot \\
98 \\
99 \\
+100 \\
\hline
5050
\end{array}
$$

Method 2 - Groups: Arrange the numbers in groups that sum to 101 and multiply the number of groups by 101

$$
\left.
\begin{array}{l}
1 + 100 = 101 \\
2 + 99 = 101 \\
3 + 98 = 101 \\
4 + 97 = 101 \\
\cdot \quad \cdot \\
\cdot \quad \cdot \\
49 + 52 = 101 \\
50 + 51 = 101
\end{array}
\right\}
50 \text{ groups}
$$

$(50 \times 101 = 5050)$

Method 3 - Formula: Use the formula

$$
\text{sum} = \frac{n(a + b)}{2}
$$

where

n= number of terms to added (100)
a= first number to be added (1)
b= last number to be added (100)

$$
\text{sum} = \frac{100(1 + 100)}{2} = 5050
$$

Figure 1.2   Summing the numbers 1 through 100

Introduction to Programming

Symbol	Name	Description
	Terminal	Indicates the beginning or end of a program
	Input/output	Indicates an input or output operation
	Process	Indicates computation or data manipulation
	Flow lines	Used to connect the other flowchart symbols and indicate the logic flow
	Decision	Indicates a program branch point
	Loop	Indicates the initial, limit, and increment values of a loop
	Predefined process	Indicates a predefined process, as in calling a function
	Connector	Indicates an entry to, or exit from, another part of the flowchart or a connection point
	Report	Indicates a written output report

Figure 1.3 Flowchart symbols

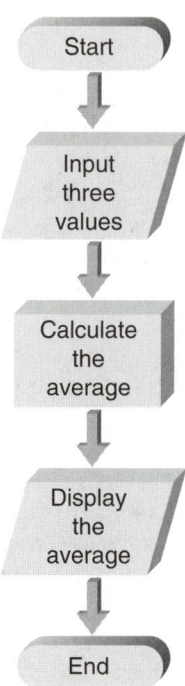

Figure 1.4   Flowchart for calculating the average of three numbers

Except for illustrating extremely simple program structures, flowcharts have fallen out of favor among professional programmers because they're cumbersome to revise and can support unstructured programming practices. In their place, pseudocode has gained increasing acceptance, which uses short English phrases to describe an algorithm. Here's an example of acceptable pseudocode for describing the steps to compute the average of three numbers:

Input the three numbers into the computer's memory
Calculate the average by adding the numbers and dividing the sum by 3
Display the average

As mentioned, before you can write an algorithm by using computer-language statements, you must first select an algorithm and understand the required steps. Writing an algorithm with computer-language statements is called **coding** the algorithm (see Figure 1.5).

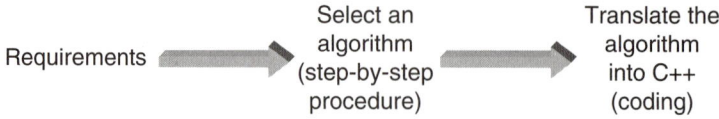

Figure 1.5   Coding an algorithm

Classes and Objects

We live in a world full of objects—planes, trains, cars, cell phones, books, computers, and so on—so it shouldn't be surprising that programming languages would eventually be based on objects. The most basic object in object-oriented C++ programming is a **data object**, a set of one or more values packaged as a single unit. For example, a student's name and grade point average can be considered a data object; in this case, the object consists of two pieces of data. Similarly, a name, street address, city, state, and zip code can be packaged as an object, one that would be useful for a program used to print address labels. Finally, a multiplication table, such as the 10s table, can be considered a data object—in this case, a specific instance of one table in a set of multiplication tables.

A central concept in all object-oriented programming languages is the difference between a specific object and the larger set of which it's a member. To make this concept clearer, consider a car. From an object viewpoint, a specific car is simply an object of a more general class of car. Therefore, a particular Ford Taurus with its own specific attributes of color, engine size, body type, and so on can be considered one car object from the broader class of all possible Ford Tauruses that could have been built. The manufacturer holds the plan for building a particular car. Only when this plan is put into action and a car is actually built does a specific object come into existence. The concept of creating an object from a larger defining set, or class, of object types is fundamental to all object-oriented programming languages, such as C++. A specific object is created from the object type or, more accurately speaking, from a class.

This book discusses both aspects of the C++ language: procedural and object oriented. You start with procedural aspects because C++ is based on the procedural language C; you can't write a C++ program without relying on some procedural code. In fact, many useful programs can be written entirely as procedural programs. After you have a firm grasp of C++'s procedural elements, you can extend these elements to create object-oriented programs with classes and objects.

As you become more fluent in C++, you'll begin creating your own classes and objects. However, as you see later in this chapter and in Chapter 3, two objects—`cin` for input of data values and `cout` for output of data values—are provided in C++. You use these two objects extensively in your early work.

Program Translation

After an algorithm or a class is written in C++, it still can't be run on a computer without further translation because all computers' internal language consists of a series of 1s and 0s, called **machine language**. Generating a machine-language program that the computer can run requires translating the C++ program, referred to as a **source program**, into the computer's machine language (see Figure 1.6).

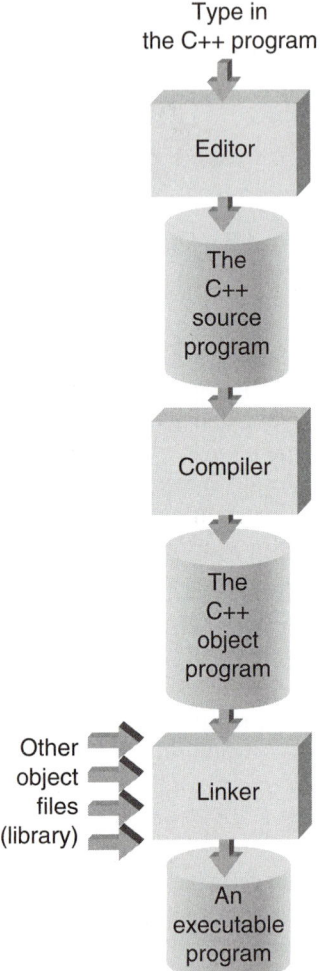

Figure 1.6 Creating an executable C++ program

The translation into machine language can be done in two ways. When each statement in the source program is translated separately and executed immediately after translation, the programming language is called an **interpreted language**, and the program doing the translation is an **interpreter**. Examples of interpreted languages are BASIC and Perl.

When all statements in a source program are translated as a complete unit before any statement is executed, the programming language is called a **compiled language**. In this case, the program doing the translation is called a **compiler**. Because C++ is a compiled language, a C++ source program is translated as a unit into machine language.

Figure 1.7 shows the relationship between a program in C++ source code and its compilation into a machine-language object program. The source code is entered by using an editor program, a word-processing tool that's part of the development environment a compiler provides.[3] Remember, however, that you begin entering code only after you have analyzed an application and planned the program's design carefully.

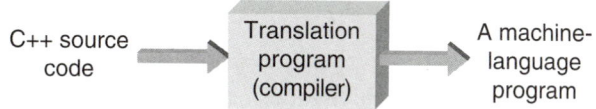

C++ source
code

→

Translation
program
(compiler)

→

A machine-
language
program

Figure 1.7   Source programs must be translated

After the C++ source code has been entered, translating the program into a machine-language program begins with the compiler. The output the compiler produces is called an **object program** (shown in Figure 1.6). It's simply a machine-language version of the source program that the computer can run, with one more processing step required.

Most C++ programs contain statements using preprogrammed routines for input and output and other machine-dependent services. Additionally, a large C++ program might be stored in two separate program files, with each file compiled separately. Any additional code must be combined to form a single program before the program can be run, and a linker program performs this step. The result of the linking process is a machine-language program, ready for execution and containing all the code your program requires. This final program is called an **executable program**.

EXERCISES 1.1

1. **(Definitions)** Define the following terms:
   - **a.** Computer program
   - **b.** Programming language
   - **c.** Programming
   - **d.** Algorithm
   - **e.** Pseudocode
   - **f.** Flowchart
   - **g.** Procedure
   - **h.** Object
   - **i.** Method
   - **j.** Message
   - **k.** Response
   - **l.** Class
   - **m.** Source program
   - **n.** Compiler
   - **o.** Object program
   - **p.** Executable program
   - **q.** Interpreter

2. **(Practice)** Determine a step-by-step procedure (list the steps) for each of the following tasks:

NOTE   **Note:** There's no single correct answer for each task. This exercise is designed to give you practice in converting heuristic commands into equivalent algorithms and understanding the differences between the thought processes involved.

---

[3]The source code you enter is manipulated and stored as ASCII text (see Section 2.1), so if you're using a commercial word-processing program, you must save source code files in text format.

a. Fix a flat tire.

b. Make a phone call.

c. Go to the store and purchase a loaf of bread.

d. Roast a turkey.

3. (Practice) Determine and write an algorithm (list the steps) to interchange the contents of two cups of liquid. Assume that a third cup is available to hold the contents of either cup temporarily. Each cup should be rinsed before any new liquid is poured into it.

4. (Practice) Write a detailed set of instructions in English to calculate the dollar amount of money in a piggybank that contains h half-dollars, q quarters, n nickels, d dimes, and p pennies.

5. (Practice) Write a set of detailed, step-by-step instructions in English to find the smallest number in a group of three integer numbers.

6. (Practice) a. Write detailed, step-by-step instructions in English to calculate the fewest number of dollar bills needed to pay a bill of amount TOTAL. For example, if TOTAL were $98, the bills would consist of one $50 bill, two $20 bills, one $5 bill, and three $1 bills. For this exercise, assume that only $100, $50, $20, $10, $5, and $1 bills are available.

   b. Repeat Exercise 6a, but assume the bill is to be paid only in $1 bills.

7. (Practice) a. Write an algorithm to locate the first occurrence of the name JEAN in a list of names arranged in random order.

   b. Discuss how you could improve your algorithm for Exercise 7a if the list of names were arranged in alphabetical order.

8. (Practice) Determine and write an algorithm to sort three numbers in ascending (from lowest to highest) order. How would you solve this problem heuristically?

9. (Practice) Define an appropriate class for each of the following specific objects:
   a. The number 5
   b. A square measuring 4 inches by 4 inches
   c. This C++ book
   d. A 1955 Ford Thunderbird car
   e. The last ballpoint pen you used

10. (Practice) a. What operations should the following objects be capable of doing?
    i. A 1955 Ford Thunderbird car
    ii. The last ballpoint pen you used

    b. Do the operations determined for Exercise 10a apply only to the particular object listed, or are they more general and applicable to all objects of the type listed?

1.2 Function and Class Names

A well-designed program is constructed by using a design philosophy similar to one for constructing a well-designed building. It doesn't just happen; it depends on careful planning and execution. As with buildings, an integral part of designing a program is its structure. Programs with a structure consisting of interrelated segments (called **modules**), arranged in a logical order to form an integrated and complete unit, are referred to as **modular programs** (see Figure 1.8). Modular programs are easier to develop, correct, and modify than programs constructed in some other manner.

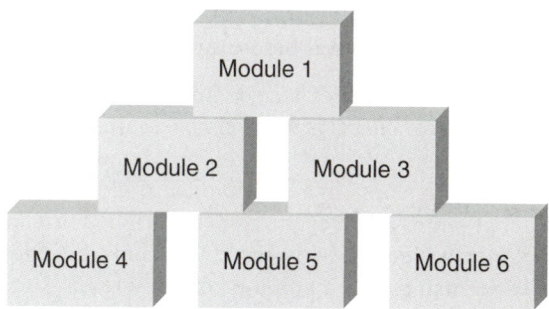

Figure 1.8   A well-designed program is built by using modules

In C++, modules can be classes or functions. A function, as you have seen, is the name given to a procedure in C++. It's composed of a sequence of C++ language instructions. It helps to think of a function as a small machine that transforms the data it receives into a finished product. For example, Figure 1.9 illustrates a function that accepts two numbers as inputs and multiplies the two numbers to produce a result. The interface to the function is its inputs and results. The method by which inputs are converted to results is encapsulated and hidden within the function. In this regard, the function can be thought of as a single unit providing a special-purpose operation.

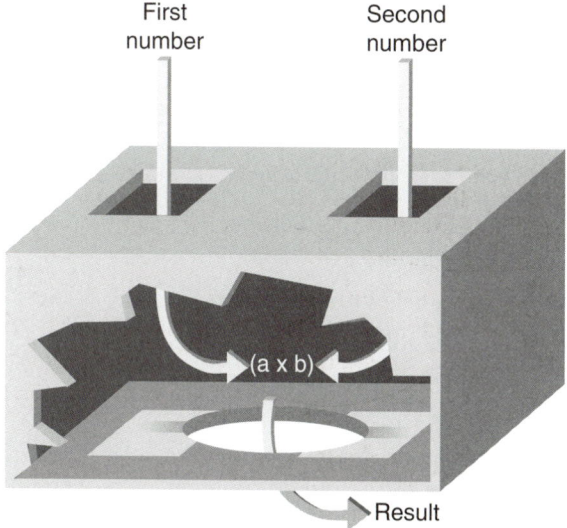

Figure 1.9   A multiplying function

A similar analogy is suitable for a class. A class, which encapsulates both data and operations, can be thought of as a complete processing plant containing all the raw materials (the data being operated on) and all the machines (functions) needed for input, output, and processing of these materials.

An important requirement for designing a good function or class is giving it a name that conveys some idea of what the function or class does. The names allowed for functions and classes are also used to name other elements of the C++ language and are collectively referred to as **identifiers**. Identifiers can be made up of any combination of letters, digits, and underscores (_) selected according to the following rules:

1. The first character of the name must be a letter or an underscore.
2. Only letters, digits, or underscores can follow the first letter. Blank spaces aren't allowed; separate words in a multiple-word identifier are indicated by capitalizing the first letter of one or more of the words. (Although underscores can also be used for this purpose, they are increasingly being used only for compiler-dependent identifiers.)
3. An identifier name can't be one of the keywords listed in Table 1.1. (A **keyword** is a word the language sets aside for a special purpose and can be used only in a specified manner.[4])
4. The maximum number of characters in an identifier is 1024.[5]

Table 1.1   Keywords in C++

auto	delete	goto	public	this
break	do	if	register	template
case	doubles	inline	return	typedef
catch	else	int	short	union
char	enum	long	signed	unsigned
class	extern	new	sizeof	virtual
const	float	overload	static	void
continue	for	private	struct	volatile
default	friend	protected	switch	while

Examples of valid C++ identifiers are the following:

```
grosspay     taxCalc      addNums     degToRad
multByTwo    salestax     netpay      bessel
```

These are examples of invalid identifiers:

```
4ab3   (Begins with a number, which violates rule 1.)
e*6    (Contains a special character, which violates rule 2.)
while  (Consists of a keyword, which violates rule 3.)
```

In addition to conforming to C++'s identifier rules, a C++ function name must *always* be followed by parentheses. Also, a good function name should be a **mnemonic** (pronounced

---

[4]Keywords in C++ are also reserved words, which means they must be used only for their specified purpose. Attempting to use them for any other purpose generates an error message.

[5]The ANSI standard requires that C++ compilers provide at least this number of characters.

Point of Information

Tokens

In a computer language, a **token** is the smallest unit of the language that has a unique meaning to the compiler. Therefore, keywords, programmer-defined identifiers, and all special mathematical symbols, such as + and -, are considered tokens of the C++ language. Separating characters in a multicharacter token with intervening characters or white space results in a compiler error.

"knee-*mon*-ic"), which is a word designed as a memory aid. For example, the function name `degToRad()` is a mnemonic for a function that converts degrees to radians. The name helps identify what the function does. Function names that aren't mnemonics should not be used because they convey no information about what the function does. Following are some examples of valid function names, including their required parentheses, that don't convey any useful information about their purpose. Names of this sort should *never* be used in a C++ program.

```
easy()    arf()    tinker()    theForce()    mike()
```

Function names can also consist of mixed uppercase and lowercase letters, as in `locateMaximum()`. This convention is becoming increasingly common in C++, although it's not required. Identifiers in all uppercase letters are usually reserved for symbolic constants, covered in Section 3.5.

If you do mix uppercase and lowercase letters, be aware that C++ is a **case-sensitive** language, meaning the compiler distinguishes between uppercase and lowercase letters. Therefore, in C++, the names TOTAL, total, and TotaL are three different identifiers.

The `main()` Function

A distinct advantage of using functions—and, as you see in Part II, classes—is that you can plan the program's overall structure in advance. You can also test and verify each function's operation separately to ensure that it meets its objectives.

For functions to be placed and executed in an orderly fashion, each C++ program must have one, and only one, function named `main`. The `main()` function is referred to as a **driver function** because it tells the other functions the sequence in which they execute (see Figure 1.10).[6]

Figure 1.11 shows the `main()` function's structure. The first line of the function—in this case, `int main()`—is referred to as a **function header line**. This line is always the first line of a function and contains three pieces of information:

- What type of data, if any, is returned from the function
- The name of the function
- What type of data, if any, is sent to the function

---

[6]Functions executed from `main()` can, in turn, execute other functions. Each function, however, always returns to the function that initiated its execution. This is true even for `main()`, which returns control to the operating system that was in effect when `main()` was initiated.

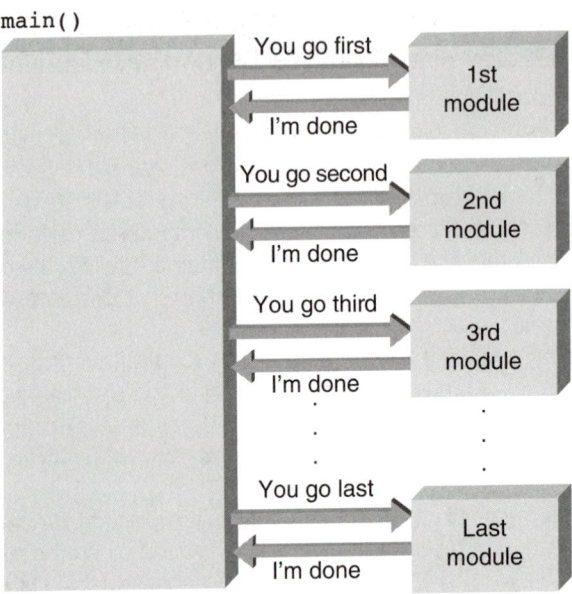

Figure 1.10   The `main()` function directs all other functions

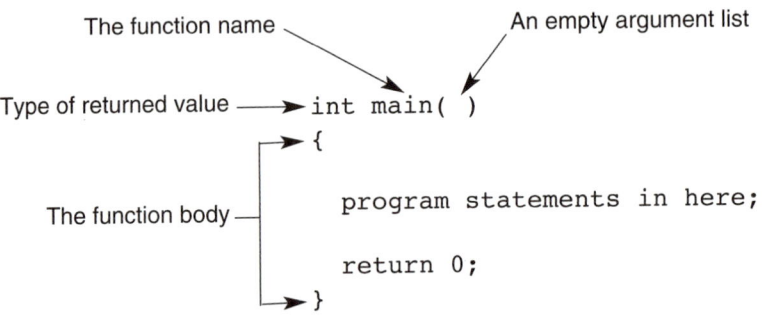

Figure 1.11   The structure of a `main()` function

The keyword before the function name defines the type of value the function returns when it has finished operating. When placed before the function's name, the keyword `int` (listed in Table 1.1), for example, means the function returns an integer value. Similarly, empty parentheses following the function name indicate that no data is transmitted to the function when it runs. (Data transmitted to a function at runtime is referred to as an **argument** of the function.) The braces, { and }, determine the beginning and end of the function body and enclose the statements making up the function.

You'll be naming and writing many of your own C++ functions. In fact, the rest of Part I is primarily about the statements required to construct useful functions and how to combine functions and data into useful programs. Each program, however, must have one and only one `main()` function. Until you learn how to pass data to a function and return data from a function

Point of Information

Executable and Nonexecutable Statements

You'll be introduced to many C++ statements in this book that can be used to create functions and programs. All statements in a function, however, belong to two broad categories: executable statements and nonexecutable statements.

An **executable statement** causes the computer to perform some specific action when the program runs. For example, a statement telling the computer to display output or add numbers is an executable statement. Executable statements must always end with a semicolon.

A **nonexecutable statement** describes some feature of the program or its data but doesn't cause the computer to perform any action when a program runs. An example of a nonexecutable statement is a comment (described in Section 1.4). A comment is intended for use by anyone reading the program. The compiler ignores all comments when it translates source code.

The statements inside the braces determine what the function does. All statements causing the computer to perform a specific action when the function is executed must end with a semicolon (;). These statements are executable statements and are described in more detail as you progress in your understanding of C++.

(the topics of Chapter 6), the header line shown in Figure 1.11 serves for all the programs you need to write. Until they're explained more fully, simply regard the first two lines

```
int main()
{
```

as indicating "the program begins here," and regard the last two lines

```
    return 0;
}
```

as designating the end of the program. Fortunately, many useful functions and classes have already been written for you. Next, you see how to use an object created from one of these classes to create your first working C++ program.

EXERCISES 1.2

1. **(Practice)** State whether the following are valid identifiers and if so, whether they're mnemonic names that convey some idea of their purpose. If the identifier names are invalid, state why.

1m1234	newBal	abcd	A12345	1A2345
power	absVal	invoices	do	while
add_5	taxes	netPay	12345	int
newBalance	a2b3c4d5	sales_tax	amount	$taxes

2. **(Practice)** Assume the following functions have been written:

   `getLength(), getWidth(), calcArea(), displayArea()`

   a. Based on their names, what do you think each function might do?
   b. In what order do you think a `main()` function might execute these functions (based on their names)?

3. **(Practice)** Assume the following functions have been written:

   `inputPrice(), calcSalestax(), calcTotal()`

   a. Based on their names, what do you think each function might do?
   b. In what order do you think a `main()` function might execute these functions (based on their names)?

4. **(Practice)** Determine names for functions that do the following:
   a. Find the average of a set of numbers.
   b. Find the area of a rectangle.
   c. Find the circumference of a circle.
   d. Find the maximum value in a set of numbers.
   e. Convert an uppercase letter to a lowercase letter.
   f. Sort a set of numbers from lowest to highest.
   g. Alphabetize a list of names.

5. **(Practice)** Just as the keyword `int` can be used to signify that a function returns an integer, the keywords `void`, `char`, `float`, and `double` can be used to signify that a function returns no value, a character, a floating-point number, and a double-precision number, respectively. Using this information, write header lines for a function named `abs()` that receives no arguments but returns the following:
   a. No value
   b. A character
   c. A floating-point number
   d. A double-precision number

1.3 The `cout` Object

One of the most versatile and commonly used objects in C++ is `cout` (pronounced "see out" and derived from *c*onsole *out*put). It's an output object that sends whatever data is passed to it to the standard display device, which is a computer screen in most systems. For example, if the data `Hello there world!` is passed to `cout`, this data is printed (displayed) on your screen. To pass this data to the `cout` object, simply place the insertion symbol, `<<`, after the object's name and before the message, as shown:

`cout << "Hello there world!"`

Now try putting all this together. Take a look at Program 1.1, which is a working C++ program that can be run on your computer.

Program 1.1

```
#include <iostream>
using namespace std;

int main()
{
  cout << "Hello there world!";

  return 0;
}
```

The first line of the program is a preprocessor command that uses the reserved word include:

```
#include <iostream>
```

Preprocessor commands begin with a pound sign (#) and perform some action *before* the compiler translates the source program into machine code. Specifically, the #include preprocessor command causes the contents of the named file—in this case, iostream—to be inserted wherever the #include command appears in the program. The iostream file is part of the standard library that contains, among other code, two classes: istream and ostream. These two classes provide data declarations and methods used for data input and output, respectively. The iostream file is called a **header file** because a reference to it is always placed at the top, or head, of a C++ program by using the #include command. You might be wondering what the iostream file has to do with this simple program. The answer is that the cout object is created from the ostream class. Therefore, the iostream header file must be included in all programs using cout. As shown in Program 1.1, preprocessor commands don't end with a semicolon.

Following the preprocessor #include command is a statement containing the reserved word using. The following statement, for example, tells the compiler where to find header files in the absence of an explicit designation:

```
using namespace std;
```

You can think of a **namespace** as a file the compiler accesses when it's looking for prewritten classes or functions. Because the iostream header file is contained in a file named std (for the standard library), the compiler automatically uses iostream's cout object from this namespace whenever cout is referenced.[7] By using namespaces, you can create your own classes and functions with the same names the standard library provides and place them in differently named namespaces. You can then tell the program which class or function to use by specifying the namespace where you want the compiler to look for the class or function.

The using statement is followed by the start of the program's main() function, which begins with the header line described previously. The body of the function, enclosed in braces,

---

[7]Section 14.8 describes how to create your own namespace.

consists of only two statements. The first statement in `main()` sends one message to the `cout` object: the string `"Hello there world!"`.

Because `cout` is an object of a prewritten class, you don't have to create it; it's available for use just by activating it correctly. Like all C++ objects, `cout` can perform only certain well-defined actions. For `cout`, this action is to assemble data for output display. When a string of characters is passed to `cout`, the object makes sure the string is displayed onscreen correctly, as shown in this output from Program 1.1:

```
Hello there world!
```

Strings in C++ are any combination of letters, numbers, and special characters enclosed in quotation marks (`"string in here"`). The quotation marks are used to delimit (mark) the beginning and ending of the string and aren't considered part of the string. Therefore, the string of characters making up the message sent to `cout` must be enclosed in quotation marks, as was done in Program 1.1.

Now examine another program to understand `cout`'s versatility. Read Program 1.2 to determine what it does.

 Program 1.2

```cpp
#include <iostream>
using namespace std;

int main()
{
  cout << "Computers, computers everywhere";
  cout << "\n  as far as I can C";

  return 0;
}
```

When Program 1.2 is run, the following is displayed:

```
Computers, computers everywhere
    as far as I can C
```

You might be wondering why the \n didn't appear in the output. The characters \ and n, when used together, are called a **newline escape sequence**. They tell cout to send instructions to the display device to move to the beginning of a new line. In C++, the backslash (\) character provides an "escape" from the normal interpretation of the character following it and alters its meaning. If the backslash were omitted from the second cout statement in Program 1.2, the n would be printed as the letter "n," and the program would output the following:

```
Computers, computers everywheren as far as I can C
```

Newline escape sequences can be placed anywhere in the message passed to cout. See whether you can determine the display Program 1.3 produces.

 **Program 1.3**

```cpp
#include <iostream>
using namespace std;

int main()
{
  cout << "Computers everywhere\n as far as\n\nI can see.";

  return 0;
}
```

This is the output for Program 1.3:

```
Computers everywhere
 as far as

    I can see.
```

 EXERCISES 1.3

1. **(Program)** Enter and run Program 1.1 on a computer. (*Note*: You must understand the procedures for entering and running a C++ program on the particular computer installation you're using.)

2. **(Program) a.** Using cout, write a C++ program that prints your name on one line, your street address on a second line, and your city, state, and zip code on the third line.
   b. Run the program you wrote for Exercise 2a on a computer.

3. (**Program**) **a.** Write a C++ program to display the following verse:

```
Computers, computers everywhere
  as far as I can see.
I really, really like these things,
  Oh joy, Oh joy for me!
```

   b. Run the program you wrote for Exercise 3a on a computer.

4. (**Practice**) **a.** How many cout statements would you use to display the following?

```
PART NO.      PRICE
T1267         $6.34
T1300         $8.92
T2401         $65.40
T4482         $36.99
```

   b. What's the minimum number of cout statements that could be used to print the table in Exercise 4a?

   c. Write a complete C++ program to produce the output shown in Exercise 4a.

   d. Run the program you wrote for Exercise 4c on a computer.

5. (**For thought**) In response to a newline escape sequence, cout positions the next displayed character at the beginning of a new line. This positioning of the next character actually represents two distinct operations. What are they?

1.4 Programming Style

C++ programs start execution at the beginning of the main() function. Because a program can have only one starting point, every C++ program must contain one and only one main() function. As you have seen, all the statements making up the main() function are then included within the braces following the function name. Although the main() function must be present in every C++ program, C++ doesn't require placing the word main, the parentheses, or the braces in any particular form. The form used in the previous section

```
int main()
{
  program statements in here;
  return 0;
}
```

was chosen strictly for clarity and ease in reading the program but is not required. For example, this general form of a main() function also works:

```
int main
(
) {  first statement;second statement;
            third statement;fourth
statement;
return 0;}
```

Notice that you can put more than one statement on a line or place a statement on more than one line. Except for strings, quotation marks, identifiers, and keywords, C++ ignores all **white space**. (White space refers to any combination of blank spaces, tabs, or new lines.) For example, changing the white space in Program 1.1 and making sure not to split the string `Hello there world!` across two lines results in the following valid program:

```cpp
#include <iostream>
using namespace std;
int main
(
){
cout <<
"Hello there world!";
  return 0;
}
```

Although this version of `main()` does work, it's an example of poor programming style because it's difficult to read and understand. For readability, the `main()` function should always be written in this standard form:

```cpp
int main()
{
  program statements in here;
  return 0;
}
```

In this standard form, the function name starts at the left margin (call this column 1) and is placed with the required parentheses on a line by itself. The opening brace of the function body follows in column 1 on the next line, directly under the first letter of the line containing the function's name. Similarly, the closing function brace is placed by itself in column 1 (lined up with the opening brace) as the last line of the function. This structure highlights the function as a single unit.

Within the function, all program statements are indented at least two spaces. Indentation is another sign of good programming practice, especially if the same indentation is used for similar groups of statements. Notice in Program 1.2 that the same indentation was used for both `cout` statements.

As you progress in your understanding and mastery of C++, you'll develop your own indentation standards. Just keep in mind that the final form of your programs should be consistent and always aid others in reading and understanding your programs.

Comments

Comments are explanatory remarks made in a program. When used carefully, comments can be helpful in clarifying the overall program's purpose, explaining what a group of statements is meant to accomplish, or explaining what one line is intended to do. C++ supports two types of comments: line and block. Both types can be placed anywhere in a program and have no effect on program execution. The compiler ignores all comments—they are there only for the convenience of those reading the program.

A **line comment** begins with two slashes (//) and continues to the end of the line. For example, the following are line comments:

```
// this is a comment
// this program prints out a message
// this program calculates a square root
```

The symbols //, with no white space between them, designate the start of the line comment. The end of the line on which the comment is written designates the end of the comment.

A line comment can be written on a line by itself or at the end of the line containing a program statement. Program 1.4 shows using line comments in a program.

 Program 1.4

```
// this program displays a message
#include <iostream>
using namespace std;

int main()
{
  cout << "Hello there world!"; // this produces the display
  return 0;
}
```

The first comment appears on a line by itself at the top of the program and describes what the program does. This location is generally a good place to put a short comment describing the program's purpose. If more comments are required, they can be added, one per line. When a comment is too long to be contained on one line, it can be separated into two or more line comments, with each comment preceded by two slashes (//). For example, the following comment generates a C++ error message because the second line doesn't start with the // symbols:

```
// this comment is invalid because it
   extends over two lines
```

This comment is correct, written as follows:

```
// this comment is used to illustrate a
// comment that extends across two lines
```

Comments extending across two or more lines are, however, more conveniently written as **block comments** than as multiple-line comments. Block comments begin with the symbols /* and end with the symbols */, as in this example:

```
/* This is a block comment that
   spans
   three lines */
```

In C++, a program's structure is intended to make it readable and understandable, so extensive comments aren't necessary. This guideline is reinforced by selecting function names carefully to convey their purpose, as discussed previously. However, if the program element's purpose still isn't clear from its structure, name, or context, include comments where clarification is needed.

Obscure code with no comments is a sure sign of bad programming, especially when other people must maintain or read the program. Similarly, excessive comments are a sign of bad programming because not enough thought was given to making the code self-explanatory. Typically, any program you write should begin with comments including a short program description, your name, and the date the program was written or last modified. For space considerations and because all programs in this book were written by the author, these initial comments are used only for short program descriptions when they aren't provided as part of the accompanying text.

EXERCISES 1.4

1. **(Debug) a.** Will the following program work?

```
#include <iostream>
using namespace std;
int main() {cout << "Hello there world!"; return 0;}
```

b. Even if the program in Exercise 1a works, explain why it's not a good program.

2. **(Modify)** Rewrite the following programs to conform to good programming practice and correct syntax:

a.
```
#include <iostream>
int main(
){
cout            <<
"The time has come"
; return 0;}
```

b.
```
#include <iostream>
using namespace std;
int main
(    ){cout << "Newark is a city\n";cout <<
"In New Jersey\n"; cout <<
"It is also a city\n"
; cout << "In Delaware\n"
; return 0;}
```

c.
```
#include <iostream>
using namespace std;
int main() {cout << Reading a program\n";cout <<
"is much easier\n"
; cout << "if a standard form for main() is used\n")
; cout
```

```
        <<"and each statement is written\n";cout
        <<           "on a line by itself\n")
        ; return 0;}
d.    #include <iostream.h>
      using namespace std;
      int main
      (     ){ cout << "Every C++ program"
      ; cout
      <<"\nmust have one and only one"
      ;
      cout << "main() function"
      ;
      cout <<
      "\n the escape sequence of characters")
      ; cout <<
        "\nfor a newline can be placed anywhere"
      ; cout
      <<"\n within the message passed to cout"
      ; return 0;}
```

3. **(For thought) a.** When used in a message, the backslash character alters the meaning of the character immediately following it. If you want to print the backslash character, you have to tell cout to escape from the way it normally interprets the backslash. What character do you think is used to alter the way a single backslash character is interpreted?

   b. Using your answer to Exercise 3a, write the escape sequence for printing a backslash.

4. **(For thought) a.** A **token** of a computer language is any sequence of one or more characters that has a unique meaning to the compiler. Separating characters with intervening characters or white space results in a compiler error. Using this definition of a token, determine whether escape sequences, function names, and keywords listed in Table 1.1 are tokens of the C++ language.

   b. Discuss whether adding white space to a message alters the message and whether messages can be considered tokens of C++.

   c. Using the definition of a token in Exercise 4a, determine whether the following statement is true: "Except for tokens of the language, C++ ignores all white space."

1.5 Common Programming Errors

Part of learning any programming language is making the elementary mistakes commonly encountered when you begin using the language. These mistakes tend to be frustrating because each language has its own set of common programming errors lying in wait for the unwary. The errors commonly made when first programming in C++ include the following:

1. Omitting the parentheses after main().
2. Omitting or incorrectly typing the opening brace, {, that signifies the start of a function body.

3. Omitting or incorrectly typing the closing brace, }, that signifies the end of a function.
4. Omitting the semicolon at the end of each C++ executable statement.
5. Adding a semicolon after the #include <iostream> preprocessor command.
6. Misspelling the name of an object or function, such as typing cot instead of cout.
7. Forgetting to enclose a string sent to cout with double quotation marks.
8. Forgetting the \n to indicate a new line.

The third, fourth, fifth, and sixth errors in this list tend to be the most common. A worthwhile practice is writing a program and introducing each error, one at a time, to see what error messages your compiler produces. When these error messages appear as a result of inadvertent errors, you'll have had experience in understanding the messages and correcting the errors.

1.6 Chapter Summary

1. A computer program is a self-contained unit of instructions and data used to operate a computer to produce a specific result.

2. An algorithm is a step-by-step procedure that must terminate; it describes how a computation or task is to be performed.

3. A C++ program consists of one or more modules called functions. One of these functions must be called main(). The main() function identifies the starting point of a C++ program.

4. The simplest C++ program consists of the single function main() and has this form:

```
#include <iostream>
using namespace std;

int main()
{
  program statements in here;

  return 0;
}
```

This program consists of a preprocessor #include statement, a using statement, a header line for the main() function, and the body of the main() function. The body of the function begins with the opening brace, {, and ends with the closing brace, }.

5. All executable C++ statements within a function body must be terminated by a semicolon.

6. Many functions and classes are supplied in a standard library provided with each C++ compiler. One set of classes, used to create input and output capabilities, is defined in the iostream header file.

7. The cout object is used to display text or numerical results. A stream of characters can be sent to cout by enclosing the characters in quotation marks and using the insertion symbol, <<, as in the statement cout << "Hello World!";. The text in the string is displayed onscreen and can include newline escape sequences for controlling the format.

1.7 Chapter Supplement: Software Development

At its most basic level, a program is a solution developed to solve a particular problem, written in a form that can be run on a computer. Therefore, writing a program is almost the last step in a process that first determines the problem to be solved and the method to be used in the solution. Each field of study has its own name for the systematic method of designing solutions to solve problems. In science and engineering, the approach is referred to as the **scientific method**, and in quantitative analysis, the approach is called the **systems approach**. Professional software developers use the **software development procedure** for understanding the problem to be solved and for creating an effective, suitable software solution. This procedure, shown in Figure 1.12, consists of three overlapping phases:

1. Development and design
2. Documentation
3. Maintenance

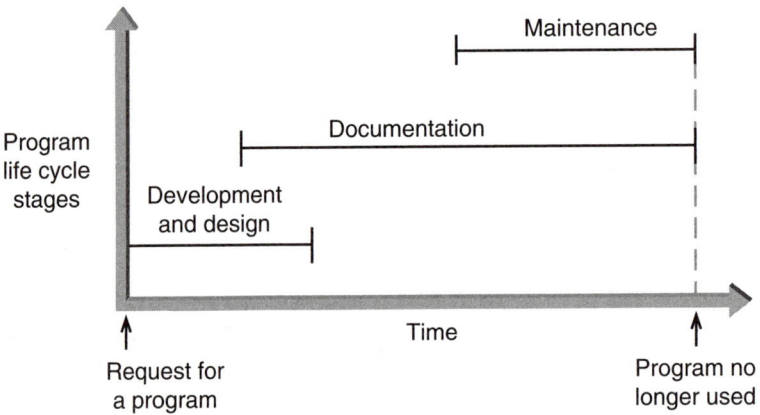

Figure 1.12   The three phases of software development

As a discipline, **software engineering** is concerned with creating readable, efficient, reliable, and maintainable programs and systems, and it uses the software development procedure to achieve this goal.

Phase I: Development and Design

Phase I begins with a statement of a problem or a specific request for a program, which is referred to as a **program requirement**. After a problem has been stated or a specific request for a program solution has been made, the development and design phase begins. This phase consists of four well-defined steps, as illustrated in Figure 1.13 and summarized in the following sections.

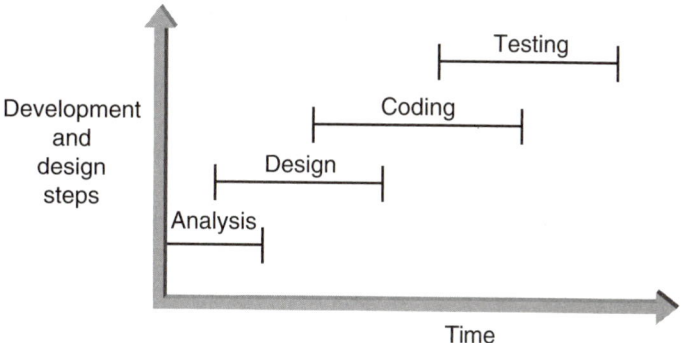

Figure 1.13   The development and design steps

Step 1: Analyze the Problem

The analysis of a problem can consist of up to two parts. The first part is a **basic analysis** that must be performed on all problems; it consists of extracting the complete input and output information supplied by the problems. For this analysis, you must:

1. Determine and understand the output items the program must produce.
2. Determine the input items.

Together, these two items are referred to as the problem's **input/output (I/O)**. Only after determining a problem's I/O can you select specific steps for transforming inputs into outputs. At this point, doing a hand calculation to verify that the output can indeed be obtained from the inputs is sometimes necessary and/or useful. Clearly, if you have a formula that relates inputs to the output, you can omit this step. If the required inputs are available and the desired outputs can be produced, the problem is said to be clearly defined and can be solved.

For a variety of reasons, completing a basic analysis might not be possible. If so, an extended analysis might be necessary. An **extended analysis** simply means you must gather more information about the problem so that you thoroughly understand what's being asked for and how to achieve the result. In this book, any additional information required to understand the problem is supplied along with the problem statement.

Step 2: Develop a Solution

Next, you select the exact set of steps, called the algorithm, to use for solving the problem. Typically, you find the solution by a series of refinements, starting with the initial algorithm you find in the analysis step, until you have an acceptable and complete algorithm. This algorithm must be checked, if it wasn't in the analysis step, to make sure it produces the required outputs correctly. The check is usually carried out by doing one or more hand calculations that haven't been done already.

For small programs, the selected algorithm might be extremely simple and consist of only one or more calculations. More typically, you need to refine the initial solution and organize it into smaller subsystems, with specifications for how the subsystems interface with each other. To achieve this goal, the algorithm's description starts from the highest level (top) requirement and proceeds downward to the parts that must be constructed to meet this requirement. To make this explanation more meaningful, think of a computer program that must track the number of parts in inventory. The required output for this program is a description of all parts carried in inventory and the number of units of each item in stock; the given inputs are the initial inventory quantity of each part, the number of items sold, the number of items returned, and the number of items purchased.

For these specifications, a designer could initially organize the program's requirements into the three sections shown in Figure 1.14. This figure is referred to as both a **top-level structure diagram** and a **first-level structure diagram** because it represents the first overall structure of the program the designer has selected.

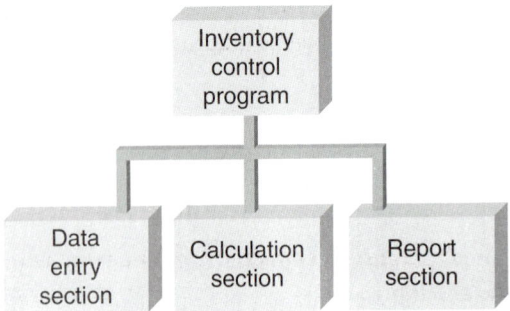

Figure 1.14   A first-level structure diagram

After an initial structure is developed, it's refined until the tasks in the boxes are completely defined. For example, the data entry and report modules shown in Figure 1.14 would be refined further. The data entry module certainly must include provisions for entering data. Because planning for contingencies and human error is the system designer's responsibility, provisions must also be made for changing incorrect data after an entry is made and for deleting previous entries. Similar subdivisions for the report module can be made. Figure 1.15 is a **second-level structure diagram** for an inventory-tracking system that includes these further refinements.

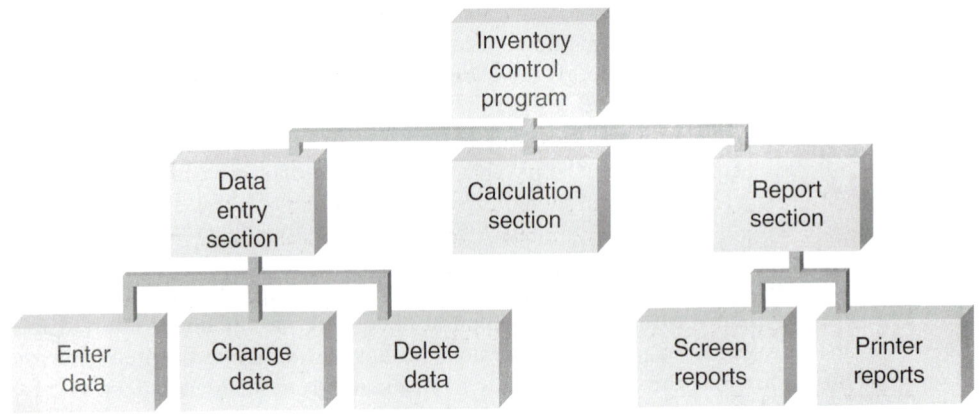

Figure 1.15   A second-level structure diagram with refinements

The process of refining a solution continues until the smallest requirement is included. Notice that the design produces a treelike structure, in which the levels branch out as you move from the top of the structure to the bottom. When the design is finished, each task designated in a box is typically coded with separate sets of instructions that are executed as they're called on by tasks higher up in the structure.

Step 3: Code the Solution (Write the Program)

This step consists of actually writing a C++ program that corresponds to the solution developed in Step 2. If the analysis and solution steps have been performed correctly, the coding step becomes rather mechanical in nature. In a well-designed program, the statements making up the program, however, conform to certain well-defined patterns or structures that have been defined in the solution step. These structures control how the program executes and consist of the following types:

- Sequence
- Selection
- Iteration
- Invocation

Sequence defines the order in which the program executes instructions. Specifying which instruction comes first, which comes second, and so on is essential if the program is to achieve a well-defined purpose.

Selection provides the capability to make a choice between different operations, depending on the result of some condition. For example, the value of a number can be checked before a division is performed. If the number isn't zero, it can be used as the denominator of a division operation; otherwise, the division isn't performed and the user is issued a warning message.

Iteration, also referred to as "looping" and "repetition," makes it possible to repeat the same operation based on the value of a condition. For example, grades might be entered and added repeatedly until a negative grade is entered. In this case, the entry of a negative grade is the condition that signifies the end of the repetitive input and addition of grades. At that point, an average for all grades entered could be calculated.

Invocation involves invoking, or summoning, a set of statements as it's needed. For example, computing a person's net pay involves the tasks of obtaining pay rates and hours worked, calculating the net pay, and providing a report or check for the required amount. Each task is typically coded as a separate unit that's called into execution, or invoked, as it's needed.

Step 4: Test and Correct the Program

The purpose of testing is to verify that a program works correctly and actually fulfills its requirements. In theory, testing would reveal all existing program errors. (In computer terminology, a program error is called a **bug**.[8]) In practice, finding all errors would require checking all possible combinations of statement execution. Because of the time and effort required, this goal is usually impossible, except for extremely simple programs. (Section 4.7 explains why this goal is generally considered impossible.)

---

[8]The derivation of this term is rather interesting. When a program stopped running on the Mark I at Harvard University in September 1945, Grace Hopper traced the malfunction to a dead insect that had gotten into the electrical circuits. She recorded the incident in her logbook as "Relay #70. . . . (moth) in relay. First actual case of bug being found."

Because exhaustive testing isn't feasible for most programs, different philosophies and methods of testing have evolved. At its most basic level, however, testing requires a conscious effort to make sure a program works correctly and produces meaningful results. This effort means giving careful thought to what the test is meant to achieve and to the data used in the test. If testing reveals an error (bug), the process of debugging, which includes locating, correcting, and verifying the correction, can be initiated. Realize that although testing might reveal the presence of an error, *it doesn't necessarily indicate the absence of one.* Therefore, the fact that a test revealed one bug *does not* indicate that another one isn't lurking somewhere else in the program.

To catch and correct errors in a program, developing a set of test data for determining whether the program produces correct answers is important. In fact, often an accepted step in formal software development is to plan test procedures and create meaningful test data *before* writing the code. Doing this step first helps you be more objective about what the program must do because it circumvents the subconscious temptation after coding to avoid test data that would reveal a problem with your program. The procedures for testing a program should examine every possible situation in which the program will be used. The program should be tested with data in a reasonable range as well as at the limits and in areas where the program should tell users the data is invalid. Developing good test procedures and data for sophisticated problems can be more difficult than writing the program code.

Table 1.2 lists the comparative amount of effort that's typically expended on each development and design step in large commercial programming projects. As this listing shows, coding is not the major effort in Phase I. Many new programmers have trouble because they spend most of their time writing the program and don't spend enough time understanding the problem or designing a suitable solution. (Note in the table that 50% of total development time is spent on testing, with many programmers testing only code that others have written.) To help you avoid making the same mistake, remember the programming proverb "It's impossible to write a successful program for a problem or application that's not fully understood." An equally valuable proverb is "The sooner you start coding a program, the longer it usually takes to complete."

Table 1.2   Effort Expended in Phase I

Step	Effort
Analyze the problem	10%
Develop a solution	20%
Code the solution (write the program)	20%
Test the program	50%

Phase II: Documentation

Because of inadequate documentation, so much work becomes useless or lost and many tasks must be repeated, so documenting your work is one of the most important steps in problem solving. Many critical documents are created during the analysis, design, coding, and testing steps. Completing the documentation phase requires collecting these documents, adding user-operating material, and presenting documentation in a form that's most useful to you and your organization.

Although not everybody classifies them in the same way, every problem solution has five main documents:

- Program description
- Algorithm development and changes
- Well-commented program listing
- Sample test runs
- Users' manual

Putting yourself in the shoes of a person who might use your work—anyone from assistants to programmers/analysts and management—should help you strive to make the content of important documentation clear. The documentation phase formally begins in the development and design phase and continues into the maintenance phase.

Phase III: Maintenance

This phase is concerned with the ongoing correction of problems, revisions to meet changing needs, and addition of new features. Maintenance is often the major effort, the primary source of revenue, and the longest lasting of all the phases. Development might take days or months, but maintenance could continue for years or decades. The better the documentation is, the more efficiently maintenance can be performed, and the happier customers and end users will be.

Backup

Although not part of the formal design process, making and keeping backup copies of the program at each step of the programming and debugging process are critical. Deleting or changing a program's current working version beyond recognition can happen quite easily. With backup copies, you can recover the last stage of work with little effort. The final working version of a useful program should be backed up at least twice. In this regard, another useful programming proverb is "Backup is unimportant if you don't mind starting over again." Many organizations keep at least one backup on site, where it can be retrieved easily, and another backup copy in a fireproof safe or at a remote location.

 **EXERCISES FOR SECTION 1.7**

Note: In each of these exercises, a programming problem is given. Read the problem statement first and then answer the questions pertaining to the problem. *Do not* attempt to write a program to solve the problems. Instead, simply answer the questions following the program specifications.

1. **(Practice)** A C++ program is required that calculates the amount, in dollars, contained in a piggybank. The bank contains half dollars, quarters, dimes, nickels, and pennies.
   a. For this programming problem, how many outputs are required?
   b. How many inputs does this problem have?
   c. Write an algorithm for converting the input items into output items.
   d. Test the algorithm written for Exercise 1c using the following sample data: half dollars 0, quarters 17, dimes 24, nickels 16, and pennies 12.

2. **(Practice)** A C++ program is required to calculate the value of distance, in miles, given this relationship:

distance = average - speed × time

   a. For this programming problem, how many outputs are required?
   b. How many inputs does this problem have?
   c. Write an algorithm for converting the input items into output items.
   d. Test the algorithm written for Exercise 2c using the following sample data: speed is 55 miles per hour and time is 2.5 hours.
   e. How must the algorithm you wrote in Exercise 2c be modified if the elapsed time is given in minutes instead of hours?

3. **(Practice)** A C++ program is required to determine the value of Ergies, given this relationship:

Ergies = Fergies × Lergies

   a. For this programming problem, how many outputs are required?
   b. How many inputs does this problem have?
   c. Determine an algorithm for converting the input items into output items.
   d. Test the algorithm written for Exercise 3c using the following sample data: Fergies = 14.65 and Lergies = 4.

4. **(Practice)** A C++ program is required to display the following name and address:
   Mr. S. Hazlet
   63 Seminole Way
   Dumont, NJ 07030
   a. For this programming problem, how many lines of output are required?
   b. How many inputs does this problem have?
   c. Write an algorithm for converting the input items into output items.

5. **(Practice)** A C++ program is required to determine how far a car has traveled after 10 seconds, assuming the car is initially traveling at 60 mph and the driver applies the brakes to decelerate at a uniform rate of 12 miles/sec^2. Use the following formula:

distance = st - (1/2)dt^2

     s is the initial speed of the car.
     d is the deceleration.
     t is the elapsed time.
   a. For this programming problem, how many outputs are required?
   b. How many inputs does this problem have?
   c. Write an algorithm for converting the input items into output items.
   d. Test the algorithm written for Exercise 5c by using the data given in the problem.

6. **(Practice)** In 1627, Manhattan Island was sold to Dutch settlers for approximately $24. If the proceeds of that sale had been deposited in a Dutch bank paying 5% interest, compounded

annually, what would the principal balance be at the end of 2012? The following display is required; xxxxxx is the amount calculated by the program:

```
Balance as of December 31, 2012 is: xxxxxx
```

a. For this programming problem, how many outputs are required?
b. How many inputs does this problem have?
c. Is the algorithm for converting the input items into output items provided?

7. **(Practice)** A C++ program is required that calculates and displays the weekly gross pay and net pay of two employees. The first employee is paid an hourly rate of $16.43, and the second is paid an hourly rate of $12.67. Both employees have 20% of their gross pay withheld for income tax, and both pay 2% of their gross pay, before taxes, for medical benefits.
   a. For this programming problem, how many outputs are required?
   b. How many inputs does this problem have?
   c. Write an algorithm for converting the input items into output items.
   d. Test the algorithm written for Exercise 7c, using the following sample data: The first employee works 40 hours during the week, and the second employee works 35 hours.

8. **(Program)** This is the formula for the standard normal deviate, z, used in statistical applications:

$$z = (X - \mu)/\sigma$$

   X is a single value.
   μ refers to a mean value.
   σ refers to a standard deviation.

   Using this formula, write a program that calculates and displays the value of the standard normal deviate when $X = 85.3$, $\mu = 80$, and $\sigma = 4$.
   a. For this programming problem, how many outputs are required?
   b. How many inputs does this problem have?
   c. Write an algorithm for converting the input items into output items.
   d. Test the algorithm written for Exercise 8c, using the data given in the problem.

9. **(Practice)** The equation describing exponential growth is as follows:

$$y = e^x$$

   Using this equation, a C++ program is required to calculate the value of y.
   a. For this programming problem, how many outputs are required?
   b. How many inputs does this problem have?
   c. Write an algorithm for converting the input items into output items.
   d. Test the algorithm written for Exercise 9c, assuming e is 2.718 and x is 10.

Chapter 2

Data Types, Declarations, and Displays

C++ programs can process different types of data in different ways. For example, calculating the bacteria growth in a polluted pond requires mathematical operations on numerical data, whereas sorting a list of names requires comparison operations with alphabetical data. This chapter introduces C++'s elementary data types and the operations that can be performed on them. You also see how to use the cout *object to display the results of these operations.*

2.1 Data Types

The objective of all programs is to process data, be it numerical, alphabetical, audio, or video. Central to this objective is classifying data into specific types. For example, calculating the interest due on a bank balance requires mathematical operations on numerical data, and alphabetizing a list of names requires comparison operations on character-based data. Additionally, some operations aren't applicable to certain types of data. For example, it makes no sense to add names together. To prevent programmers from attempting to perform an inappropriate operation, C++ allows performing only certain operations on certain types of data.

The types of data permitted and the operations allowed for each type are referred to as a data type. Formally, a **data type** is defined as a set of values *and* a set of operations that can be applied to these values. For example, the set of all integer (whole) numbers constitutes a set of values. This set of numbers, however, doesn't constitute a data type until a set of operations is included. These operations, of course, are the familiar mathematical and comparison operations. The combination of a set of values *plus* operations results in a true data type.

C++ categorizes data types as class or built-in types. A **class data type** (referred to as a "class," for short) is a programmer-created data type. This means the programmer defines both acceptable values and operations, and this type is discussed in Part II of this book.

A **built-in data type** is provided as an integral part of the programming language. Built-in data types are also referred to as **primitive types**. C++'s built-in numerical data types consist of the basic numerical types shown in Figure 2.1 and the operations listed in Table 2.1. As Table 2.1 shows, the majority of operations for built-in data types use conventional mathematical symbols. For class data types, most operations, as you see in Part II, are provided as functions.

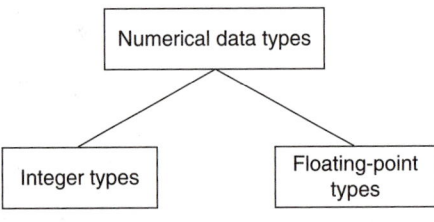

Figure 2.1   Built-in data types

Table 2.1   Built-In Data Type Operations

Built-in Data Type	Operations
Integer	+, -, *, /, %, =, ==, !=, <=, >=, sizeof(), and bit operations (see Appendix C, available online)
Floating-point	+, -, *, /, =, ==, !=, <=, >=, sizeof()

Literal values are used to introduce the built-in data types in C++. A **literal value** means the value identifies itself. (Another name for a literal value is a **literal** or **constant**.) For example, all numbers, such as 2, 3.6, and -8.2, are referred to as literal values because they literally display their values. Text, such as "Hello World!", is also referred to as a literal value because the text itself is displayed. You have been using literal values throughout your life but have known them as numbers and words. In Section 2.3, you see some examples of nonliteral values—that is, values that don't display themselves but are stored and accessed by using identifiers.

Integer Data Types

C++ provides nine built-in integer data types, as shown in Figure 2.2. The essential difference between these integer data types is the amount of storage used for each type, which affects the range of values each type is capable of representing. The three most important and common types used in many applications are int, char, and bool. The other types were provided to accommodate special situations (such as a very small or large range of numbers) and have been retained for historical reasons. They enabled programmers to maximize memory usage by selecting the data type using the smallest amount of memory, consistent with an application's requirements. When computer memories were small and expensive, compared with today's computers, the amount of memory used was a major concern. Although no longer a concern for most programs, these types still allow programmers to optimize memory usage when necessary. This optimization is often required in engineering applications, such as control systems used in home appliances and automobiles.

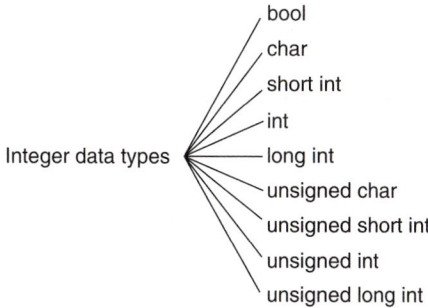

Figure 2.2   C++ integer data types

The int Data Type   The values supported by the int data type are whole numbers, which are mathematically known as **integers**. An integer value consists of digits only and can optionally be preceded by a plus (+) or minus (–) sign. Therefore, an integer value can be the number 0 or any positive or negative number without a decimal point. The following are examples of valid integers:

```
0       -10      1000       -26351
5       +25       253         +36
```

As these examples show, integers can contain an explicit sign. However, no commas, decimal points, or special symbols, such as the dollar sign, are allowed, as in these examples of invalid integers:

```
$255.62     3.          1,492.89
2,523       6,243,892    +6.0
```

Compilers differ in their internal limit on the largest (most positive) and smallest (most negative) integer values that can be stored in each data type.[1] The most common storage allocation is 4 bytes for the int data type, which restricts the values used to represent integers from -2,147,483,648 to 2,147,483,647.[2]

---

[1]The limits the compiler imposes are found in the limits header file and defined as the constants INT_MIN and INT_MAX.
[2]The magnitude of the most negative number is always one more than the magnitude of the most positive number. The reason is the twos complement method of integer storage, described in Section 2.6.

The char Data Type   The char data type is used to store single characters, including the letters of the alphabet (uppercase and lowercase), the digits 0 through 9, and special symbols, such as + $. , - and !. A character value is any single letter, digit, or special symbol enclosed by single quotation marks, as shown in these examples:

'A'   '$'   'b'   '7'   'y'   '!'   'M'   'q'

Character values are typically stored in a computer with the ASCII or Unicode codes. ASCII (pronounced "*as*-key") is the acronym for American Standard Code for Information Interchange. Both ASCII and Unicode codes assign characters to specific patterns of 0s and 1s. Table 2.2 lists the correspondence between ASCII bit patterns and the lowercase and uppercase letters.

Table 2.2   The ASCII Letter Codes

Lowercase Letter	Binary Code	Lowercase Letter	Binary Code	Uppercase Letter	Binary Code	Uppercase Letter	Binary Code
a	01100001	n	01101110	A	01000001	N	01001110
b	01100010	o	01101111	B	01000010	O	01001111
c	01100011	p	01110000	C	01000011	P	01010000
d	01100100	q	01110001	D	01000100	Q	01010001
e	01100101	r	01110010	E	01000101	R	01010010
f	01100110	s	01110011	F	01000110	S	01010011
g	01100111	t	01110100	G	01000111	T	01010100
h	01101000	u	01110101	H	01001000	U	01010101
i	01101001	v	01110110	I	01001001	V	01010110
j	01101010	w	01110111	J	01001010	W	01010111
k	01101011	x	01111000	K	01001011	X	01011000
l	01101100	y	01111001	L	01001100	Y	01011001
m	01101101	z	01111010	M	01001101	Z	01011010

The newer Unicode code is used for international applications because it accommodates character sets for almost all languages, in addition to English. As the first 256 Unicode codes are the same binary codes as the complete set of 256 ASCII codes (with the addition of eight leading 0s), you needn't be concerned with which storage code is used for English-language characters.

Using Table 2.2, you can determine how the characters 'B', 'A', 'R', 'T', 'E', and 'R', for example, are stored in a computer by using ASCII codes. This sequence of six characters requires 6 bytes of storage (1 byte for each letter) and is stored as shown in Figure 2.3. (Review Section 2.6 if you're unfamiliar with the concept of a byte.)

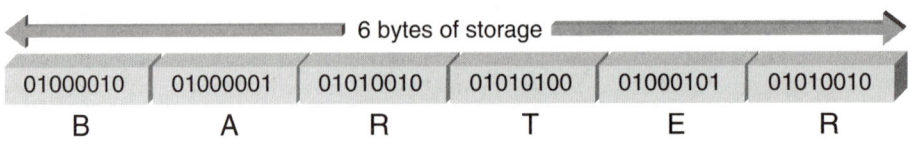

Figure 2.3   The letters BARTER stored in a computer

The Escape Character As you've seen in Section 1.3, the backslash (\) has a special meaning in C++ as the escape character. When a backslash is placed in front of a group of characters, it tells the compiler to escape from the way these characters are normally interpreted. The combination of a backslash and these characters is called an **escape sequence**. Table 2.3 lists C++'s most common escape sequences.

Table 2.3 Escape Sequences

Escape Sequence	Character Represented	Meaning	ASCII Code
\n	Newline	Move to a new line	00001010
\t	Horizontal tab	Move to the next horizontal tab setting	00001001
\v	Vertical tab	Move to the next vertical tab setting	00001011
\b	Backspace	Move back one space	00001000
\r	Carriage return	Move the cursor to the start of the current line; used for overprinting	00001101
\f	Form feed	Issue a form feed	00001100
\a	Alert	Issue an alert (usually a bell sound)	00000111
\\	Backslash	Insert a backslash character (used to place an actual backslash character in a string)	01011100
\?	Question mark	Insert a question mark character	00111111
\'	Single quotation	Insert a single-quote character (used to place an inner single quote inside a set of outer single quotes)	00100111
\"	Double quotation	Insert a double-quote character (used to place an inner double quote inside a set of outer double quotes)	00100010
\nnn	Octal number	Consider the number nnn (n is a digit) an octal number	Dependent on nnn
\xhhhh	Hexadecimal number	Consider the number hhhh (h is a digit) a hexadecimal number	Dependent on hhhh
\0	Null character	Insert the null character, which is defined as having the value 0	00000000

Although each escape sequence in Table 2.3 is made up of two characters, the combination of these characters, with no intervening white space, causes the compiler to create the single ASCII code listed in the table.

The bool Data Type In C++, the bool data type is used to represent Boolean (logical) data, so it's restricted to one of two values: true or false. This data type is most useful when a program must examine a condition and take a prescribed course of action, based on whether the condition is true or false. For example, in a sales application, the condition being examined might be "is the total purchase for $100 or more." Only when this condition is true is a discount applied. Because the `bool` data type uses an integer storage code, however, it has useful implications that most professional C++ programmers utilize. Chapter 4 covers the practical uses of Boolean conditions, so the `bool` data type is discussed in more detail in that chapter.

Determining Storage Size

A unique feature of C++ is that you can see where and how values are stored. As an example, the C++ operator `sizeof()` provides the number of bytes (discussed in Section 2.6) used to store values for the data type given in the parentheses. This built-in operator doesn't use an arithmetic symbol to perform its operation. Program 2.1 uses this operator to determine the amount of storage reserved for the `int`, `char`, and `bool` data types.

 **Program 2.1**

```cpp
#include <iostream>
using namespace std;

int main()
{
  cout << "\nData Type  Bytes";
  cout << "\n---------  -----";
  cout << "\nint        " << sizeof(int);
  cout << "\nchar       " << sizeof(char);
  cout << "\nbool       " << sizeof(bool);
  cout << '\n';

  return 0;
}
```

In reviewing Program 2.1, notice that the `\n` character is included at the start of each output string in the first five `cout` statements. Each time the compiler encounters the newline escape sequence, as part of a string or as one character, it's translated as a single character that forces the display to start at the beginning of a new line. In the final `cout` statement, the newline escape sequence is inserted as a single `'\n'` character. Although quotation marks can be used for this final newline insertion, as `"\n"`, doing so designates a string. The single quotes, as in `'\n'`, clearly indicate that a single character is being transmitted. From a practical standpoint, however, both notations (`'\n'` and `"\n"`) force a new line in the display.

> ## Point of Information
>
> ### The Character '\n' and the String "\n"
>
> The compiler recognizes both '\n' and "\n" as containing the newline character. The difference is in the data type used. Formally, '\n' is a character literal, and "\n" is a string literal. From a practical standpoint, both cause the same thing to happen: A new line is forced in the output display. In encountering the character value '\n', however, the compiler translates it by using the ASCII code 00001010 (see Table 2.3). In encountering the string value "\n", the compiler translates it by using the same character code but adds the code for the end-of-string character, '\0', which is 00000000.
>
> Good programming practice requires ending the last output display with a newline escape sequence. This practice ensures that the first line of output from one program doesn't end up on the last line displayed by the previously executed program.

The output of Program 2.1 is compiler dependent, meaning each compiler reports the amount of storage it provides for the data type under consideration. When run on a computer using Microsoft's current Visual C++ compiler, for example, the following output is produced:

```
Data Type  Bytes
---------  -----
int          4
char         1
bool         1
```

For this output, which is the typical storage almost all current C++ compilers provide, you can determine the range of values that can be stored in each data type. Doing so, however, requires understanding the difference between a signed and an unsigned data type, discussed in the next section.

Signed and Unsigned Data Types A **signed data type** allows storing negative values, the value 0, and positive values, so int is a signed data type. An **unsigned data type** provides for only non-negative values (that is, 0 and positive values). Some applications require only unsigned numerical values. For example, many date applications store dates in the numerical form *yearmonthday* (storing 12/25/2011 as 20111225, for example) and are concerned only with dates after 0 CE. For these applications, which never require a negative value, an unsigned data type can be used.

All unsigned integer types, such as unsigned int, provide a range of positive values that, for all practical purposes, is double the range for their signed counterparts. This extra positive range is made available by using the negative range of its signed version for additional positive numbers.

Table 2.4 lists the range of integer values supported by current C++ compilers for its signed and unsigned integer data types. As you can see, a long int uses the same amount of storage (4 bytes) as an int. The only requirement of the ANSI C++ standard is that an int must provide at least as much storage as a short int, and a long int must provide at least as much storage as an int. On early desktop computers with a memory capacity limited to thousands of bytes, a `short int` typically used 1 byte of storage, an `int` 2 bytes, and a `long int` 4 bytes. This storage limited the range of `int` values from -32,768 to +32,767 and `unsigned int` values from 0 to 65,535, thus doubling the number of possible positive values, which was significant. With the current range of `int` values in the -2 billion to +2 billion range, doubling positive values is rarely a consideration. Additionally, a `long int` is unnecessary now because it uses the same storage capacity as an `int`.

Table 2.4   Integer Data Type Storage

Name of Data Type	Storage Size	Range of Values
char	1	256 characters
bool	1	true (considered as any positive value) and false (which is a 0)
short int	2	-32,768 to +32,767
unsigned short int	2	0 to 65,535
int	4	-2,147,483,648 to +2,147,483,647
unsigned int	4	0 to 4,294,967,295
long int	4	-2,147,483,648 to +2,147,483,647
unsigned long int	4	0 to 4,294,967,295

Floating-Point Types

A **floating-point number**, more commonly known as a **real number**, can be the number 0 or any positive or negative number containing a decimal point. The following are examples of floating-point numbers:

```
+10.625    5.0    -6.2    3251.92    0.0    0.33    -6.67    +2.
```

Notice that the numbers 5.0, 0.0, and +2. are classified as floating-point values, but the same numbers written without a decimal point (5, 0, +2) would be integer values. As with integer values, special symbols, such as the dollar sign and comma, aren't permitted in real numbers. Examples of invalid real numbers are as follows:

```
5,326.25    24    6,459    $10.29    7.007.645
```

C++ supports three floating-point data types: `float`, `double`, and `long double`. The difference between these data types is the amount of storage the compiler uses for each type. Most compilers use twice the amount of storage for `doubles` as for `floats`, which allows a `double` to have approximately twice the precision of a `float`. For this reason, a `float` value is sometimes referred to as a **single-precision number** and a `double` value as a **double-precision number**. The actual storage allocation for each data type, however, depends on the compiler. The ANSI C++ standard requires only that a `double` have at least the same amount of precision as a `float`, and a `long double` have at least the same amount of storage as a `double`. Currently, most C++ compilers allocate 4 bytes for `floats` and 8 bytes for `doubles` and `long doubles`, which produces the range of numbers listed in Table 2.5.

Table 2.5 Floating-Point Data Types

Type	Storage	Absolute Range of Values (+ and -)
float	4 bytes	$1.40129846432481707 \times 10^{-45}$ to $3.40282346638528860 \times 10^{+38}$
double and long double	8 bytes	$4.94065645841246544 \times 10^{-324}$ to $1.79769313486231570 \times 10^{+308}$

In compilers using the same amount of storage for double and long double numbers, these two data types are identical. (The sizeof() operator in Program 2.1 can always be used to determine the amount of storage your compiler reserves for these data types.) A float literal is indicated by appending an f or F to the number, and a long double is created by appending an l or L to the number. In the absence of these suffixes, a floating-point number defaults to a double. For example, take a look at the following:

9.234 indicates a double literal.
9.234F indicates a float literal.
9.234L indicates a long double literal.

The only difference in these numbers is the amount of storage the computer can use for them. Appendix D (available online) describes the binary storage format used for floating-point numbers and its impact on number precision.

Exponential Notation

Floating-point numbers can also be written in **exponential notation**, which is similar to scientific notation and is commonly used to express both very large and very small values in compact form. The following examples show how numbers with decimals can be expressed in exponential and scientific notation:

Decimal Notation	Exponential Notation	Scientific Notation
162.5	1.625e2	1.625×10^2
63421.	6.3421e4	6.3421×10^4
.00731	7.31e-3	7.31×10^{-3}
.000625	6.25e-4	6.25×10^{-4}

In exponential notation, the letter e stands for "exponent." The number following the e represents a power of 10 and indicates the number of places the decimal point should be moved to obtain the standard decimal value. The decimal point is moved to the right if the number after the e is positive or moved to the left if the number after the e is negative. For example, the e2 in 1.625e2 means move the decimal place two places to the right, so the number becomes 162.5. The e-3 in 7.31e-3 means move the decimal point three places to the left, so 7.31e-3 becomes .00731.

Certain notations occur frequently enough in computer applications that they have their own symbols. Table 2.6 lists the most commonly used of these symbols.

Point of Information

What Is Precision?

In numerical theory, the term **precision** typically refers to numerical accuracy. In this context, the statement "This computation is accurate, or precise, to the fifth decimal place" means the fifth digit after the decimal point has been rounded, and the number is accurate to within ±0.00005.

In computer programming, "precision" can refer to a number's accuracy or the number of significant digits; **significant digits** are defined as the number of clearly correct digits plus 1. For example, if the number 12.6874 has been rounded to the fourth decimal place, it's correct to say that this number is precise to the fourth decimal place. In other words, all digits in the number are accurate except the fourth decimal digit, which has been rounded. Similarly, this same number has a precision of six digits, which means the first five digits are correct and the sixth digit has been rounded. Another way of saying this is that the number 12.6874 has six significant digits.

The significant digits in a number need not have any relation to the number of displayed digits. For example, if the number 687.45678921 has five significant digits, it's accurate only to the value 687.46; the last digit is assumed to be rounded. Similarly, dollar values in large financial applications are often rounded to the nearest hundred thousand dollars. In these applications, a displayed dollar value of $12,400,000, for example, isn't accurate to the closest dollar. If this value is specified as having three significant digits, it's accurate only to the hundred-thousand digit.

Table 2.6   Exponential and Scientific Symbol Names

Exponential Notation	Scientific Notation	Symbol	Name
e-12	10^{-12}	p	pico
e-9	10^{-9}	n	nano
e-6	10^{-6}	μ	micro
e-3	10^{-3}	m	milli
e3	10^{3}	k	kilo
e6	10^{6}	M	mega
e9	10^{9}	G	giga
e12	10^{12}	T	tera

For example, the storage capacities of flash drives are currently specified in gigabytes (GB), meaning they contain trillions (10^9) of bytes. Similarly, computer processing speeds are specified in the nanosecond (nsec) range, which means a billionth (10^{-9}) of a second.

EXERCISES 2.1

1. **(Practice)** Determine data types suitable for the following data:
   a. The average of four grades
   b. The number of days in a month
   c. The length of the Golden Gate Bridge
   d. The numbers in a state lottery
   e. The distance from Brooklyn, N.Y. to Newark, N.J.
   f. The single-character prefix that specifies a component type

2. **(Practice)** Compile and run Program 2.1.

3. **(Modify)** Modify Program 2.1 to determine the storage your compiler uses for all the C++ integer data types.

4. **(Practice)** Show how the name KINGSLEY is stored in a computer that uses the ASCII code by drawing a diagram similar to Figure 2.3, shown previously.

5. **(Practice)** Repeat Exercise 4, using the letters of your own last name.

6. **(Modify)** Modify Program 2.1 to determine how many bytes your compiler assigns to the `float`, `double`, and `long double` data types.

7. **(Practice)** Convert the following numbers from exponential form to standard decimal form:
   a. 6.34e5
   b. 1.95162e2
   c. 8.395e1
   d. 2.95e-3
   e. 4.623e-4

8. **(Practice)** Convert the following numbers from scientific notation to standard decimal form:
   a. 2.67×10^3
   b. 2.67×10^{-3}
   c. 1.872×10^9
   d. 1.872×10^{-9}
   e. 6.6256×10^{-34}

9. **(Practice)** Write the following decimal numbers in scientific notation:
   a. 126.
   b. 656.23
   c. 3426.95
   d. 4893.2
   e. .321
   f. .0123
   g. .006789

10. **(For thought)** Because computers use different representations for storing integer, floating-point, double-precision, and character values, discuss how a program might alert the computer to the data types of different values it will be using.

11. **(For thought)** Although you have concentrated on operations involving integer and floating-point numbers, C++ allows adding and subtracting characters and integers. (These operations are possible with characters because they're integer data types and are stored by using integer codes.) Therefore, characters and integers can be mixed in arithmetic expressions. For example, if your computer uses the ASCII code, the expression `'a' + 1` equals `'b'` and `'z' - 1` equals `'y'`. Similarly, `'A' + 1` is `'B'` and `'Z' - 1` is `'Y'`. With this information as background, determine the character results of the following expressions. (Assume all characters are stored by using ASCII codes.)

a. `'m' - 5`

b. `'m' + 5`

c. `'G' + 6`

d. `'G' - 6`

e. `'b' + 7`

f. `'g' - 1`

g. `'G' - 1`

Note: To complete the following exercise, you need to understand basic computer storage concepts. Specifically, if you're unfamiliar with the concepts of bytes and words, refer to Section 2.6 before doing the next exercise.

12. **(Practice)** Although the total number of bytes varies from computer to computer, memory sizes of 65,536 to more than several million bytes are common. In computer language, the letter K represents the number 1024, which is 2 raised to the 10th power, and M represents the number 1,048,576, which is 2 raised to the 20th power. Therefore, a memory size of 640 KB is really 640 times 1024 (655,360 bytes), and a memory size of 4 MB is really 4 times 1,048,576 (4,194,304 bytes). Using this information, calculate the actual number of bytes in the following:

a. A memory containing 512 MB

b. A memory consisting of 256 MB words, with each word consisting of 2 bytes

c. A memory consisting of 256 MB words, with each word consisting of 4 bytes

d. A thumb drive that specifies 2 MB

e. A disk that specifies 250 MB

f. A disk that specifies 8 GB (*Hint:* See Table 2.6.)

2.2 Arithmetic Operations

The previous section presented the data values corresponding to C++'s built-in data types. This section explains the arithmetic operations that can be applied to these values.

Integers and real numbers can be added, subtracted, multiplied, and divided. Although it's usually better not to mix integers and real numbers when performing arithmetic operations, you can get predictable results when using different data types in the same arithmetic expression.

Surprisingly, you can add and subtract character data and mix it with integer data to produce useful results. (For example, `'A' + 1` results in the character `'B'`.) These operations are possible because characters are stored by using integer codes.

The following operators used for arithmetic operations are called **arithmetic operators**:

Operation	Operator
Addition	+
Subtraction	–
Multiplication	*
Division	/
Modulus division[3]	%

These operators are also called **binary operators**, which means the operator requires two operands to produce a result. An **operand** can be a literal value or an identifier with an associated value. A **simple binary arithmetic expression** consists of a binary operator connecting two literal values in this form:

literalValue operator literalValue

Examples of simple binary arithmetic expressions include the following:

```
3 + 7
8 - 3
12.62 + 9.8
0.08 * 12.2
12.6 / 2
```

The spaces around arithmetic operators in these examples are inserted strictly for clarity and can be omitted without affecting the value of the expression. However, an expression in C++ must be entered in a straight-line form, as shown in these examples. For example, the C++ expression equivalent to 12.6 divided by 2 must be entered as `12.6 / 2`, not as the algebraic expression shown here:

$$\frac{12.6}{2}$$

You can use `cout` to display the value of any arithmetic expression. To do this, the value must be sent to the object. For example, the following statement yields the display 21:

```
cout << (6 + 15);
```

Strictly speaking, the parentheses surrounding the expression 6 + 15 aren't required to indicate that the value of the expression (that is, 21) is being displayed.[4] In addition to

---

[3]Don't be concerned at this stage if you don't understand the term "modulus division." You learn more about this operator later in the section "Integer Division."

[4]The parentheses aren't required because the + operator has a higher precedence than the << operator; therefore, the addition is performed before the insertion.

displaying a numerical value, cout can display a string identifying the output, as was done in Section 2.1. For example, the following statement sends two pieces of data, a string and a value, to cout:

```
cout << "The sum of 6 and 15 is "  <<   (6 + 15);
```

Each set of data sent to cout must be preceded by its own insertion operator, <<. In the preceding example, the first data sent for display is the string "The sum of 6 and 15 is ", and the second item sent is the value of the expression 6 + 15. This statement produces the following display:

```
The sum of 6 and 15 is 21
```

The space between the word "is" and the number 21 is caused by the space in the string sent to cout. As far as cout is concerned, its input is a set of characters sent to be displayed in the order they're received. Characters from the input are queued, one behind the other, and sent to the screen for display. Placing a space in the input makes the space part of the stream of characters that's displayed. For example, the statement

```
cout << "The sum of 12.2 and 15.754 is "  <<   (12.2 + 15.754);
```

yields the following display:

```
The sum of 12.2 and 15.754 is 27.954
```

When multiple insertions are sent to cout, the code can be spread across multiple lines. Only one semicolon, however, must be used, which is placed after the last insertion and terminates the complete statement. Therefore, the preceding display is also produced by the following statement, which spans two lines:

```
cout << "The sum of 12.2 and 15.754 is "
        <<   (12.2 + 15.754);
```

When you allow a statement to span multiple lines, two rules must be followed: A string contained in quotation marks can't be split across lines, and the terminating semicolon should appear only on the last line. You can always place multiple insertion symbols within a line.

If floating-point numbers have six or fewer decimal digits, they're displayed with enough decimal places to accommodate the fractional part of the number. If the number has more than six decimal digits, the fractional part is rounded to six decimal digits, and if the number has no decimal digits, neither a decimal point nor any decimal digits are displayed.[5]

Program 2.2 illustrates using cout to display the results of arithmetic expressions in the context of a complete program.

---

[5]None of this output is defined as part of the C++ language. Rather, it's defined by a set of classes and routines provided with each C++ compiler.

 **Program 2.2**

```cpp
#include <iostream>
using namespace std;

int main()
{
  cout << "15.0 plus 2.0 equals " << (15.0 + 2.0) << endl
       << "15.0 minus 2.0 equals " << (15.0 - 2.0) << endl
       << "15.0 times 2.0 equals " << (15.0 * 2.0) << endl
       << "15.0 divided by 2.0 equals " << (15.0 / 2.0) << endl;

  return 0;
}
```

The output of Program 2.2 is the following:

```
15.0 plus 2.0 equals 17
15.0 minus 2.0 equals 13
15.0 times 2.0 equals 30
15.0 divided by 2.0 equals 7.5
```

The only new item used in Program 2.2 is endl, which is an example of a C++ manipulator. A **manipulator** is an item used to change how an output stream of characters is displayed. In particular, the endl manipulator causes a newline character ('\n') to be inserted in the display first, and then forces all current insertions to be displayed immediately, instead of waiting for more data. (Section 3.2 lists the most commonly used manipulators.)

Expression Types

An **expression** is any combination of operators and operands that can be evaluated to yield a value. An expression containing only integer values as operands is called an **integer expression**, and the result of the expression is an integer value. Similarly, an expression containing only floating-point values (single-precision and double-precision) as operands is called a **floating-point expression** (also called a "real expression"), and the result of the expression is a floating-point value. An expression containing integer and floating-point values is called a **mixed-mode expression**. When mixing integer and floating-point values in an arithmetic operation, each operation's data type is determined by the following rules:

- If both operands are integers, the result of the operation is an integer.
- If one operand is a real value, the result of the operation is a double-precision value.

The result of an arithmetic expression is never a single-precision (float) number. This is because during execution, a C++ program temporarily converts all single-precision numbers to double-precision numbers when an arithmetic expression is evaluated.

Point of Information

The endl Manipulator

On many systems, the `endl` manipulator (derived from the term "end line") and the \n escape sequence are processed in the same way and produce the same effect. The one exception is on systems where output is accumulated internally until enough characters collect to make it advantageous to display them all in one burst onscreen. In these systems, referred to as "buffered," the `endl` manipulator forces all accumulated output to be displayed immediately, without waiting for additional characters to fill the buffer area before being printed. As a practical matter, you wouldn't notice a difference in the final display. As a general rule, however, use the \n escape sequence whenever it can be included in an existing string, and use the `endl` manipulator whenever a \n would appear by itself or to formally signify the end of a specific group of output.

Although this point has no direct bearing on your work in this chapter, it's worth noting that the arithmetic operations of addition, subtraction, multiplication, and division are actually implemented differently for integer and floating-point values. In this sense, arithmetic operators are considered to be "overloaded." More formally, an **overloaded operator** is an operator whose actual implementation depends on the types of operands encountered. In Part II, when you see how to modify an operator's execution, you'll need this overloading capability.

Integer Division

The division of two integer values can produce rather strange results for the unwary. For example, the expression 15/2 yields the integer result 7. Because integers can't contain a fractional part, the value 7.5 can't be obtained. The fractional part resulting when two integers are divided—the remainder—is always dropped (truncated). Therefore, the value of 9/4 is 2 and 20/3 is 6.

Often, however, you need to retain the remainder of an integer division. To do this, C++ provides the **modulus operator** (also referred to as the "remainder operator"), which has the symbol %. This operator captures the remainder when an integer is divided by an integer; using a noninteger value with the modulus operator results in a compiler error. The following examples show how the modulus operator is used:

    9 % 4 is 1 (the remainder when 9 is divided by 4 is 1)
    17 % 3 is 2 (the remainder when 17 is divided by 3 is 2)
    15 % 4 is 3 (the remainder when 15 is divided by the 4 is 3)
    14 % 2 is 0 (the remainder when 14 is divided by 2 is 0)

Negation

In addition to binary operators, C++ provides **unary operators**, which operate on a single operand. One of these unary operators uses the same symbol as binary subtraction (-). With this unary operator, the minus sign in front of a single numerical value negates (reverses the sign of) the number.

Table 2.7 summarizes the six arithmetic operations described so far and lists the data type for the result each operator produces, based on the data type of the operands involved.

Table 2.7 Summary of Arithmetic Operators

Operation	Operator Symbol	Type	Operand(s)	Result
Addition	+	Binary	Both are integers One operand is not an integer	Integer Double-precision
Subtraction	–	Binary	Both are integers One operand is not an integer	Integer Double-precision
Multiplication	*	Binary	Both are integers One operand is not an integer	Integer Double-precision
Division	/	Binary	Both are integers One operand is not an integer	Integer Double-precision
Modulus	%	Binary	Both are integers One operand is not an integer	Integer Compiler error
Negation	–	Unary	Integer or double	Same as operand

Operator Precedence and Associativity

In addition to simple expressions, such as 5 + 12 and .08 * 26.2, you can create more complex arithmetic expressions. C++, like most other programming languages, requires following certain rules when writing expressions containing more than one arithmetic operator:

- Two binary operator symbols must never be placed side by side. For example, 5 * % 6 is invalid because two operators, * and %, are placed next to each other.
- Parentheses can be used to form groupings, and all expressions enclosed in parentheses are evaluated first. In this way, you can use parentheses to alter the evaluation to any order. For example, in the expression (6 + 4) / (2 + 3), the 6 + 4 and 2 + 3 are evaluated first to yield 10 / 5. The 10 / 5 is then evaluated to yield 2.
- Parentheses can be enclosed by other parentheses. For example, the expression (2 * (3 + 7)) / 5 is valid and evaluates to 4. When parentheses are included within parentheses, expressions in the innermost parentheses are always evaluated first. The evaluation continues from innermost to outermost parentheses until all expressions in parentheses have been evaluated. The number of closing parentheses,), must always equal the number of opening parentheses, (, so that no unpaired sets exist.
- Parentheses can't be used to indicate multiplication; instead, the multiplication operator, *, must be used. For example, the expression (3 + 4) (5 + 1) is invalid. The correct expression is (3 + 4) * (5 + 1).

Parentheses should specify logical groupings of operands and indicate the intended order of arithmetic operations clearly to the compiler and programmers. Although expressions in parentheses are always evaluated first, expressions containing multiple operators, whether enclosed in parentheses or not, are evaluated by the priority, or **precedence**, of the operators. There are three levels of precedence:

1. *P1*—All negations are done first.
2. *P2*—Multiplication, division, and modulus operations are computed next. Expressions containing more than one multiplication, division, or modulus operator are evaluated from left to right as each operator is encountered. For example, in the expression 35 / 7 % 3 * 4, all operations have the same priority, so the operations are performed from left to right as each operator is encountered. The division is done first, yielding the expression 5 % 3 * 4. The modulus operation, 5 % 3, is performed next, yielding a result of 2. Finally, the expression 2 * 4 is computed to yield 8.
3. *P3*—Addition and subtraction are computed last. Expressions containing more than one addition or subtraction are evaluated from left to right as each operator is encountered.

In addition to precedence, operators have an **associativity,** which is the order in which operators of the same precedence are evaluated, as described in rule P2. For example, does the expression 6.0 * 6 / 4 yield 9.0, which is (6.0 * 6) / 4, or 6.0, which is 6.0 * (6 / 4)? The answer is 9.0 because C++'s operators use the same associativity as in general mathematics, which evaluates multiplication from left to right, as rule P2 indicates.

Table 2.8 lists the precedence and associativity of the operators discussed in this section. As you have seen, an operator's precedence establishes its priority in relation to all other operators. Operators at the top of Table 2.8 have a higher priority than operators at the bottom of the table. In expressions with multiple operators of different precedence, the operator with the higher precedence is used before an operator with lower precedence. For example, in the expression 6 + 4 / 2 + 3, because the division operator has a higher precedence (P2) than the addition operator, the division is done first, yielding an intermediate result of 6 + 2 + 3. The additions are then performed, left to right, to yield a final result of 11.

Table 2.8   Operator Precedence and Associativity

Operator	Associativity
Unary –	Right to left
* / %	Left to right
+ –	Left to right

Finally, take a look at using the precedence rules shown in Table 2.8 to evaluate an expression containing operators of different precedence, such as 8 + 5 * 7 % 2 * 4. Because the multiplication and modulus operators have a higher precedence than the addition operator, these two operations are evaluated first (P2), using their left-to-right associativity, before the addition is evaluated (P3). Therefore, the complete expression is evaluated as follows:

```
8 + 5 * 7 % 2 * 4 =
    8 + 35 % 2 * 4 =
        8 + 1 * 4 =
            8 + 4 = 12
```

EXERCISES 2.2

1. **(Practice)** For the following correct algebraic expressions and corresponding incorrect C++ expressions, find the errors and write corrected C++ expressions:

Algebra	**C++ Expression**
a. $(2)(3) + (4)(5)$	$(2)(3) + (4)(5)$
b. $\dfrac{6 + 18}{2}$	$6 + 18 / 2$
c. $\dfrac{4.5}{12.2 - 3.1}$	$4.5 / 12.2 - 3.1$
d. $4.6(3.0 + 14.9)$	$4.6 (3.0 + 14.9)$
e. $(12.1 + 18.9)(15.3 - 3.8)$	$(12.1 + 18.9) (15.3 - 3.8)$

2. **(Practice)** Determine the values of the following integer expressions:

a. 3 + 4 * 6
b. 3 * 4 / 6 + 6
c. 2 * 3 / 12 * 8 / 4
d. 10 * (1 + 7 * 3)
e. 20 - 2 / 6 + 3
f. 20 - 2 / (6 + 3)
g. (20 - 2) / 6 + 3
h. (20 - 2) / (6 + 3)
i. 50 % 20
j. (10 + 3) % 4

3. **(Practice)** Determine the value of the following floating-point expressions:

a. 3.0 + 4.0 * 6.0
b. 3.0 * 4.0 / 6.0 + 6.0
c. 2.0 * 3.0 / 12.0 * 8.0 / 4.0
d. 10.0 * (1.0 + 7.0 * 3.0)
e. 20.0 - 2.0 / 6.0 + 3.0
f. 20.0 - 2.0 / (6.0 + 3.0)
g. (20.0 - 2.0) / 6.0 + 3.0
h. (20.0 - 2.0) / (6.0 + 3.0)

4. (Practice) Evaluate the following mixed-mode expressions and list the data type of the result. In evaluating the expressions, be aware of the data types of all intermediate calculations.

a. `10.0 + 15 / 2 + 4.3`
b. `10.0 + 15.0 / 2 + 4.3`
c. `3.0 * 4 / 6 + 6`
d. `3 * 4.0 / 6 + 6`
e. `20.0 - 2 / 6 + 3`
f. `10 + 17 * 3 + 4`
g. `10 + 17 / 3.0 + 4`
h. `3.0 * (4 % 6) + 6`
i. `10 + 17 % 3 + 4`

5. (Practice) Assume that `amount` stores the integer value 1, `m` stores the integer value 50, `n` stores the integer value 10, and `p` stores the integer value 5. Evaluate the following expressions:

a. `n / p + 3`
b. `m / p + n - 10 * amount`
c. `m - 3 * n + 4 * amount`
d. `amount / 5`
e. `18 / p`
f. `-p * n`
g. `-m / 20`
h. `(m + n) / (p + amount)`
i. `m + n / p + amount`

6. (Practice) Repeat Exercise 5, assuming that `amount` stores the value 1.0, `m` stores the value 50.0, `n` stores the value 10.0, and `p` stores the value 5.0.

7. (Practice) Enter, compile, and run Program 2.2.

8. (Desk check) Determine the output of the following program:

```
#include <iostream>
using namespace std;
int main()   // a program illustrating integer truncation
{
   cout << "answer1 is the integer " << 9/4;
   cout << "\nanswer2 is the integer " << 17/3;

   return 0;
}
```

9. (**Desk check**) Determine the output of the following program:

```
#include <iostream>
using namespace std;
int main()  // a program illustrating the % operator
{
  cout << "The remainder of 9 divided by 4 is " << 9 % 4;
  cout << "\nThe remainder of 17 divided by 3 is " << 17 % 3;

  return 0;
}
```

10. (**Program**) Write a C++ program that displays the results of the expressions `3.0 * 5.0`, `7.1 * 8.3 - 2.2`, and `3.2 / (6.1 * 5)`. Calculate the value of these expressions manually to verify that the displayed values are correct.

11. (**Program**) Write a C++ program that displays the results of the expressions `15 / 4`, `15 % 4`, and `5 * 3 - (6 * 4)`. Calculate the value of these expressions manually to verify that the displayed values are correct.

2.3 Variables and Declarations

All integer, floating-point, and other values used in a program are stored in and retrieved from the computer's memory. Conceptually, locations in memory are arranged like the rooms in a large hotel, and each memory location has a unique address, like room numbers in a hotel. Before high-level languages such as C++, memory locations were referenced by their addresses. For example, storing the integer values 45 and 12 in the memory locations 1652 and 2548 (see Figure 2.4) required instructions equivalent to the following:

> ***Put a 45 in location 1652***
> ***Put a 12 in location 2548***

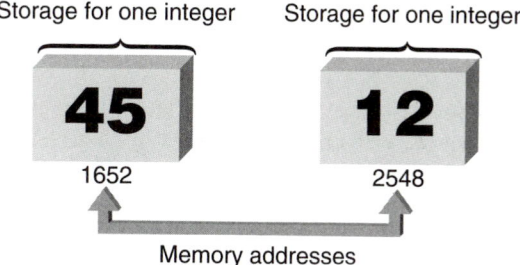

Figure 2.4   Enough storage for two integers

To add the two numbers just stored and save the result in another memory location, such as 3000, you need an instruction such as the following:

Add the contents of location 1652
to the contents of location 2548
and store the result in location 3000

Clearly, this method of storage and retrieval is cumbersome. In high-level languages such as C++, symbolic names, called **variables**, are used in place of memory addresses. A variable is simply a name the programmer assigns to refer to computer storage locations. The term "variable" is used because the value stored in the memory locations assigned to the variable can change, or vary. For each name the programmer uses, the computer keeps track of the memory address corresponding to that name. In the hotel room analogy, it's equivalent to putting a name on a room's door and referring to the room by this name, such as calling it the Blue Room instead of Room 205.

In C++ the selection of variable names is left to the programmer, as long as the following rules are observed:

- The variable name must begin with a letter or underscore (_) and can contain only letters, underscores, or digits. It can't contain blank spaces, commas, or special symbols, such as ( ) & , $ # . ! ?. Use initial uppercase letters to separate names consisting of multiple words.
- A variable name can't be a keyword (see Table 1.1).

These rules are similar to those for selecting function names. Like function names, variable names should be mnemonics that give some indication of the variable's purpose. For a variable used to store a value that's the total of other values, a good name is `sum` or `total`. Variable names giving no indication of the value stored, such as `r2d2`, `linda`, and `getum`, shouldn't be used. As with function names, variable names can consist of uppercase and lowercase letters.

Assume the first memory location shown in Figure 2.5, which has the address 1652, is given the name `num1`. The memory location 2548 is given the variable name `num2`, and memory location 3000 is given the variable name `total`.

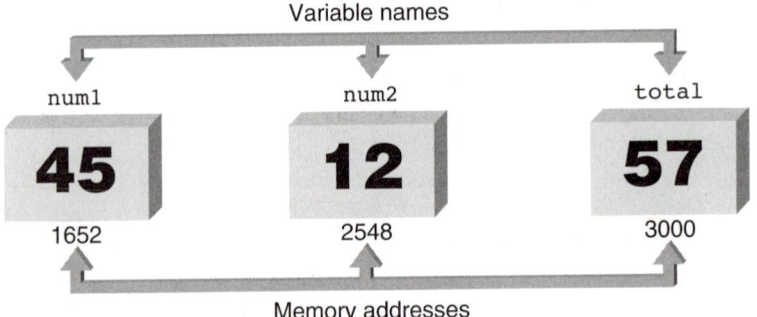

Figure 2.5 Naming storage locations

> ### Point of Information
>
> **Atomic Data**
>
> All the variables declared so far have been used to store atomic data values. An **atomic data value** is considered a complete entity and can't be decomposed into a smaller data type supported by the language. For example, although an integer can be decomposed into separate digits, C++ doesn't have a numerical digit type. Instead, each integer is regarded as a complete value and, therefore, is considered atomic data. Because the integer data type supports only atomic data values, it's said to be an **atomic data type**. As you might expect, `doubles`, `chars`, and `bools` are atomic data types, too.

Using these variable names, the operation of storing 45 in location 1652, storing 12 in location 2548, and adding the contents of these two locations is accomplished with these C++ statements:

```
num1 = 45;
num2 = 12;
total = num1 + num2;
```

Each of these statements is called an **assignment statement** because it tells the computer to assign (store) a value in a variable. Assignment statements always have an equals sign (=) and one variable name immediately to the left of the =. The value to the right of the equals sign is determined first; this value is then assigned to the variable to the left of the equals sign. The blank spaces in assignment statements are inserted for readability. Assignment statements are explained in more detail in Chapter 3, but for now, just know that you can use them to store values in variables.

A variable name is useful because it frees programmers from having to think about where data is physically stored in the computer. You simply use the variable name and let the compiler worry about where in memory the data is actually stored. Before storing a value in a variable, however, C++ requires clearly declaring the type of data to be stored in it. You must tell the compiler, in advance, the names of variables used for characters, the names used for integers, and the names used to store other C++ data types.

Declaration Statements

To name a variable and specify the data type that can be stored in it, you use a **declaration statement**, which has this general form:

```
dataType variableName;
```

In this form, `dataType` designates a valid C++ data type, and `variableName` is the name you select for the variable. For example, variables used to hold integer values are declared by using the keyword `int` to specify the data type and have this form:

```
int variableName;
```

Therefore, the following declaration statement declares `sum` as the name of a variable capable of storing an integer value:

```
int sum;
```

In addition, the keyword `long` is used to specify a `long` integer.[6] For example, the statement

```
long datenum;
```

declares `datenum` as a variable used to store a `long` integer. When you're using the `long` qualifier, you can also include the keyword `int`, so the previous declaration can also be written as follows:

```
long int datenum;
```

Variables used to hold single-precision values are declared by using the keyword `float`, and variables used to hold double-precision values are declared by using the keyword `double`. For example, the following statement declares `firstnum` as a variable used to store a single-precision number:

```
float firstnum;
```

Similarly, the following statement declares that the variable `secnum` is used to store a double-precision number:

```
double secnum;
```

Although declaration statements can be placed anywhere in a function, typically they're grouped together and placed after the function's opening brace. However, a variable must *always* be declared before using it, and like all C++ statements, declaration statements must end with a semicolon. A simple `main()` function containing declaration statements right after the opening function brace has this general form:

```
#include <iostream>
using namespace std;

int main()
{
  declaration statements;

  other statements;

  return 0;
}
```

Program 2.3 uses this form in declaring and using four double-precision variables, with the `cout` object used to display one of the variable's contents.

---

[6]Additionally, the keywords `unsigned int` are used to specify an integer that can store only non-negative numbers, and the keyword `short` specifies a `short` integer.

 **Program 2.3**

```cpp
#include <iostream>
using namespace std;
int main()
{
  double grade1;  // declare grade1 as a double variable
  double grade2;  // declare grade2 as a double variable
  double total;   // declare total as a double variable
  double average; // declare average as a double variable

  grade1 = 85.5;
  grade2 = 97.0;
  total = grade1 + grade2;
  average = total/2.0;  // divide the total by 2.0
  cout << "The average grade is " << average << endl;

  return 0;
}
```

The placement of the declaration statements in Program 2.3 is straightforward, although you'll see shortly that these four declarations can be combined into a single declaration statement. When Program 2.3 runs, the following output is displayed:

```
The average grade is 91.25
```

Notice that when a variable name is inserted in a cout statement, the value stored in the variable is placed on the output stream and displayed.

Just as integer and real (single-precision, double-precision, and long double) variables must be declared before they can be used, a variable used to store a single character must also be declared. Character variables are declared by using the keyword char. For example, the following declaration specifies that ch is a character variable:

```
char ch;
```

Program 2.4 illustrates this declaration and the use of cout to display the value stored in a character variable.

 Program 2.4

```
#include <iostream>
using namespace std;

int main()
{
  char ch;      // this declares a character variable

  ch = 'a';     // store the letter a in ch
  cout << "The character stored in ch is " << ch << endl;
  ch = 'm';     // now store the letter m in ch
  cout << "The character now stored in ch is "<< ch << endl;

  return 0;
}
```

When Program 2.4 runs, this output is produced:

```
The character stored in ch is a
The character now stored in ch is m
```

Notice that the first letter stored in the variable ch is a and the second letter stored is m. Because a variable can be used to store only one value at a time, assigning m to the variable overwrites the a value automatically.

Multiple Declarations

Variables of the same data type can always be grouped together and declared by using a single declaration statement, which has this common form:

dataType variableList;

For example, the four separate declarations used in Program 2.3

```
double grade1;
double grade2;
double total;
double average;
```

can be replaced with this single declaration statement:

```
double grade1, grade2, total, average;
```

Similarly, the two character declarations

```
char ch;
char key;
```

can be replaced with this single declaration statement:

```
char ch, key;
```

Declaring multiple variables in a single declaration statement requires giving the data type of variables only once, separating all variable names by commas, and using only one semicolon to terminate the declaration. The space after each comma is inserted for readability and isn't required.

Declaration statements can also be used to store a value in declared variables. For example, the declaration statement

```
int num1 = 15;
```

both declares the variable num1 as an integer variable and sets the value of 15 in the variable. When a declaration statement is used to store a value in a variable, the variable is said to be **initialized**. Therefore, in this example, it's correct to say the variable num1 has been initialized to 15.

Similarly, the following declaration statements declare three double-precision variables and initialize two of them:

```
double grade1 = 87.0;
double grade2 = 93.5;
double total;
```

Expressions using constants and/or previously initialized variables can also be used as initializers. Therefore, the expression 87.5 - 3.0 * factor is a valid initializer only if factor has been declared and initialized previously. Additionally, multiple initializations can be made by using a single declaration statement. These declarations, however, should be clear and, if possible, short, as in the declaration int x, y=0, z=0;. Program 2.3 with declaration initialization becomes Program 2.3a.

Program 2.3a

```cpp
#include <iostream>
using namespace std;

int main()
{
  double grade1 = 85.5;
  double grade2 = 97.0;
  double total, average;

  total = grade1 + grade2;
  average = total/2.0;   // divide the total by 2.0
  cout << "The average grade is " << average << endl;

  return 0;
}
```

Notice the blank line after the last declaration statement. Inserting a blank line after variable declarations placed at the top of a function body is a good programming practice. It improves a program's appearance and readability.

An interesting feature of C++ is that variable declarations can be intermixed and even contained in other statements; the only requirement is that a variable must be declared before its use. For example, the variable `total` in Program 2.3a could have been declared when it's first used with the statement `double total = grade1 + grade2;`. In restricted situations (such as debugging, described in Section 4.7, or in a `for` loop, described in Section 5.3), declaring a variable at its first use can be helpful. In general, however, it's preferable not to spread out declarations; instead, group them as concisely and clearly as possible at the top of each function.

Memory Allocation

The declaration statements you have seen so far have performed both software and hardware tasks. From a software perspective, declaration statements always provide a list of variables and their data types. In this software role, variable declarations also help control an otherwise common and troublesome error caused by misspelling a variable's name in a program. For example, assume a variable named `distance` is declared and initialized by using this statement:

```
int distance = 26;
```

Later in the program, say the variable is inadvertently misspelled in this statement:

```
mpg = distnce / gallons;
```

In languages that don't require variable declarations, the program treats `distnce` as a new variable and assigns it an initial value of 0 or uses whatever value happens to be in the variable's storage area. In either case, a value is calculated and assigned to `mpg`, and finding the error or even knowing an error occurred could be difficult. These errors are impossible in C++, however, because the compiler flags `distnce` as an undeclared variable. The compiler can't, of course, detect when one declared variable is mistakenly typed in place of another declared variable.

In addition to their software role, declaration statements can also perform a hardware task. Because each data type has its own storage requirements, the computer can allocate enough storage for a variable only after knowing the variable's data type. Variable declarations provide this information, so they can be used to force the compiler to reserve enough physical memory storage for each variable. Declaration statements used for this hardware task are also called **definition statements** because they define or tell the compiler how much memory is needed for data storage.

All the declaration statements you have encountered so far have also been definition statements. Later, you'll see declaration statements that don't allocate storage and are used simply to alert the program to the data types of variables created elsewhere in the program.

Figures 2.6a through 2.6d illustrate the operations set in motion by definition statements. The figures show that definition statements (or declaration statements that also allocate memory) "tag" the first byte of each set of reserved bytes with a name. This name is, of course, the variable's name, and the computer uses it to locate the starting point of a variable's reserved memory area.

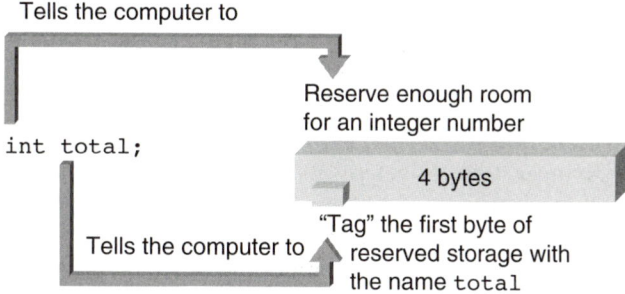

Figure 2.6a Defining the integer variable named `total`

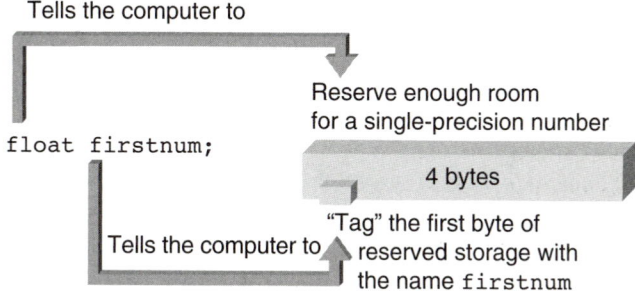

Figure 2.6b Defining the floating-point variable named `firstnum`

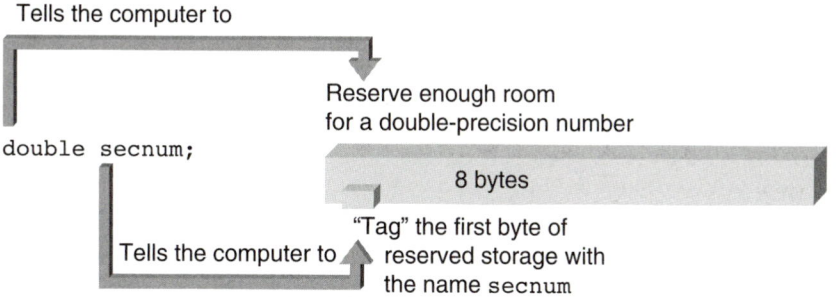

Figure 2.6c Defining the double-precision variable named `secnum`

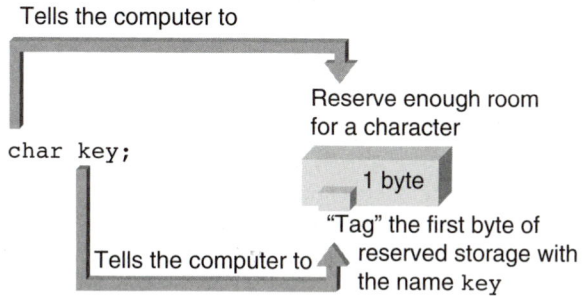

Figure 2.6d Defining the character variable named `key`

After a variable has been declared in a program, typically a programmer uses it to refer to the variable's contents (its value). The value's memory location is generally of little concern to programmers. The compiler, however, must know where each value is stored and locate each variable correctly. For this task, the compiler uses the variable name to locate the first byte of storage previously allocated to the variable. Knowing the variable's data type then allows the compiler to store or retrieve the correct number of bytes.

EXERCISES 2.3

1. **(Practice)** State whether the following variable names are valid. If they're invalid, state the reason.

prod_a	c1234	abcd	_c3	12345
newbal	while	$total	new bal	a1b2c3d4
9ab6	sum.of	average	grade1	finGrade

2. **(Practice)** State whether the following variable names are valid. If they're invalid, state the reason. Also, indicate which of the valid variable names shouldn't be used because they convey no information about the variable.

salestax	a243	r2d2	firstNum	cc_al
harry	sue	c3p0	average	sum
maximum	okay	a	awesome	goforit
3sum	for	tot.al	c$five	netpay

3. **(Practice) a.** Write a declaration statement to declare that the variable `count` will be used to store an integer.
   b. Write a declaration statement to declare that the variable `grade` will be used to store a floating-point number.
   c. Write a declaration statement to declare that the variable `yield` will be used to store a double-precision number.
   d. Write a declaration statement to declare that the variable `initial` will be used to store a character.

4. **(Practice)** Write a single declaration statement for each set of variables:
   a. num1, num2, and num3 used to store integer numbers
   b. grade1, grade2, grade3, and grade4 used to store double-precision numbers
   c. temp1, temp2, and temp3 used to store double-precision numbers
   d. let1, let2, let3, and let4 used to store characters

5. **(Practice)** Write a single declaration statement for each set of variables:
   a. firstnum and secnum used to store integers
   b. price, yield, and coupon used to store double-precision numbers
   c. average used to store a double-precision number

6. (**Modify**) Rewrite each of these declaration statements as three separate declarations:

a. `int month, day = 30, year;`

b. `double hours, volt, power = 15.62;`

c. `double price, amount, taxes;`

d. `char inKey, ch, choice = 'f';`

7. (**Desk check**) a. Determine what each statement causes to happen in the following program:

```cpp
#include <iostream>
using namespace std;
int main()
{
  int num1, num2, total;

  num1 = 25;
  num2 = 30;
  total = num1 + num2;
  cout << "The total of " << num1 << " and "
       << num2 << " is " << total << endl;

  return 0;
}
```

b. What output will be displayed when the program in Exercise 7a runs?

8. (**Program**) Write a C++ program that stores the sum of the integer numbers 12 and 33 in a variable named `sum`. Have your program display the value stored in `sum`.

9. (**Program**) Write a C++ program that stores the integer value 16 in the variable `length` and the integer value 18 in the variable `width`. Have your program calculate the value assigned to the `perimeter` variable, using this formula:

perimeter = 2 × (length + width)

Your program should then display the value stored in `perimeter`. Be sure to declare all variables as integers at the beginning of the `main()` function.

10. (**Program**) Write a C++ program that stores the integer value 16 in the variable `num1` and the integer value 18 in the variable `num2`. (Be sure to declare the variables as integers.) Have your program calculate the total of these numbers and their average. Store the total in an integer variable named `total` and the average in an integer variable named `average`. (Use the statement `average = total/2.0;` to calculate the average.) Use a `cout` statement to display the total and average.

11. **(Debug)** Enter, compile, and run the following program. Determine why an incorrect average is displayed and correct the error.

```cpp
#include <iostream>
using namespace std;

int main()
{

  int num1 = 15;
  int num2 = 18;
  int total, average;

  total = num1 + num2;
  average = total / 2.0;
  cout << "The average of " << num1
       << " and " << num2 << " is "
       << average << endl;

  return 0;
}
```

12. **(Debug)** The following program was written to correct the error produced by the program in Exercise 11. Determine why this program also doesn't provide the correct result and correct the error.

```cpp
#include <iostream>
using namespace std;

int main()
{

  int num1 = 15;
  int num2 = 18;
  int total;
  double average;

  total = num1 + num2;
  average = total / 2;
  cout << "The average of " << num1
       << " and " << num2 << " is "
       << average << endl;

  return 0;
}
```

13. **(Program)** Write a C++ program that stores the number 105.62 in the variable `firstnum`, 89.352 in the variable `secnum`, and 98.67 in the variable `thirdnum`. (Be sure to declare the variables first as `float` or `double`.) Have your program calculate the total of the three numbers and their average. The total should be stored in the variable `total` and the average in the variable `average`. (Use the statement `average = total /3.0;` to calculate the average.) Use a `cout` statement to display the total and average.

14. **(For thought) a.** A statement used to clarify the relationship between squares and rectangles is "All squares are rectangles but not all rectangles are squares." Write a similar statement that describes the relationship between definition and declaration statements.

 b. Why must a variable be defined before any other C++ statement that uses the variable?

NOTE   **Note for Exercises 15 to 17:** Assume that a character requires 1 byte of storage, an integer requires 4 bytes, a single-precision number requires 4 bytes, and a double-precision number requires 8 bytes. Variables are assigned storage in the order they're declared. (Review Section 2.6 if you're unfamiliar with the concept of a byte.) Refer to Figure 2.7 for these exercises.

Addresses

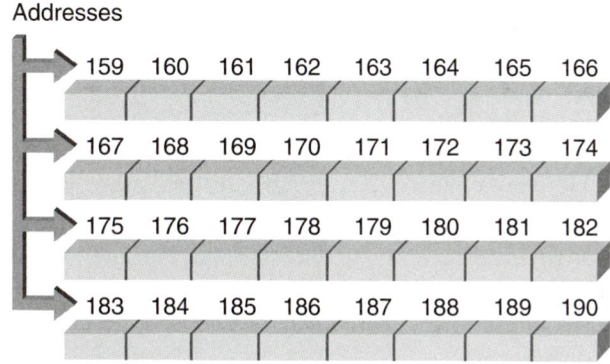

Figure 2.7 Memory bytes for Exercises 15 to 17

15. **(Practice) a.** Using Figure 2.7 and assuming the variable name `rate` is assigned to the byte at memory address 159, determine the addresses corresponding to each variable declared in the following statements. Also, fill in the correct number of bytes with the initialization data included in the declaration statements. (Use letters for the characters, not the computer codes that would actually be stored.)

```
float rate;
char ch1 = 'M', ch2 = 'E', ch3 = 'L', ch4 = 'T';
double taxes;
int num, count = 0;
```

 b. Repeat Exercise 15a, but substitute the actual byte patterns that a computer using the ASCII code would use to store characters in the variables `ch1`, `ch2`, `ch3`, and `ch4`. (*Hint*: Use Table 2.2.)

16. **(Practice)** **a.** Using Figure 2.7 and assuming the variable named `cn1` is assigned to the byte at memory address 159, determine the addresses corresponding to each variable declared in the following statements. Also, fill in the correct number of bytes with the initialization data included in the declaration statements. (Use letters for the characters, not the computer codes that would actually be stored.)

```
char cn1 = 'P', cn2 = 'E', cn3 = 'R', cn4 = 'F', cn5 = 'E';
char cn6 = 'C', cn7 = 'T', key = '\\', sch = '\'', inc = 'A';
char incl = 'T';
```

   b. Repeat Exercise 16a, but substitute the actual byte patterns a computer using the ASCII code would use to store characters in each declared variable. (*Hint:* Use Tables 2.2 and 2.3.)

17. **(Practice)** Using Figure 2.7 and assuming the variable name `miles` is assigned to the byte at memory address 159, determine the addresses corresponding to each variable declared in the following statements:

```
float miles;
int count, num;
double dist, temp;
```

2.4 Common Programming Errors

The common programming errors associated with the material in this chapter are as follows:

1. Forgetting to declare all variables used in a program. The compiler detects this error, and an error message is generated for all undeclared variables.
2. Attempting to store one data type in a variable declared for a different type. The compiler doesn't detect this error. The value is converted to the data type of the variable it's assigned to.
3. Using a variable in an expression before a value has been assigned to the variable. Whatever value happens to be in the variable is used when the expression is evaluated and, therefore, the result of the expression is meaningless.
4. Dividing integer values incorrectly. This error is usually hidden in a larger expression and can be troublesome to detect. For example, the expression

   `3.425 + 2/3 + 7.9`

   yields the same result as the expression

   `3.425 + 7.9`

   because the integer division of 2/3 is 0.
5. Mixing data types in the same expression without understanding the effect clearly. Because C++ allows expressions with "mixed" data types, understanding the order of

evaluation and the data type of all intermediate calculations is important. These are the rules for evaluating the result of each binary operation:

- If both operands are integers, the result is an integer.
- If any operand is a real value, the result is a double-precision value.

As a general rule, it's better not to mix data types in an expression unless you want a specific effect.

6. Forgetting to separate data streams passed to cout with an insertion symbol, <<.

2.5 Chapter Summary

1. The four basic types of data C++ recognizes are integer, floating-point, character, and Boolean. Each data type is typically stored in a computer by using different amounts of memory.

2. The cout object can be used to display all C++ data types.

3. Every variable in a C++ program must be declared, and the type of value it can store must be specified. Declarations in a function can be placed anywhere in the function, although a variable can be used only after it's declared. Variables can also be initialized when they're declared. Additionally, variables of the same type can be declared with a single declaration statement. Variable declaration statements have this general form:

```
dataType variableName(s);
```

4. A simple C++ program containing declaration statements has this typical form:

```
#include <iostream>
using namespace std;

int main()
{
   declaration statements;

   other statements;

   return 0;
}
```

5. Declaration statements always play the software role of informing the compiler of a function's valid variable names. When a variable declaration also causes the computer to set aside memory locations for the variable, the declaration statement is called a definition statement. (All declarations used in this chapter have also been definition statements.)

6. The sizeof() operator can be used to determine the amount of storage reserved for variables.

2.6 Chapter Supplement: Bits, Bytes, and Binary Number Representations

This section explains how numbers are stored in a computer's memory and different means of representing them.

Bits and Bytes

The physical components used in manufacturing a computer require that numbers and letters in its memory not be stored with the same symbols people use. For example, the number 126 isn't stored with the symbols 1, 2, and 6, nor is the letter you recognize as an "A" stored with this symbol. This section explains the reasons for these storage requirements and how computers store numbers.

The smallest and most basic data item in a computer is called a bit (derived from the term "*bi*nary dig*it*"). Physically, a **bit** is actually a switch that can be open or closed. The convention followed in this book is that the open position is represented as a 0, and the closed position is represented as a 1.

A single bit that can represent the values 0 and 1 has limited usefulness. All computers, therefore, group a set number of bits together for storage and transmission. Grouping 8 bits to form a larger unit, called a **byte**, is an almost universal computer standard. A single byte consisting of 8 bits, with each bit being a 0 or 1, can represent any one of 256 distinct patterns. These patterns consist of 00000000 (all eight switches open) to 11111111 (all eight switches closed) and all possible combinations of 0s and 1s in between. Each pattern can be used to represent a letter of the alphabet, a character (such as a dollar sign or comma), a single digit, or a number containing more than one digit. A collection of patterns used to represent letters, single digits, and other characters is called a **character code**. (One character code, called ASCII, was discussed in Section 2.1.) The patterns used to store numbers are called **number codes**, one of which, known as twos complement representation, is explained at the end of this section.

Words and Addresses   In a computer's memory, bytes can be grouped into larger units, called **words**, to facilitate storage of larger values and to allow faster and more extensive data access. For example, retrieving a word consisting of 4 bytes from a computer's memory results in more information than retrieving a word consisting of a single byte. This type of retrieval is also much faster than four separate 1-byte retrievals. Achieving this increase in speed and capacity, however, requires increasing the computer's cost and complexity. Desktop and laptop computers currently use word sizes of 4 and 8 bytes.

The arrangement of words in a computer's memory can be compared with the arrangement of standard rooms in a large hotel. Just as each room has a unique room number to locate and identify it, each word has a unique numeric address. (In computers that allow accessing each byte separately, each byte has its own address.) Like room numbers, word and byte addresses are always unsigned whole numbers used for location and identification purposes. In addition, in the same way hotel rooms with connecting doors form larger suites, words can be combined to form larger units for accommodating data types of different sizes.

You can check the storage allocated for each integer data type discussed in this chapter and the range of values your compiler provides by using the identifier names listed in Table 2.9. To do this, you can inspect the `limits` header file for the definition of these identifiers or construct a C++ program to display these values. Program 2.5 shows how this storage check is accomplished.

Table 2.9   Integer Data Type Storage

Data Type	Range of Values	Identifier (in `limits` header file)	Storage Size (in bytes)
char	-128 to +127	SCHAR_MIN, SCHAR_MAX	1
short int	-32,768 to +32,767	SHRT_MIN, SHRT_MAX	2
int	-2,147,483,648 to +2,147,483,647	INT_MIN, INT_MAX	4
long int	-2,147,483,648 to +2,147,483,647	LONG_MIN, LONG_MAX	4
unsigned short int	0 to 65,535	USHRT_MAX	2
unsigned int	0 to 4,294,967,295	UINT_MAX	4
unsigned long int	0 to 4,294,967,295	ULONG_MAX	4

Program 2.5

```cpp
#include <iostream>
#include <limits> //contains the maximum and minimum specifications
using namespace std;

int main()
{

  cout << "The smallest character code is " << SCHAR_MIN << endl;
  cout << "The largest character code is " << SCHAR_MAX << endl;
  cout <<  sizeof(char) << " byte(s) are used to store characters\n";

  cout << "\nThe smallest integer value is " << INT_MIN << endl;
  cout << "The largest integer value is " << INT_MAX << endl;
  cout <<  sizeof(int) << " byte(s) are used to store integers\n";

  cout << "\nThe smallest short integer value is " << SHRT_MIN <<endl;
  cout << "The largest short integer value is " << SHRT_MAX << endl;
  cout <<  sizeof(short) << " byte(s) are used to store short integers\n";
```

☞

```
cout << "The smallest long integer value is " << LONG_MIN << endl;
cout << "The largest long integer value is " << LONG_MAX << endl;
cout <<  sizeof(long) << " byte(s) are used to store long integers\n";

return 0;
}
```

Program 2.5 produces the following output:

```
The smallest character code is -128
The largest character code is 127
    1 byte(s) are used to store characters

The smallest integer value is -2147483648
The largest integer value is 2147483647
    4 byte(s) are used to store integers

The smallest short integer value is -32768
The largest short integer value is 32767
    2 byte(s) are used to store short integers

The smallest long integer value is -2147483648
The largest long integer value is 2147483647
    4 byte(s) are used to store long integers
```

Notice that the displayed values correspond with those listed previously in Table 2.9.

Binary, Hexadecimal, and Octal Numbers

The most common binary number code for storing integer values in a computer is called the **twos complement** representation. With this code, the integer decimal equivalent of any bit pattern, such as 10001101, is easy to determine and can be found for positive or negative integers with no change in the conversion method. For convenience, assume byte-sized bit patterns consisting of 8 bits each, although the procedure carries over to larger bit patterns.

The easiest way to determine the decimal integer each bit pattern represents is to construct a simple device called a **value box**. Figure 2.8 shows a value box for a single byte. Mathematically, each value in this box represents an increasing power of 2. Because twos complement numbers must be capable of representing both positive and negative integers, the leftmost position, in addition to having the largest absolute magnitude, has a negative sign.

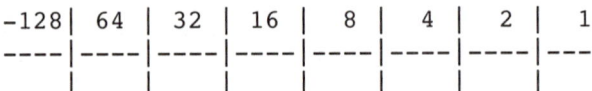

Figure 2.8 An 8-bit value box

Chapter Supplement: Bits, Bytes, and Binary
Number Representations

To convert any binary number, such as 10001101, into its decimal integer value, simply insert the bit pattern into the value box and add the values having 1s under them. Therefore, as shown in Figure 2.9, the bit pattern 10001101 represents the decimal integer number -115.

```
-128 |  64 |  32 |  16 |   8 |   4 |   2 |   1
---- |---- |---- |---- |---- |---- |---- |---
   1 |   0 |   0 |   0 |   1 |   1 |   0 |   1
-128 +   0 +   0 +   0 +   8 +   4 +   0 +   1 = -115
```

Figure 2.9   Converting 10001101 to a decimal number

The value box can also be used in reverse to convert a decimal integer number into its equivalent binary bit pattern. Some conversions, in fact, can be made by inspection. For example, the decimal integer -125 is obtained by adding 3 to -128. Therefore, the binary representation of -125 is 10000011, which equals -128 + 2 + 1. Similarly, the twos complement representation of the number 40 is 00101000, which is 32 + 8.

Although the value box conversion method is deceptively simple, it's related to the underlying mathematical basis of twos complement binary numbers. The original name of the twos complement code was the **weighted-sign code**, which correlates to the value box. As the name "weighted sign" implies, each bit position has a weight, or value, of 2 raised to a power and a sign. The signs of all bits except the leftmost bit are positive, and the sign of the leftmost bit is negative.

In reviewing the value box, you can see that any twos complement binary number with a leading 1 represents a negative number, and any bit pattern with a leading 0 represents a positive number. Using the value box, it's easy to determine the most positive and most negative values capable of being stored. The most negative value that can be stored in a single byte is the decimal number -128, which has the bit pattern 10000000. Any other non-zero bit simply adds a positive amount to the number. Additionally, a positive number must have a 0 as its leftmost bit. From this, you can see that the largest positive 8-bit twos complement number is 01111111, or 127.

In addition to representing integer values, computers must store and transmit numbers containing decimal points, which are mathematically referred to as "real numbers." Appendix D (available online) lists the binary codes used to represent real numbers.

Hexadecimal Representation   Because binary numbers tend to be lengthy, the more compact hexadecimal representation is often used. For example, the hexadecimal representation of the 16-bit binary number 11110000101011001110001101111011 is F0ACE37B.

Each hexadecimal symbol represents a specific 4-bit binary pattern. The correspondence between each hexadecimal symbol and its 4-bit binary pattern is listed in the first two columns of Table 2.10. For convenience, the equivalent decimal value of each hexadecimal symbol and the binary number it represents are also provided. Using this table, you can convert any hexadecimal number to its binary equivalent by substituting the correct 4-bit binary sequence for each hexadecimal symbol in the hexadecimal number. For example, Figure 2.10 shows how the hexadecimal number 2D1F is converted to its binary equivalent by using the corresponding values from Table 2.10.

Table 2.10   Hexadecimal to Binary Conversion

Hexadecimal Symbol	Binary Pattern	Decimal Symbol
0	0000	0
1	0001	1
2	0010	2
3	0011	3
4	0100	4
5	0101	5
6	0110	6
7	0111	7
8	1000	8
9	1001	9
A	1010	10
B	1011	11
C	1100	12
D	1101	13
E	1110	14
F	1111	15

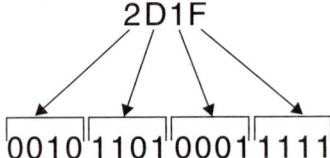

Figure 2.10   Converting a hexadecimal number to binary

To do the reverse conversion, from binary to hexadecimal, first group the binary digits in units of four, starting from the right of the binary number. Next, using Table 2.10, assign each group of four binary digits its corresponding hexadecimal symbol. Figure 2.11 shows an example of converting the 16-bit binary number 0111111100001010 to its hexadecimal representation.

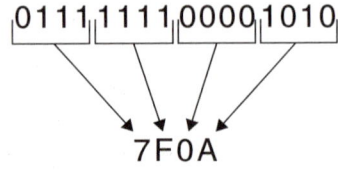

Figure 2.11   Converting a binary number to hexadecimal

Hexadecimal symbols work well for representing the 8 bits in a byte because each byte consists of two groups of 4 bits. (Sometimes 4-bit patterns are referred to as **nibbles**.) Therefore, a byte's binary code can be represented conveniently with two hexadecimal symbols.

In reviewing the hexadecimal symbols in Table 2.10, notice that the first 10 are the same as those used in the decimal system. After using the familiar 0 to 9 symbols, however, unique symbols are needed for the last six binary patterns in the table. The symbols you recognize as 10 through 15 can't be used because they consist of two symbols, so the letters A through F are used for these six additional symbols. To indicate clearly that hexadecimal numbers are being used, often they're preceded by 0X or 0x, as in 0xF0ACE37B.

Octal Representation   Although they have almost been superseded by hexadecimal numbers, you might still encounter binary numbers represented in their octal form. Octal numbers group binary numbers in units of three. Table 2.11 shows the correspondence between octal symbols and their 3-bit binary values.

Table 2.11   Octal to Binary Conversion

Octal Symbol	Binary Value
0	000
1	001
2	010
3	011
4	100
5	101
6	110
7	111

Using the values listed in Table 2.11, the octal number 541 represents the binary number 101100001. This is done by replacing the octal value 5 with its equivalent 101 binary bit pattern, replacing the 4 with its corresponding 100 binary bit pattern, and replacing the 1 with its corresponding 001 binary bit pattern.

To convert from binary to octal, first group the binary digits in units of three, proceeding from right to left. In doing this, you might have to add one or two leading zeros to the binary number to pad out the leftmost bit pattern to three binary digits. For example, the 8-bit binary number 11111010 is padded out to nine binary digits by adding a leading zero. The resulting number, 011111010, is then grouped in units of three, as |011|111|010|. The bar symbol, |, has been used to separate each group of three binary digits clearly. Using the correspondence between 3-bit patterns and octal symbols in Table 2.11, this binary number becomes the octal number 372.

Before a byte was standardized to consist of 8 bits, octal numbers were typically used to represent binary values. This method had the added advantage of using numeric symbols that were familiar to people used to dealing with decimal numbers. With the standardization of 8-bit bytes, however, the use of hexadecimal symbols and their correspondence with 4-bit binary numbers became the numbering system of choice for representing binary numbers.

Chapter

3

Assignment and Interactive Input

In Chapter 2, you were introduced to the concepts of data storage, variables, and their associated declaration statements. You also saw how the cout *object is used to display output data. This chapter continues your introduction to C++ by explaining how data is processed with both assignment statements and mathematical functions. Additionally, it discusses the* cin *object, which makes it possible for a user to enter data while a program is running. You also learn more about the* cout *object, which can be used for precise formatting of output data.*

3.1 Assignment Operators

You learned about simple assignment statements in Chapter 2. An assignment statement is the most basic C++ statement for assigning values to variables and performing computations. This statement has the following syntax:

```
variable = expression;
```

The simplest expression in C++ is a <u>single constant.</u> In the following assignment statements, the operand to the right of the equals sign is a constant:

```
length = 25;
width = 17.5;
```

In these assignment statements, the value of the constant to the right of the equals sign is assigned to the variable on the left of the equals sign. Note that the equals sign in C++ doesn't have the same meaning as an equals sign in algebra. The equals sign in an assignment statement tells the computer first to determine the value of the operand to its right, and then to store (or assign) this value in the locations associated with the variable on its left. For example, the C++ statement `length = 25;` formally means "length is assigned the value 25." The blank spaces in the assignment statement are inserted for readability only.

Recall that a variable can be initialized when it's declared. If an initialization isn't done in the declaration statement, the variable should be assigned a value with an assignment statement or input operation before it's used in any computation. Subsequent assignment statements can, of course, be used to change the value assigned to a variable. For example, assume the following statements are executed one after another, and `slope` wasn't initialized when it was declared:

```
slope = 3.7;
slope = 6.28;
```

The first assignment statement assigns the value of 3.7 to the variable named `slope`.[1] The next assignment statement causes the computer to assign a value of 6.28 to `slope`. The 3.7 that was in `slope` is overwritten with the new value of 6.28 because a variable can store only one value at a time. Sometimes it's useful to think of the variable to the left of the equals sign as a temporary parking spot in a huge parking lot. Just as a parking spot can be used by only one car at a time, each variable can store only one value at a time. "Parking" a new value in a variable automatically causes the program to remove any value parked there previously.

In addition to being a constant, the operand to the right of the equals sign in an assignment statement can be a variable or any other valid C++ expression. An **expression** is any combination of constants, variables, and function calls that can be evaluated to yield a result. Therefore, the expression in an assignment statement can be used to perform calculations by using the arithmetic operators introduced in Section 2.2. The following are examples of assignment statements using expressions containing these operators:

```
sum = 3 + 7;
diff = 15 - 6;
product = .05 * 14.6;
tally = count + 1;
newtotal = 18.3 + total;
taxes = .06 * amount;
```

---

[1]Because it's the first time a value is explicitly assigned to this variable, it's often referred to as an "initialization." This term stems from historical usage that said a variable was initialized the first time a value was assigned to it. Under this usage, it's correct to say that "slope is initialized to 3.7." From an implementation viewpoint, however, this statement is incorrect because the C++ compiler handles an assignment operation differently from an initialization; an initialization can happen only when a variable is created by a declaration statement. This difference is important only when using C++'s class features and is explained in detail in Section 10.1.

Assignment Operators

```
totalWeight = factor * weight;
average = sum / items;
slope = (y2 - y1) / (x2 - x1);
```

As always in an assignment statement, the program first calculates the value of the expression to the right of the equals sign and then stores this value in the variable to the left of the equals sign. For example, in the assignment statement `totalWeight = factor * weight;`, the arithmetic expression `factor * weight` is evaluated first to yield a result. This result, which is a number, is then stored in the variable `totalWeight`.

In writing assignment statements, you must be aware of two important considerations. Because the expression to the right of the equals sign is evaluated first, all variables used in the expression must have been given valid values previously if the result is to make sense. For example, the assignment statement `totalWeight = factor * weight;` causes a valid number to be stored in `totalWeight` only if the programmer takes care to assign valid numbers first to both `factor` and `weight`. Therefore, the following sequence of statements tells you the values used to obtain the result to be stored in `totalWeight`:

```
factor = 1.06;
weight = 155.0;
totalWeight = factor * weight;
```

Figure 3.1 shows the values stored in the variables `factor`, `weight`, and `totalWeight`.

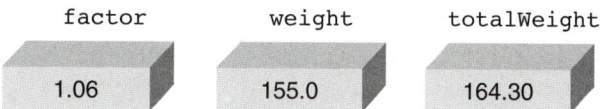

    factor   weight   totalWeight

    1.06   155.0   164.30

Figure 3.1 Values stored in variables

The second consideration is that because the value of an expression is stored in the variable to the left of the equals sign, only one variable can be listed in this position. For example, this assignment statement is invalid:

```
amount + 1892 = 1000 + 10 * 5;
```

The expression on the right evaluates to the integer 1050, which can only be stored in a variable. Because `amount + 1892` isn't a valid variable name, the compiler has no means of knowing where to store the calculated value and issues a syntax error message.

Program 3.1 shows using assignment statements to calculate the area of a rectangle.

Program 3.1

```cpp
// this program calculates the area of a rectangle,
// given its length and width

#include <iostream>
using namespace std;

int main()
{
  double length, width, area;

  length = 27.2;
  width = 13.6;
  area = length * width;
  cout << "The length of the rectangle is " << length << endl;
  cout << "The width of the rectangle is " << width << endl;
  cout << "The area of the rectangle is " << area << endl;

  return 0;
}
```

When Program 3.1 is run, this is the output:

```
The length of the rectangle is 27.2
The width of the rectangle is 13.6
The area of the rectangle is 369.92
```

Take a look at the flow of control the computer uses in executing Program 3.1. Program execution begins with the first statement and continues sequentially, statement by statement, until the closing brace of `main()` is encountered. This flow of control is true for all programs. The computer works on one statement at a time, executing the statement with no knowledge of what the next statement will be. This sequential execution explains why all operands used in an expression must have values assigned to them before the expression is evaluated.

When the computer executes the statement `area = length * width;` in Program 3.1, it uses whatever values are stored in the variables `length` and `width` at the time the assignment is executed. If no values have been specifically assigned to these variables before they're used in the expression `length * width`, the computer uses whatever values happen to occupy these variables when they're referenced. (Most C++ compilers initialize all variables to zero automatically; most also give you a warning that the variable hasn't been explicitly initialized.) The computer doesn't "look ahead" to see whether you assign values to these variables later in the program.

It's important to realize that in C++, the equals sign (=) used in assignment statements is an operator, which differs from the way most other high-level languages process this symbol. In C++, the = symbol is called the **assignment operator**, and an expression using this operator,

Assignment Operators

such as interest = principal * rate, is an **assignment expression**. Because the assignment operator has a lower precedence than any other arithmetic operator, the value of any expression to the right of the equals sign is evaluated first, before the assignment.

Like all expressions, an assignment expression has a value, which is the value assigned to the variable on the left of the assignment operator. For example, the expression a = 5 assigns a value of 5 to the variable a and results in the expression also having a value of 5. The expression's value can always be verified by using a statement such as the following:

```
cout << "The value of the expression is " << (a = 5);
```

This statement displays the expression's value, not the contents of the variable a. Although both the variable's contents and the expression have the same value, you should realize that you're dealing with two distinct entities.

From a programming perspective, it's the actual assignment of a value to a variable that's important in an assignment expression; the final value of the assignment expression is of little consequence. However, the fact that assignment expressions have a value has implications that must be considered when you learn about C++'s relational operators in Chapter 4.

Any expression terminated by a semicolon becomes a C++ statement. The most common example is the assignment statement, which is simply an assignment expression terminated with a semicolon. For example, terminating the assignment expression a = 33 with a semicolon results in the assignment statement a = 33;, which can be used in a program on a line by itself.

Because the equals sign is an operator in C++, multiple assignments are possible in the same expression or in its equivalent statement. For example, in the expression a = b = c = 25, all the assignment operators have the same precedence. The assignment operator has a right-to-left associativity, so the final evaluation proceeds in this sequence:

```
c = 25
b = c
a = b
```

In this example, this sequence of expressions has the effect of assigning the number 25 to each variable and can be represented as follows:

```
a = (b = (c = 25))
```

Appending a semicolon to the original expression results in this multiple assignment statement:

```
a = b = c = 25;
```

This statement assigns the value 25 to the three variables, equivalent to the following order:

```
c = 25;
b = 25;
a = 25;
```

Point of Information

lvalues **and** rvalues

The terms `lvalue` and `rvalue` are used often in almost all programming languages that define assignment with an operator that permits multiple assignments in the same statement. An `lvalue` refers to any quantity that's valid on the left side of an assignment operator, and an `rvalue` refers to any quantity that's valid on the right side of an assignment operator.

For example, each variable you've encountered so far can be an `lvalue` or `rvalue` (that is, a variable, by itself, can appear on both sides of an assignment operator), but a number can be only an `rvalue`. More generally, an expression is an `rvalue`. Not all variables, however, can be used as `lvalues` or `rvalues`. For example, an array type, introduced in Chapter 7, can't be an `lvalue` or `rvalue`, but elements in an array can be both.

Coercion

When working with assignment statements, keep in mind the data type assigned to the values on both sides of the expression because data type conversions take place across assignment operators. In other words, the value of the expression to the right of the assignment operator is converted to the data type of the variable to the left of the assignment operator. This type of conversion is referred to as a **coercion** because the value assigned to the variable on the left of the assignment operator is forced into the data type of the variable it's assigned to.

An example of a coercion occurs when an integer value is assigned to a real variable; this assignment causes the integer to be converted to a real value. Similarly, assigning a real value to an integer variable forces conversion of the real value to an integer. This conversion always results in losing the fractional part of the number because of truncation. For example, if `temp` is an integer variable, the assignment `temp = 25.89` causes the integer value 25 to be stored in the integer variable `temp`.[2]

Another example of data type conversions, which includes both mixed-mode and assignment conversions, is evaluation of the expression

```
a = b * d
```

where a and b are integer variables and d is a double-precision variable. When the mixed-mode expression b * d is evaluated,[3] the value of b used in the expression is converted to a double-precision number for purposes of computation. (Note that the value stored in b remains an integer number, and the resulting value of the expression b * d is a double-precision number.) Finally, data type conversion across the assignment operator comes into play. The left side of the assignment operator is an integer variable, so the double-precision value of the expression b * d is truncated to an integer value and stored in the variable a.

---

[2]The correct integer portion is retained only when it's within the range of integer values allowed by the compiler.
[3]Review the rules in Table 2.8, Section 2.2, for evaluating mixed-mode expressions, if necessary.

Assignment Variations

Although only one variable is allowed immediately to the left of the equals sign in an assignment expression, the variable to the left of the equals sign can also be used to the right of the equals sign. For example, the assignment expression sum = sum + 10 is valid. Clearly, as an algebraic equation, sum could never be equal to itself plus 10. In C++, however, sum = sum + 10 is *not* an equation—it's an expression evaluated in two major steps: First, the value of sum + 10 is calculated, and second, the computed value is stored in sum. See whether you can determine the output of Program 3.2.

Program 3.2

```
#include <iostream>
using namespace std;

int main()
{
  int sum;

  sum = 25;
  cout << "The number stored in sum is " << sum << endl;
  sum = sum + 10;
  cout << "The number now stored in sum is "
       << sum << endl;

  return 0;
}
```

In Program 3.2, the assignment statement sum = 25; tells the computer to store the number 25 in sum, as shown in Figure 3.2.

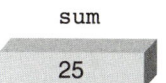

sum

25

Figure 3.2   The integer 25 is stored in sum

The first cout statement displays the value stored in sum with the message The number stored in sum is 25. The second assignment statement, sum = sum + 10;, causes the program to retrieve the 25 stored in sum and add 10 to this number, yielding 35. The number 35 is then stored in the variable to the left of the equals sign, which is the variable sum. The 25 that was in sum is simply overwritten with the new value of 35 (see Figure 3.3).

Figure 3.3 sum = sum + 10; causes a new value to be stored in sum

Assignment expressions such as sum = sum + 10, which use the same variable on both sides of the assignment operator, can be written by using the following **shortcut assignment operators**:

+=   -=   *=   /=   %=

For example, the expression sum = sum + 10 can be written as sum += 10. Similarly, the expression price *= rate is equivalent to the expression price = price * rate. In using shortcut assignment operators, note that the variable to the left of the assignment operator is applied to the complete expression on the right. For example, the expression price *= rate + 1 is equivalent to the expression price = price * (rate + 1), not price = price * rate + 1.

Accumulating

Assignment expressions, such as sum += 10 or its equivalent, sum = sum + 10, are common in programming. These expressions are required in accumulating subtotals when data is entered one number at a time. For example, if you want to add the numbers 96, 70, 85, and 60 in calculator fashion, the following statements could be used:

Statement	Value in sum
sum = 0;	0
sum = sum + 96;	96
sum = sum + 70;	166
sum = sum + 85;	251
sum = sum + 60;	311

The first statement initializes sum to 0, which removes any number stored in sum that would invalidate the final total (a "garbage value"). As each number is added, the value stored in sum is increased accordingly. After completion of the last statement, sum contains the total of all the added numbers. Program 3.3 shows the effect of these statements by displaying sum's contents after each addition.

Program 3.3

```cpp
#include <iostream>
using namespace std;

int main()
{
  int sum;

  sum = 0;
  cout << "The value of sum is initially set to "
      << sum << endl;
  sum = sum + 96;
  cout << "  sum is now " << sum << endl;
  sum = sum + 70;
  cout << "  sum is now " << sum << endl;
  sum = sum + 85;
  cout << "  sum is now " << sum  << endl;
  sum = sum + 60;
  cout << "  The final sum is " << sum << endl;

  return 0;
}
```

Program 3.3 displays this output:

```
The value of sum is initially set to 0
   sum is now 96
   sum is now 166
   sum is now 251
   The final sum is 311
```

Although Program 3.3 isn't a practical program (because adding the numbers by hand is easier), it does illustrate the subtotaling effect of repeated use of statements having this form:

variable = variable + newValue;

This type of statement is called an **accumulation statement.** You'll find many uses for accumulation statements when you become more familiar with the repetition statements introduced in Chapter 5.

Counting

The **counting statement**, which is an assignment statement similar to the accumulating statement, has the following form:

variable = variable + fixedNumber;

Examples of counting statements are as follows:

```
i = i + 1;
n = n + 1;
count = count + 1;
j = j + 2;
m = m + 2;
kk = kk + 3;
```

In these examples, the same variable is used on both sides of the equals sign. After the statement is executed, the variable's value is increased by a fixed amount. In the first three examples, the variables i, n, and count have been increased by 1. In the next two examples, the variables have been increased by 2, and in the final example, the variable kk has been increased by 3.

For a variable that's increased or decreased by only 1, C++ provides two unary operators: increment and decrement operators. Using the **increment operator**,[4] ++, the expression variable = variable + 1 can be replaced by the expression variable++ or the expression ++variable. Here are examples of the increment operator:

Expression	Alternative
i = i + 1	i++ or ++i
n = n + 1	n++ or ++n
count = count + 1	count++ or ++count

Program 3.4 illustrates the use of the increment operator. It displays the following output:

```
The initial value of count is 0
    count is now 1
    count is now 2
    count is now 3
    count is now 4
```

---

[4]As a historical note, the ++ in C++'s name was inspired by the increment operator symbol. It was used to indicate that C++ was the next increment to the C language.

Program 3.4

```cpp
#include <iostream>
using namespace std;

int main()
{
  int count;

  count = 0;
  cout << "The initial value of count is " << count << endl;
  count++;
  cout << "   count is now " << count << endl;
  count++;
  cout << "   count is now " << count << endl;
  count++;
  cout << "   count is now " << count << endl;
  count++;
  cout << "   count is now " << count << endl;

  return 0;
}
```

When the ++ operator appears before a variable, it's called a **prefix increment operator**; when it appears after a variable, it's called a **postfix increment operator**. The distinction between a prefix and postfix increment operator is important when the variable being incremented is used in an assignment expression. For example, k = ++n, which uses a prefix increment operator, does two things in one expression: The value of n is incremented by 1, and then the new value of n is assigned to the variable k. Therefore, the statement k = ++n; is equivalent to these two statements:

```cpp
n = n + 1;   // increment n first
k = n;       // assign n's value to k
```

The assignment expression k = n++, which uses a postfix increment operator, reverses this procedure. A postfix increment operator works after the assignment is completed. Therefore, the statement k = n++; first assigns the current value of n to k, and then increments the value of n by 1. This process is equivalent to these two statements:

```cpp
k = n;       // assign n's value to k
n = n + 1;   // and then increment n
```

C++ also provides the decrement operator, --, in prefix and postfix variations. As you might expect, both the expressions variable-- and --variable are equivalent to the expression variable = variable - 1. Here are examples of the decrement operator:

Expression	Alternative
i = i - 1	i-- or --i
n = n - 1	n-- or --n
count = count - 1	count-- or --count

When the -- operator appears before a variable, it's called a **prefix decrement operator**. When this operator appears after a variable, it's called a **postfix decrement operator**. For example, both the expressions n-- and --n reduce the value of n by 1 and are equivalent to the longer expression n = n - 1.

As with the increment operators, however, the prefix and postfix decrement operators produce different results when used in assignment expressions. For example, the expression k = --n first decrements the value of n by 1 before assigning the value of n to k, and the expression k = n-- first assigns the current value of n to k, and then reduces the value of n by 1.

EXERCISES 3.1

1. **(Practice)** Write an assignment statement to calculate the circumference of a circle having a radius of 3.3 inches. The formula for determining the circumference, c, of a circle is $c = 2\pi r$, where r is the radius and π equals 3.1416.

2. **(Practice)** Write an assignment statement to calculate the area of a circle. The formula for determining the area, a, of a circle is $a = \pi r^2$, where r is the radius and $\pi = 3.1416$.

3. **(Practice)** Write an assignment statement to convert temperature in degrees Fahrenheit to degrees Celsius. The formula for this conversion is *Celsius = 5.0 / 9.0 (Fahrenheit - 32)*.

4. **(Practice)** Write an assignment statement to calculate the round-trip distance, d, in feet, of a trip that's s miles long one way.

5. **(Practice)** Write an assignment statement to calculate the elapsed time, in minutes, it takes to make a trip. The formula for computing elapsed time is *elapsed time = total distance / average speed*. Assume the distance is in miles and the average speed is in miles per hour (mph).

6. **(Practice)** Write an assignment statement to calculate the value, v, of the *n*th term in an arithmetic sequence. The formula for calculating this value is as follows:

v = a + (n - 1)d

   a is the first number in the sequence.
   d is the difference between any two numbers in the sequence.

Assignment Operators

7. **(Practice)** Write an assignment statement to determine the maximum bending moment, M, of a beam, given this formula:

$M = X W (L - X) / L$

X is the distance from the end of the beam that a weight, W, is placed.
L is the length of the beam.

8. **(Debug)** Determine and correct the errors in the following programs.

a.
```cpp
#include <iostream>
using namespace std;
int main()
{
  width = 15
  area = length * width;
  cout << "The area is " << area


}
```

b.
```cpp
#include <iostream>
using namespace std;
int main()
{
  int length, width, area;
  area = length * width;
  length = 20;
  width = 15;
  cout << "The area is " << area;

  return 0;
```

c.
```cpp
#include <iostream>

int main()
{
  int length = 20; width = 15, area;
  length * width = area;
  cout << "The area is " , area;

  return 0;
}
```

9. **(Debug)** By mistake, a student reordered the statements in Program 3.3 as follows:

```cpp
#include <iostream>
using namespace std;
```

```
int main()
{
  int sum;
  sum = 0;
  sum = sum + 96;
  sum = sum + 70;
  sum = sum + 85;
  sum = sum + 60;
  cout << "The value of sum is initially set to "
       << sum << endl;
  cout << "  sum is now " << sum << endl;
  cout << "  sum is now " << sum << endl;
  cout << "  sum is now " << sum << endl;
  cout << "  The final sum is " << sum << endl;

  return 0;
}
```

Determine the output this program produces.

10. **(Practice)** Using Program 3.1, complete the following chart by determining the area of a rectangle having these lengths and widths:

Length (in.)	Width (in.)	Area
1.62	6.23	
2.86	7.52	
4.26	8.95	
8.52	10.86	
12.29	15.35	

11. **(Program)** The area of an ellipse (see Figure 3.4) is given by this formula:

Area = π *a b*

Using this formula, write a C++ program to calculate the area of an ellipse having a minor axis, *a*, of 2.5 inches and a major axis, *b*, of 6.4 inches.

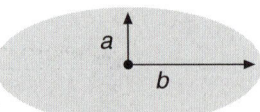

Figure 3.4   The minor axis, a, and the major axis, b, of an ellipse

12. **(Program) a.** Write a C++ program to calculate the dollar amount contained in a piggybank. The bank currently contains 12 half-dollars, 20 quarters, 32 dimes, 45 nickels, and 27 pennies.
b. Run the program written for Exercise 12a on a computer.

13. **(Program) a.** Write a C++ program to calculate the distance, in feet, of a trip that's 2.36 miles long. One mile is equal to 5280 feet.

    b. Run the program written for Exercise 13a on a computer.

14. **(Program) a.** Write a C++ program to calculate the elapsed time it takes to make a 183.67-mile trip. The equation for computing elapsed time is *elapsed time = total distance / average speed*. Assume that the average speed during the trip is 58 miles per hour.

    b. Run the program written for Exercise 14a on a computer.

15. **(Program) a.** Write a C++ program to calculate the sum of the numbers from 1 to 100. The formula for calculating this sum is *sum = (n / 2) × (2 × a + (n - 1) × d)*, where *n* = number of terms to be added, *a* = the first number, and *d* = the difference between each number and the next number (*d* = 1).

    b. Run the program written for Exercise 15a on a computer.

16. **(For thought)** Determine why the expression a - b = 25 is invalid but the expression a - (b = 25) is valid.

3.2 Formatted Output

Besides displaying correct results, a program should present its results attractively. In fact, most programs are judged on the perceived ease of data entry and the style and presentation of the output. For example, displaying a monetary result as 1.897 isn't in keeping with accepted report conventions. The display should be $1.90 or $1.89, depending on whether rounding or truncation is used.

To control the format of numbers displayed by cout, you can include **field width manipulators** in an output stream. Table 3.1 lists the most common stream manipulators for this purpose.[5]

Table 3.1 Commonly Used Stream Manipulators

Manipulator	Action
setw(*n*)	Set the field width to *n*.
setprecision(*n*)	Set the floating-point precision to *n* places. If the **fixed** manipulator is designated, *n* specifies the total number of displayed digits after the decimal point; otherwise, *n* specifies the total number of significant digits displayed (integer plus fractional digits).
setfill('*x*')	Set the default leading fill character to *x*. (The default leading fill character is a space, which is used to fill the beginning of an output field when the field width is larger than the value being displayed.)
setiosflags(*flags*)	Set the format flags. (See Table 3.3 for flag settings.)
scientific	Set the output to display real numbers in scientific notation.
showbase	Display the base used for numbers. A leading 0 is displayed for octal numbers and a leading 0x for hexadecimal numbers.

---

[5]As noted in Chapter 2, the endl manipulator inserts a new line and then forces all current insertions to be displayed immediately, called "flushing the stream."

Table 3.1   Commonly Used Stream Manipulators (*continued*)

Manipulator	Action
showpoint	Always display six digits total (combination of integer and fractional parts). Fill with trailing zeros, if necessary. For larger integer values, revert to scientific notation.
showpos	Display all positive numbers with a leading + sign.
boolalpha	Display Boolean values as **true** and **false** rather than 1 and 0.
dec	Set the output for decimal display, which is the default.
endl	Output a newline character and display all characters in the buffer.
fixed	Always show a decimal point and use a default of six digits after the decimal point. Fill with trailing zeros, if necessary.
flush	Display all characters in the buffer.
left	Left-justify all numbers.
hex	Set the output for hexadecimal display.
oct	Set the output for octal display.
uppercase	Display hexadecimal digits and the exponent in scientific notation in uppercase.
right	Right-justify all numbers (the default).
noboolalpha	Display Boolean values as 1 and 0 rather than **true** and **false**.
noshowbase	Don't display octal numbers with a leading 0 and hexadecimal numbers with a leading 0x.
noshowpoint	Don't use a decimal point for real numbers with no fractional parts, don't display trailing zeros in the fractional part of a number, and display a maximum of six decimal digits only.
noshowpos	Don't display leading + signs (the default).
nouppercase	Display hexadecimal digits and the exponent in scientific notation in lowercase.

For example, the statement

```
cout << "The sum of 6 and 15 is" << setw(3) << 21;
```

creates this printout:

```
The sum of 6 and 15 is 21
```

The setw(3) field width manipulator included in the data stream sent to cout is used to set the displayed field width. The 3 in this manipulator sets the default field width for the next number in the stream to be three spaces. This field width setting causes the 21 to be printed in a field of three spaces, which includes one blank and the number 21. As shown in this output, integers are right-justified in the specified field.

Field width manipulators are useful in printing columns of numbers so that the numbers align correctly in each column. For example, Program 3.5 shows how a column of integers aligns in the absence of field width manipulators.

Program 3.5

```cpp
#include <iostream>
using namespace std;

int main()
{
  cout << 6 << endl
       << 18 << endl
       << 124 << endl
       << "---\n"
       << (6+18+124) << endl;

  return 0;
}
```

The output of Program 3.5 is the following:

```
6
18
124
---
148
```

Because no field width manipulators are used in Program 3.5, the cout object allocates enough space for each number as it's received. Forcing numbers to align on the units digit requires a field width wide enough for the largest displayed number, which is three for the numbers in Program 3.5. Program 3.6 shows the use of this field width.

Program 3.6

```cpp
#include <iostream>
#include <iomanip>
using namespace std;

int main()
{
  cout << setw(3) << 6 << endl
       << setw(3) << 18 << endl
       << setw(3) << 124 << endl
       << "---\n"
       << (6+18+124) << endl;

  return 0;
}
```

The output of Program 3.6 is as follows:

```
  6
 18
124
---
148
```

The field width manipulator must be included for each occurrence of a number inserted in the data stream sent to `cout`. This manipulator applies only to the next insertion of data immediately following it.

When a manipulator requiring an argument is used, the `iomanip` header file must be included as part of the program. To do this, you use the preprocessor command `#include <iomanip>`, which is the second line in Program 3.6.

Formatting floating-point numbers requires using three field width manipulators. The first manipulator sets the total width of the display, the second manipulator forces the display of a decimal point, and the third manipulator determines how many significant digits are displayed to the right of the decimal point. (See the "Point of Information" box in Chapter 2 for a review of significant digits.) For example, examine the following statement:

```
cout << "|" << setw(10) << fixed << setprecision(3) << 25.67 << "|";
```

It causes the following printout:

```
|    25.670|
```

The bar symbol, |, in this example is used to delimit (mark) the beginning and end of the display field. The `setw` manipulator tells `cout` to display the number in a total field of 10. (With real numbers, the decimal point takes up one of these field locations.) The `fixed` manipulator forces the display of a decimal point, and the `setprecision` manipulator designates the number of digits displayed after the decimal point. In this case, `setprecision` specifies a display of three digits after the decimal point. Without the explicit designation of a decimal point (which can also be designated as `setiosflags(ios::fixed)`, explained shortly), the `setprecision` manipulator specifies the total number of displayed digits, which includes the integer and fractional parts of the number.

For all numbers (integers, single-precision, and double-precision), `cout` ignores the `setw` manipulator specification if the total specified field width is too small, and it allocates enough space for printing the integer part of the number. The fractional part of single-precision and double-precision numbers is displayed up to the precision set with the `setprecision` manipulator. (In the absence of `setprecision`, the default precision is set to six decimal places.) If the fractional part of the number to be displayed contains more digits than are called for in the `setprecision` manipulator, the number is rounded to the indicated number of decimal places; if the fractional part contains fewer digits than specified, the number is displayed with fewer digits. Table 3.2 shows the effect of several format manipulator combinations. For clarity, the bar symbol delimits the beginning and end of output fields.

Table 3.2 Effect of Format Manipulators

Manipulators	Number	Display	Comments
setw(2)	3	| 3|	Number fits in the field.
setw(2)	43	|43|	Number fits in the field.
setw(2)	143	|143|	Field width is ignored.
setw(2)	2.3	|2.3|	Field width is ignored.
setw(5) fixed setprecision(2)	2.366	| 2.37|	Field width of five with two decimal digits.
setw(5) fixed setprecision(2)	42.3	|42.30|	Number fits in the field with the specified precision. Note that the decimal point takes up one location in the field width.
setw(5) setprecision(2)	142.364	|1.4e+002|	Field width is ignored, and scientific notation is used with the setprecision manipulator.
setw(5) fixed setprecision(2)	142.364	|142.36|	Field width is ignored, but precision specification is used. The setprecision manipulator specifies the number of fractional digits.
setw(5) fixed setprecision(2)	142.366	|142.37|	Field width is ignored, but precision specification is used. The setprecision manipulator specifies the number of fractional digits. (Note the rounding of the last decimal digit.)
setw(5) fixed setprecision(2)	142	| 142|	Field width is used; fixed and setprecision manipulators are irrelevant because the number is an integer that specifies the total number of significant digits (integer plus fractional digits).

The setiosflags() Manipulator[6]

In addition to the setw and setprecision manipulators, a field justification manipulator is available. As you have seen, numbers sent to cout are normally right-justified in the display field, and strings are left-justified. To alter the default justification for a stream of data, you use the setiosflags manipulator. For example, the statement

```
cout << "|" << setw(10) << setiosflags(ios::left) << 142 << "|";
```

causes the following left-justified display:

```
|142       |
```

---

[6]This topic can be omitted on first reading without loss of subject continuity.

Point of Information

What Is a Flag?

In current programming usage, the term **flag** refers to an item, such as a variable or an argument, that sets a condition usually considered active or nonactive. Although the exact origin of this term in programming is unknown, it probably came from using real flags to signal a condition, such as the Stop, Go, Caution, and Winner flags commonly used at car races.

In a similar manner, each flag argument for the `setiosflags()` manipulator function activates a specific condition. For example, the `ios::dec` flag sets the display format to decimal, and the `ios::oct` flag activates the octal display format. Because these conditions are mutually exclusive (only one can be active at a time), activating this type of flag deactivates the other flags automatically.

Flags that aren't mutually exclusive, such as `ios::dec`, `ios::showpoint`, and `ios::fixed`, can be set simultaneously. You can do this by using three separate `setiosflag()` calls or combining all arguments into one call as follows:

```
cout << setiosflags(ios::dec | ios::fixed | ios::showpoint);
```

Because data passed to `cout` can be continued across multiple lines, the previous display is also produced by this statement:

```
cout << "|" << setw(10)
     << setiosflags(ios::left)
     << 142 << "|";
```

To right-justify strings in a stream, you use the `setiosflags(ios::right)` manipulator. The letters "ios" in the function name and the `ios::right` argument come from the first letters of the words "input output stream."

In addition to the `left` and `right` flags that can be used with `setiosflags()`, other flags can be used to affect output. Table 3.3 lists the most commonly used flags for this manipulator function. The flags in this table provide another way of setting the manipulators listed in Table 3.1.

Table 3.3   Format Flags for Use with `setiosflags()`

Flag	Meaning
`ios::fixed`	Always show the decimal point with six digits following it. Fill with trailing zeros after the decimal point, if necessary. This flag takes precedence if it's set with the `ios::showpoint` flag.
`ios::scientific`	Use exponential display in the output.
`ios::showpoint`	Always display a decimal point and six significant digits total (combination of integer and fractional parts). For larger integer values, revert to scientific notation unless the `ios::fixed` flag is set.
`ios::showpos`	Display a leading + sign when the number is positive.

Table 3.3   Format Flags for Use with `setiosflags()` (*continued*)

Flag	Meaning
`ios::left`	Left-justify the output.
`ios::right`	Right-justify the output.

Because the flags in Table 3.3 are used as arguments to `setiosflags()` and the terms "argument" and "parameter" are synonymous, another name for a manipulator method that uses arguments is a **parameterized manipulator**. The following is an example of a parameterized manipulator method:

```
cout << setiosflags(ios::fixed) << setprecision(4);
```

This statement forces all subsequent floating-point numbers sent to the output stream to be displayed with a decimal point and four decimal digits. If the number has fewer than four decimal digits, it's padded with trailing zeros.

Hexadecimal and Octal I/O[7]

In addition to outputting integers in decimal notation, the `oct` and `hex` manipulators are used for conversions to octal and hexadecimal. (Review Section 2.6 if you're unfamiliar with hexadecimal or octal numbers.) Program 3.7 uses these flags in an example of converting a decimal number to its equivalent hexadecimal and octal values. Because decimal is the default display, the `dec` manipulator isn't required in the first output stream.

 **Program 3.7**

```cpp
// a program that illustrates output conversions
#include <iostream>
#include <iomanip>
using namespace std;

int main()
{
  cout << "The decimal (base 10) value of 15 is "
       << 15 << endl;
  cout << "The octal (base 8) value of 15 is "
       << showbase << oct << 15 <<endl;
  cout << "The hexadecimal (base 16) value of 15 is "
       << showbase << hex << 15 << endl;

  return 0;
}
```

---

[7]This topic can be omitted on first reading without loss of subject continuity.

Point of Information

Formatting `cout` Stream Data

Floating-point data in a `cout` output stream can be formatted in precise ways. For example, a common format requirement is to display monetary amounts with two digits after the decimal point, such as 123.45. You can do this with the following statement:

```
cout << setiosflags(ios::fixed)
     << setiosflags(ios::showpoint)
     << setprecision(2);
```

The first manipulator flag, `ios::fixed`, forces all floating-point numbers in the `cout` stream to be displayed in decimal notation. This flag also prevents using scientific notation. The next flag, `ios::showpoint`, tells the stream to always display a decimal point. Finally, the `setprecision` manipulator tells the stream to always display two digits after the decimal point. Instead of using manipulators, you can use the `cout` stream methods `setf()` and `precision()`. For example, the previous formatting can also be accomplished with this code:

```
cout.setf(ios::fixed);
cout.setf(ios::showpoint);
cout.precision(2);
```

Note the syntax: The name of the object, `cout`, is separated from the method with a period. This format is the standard way of specifying a method and connecting it to a specific object.

Additionally, the flags used in both the `setf()` method and the `setiosflags()` manipulator method can be combined by using the bitwise OR operator, | (explained in Appendix C, available online). Using this operator, the following two statements are equivalent:

```
cout <<  setiosflags(ios::fixed | ios::showpoint);
cout.setf(ios::fixed | ios::showpoint);
```

The statement you select is a matter of personal preference or a predefined standard.

This is the output produced by Program 3.7:

```
The decimal (base 10) value of 15 is 15
The octal (base 8) value of 15 is 017
The hexadecimal (base 16) value of 15 is 0xf
```

The display of integer values in one of three possible numbering systems (decimal, octal, and hexadecimal) doesn't affect how the number is stored in a computer. All numbers are stored by using the computer's internal codes. The manipulators sent to cout tell the object how to convert the internal code for output display purposes.

Besides integers being displayed in octal or hexadecimal form, they can also be written in a program in these forms. To designate an octal integer, the number must have a leading zero. The number 023, for example, is an octal number in C++. Hexadecimal numbers are denoted with a leading 0x. Program 3.8 shows how octal and hexadecimal integer numbers are used.

 **Program 3.8**

```cpp
#include <iostream>
using namespace std;

int main()
{
  cout << "The decimal value of 025 is " << 025 << endl
       << "The decimal value of 0x37 is "<< 0x37 << endl;

  return 0;
}
```

Program 3.8 produces the following output:

```
The decimal value of 025 is 21
The decimal value of 0x37 is 55
```

Figure 3.5 shows the relationship between input, storage, and display of integers.

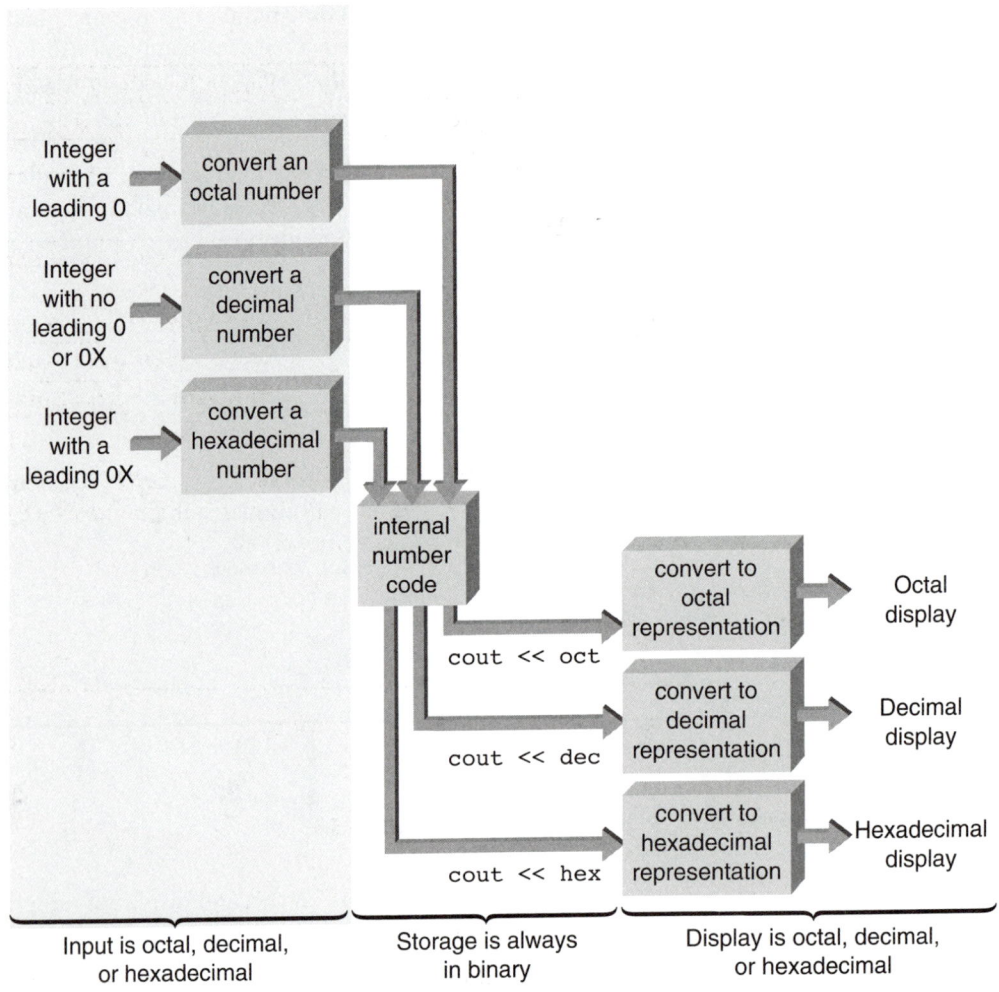

Figure 3.5   Input, storage, and display of integers

Finally, you can set the manipulators listed in Tables 3.1 and 3.2 by using the `ostream` class methods listed in Table 3.4.

Table 3.4 `ostream` Class Methods

Method	Comment	Example
`precision(n)`	Equivalent to `setprecision()`	`cout.precision(2)`
`fill('x')`	Equivalent to `setfill()`	`cout.fill('*')`
`setf(ios::fixed)`	Equivalent to `cout.setf(ios::fixed)`	`setiosflags(ios::fixed)`
`setf(ios::showpoint)`	Equivalent to `cout.setf(ios::showpoint)`	`setiosflags(ios::showpoint)`
`setf(iof::left)`	Equivalent to `left`	`cout.setf(ios::left)`
`setf(ios::right)`	Equivalent to `right`	`cout.setf(ios::right)`
`setf(ios::flush)`	Equivalent to `endl`	`cout.setf(ios::flush)`

In the Example column of Table 3.4, notice that the name of the object, cout, is separated from the method with a period. As mentioned, this format is the standard way of calling a class method and providing an object for it to operate on.

EXERCISES 3.2

1. **(Debug)** Determine the errors in the following statements:
   a. `cout << "\n << " 15)`
   b. `cout << "setw(4)" << 33;`
   c. `cout << "setprecision(5)" << 526.768;`
   d. `"Hello World!" >> cout;`
   e. `cout << 47 << setw(6);`
   f. `cout << set(10) << 526.768 << setprecision(2);`

2. **(Desk check)** Determine and write out the display produced by the following statements:
   a. `cout << "|" << 5 <<"|";`
   b. `cout << "|" << setw(4) << 5 << "|";`
   c. `cout << "|" << setw(4) << 56829 << "|";`
   d. `cout << "|" << setw(5)  << setiosflags(ios::fixed)`
      `     << setprecision(2) << 5.26 << "|";`
   e. `cout << "|" << setw(5)  << setiosflags(ios::fixed)`
      `     << setprecision(2) << 5.267 << "|";`
   f. `cout << "|" << setw(5)  << setiosflags(ios::fixed)`
      `     << setprecision(2) << 53.264 << "|";`
   g. `cout << "|" << setw(5)  << setiosflags(ios::fixed)`
      `     << setprecision(2) << 534.264 << "|";`
   h. `cout << "|" << setw(5)  << setiosflags(ios::fixed)`
      `     << setprecision(2) << 534. << "|";`

3. (Desk check) Write out the display produced by the following statements:

   a. ```
   cout << "The number is " << setw(6) << setiosflags(ios::fixed)
         << setprecision(2)   << 26.27 << endl;
   cout << "The number is " << setw(6) << setiosflags(ios::fixed)
         << setprecision(2)   << 682.3 << endl;
   cout << "The number is " << setw(6) << setiosflags(ios::fixed)
         << setprecision(2)   << 1.968 << endl;
   ```

   b. ```
   cout << setw(6) << setiosflags(ios::fixed)
         << setprecision(2) << 26.27 << endl;
   cout << setw(6) << setiosflags(ios::fixed)
         << setprecision(2) << 682.3 << endl;
   cout << setw(6) << setiosflags(ios::fixed)
         << setprecision(2) << 1.968 << endl;
   cout << "------\n";
   cout << setw(6) << setiosflags(ios::fixed)
         << setprecision(2)
         << 26.27 + 682.3 + 1.968 << endl;
   ```

   c. ```
   cout << setw(5) << setiosflags(ios::fixed)
         << setprecision(2) << 26.27 << endl;
   cout << setw(5) << setiosflags(ios::fixed)
         << setprecision(2) << 682.3 << endl;
   cout << setw(5) << setiosflags(ios::fixed)
         << setprecision(2) << 1.968 << endl;
   cout << "-----\n";
   cout << setw(5) << setiosflags(ios::fixed)
         << setprecision(2)
         << 26.27 + 682.3 + 1.968 << endl;
   ```

   d. ```
   cout << setw(5) << setiosflags(ios::fixed)
         << setprecision(2) << 36.164 << endl;
   cout << setw(5) << setiosflags(ios::fixed)
         << setprecision(2) << 10.003 << endl;
   cout << "-----" << endl;
   ```

4. (Desk check) The following chart lists the equivalent octal and hexadecimal representations for the decimal numbers 1 through 15:

Decimal:	1	2	3	4	5	6	7	8	9	10	11	12	13	14	15
Octal:	1	2	3	4	5	6	7	10	11	12	13	14	15	16	17
Hexadecimal:	1	2	3	4	5	6	7	8	9	a	b	c	d	e	f

Using this chart, determine the output of the following program:

```
#include <iostream>
#include <iomanip>
using namespace std;

int main()
{
```

```
    cout << "\nThe value of 14 in octal is " << oct << 14
         << "\nThe value of 14 in hexadecimal is " << hex << 14
         << "\nThe value of 0xA in decimal is " << dec << 0xA
         << "\nThe value of 0xA in octal is " << oct << 0xA
         << endl;

    return 0;
}
```

5. **(Program)** Write a C++ program to calculate and display the value of the slope of the line connecting two points with the coordinates (3,7) and (8,12). Use the fact that the slope between two points at the coordinates (x_1,y_1) and (x_2,y_2) is slope = $(y_2 - y_1) / (x_2 - x_1)$. Your program should produce this display:

```
The value of the slope is xxx.xx
```

The **xxx.xx** denotes placing the calculated value in a field wide enough for three places to the left of the decimal point and two places to the right of it.

6. **(Program)** Write a C++ program to calculate and display the midpoint coordinates of the line connecting the two points with coordinates of (3,7) and (8,12). Use the fact that the midpoint coordinates between two points with the coordinates (x_1,y_1) and (x_2,y_2) are $((x_2 + x_1) / 2,$ $(y_2 + y_1) / 2)$. Your program should produce this display:

```
The x coordinate of the midpoint is xxx.xx
The y coordinate of the midpoint is xxx.xx
```

The **xxx.xx** denotes placing the calculated value in a field wide enough for three places to the left of the decimal point and two places to the right of it.

Verify your program using the following test data:

    Test data set 1: Point 1 = (0,0) and Point 2 = (16,0)
    Test data set 2: Point 1 = (0,0) and Point 2 = (0,16)
    Test data set 3: Point 1 = (0,0) and Point 2 = (-16,0)
    Test data set 4: Point 1 = (0,0) and Point 2 = (0,-16)
    Test data set 5: Point 1 = (-5,-5) and Point 2 = (5,5)

When you have completed your verification, use your program to complete the following table.

```
Point 1        Point 2        Midpoint
-------        -------        --------
(4,6)          (16,18)
(22,3)         (8,12)
(-10,8)        (14,4)
(-12,2)        (14,3.1)
(3.1,-6)       (20,16)
(3.1,-6)       (-16,-18)
```

7. **(Program)** The change remaining after an amount is used to pay a restaurant bill of amount check can be calculated by using the following C++ statements:

```
// determine the number of pennies in the change
    change = (paid - check) * 100;
// determine the number of dollars in the change
    dollars = (int) (change/100);
```

   a. Using the previous statements as a starting point, write a C++ program that calculates the number of dollar bills, quarters, dimes, nickels, and pennies in the change when $10 is used to pay a bill of $6.07.

   b. Without compiling or running your program, check the effect, by hand, of each statement in the program and determine what's stored in each variable as each statement is encountered.

   c. When you have verified that your algorithm works correctly, compile and run your program. Verify that the result produced by your program is correct, and then use your program to determine the change when a check of $12.36 is paid with a 20-dollar bill.

8. **(Program)** Write a C++ program to calculate and display the maximum bending moment, M, of a beam that's supported on both ends (see Figure 3.6). The formula is $M = XW (L - X) / L$, where X is the distance from the end of the beam that a weight, W, is placed, and L is the length of the beam. Your program should produce this display:

`The maximum bending moment is xxxx.xxxx`

The xxxx.xxxx denotes placing the calculated value in a field wide enough for four places to both the right and left of the decimal point.

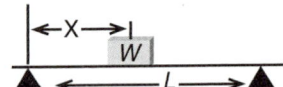

Figure 3.6   Calculating the maximum bending moment

3.3 Mathematical Library Functions

As you have seen, assignment statements can be used to perform arithmetic computations. For example, the following assignment statement multiplies the value in `unitPrice` times the value in `amount` and assigns the resulting value to `totalPrice`:

`totalPrice = unitPrice * amount;`

Although addition, subtraction, multiplication, and division are easily accomplished with C++'s arithmetic operators, no operators exist for raising a number to a power, finding a number's square root, or determining trigonometric values. To perform these calculations, C++ provides standard preprogrammed functions that can be included in a program. Before using one of these mathematical functions, you need to know the following:

- The name of the mathematical function
- What the mathematical function does

- The type of data the mathematical function requires
- The data type of the result the mathematical function returns
- How to include the mathematical library

To illustrate the use of C++'s mathematical functions, take a look at the mathematical function sqrt(), which calculates a number's square root and uses this form:

sqrt(*number*)

The function's name—in this case, sqrt—is followed by parentheses containing the number for which the square root should be calculated. The purpose of the parentheses after the function name is to provide a funnel through which data can be passed to the function (see Figure 3.7). The items passed to the function through the parentheses are called **arguments** of the function, as you learned in Chapter 1, and constitute its input data. For example, the following expressions are used to compute the square root of the arguments 4., 17.0, 25., 1043.29, and 6.4516:

sqrt(4.)
sqrt(17.0)
sqrt(25.)
sqrt(1043.29)
sqrt(6.4516)

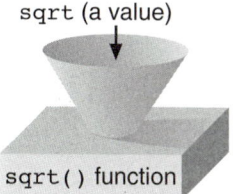

Figure 3.7 Passing data to the sqrt() function

Notice that the argument to the sqrt() function must be a real value, which is an example of C++'s function-overloading capabilities. **Function overloading** permits using the same function name for arguments of different data types.[8] C++ has three functions named sqrt()—defined for float, double, and long double arguments. The correct sqrt() function is called depending on the type of value passed to the function when the call is made. When one of the functions named sqrt() is called (again, the selection is automatic, based on

---

[8]If overloading wasn't supported, three separate square root functions, each with a different name, would have to be defined—one for each type of argument.

the passed argument), the function determines the square root of its argument and returns the result as a `double`. The previous expressions return these values:

Expression	Value Returned
`sqrt(4.)`	2.
`sqrt(17.0)`	4.12311
`sqrt(25.)`	5.
`sqrt(1043.29)`	32.3
`sqrt(6.4516)`	2.54

In addition to the `sqrt()` function, Table 3.5 lists commonly used mathematical functions provided in C++. Accessing these functions in a program requires including the mathematical header file `cmath`, which contains declarations for the mathematical function. To use this header file, place the following preprocessor statement at the top of any program using a mathematical function:

```
#include <cmath>
```

Although some mathematical functions in Table 3.5 require more than one argument, all functions, by definition, can return at most one value. Additionally, all the functions listed are overloaded, which means the same function name can be used with different argument data types. Table 3.6 shows the value returned by selected functions, using sample arguments.

Table 3.5 Common C++ Functions

Function Name	Description	Returned Value
`abs(a)`	Absolute value	Same data type as argument
`pow(a1,a2)`	a1 raised to the a2 power	Same data type as argument a1
`sqrt(a)`	Square root of a real number (*Note*: An integer argument results in a compiler error.)	Double-precision
`sin(a)`	Sine of a (a in radians)	Double-precision
`cos(a)`	Cosine of a (a in radians)	Double-precision
`tan(a)`	Tangent of a (a in radians)	Double-precision
`log(a)`	Natural logarithm of a	Double-precision
`log10(a)`	Common log (base 10) of a	Double-precision
`exp(a)`	e raised to the a power	Double-precision

Table 3.6 Selected Function Examples

Example	Returned Value
abs(-7.362)	7.362
abs(-3)	3
pow(2.0,5.0)	32.
pow(10,3)	1000
log(18.697)	2.92836
log10(18.697)	1.27177
exp(-3.2)	0.040762

Each time a mathematical function is used, it's called into action (referred to as **invoking** or **calling** the function) by giving the name of the function and passing to it any data in the parentheses following the function's name (see Figure 3.8).

function-name (data passed to the function);

This identifies   This passes data to
the called   the function
function

Figure 3.8 Using and passing data to a function

The arguments passed to a function need not be single constants. Expressions can also be arguments, provided the expression can be computed to yield a value of the required data type. For example, the following arguments are valid for the given functions:

```
sqrt(4.0 + 5.3 * 4.0)          abs(2.3 * 4.6)
sqrt(16.0 * 2.0 - 6.7)         sin(theta - phi)
sqrt(x * y - z/3.2)            cos(2.0 * omega)
```

The expressions in parentheses are evaluated first to yield a specific value. Therefore, values have to be assigned to the variables theta, phi, x, y, z, and omega before their use in the preceding expressions. After the value of the argument is calculated, it's passed to the function.

Functions can also be included as part of larger expressions, as shown in this example:

```
4 * sqrt(4.5 * 10.0 - 9.0) - 2.0
=   4 * sqrt(36.0) - 2.0
=   4 * 6.0 - 2.0
=   24.0 - 2.0
=   22.0
```

The step-by-step evaluation of an expression such as

```
3.0 * sqrt(5 * 33 - 13.71) / 5
```

is as follows:

Step	Result
1. Perform multiplication in the argument.	`3.0 * sqrt(165 - 13.71) / 5`
2. Complete the argument calculation.	`3.0 * sqrt(151.29) / 5`
3. Return a function value.	`3.0 * 12.3 / 5`
4. Perform the multiplication.	`36.9 / 5`
5. Perform the division.	`7.38`

Program 3.9 shows using the `sqrt()` function to determine the time it takes a ball to hit the ground after it has been dropped from an 800-foot tower. The mathematical formula for calculating the time in seconds it takes for the ball to fall a given distance in feet is as follows, where g is the gravitational constant equal to 32.2 ft/sec^2:

$time = sqrt(2 \times distance / g)$

Program 3.9

```cpp
#include <iostream> // this line can be placed second instead of first
#include <cmath>    // this line can be placed first instead of second
using namespace std;

int main()
{
  int height;
  double time;

  height = 800;
  time = sqrt(2 * height / 32.2);
  cout << "It will take " << time << " seconds to fall "
       << height << " feet.\n";

  return 0;
}
```

Program 3.9 produces this output:

```
It will take 7.04907 seconds to fall 800 feet.
```

As used in Program 3.9, the value that the `sqrt()` function returns is assigned to the variable `time`. In addition to assigning a function's returned value to a variable, the returned value can be included in a larger expression or even used as an argument to another function. For example, the following expression is valid:

```
sqrt( sin( abs(theta) ) )
```

Because parentheses are present, the computation proceeds from the inner to outer pairs of parentheses. Therefore, the absolute value of `theta` is computed first and used as an argument to the `sin()` function. The value the `sin()` function returns is then used as an argument to the `sqrt()` function.

Note that the arguments of all trigonometric functions (`sin()`, `cos()`, and so forth) must be in radians. Therefore, to calculate the sine of an angle given in degrees, the angle must be converted to radians first. You can do this easily by multiplying the angle by the term (`3.1416/180.`). For example, to obtain the sine of 30 degrees, use the expression `sin (30 * 3.1416/180.)`.

Casts

You have already seen the conversion of an operand's data type in mixed-mode arithmetic expressions (Section 2.2) and with different operators (Section 3.1). In addition to these implicit data type conversions made automatically in mixed-mode arithmetic and assignment expressions, C++ provides for explicit user-specified type conversions. The operator used to force converting a value to another type is the **cast operator**. C++ provides compile-time and runtime cast operators. The compile-time cast is a unary operator with this syntax:

```
dataType (expression)
```

The `dataType` is the data type to which the expression in parentheses is converted. For example, the following expression converts the value of the expression `a * b` to an integer value:[9]

```
int (a * b)
```

Runtime casts are also included in C++. In this type of cast, the requested type conversion is checked at runtime and applied if the conversion results in a valid value. Although four types of runtime casts are available, the most commonly used cast and the one corresponding to the compile-time cast has the following syntax:

```
staticCast<dataType> (expression)
```

For example, the runtime cast `staticCast<int>(a * b)` is equivalent to the compile-time cast `int (a* b)`.

---

[9]The C type cast syntax, in this case `(int)(a * b)`, also works in C++.

EXERCISES 3.3

1. **(Practice)** Write function calls to determine the following:
   a. The square root of 6.37
   b. The square root of x - y
   c. The sine of 30 degrees
   d. The sine of 60 degrees
   e. The absolute value of $a^2 - b^2$
   f. The value of e raised to the third power

2. **(Practice)** For a = 10.6, b = 13.9, and c = -3.42, determine the following values:
   a. `int (a)`
   b. `int (b)`
   c. `int (c)`
   d. `int (a + b)`
   e. `int (a) + b + c`
   f. `int (a + b) + c`
   g. `int (a + b + c)`
   h. `double (int (a)) + b`
   i. `double (int (a + b))`
   j. `abs(a) + abs(b)`
   k. `sqrt(abs(a - b))`

3. **(Practice)** Write C++ statements for the following:
   a. $area = (c \times b \times \sin a) / 2$
   b. $c = \sqrt{a^2 + b^2}$
   c. $p = \sqrt{|m - n|}$
   d. $sum = \dfrac{a\left(r^n - 1\right)}{r - 1}$
   e. $b = \sin^2 x - \cos^2 x$

4. **(Program)** Write, compile, and run a C++ program that calculates and returns the fourth root of the number 81.0, which is 3. After verifying that your program works correctly, use it to determine the fourth root of 1,728.896400. Your program should make use of the `sqrt()` function or use the fact that the fourth root of a value can be obtained by raising the value to the 1/4 power.

5. **(Program)** The volume of oil stored in an underground 200-foot deep cylindrical tank is determined by measuring the distance from the top of the tank to the surface of the oil. Knowing this distance and the radius of the tank, the volume of oil in the tank can be determined by using this formula:

   volume = π radius² (200 - distance)

Using this information, write, compile, and run a C++ program that determines the volume of oil in a 200-foot tank that has a radius of 10 feet and measures 12 feet from the top of the tank to the top of the oil. Your program should display the radius, distance from the top of the tank to the oil, and the calculated volume.

6. **(Program)** The circumference of an ellipse (review Figure 3.4) is given by this formula:

$$Circumference = \pi\sqrt{\left(a+b\right)^2}$$

Using this formula, write a C++ program to calculate the circumference of an ellipse with a minor radius, a, of 2.5 inches and a major radius, b, of 6.4 inches.

7. **(Program)** Write, compile, and run a C++ program to calculate the distance between two points with the coordinates (7, 12) and (3, 9). Use the fact that the distance between two points with the coordinates (x_1, y_1) and (x_2, y_2) is given by this formula:

$$distance = \sqrt{\left(x_2 - x_1\right)^2 + \left(y_2 - y_1\right)^2}$$

After verifying that your program works correctly by calculating the distance between the two points manually, use your program to determine the distance between the points (-12, -15) and (22, 5).

8. **(Program)** If a 20-foot ladder is placed on the side of a building at a 85-degree angle, as shown in Figure 3.9, the height at which the ladder touches the building can be calculated as *height* = 20 × sin 85°. Calculate this height by hand, and then write, compile, and run a C++ program that determines and displays the value of the height. After verifying that your program works correctly, use it to determine the height of a 25-foot ladder placed at an angle of 85 degrees.

Figure 3.9 Calculating the height of a ladder against a building

9. **(Program)** The maximum height reached by a ball thrown with an initial velocity, v, in meters/sec, at an angle of θ is given by this formula:

$$height = (.5 \times v^2 \times sin^2 \theta) / 9.8$$

Using this formula, write, compile, and run a C++ program that determines and displays the maximum height reached when the ball is thrown at 5 mph at an angle of 60 degrees. (*Hint*: Make sure to convert the initial velocity into the correct units. There are 1609 meters in a mile.) Calculate the maximum height manually, and verify the result your program produces. After verifying the result, use your program to determine the height reached by a ball thrown at 7 mph at an angle of 45 degrees.

10. **(Program)** A model of worldwide population growth, in billions of people, since 2000 is given by this formula:

$$Population = 7.5 \ e^{0.02[Year - 2010]}$$

Using this formula, write, compile, and run a C++ program to estimate the worldwide population in the year 2012. Verify the result your program produces by calculating the answer manually, and then use your program to estimate the world's population in the year 2020.

11. **(Program)** The roads of Kansas are laid out in a rectangular grid at exactly one-mile intervals, as shown in Figure 3.10. Farmer Pete drives his 1939 Ford pickup x miles east and y miles north to get to farmer Joe's farm. Both x and y are integer numbers. Using this information, write, test, and run a C++ program that prompts the user for the values of x and y, and then uses this formula to find the shortest driving distance across the fields to Joe's farm:

$$distance = sqrt(x^2 + y^2);$$

Round the answer to the nearest integer value before it's displayed.

12. **(Program)** A model to estimate the number of grams of a radioactive isotope left after t years is given by this formula:

$$remaining \ material = (original \ material) \ e^{-0.00012t}$$

Using this formula, write, compile, and run a C++ program to determine the amount of radioactive material remaining after 1000 years, assuming an initial amount of 100 grams. Verify the display your program produces by using a hand calculation. After verifying that your program is working correctly, use it to determine the amount of radioactive material remaining after 275 years, assuming an initial amount of 250 grams.

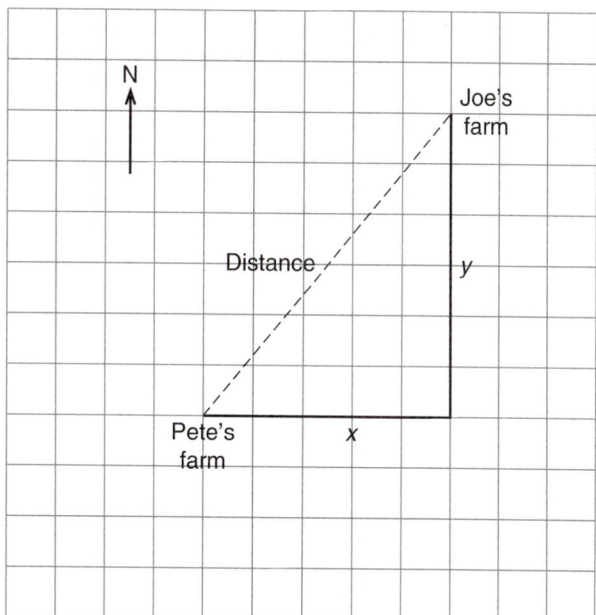

Figure 3.10   Illustration for Exercise 11

13. **(Program)** The number of years it takes for an isotope of uranium to decay to one-half an original amount is given by this formula, where λ, the decay constant (which is equal to the inverse of the mean lifetime), equals 0.00012:

half-life - ln(2) / λ

Using this formula, write, compile, and run a C++ program that calculates and displays the half-life of this uranium isotope. Verify the result your program produces by using a hand calculation. After verifying that your program is working correctly, use it to determine the half-life of a uranium isotope with λ = 0.00026.

14. **(Program) a.** Appendix B lists the integer values corresponding to each letter stored with the ASCII code. Note that uppercase letters consist of contiguous codes, starting with an integer value of 65 for the letter A and ending with 90 for the letter Z. Similarly, lowercase letters begin with the integer value of 97 for the letter a and end with 122 for the letter z. With this information as background, determine the character value of the expressions char ('A' + 32) and char ('Z' + 32).

   b. Using Appendix B, determine the integer value of the expression 'a' - 'A'.

   c. Using the results of Exercises 14a and 14b, determine the character value of the following expression, where *uppercase letter* can be any uppercase letter from A to Z: char (*uppercase letter* + 'a' - 'A').

15. (**Desk check and program**) **a.** For display purposes, the `setprecision()` manipulator allows rounding all outputs to the specified number of decimal places. Doing so can, however, yield seemingly incorrect results when used in financial programs that require displaying all monetary values to the nearest penny. For example, examine this program:

```cpp
#include <iostream>
#include <iomanip>
using namespace std;
int main()
{
   double a, b, c;

   a = 1.674;
   b = 1.322;
   cout << setiosflags(ios::fixed) << setprecision(2);
   cout << a << endl;
   cout << b << endl;
   cout << "----\n";
   c = a + b;
   cout << c << endl;

   return 0;
}
```

It produces the following display:

```
1.67
1.32
----
3.00
```

Clearly, the sum of the displayed numbers should be 2.99, not 3.00. The problem is that although the values in a and b have been displayed with two decimal digits, they were added internally in the program as three-digit numbers. The solution is to round the values in a and b before they're added with the statement c = a + b;. Using the int cast, devise a method to round the values in the variables a and b to the nearest hundredth (penny value) before they're added.

b. Include the method you devised for Exercise 15a in a working program that produces the following display:

```
1.67
1.32
----
2.99
```

3.4 Interactive Keyboard Input

Data for programs to be run only once can be included in the program. For example, if you want to multiply the numbers 30.0 and 0.05, you could use Program 3.10.

Program 3.10

```
#include <iostream>
using namespace std;

int main()
{
  double num1, num2, product;

  num1 = 30.0;
  num2 = 0.05;
  product = num1 * num2;
  cout << "30.0 times 0.05 is " << product << endl;

  return 0;
}
```

This is the output displayed by Program 3.10:

```
30.0 times 0.05 is 1.5
```

Program 3.10 can be shortened, as shown in Program 3.11. Both programs, however, suffer from the same basic problem: They must be rewritten to multiply different numbers. Neither program allows entering different numbers to operate on.

Program 3.11

```
#include <iostream>
using namespace std;

int main()
{

  cout << "30.0 times 0.05 is " << 30.0 * 0.05 << endl;

  return 0;
}
```

Except for the programming practice you get by writing, entering, and running the program, programs that do the same calculation only once, on the same set of numbers, clearly aren't very useful. After all, using a calculator to multiply two numbers is simpler than entering and running Program 3.10 or Program 3.11.

This section explains the `cin` object, which is used to enter data in a program while it's running. Just as the `cout` object displays a copy of the value stored in a variable, the `cin` object allows the user to enter a value at the keyboard (see Figure 3.11). The value is then stored in a variable.

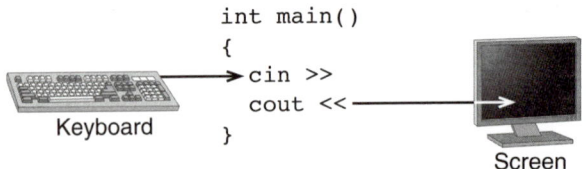

Figure 3.11   `cin` is used to enter data; `cout` is used to display data

When a statement such as `cin >> num1;` is encountered, the computer stops program execution and accepts data from the keyboard. When a data item is typed, the `cin` object stores the item in the variable listed after the extraction ("get from") operator, `>>`. The program then continues execution with the next statement after the call to `cin`. To see how this object works, take a look at Program 3.12.

Program 3.12

```
#include <iostream>
using namespace std;

int main()
{
  double num1, num2, product;

  cout << "Please type in a number: ";
  cin  >> num1;
  cout << "Please type in another number: ";
  cin  >> num2;
  product = num1 * num2;
  cout << num1 << " times " << num2 << " is " << product << endl;

  return 0;
}
```

The first `cout` statement in Program 3.12 prints a string that tells the person at the keyboard what should be typed. When an output string is used in this manner, it's called a **prompt**.

In this case, the prompt tells the user to type a number. The computer then executes the next statement, which activates `cin`. The `cin` object puts the computer into a temporary pause (or wait) state while the user types a value, and then the user signals the `cin` object that the data entry is finished by pressing the Enter key. The entered value is stored in the variable to the right of the extraction operator (`num1`), and the computer is taken out of its paused state.

Program execution proceeds with the next statement, which in Program 3.12 is another `cout` activation that displays a message asking the user to enter another number. The second `cin` statement again puts the computer into a temporary wait state while the user types a second value. This second number is stored in the variable `num2`.

The following sample run was made with Program 3.12; the bold code indicates what the user enters:

```
Please type in a number: 30
Please type in another number: 0.05
30 times 0.05 is 1.5
```

In Program 3.12, each time `cin` is invoked, it's used to store one value in a variable. The `cin` object, however, can be used to enter and store as many values as there are extraction operators and variables to hold the entered data. For example, the statement

```
cin >> num1 >> num2;
```

results in two values being read from the keyboard and assigned to the variables **num1** and **num2**. If the data entered at the keyboard is

```
0.052     245.79
```

the variables **num1** and **num2** contain the values 0.052 and 245.79, respectively. Note that there must be at least one space between numbers when they're entered to clearly indicate where one number ends and the next begins. Inserting more than one space between the numbers has no effect on `cin`.

The same spacing is applicable to entering character data; that is, the extraction operator, >>, skips blank spaces and stores the next nonblank character in a character variable. For example, in response to these statements,

```
char ch1, ch2, ch3; // declare three character variables
cin >> ch1 >> ch2 >> ch3; // accept three characters
```

the input

```
a  b  c
```

causes the letter a to be stored in the variable `ch1`, the letter b to be stored in the variable `ch2`, and the letter c to be stored in the variable `ch3`. Because a character variable can be used to store only one character, the following input, without spaces, can also be used:

```
abc
```

You can make any number of statements with the `cin` object in a program, and any number of values can be entered with a single `cin` statement. Program 3.13 shows using the `cin` object to input three numbers from the keyboard. The program then calculates and displays the average of the entered numbers.

Program 3.13

```cpp
#include <iostream>
using namespace std;

int main()
{
  int num1, num2, num3;
  double average;

  cout << "Enter three integer numbers: ";
  cin  >> num1 >> num2 >> num3;
  average = (num1 + num2 + num3) / 3.0;
  cout << "The average of the numbers is " << average << endl;

  return 0;
}
```

Program 3.13 produces the following output:

```
Enter three integer numbers: 22 56 73
The average of the numbers is 50.3333
```

Note that the data entered at the keyboard for this sample run consists of this input:

```
22   56   73
```

In response to this stream of input, Program 3.13 stores the value 22 in the variable num1, the value 56 in the variable num2, and the value 73 in the variable num3 (see Figure 3.12). Because the average of three integer numbers can be a floating-point number, the variable average, used to store the average, is declared as a double-precision variable. Note also that parentheses are needed in the assignment statement average = (num1 + num2 + num3) / 3.0;. Without the parentheses, the only value divided by 3 would be the integer in num3 (because division has a higher precedence than addition).

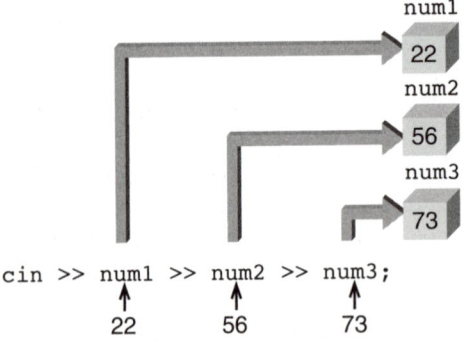

Figure 3.12　Inputting data in the variables num1, num2, and num3

The `cin` extraction operation, like the `cout` insertion operation, is "clever" enough to make a few data type conversions. For example, if an integer is entered in place of a double-precision number, the integer is converted to the correct data type.[10] Similarly, if a double-precision number is entered when an integer is expected, only the integer part of the number is used. For example, assume the following numbers are typed in response to the statement `cin >> num1 >> num2 >> num3;`, where `num1` and `num3` have been declared as double-precision variables and `num2` is an integer variable:

```
56     22.879     33.923
```

The 56 is converted to 56.0 and stored in the variable `num1`. The extraction operation continues, extracting data from the input stream and expecting an integer value. As far as `cin` is concerned, the decimal point in 22.879 indicates the end of an integer and the start of a decimal number. Therefore, the number 22 is assigned to `num2`. Continuing to process its input stream, `cin` takes the .879 as the next double-precision number and assigns it to `num3`. As far as `cin` is concerned, 33.923 is extra input and is ignored. If, however, you don't enter enough data initially, the `cin` object continues to make the computer pause until enough data has been entered.

A First Look at User-Input Validation

A well-constructed program should validate user input and ensure that a program doesn't crash or produce nonsensical output caused by unexpected input. The term **validate** means checking that the entered value matches the data type of the variable it's assigned to in a `cin` statement and the value is within an acceptable range for the application. Programs that detect and respond effectively to unexpected user input are formally called **robust programs** and informally referred to as "bulletproof" programs. One of your jobs as a programmer is to produce robust programs. As written, Programs 3.12 and 3.13 aren't robust programs, and in the following discussion, you see why.

The first problem with these programs becomes evident when a user enters a nonnumerical value. For example, examine the following sample run of Program 3.13:

```
Enter three integer numbers: 10 20.68 20
The average of the numbers is -2.86331e+008
```

This output occurs because the conversion of the second input number results in assigning the integer value 20 to `num2` and the value -858993460 to `num3`. The -858993460 value results because an invalid character, the decimal point, is assigned to a variable that expects an integer value. The average of the numbers 10, 20, and -858993460 is computed correctly as -286331143.3, which is displayed in scientific notation with six significant digits as -2.86331e+008. As far as the average user is concerned, this result would be reported as a program error.

This same problem occurs whenever a noninteger value is entered for either of the first two inputs. (It doesn't occur for any numerical value entered as the third input because the integer part of the last input is accepted, and the remaining input is ignored.) As a programmer,

---

[10]Strictly speaking, what comes in from the keyboard isn't any data type, such as an `int` or a `double`, but is simply a sequence of characters. The extraction operation handles the conversion from the character sequence to a defined data type.

your first response might be "The program clearly asks you to enter integer values." Experienced programmers, however, understand that their responsibility is to ensure that a program anticipates and appropriately handles all inputs users can possibly enter. To achieve this goal, think about what can go wrong with your program as you develop it, and then have another person or group test the program thoroughly.[11]

The basic approach to handling invalid data input is called **user-input validation**, which means checking the entered data during or immediately after it has been entered, and then giving users a way to reenter any invalid data. User-input validation is an essential part of any commercially viable program; if done correctly, it protects a program from attempting to process data that can cause computational problems. You see how to do this type of validation in Chapters 4 and 5, when you learn about C++'s selection and repetition statements.

EXERCISES 3.4

1. **(Practice)** For the following declaration statements, write one or more statements using the `cin` object that causes the computer to pause while the user enters the appropriate data:

   a. `int firstnum;`

   b. `double grade;`

   c. `double secnum;`

   d. `char keyval;`

   e. `int month, years;`
      `double average;`

   f. `char ch;`
      `int num1,num2;`
      `double grade1,grade2;`

   g. `double interest, principal, capital;`
      `double price, yield;`

   h. `char ch,letter1,letter2;`
      `int num1,num2,num3;`

   i. `double temp1,temp2,temp3;`
      `double volts1,volts2;`

2. **(Program) a.** Write, compile, and run a C++ program that displays the following prompts:

   `Enter the length of the room:`
   `Enter the width of the room:`

   After each prompt is displayed, your program should use a `cin` object call to accept data from the keyboard for the displayed prompt. After the width of the room is entered, your program should calculate and display the area of the room. The area displayed should be calculated by using the formula *area = length × width* and should be included in an appropriate message.

   b. Check the area displayed by the program written for Exercise 2a by calculating the result manually.

---

[11] Test specifications are often provided before a program is written, and a team of programmers is assigned to test programs after they're written.

Interactive Keyboard Input

3. **(Program) a.** Write, compile, and run a C++ program that displays the following prompts:

```
Enter the length of the swimming pool:
Enter the width of the swimming pool:
Enter the average depth of the swimming pool:
```

After each prompt is displayed, your program should use a `cin` statement to accept data from the keyboard for the displayed prompt. After the depth of the swimming pool is entered, your program should calculate and display the volume of the pool. The volume should be calculated with the formula *volume = length × width × average depth* and be displayed in an output message.

b. Check the volume displayed by the program written for Exercise 3a by calculating the result manually.

4. **(Program)** Write, compile, and run a C++ program that displays the following prompt:

```
Enter the radius of a circle:
```

After accepting a value for the radius, your program should calculate and display the area of the circle. (*Hint: Area = 3.1416 × radius².*) For testing purposes, verify your program by using an input radius of 3 inches. After manually determining that your program's result is correct, use your program to complete the following chart:

Radius (in)	Area (sq. in)
1.0	
1.5	
2.0	
2.5	
3.0	
3.5	

5. **(Program) a.** Write a C++ program that first displays the following prompt:

```
Enter the temperature in degrees Celsius:
```

Have your program accept a value entered from the keyboard and convert the temperature entered to degrees Fahrenheit, using this formula:

Fahrenheit = (9.0 / 5.0) × Celsius + 32.0

Your program should then display the temperature in degrees Fahrenheit with an output message.

b. Compile and run the program written for Exercise 5a. To verify your program, use the following test data and calculate the Fahrenheit equivalents by hand, and then use your program to see whether you get the same results:

> Test data set 1: 0 degrees Celsius
> Test data set 2: 50 degrees Celsius
> Test data set 3: 100 degrees Celsius

When you're sure your program is working correctly, use it to complete the following chart:

Celsius	Fahrenheit
45	
50	
55	
60	
65	
70	

6. (**Program**) **a.** Write, compile, and run a C++ program that displays the following prompts:

```
Enter the miles driven:
Enter the gallons of gas used:
```

After each prompt is displayed, your program should use a cin statement to accept data from the keyboard for the displayed prompt. After the number for gallons of gas used has been entered, your program should calculate and display the miles per gallon (mpg). This value should be calculated with the formula *miles per gallon = miles / gallons used* and displayed in an output message. Verify your program by using the following test data:

> Test data set 1: miles = 276, gas = 10 gallons
> Test data set 2: miles = 200, gas = 15.5 gallons

After finishing your verification, use your program to complete the following chart. (Make sure to convert the miles driven to kilometers driven, convert gallons used to liters used, and then compute the kilometers per liter. There are 1.61 kilometers per mile and 4.54609 liters per gallon.)

Miles Driven	Gallons Used	Mpg	Km Driven	Liters Used	Km/L
250	16.00				
275	18.00				
312	19.54				
296	17.39				

b. For the program written for Exercise 6a, determine how many verification runs are required to make sure the program is working correctly, and give a reason to support your answer.

7. (**Program**) **a.** Write, compile, and run a C++ program that displays the following prompts:

```
Enter a number:
Enter a second number:
Enter a third number:
Enter a fourth number:
```

After each prompt is displayed, your program should use a cin statement to accept a number from the keyboard for the displayed prompt. After the fourth number has been entered, your program should calculate and display the average of the numbers. The average should be displayed in an output message. Check the average your program calculates by using the following test data:

    Test data set 1: 100, 100, 100, 100
    Test data set 2: 100, 0, 100, 0

After finishing your verification, use your program to complete the following chart:

Numbers	Average
92, 98, 79, 85	
86, 84, 75, 86	
63, 85, 74, 82	

    b. Repeat Exercise 7a, making sure you use the same variable name, number, for each number input. Also, use the variable sum for the sum of the numbers. (*Hint*: To do this, you can use the statement sum = sum + number; after each number is accepted. Review the material on accumulating in Section 3.1.)

8. **(Program)** The perimeter, approximate surface area, and approximate volume of an in-ground pool are given by the following formulas:

perimeter = 2 × (length + width)
volume = length × width × average depth
underground surface area = 2 × (length + width) × average depth + length × width

Using these formulas as a basis, write a C++ program that accepts the length, width, and average depth measurements, and then calculates the pool's perimeter, volume, and underground surface area. In writing your program, make these two calculations immediately after entering the input data: *length × width* and *length + width*. The results of these two calculations should be used, as needed, in the assignment statements for determining the perimeter, volume, and underground surface area without recalculating them for each equation. Verify your program's results by doing a hand calculation, using the following test data: *length* = 25 feet, *width* = 15 feet, and *average depth* = 5.5 feet. After verifying that your program is working, use it to complete the following chart:

Length	Width	Average Depth	Perimeter	Volume	Underground Surface Area
25	10	5.0			
25	10	5.5			
25	10	6.0			
25	10	6.5			
30	12	5.0			
30	12	5.5			
30	12	6.0			
30	12	6.5			

9. **(Program) a.** Write, compile, and run a C++ program to compute and display the value of the second-order polynomial $ax^2 + bx + c$ for any user-entered values of the coefficients a, b, and c and the variable x. Have your program display a message first to inform users what the program does, and then display suitable prompts to alert users to enter data. (*Hint*: Use a prompt such as `Enter the coefficient of the x-squared term:`.)

   b. Check the result of your program written for Exercise 9a by using the following test data:

   Test data set 1: $a = 0$, $b = 0$, $c = 22$, $x = 56$
   Test data set 2: $a = 0$, $b = 22$, $c = 0$, $x = 2$
   Test data set 3: $a = 22$, $b = 0$, $c = 0$, $x = 2$
   Test data set 4: a = 2, b = 4, c = 5, x = 2

   After finishing your verification, use your program to complete the following chart:

a	b	c	x	Polynomial Value ($ax^2 + bx + c$)
2.0	17.0	-12.0	1.3	
3.2	2.0	15.0	2.5	
3.2	2.0	15.0	-2.5	
-2.0	10.0	0.0	2.0	
-2.0	10.0	0.0	4.0	
-2.0	10.0	0.0	5.0	
-2.0	10.0	0.0	6.0	
5.0	22.0	18.0	8.3	
4.2	-16	-20	-5.2	

10. **(Program)** Write, compile, and run a program that calculates and displays the square root value of a user-entered real number. Verify your program by calculating the square roots of this test data: 25, 16, 0, and 2. After finishing your verification, use your program to determine the square roots of 32.25, 42, 48, 55, 63, and 79.

11. **(Program)** Write, compile, and run a program to calculate and display the fourth root of a user-entered number. Recall from elementary algebra that you find the fourth root of a number by raising the number to the 1/4 power. (*Hint*: Don't use integer division—can you see why?) Verify your program by calculating the fourth root of this test data: 81, 16, 1, and 0. When you're finished, use your program to determine the fourth root of 42, 121, 256, 587, 1240, and 16,256.

12. **(Program)** Program 3.12 prompts users to input two numbers; the first value entered is stored in `num1`, and the second value is stored in `num2`. Using this program as a starting point, write a program that swaps the values stored in the two variables.

13. **(Program)** Write a C++ program that prompts users to enter a number. Have your program accept the number as an integer and display the integer immediately by using a `cout` statement. Run your program three times. The first time, enter a valid integer number; the second time, enter a double-precision number; and the third time, enter a character. Using the output display, see what number your program actually accepted from the data you entered.

14. **(Program)** Repeat Exercise 13, but have your program declare the variable used to store the number as a double-precision variable. Run the program three times. The first time, enter an integer; the second time, enter a double-precision number; and the third time, enter a character. Using the output display, keep track of what number your program actually accepted from the data you entered. What happened, if anything, and why?

15. **(For thought) a.** Why do you think successful programs contain extensive data-input validity checks? (*Hint*: Review Exercises 13 and 14.)

    b. What do you think is the difference between a data-type check and a data-reasonableness check?

    c. Assume that a program requests users to enter a month, day, and year. What are some checks that could be made on the data entered?

3.5 Symbolic Constants

Certain constants used in a program have more general meanings that are recognized outside the program's context. Examples of these types of constants include the number 3.1416, which is π accurate to four decimal places; 32.2 ft/sec², which is the gravitational constant; and the number 2.71828, which is Euler's number accurate to five decimal places.

    The meanings of certain other constants used in a program are defined strictly in the context of the application being programmed. For example, in a program used to determine bank interest charges, the interest rate typically appears in a number of different places throughout the program. Similarly, in a program used to calculate taxes, the tax rate might appear in many instructions. Programmers refer to these types of numbers as **magic numbers**. By themselves, the numbers are ordinary, but in the context of a particular application, they have a special ("magical") meaning. When a magic number appears repeatedly in the same program, it becomes a potential source of error if the constant has to be changed. For example, if the interest rate or the sales tax rate changes, as these rates are likely to do, the programmer has the cumbersome task of changing the value everywhere it appears in the program. Multiple changes are subject to error: If just one value is overlooked and remains unchanged, when the program runs the result will be incorrect, and the source of the error will be difficult to locate.

    To avoid the problem of having a magic number spread throughout a program in many places and to identify more universal constants clearly, such as π, C++ enables programmers to give these constants symbolic names. Then the symbolic name instead of the magic number can be used throughout the program. If the number ever has to be changed, the change need be made only once, at the point where the symbolic name is equated to the actual number value. To equate numbers to symbolic names, you use the `const` declaration qualifier, which specifies that the declared identifier is read-only after it's initialized; it can't be changed. Here are three examples of using this qualifier:

```
const double PI = 3.1416;
const double SALESTAX = 0.05;
const int MAXNUM = 100;
```

    The first declaration statement creates a double-precision variable named `PI` and initializes it with the value 3.1416. The second declaration statement creates the double-precision constant named SALESTAX and initializes it to 0.05. Finally, the third declaration creates an integer constant named MAXNUM and initializes it with the value 100.

After a const identifier is created and initialized, the value stored in it *can't* be changed. For all practical purposes, the name of the constant and its value are linked together for the duration of the program that declares them.

Although the const identifiers have been shown in uppercase letters, lowercase letters could have been used. Using uppercase letters is customary in C++, however, to make const identifiers easy to identify. When programmers see uppercase letters in a program, they know a constant is being used, and its value can't be changed in the program.

After it's declared, a const identifier can be used in any C++ statement in place of the number it represents. For example, both these assignment statements are valid:

```
circum = 2 * PI * radius;
amount = SALESTAX * purchase;
```

These statements must, of course, appear after the declarations for all their variables and constants. Because a const declaration equates a constant value to an identifier, and the identifier can be used as a replacement for its initializing constant, these identifiers are commonly referred to as **symbolic constants** or **named constants**. These terms are used interchangeably in this book.

Placement of Statements

At this stage, you have been introduced to a variety of statement types. The general rule in C++ for statement placement is simply that a variable or symbolic constant must be declared before it can be used. Although this rule permits placing both preprocessor directives and declaration statements throughout a program, doing so results in a poor program structure. As a matter of good programming form, the following statement order should be used:

```
preprocessor directives

int main()
{
  // symbolic constants
  // variable declarations

  // other executable statements

  return 0;
}
```

As new statement types are introduced, this placement structure will be expanded to accommodate them. Note that comment statements can be intermixed anywhere in this basic structure. Program 3.14 illustrates this structure and uses a symbolic constant to calculate the sales tax due on a purchased item.

Program 3.14

```cpp
#include <iostream>
#include <iomanip>
using namespace std;

int main()
{
  const double SALESTAX = 0.05;
  double amount, taxes, total;

  cout << "\nEnter the amount purchased: ";
  cin  >> amount;
  taxes = SALESTAX * amount;
  total = amount + taxes;
  cout << setiosflags(ios::fixed)
       << setiosflags(ios::showpoint)
       << setprecision(2);
  cout << "The sales tax is " << setw(4) << taxes << endl;
  cout << "The total bill is " << setw(5) << total << endl;

  return 0;
}
```

The following sample run was made with Program 3.14:

```
Enter the amount purchased: 36.00
The sales tax is 1.80
The total bill is 37.80
```

Although the const qualifier has been used to construct symbolic constants, you encounter this data type again in Chapter 11, where you learn that it's useful as a function argument to make sure the argument isn't modified in the function.

EXERCISES 3.5

1. **(Modify)** Rewrite the following program to use the symbolic constant PI in place of the value 3.1416 used in the program:

```cpp
#include <iostream>
using namespace std;
int main()
{
  double radius, circum;
```

```
   cout << "Enter a radius: ";
   cin  >> radius;
   circum = 2.0 * 3.1416 * radius;
   cout << "\nThe circumference of the circle is "
        << circum << endl;

   return 0;
}
```

2. **(Modify)** Rewrite the following program to use the named constant FACTOR in place of the expression (5.0/9.0) used in the program:

```
#include <iostream>
using namespace std;

int main()
{
   double fahren, celsius;
   cout << "Enter a temperature in degrees Fahrenheit: ";
   cin  >> fahren;
   celsius = (5.0/9.0) * (fahren - 32.0);
   cout << "The equivalent Celsius temperature is "
        << celsius << endl;

   return 0;
}
```

3. **(Modify)** Rewrite the following program to use the symbolic constant PRIME in place of the value 0.04 used in the program:

```
#include <iostream>
using namespace std;

int main()
{
   double prime, amount, interest;
   prime = 0.04;        // prime interest rate
   cout << Enter the amount: ";
   cin  >> amount;
   interest = prime * amount;
   cout << "The interest earned is "
        << interest << " dollars" << endl;

   return 0;
}
```

4. (Program) Heat is radiated from the sun and all planets orbiting the sun. The heat that's radiated can be calculated by using the following formula:

$$E = e \, \sigma \, T^4$$

     E is the energy radiated per second in units of watts per meter squared (watts/m^2).
     e is the emissivity of the substance, which is 1 for the sun and all the planets.
     σ is the constant (.000000056697 = 5.6697e-8).
     T is the surface temperature in degrees Celsius.

For example, the heat radiated from the sun, which has an emissivity of 1 and a surface temperature of approximately 6000° C, is as follows:

$$E = (1) \times (.000000056697) \times (6000)^4 \text{ watts/m}^2$$
$$= 73,479,300 \text{ watts/m}^2$$

Using the formula, write a C++ program that accepts a planet's temperature and provides the heat generated from the planet as its output. Your program should assign the value 5.6697e-8 to a symbolic constant named **HEATFACTOR**. After determining that your program is working correctly (make sure it produces the correct radiation for the sun), use it to complete the following chart:

Planet (emissivity = 1)	Average Surface Temperature (° Celsius)	Heat Radiated (watts/m^2)
Mercury	270	
Venus	462	
Earth	14	

5. (Program) During the day, heat is absorbed by many objects, such as cars, roofs, and brick walls. This heat is then radiated back into the environment during the cooler evening hours. Using the formula $E = e \, \sigma \, T^4$ (see Exercise 4), write a C++ program that determines the amount of heat radiated for the objects listed in the following table. Your program should request the object's average surface temperature and emissivity, and then calculate and display the heat radiated. Make sure to use a symbolic constant named **HEATFACTOR** for the value of σ. Complete the following chart, making three runs of the program:

Substance	Average Surface Temperature (° Celsius)	Emissivity	Heat Radiated (watts/m^2)
Automobile	47	.3	
Brick	45	.9	
Commercial roof	48	.05	

3.6 Common Programming Errors

When using the material in this chapter, be aware of the following possible errors:

1. Forgetting to assign or initialize values for all variables before using them in an expression. Values can be assigned by assignment statements, initialized in a declaration statement, or assigned interactively by entering values with the `cin` object.
2. Using a mathematical library function without including the preprocessor statement `#include <cmath>` (and on a UNIX-based system, forgetting to include the `-lm` argument on the `cc` command line).
3. Using a library function without providing the correct number of arguments of the proper data type.
4. Applying the increment or decrement operator to an expression. For example, the expression `(count + n)++` is incorrect. The increment and decrement operators can be applied only to variables.
5. Forgetting to use the extraction operator, `>>`, to separate variables in a `cin` statement.
6. A more unusual error occurs when increment and decrement operators are used with variables appearing more than once in the same expression. This error occurs because C++ doesn't specify the order in which operands are accessed in an expression. For example, the value assigned to `result` in the following statement depends on the compiler:

    ```
    result = i + i++;
    ```

    If your compiler accesses the first operand (`i`) first, the preceding statement is equivalent to

    ```
    result = 2 * i;
    i++;
    ```

    However, if your compiler accesses the second operand (`i++`) first, the value of the first operand is altered before it's used the second time, and the value `2i + 1` is assigned to `result`. As a general rule, don't use the increment or decrement operator in an expression when the variable it operates on appears more than once in the expression.
7. Being unwilling to test a program in depth. Being objective about testing your own software is difficult, but as a programmer, you must remind yourself that just because you think your program is correct doesn't make it so.

3.7 Chapter Summary

1. An expression is a sequence of one or more operands separated by operators. An operand is a constant, a variable, or another expression. A value is associated with an expression.

2. Expressions are evaluated according to the precedence and associativity of the operators used in the expression.

3. The assignment operator is the = symbol. Expressions using this operator assign a value to a variable, and the expression also takes on a value. Because assignment is a C++ operation, the assignment operator can be used more than once in the same expression.

4. The increment operator, ++, adds 1 to a variable, and the decrement operator, --, subtracts 1 from a variable. Both operators can be used as prefixes or postfixes. In a prefix operation, the variable is incremented (or decremented) before its value is used. In a postfix operation, the variable is incremented (or decremented) after its value is used.

5. C++ provides library functions for calculating square root, logarithmic, and other mathematical computations. Programs using a mathematical function must include the statement `#include <cmath>` or have a function declaration before calling the mathematical function.

6. Every mathematical library function operates on its arguments to calculate a single value. To use a library function effectively, you must know the function name, what the function does, the number and data types of arguments the function expects, and the data type of the returned value.

7. Data passed to a function is called an argument of the function. Arguments are passed to a library function by including each argument, separated by commas, in the parentheses following the function's name. Each function has its own requirements for the number and data types of the arguments that must be provided.

8. Functions can be included in larger expressions.

9. The `cin` object is used for data input. It accepts a stream of data from the keyboard and assigns the data to variables. This is the general form of a statement using `cin`:

```
cin >> var1 >> var2 . . . >> varn;
```

The extraction operator, >>, must be used to separate variable names in a `cin` statement.

10. When a `cin` statement is encountered, the computer temporarily suspends further execution until enough data has been entered for the number of variables in the `cin` statement.

11. It's a good programming practice to display a message before a `cin` statement that alerts users to the type and number of data items to be entered. This message is called a prompt.

12. Values can be equated to a single constant by using the `const` keyword. This keyword creates a named constant that's read-only after it's initialized in the declaration statement. This declaration has the syntax

```
const dataType symbolicName = initialValue;
```

and permits using the constant instead of *initialValue* anywhere in the program after the declaration. Generally, these declarations are placed before variable declarations in a program.

3.8 Chapter Supplement: Errors, Testing, and Debugging

The ideal in programming is to produce readable, error-free programs that work correctly and can be modified or changed with a minimum of testing. You can work toward this ideal by keeping in mind the different types of errors that can occur, when they're typically detected, and how to correct them.

Program errors can be detected at any of the following times:

- Before a program is compiled
- While the program is being compiled
- While the program is running
- After the program has been run and the output is being examined

The method for detecting errors before a program is compiled is called **desk checking** because you're usually sitting at a desk with the code in front of you. It refers to the process of examining source code for syntax and logic errors. The method for detecting errors after a program has run is called **program verification and testing.**

Compile-Time and Runtime Errors

Errors detected while a program is being compiled are called **compile-time errors**, and errors that occur while a program is running are called **runtime errors**. These terms describe when errors occur, not what caused them. Most compile-time errors, however, are caused by syntax errors, and the majority of runtime errors are caused by logic errors.

By now, you have probably encountered numerous compile-time errors. Beginning programmers tend to be frustrated by them, but experienced programmers understand the compiler is doing a lot of valuable checking, and correcting errors the compiler does detect is usually easy. Because these errors occur while the program is being developed, not while a user is performing an important task, no one but the programmer ever knows they occurred. You fix them, and they go away.

Runtime errors are more troubling because they occur while a user is running the program. Because the user in most commercial systems isn't the programmer, typically the error can't be assessed and corrected immediately. Runtime errors can be caused by program or hardware failures. From a programming standpoint, however, most runtime errors are caused by logic errors.

Syntax and Logic Errors

Computer literature distinguishes between two main types of errors: syntax and logic errors. A **syntax error** is an error in ordering valid language elements in a statement or the attempt to use invalid language elements. For example, examine the following statements:

```
cout << "There are four syntax errors here\n
cot " Can you find tem";
```

They contain the following syntax errors:

1. A closing quotation mark is missing in line 1.
2. A terminating semicolon (;) is missing in line 1.
3. The keyword cout is misspelled in line 2.
4. The insertion symbol, <<, is missing in line 2.

If these errors aren't discovered by desk checking, the compiler detects them and displays an error message.[12] Sometimes the error message is clear and the error is obvious; at other times, understanding the compiler's error message takes a little detective work. Because

---

[12]Generally, not all syntax errors might be detected at the same time, however. Frequently, one syntax error masks another error, and the second error is detected after the first one is corrected.

syntax errors are detected only at compile time, the terms "compile-time errors" and "syntax errors" are used interchangeably. Strictly speaking, however, "compile time" refers to when the error is detected, and "syntax" refers to the type of error detected.

Note that the misspelling of "them" in the second statement isn't a syntax error. Although this spelling error results in displaying an undesirable output line, it's not a violation of C++'s syntax rules. It's simply a **typographical error**, commonly referred to as a "typo." The compiler doesn't catch this type of typographical error.[13]

Another error the compiler doesn't catch is a **logic error**, which is characterized by erroneous, unexpected, or unintentional output that's a result of some flaw in the program's logic. These errors can be detected by desk checking, by program testing, by accident when a user gets erroneous output while the program is running, or not at all.

The most serious logic error is caused by not fully understanding the program's requirements because the logic in a program reflects the logic on which it's coded. For example, if a program's purpose is to calculate a mortgage payment on a house or the load-bearing strength of a steel beam and the programmer doesn't fully understand how to make the calculation, what inputs are needed to perform the calculation, or what special conditions exist (such as what happens when someone makes an extra mortgage payment or how temperature affects the beam), a logic error occurs. Because the compiler doesn't detect these errors and they often go undetected at runtime, they are always more difficult to detect than syntax errors.

If logic errors *are* detected, typically they're revealed in one of two main ways. First, the program executes to completion but produces incorrect results, such as the following:

- *No output*—This result is caused by omitting an output statement or using a sequence of statements that inadvertently bypasses an output statement.
- *Unappealing or misaligned output*—This result is caused by an error in an output statement.
- *Incorrect numerical results*—This result is caused by assigning incorrect values to variables in an expression, coding an incorrect or incomplete algorithm, coding a correct algorithm incorrectly, omitting a statement, making a round-off error, or using an improper sequence of statements.

Second, a logic error can cause a runtime error. Examples of this type of logic error are attempts to divide by zero or take the square root of a negative number. Typically, these errors are caused by incorrect user input. Although beginning programmers tend to blame users for runtime errors caused by entering incorrect data, professionals don't. They understand that a runtime error is a basic flaw in the program's construction that can damage the reputation of both the program and the programmer. They also understand that determining the error and correcting what caused it are more fruitful than determining who caused it.

Testing and Debugging

Program testing should be well thought out to maximize the possibility of locating errors. In this regard, an important programming realization is that although a single test can reveal the presence of an error, it *does not* verify the absence of one. In other words, the fact that a

---

[13]The misspelling of a C++ keyword or a declared variable name that results in an undeclared name *is* caught, however, because it results in a syntax error.

verification run reveals one error *does not* mean another error isn't lurking somewhere else in the program. Furthermore, the fact that one test revealed no errors *does not* mean there are no errors.

After you discover an error, however, you must locate where it occurs and fix it. In computer jargon, a program error is referred to as a **bug**, and the process of isolating and correcting the error and verifying the correction is called **debugging**.

Although no hard-and-fast rules exist for isolating a bug, some useful techniques can be applied. The first is preventive. Often programmers introduce errors in the rush to code and run a program before understanding what's required and how to achieve the required results. Symptoms of this haste include lacking an outline of the proposed program or not having a detailed understanding of the program's requirements. Many errors can be eliminated by desk checking the program before entering or compiling it.

A second useful technique is imitating the computer by executing each statement by hand as the computer would. This technique, called **program tracing**, involves writing down each variable, as it's encountered in the program, and listing the value that should be stored in the variable as each input and assignment statement is encountered. Doing this sharpens your programming skills because it helps you understand what each statement in your program causes to happen.

A third useful technique is including some temporary code in your program that displays the values of selected variables. If the displayed values are incorrect, you can determine what part of your program generated them and make the necessary corrections. You can also add temporary code that displays the values of all input data. This technique, called **echo printing**, is useful in establishing that the program is receiving and interpreting input data correctly.

The most powerful technique is using a special program called a **debugger**. A debugger program can control the execution of a C++ program, interrupt the C++ program at any point in its execution, and display the values of all variables at the point of interruption.

Finally, no discussion of debugging is complete without mentioning the main ingredient needed for isolating and correcting errors successfully: the attitude you bring to the task. After you write a program, you naturally assume it's correct. Taking a step back to be objective about testing and finding errors in your own software is difficult. As a programmer, you must remind yourself that just because you think your program is correct doesn't make it so. Finding errors in your own programs is a sobering experience but one that helps you become a better programmer. The process can be exciting and fun if you approach it as a detection problem, with you as the master detective.

Chapter 4

Selection

The term flow of control refers to the order in which a program's statements are executed. Unless directed otherwise, the normal flow of control for all programs is sequential. This term means statements are executed in sequence, one after another, in the order in which they're placed in the program.

Both selection and repetition statements enable programmers to alter this normal sequential flow of control. As their names imply, selection statements make it possible to select which statement, from a well-defined set, is executed next, and repetition statements make it possible to go back and repeat a set of statements. In this chapter, you learn about C++'s selection statements. Because selection requires choosing between alternatives, this chapter begins with a description of C++'s selection criteria.

4.1 Relational Expressions

Besides providing addition, subtraction, multiplication, and division capabilities, all computers have the capability to compare numbers. Because many seemingly "intelligent" decision-making situations can be reduced to choosing between two values, a computer's comparison capability can be used to create a remarkable intelligence-like facility.

The expressions used to compare operands are called **relational expressions**. A **simple relational expression** consists of a relational operator connecting two variable and/or constant operands, as shown in Figure 4.1. Table 4.1 lists the relational operators available in C++. They can be used with integer, Boolean, double, or character data, but they must be typed exactly as shown in Table 4.1.

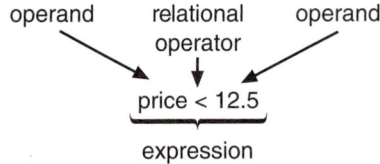

Figure 4.1   Anatomy of a simple relational expression

Table 4.1   C++'s Relational Operators

Operator	Meaning	Example
<	Less than	`age < 30`
>	Greater than	`height > 6.2`
<=	Less than or equal to	`taxable <= 20000`
>=	Greater than or equal to	`temp >= 98.6`
==	Equal to	`grade == 100`
!=	Not equal to	`number != 250`

The following are examples of valid relational expressions:

```
age > 40    length <= 50   width > 7
3 < 4       flag == done   idNum == 682
day != 5    2.0 > 3.3      hours > 40
```

The following examples are invalid:

```
length =< 50     // incorrect symbol
2.0 >> 3.3       // invalid relational operator
flag = = done    // spaces are not allowed
```

Relational expressions are sometimes called **conditions**, and both terms are used in this book. Like all C++ expressions, relational expressions are evaluated to yield a numerical result.[1] *A condition that's interpreted as true evaluates to an integer value of 1, and a false condition evaluates to an integer value of 0.*

For example, because the relationship 3 < 4 is always true, this expression has a value of 1, and because the relationship 2.0 > 3.3 is always false, the value of the expression is 0. This can be verified by these statements:

```
cout << "The value of 3 < 4 is " << (3 < 4);
cout << "\nThe value of 2.0 > 3.3 is " << (2.0 > 3.3);
```

---

[1] In this regard, C++ differs from most other high-level languages, which yield a Boolean (true or false) result.

These statements result in the following display:

```
The value of 3 < 4 is 1
The value of 2.0 > 3.3 is 0
```

The value of a relational expression, such as hours > 40, depends on the value stored in the variable hours. In a C++ program, a relational expression's value isn't as important as the interpretation C++ places on the value when the expression is used as part of a selection statement. In these statements, which are explained in the next section, you'll see that C++ uses a zero value to represent a false condition and any non-zero value to represent a true condition. The selection of which statement to execute next is then based on this value.

In addition to numerical operands, character data can be compared by using relational operators. For example, in the ASCII code, the letter 'A' is stored by using a code with a lower numerical value than the letter 'B', the code for 'B' has a lower value than the code for 'C', and so on. For character sets coded in this manner, the following conditions are evaluated as shown:

Expression	Value	Interpretation
'A' > 'C'	0	false
'D' <= 'Z'	1	true
'E' == 'F'	0	false
'g' >= 'm'	0	false
'b' != 'c'	1	true
'a' == 'A'	0	false

Comparing letters is essential in alphabetizing names or in using characters to select a choice in decision-making situations.

Logical Operators

In addition to using simple relational expressions as conditions, more complex conditions can be created by using the **logical operators** AND, OR, and NOT. These operators are represented by the symbols &&, ||, and !.

When the AND operator, &&, is used with two simple expressions, the condition is true only if both expressions are true by themselves. Therefore, the logical condition

```
(age > 40) && (term < 10)
```

is true only if age is greater than 40 and term is less than 10. Because relational operators have a higher precedence than logical operators, the parentheses in this logical expression could have been omitted.

The OR operator, ||, is also used with two expressions. When using the OR operator, the condition is satisfied if one or both of the two expressions are true. Therefore, the condition

```
(age > 40) || (term < 10)
```

is true if `age` is greater than 40, `term` is less than 10, or both conditions are true. Again, the parentheses surrounding the relational expressions are included to make the statement easier to read. Because relational operators have a higher precedence than logical operators, the same evaluation is made even if the parentheses are omitted.

For the declarations

```
int i, j;
double a, b, complete;
```

the following are valid conditions:

```
a > b
(i == j) || (a < b) || complete
(a/b > 5) && (i <= 20)
```

Before these conditions can be evaluated, the values of a, b, i, j, and `complete` must be known. For the assignments

```
a = 12.0;
b = 2.0;
i = 15;
j = 30;
complete = 0.0;
```

the previous expressions yield the following results:

Expression	Value	Interpretation
`a > b`	1	`true`
`(i == j) || (a < b) || complete`	0	`false`
`(a/b > 5) && (i <= 20)`	1	`true`

The NOT operator, `!`, is used to change an expression to its opposite state; that is, if the expression has a non-zero value (`true`), the statement `!expression` produces a zero value (`false`). If an expression is false to begin with (has a zero value), `!expression` is true and evaluates to 1. For example, if the number 26 is stored in the variable `age`, the expression `age > 40` has a value of 0 (`false`), and the expression `!(age > 40)` has a value of 1 (`true`). Because the NOT operator is used with only one expression, it's a unary operator.

Relational and logical operators have a hierarchy of execution similar to arithmetic operators. Table 4.2 lists the precedence of these operators in relation to the other operators you have used.

Table 4.2 Operator Precedence and Associativity

Operator	Associativity
! unary - ++ --	Right to left
* / %	Left to right
+ -	Left to right
< <= > >=	Left to right
== !=	Left to right
&&	Left to right
||	Left to right
= += -= *= /=	Right to left

The following chart illustrates using an operator's precedence and associativity to evaluate relational expressions, assuming the following declarations:

```
char key = 'm';
int i = 5, j = 7, k = 12;
double x = 22.5;
```

Expression	Equivalent Expression	Value	Interpretation
i + 2 == k - 1	(i + 2) == (k - 1)	0	false
3 * i - j < 22	((3 * i) - j) < 22	1	true
i + 2 * j > k	(i + (2 * j)) > k	1	true
k + 3 <= -j + 3 * i	(k + 3) <= ((-j) + (3*i))	0	false
'a' + 1 == 'b'	('a' + 1) == 'b'	1	true
key - 1 > 'p'	(key - 1) > 'p'	0	false
key + 1 == 'n'	(key + 1) == 'n'	1	true
25 >= x + 1.0	25 >= (x + 1.0)	1	true

As with all expressions, parentheses can be used to alter the assigned operator priority and improve the readability of relational expressions. By evaluating the expressions in parentheses first, the following compound condition is evaluated as shown:

```
(6 * 3 == 36 / 2) || (13 < 3 * 3 + 4) && !(6 - 2 < 5)
      (18 == 18) ||    (13 < 9 + 4)    && !(4 < 5)
             1 ||    (13 < 13)    && !1
             1 ||         0       && 0
             1 ||         0
                    1
```

A Numerical Accuracy Problem

In C++'s relational expressions, a subtle numerical accuracy problem related to single-precision and double-precision numbers can occur. Because of the way computers store these numbers, you should avoid testing for equality of single-precision and double-precision values and variables with the relational operator ==.

The reason is that many decimal numbers, such as 0.1, can't be represented exactly in binary with a finite number of bits, so testing for exact equality for these numbers can fail. When you want equality of noninteger values, it's better to require that the absolute value of the difference between operands be less than some extremely small value. Therefore, for single-precision and double-precision operands, the general expression

```
operand_1 == operand_2
```

should be replaced by this condition:

```
abs(operand_1 - operand_2) < EPSILON
```

EPSILON can be a constant set to any acceptably small value, such as 0.000001.[2] Therefore, if the difference between the two operands is less than the value of EPSILON, the two operands are considered essentially equal. For example, if x and y are double-precision variables, a condition such as

```
x/y == 0.35
```

should be programmed as the following:

```
abs(x/y - 0.35) < EPSILON
```

This condition ensures that slight inaccuracies in representing noninteger numbers in binary don't affect evaluation of the tested condition. Because all computers have an exact binary representation of 0, comparisons for exact equality to 0 don't have this numerical accuracy problem.

EXERCISES 4.1

1. **(Practice)** Determine the value of the following expressions, assuming a = 5, b = 2, c = 4, d = 6, and e = 3:

   a. a > b

   b. a != b

   c. d % b == c % b

   d. a * c != d * b

   e. d * b == c * e

   f. a * b

   g. a % b * c

   h. c % b * a

   i. b % c * a

---

2. **(Practice)** Using parentheses, rewrite the following expressions to indicate their order of evaluation correctly. Then evaluate each expression, assuming a = 5, b = 2, and c = 4.

a. `a % b * c && c % b * a`
b. `a % b * c || c % b * a`
c. `b % c * a && a % c * b`
d. `b % c * a || a % c * b`

3. **(Practice)** Write relational expressions to express the following conditions (using variable names of your choosing):

a. A person's age is equal to 30.
b. A person's temperature is greater than 98.6 degrees.
c. A person's height is less than 6 feet.
d. The current month is 12 (December).
e. The letter input is m.
f. A person's age is equal to 30, and the person is taller than 6 feet.
g. The current day is the 15th day of the 1st month.
h. A person is older than 50 or has been employed at the company for at least 5 years.
i. A person's identification number is less than 500 and the person is older than 55.
j. A length is greater than 2 feet and less than 3 feet.

4. **(Practice)** Determine the value of the following expressions, assuming a = 5, b = 2, c = 4, and d = 5:

a. `a == 5`
b. `b * d == c * c`
c. `d % b * c > 5 || c % b * d < 7`

4.2 The `if-else` Statement

The `if-else` statement directs the computer to select between two statements based on the result of a comparison. For example, if a New Jersey resident's income is less than or equal to $20,000, the applicable state tax rate is 2%. If the person's income is greater than $20,000, a different rate is applied to the amount over $20,000. The `if-else` statement can be used in this situation to determine the tax rate based on whether the person's income is less than or equal to $20,000. This is the general form of the `if-else` statement:

```
if (expression) statement1;
  else statement2;
```

The *expression* is evaluated first. If its value is non-zero, *statement1* is executed. If its value is zero, the statement after the keyword `else` is executed. Therefore, one of the two statements (*statement1* or *statement2* but not both) is always executed, depending on the expression's value. Notice that the tested expression must be enclosed by parentheses, and a semicolon is placed after each statement.

For clarity, the `if-else` statement is typically written on four lines in this form:

```
if (expression)  ◄─────────── no semicolon here
   statement1;
else  ◄─────────── no semicolon here
   statement2;
```

The form of the `if-else` statement that's used typically depends on the length of *statement1* and *statement2*. However, when using this four-line form, don't put a semicolon after the parentheses or the `else` keyword. The semicolons are placed only at the ends of statements. Figure 4.2 shows the flowchart for the `if-else` statement.

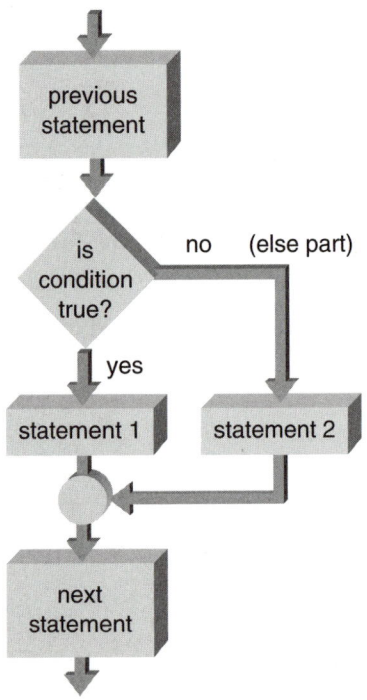

Figure 4.2   The `if-else` flowchart

As an example, take a look at writing an income tax computation program containing an `if-else` statement. As stated, the New Jersey state income tax is assessed at 2% of taxable income for incomes less than or equal to $20,000. For taxable incomes greater than $20,000, state taxes are 2.5% of the income exceeding $20,000 plus a fixed amount of $400. The expression to be tested is whether taxable income is less than or equal to $20,000, so the following is a suitable `if-else` statement for this program:[3]

```
if (taxable <= 20000.0)
   taxes = 0.02 * taxable;
else
   taxes = 0.025 * (taxable - 20000.0) + 400.0;
```

---

[3]Note that in actual practice, the numerical values in this statement would be defined as named constants.

The relational operator <= is used to represent the condition "is less than or equal to." If the value of taxable is less than or equal to 20000.0, the condition is true (has a value of 1) and the statement taxes = 0.02 * taxable; is executed. If the condition isn't true, the expression's value is zero, and the statement after the else keyword is executed. Program 4.1 shows using this statement in a complete program.

Program 4.1

```cpp
#include <iostream>
#include <iomanip>
using namespace std;

int main()
{
  double taxable, taxes;

  cout << "Please type in the taxable income: ";
  cin  >> taxable;

  if (taxable <= 20000.0)
    taxes = 0.02 * taxable;
  else
    taxes = 0.025 * (taxable - 20000.0) + 400.0;

  cout << setiosflags(ios::fixed)
       << setiosflags(ios::showpoint)
       << setprecision(2)
       << "Taxes are $ " << taxes << endl;

  return 0;
}
```

A blank line is inserted before and after the if-else statement to highlight it in the program. This format is used throughout the book to emphasize the statement being discussed.

To illustrate selection in action, Program 4.1 was run twice with different input data. These are the results:

```
Please type in the taxable income: 10000.
Taxes are $ 200.00
```

and

```
Please type in the taxable income: 30000.
Taxes are $ 650.00
```

In reviewing this output, observe that the taxable income input in the first run was less than $20,000, and the tax rate was calculated correctly as 2% of the number entered. In the second run, the taxable income was more than $20,000, and the `else` part of the `if-else` statement was used to yield this correct tax rate computation:

```
0.025 * ($30,000. - $20,000.) + $400. = $650.
```

Although any expression can be tested by an `if-else` statement, only relational expressions are generally used. However, statements such as the following are valid:

```
if (num)
  cout << "Bingo!";
else
  cout << "You lose!";
```

Because `num` is a valid expression by itself, the message `Bingo!` is displayed if `num` has any non-zero value, and the message `You lose!` is displayed if `num` has a value of zero.

Compound Statements

Although only a single statement is permitted in the `if` and `else` parts of the `if-else` statement, each single statement can be a compound statement. A **compound statement** is a sequence of single statements between braces, as shown in this example:

```
{
    statement1;
    statement2;
    statement3;
        .
        .
        .
    last statement;
}
```

Using braces to enclose a set of statements creates a single block of statements, which can be used anywhere in a C++ program in place of a single statement. The next example shows using a compound statement in the general form of an `if-else` statement:

```
if (expression)
{
  statement1;      // as many statements as necessary
  statement2;      // can be put inside the braces
  statement3;      // each statement must end with a ;
}
else
{
  statement4;
  statement5;
      .
      .
  last statement;
}
```

Program 4.2 shows using a compound statement in an actual program. This program checks whether the value in tempType is f. If so, the compound statement corresponding to the if part of the if-else statement is executed. Any other letter in tempType results in executing the compound statement corresponding to the else part.

Program 4.2

```cpp
#include <iostream>
#include <iomanip>
using namespace std;

// a temperature conversion program
int main()
{
  char tempType;
  double temp, fahren, celsius;

  cout << "Enter the temperature to be converted: ";
  cin  >> temp;
  cout << "Enter an f if the temperature is in Fahrenheit";
  cout << "\n or a c if the temperature is in Celsius: ";
  cin  >> tempType;

  // set output formats
  cout << setiosflags (ios::fixed)
       << setiosflags (ios::showpoint)
       << setprecision(2);

  if (tempType == 'f')
  {
    celsius = (5.0 / 9.0) * (temp - 32.0);
    cout << "\nThe equivalent Celsius temperature is "
         << celsius << endl;
  }
  else
  {
    fahren = (9.0 / 5.0) * temp + 32.0;
    cout << "\nThe equivalent Fahrenheit temperature is "
         << fahren << endl;
  }

  return 0;
}
```

A sample run of Program 4.2 follows.

```
Enter the temperature to be converted: 212
Enter an f if the temperature is in Fahrenheit
    or a c if the temperature is in Celsius: f

The equivalent Celsius temperature is 100.00
```

Block Scope

All statements contained in a compound statement constitute a single block of code, and any variable declared in this block has meaning only between its declaration and the closing braces defining the block. For example, take a look at the following example, which consists of two blocks of code:

```
{   // start of outer block
    int a = 25;
    int b = 17;
    cout << "The value of a is " << a
        << " and b is " << b << endl;

    {   // start of inner block
        double a = 46.25;
        int c = 10;
            cout << "a is now " << a
                << " b is now " << b
                << " and c is " << c << endl;
    }   // end of inner block

    cout << "a is now " << a << " and b is " << b << endl;
}   // end of outer block
```

This section of code produces the following output:

```
The value of a is 25 and b is 17
a is now 46.25 b is now 17 and c is 10
a is now 25 and b is 17
```

This output is produced as follows: The first block of code defines two variables named a and b, which can be used anywhere in this block after their declarations, including any block inside this outer block. In the inner block, two new variables have been declared, named a and c. Therefore, at this stage, four different variables have been created, two with the same name. When a variable is referenced, the compiler first attempts to access a variable with the correct name that has been declared in the block containing the reference. If the referenced variable hasn't been defined in the block, the compiler attempts to access the variable declared in the next outer block, until a valid access results.

Point of Information

Placement of Braces in a Compound Statement

A common practice for some C++ programmers is placing the opening brace of a compound statement on the same line as the `if` and `else` statements. Using this convention, the `if` statement in Program 4.2 would look like the following example. (This placement is a matter of style only—both styles are used, and both are acceptable.)

```
if (tempType == 'f') {
  celsius = (5.0 / 9.0) * (temp - 32.0);
  cout << "\nThe equivalent Celsius temperature is "
      << celsius << endl;
}
else {
  fahren =  (9.0 / 5.0) * temp + 32.0;
  cout << "\nThe equivalent Fahrenheit temperature is "
      << fahren << endl;
}
```

Therefore, the values of the variables a and c referenced in the inner block use the values of the variables a and c declared in that block. Because no variable named b was declared in the inner block, the value of b displayed from inside the inner block is obtained from the outer block. Finally, the last cout object, which is outside the inner block, displays the value of the variable a declared in the outer block. If an attempt is made to display the value of c anywhere in the outer block, the compiler issues an error message stating that c is an undefined symbol.

The area in a program where a variable can be used is formally referred to as the **scope of the variable**, and you delve into this subject in Chapter 6.

One-Way Selection

A useful modification of the if-else statement involves omitting the else part of the statement and has this shortened and often useful form:

```
if (expression)
    statement;
```

The statement following if (*expression*) is executed only if the expression has a non-zero value (a true condition). As before, the *statement* can be a compound statement. Figure 4.3 shows the flowchart for this statement.

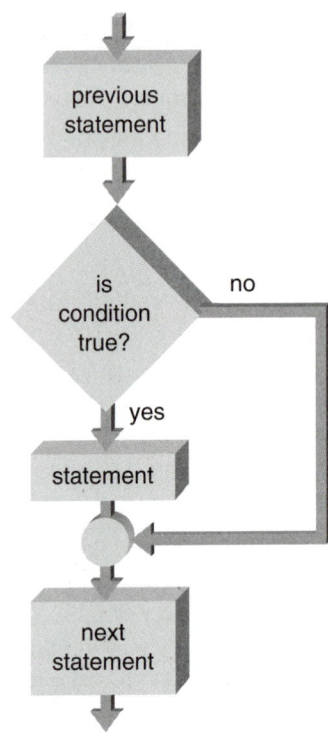

Figure 4.3 A one-way if statement

This modified form of the if statement is called a **one-way if statement**. Program 4.3 uses this statement to check a car's mileage and display a message only for cars that have been driven more than 3000.0 miles.

 **Program 4.3**

```
#include <iostream>
using namespace std;

int main()
{

  const double LIMIT = 3000.0;
  int idNum;
  double miles;

  cout << "Please type in car number and mileage: ";
  cin  >> idNum >> miles;
```

```
if(miles > LIMIT)
  cout << " Car " << idNum << " is over the limit." << endl;

cout << "End of program output." << endl;

return 0;
}
```

To show the one-way selection criteria in action, Program 4.3 was run twice, each time with different input data. Only the input data for the first run causes the message Car 256 is over the limit to be displayed.

```
Please type in car number and mileage: 256 3562.8
  Car 256 is over the limit.
End of program output.
```

and

```
Please type in car number and mileage: 23 2562.3
End of program output.
```

Problems Associated with the if-else Statement

Two of the most common problems encountered in using C++'s if-else statement are the following:

- Misunderstanding the full implications of what an expression is
- Using the assignment operator, =, in place of the relational operator ==

Recall that an expression is any combination of operands and operators that yields a result. This definition is much broader and more encompassing than is apparent at first. For example, all the following are valid C++ expressions:

```
age + 5
age = 30
age == 40
```

Assuming the variables are declared correctly, each of these expressions yields a result. The following example uses the cout object to display the value of these expressions when age is initially assigned the value 18:

```
age = 18;
cout << "The value of the first expression is " << (age + 5) << endl;
cout << "The value of the second expression is " << (age = 30) << endl;
cout << "The value of the third expression is " << (age == 40) << endl;
```

This code produces the following display:

```
The value of the first expression is 23
The value of the second expression is 30
The value of the third expression is 0
```

As this output shows, each expression has a value associated with it. The value of the first expression is the sum of the variable age plus 5, which is 23. The value of the second expression is 30, which is also assigned to the variable age. The value of the third expression is 0 because age is not equal to 40, and a false condition is represented in C++ with the value 0. If the value in age had been 40, the relational expression a == 40 would be true and have the value 1.

Say the relational expression age == 40 was intended to be used in the if statement

```
if (age == 40)
  cout << "Happy Birthday!";
```

but was mistyped as age = 40, resulting in the following:

```
if (age = 40)
  cout << "Happy Birthday!";
```

Because the mistake results in a valid C++ expression, and any C++ expression can be tested by an if statement, the resulting if statement is valid and causes the message Happy Birthday! to be displayed regardless of what value was previously assigned to age. Can you see why?

The condition tested by the if statement doesn't compare the value in age to the number 40. It assigns the number 40 to age. That is, the expression age = 40 isn't a relational expression at all; it's an assignment expression. At the completion of the assignment, the expression itself has a value of 40. Because C++ treats any non-zero value as true, the cout statement is executed. Another way of looking at it is to realize that the if statement is equivalent to the following statements:

```
age = 40;  // assign 40 to age
if (age)   // test the value of age
  cout << "Happy Birthday!";
```

Because a C++ compiler has no means of knowing that the expression being tested isn't the one you want, you must be especially careful when writing conditions.

Point of Information

The Boolean Data Type

Before the current ANSI/ISO C++ standard, C++ didn't have a built-in Boolean data type with its two Boolean values, `true` and `false`. Because this data type wasn't originally part of the language, a tested expression could not evaluate to a Boolean value. Therefore, the syntax

```
if (Boolean expression is true)
    execute this statement;
```

also wasn't built into C or C++. Instead, C++ uses the more encompassing syntax,

```
if (expression)
    execute this statement;
```

where *expression* is any expression that evaluates to a numeric value. If the value of the tested expression is a non-zero value, it's considered true, and only a zero value is considered false.

As the ANSI/ISO C++ standard specifies, C++ has a built-in Boolean data type containing the values `true` and `false`. Boolean variables are declared with the `bool` keyword. As currently implemented, the actual values that the Boolean values `true` and `false` represent are the integer values 1 and 0. For example, examine the following program, which declares two Boolean variables:

```
#include <iostream>
using namespace std;
int main()
{
  bool t1, t2;

  t1 = true;
  t2 = false;
  cout << "The value of t1 is " << t1
       << "\nand the value of t2 is " << t2 << endl;

  return 0;
}
```

This program produces the following output:

```
The value of t1 is 1
and the value of t2 is 0
```

continued

Point of Information

The Boolean Data Type (*continued*)

As shown by this output, the Boolean values `true` and `false` are represented by the integer values 1 and 0 and have the following relationships:

```
!true= is false
!false= is true
```

Additionally, applying a postfix or prefix ++ operator to a variable of type `bool` sets the Boolean value to `true`. The postfix and prefix -- operators can't be applied to Boolean variables.

Boolean values can also be compared, as shown in the following code:

```
if (t1 == t2)
    cout << "The values are equal" << endl;
else
    cout << "The values are not equal" << endl;
```

Last, assigning any non-zero value to a Boolean variable results in the variable being set to `true` (a value of 1), and assigning a zero value to a Boolean results in the variable being set to `false` (a value of 0).

EXERCISES 4.2

1. **(Practice)** Write suitable `if` statements for the following conditions:

   a. If an angle is equal to 90 degrees, print the message "The angle is a right angle."; else, print the message "The angle is not a right angle."

   b. If the temperature is above 100 degrees, display the message "above the boiling point of water"; else, display the message "below the boiling point of water."

   c. If the number is positive, add the number to the variable `positivesum`; else, add the number to the variable `negativesum`.

   d. If the slope is less than 0.5, set the variable `flag` to 0; else, set `flag` to 1.

   e. If the difference between `slope1` and `slope2` is less than 0.001, set the variable `approx` to 0; else, calculate `approx` as the quantity `(slope1 - slope2) / 2.0`.

   f. If the frequency is above 60, display the message "The frequency is too high."

   g. If the difference between `temp1` and `temp2` exceeds 2.3, calculate the variable `error` as `(temp1 - temp2) * factor`.

   h. If `x` is greater than `y` and `z` is less than 20, request that the user input a value for the variable `p`.

   i. If distance is greater than 20 and less than 35, request that the user input a value for the variable `time`.

2. **(Practice)** Write `if` statements corresponding to the conditions shown in the following flowcharts:

a.

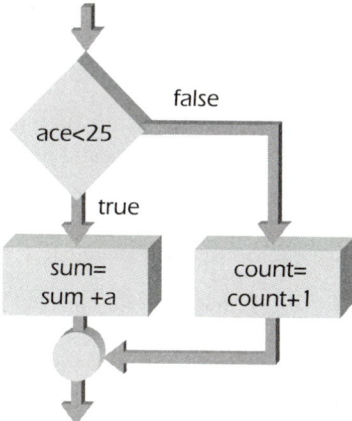

b.

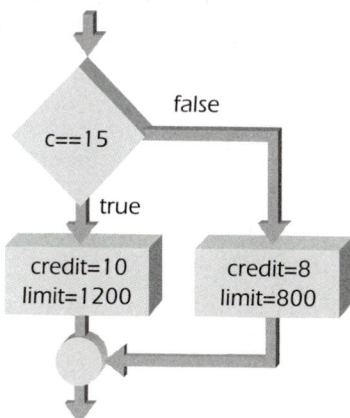

c.

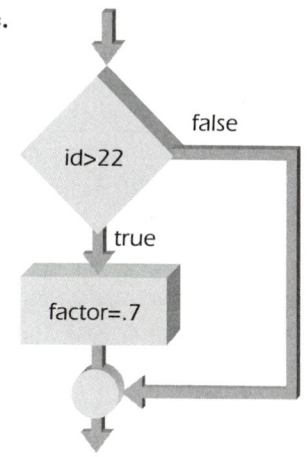

d.

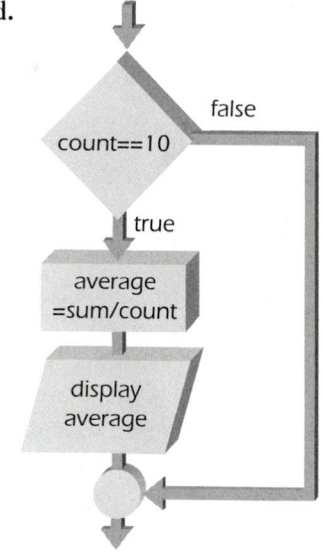

3. **(Practice)** Write a C++ program that asks the user to input two numbers. If the first number entered is greater than the second number, the program should print the message "The first number is greater."; else, it should print the message "The first number is smaller." Test your program by entering the numbers 5 and 8 and then using the numbers 11 and 2. What do you think your program will display if the two numbers entered are equal? Test this case.

4. **(Program) a.** In a pass/fail course, a student passes if the grade is greater than or equal to 70 and fails if the grade is lower than 70. Write a C++ program that accepts a grade and prints the message "A passing grade" or "A failing grade," as appropriate.

   b. How many runs should you make for the program written in Exercise 4a to verify that it's operating correctly? What data should you input in each program run?

5. **(Program) a.** If money is left in a particular bank for more than 5 years, the bank pays interest at a rate of 4.5%; otherwise, the interest rate is 3.0%. Write a C++ program that uses the `cin` object to accept the number of years in the variable `numYears` and display the correct interest rate, depending on the value input into `numYears`.

   b. How many runs should you make for the program written in Exercise 5a to verify that it's operating correctly? What data should you input in each program run?

6. **(Practice) a.** Write a C++ program to display the message "PROCEED WITH TAKEOFF" or "ABORT TAKEOFF" depending on the input. If the character g is entered in the variable `code`, the first message should be displayed; otherwise, the second message should be displayed.

   b. How many runs should you make for the program written in Exercise 6a to verify that it's operating correctly? What data should you input in each program run?

7. **(Program)** Write, compile, and run a C++ program that accepts a user-input integer number and determines whether it's even or odd. The output should display the message "The entered number is even." or "The entered number is odd." corresponding to the number the user entered. (*Hint*: An even number has a 0 remainder when divided by 2.)

8. **(Program)** Write, compile, and run a C++ program that accepts a user-entered number and calculates the square root and the reciprocal. Before calculating the square root, validate that the number isn't negative, and before calculating the reciprocal, check that the number isn't zero. If either condition occurs, display a message stating that the operation can't be calculated.

9. **(Program)** Years that are evenly divisible by 400 or are evenly divisible by 4 but not by 100 are leap years. For example, because 1600 is evenly divisible by 400, 1600 was a leap year. Similarly, because 1988 is evenly divisible by 4 but not by 100, it was also a leap year. Using this information, write a C++ program that accepts the year as user input, determines whether the year is a leap year, and displays a message telling the user whether the entered year is or is not a leap year.

10. **(Program) a.** Write, compile, and run a C++ program to compute and display a person's weekly salary as determined by the following conditions: If the hours worked are less than or equal to 40, the person receives $12.00 per hour; otherwise, the person receives $480.00 plus

$18.00 for each hour worked over 40 hours. The program should request the hours worked as input and display the salary as output.

b. How many runs should you make for the program written in Exercise 10a to verify that it's operating correctly? What data should you input in each program run?

11. **(Program) a.** A senior salesperson is paid $800 a week, and a junior salesperson, $500 a week. Write a C++ program that accepts as input a salesperson's status in the character variable `status`. If `status` equals s, the senior salesperson's salary should be displayed; otherwise, the junior salesperson's salary should be displayed.

b. How many runs should you make for the program written in Exercise 11a to verify that it's operating correctly? What data should you input in each program run?

12. **(Program) a.** Write a C++ program that displays the message "I feel great today!" or "I feel down today #$*!" depending on the input. If the character u is entered in the variable ch, the first message should be displayed; otherwise, the second message should be displayed.

b. How many runs should you make for the program written in Exercise 12a to verify that it's operating correctly? What data should you input in each program run?

13. **(Program) a.** Write a program to display the following two prompts:

```
Enter a month (use a 1 for Jan, etc.):
Enter a day of the month:
```

Have your program accept and store a number in the variable `month` in response to the first prompt and accept and store a number in the variable `day` in response to the second prompt. If the month entered isn't between 1 and 12, display a message informing the user that an invalid month has been entered. If the day entered isn't between 1 and 31, display a message informing the user that an invalid day has been entered.

b. What will your program do if the user enters a number with a decimal point for the month? How can you make sure your `if` statements check for an integer number?

14. **(Program) a.** Write, compile, and run a C++ program that accepts a character as input data and determines whether the character is a lowercase letter. A lowercase letter is any character that's greater than or equal to "a" and less than or equal to "z." If the entered character is a lowercase letter, display the message "The character just entered is a lowercase letter." If the entered letter isn't lowercase, display the message "The character just entered is not a lowercase letter."

b. Modify the program written for Exercise 14a to also determine whether the entered character is an uppercase letter. An uppercase letter is any character greater than or equal to "A" and less than or equal to "Z."

15. **(Program)** Write, compile, and run a C++ program that first determines whether an entered character is a lowercase or an uppercase letter (see Exercise 14). If the letter is lowercase, determine and print its position in the alphabet. For example, if the entered letter is c, the program should print 3 because c is the third letter in the alphabet. (*Hint:* If the entered character is lowercase, its position can be determined by subtracting `'a'` from the letter and adding 1.) Similarly, if the letter is uppercase, determine and print its position in the alphabet. For example, if the entered letter is G, the program should print 7 because G is the seventh letter in the alphabet. (*Hint:* If the entered character is uppercase, its position can be determined by subtracting `'A'` from the letter and adding 1.)

16. **(Program)** Write, compile, and run a C++ program that asks the user to input two numbers. After your program accepts these numbers by using one or more `cin` object calls, have it check the numbers. If the first number entered is greater than the second number, the program should print the message "The first number is greater."; otherwise, it should print the message "The first number is not greater than the second." Test your program by entering the numbers 5 and 8 and then using the numbers 11 and 2. What will your program display if the two numbers entered are equal?

17. **(Debug)** The following program displays the message `Hello there!` regardless of the letter input. Determine where the error is and why the program always causes the message to be displayed.

```cpp
#include <iostream>
using namespace std;
int main()
{
  char letter;

  cout << "Enter a letter: ";
  cin  >> letter;
  if (letter = 'm')
    cout << "Hello there!" << endl;

  return 0;
}
```

4.3 Nested `if` Statements

As you have seen, an `if-else` statement can contain any valid C++ simple or compound statements, including another `if-else` statement. Therefore, one or more `if-else` statements can be included in either part of an `if-else` statement. Including one or more `if` statements inside an existing `if` statement is called a **nested `if` statement**. For example, substituting the one-way `if` statement

```cpp
if (distance > 500)
  cout << "snap";
```

for `statement1` in this `if` statement

```cpp
if (hours < 9)
  statement1;
else
  cout << "pop";
```

results in the following nested if statement:

```
if (hours < 9)
{
  if (distance > 500)
    cout << "snap";
}
else
  cout << "pop";
```

The braces around the inner one-way if statement are essential because in their absence, C++ associates an else with the closest unpaired if. Therefore, without the braces, the preceding statement is equivalent to the following:

```
if (hours < 9)
  if (distance > 500)
    cout << "snap";
  else
    cout << "pop";
```

In this example, the else is paired with the inner if, which destroys the meaning of the original if-else statement. Notice also that the indentation is irrelevant, as far as the compiler is concerned. Whether the indentation exists or not, the statement is compiled by associating the last else with the closest unpaired if, *unless braces are used to alter the default pairing.* The process of nesting if statements can be extended indefinitely, so the cout << "snap"; statement could be replaced by a complete if-else statement or another one-way if statement.

The if-else Chain

In general, nesting in which one if-else statement is placed inside the if part of another if-else statement tends to be confusing and is best avoided in practice. However, an extremely useful construction is placing one if-else statement inside the else part of another if-else statement. Typically, this nesting is written in the following form:

```
if (expression_1)
  statement1;
else if (expression_2)
  statement2;
else
  statement3;
```

This useful construction, called an **if-else chain**, is used extensively in programming applications. Each condition is evaluated in order, and if any condition is true, the corresponding statement is executed, and the remainder of the chain is terminated. The statement associated with the final else is executed only if no previous condition is satisfied. This final else serves as a default or catch-all case that's useful for detecting an impossible condition or an error condition.

The chain can be continued indefinitely by repeatedly making the last statement another `if-else` statement. Therefore, the general form of an `if-else` chain is as follows:

```
if (expression_1)
   statement1;
else if (expression_2)
   statement2;
else if (expression_3)
   statement3;
         .
         .
         .
else if (expression_n)
   statement_n;
else
   last_statement;
```

As with all C++ statements, each statement can be a compound statement bounded by braces. To illustrate using an `if-else` chain, Program 4.4 displays a person's marital status corresponding with a letter input. The following letter codes are used:

Input Code	Marital Status
M	Married
S	Single
D	Divorced
W	Widowed

Program 4.4

```cpp
#include <iostream>
using namespace std;

int main()
{
  char marcode;

  cout << "Enter a marital code: ";
  cin  >> marcode;

  if (marcode == 'M')
    cout << "Individual is married." << endl;
  else if (marcode == 'S')
    cout << "Individual is single." << endl;
```

☞

```
else if (marcode == 'D')
  cout << "Individual is divorced." << endl;
else if (marcode == 'W')
  cout << "Individual is widowed." << endl;
else
  cout << "An invalid code was entered." << endl;

return 0;
}
```

As another example of an if-else chain, take a look at determining the monthly income of a salesperson by using the following commission schedule:

Monthly Sales	Income
Greater than or equal to $50,000	$375 plus 16% of sales
Less than $50,000 but greater than or equal to $40,000	$350 plus 14% of sales
Less than $40,000 but greater than or equal to $30,000	$325 plus 12% of sales
Less than $30,000 but greater than or equal to $20,000	$300 plus 9% of sales
Less than $20,000 but greater than or equal to $10,000	$250 plus 5% of sales
Less than $10,000	$200 plus 3% of sales

The following if-else chain can be used to determine the correct monthly income; the monthlySales variable is used to store the salesperson's current monthly sales:

```
if (monthlySales >= 50000.00)
  income = 375.00 + .16 * monthlySales;
else if (monthlySales >= 40000.00)
  income = 350.00 + .14 * monthlySales;
else if (monthlySales >= 30000.00)
  income = 325.00 + .12 * monthlySales;
else if (monthlySales >= 20000.00)
  income = 300.00 + .09 * monthlySales;
else if (monthlySales >= 10000.00)
  income = 250.00 + .05 * monthlySales;
else
  income = 200.000 + .03 * monthlySales;
```

Notice that this example makes use of the chain stopping after a true condition is found by checking for the highest monthly sales first. If the salesperson's monthly sales are less than $50,000, the if-else chain continues checking for the next highest sales amount, and so on, until the correct category is obtained. Program 4.5 uses this if-else chain to calculate and display the income corresponding with the value of monthly sales input in the cin object.

Program 4.5

```cpp
#include <iostream>
#include <iomanip>
using namespace std;

int main()
{
  double monthlySales, income;

  cout << "Enter the value of monthly sales: ";
  cin  >> monthlySales;
  if (monthlySales >= 50000.00)
    income = 375.00 + .16 * monthlySales;
  else if (monthlySales >= 40000.00)
    income = 350.00 + .14 * monthlySales;
  else if (monthlySales >= 30000.00)
    income = 325.00 + .12 * monthlySales;
  else if (monthlySales >= 20000.00)
    income = 300.00 + .09 * monthlySales;
  else if (monthlySales >= 10000.00)
    income = 250.00 + .05 * monthlySales;
  else
    income = 200.00 + .03 * monthlySales;

  cout << setiosflags(ios::showpoint)
       << setiosflags(ios:: fixed)
       << setprecision(2)
       << "The income is $" << income << endl;

  return 0;
}
```

A sample run of Program 4.5 follows:

```
Enter the value of monthly sales: 36243.89
The income is $4674.27
```

EXERCISES 4.3

1. **(Practice)** An acute angle is less than 90 degrees, an obtuse angle is greater than 90 degrees, and a right angle is equal to 90 degrees. Using this information, write a C++ program that accepts an angle, in degrees, and displays the type of angle corresponding to the degrees entered.

2. **(Program)** The grade level of undergraduate college students is typically determined according to the following schedule:

Number of Credits Completed	Grade Level
Less than 32	Freshman
32 to 63	Sophomore
64 to 95	Junior
96 or more	Senior

Using this information, write a C++ program that accepts the number of credits a student has completed, determines the student's grade level, and displays the grade level.

3. **(Program)** A student's letter grade is calculated according to the following schedule:

Numerical Grade	Letter Grade
Greater than or equal to 90	A
Less than 90 but greater than or equal to 80	B
Less than 80 but greater than or equal to 70	C
Less than 70 but greater than or equal to 60	D
Less than 60	F

Using this information, write, compile, and run a C++ program that accepts a student's numerical grade, converts the numerical grade to an equivalent letter grade, and displays the letter grade.

4. **(Program)** The interest rate paid on funds deposited in a bank is determined by the amount of time the money is left on deposit. For a particular bank, the following schedule is used:

Time on Deposit	Interest Rate
Greater than or equal to 5 years	.040
Less than 5 years but greater than or equal to 4 years	.035
Less than 4 years but greater than or equal to 3 years	.030
Less than 3 years but greater than or equal to 2 years	.025
Less than 2 years but greater than or equal to 1 year	.020
Less than 1 year	.015

Write, compile, and run a C++ program that accepts the time funds are left on deposit and displays the interest rate corresponding with the time entered.

5. **(Program)** Fluid flowing through a pipe can flow in a smooth, constant manner, called laminar flow; in a chaotic manner, called turbulent flow; or in an intermediate stage between smooth and turbulent flow, which is called transitional flow. In practice, a value known as the Reynolds number can be used to determine the type of flow. For a Reynolds number below 2000, the flow is laminar, and for a Reynolds number above 3000, the flow is turbulent. For a Reynolds number between 2000 and 3000, the flow is transitional.

Using this information, write, compile, and run a C++ program that accepts a Reynolds number as user input and displays a message indicating whether the flow is laminar, turbulent, or transitional.

6. **(Program)** The tolerance of critical components in a system is determined according to the following schedule:

Specification Status	Tolerance
Space exploration	Less than 0.1%
Military grade	Greater than or equal to 0.1% and less than 1%
Commercial grade	Greater than or equal to 1% and less than 10%
Toy grade	Greater than or equal to 10%

Using this information, write, compile, and run a C++ program that accepts a component's tolerance reading and determines the specification that should be assigned to it.

7. **(Program) a.** Write, compile, and run a program that accepts two real numbers and a select code from a user. If the entered select code is 1, have the program add the two previously entered numbers and display the result; if the select code is 2, the numbers should be multiplied; and if the select code is 3, the first number should be divided by the second number.

   b. Determine what the program written in Exercise 7a does when the entered numbers are 3 and 0 and the select code is 3.

   c. Modify the program written in Exercise 7a so that division by 0 isn't allowed, and a message is displayed when this division is attempted.

8. **(Program)** The quadrant in which a line starting from the origin is located is determined by the angle the line makes with the positive x axis, as follows:

Angle from the Positive x Axis	Quadrant
Between 0 and 90 degrees	I
Between 90 and 180 degrees	II
Between 180 and 270 degrees	III
Between 270 and 360 degrees	IV

   a. Using this information, write, compile, and run a C++ program that accepts the angle of the line as user input and determines and displays the correct quadrant for the input data. (*Note:* If the angle is exactly 0, 90, 180, or 270 degrees, the corresponding line doesn't reside in any quadrant but lies on an axis.)

   b. Modify the program written for Exercise 8a to display a message that identifies an angle of 0 degrees as the positive x axis, an angle of 90 degrees as the positive y axis, an angle of 180 degrees as the negative x axis, and an angle of 270 degrees as the negative y axis.

9. **(Program)** Write, compile, and run a C++ program that accepts a number followed by one space and then a letter. If the letter following the number is f, the program is to treat the number entered as a temperature in degrees Fahrenheit, convert the number to the equivalent degrees Celsius, and display a suitable message. If the letter following the number is c, the program is to treat the number entered as a temperature in degrees Celsius, convert the number to the equivalent degrees Fahrenheit, and display a suitable message. If the letter is neither f nor c, the program is to display a message that the data entered is incorrect and then terminate. Use an `if-else` chain in your program and make use of these conversion formulas:
Celsius = (5.0 / 9.0) × (Fahrenheit - 32.0)
Fahrenheit = (9.0 / 5.0) × Celsius + 32.0

10. **(Program)** Many states base yearly car registration fees on an automobile's model year and weight, using a schedule similar to the following:

Model Year	Weight	Weight Class	Registration Fee
1990 or earlier	Less than 2700 lbs	1	26.50
	2700 to 3800 lbs	2	35.50
	More than 3800 lbs	3	56.50
1991 to 1999	Less than 2700 lbs	4	35.00
	2700 to 3800 lbs	5	45.50
	More than 3800 lbs	6	62.50
2000 or later	Less than 3500 lbs	7	49.50
	3500 or more lbs	8	62.50

Using this information, write, compile, and run a C++ program that accepts an automobile's year and weight and determines and displays its weight class and registration fee.

11. **(Debug)** Using the commission schedule from Program 4.5, the following program calculates monthly income:

```
#include <iostream>
#include <iomanip>
using namespace std;

int main()
{
    double monthlySales, income;

    cout << "Enter the value of monthly sales: ";
    cin  >> monthlySales;
    if (monthlySales >= 50000.00)
        income = 375.00 + .16 * monthlySales;
    if (monthlySales >= 40000.00 && monthlySales < 50000.00)
        income = 350.00 + .14 * monthlySales;
    if (monthlySales >= 30000.00 && monthlySales < 40000.00)
        income = 325.00 + .12 * monthlySales;
```

```
    if (monthlySales >= 20000.00 && monthlySales < 30000.00)
      income = 300.00 + .09 * monthlySales;
    if (monthlySales >= 10000.00 && monthlySales < 20000.00)
      income = 250.00 + .05 * monthlySales;
    if (monthlySales < 10000.00)
      income = 200.00 + .03 * monthlySales;

    cout << setiosflags(ios::showpoint)
         << setiosflags(ios:: fixed)
         << setprecision(2)
         << "\n\nThe income is $" << income << endl;

    return 0;
  }
```

a. Will this program produce the same output as Program 4.5?

b. Which program is better? Why?

12. **(Debug)** The following program was written to produce the same result as Program 4.5:

```
#include <iostream>
#include <iomanip>
using namespace std;

int main()
{
  double monthlySales, income;

  cout << "Enter the value of monthly sales: ";
  cin  >> monthlySales;

  if (monthlySales < 10000.00)
    income = 200.00 + .03 * monthlySales;
  else if (monthlySales >= 10000.00)
    income = 250.00 + .05 * monthlySales;
  else if (monthlySales >= 20000.00)
    income = 300.00 + .09 * monthlySales;
  else if (monthlySales >= 30000.00)
    income = 325.00 + .12 * monthlySales;
  else if (monthlySales >= 40000.00)
    income = 350.00 + .14 * monthlySales;
  else if (monthlySales >= 50000.00)
    income = 375.00 + .16 * monthlySales;

  cout << setiosflags(ios::showpoint)
       << setiosflags(ios:: fixed)
```

```
          << setprecision(2)
          << "The income is $" << income << endl;

     return 0;
 }
```

a. What does this program do?

b. For what values of monthly sales does this program calculate the correct income?

4.4 The switch Statement

An if-else chain is used in programming applications in which one set of instructions must be selected from many possible alternatives. A **switch statement** is an alternative to the if-else chain for cases that involve comparing an integer expression with a specific value. It has this general form:

```
switch (integer_expression)
{    // start of compound statement
  case value_1:  // terminated with a colon
    statement1;
    statement2;

       .

       .

    break;
  case value_2:  // terminated with a colon
    statementm;
    statementn;

       .

       .

    break;

    .

    .

  case value_n:  // terminated with a colon
    statementw;
    statementx;

       .

       .

    break;
  default:  // terminated with a colon
    statementaa;
    statementbb;

       .

       .

 }    // end of switch and compound statement
```

The `switch` statement uses four new keywords: `switch`, `case`, `default`, and `break`. The following discussion explains what each of these keywords does.

The `switch` keyword identifies the start of the `switch` statement. The expression in parentheses after `switch` is then evaluated, and the result is compared with alternative values contained in the compound statement. The expression in the `switch` statement must evaluate to an integer result, or a compilation error results.

In the `switch` statement, the `case` keyword identifies values that are compared with the `switch` expression's value. The `case` values are compared in the order in which they're listed until a match is found, and then execution begins with the statement following the match. As shown in Figure 4.4, the `switch` expression's value determines where execution actually begins.

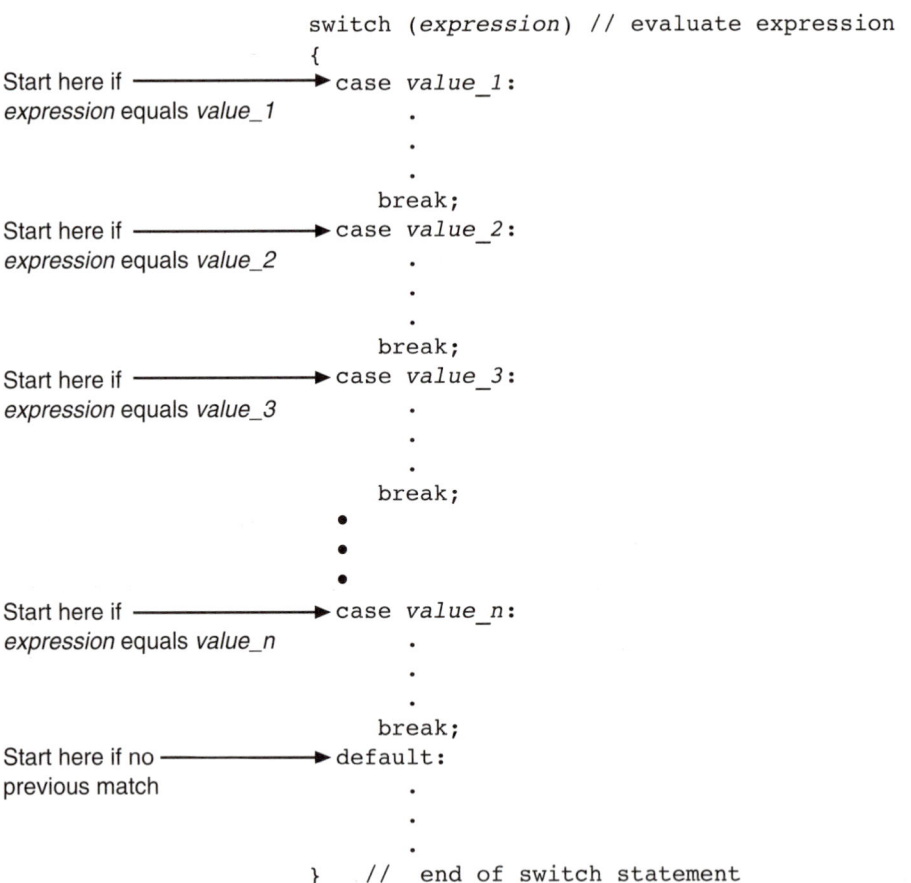

Figure 4.4   The expression determines an entry point for execution

A `switch` statement can contain any number of `case` labels in any order. If the value of the expression doesn't match any of the `case` values, however, no statement is executed unless the `default` keyword is encountered. (The `default` keyword is optional and operates just like the last `else` in an `if-else` chain.) If the value of the expression doesn't match any `case` value, program execution begins with the statement following the `default` keyword.

After the switch statement has located an entry point, all further case value evaluations are ignored. Execution continues through the end of the compound statement unless the break keyword is encountered, which identifies the end of a case and causes an immediate exit from the switch statement. Just as the case keyword identifies possible entry points in the compound statement, the break keyword determines terminating points. If break statements are omitted, all cases following the matching case value, including the default case, are executed.

When writing a switch statement, you can use multiple case values to refer to the same set of statements; the default keyword is optional, as mentioned. For example, take a look at the following:

```
switch (number)
{
  case 1:
    cout << "Have a Good Morning\n";
    break;
  case 2:
    cout << "Have a Happy Day\n";
    break;
  case 3:
  case 4:
  case 5:
    cout << "Have a Nice Evening\n";
}
```

If the value stored in the number variable is 1, the message Have a Good Morning is displayed. Similarly, if the value of number is 2, the second message is displayed. Finally, if the value of number is 3, 4, or 5, the last message is displayed. Because the statement to be executed for the last three cases is the same, the case statements for these values can be "stacked together," as shown in the example. Also, because there's no default keyword, no message is printed if the value of number isn't one of the listed case values. Although listing case values in increasing order is a good programming practice, it's not required by the switch statement. A switch statement can have any number of case values, in any order; only the values you're testing for must be listed.

Program 4.6 uses a switch statement to select the arithmetic operation (addition, multiplication, or division) to perform on two numbers, depending on the value of the opselect variable.

Program 4.6

```
#include <iostream>
using namespace std;
int main()
{
  int opselect;
```

```
    double fnum, snum;

    cout << "Please type in two numbers: ";
    cin  >> fnum >> snum;
    cout << "Enter a select code: ";
    cout << "\n          1 for addition";
    cout << "\n          2 for multiplication";
    cout << "\n          3 for division : ";
    cin  >> opselect;

    switch (opselect)
    {
      case 1:
        cout << "The sum of the numbers entered is "
             << fnum+snum << endl;
        break;
      case 2:
        cout << "The product of the numbers entered is "
             << fnum*snum << endl;
        break;
      case 3:
        cout << "The first number divided by the second is "
             << fnum/snum << endl;
        break;
    }      // end of switch

    return 0;
}   // end of main()
```

In the following two sample runs, the display clearly identifies the `case` that was selected:

```
    Please type in two numbers: 12 3
    Enter a select code:
            1 for addition
            2 for multiplication
            3 for division : 2
    The product of the numbers entered is 36
```

and

```
    Please type in two numbers: 12 3
    Enter a select code:
            1 for addition
            2 for multiplication
            3 for division : 3
    The first number divided by the second is 4
```

In reviewing Program 4.6, notice the `break` statement in the last `case` statement. Although it's not necessary, terminating the last `case` in a `switch` statement with a `break` is a good programming practice. It prevents a possible program error later if another `case` statement is added to the `switch` statement. With the addition of a new `case`, the `break` keyword between cases ensures that you won't forget to include the `break` at the time of the modification.

Because character data types are always converted to integers in an expression, a `switch` statement can also be used to "switch" based on the value of a character expression. For example, assuming `choice` is a character variable, the following `switch` statement is valid:

```
switch(choice)
{
  case 'a': case 'e': case 'i': case 'o': case 'u':
    cout << "The character in choice is a vowel\n";
    break;
  default:
    cout << "The character in choice is not a vowel\n";
    break;    // this break is optional
}    // end of switch statement
```

EXERCISES 4.4

1. **(Modify)** Rewrite the following `if-else` chain by using a `switch` statement:

```
if (letterGrade == 'A')
  cout << "The numerical grade is between 90 and 100\n";
else if (letterGrade == 'B')
  cout << "The numerical grade is between 80 and 89.9\n";
else if (letterGrade == 'C')
  cout << "The numerical grade is between 70 and 79.9\n";
else if (letterGrade == 'D')
  cout << "How are you going to explain this one?\n";
else
{
  cout << "Of course I had nothing to do with my grade.\n";
  cout << "It must have been the professor's fault.\n";
}
```

2. **(Modify)** Rewrite the following `if-else` chain by using a `switch` statement:

```
if (bondType == 1)
{
  inData();
  check();
}
else if (bondType == 2)
{
```

☞

```
    dates();
    leapYr();
}
else if (bondType == 3)
{
   yield();
   maturity();
}
else if (bondType == 4)
{
   price();
   roi();
}
else if (bondType == 5)
{
   files();
   save();
}
else if (bondType == 6)
{
   retrieve();
   screen();
}
```

3. (**Program**) Each storage drive in a shipment is stamped with a code from 1 to 4, indicating the following storage capacities:

Code	Capacity
1	2 GB
2	4 GB
3	16 GB
4	32 GB

Write, compile, and run a C++ program that accepts the code number as an input value and, based on the value entered, displays the correct storage drive capacity.

4. (**Modify**) Rewrite Program 4.4 by using a `switch` statement.

5. (**Modify**) Repeat Exercise 9 in Section 4.3, using a `switch` statement instead of an `if-else` chain.

6. (**Modify**) Rewrite Program 4.6 by using a character variable for the select code.

7. (**For thought**) Determine why the `if-else` chain in Program 4.5 can't be replaced with a `switch` statement.

4.5 Common Programming Errors

Three programming errors are common with C++'s selection statements:

1. Using the assignment operator, =, in place of the relational operator ==. This error can cause frustration because any expression can be tested by an if-else statement, so it's not a syntax error that the compiler will pick up. Rather, it's a logic error, which can be difficult to locate. For example, the statement

```
if (opselect = 2)
    cout << "Happy Birthday";
else
    cout << "Good Day";
```

always results in the message Happy Birthday being displayed, regardless of the initial value in the opselect variable. The reason is that the assignment expression opselect = 2 has a value of 2, which is considered a true value in C++. The correct expression to determine the value in opselect is opselect == 2.

2. Letting the if-else statement appear to select an incorrect choice. In this typical debugging problem, the programmer mistakenly concentrates on the tested condition as the source of the problem. For example, assume the following if-else statement is part of your program:

```
if (key == 'F')
{
    contemp = (5.0/9.0) * (intemp - 32.0);
    cout << "Conversion to Celsius was done";
}
else
{
    contemp = (9.0/5.0) * intemp + 32.0;
    cout << "Conversion to Fahrenheit was done";
}
```

This statement always displays Conversion to Celsius was done when the variable key contains an F. Therefore, if this message is displayed when you believe key doesn't contain F, you should investigate key's value. As a general rule, whenever a selection statement doesn't act as you think it should, test your assumptions about the values assigned to the tested variables by displaying their values. If an unanticipated value is displayed, you have at least isolated the source of the problem to the variables rather than the structure of the if-else statement. From there, you have to determine where and how the incorrect value was produced.

3. Using nested `if` statements without including braces to indicate the structure. Without braces, the compiler defaults to pairing `else`s with the closest unpaired `if`s, which sometimes destroys the selection statement's original intent. To avoid this problem and create code that's adaptable to change, writing all `if-else` statements as compound statements in this form is useful:

```
if (expression)
{
    one or more statements in here
}
else
{
    one or more statements in here

}
```

No matter how many statements are added later, this form maintains the `if` statement's original intent.

4.6 Chapter Summary

1. Relational expressions, also called conditions, are used to compare operands. If a relational expression is true, the value of the expression is the integer 1. If the relational expression is false, it has an integer value of 0. Relational expressions are created by using the following relational operators:

Relational Operator	Meaning	Example
<	Less than	`age < 30`
>	Greater than	`height > 6.2`
<=	Less than or equal to	`taxable <= 20000`
>=	Greater than or equal to	`temp >= 98.6`
==	Equal to	`grade == 100`
!=	Not equal to	`number != 250`

2. More complex conditions can be constructed from relational expressions by using C++'s logical operators, `&&` (AND), `||` (OR), and `!` (NOT).

3. An `if-else` statement is used to select between two alternative statements based on an expression's value. Although relational expressions are usually used for the tested expression, any valid expression can be used. In testing an expression, `if-else` statements interpret a non-zero value as true and a zero value as false. The general form of an `if-else` statement is as follows:

```
if (expression)
    statement1;
else
    statement2;
```

This form is a two-way selection statement. If the expression has a non-zero value, it's considered true and *statement1* is executed; otherwise, *statement2* is executed.

4. An `if-else` statement can contain other `if-else` statements. In the absence of braces, each `else` is associated with the closest preceding unpaired `if`.

5. The `if-else` chain is a multiway selection statement with this general form:

```
if (expression_1)
   statement_1;
else if (expression_2)
   statement_2;
else if (expression_3)
   statement_3;

         .

         .

         .

else if (expression_m)
   statement_m;
else
   statement_n;
```

Each expression is evaluated in the order in which it appears in the chain. If an expression is true (has a non-zero value), only the statement between this expression and the next `else if` or `else` is executed, and no further expressions are tested. The final `else` is optional, and the statement corresponding to the final `else` is executed only if no previous expressions are true.

6. A compound statement consists of any number of single statements enclosed by the brace pair { and }. Compound statements are treated as a single unit and can be used anywhere a single statement is used.

7. Variables have meaning only in the block in which they're declared, which includes any inner block contained in the declaring block.

8. The `switch` statement is a multiway selection statement with this general form:

```
switch (integer_expression)
{     // start of compound statement
  case value_1:  // terminated with a colon
     statement1;
     statement2;

        .

        .

     break;
  case value_2:  // terminated with a colon
     statementm;
     statementn;
```

```
        .
        .
    break;
        .
        .
  case value_n:  // terminated with a colon
     statementw;
     statementx;
        .
        .
    break;
  default:  // terminated with a colon
     statementaa;
     statementbb;
        .
        .

}    // end of switch and compound statement
```

For this statement, the value of an integer expression is compared with integer or character constants or constant expressions. Program execution is transferred to the first matching case and continues through the end of the switch statement, unless an optional break statement is encountered. The case values in a switch statement can appear in any order, and an optional default case can be included. The default case is executed if no other cases are matched.

4.7 Chapter Supplement: A Closer Look at Testing

In theory, a comprehensive set of test runs would reveal all possible program errors and ensure that a program works correctly for any combination of input and computed data. In practice, this level of testing requires checking all possible combinations of statement execution. Because of the time and effort required, this goal is usually impossible except for extremely simple programs. To see why this is so, take a look at Program 4.7.

 **Program 4.7**

```cpp
#include <iostream>
using namespace std;

int main()
{
  int num;
  cout << "Enter a number: ";
  cin  >> num;
```

☞

```
if (num == 5)
   cout << "Bingo!\n";
else
   cout << "Bongo!\n";

return 0;
}
```

Program 4.7 has two paths that can be traversed as the program progresses from its opening brace to its closing brace. The first path, which is executed when the input number is 5, is in this sequence:

```
cout << "Enter a number";
cin  >> num;
cout << "Bingo!\n";
```

The second path, which is executed when any number except 5 is input, includes this sequence of instructions:

```
cout << "Enter a number";
cin  >> num;
cout << "Bongo!\n";
```

Testing each possible path through Program 4.7 requires two runs with a judicious selection of test input data to make sure both paths of the if statement are exercised. Adding one more if statement in the program increases the number of possible execution paths by a factor of two and requires four (that is, 2^2) runs for complete testing. Similarly, a program consisting of three unnested if-else statements requires eight (that is, 2^3) runs for complete testing, and a program containing four unnested if-else statements requires 16 (that is, 2^4) test runs.

Now consider a program consisting of only 10 modules, with each module containing five if statements. Assuming the modules are always called in the same sequence, there are 32 possible paths through each module (2^5) and more than 1,000,000,000,000,000 (2^{50}, representing the number of modules multiplied by the number of if statements per module) possible paths through the complete program (all modules executed in sequence). The time needed to create test data and the computer runtime required to exercise each path with the test data make complete testing of this program virtually impossible.

The inability to test all combinations of statement execution sequences fully has led to the programming proverb "There is no error-free program." It has also led to the realization that any testing should be well thought out to maximize the possibility of locating errors. At a minimum, test data should include suitable values for input data, illegal input values that the program should reject, and limiting values that are checked by selection statements in the program.

Chapter

5

Repetition

The programs you've examined so far have illustrated the programming concepts involved in input, output, assignment, and selection capabilities. By this time, you should have gained enough experience to be comfortable with these concepts and the mechanics of implementing them in C++. Many problems, however, require a repetition capability, in which the same calculation or sequence of instructions is repeated, over and over, using different sets of data. Examples of this type of repetition include continual checking of user data entries until an acceptable entry, such as a valid password, is entered; counting and accumulating running totals; and constant acceptance of input data and recalculation of output values that stop only at entry of a sentinel value.

This chapter explores the different methods programmers use in constructing repeating sections of code and explains how they can be implemented in C++. More commonly, a section of code that's repeated is referred to as a loop because after the last statement in the code is executed, the program can branch, or loop, back to the first statement and start another repetition through the code. Each repetition is also referred to as an iteration or a pass through the loop. In this chapter, you explore the C++ statements used to create loops: `while`, `for`, *and* `do-while`.

5.1 The `while` Statement

A **while statement** is a general repetition statement that can be used in a variety of programming situations. It has this general form:

```
while (expression)
  statement;
```

The *expression* in parentheses is evaluated in exactly the same manner as one in an `if-else` statement; the difference is in how the expression is used. As you have seen, when the expression in an `if-else` statement is true (has a non-zero value), the statement following the expression is executed once. In a `while` statement, the statement following the expression is executed repeatedly as long as the expression evaluates to a non-zero value. Naturally, this means that somewhere in the `while` statement must be a statement altering the tested expression's value. As you'll see, this is indeed the case. For now, however, considering just the expression and the statement following the parentheses, the computer uses this process in evaluating a `while` statement:

1. Test the expression
2. If the expression has a non-zero (true) value
    a. execute the statement following the parentheses
    b. go back to Step 1
  else
    exit the `while` statement and execute the next executable statement following the `while` statement

Notice that Step 2b forces program control to be transferred back to Step 1. This transfer of control back to the start of a `while` statement to reevaluate the expression is what forms the program loop. The `while` statement literally loops back on itself to recheck the expression until it evaluates to zero (becomes false). This rechecking means the loop must contain a provision that permits altering the tested expression's value. As you'll see, this provision is indeed made.

Figure 5.1 shows the looping process a `while` statement produces. A diamond shape is used to show the two entry and two exit points required in the decision part of the `while` statement.

To make this looping process more tangible, consider the relational expression `count <= 10` and the statement `cout << count;`. Using these elements, you can write the following valid `while` statement:

```
while (count <= 10)
  cout << count;
```

Although this statement is valid, the alert reader will realize that it creates a situation in which the `cout` statement is called forever (or until you stop the program) or not called at all. Here's why this happens: If `count` has a value less than or equal to 10 when the expression is first evaluated, a call to `cout` is made. The `while` statement then automatically loops back on itself and retests the expression. Because you haven't changed the value stored in `count`, the expression is still true, and another call to `cout` is made. This process continues forever, or until the program containing this statement is stopped prematurely by the user. However, if count starts with a value greater than 10, the expression is false to begin with, and the call to cout is never made.

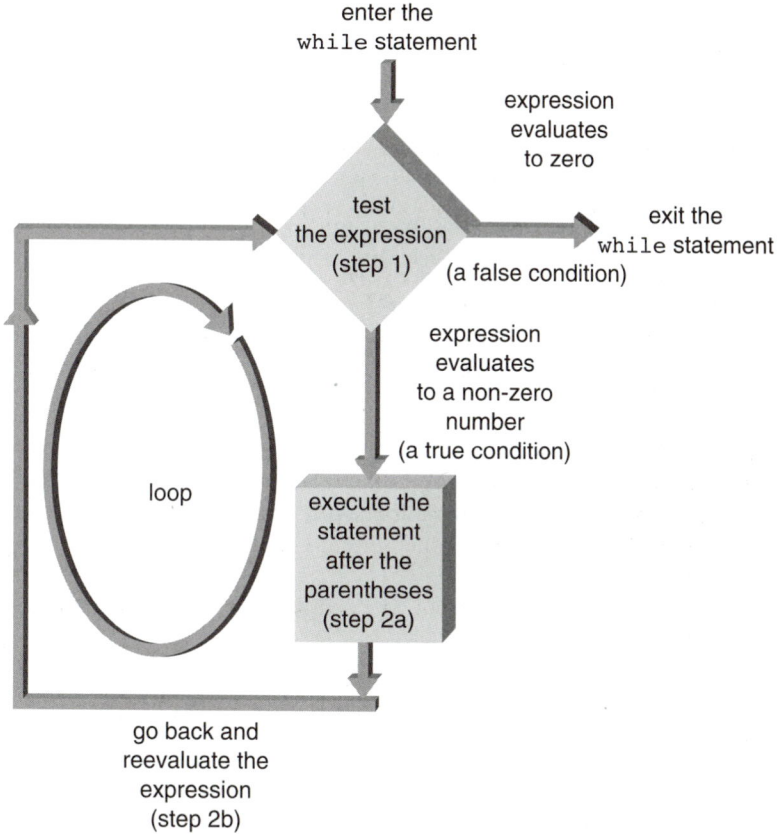

enter the
while statement

expression
evaluates
to zero

test
the expression
(step 1)

exit the
while statement
(a false condition)

expression
evaluates
to a non-zero
number
(a true condition)

loop

execute the
statement
after the
parentheses
(step 2a)

go back and
reevaluate the
expression
(step 2b)

Figure 5.1 Anatomy of a while loop

How do you set an initial value in count to control what the while statement does the first time the expression is evaluated? The answer, of course, is to assign values to each variable in the tested expression before the while statement is encountered. For example, the following sequence of instructions is valid:

```
count = 1;
while (count <= 10)
  cout << count << " ";
```

Using this sequence of instructions ensures that count starts with a value of 1. You could assign any value to count in the assignment statement. What's important is to assign *some* value. In practice, the assigned value depends on the application.

You must still change the value of count so that you can finally exit the while statement. Doing so requires an expression such as count = count + 1 to increment the value of count each time the while statement is executed. The fact that a while statement provides for repetition of a single statement doesn't prevent including an additional statement to change the value of count. All you have to do is replace the single statement with a compound statement, as in this example:

```
count = 1;            // initialize count
while (count <= 10)
{
  cout << count << " ";
  count++;            // increment count
}
```

Note that, for clarity, each statement in the compound statement is placed on a different line. This format is consistent with the convention adopted for compound statements in Chapter 4.

Now analyze the preceding sequence of instructions. The first assignment statement sets count equal to 1. The while statement is then entered, and the expression is evaluated for the first time. Because the value of count is less than or equal to 10, the expression is true, and the compound statement is executed. The first statement in the compound statement uses the cout object to display the value of count. The next statement adds 1 to the value currently stored in count, making this value equal to 2. The while statement then loops back to retest the expression. Because count is still less than or equal to 10, the compound statement is executed again. This process continues until the value of count reaches 11. Program 5.1 shows these statements in an actual program.

 **Program 5.1**

```
#include <iostream>
using namespace std;

int main()
{
  int count;

  count = 1;                  // initialize count
  while (count <= 10)
  {
    cout << count << " ";
    count++;                  // increment count
  }

  return 0;
}
```

This is the output for Program 5.1:

    1   2   3   4   5   6   7   8   9   10

Note that there's nothing special about the name count used in Program 5.1. Any valid integer variable could have been used.

Before you look at other examples of the while statement, two comments on Program 5.1 are in order. First, the statement count++ can be replaced with any statement that changes the value of count. A statement such as count = count + 2;, for example, causes every second integer to be displayed. Second, it's the programmer's responsibility to ensure that count is changed in a way that leads to a normal exit from the while statement. For example, if you replace the expression count++ with the expression count--, the value of count never exceeds 10 and an infinite loop is created. An **infinite loop** is one that never ends. The computer doesn't tap you on the shoulder and say, "Excuse me. You've created an infinite loop." The program just keeps displaying numbers until you realize it isn't working as you expected.

Now that you have some familiarity with the while statement, see whether you can read and determine the output of Program 5.2.

Program 5.2

```cpp
#include <iostream>
using namespace std;

int main()
{
   int i;

   i = 10;
   while (i >= 1)
   {
     cout << i << " ";
     i--;    // subtract 1 from i
   }

   return 0;
}
```

The assignment statement in Program 5.2 initially sets the int variable i to 10. The while statement then checks whether the value of i is greater than or equal to 1. While the expression is true, the value of i is displayed by the cout object, and the value of i is decremented by 1. When i finally reaches 0, the expression is false, and the program exits the while statement. Therefore, Program 5.2 produces the following display when it runs:

        10 9 8 7 6 5 4 3 2 1

To understand the power of the while statement, consider the task of printing a table of numbers from 1 to 10 with the numbers' squares and cubes. You can do this with a simple while statement, as shown in Program 5.3.

 Program 5.3

```cpp
#include <iostream>
#include <iomanip>
using namespace std;

int main()
{
  int num;
  cout << "NUMBER    SQUARE    CUBE\n"
       << "------    ------    ----\n";

  num = 1;
  while (num < 11)
  {
    cout << setw(3) << num << "         "
         << setw(3) << num * num << "        "
         << setw(4) << num * num * num << endl;
    num++;     // increment num
  }

  return 0;
}
```

When Program 5.3 runs, the following display is produced:

NUMBER	SQUARE	CUBE
1	1	1
2	4	8
3	9	27
4	16	64
5	25	125
6	36	216
7	49	343
8	64	512
9	81	729
10	100	1000

Note that the expression used in Program 5.3 is num < 11. For the integer variable num, this expression is exactly equivalent to the expression num <= 10. The choice of which to use is entirely up to you.

If you want to use Program 5.3 to produce a table of 1000 numbers, all you do is change the expression in the while statement from num < 11 to num < 1001. Changing the 11 to 1001 produces a table of 1000 lines—not bad for a simple five-line while statement.

All the program examples of the while statement use fixed-count loops because the tested condition is a counter that checks for a fixed number of repetitions. In a variation on the fixed-count loop, the counter isn't incremented by 1 each time through the loop but by some other value. For example, suppose you have the task of producing a Celsius-to-Fahrenheit temperature conversion table. Fahrenheit temperatures corresponding to Celsius temperatures from 5 to 50 degrees are to be displayed in increments of 5 degrees, which can be done with this series of statements:

```cpp
celsius = 5;      // starting Celsius value
while (celsius <= 50)
{
   fahren = (9.0/5.0) * celsius + 32.0;
   cout << setw(4)  << celsius
        << setw(13) << fahren << endl;
   celsius = celsius + 5;
}
```

As before, the while statement consists of everything from the word while through the compound statement's closing brace. Before the program enters the while loop, you must make sure a value is assigned to the counter being evaluated, and there's a statement to alter the counter's value in the loop (in increments of 5) to ensure an exit from the while loop. Program 5.4 illustrates using similar code in a complete program.

Program 5.4

```cpp
#include <iostream>
#include <iomanip>
using namespace std;

// a program to convert Celsius to Fahrenheit
int main()
{

  const int MAXCELSIUS = 50;
  const int STARTVAL = 5;
  const int STEPSIZE = 5;
  int celsius;
  double fahren;

  cout << "DEGREES    DEGREES\n"
       << "CELSIUS   FAHRENHEIT\n"
       << "-------    ----------\n";

  celsius = STARTVAL;
```

☞

```
// set output formats for floating-point numbers only
cout << setiosflags(ios::showpoint) << setiosflags(ios::fixed)
     << setprecision(2);

while (celsius <= MAXCELSIUS)
{
 fahren = (9.0/5.0) * celsius + 32.0;
 cout << setw(4)  << celsius
      << setw(13) << fahren << endl;
 celsius = celsius + STEPSIZE;
}

return 0;
}
```

This is the display produced when Program 5.4 runs:

```
DEGREES    DEGREES
CELSIUS   FAHRENHEIT
-------   ----------
   5        41.00
  10        50.00
  15        59.00
  20        68.00
  25        77.00
  30        86.00
  35        95.00
  40       104.00
  45       113.00
  50       122.00
```

 **EXERCISES 5.1**

1. **(Modify)** Rewrite Program 5.1 to print the numbers 2 to 10 in increments of 2. The output of your program should be the following:

   2   4   6   8   10

2. **(Modify)** Rewrite Program 5.4 to produce a table starting at a Celsius value of -10 and ending with a Celsius value of 60, in increments of 10 degrees.

3. **(Desk check) a.** For the following program, determine the total number of items displayed as well as the first and last numbers printed:

   ```
   #include <iostream>
   using namespace std;
   ```

```
int main()
{
  int num = 0;
  while (num <= 20)
  {
    num++;
    cout << num << " ";
  }

  return 0;
}
```

b. Enter and run the program from Exercise 3a on a computer to verify your answers to the exercise.

c. How would the output be affected if the two statements in the compound statement were reversed (that is, if the `cout` statement were placed before the `num++` statement)?

4. **(Program)** Write, compile, and run a C++ program that converts gallons to liters. The program should display gallons from 10 to 20 in 1-gallon increments and the corresponding liter equivalents. Use the relationship that 1 gallon = 3.785 liters.

5. **(Program)** Write, compile, and run a C++ program that converts feet to meters. The program should display feet from 3 to 30 in 3-foot increments and the corresponding meter equivalents. Use the relationship that 3.28 feet = 1 meter.

6. **(Program)** A machine purchased for $28,000 is depreciated at a rate of $4000 a year for 7 years. Write, compile, and run a C++ program that computes and displays a depreciation table for 7 years. The table should have this form:

YEAR	DEPRECIATION	END-OF-YEAR VALUE	ACCUMULATED DEPRECIATION
1	4000	24000	4000
2	4000	20000	8000
3	4000	16000	12000
4	4000	12000	16000
5	4000	8000	20000
6	4000	4000	24000
7	4000	0	28000

7. **(Program)** An automobile travels at an average speed of 55 mph for 4 hours. Write, compile, and run a C++ program that displays the distance, in miles, the car has traveled after 0.5, 1.0, 1.5, and so on hours until the end of the trip.

8. **(Program) a.** The following is an approximate conversion formula for converting Fahrenheit to Celsius temperatures:

Celsius = (Fahrenheit - 30) / 2

Using this formula, and starting with a Fahrenheit temperature of 0 degrees, write a C++ program that determines when the approximate equivalent Celsius temperature differs from the exact equivalent value by more than 4 degrees. (*Hint:* Use a `while` loop that terminates when the difference between approximate and exact Celsius equivalents exceeds 4 degrees.)

b. Using the approximate Celsius conversion formula given in Exercise 8a, write a C++ program that produces a table of Fahrenheit temperatures, exact Celsius equivalent temperatures, approximate Celsius equivalent temperatures, and the difference between the exact and approximate equivalent Celsius values. The table should begin at 0 degrees Fahrenheit, use 2-degree Fahrenheit increments, and terminate when the difference between exact and approximate values is more than 4 degrees.

5.2 Interactive `while` Loops

Combining interactive data entry with the repetition capabilities of the `while` statement produces adaptable and powerful programs. To understand the concept, take a look at Program 5.5, in which a `while` statement is used to accept and then display four user-entered numbers, one at a time. Although the program uses a simple idea, it highlights the flow of control concepts needed to produce more useful programs.

 **Program 5.5**

```cpp
#include <iostream>
using namespace std;

int main()
{
  const int MAXNUMS = 4;
  int count;
  double num;

  cout << "\nThis program will ask you to enter "
       << MAXNUMS << " numbers.\n";
  count = 1;

  while (count <= MAXNUMS)
  {
    cout << "\nEnter a number: ";
    cin  >> num;
    cout << "The number entered is " << num;
    count++;
  }
  cout << endl;

  return 0;
}
```

The following is a sample run of Program 5.5. The bolded numbers were input in response to the prompts:

```
This program will ask you to enter 4 numbers.

Enter a number: 26.2
The number entered is 26.2
Enter a number: 5
The number entered is 5
Enter a number: 103.456
The number entered is 103.456
Enter a number: 1267.89
The number entered is 1267.89
```

Review the program so that you understand clearly how the output was produced. The first message displayed is caused by execution of the first cout statement. This statement is outside and before the while statement, so it's executed once, before any statement in the while loop.

After the while loop is entered, the statements in the compound statement are executed while the tested condition is true. The first time through the compound statement, the message Enter a number: is displayed. The program then calls cin, which forces the computer to wait for a number to be entered at the keyboard. After a number is typed and the Enter key is pressed, the cout object displays the number. The variable count is then incremented by 1. This process continues until four passes through the loop have been made and the value of count is 5. Each pass causes the message Enter a number: to be displayed, causes one call to cin to be made, and causes the message The number entered is to be displayed. Figure 5.2 shows this flow of control.

Instead of simply displaying the entered numbers, Program 5.5 can be modified to use the entered data. For example, you can add the numbers entered and display the total. To do this, you must be careful about how you add the numbers because the same variable, num, is used for each number entered. For this reason, the entry of a new number in Program 5.5 automatically causes the previous number stored in num to be lost. Therefore, each number entered must be added to the total before another number is entered. This is the required sequence:

Enter a number
Add the number to the total

How do you add a single number to a total? A statement such as total = total + num; does the job perfectly. It's the accumulation statement introduced in Section 3.1. After each number is entered, the accumulating statement adds the number to the total, as shown in Figure 5.3. Figure 5.4 illustrates the flow of control for adding the numbers.

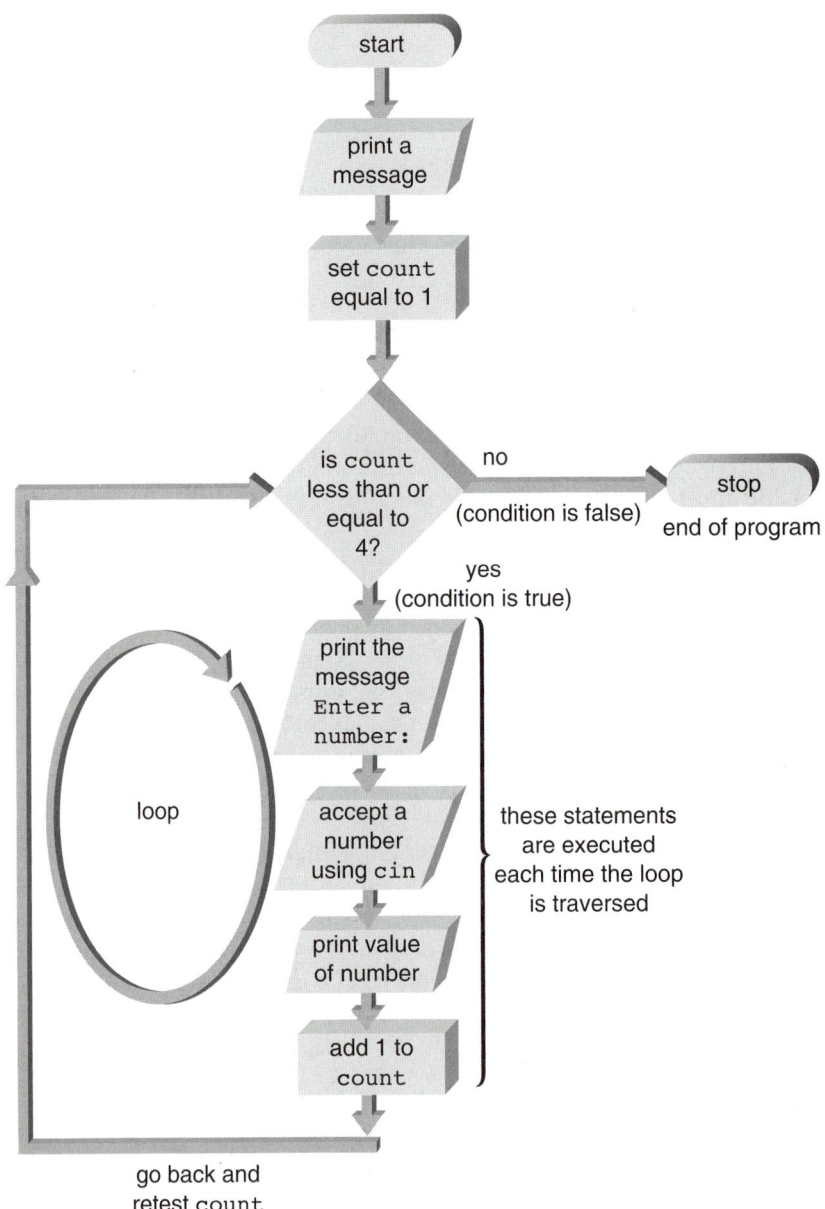

Figure 5.2 Flow of control diagram for Program 5.5

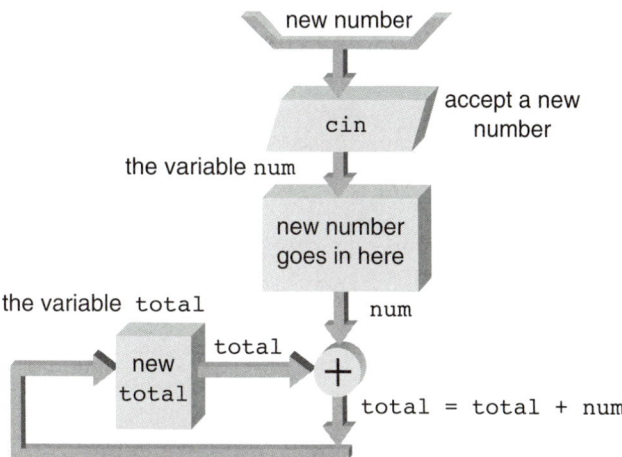

Figure 5.3   Accepting and adding a number to a total

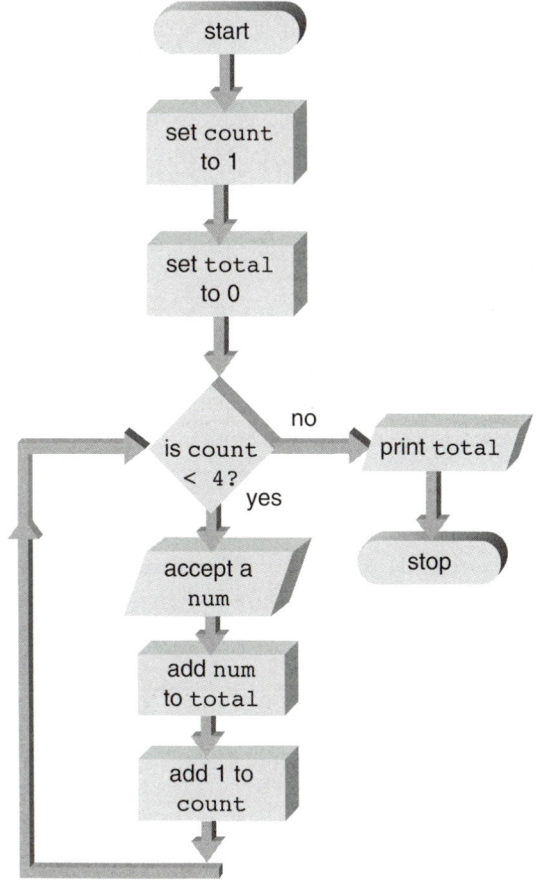

Figure 5.4   Accumulation flow of control

In reviewing Figure 5.4, observe that a provision has been made for initially setting the total to 0 before the while loop is entered. If you cleared the total inside the while loop, it would be set to 0 each time the loop was executed, and any value stored previously would be erased.

Program 5.6 incorporates the necessary modifications to Program 5.5 to total the numbers entered. As shown, the statement total = total + num; is placed immediately after the call to cin. Putting the accumulating statement at this point in the program ensures that the entered number is "captured" immediately into the total.

 **Program 5.6**

```
#include <iostream>
using namespace std;

int main()
{
  const int MAXNUMS = 4;
  int count;
  double num, total;

  cout << "\nThis program will ask you to enter "
       << MAXNUMS << " numbers.\n";
  count = 1;
  total = 0;

  while (count <= MAXNUMS)
  {
    cout << "\nEnter a number: ";
    cin  >> num;
    total = total + num;
    cout << "The total is now " << total;
    count++;
  }

  cout   << "\n\nThe final total is " << total << endl;

  return 0;
}
```

To make sure you understand, review Program 5.6. The variable total was created to store the total of the numbers entered. Before entering the while statement, the value of total is set to 0 to make sure any previous value in the storage location(s) assigned to this variable is erased. Inside the while loop, the statement total = total + num; is used to add the value of the entered number to total. As each value is entered, it's added to the existing total to create a new total. Therefore, total becomes a running subtotal of all the values entered. Only after all numbers are entered does total contain the final sum of all the numbers. After the while loop is finished, a cout statement is used to display this sum.

Using the same data entered in the sample run for Program 5.5, the following sample run of Program 5.6 was made:

```
This program will ask you to enter 4 numbers.

Enter a number: 26.2
The total is now 26.2
Enter a number: 5
The total is now 31.2
Enter a number: 103.456
The total is now 134.656
Enter a number: 1267.89
The total is now 1402.546


The final total is 1402.546
```

Having used an accumulating assignment statement to add the numbers entered, you can go further and calculate the average of the numbers. Where do you calculate the average—inside the while loop or outside it? In the case at hand, calculating an average requires that both a final sum and the number of items in that sum be available. The average is then computed by dividing the final sum by the number of items. At this stage, you must ask, "At what point in the program is the correct sum available, and at what point is the number of items available?"

In reviewing Program 5.6, you can see that the correct sum needed for calculating the average is available after the while loop is finished. In fact, the whole purpose of the while loop is to ensure that the numbers are entered and added correctly to produce a correct sum. After the loop is finished, you also have a count of the number of items used in the sum. However, because of the way the while loop was constructed, the number in count (5) when the loop is finished is 1 more than the number of items (4) used to obtain the total. Knowing this, you simply subtract 1 from count before using it to determine the average. With this information as background, see whether you can read and understand Program 5.7.

 **Program 5.7**

```cpp
#include <iostream>
using namespace std;

int main()
{
  const int MAXNUMS = 4;
  int count;
  double num, total, average;
```

```
cout << "\nThis program will ask you to enter "
     << MAXNUMS << " numbers.\n\n";
count = 1;
total = 0;

while (count <= MAXNUMS)
{
  cout << "Enter a number: ";
  cin  >> num;
  total = total + num;
  count++;
}

count--;
average = total / count;
cout << "\nThe average of the numbers is "
     << average << endl;

return 0;
}
```

Program 5.7 is almost identical to Program 5.6, except for the calculation of the average. The constant display of the total inside and after the while loop has also been removed. The loop in Program 5.7 is used to enter and add four numbers. Immediately after the loop is exited, the average is computed and displayed. A sample run of Program 5.7 follows:

```
This program will ask you to enter 4 numbers.

Enter a number: 26.2
Enter a number: 5
Enter a number: 103.456
Enter a number: 1267.89

The average of the numbers is 350.637
```

Sentinels

All the loops created so far have been examples of fixed-count loops, in which a counter is used to control the number of loop iterations. By means of a while statement, variable-condition loops can also be constructed. For example, when entering grades, you might not want to count the number of grades that will be entered. Instea l, you prefer to enter grades continuously, and at the end, type a special data value to signal the end of data input.

In programming, data values used to signal the start or end of a data series are called **sentinels**. Sentinel values must, of course, be selected so as not to conflict with legitimate data values. For example, if you're constructing a program to process a student's grades, and assuming no extra credit is given that could produce a grade higher than 100, you could use any grade higher than 100 as a sentinel value. Program 5.8 illustrates this concept: Data is requested and accepted continuously until a number larger than 100 is entered. Entering a number higher than 100 alerts the program to exit the while loop and display the sum of the numbers entered.

 **Program 5.8**

```cpp
#include <iostream>
using namespace std;

int main()
{
  const int HIGHGRADE = 100;
  double grade, total;

  grade = 0;
  total = 0;
  cout << "\nTo stop entering grades, type in any number";
  cout << "\n greater than 100.\n\n";
  cout << "Enter a grade: ";
  cin  >> grade;

  while (grade <= HIGHGRADE)
  {
    total = total + grade;
    cout << "Enter a grade: ";
    cin  >> grade;
  }

  cout << "\nThe total of the grades is " << total << endl;

  return 0;
}
```

Point of Information

Loop Types

A loop that evaluates a condition before any statements in the loop are executed is referred to as a **pretest loop** or an **entrance-controlled loop**. In C++, these loops are created by using `while` or `for` statements.

A loop that evaluates a condition at the end of the repeating section of code is referred to as a **posttest loop** or an **exit-controlled loop**. These loops always execute the loop statements at least once before the condition is tested. The `do-while` statement is used to construct this type of loop.

In addition to where the condition is tested (pretest or posttest), repeating sections of code are classified by the type of condition being tested. In a **fixed-count loop**, the condition is used to keep track of how many repetitions have occurred. In this type of loop, a fixed number of calculations are performed or a fixed number of lines are printed, at which point the repeating section of code is exited. All of C++'s repetition statements can be used to create fixed-count loops.

In a **variable-condition loop**, the tested condition doesn't depend on a count being reached, but on a variable that can change interactively with each pass through the loop. When a specified value is encountered, regardless of how many iterations have occurred, repetitions stop. All of C++'s repetition statements can be used to create variable-condition loops.

The following lines show a sample run of Program 5.8. As long as grades less than or equal to 100 are entered, the program continues to request and accept additional data. When a number less than or equal to 100 is entered, the program adds this number to the total. When a number greater than 100 is entered, the loop is exited, and the sum of the grades that were entered is displayed.

```
To stop entering grades, type in any number
 greater than 100.

Enter a grade: 95
Enter a grade: 100
Enter a grade: 82
Enter a grade: 101

The total of the grades is 277
```

break and continue Statements

Two useful statements in connection with repetition statements are the break and continue statements. You encountered the break statement in Section 4.4 when learning about the switch statement. This is the format of the break statement:

```
break;
```

A break statement, as its name implies, forces an immediate break, or exit, from the switch, while, for, and do-while statements (discussed in the next sections). For example, execution of the following while loop is terminated immediately if a number greater than 76 is entered:

```
while(count <= 10)
{
  cout << "Enter a number: ";
  cin  >> num;
  if (num > 76)
  {
    cout << "You lose!\n";
    break;       // break out of the loop
  }
  else
    cout << "Way to go!\n";
  count++;
}
// break jumps to here
```

The break statement violates structured programming principles because it provides a second, nonstandard exit from a loop. Nevertheless, the break statement is extremely useful for breaking out of loops when an unusual condition is detected. It's also used to exit from a switch statement, but it's because the matching case value has been detected and processed.

The continue statement is similar to the break statement but applies only to loops created with while, do-while, and for statements. This is the general format of a continue statement:

```
continue;
```

When continue is encountered in a loop, the next iteration of the loop begins immediately. For while loops, this means execution is transferred automatically to the top of the loop, and reevaluation of the tested expression is initiated. Although the continue statement has no direct effect on a switch statement, it can be included in a switch statement, which is also contained in a loop. The effect of continue is the same: The next loop iteration begins.

As a general rule, the `continue` statement is less useful than the `break` statement, but it's convenient for skipping over data that shouldn't be processed while remaining in a loop. For example, invalid grades are simply ignored in the following section of code, and only valid grades are added to the total:[1]

```
while (count < 30)
{
cout << "Enter a grade: ";
  cin  >> grade;
  if(grade < 0 || grade > 100)
    continue;
  total = total + grade;
  count++;
}
```

The Null Statement

All statements must be terminated by a semicolon. A semicolon with nothing preceding it is also a valid statement, called the **null statement**, as shown:

```
;
```

It's a do-nothing statement used where a statement is required syntactically, but no action is called for. Typically, null statements are used with `while` or `for` statements. Program 5.9c in Section 5.3 shows an example of a `for` statement using a null statement.

EXERCISES 5.2

1. **(Modify)** Rewrite Program 5.6 to compute the total of eight numbers.

2. **(Modify)** Rewrite Program 5.6 to display this prompt:

Please type in the total number of data values to be added:

In response to this prompt, the program should accept a user-entered number, and then use it to control the number of times the `while` loop is executed. So if the user enters 5 in response to the prompt, the program should request the input of five numbers and display the total after five numbers have been entered.

3. **(Modify)** Rewrite Program 5.7 to compute the average of 10 numbers.

---

[1]Although this section of code illustrates the flow of control the `continue` statement provides, it's not the preferred way of achieving the correct result. Instead of using an `if` statement and a `continue` statement to exclude invalid data, a better method is including valid data with these statements:

```
        if (grade >= 0 && grade <= 100)
        {
          total = total + grade;
          count++;
        }
```

4. **(Modify)** Rewrite Program 5.7 to display the following prompt:

```
Please type in the total number of data values to be averaged:
```

In response to this prompt, the program should accept a user-entered number, and then use it to control the number of times the `while` loop is executed. So if the user enters 6 in response to the prompt, the program should request an input of six numbers and display the average of the next six numbers entered.

5. **(Debug)** By mistake, a programmer puts the statement `average = total / count;` in the `while` loop immediately after the statement `total = total + num;` in Program 5.7. As a result, the `while` loop becomes the following:

```
while (count <= MAXNUMS)
{
  cout << "Enter a number: ";
  cin  >> num;
  total = total + num;
  average = total / count;
  count++;
}
```

   a. Will the program yield the correct result with this `while` loop?

   b. From a programming perspective, which `while` loop is better to use, and why?

6. **(Program) a.** Write a C++ program to convert meters to feet. The program should request the starting meter value, the number of conversions to be made, and the increment between metric values. The display should have appropriate headings and list the meters and corresponding feet value. If the number of iterations is greater than 10, have your program substitute a default increment of 10. Use the relationship that 1 meter = 3.281 feet.

   b. Run the program written in Exercise 6a on a computer. Verify that your program begins at the correct starting meter value and contains the exact number of conversions specified in your input data.

7. **(Modify) a.** Modify the program written in Exercise 6a to request the starting meter value, the ending meter value, and the increment. Instead of the condition checking for a fixed count, it checks for the ending meter value. If the number of iterations is greater than 20, have your program substitute a default increment of *(ending value - starting value) / 19*.

   b. Run the program written in Exercise 7a on a computer. Verify that your output starts at the correct beginning value and ends at the correct ending value.

8. **(Program) a.** Write a C++ program to convert Celsius degrees to Fahrenheit. The program should request the starting Celsius value, the number of conversions to be made, and the increment between Celsius values. The display should have appropriate headings and list the Celsius value and the corresponding Fahrenheit value. Use the relationship that *Fahrenheit = (9.0 / 5.0) * Celsius + 32.0.*

   b. Compile and run the program written in Exercise 8a on a computer. Verify that your program begins at the correct starting Celsius value and contains the exact number of conversions specified in your input data.

9. (**Program**) An arithmetic series is defined by the following:

$$a + (a + d) + (a + 2d) + (a + 3d) + \cdots + [(a + (n - 1)d)]$$

> a is the first term.
> d is the "common difference."
> n is the number of terms to be added.

Using this information, write a C++ program that uses a while loop to display each term and determine the sum of the arithmetic series having $a = 1$, $d = 3$, and $n = 100$. Make sure your program displays the value it has calculated.

10. (**Program**) A geometric series is defined by the following:

$$a + ar + ar^2 + ar^3 + \cdots + ar^{n-1}$$

> a is the first term.
> r is the "common ratio."
> n is the number of terms in the series.

Using this information, write a C++ program that uses a while loop to display each term and determine the sum of a geometric series having $a = 1$, $r = .5$, and $n = 10$. Make sure your program displays the value it has calculated.

11. (**Program**) a. The data in the following chart was collected on a recent automobile trip:

Mileage	Gallons
22,495	Full tank
22,841	12.2
23,185	11.3
23,400	10.5
23,772	11.0
24,055	12.2
24,434	14.7
24,804	14.3
25,276	15.2

Write, compile, and run a C++ program that accepts a mileage and gallons value and calculates the miles per gallon (mpg) for that segment of the trip. The mpg is calculated as the difference in mileage between fill-ups divided by the number of gallons of gasoline used in the fill-up.

b. Modify the program written for Exercise 11a to also compute and display the cumulative mpg after each fill-up. The cumulative mpg is calculated as the difference between mileage at each fill-up and mileage at the start of the trip divided by the sum of gallons used to that point in the trip.

12. **(Program) a.** A bookstore summarizes its monthly transactions by keeping the following information for each book in stock:

> Book identification number
> Inventory balance at the beginning of the month
> Number of copies received during the month
> Number of copies sold during the month

Write a C++ program that accepts this data for each book and then displays the book identification number and an updated book inventory balance, using this relationship:

> New balance = Inventory balance at the beginning of the month
>   + Number of copies received during the month
>   - Number of copies sold during the month

Your program should use a `while` statement with a fixed-count condition so that information on only three books is requested.

     b. Compile and run the program written in Exercise 12a. Review the display your program produces and verify that the output is correct.

13. **(Modify)** Modify the program you wrote for Exercise 12 to keep requesting and displaying results until a sentinel value of 999 is entered. Compile and run your program. Review the display your program produces and verify that the output is correct.

5.3 The for Statement

A **for statement** performs the same functions as the `while` statement but uses a different form. In many situations, especially those using a fixed-count condition, the `for` statement's format is easier to use than the `while` statement equivalent. This is the general form of the `for` statement:

```
for (initializing list; expression; altering list)
   statement;
```

Although the `for` statement looks a little complicated, it's really quite simple if you consider each part separately. Inside the parentheses of the `for` statement are three items, separated by semicolons. Each item is optional and can be described separately, but the semicolons must always be present, even if you don't use the items. As you'll see, the items in parentheses correspond to the initialization, expression evaluation, and expression altering values you've already used with the `while` statement.

Typically, variables need to be initialized or other evaluations need to be made before entering a repetition loop, so the `for` statement allows grouping all initializing statements as the first set of items inside `for`'s parentheses. The items in this *initializing list* are executed only once, before the expression is evaluated for the first time.

The middle item in parentheses, *expression*, is any valid C++ expression, and there's no difference in the way `for` and `while` statements use this expression. In both statements, as long as the expression has a non-zero (true) value, the statement following the parentheses is executed. So before the first check of the expression, initial values for the tested expression's variables must be assigned, and before the expression is reevaluated, there must be one or more statements that alter these values.

The for statement also provides a single place for all expression-altering statements: the *altering list*, the last item inside for's parentheses. All items in this list are executed by the for statement at the end of the loop, just before the expression is reevaluated.

Figure 5.5 illustrates the internal workings of a for loop. As shown, when the for loop is completed, control is transferred to the first executable statement following the loop.

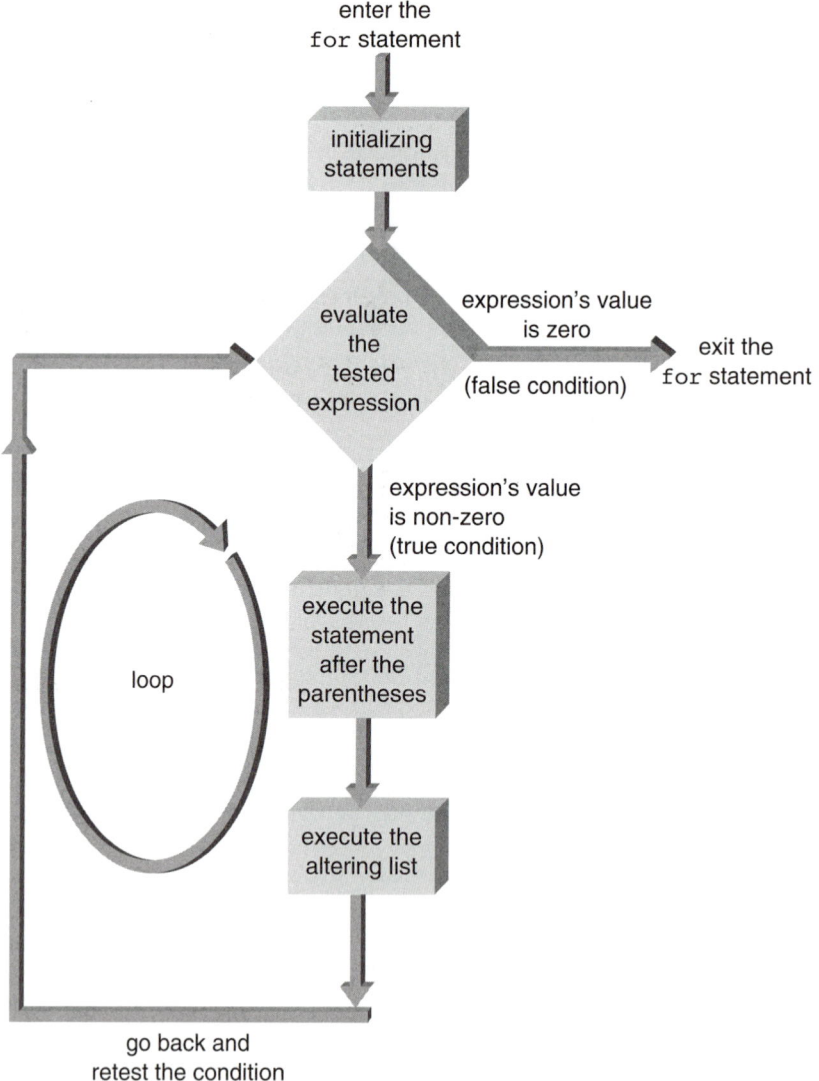

Figure 5.5   The for statement's flow of control

To avoid having to show every step, you can use a simplified set of flowchart symbols to describe for loops. If you use the following flowchart symbol to represent a for statement,

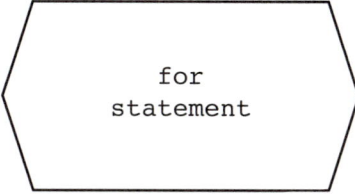

you can then illustrate a complete for loop, as shown in Figure 5.6.

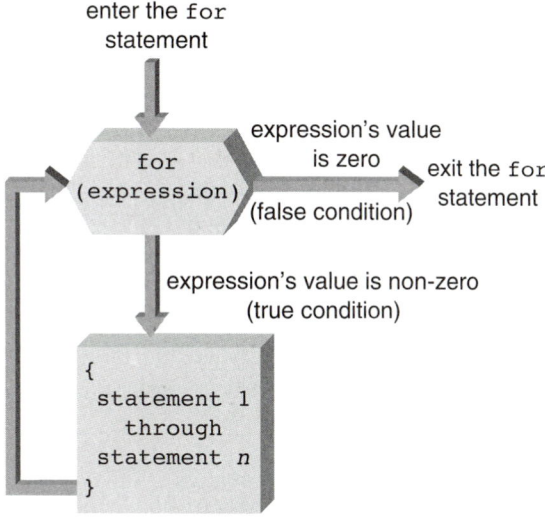

Figure 5.6 A simplified for loop flowchart

The following examples show the correspondence between while and for statements. First, take a look at this while statement:

```
count = 1;
while (count <= 10)
{
  cout << count  << " ";
  count++;
}
```

Here's the corresponding for statement:

```
for (count = 1; count <= 10; count++)
  cout << count  << " ";
```

Point of Information

Where to Place the Opening Braces

When the `for` loop contains a compound statement, professional C++ programmers use two styles of writing `for` loops. The style used in this book takes the following form:

```
for (expression)
{
  compound statement in here
}
```

An equally acceptable style places the compound statement's opening brace on the first line. Using this style, a `for` loop looks like the following:

```
for (expression) {
  compound statement in here
}
```

The advantage of the first style is that the braces line up under one another, making it easier to locate brace pairs. The advantage of the second style is that it makes the code more compact and saves a line, so more code can be viewed in the same display area. Both styles are used but are almost never intermixed. Select whichever style appeals to you and be consistent in its use. As always, the indentation you use in the compound statement (two or four spaces or a tab) should also be consistent throughout all your programs. The combination of styles you select becomes a "signature" for your programming work.

As this example shows, the only difference between the `for` and `while` statements is the placement of equivalent expressions. Grouping the initialization, expression test, and altering list in the `for` statement is convenient, especially when you're creating fixed-count loops. Now look at this `for` statement:

```
for (count = 2; count <= 20; count = count + 2)
  cout << count << " ";
```

In this statement, all the loop control information is contained in the parentheses. The loop starts with a count of 2, stops when the count exceeds 20, and increments the loop counter in steps of 2. Program 5.9 shows this `for` statement in an actual program. A blank space is placed between output values for readability.

Program 5.9

```cpp
#include <iostream>
using namespace std;
int main()
{
  int count;
  for (count = 2; count <= 20; count = count + 2)
    cout << count << " ";

  return 0;
}
```

This is the output of Program 5.9:

    2 4 6 8 10 12 14 16 18 20

The `for` statement doesn't require having any of the items inside `for`'s parentheses or using them for initializing or altering the values in the expression statements; however, the two semicolons must be included in these parentheses. For example, the construction `for ( ; count <= 20 ;)` is valid.

If the initializing list is missing, the initialization step is omitted when the `for` statement is executed. Therefore, the programmer must provide the required initializations before the `for` statement is encountered. Similarly, if the altering list is missing, any expressions needed to alter the evaluation of the tested expression must be included in the statement part of the loop. The `for` statement only ensures that all expressions in the initializing list are executed once, before evaluation of the tested expression, and all expressions in the altering list are executed at the end of the loop, before the tested expression is rechecked. Program 5.9 can be rewritten in any of the three ways shown in Programs 5.9a, 5.9b, and 5.9c.

Program 5.9a

```cpp
#include <iostream>
using namespace std;

int main()
{
  int count;

  count = 2;     // initialized outside the for statement
  for ( ; count <= 20; count = count + 2)
    cout << count << " ";

  return 0;
}
```

Program 5.9b

```cpp
#include <iostream>
using namespace std;
int main()
{
  int count;

  count = 2;    // initialized outside the for statement
  for( ; count <= 20; )
  {
    cout << count << " ";
    count = count + 2;    // alteration statement
  }

  return 0;
}
```

Program 5.9c

```cpp
#include <iostream>
using namespace std;
int main()    // all expressions inside for's parentheses
{
  int count;

  for (count = 2; count <= 20; cout << count << " ", count = count + 2);

  return 0;
}
```

In Program 5.9a, count is initialized outside the for statement, and the first list inside the parentheses is left blank. In Program 5.9b, both the initializing list and the altering list are outside the parentheses. Program 5.9b also uses a compound statement in the for loop, with the expression-altering statement included in the compound statement. Finally, Program 5.9c has included all items inside the parentheses, so there's no need for any useful statement following the parentheses. In this example, the null statement (;) satisfies the syntax requirement of one statement to follow for's parentheses.

Also, observe in Program 5.9c that the altering list (the last set of items in parentheses) consists of two items, and a comma has been used to separate these items. Using commas to separate items in both the initializing and altering lists is required if either of these lists contains more than one item.

Last, note that these three programs are all inferior to Program 5.9, and although you might encounter them in your programming career, you shouldn't use them. The `for` statement in Program 5.9 is much clearer because all items pertaining to the tested expression are grouped together inside the parentheses. Keeping the `for` loop structure "clean," as in Program 5.9, is important and a good programming practice.

Although the initializing and altering lists can be omitted from a `for` statement, omitting the tested expression results in an infinite loop. For example, this statement creates an infinite loop:

```
for (count = 2; ; count++)
  cout << count << " ";
```

As with the `while` statement, both `break` and `continue` statements can be used in a `for` loop. A `break` forces an immediate exit from the `for` loop, as it does in the `while` loop. A `continue`, however, forces control to be passed to the altering list in a `for` statement, after which the tested expression is reevaluated. This action differs from `continue`'s action in a `while` statement, where control is passed directly to reevaluation of the tested expression.

Finally, many programmers use the initializing list of a `for` statement to both declare and initialize the counter variable and any other variables used primarily in the `for` loop. For example, in this `for` statement, the variable `count` is both declared and initialized inside the `for` statement:

```
for(int count = 0; count < 10; count++)
  cout << count  << " ";
```

As always, having been declared, `count` can now be used anywhere after its declaration in the body of the function containing the declaration.

To understand the enormous power of `for` loops, consider the task of printing a table of numbers from 1 to 10, including their squares and cubes, by using a `for` statement. This table was produced previously by using a `while` loop in Program 5.3. You might want to review Program 5.3 and compare it with Program 5.10 to get a better sense of the equivalence between `for` and `while` statements.

Program 5.10

```cpp
#include <iostream>
#include <iomanip>
using namespace std;

int main()
{
  const int MAXNUMS = 10;
  int num;
  cout << endl;       // print a blank line
  cout << "NUMBER    SQUARE    CUBE\n"
       << "------    ------    ----\n";
```

```
    for (num = 1; num <= MAXNUMS; num++)
      cout << setw(3) << num << "          "
           << setw(3) << num * num << "       "
           << setw(4) << num * num * num << endl;

    return 0;
}
```

When Program 5.10 is run, this is the display produced:

NUMBER	SQUARE	CUBE
1	1	1
2	4	8
3	9	27
4	16	64
5	25	125
6	36	216
7	49	343
8	64	512
9	81	729
10	100	1000

Simply changing the number 10 in the for statement of Program 5.10 to 1000 creates a loop that's executed 1000 times and produces a table of numbers from 1 to 1000. As with the while statement, this small change produces an immense increase in the program's processing and output. Notice also that the expression num++ was used in the altering list in place of the equivalent num = num + 1.

Interactive for Loops

Using the cin object inside a for loop creates an interactive for loop, much like using this object in a while loop. For example, in Program 5.11, a cin object is used to input a set of numbers. As each number is input, it's added to a total. When the for loop is exited, the average is calculated and displayed.

 **Program 5.11**

```
#include <iostream>
using namespace std;

// This program calculates the average
// of MAXCOUNT user-entered numbers
int main()
{
```

```
const int MAXCOUNT = 5;
int count;
double num, total, average;

total = 0.0;

for (count = 0; count < MAXCOUNT; count++)
{
  cout << "Enter a number: ";
  cin  >> num;
  total = total + num;
}

average = total / count;
cout << "The average of the data entered is " << average
     << endl;

return 0;
}
```

The for statement in Program 5.11 creates a loop that's executed five times. The user is prompted to enter a number each time through the loop. After each number is entered, it's added to the total immediately. Although total was initialized to 0 before the for statement, this initialization could have been included with the initialization of count, as follows:

```
for (total = 0.0, count = 0; count < MAXCOUNT; count++)
```

Additionally, the declarations for both total and count could have been included with their initializations inside the initializing list, as follows:

```
for (double total = 0.0, int count = 0; count < MAXCOUNT; count++)
```

Any of these for constructs is considered a good programming practice. Which one you choose is simply a matter of your own programming style.

Nested Loops

In many situations, using a loop within another loop, called a **nested loop**, is convenient. Here's a simple example of a nested loop:

```
for(i = 1; i <= 5; i++) // start of outer loop  <-----+
{                                        //             |
   cout << "\ni is now " << i << endl;   //             |
                                         //             |
   for(j = 1; j <= 4; j++)  // start of inner loop      |
     cout << " j = " << j;  // end of inner loop        |
}                           // end of outer loop   <-----+
```

The first loop, controlled by the value of i, is called the **outer loop**. The second loop, controlled by the value of j, is called the **inner loop**. Notice that all statements in the inner loop are contained in the boundaries of the outer loop, and a different variable is used to control each loop. For each trip through the outer loop, the inner loop runs through its entire sequence. Therefore, each time the i counter increases by 1, the inner for loop executes completely and goes through four values (j takes on the values 1 to 4), as shown in Figure 5.7. Program 5.12 includes this type of loop in a working program.

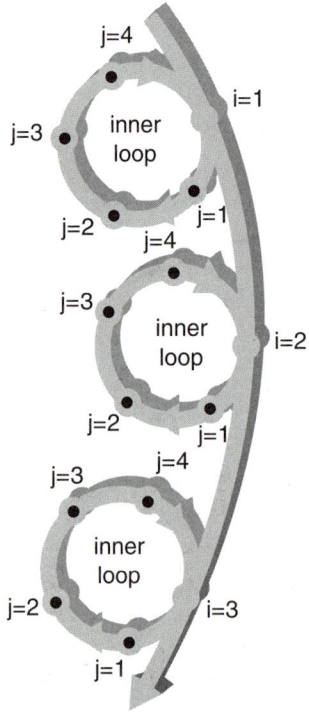

Figure 5.7   For each value of i, j loops four times

Program 5.12

```
#include <iostream>
using namespace std;

int main()
{
    int i,j;
```

```
for(i = 1; i <= 5; i++)     // start of outer loop <----+
{                                      //              |
   cout << "\ni is now " << i << endl;  //             |
                                       //              |
   for(j = 1;  j <= 4; j++)// start of inner loop      |
     cout << " j = " << j; // end of inner loop        |
}                          // end of outer loop    <----+

   return 0;
}
```

This is the output of a sample run of Program 5.12:

```
i is now 1
  j = 1  j = 2  j = 3  j = 4
i is now 2
  j = 1  j = 2  j = 3  j = 4
i is now 3
  j = 1  j = 2  j = 3  j = 4
i is now 4
  j = 1  j = 2  j = 3  j = 4
i is now 5
  j = 1  j = 2  j = 3  j = 4
```

To understand the usefulness of a nested loop, take a look at using one to compute the average grade for each student in a class of 20 students. Each student has taken four exams during the semester. The final grade is calculated as the average of these exam grades. An outer loop consisting of 20 passes is used to compute the average grade for each student. The inner loop consists of four passes, and one exam grade is entered in each inner loop pass. As each grade is entered, it's added to the total for the student, and at the end of the loop, the average is calculated and displayed. Because both the outer and inner loops are fixed-count loops of 20 and 4, respectively, for statements are used to create these loops. Program 5.13 uses a nested loop to make the required calculations.

 **Program 5.13**

```cpp
#include <iostream>
using namespace std;

int main()
{

   const int NUMGRADES = 4;
   const int NUMSTUDENTS = 20;
   int i,j;
   double grade, total, average;
```

```
for (i = 1; i <= NUMSTUDENTS; i++)  // start of outer loop
{
  total = 0;              // clear the total for this student
  for (j = 1; j <= NUMGRADES; j++)  // start of inner loop
  {
    cout << "Enter an examination grade for student: "
         << j << ":";
    cin >> grade;
    total = total + grade;      // add the grade to the total
  }                             // end of the inner for loop
  average = total / NUMGRADES;  // calculate the average
  cout << "\nThe average for student " << i
       << " is " << average << "\n\n";
}                               // end of the outer for loop

  return 0;
}
```

In reviewing Program 5.13, pay particular attention to the initialization of total in the outer loop, before the inner loop is entered: total is initialized 20 times, once for each student. Also, notice that the average is calculated and displayed immediately after the inner loop is finished. Because the statements that compute and print the average are also in the outer loop, 20 averages are calculated and displayed. The entry and addition of each grade in the inner loop uses techniques you have seen before and should be familiar with now.

EXERCISES 5.3

1. **(Practice)** Write a for statement for each of the following cases:
    a. Use a counter named i that has an initial value of 1, a final value of 20, and an increment of 1.
    b. Use a counter named icount that has an initial value of 1, a final value of 20, and an increment of 2.
    c. Use a counter named j that has an initial value of 1, a final value of 100, and an increment of 5.
    d. Use a counter named icount that has an initial value of 20, a final value of 1, and an increment of -1.
    e. Use a counter named icount that has an initial value of 20, a final value of 1, and an increment of -2.
    f. Use a counter named count that has an initial value of 1.0, a final value of 16.2, and an increment of 0.2.
    g. Use a counter named xcnt that has an initial value of 20.0, a final value of 10.0, and an increment of -0.5.

2. **(Desk check)** Determine the number of times each for loop is executed for the for statements written in Exercise 1.

3. **(Desk check)** Determine the value in total after each of the following loops is executed:

a.
```
total = 0;
for (i = 1; i <= 10; i = i + 1)
    total = total + 1;
```
b.
```
total = 1;
for (count = 1; count <= 10; count = count + 1)
    total = total * 2;
```
c.
```
total = 0;
for (i = 10; i <= 15; i = i + 1)
    total = total + i;
```
d.
```
total = 50;
for (i = 1; i <=10; i = i + 1)
    total = total - i;
```
e.
```
total = 1;
for (icnt = 1; icnt <= 8; ++icnt)
    total = total * icnt;
```
f.
```
total = 1.0;
for (j = 1; j <= 5; ++j)
    total = total / 2.0;
```

4. **(Desk check)** Determine the output of the following program:

```cpp
#include <iostream>
using namespace std;

int main()
{
    int i;

    for (i = 20; i >= 0; i -= 4)
    cout << i;

    return 0;
}
```

5. **(Modify)** Modify Program 5.10 to produce a table of the numbers 0 through 20 in increments of 2, with their squares and cubes.

6. **(Modify)** Modify Program 5.10 to produce a table of numbers from 10 to 1, instead of 1 to 10, as it currently does.

7. **(Program) a.** Write, compile, and run a C++ program that displays a table of 20 temperature conversions from Fahrenheit to Celsius. The table should start with a Fahrenheit value of 20 degrees and be incremented in values of 4 degrees. Recall that Celsius = (5.0/9.0) × (Fahrenheit - 32.0).

b. Modify the program written for Exercise 7a to request the number of conversions to be made.

8. **(Program)** Write, compile, and run a C++ program that converts Fahrenheit to Celsius temperature in increments of 5 degrees. The initial value of Fahrenheit temperature and the total conversions to be made should be requested as user input during program execution. Recall that Celsius = (5.0/9.0) × (Fahrenheit - 32.0).

9. **(Program) a.** Write, compile, and run a C++ program that accepts five values of gallons, one at a time, and converts each value entered to its liter equivalent before the next value is requested. Use a `for` loop in your program. There are 3.785 liters in 1 gallon of liquid.
   b. Modify the program written for Exercise 9a to request the number of data items to be entered and converted first.

10. **(Program) a.** An old Arabian legend has it that a fabulously wealthy but unthinking king agreed to give a beggar 1 cent and double the amount for 64 days. Using this information, write, compile, and run a C++ program that displays how much the king must pay the beggar on each day. The output of your program should appear as follows:

    ```
    Day        Amount Owed
    ---        -----------
     1            0.01
     2            0.02
     3            0.04
     .             .
     .             .
     .             .
    64             .
    ```

    b. Modify the program you wrote for Exercise 10a to determine on which day the king will have paid the beggar a total of one million dollars.

11. **(Debug)** Is the following program correct? If it is, determine its output. If it's not, determine the error and correct it so that the program will run.

    ```cpp
    #include <iostream>
    using namespace std;

    int main()
    {

      for(int i = 1; i < 10; i++)
        cout << i << '\n';

      for (j = 1; i < 5; i++)
        cout << i << endl;

      return 0;
    }
    ```

12. **(Program) a.** Write, compile, and run a C++ program that calculates and displays the amount of money available in a bank account that initially has $1000 deposited and earns interest at the rate of 3% a year. Your program should display the amount available at the end of each year for a period of 10 years. Use the relationship that the money available at the end of each year = the amount of money in the account at the start of the year + .03 × the amount available at the start of the year.

   b. Modify the program written for Exercise 12a to prompt the user for the amount of money initially deposited in the account.

   c. Modify the program written for Exercise 12a to prompt the user for both the amount of money initially deposited and the number of years to be displayed.

   d. Modify the program written for Exercise 12a to prompt the user for the amount of money initially deposited, the interest rate to be used, and the number of years to be displayed.

13. **(Program)** According to legend, the island of Manhattan was purchased from the native Indian population in 1626 for $24. Assuming this money was invested in a Dutch bank paying 4% simple interest per year, construct a table showing how much money the native population would have at the end of each 50-year period, starting in 1626 and ending 400 years later. Use the relationship that the money available at the end of each 50-year period = the amount of money in the account at the start of period × the quantity $(1 + .04)^{50}$.

14. **(Program)** A well-regarded manufacturer of widgets has been losing 4% of its sales each year. The company's annual profit is 10% of sales. This year, the company has had $10 million in sales and a profit of $1 million. Determine the expected sales and profit for the next 10 years. Your program should produce a display in the following form:

```
            SALES AND PROFIT PROJECTION
            ----------------------------


    YEAR        EXPECTED SALES      PROJECTED PROFIT
    ----        --------------      ----------------
     1           $10000000.00         $1000000.00
     2           $ 9600000.00         $ 960000.00
     3                 .                    .
     .                 .                    .
     .                 .                    .
     .                 .                    .
    10                 .                    .
    ----------------------------------------------------
    Totals:     $      .              $      .
```

15. (**Program**) Four experiments are performed, and each experiment has six test results. The results for each experiment are given in the following list. Write, compile, and run a C++ program using a nested loop to compute and display the average of the test results for each experiment.

1st experiment results:	23.2	31	16.9	27.5	25.4	28.6
2nd experiment results:	34.8	45.2	27.9	36.8	33.4	39.4
3rd experiment results:	19.4	16.8	10.2	20.8	18.9	13.4
4th experiment results:	36.9	39.5	49.2	45.1	42.7	50.6

16. (**Modify**) Modify the program written for Exercise 15 so that the number of test results for each experiment is entered by the user. Write your program so that a different number of test results can be entered for each experiment.

17. (**Program**) a. A bowling team consists of five players, and each player bowls three games. Write, compile, and run a C++ program that uses a nested loop to enter each player's scores and then computes and displays the average score for each bowler. Assume each bowler has the following scores:

1st bowler: 286	252	265
2nd bowler: 212	186	215
3rd bowler: 252	232	216
4th bowler: 192	201	235
5th bowler: 186	236	272

   b. (**Modify**) Modify the program written for Exercise 17a to calculate and display the average team score. (*Hint:* Use a second variable to store the total of all players' scores.)

   c. (**Modify**) Rewrite the program written for Exercise 17a to eliminate the inner loop. To do this, you have to input three scores for each bowler rather than enter one at a time. Each score must be stored in its own variable name before the average is calculated.

18. (**Program**) Write, compile, and run a C++ program that calculates and displays the yearly amount available if $1000 is invested in a bank account for 10 years. Your program should display the amounts available for interest rates from 6% to 12%, inclusive, in 1% increments. Use a nested loop, with the outer loop having a fixed count of 7 and the inner loop having a fixed count of 10. The first iteration of the outer loop should use an interest rate of 6% and display the amount of money available at the end of the first 10 years. In each subsequent pass through the outer loop, the interest rate should be increased by 1%. Use this relationship: money available at end of each year = amount of money in account at start of the year + interest rate × amount available at start of the year.

5.4 The `do-while` Statement

Both `while` and `for` statements evaluate an expression at the start of the repetition loop. In some cases, however, testing an expression at the end of the loop is more convenient. For example, suppose you have constructed the following `while` loop to calculate sales taxes:

```
cout << "Enter a price: ";
cin  >> price;
while (price != SENTINEL)
{
  salestax = RATE * price;
  cout << "The sales tax is $" << salestax;
  cout << "\nEnter a price: ";
  cin >> price;
}
```

Using this `while` statement requires duplicating the prompt and `cin` statement before the loop and then inside the loop, as done in this example, or resorting to another method to force execution of statements in the `while` loop first.

A `do-while` statement, as its name implies, allows you to perform some statements before an expression is evaluated at the end of the loop. In many situations, this approach can be used to eliminate the duplication shown in the previous example. It has this general form in C++:

do
  statement;
`while (expression);` ◄————————————don't forget the final semicolon, which is required here

As with all C++ programs, the single statement in the `do-while` can be replaced with a compound statement. Figure 5.8 shows a flow control diagram illustrating the operation of the do statement.

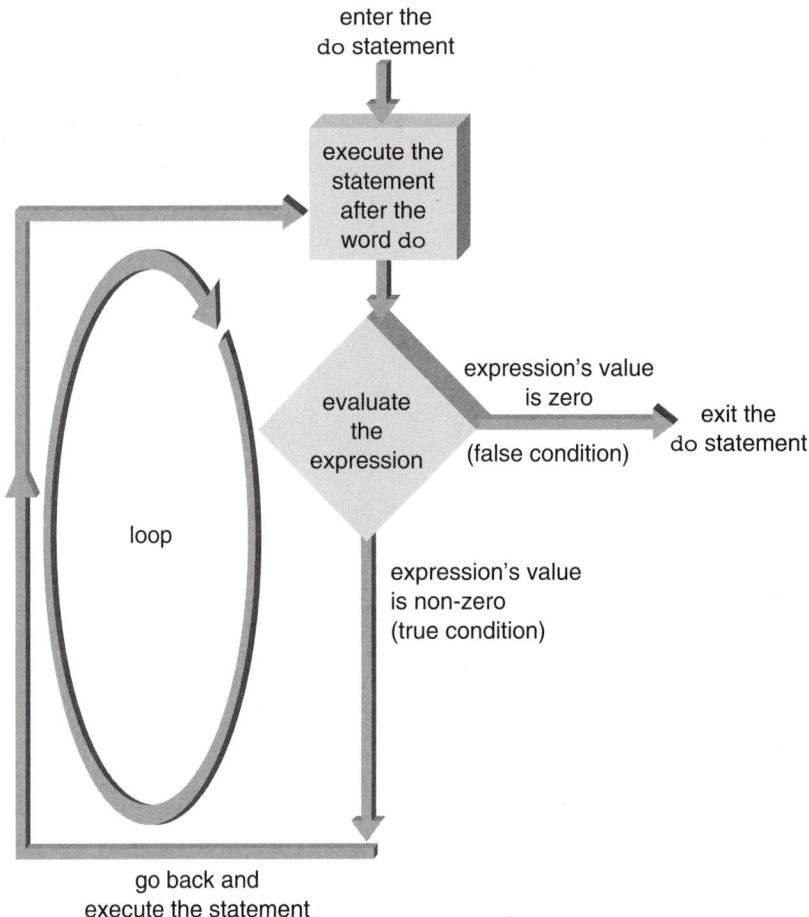

enter the
do statement

execute the
statement
after the
word do

loop

evaluate
the
expression

expression's value
is zero
(false condition)

exit the
do statement

expression's value
is non-zero
(true condition)

go back and
execute the statement

Figure 5.8   The do statement's flow of control

As shown, all statements within the do-while statement are executed at least once before the expression is evaluated. Then, if the expression has a non-zero value, the statements are executed again. This process continues until the expression evaluates to zero (becomes false). For example, take a look at the following do-while statement:

```
do
{
  cout << "\nEnter a price: ";
  cin  >> price;
  if ( abs(price - SENTINEL) < 0.0001 ) break;
  salestax = RATE * price;
  cout << "The sales tax is $" << salestax;
}
while (price != SENTINEL);
```

Observe that only one prompt and `cin` statement are used because the tested expression is evaluated at the end of the loop.

As with all repetition statements, the `do-while` statement can always replace or be replaced by an equivalent `while` or `for` statement. The choice of which statement to use depends on the application and the programmer's preferred style. In general, `while` and `for` statements are preferred because anyone reading the program can clearly see what's being tested up front, at the top of the program loop.

Validity Checks

The `do-while` statement is particularly useful in filtering user-entered input and providing data validation checks. For example, an operator is required to enter a valid customer identification number between 100 and 1999. A number outside this range is rejected, and a new request for a valid number is made. The following section of code supplies the data filter needed to verify the entry of a valid identification number:

```
do
{
  cout << "\nEnter an identification number: ";
  cin  >> idNum;
}
while (idNum < 100 || idNum > 1999);
```

In this code, a request for an identification number is repeated until a valid number is entered. This section of code is "bare bones," in that it doesn't alert the operator to the cause of the new request for data or allow premature exit from the loop if a valid identification number can't be found. The following code is an alternative for removing the first drawback:

```
do
{
  cout << "\nEnter an identification number: ";
  cin  >> idNum;
  if (idNum < 100 || idNum > 1999)
  {
    cout  << "\n An invalid number was just entered"
          << "\nPlease check the ID number and reenter";
  }
  else
    break;      // break if a valid ID number was entered
} while(1);     // this expression is always true
```

A `break` statement is used to exit from the loop. Because the expression the `do-while` statement is evaluating is always 1 (true), an infinite loop has been created that's exited only when the `break` statement is encountered.

EXERCISES 5.4

1. **(Program) a.** Using a do-while statement, write, compile, and run a C++ program to accept a grade. The program should request a grade continuously as long as an invalid grade is entered. An invalid grade is any grade less than 0 or greater than 100. After a valid grade has been entered, your program should display the value of the grade entered.

   b. Modify the program written for Exercise 1a so that the user is alerted when an invalid grade has been entered.

   c. Modify the program written for Exercise 1b so that it allows the user to exit the program by entering the number 999.

   d. Modify the program written for Exercise 1b so that it automatically terminates after five invalid grades are entered.

2. **(Program) a.** Write, compile, and run a C++ program that continuously requests a grade to be entered. If the grade is less than 0 or greater than 100, your program should print a message informing the user that an invalid grade has been entered; else, the grade should be added to a total. When a grade of 999 is entered, the program should exit the repetition loop and compute and display the average of the valid grades entered.

   b. Run the program written in Exercise 2a on a computer and verify the program by using appropriate test data.

3. **(Program) a.** Write, compile, and run a C++ program to reverse the digits of a positive integer number. For example, if the number 8735 is entered, the number displayed should be 5378. (*Hint*: Use a do-while statement and continuously strip off and display the number's units digit. If the variable num initially contains the number entered, the units digit is obtained as (num % 10)). After a units digit is displayed, dividing the number by 10 sets up the number for the next iteration. Therefore, (8735 % 10) is 5 and (8735 / 10) is 873. The do-while statement should continue as long as the remaining number is not 0.

   b. Run the program written in Exercise 3a on a computer and verify the program by using appropriate test data.

4. **(Practice)** Repeat any of the exercises in Section 5.3, using a do-while statement rather than a for statement.

5.5 Common Programming Errors

When using repetition statements, beginning C++ programmers are prone to making the following seven errors:

1. The most troublesome error for new programmers is the "off by one" error, in which the loop executes one too many or one too few times than was intended. For example, the loop created by the statement for(i = 1; i < 11; i++) executes 10 times, not 11, even though the number 11 is used in the statement. An equivalent loop can be constructed by using the statement for(i = 1; i <= 10; i++).

However, if the loop is started with an initial value of `i = 0`, using the statement `for(i = 0; i < 11; i++)`, the loop is traversed 11 times, as is a loop constructed with the statement `for(i = 0; i <= 10; i++)`. In constructing loops, you must pay particular attention to both the initial and final conditions used to control the loop to make sure the number of loop traversals isn't off by one too many or one too few executions.

The next two errors pertain to the tested expression, and you have already encountered them with the `if` and `switch` statements:

2. Inadvertently using the assignment operator, =, in place of the equality operator, ==, in the tested expression—for example, typing the assignment expression `a = 5` instead of the correct relational expression `a==5`. Because the tested expression can be any valid C++ expression, including arithmetic and assignment expressions, the compiler doesn't detect this error.

3. Using the equality operator, ==, when testing double-precision operands. For example, the expression `fnum == 0.01` should be replaced by a test requiring that the absolute value `fnum - 0.01` be less than an acceptable amount. The reason is that all numbers are stored in binary form. Using a finite number of bits, decimal numbers such as 0.01 have no exact binary equivalent, so tests requiring equality with these numbers can fail. (See Section 4.1 for a more complete description of this numerical accuracy problem.)

The next three errors are particular to the `for` statement:

4. Placing a semicolon at the end of `for`'s parentheses, which often produces a do-nothing loop. For example, take a look at these statements:

```
for(count = 0; count < 10; count++);
   total = total + num;
```

The semicolon at the end of the first line of code is a null statement. It has the effect of creating a loop that's executed 10 times with nothing done except incrementing and testing `count`. This error tends to occur because C++ programmers are used to ending most lines with a semicolon.

5. Using commas to separate items in a `for` statement instead of the required semicolons, as in this example:

```
for (count = 1, count < 10, count++)
```

Commas must be used to separate items in the initializing and altering lists, but semicolons must be used to separate these lists from the tested expression.

6. Changing the value of the control variable used in the tested condition both inside the body of a `for` loop and in its altering list. For example, take a look at this `for` loop:

```
for(int i=0; i<10; i++)
     cout << i++;
```

In this code, the value of the variable being tested (in this case, `i`) is changed in two places, which is a serious logic error.

7. The final common programming error is omitting the final semicolon from the do-while statement. This error is usually made by programmers who have learned to omit the semicolon after the parentheses of a while statement and carry over this habit when encountering the reserved word while at the end of a do-while statement.

5.6 Chapter Summary

1. A section of repeating code is referred to as a loop. A loop is controlled by a repetition statement that tests a condition to determine whether the code is to be executed. Each pass through the loop is referred to as a repetition or an iteration. The tested condition must always be set explicitly before its first evaluation by the repetition statement. Inside the loop, there must always be a statement that permits altering the condition so that the loop, after it's entered, can be exited.

2. There are three basic type of loops: while, for, and do-while. The while and for loops are pretest or entrance-controlled loops. In this type of loop, the tested condition is evaluated at the beginning of the loop, which requires setting the tested condition explicitly before loop entry. If the condition is true, loop repetitions begin; otherwise, the loop is not entered. Iterations continue as long as the condition remains true. In C++, while and for loops are constructed by using while and for statements.

   The do-while loop is a posttest or an exit-controlled loop, in which the tested condition is evaluated at the end of the loop. This type of loop is always executed at least once. As long as the tested condition remains true, do-while loops continue to execute.

3. Loops are also classified according to the type of tested condition. In a fixed-count loop, the condition is used to keep track of how many repetitions have occurred. In a variable-condition loop, the tested condition is based on a variable that can change interactively with each pass through the loop.

4. In C++, a while loop is constructed by using a while statement. This is the most commonly used form of this statement:

```
while (expression)
{
   statements;
}
```

The *expression* in parentheses is the condition that's tested to determine whether the statement following the parentheses, which is generally a compound statement, is executed. The expression is evaluated in the same manner as one in an if-else statement; the difference is how the expression is used. In a while statement, the statement following the expression is executed repeatedly as long as the expression retains a non-zero value, instead of just once, as in an if-else statement. An example of a while loop follows:

```
count = 1;              // initialize count
while (count <= 10)
{
   cout << count << "  ";
   count++;             // increment count
}
```

The first assignment statement sets count equal to 1. The while statement is then entered, and the expression is evaluated for the first time. Because the value of count is less than or equal to 10, the expression is true, and the compound statement is executed. The first statement in the compound statement uses the cout statement to display the value of count.

The next statement adds 1 to the value currently stored in count, making this value equal to 2. The while statement then loops back to retest the expression. Because count is still less than or equal to 10, the compound statement is executed again. This process continues until the value of count reaches 11.

Because the while statement always checks its expression at the top of the loop, any variables in the tested expression must have values assigned before the while is encountered. In addition, the while loop must contain a statement that alters the tested expression's value.

5. In C++, a for loop is constructed by using a for statement. This statement performs the same functions as the while statement but uses a different form. In many situations, especially those using a fixed-count condition, the for statement format is easier to use than its while statement equivalent. This is the most commonly used form of the for statement:

```
for (initializing list; expression; altering list)
{
   statements;
}
```

Inside the parentheses of the for statement are three items, separated by semicolons. Each of these items is optional, but the semicolons must be present.

The *initializing list* is used to set any initial values before the loop is entered; generally, it's used to initialize a counter. Statements in the initializing list are executed only once. The *expression* in the for statement is the condition being tested: It's tested at the start of the loop and before each iteration. The *altering list* contains loop statements that aren't within the compound statement; generally, it's used to increment or decrement a counter each time the loop is executed. Multiple statements in both initializing and altering lists are separated by commas. Here's an example of a for loop:

```
for (total = 0, count = 1; count < 10; count++)
{
    cout << "Enter a grade: ";
    total = total + grade;
}
```

In this for statement, the initializing list is used to initialize both total and count. The expression determines that the loop will execute as long as the value in count is less than 10, and the altering list specifies that the value of count is incremented by 1 each time through the loop.

6. The for statement is extremely useful in creating fixed-count loops because you can include initializing statements, the tested expression, and statements affecting the tested expression in parentheses at the top of a for loop for easy inspection and modification.

7. The do-while statement is used to create posttest loops because it checks its expression at the end of the loop. Checking at the end of the loop ensures that the body of a do loop is executed at least once. A do-while loop must contain at least one statement that alters the tested expression's value.

Chapter

6

Modularity Using Functions

Professional programs are designed, coded, and tested much like hardware: as a set of modules integrated to perform a completed whole. A good analogy is an automobile; one major module is the engine, another is the transmission, a third the braking system, a fourth the body, and so on. All these modules are linked together and placed under the driver's control, which can be compared to a main() *program module. The whole now operates as a complete unit, able to do useful work, such as driving to the store. During the assembly process, each module is constructed, tested, and found to be free of defects (bugs) before it's installed in the final product.*

In this analogy, each major car component can be compared to a function. For example, the driver calls on the engine when the gas pedal is pressed. The engine accepts inputs of fuel, air, and electricity to turn the driver's request into a useful product—power—and then sends this output to the transmission for further processing. The transmission receives the engine's output and converts it to a form the wheels can use. An additional input to the transmission is the driver's selection of gears (drive, reverse, neutral, and so on).

The engine, transmission, and other modules "know" only the universe bounded by their inputs and outputs. The driver doesn't need to know the internal operation of the modules being controlled. All that's required is knowing what each module does and how to "call" on it when the module's output is needed.

Communication between modules is restricted to passing inputs to each module as it's called on to perform its task, and each module operates in a fairly independent manner. Programmers use this same modular approach to create and maintain reliable C++ programs by using functions.

As you have seen, each C++ program must contain a main() *function. In addition to this required function, C++ programs can also contain any number of other functions. In this chapter, you learn how to write these functions, pass data to them, process the passed data, and return a result.*

6.1 Function and Parameter Declarations

In creating C++ functions, you must be concerned with the function itself and how it interacts with other functions, such as main(). Interaction with a function includes passing data to a function correctly when it's called (inputs) and returning values from a function (outputs) when it ceases operation. This section describes the first part of the interface, passing data to a function and having the function receive, store, and process the transmitted data correctly.

As you have already seen with mathematical functions, a function is called, or used, by giving the function's name and passing any data to it, as arguments, in the parentheses following the function name (see Figure 6.1). The called function must be able to accept the data passed to it by the function doing the calling. Only after the called function receives the data successfully can the data be manipulated to produce a useful result.

$$\underbrace{\textit{function-name}}\ \underbrace{(\textit{data passed to function})};$$

This identifies the   This passes data
called function   to the function

Figure 6.1 Calling and passing data to a function

To clarify the process of sending and receiving data, take a look at Program 6.1, which calls a function named findMax(). The program, as shown, is not yet complete. After the function findMax() is written and included in Program 6.1, the completed program, consisting of the functions main() and findMax(), can be compiled and run.

 Program 6.1

```
#include <iostream>
using namespace std;
void findMax(int, int);   // the function declaration (prototype)

int main()
{
  int firstnum, secnum;
```

```
cout << "\nEnter a number: ";
cin  >> firstnum;
cout << "Great! Please enter a second number: ";
cin  >> secnum;

findMax(firstnum, secnum);  // the function is called here

return 0;
}
```

First, examine the declaration and calling of the `findMax()` function from `main()`. You then see how to write `findMax()` to accept data passed to it, determine the largest or maximum value of the two passed values, and display the maximum value.

The `findMax()` function is referred to as the **called function** because it's called or summoned into action by its reference in `main()`. The function that does the calling—in this case, `main()`—is referred to as the **calling function**. The terms "called" and "calling" come from standard phone usage, in which one party calls the other: The person initiating the call is the calling party, and the person receiving the call is the called party. The same terms describe function calls. The called function—in this case, `findMax()`—is declared as a function that expects to receive two integer numbers and to return no value (a void) to `main()`. This declaration is formally called a function prototype. The function is then called by the last statement in the program.

Function Prototypes

Before a function can be called, it must be declared to the function that will do the calling. The declaration statement for a function is referred to as a **function prototype**. The function prototype tells the calling function the type of value that will be formally returned, if any, and the data type and order of the values the calling function should transmit to the called function. For example, the function prototype used in Program 6.1

```
void findMax(int, int);
```

declares that the `findMax()` function expects two integer values to be sent to it and returns no value (`void`).

Function prototypes can be placed with the variable declaration statements of the calling function, above the calling function name, as in Program 6.1, or in a separate header file specified with an `#include` preprocessor statement. The function prototype for `findMax()` could have been placed before or after the statement `#include <iostream>`, before `main()`, or within `main()`. (The reasons for the choice of placement are explained in Section 6.3.) The general form of function prototype statements is as follows:

```
returnDataType functionName(list of argument data types);
```

The *returnDataType* refers to the type of value the function returns. Here are some examples of function prototypes:

```
int fmax(int, int);
double swap(int, char, char, double);
void display(double, double);
```

The function prototype for `fmax()` declares that this function expects to receive two integer arguments and returns an integer value. The function prototype for `swap()` declares that this function requires four arguments—consisting of an integer, two characters, and a double-precision argument, in that order—and returns a double-precision number. Finally, the function prototype for `display()` declares that this function requires two double-precision arguments and doesn't return any value. This function might be used to display the results of a computation without returning any value to the called function.

Using function prototypes permits the compiler to error-check data types. If the function prototype doesn't agree with data types defined when the function is written, a warning message is displayed when the program is compiled. The prototype also serves another task: It ensures that all arguments passed to the function are converted to the declared data type when the function is called.

Calling a Function

Calling a function is rather easy. The only requirements are using the name of the function and enclosing any data passed to the function in the parentheses following the function name, using the same order and type declared in the function prototype. The items enclosed in parentheses are called **arguments** of the called function (see Figure 6.2).

findMax (*firstnum, secnum*);

This identifies   This causes two
the `findMax()`   values to be passed
function   to `findMax()`

Figure 6.2   Calling and passing two values to `findMax()`

If a variable is one of the arguments in a function call, the called function receives a copy of the value stored in the variable. For example, the statement `findMax(firstnum, secnum);` calls the `findMax()` function and causes the values stored in the variables `firstnum` and `secnum` to be passed to `findMax()`. The variable names in parentheses are arguments that provide values to the called function. After values are passed, control is transferred to the called function.

As shown in Figure 6.3, the `findMax()` function does *not* receive the variables named `firstnum` and `secnum` and has no knowledge of these variable names.[1] The function simply receives the values in these variables and must then determine where to store these values before it does anything else. Although this procedure for passing data to a function might seem surprising, it's actually a safety measure for ensuring that a called function doesn't

---

[1]In Section 6.3, you see how C++ also allows direct access to the calling function's variables by using reference variables.

inadvertently change data stored in a variable. The function gets a copy of the data to use. It can change its copy and, of course, change any variables declared inside it. However, unless specific steps to do so are taken, a function isn't allowed to change the contents of variables declared in other functions.

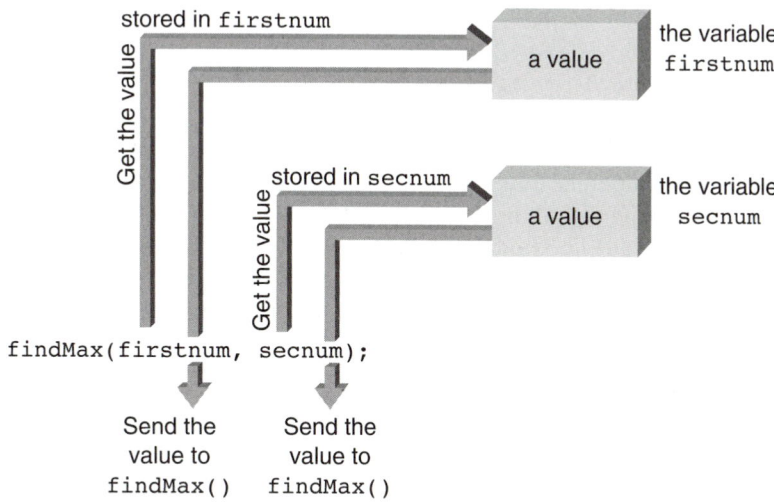

Figure 6.3 The findMax() function receives actual values

Next, you begin writing the findMax() function to process the values passed to it.

Defining a Function

A function is defined when it's written. Each function is defined once (that is, written once) in a program and can then be used by any other function in the program that declares it suitably.

Like the main() function, every C++ function consists of two parts, a **function header** and a **function body**, as shown in Figure 6.4. The function header's purpose is to identify the data type of the value the function returns, give the function a name, and specify the number, order, and type of arguments the function expects. The function body's purpose is to operate on the passed data and return, at most, one value directly back to the calling function. (In Section 6.3, you see how a function can be made to return multiple values indirectly by using its arguments.)

The function header is always the first line of a function and contains the function's return value type, its name, and the names and data types of its arguments. Because findMax() doesn't formally return any value and receives two integer values, the following function header can be used:

```
void findMax(int x, int y)  ◄————— no semicolon
```

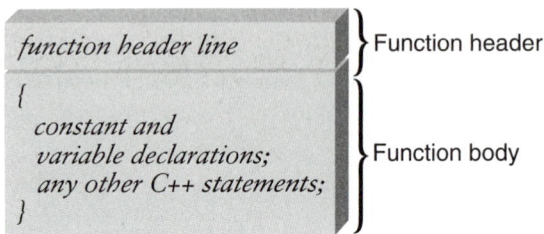

Figure 6.4 The general format of a function

The argument names in parentheses in the header are called the **formal parameters** of the function (or parameters, for short).[2] Therefore, the parameter x is used to store the first value passed to findMax() and the parameter y is used to store the second value passed at the time of the function call. The function doesn't know where the values come from when the call is made from main(). The first part of the call procedure the computer executes involves going to the variables firstnum and secnum and retrieving the stored values. These values are then passed to findMax() and stored in the parameters x and y (see Figure 6.5).

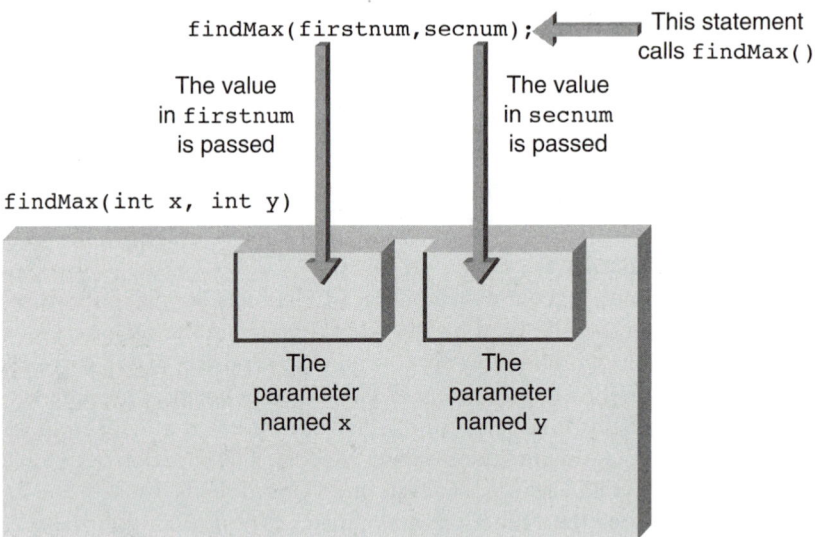

Figure 6.5 Storing values in parameters

The function name and all parameter names in the header—in this case, findMax, x, and y—are chosen by the programmer. Any names selected according to the rules for choosing variable names can be used. Each parameter listed in the function header must include a data type. If more than one parameter is declared in the function header, they must be separated by commas and have their data types declared separately.

---

[2]The portion of the function header containing function names and parameters is formally referred to as a "function declarator." The items enclosed in parentheses, the parameters, are specifications for the arguments. The arguments are the values provided when the function is called.

Point of Information

Function Definitions and Function Prototypes

When you write a function, you're formally creating a **function definition**. Each definition begins with a header line that includes a parameter list, if any, enclosed in parentheses and ends with the closing brace that terminates the function's body. The parentheses are required whether or not the function uses any parameters. The following is a commonly used syntax for a function definition:

```
returnDataType functionName(parameter list)
{
    constant declarations
    variable declarations

  other C++ statements

  return value
}
```

As you've learned, a function prototype declares a function. The syntax for a function prototype, which provides the function's return data type, the function's name, and the function's parameter list, is as follows:

```
returnDataType functionName(list of parameter data types);
```

The prototype, along with precondition and postcondition comments (see the next Point of Information box), should give users all the programming information needed to call the function successfully.

Generally, all function prototypes are placed at the top of the program, and all definitions are placed after the **main()** function. However, this placement can be changed. The only requirement in C++ is that a function can't be called before it has been declared or defined.

Now that the function header for **findMax()** has been written, you can construct its body. The function is to select and display the larger of the two numbers passed to it.

A function body begins with an opening brace, {, contains any necessary declarations and other C++ statements, and ends with a closing brace, }. This structure should be familiar because it's the same one used in all the **main()** functions you've seen so far. This required structure shouldn't be a surprise because **main()** is a function and must adhere to the rules for constructing all legitimate functions, as shown here:

```
{
  variable declarations and
  other C++ statements
}
```

Point of Information

Preconditions and Postconditions

Preconditions are any set of conditions a function requires to be true if it's to operate correctly. Similarly, a **postcondition** is a condition that will be true after the function is executed, assuming the preconditions are met.

Preconditions and postconditions are typically documented as user comments. For example, examine the following declaration and comments:

```
bool leapyr(int)
// Precondition: the integers must represent a year in a
//              : four-digit form, such as 2011
// Postcondition: a value of true is returned if the year is
//              : a leap year; otherwise, false is returned
```

Precondition and postcondition comments should be included with function prototypes and function definitions whenever clarification is needed.

In the body of the `findMax()` function, one variable is declared to store the maximum of the two numbers passed to it. An `if-else` statement is then used to find the maximum of the two numbers. Finally, a `cout` statement is used to display the maximum. The following shows the complete function definition for `findMax()`:

```
void findMax() (int x, int y)
{                       // start of function body
   int maxnum;          // variable declaration

   if (x >= y)          // find the maximum number
     maxnum = x;
   else
     maxnum = y;

   cout << "\nThe maximum of the two numbers is "
        << maxnum << endl;

   return;
}  // end of function body and end of function
```

Notice that the parameter declarations are made in the function header, and the variable declaration is made immediately after the function body's opening brace. This placement is in keeping with the concept that parameter values are passed to a function from outside the function, and variables are declared and assigned values from inside the function body. Program 6.2 includes the `findMax()` function in the program code previously listed in Program 6.1.

 **Program 6.2**

```cpp
#include <iostream>
using namespace std;
void findMax(int, int);        // the function prototype

int main()
{
  int firstnum, secnum;

  cout << "\nEnter a number: ";
  cin  >> firstnum;
  cout << "Great! Please enter a second number: ";
  cin  >> secnum;

  findMax(firstnum, secnum);  // the function is called here

  return 0;
}

// following is the function findMax()

void findMax(int x, int y)
{                      // start of function body
  int maxnum;          // variable declaration

  if (x >= y)          // find the maximum number
    maxnum = x;
  else
    maxnum = y;

  cout << "\nThe maximum of the two numbers is "
       << maxnum << endl;

  return;
}     // end of function body and end of function
```

Program 6.2 can be used to select and print the maximum of any two integer numbers the user enters. A sample run of Program 6.2 follows, with user-entered numbers shown in bold:

```
Enter a number: 25
Great! Please enter a second number: 5

The maximum of the two numbers is 25
```

The placement of the `findMax()` function after the `main()` function in Program 6.2 is a matter of choice. Usually, `main()` is listed first because it's the driver function that gives anyone reading the program an idea of what the complete program is about before encountering the details of each function. In no case, however, can the definition of `findMax()` be placed inside `main()`. This rule applies to all C++ functions, which must be defined by themselves outside any other function. Each C++ function is a separate and independent entity with its own parameters and variables; nesting functions is *never* permitted.

Placement of Statements

C++ doesn't impose a rigid statement-ordering structure on programmers. The general rule for placing statements in a C++ program is simply that all preprocessor directives, symbolic constants, variables, and functions must be declared or defined before they can be used. As noted previously, although this rule permits placing both preprocessor directives and declaration statements throughout a program, doing so results in poor program structure.

As a matter of good programming form, the following statement ordering should form the basic structure around which all C++ programs are constructed:

```
preprocessor directives
function prototypes

  int main()
  {
    // symbolic constants
    // variable declarations

    // other executable statements

    // return statement
  }

  // function definitions
```

As always, comment statements can be intermixed anywhere in this basic structure.

Function Stubs

An alternative, used by all programmers, to completing each function required in a complete program is writing the `main()` function first and then using placeholders for the final functions. To understand how this alternative works, take another look at Program 6.1. For convenience, its code has been reproduced here. As it's currently written, this program can't be compiled and run until the `findMax()` function is included.

```
#include <iostream>
using namespace std;
void findMax(int, int); // the function declaration (prototype)

int main()
{
```

```
    int firstnum, secnum;

    cout << "\nEnter a number: ";
    cin  >> firstnum;
    cout << "Great! Please enter a second number: ";
    cin  >> secnum;

    findMax(firstnum, secnum); // the function is called here

    return 0;
}
```

This program would be complete if there were a function definition for `findMax()`. However, you really don't need a *correct* `findMax()` function to test and run what has been written; you just need a function that *acts* as though it is. A "fake" `findMax()` that accepts the correct number and types of parameters and returns values of the proper form for the function call is all you need for initial testing. This fake function, called a **stub**, is the beginning of a final function and can be used as a placeholder for the final function until it's completed. A stub for `findMax()` is as follows:

```
void findMax(int x, int y)
{
  cout << "In findMax()\n";
  cout << "The value of x is " << x << endl;
  cout << "The value of y is " << y << endl;
}
```

This stub function can now be compiled and linked with the previously completed code to produce an executable program. The code for the function can then be further developed with the "real" code when it's completed, replacing the stub portion.

The minimum requirement of a stub function is that it compiles and links with its calling module. In practice, it's a good idea to have a stub display a message that it has been entered successfully and display the values of its received parameters, as in the stub for `findMax()`. As the function is refined, you let it do more, perhaps allowing it to return intermediate or incomplete results. This incremental, or stepwise, refinement is an important concept in efficient program development that gives you the means to run a program that doesn't yet meet all its final requirements.

Functions with Empty Parameter Lists

Although useful functions having an empty parameter list are extremely limited, they can occur. (You see one such function in Exercise 15 at the end of this section.) The function prototype for this type of function requires writing the keyword `void` or nothing at all between the parentheses following the function's name. For example, both these prototypes

```
int display();
```

and

```
int display(void);
```

Point of Information

Isolation Testing

One of the most successful software testing methods is always embedding the code being tested in an environment of working code. For example, you have two untested functions called in the following order, and the result the second function returns is incorrect:

From the information shown in this figure, one or possibly both of the functions could be operating incorrectly. The first order of business is to isolate the problem to a specific function.

One powerful method of performing this code isolation is to decouple the functions. You do this by testing each function separately or by testing one function first and, only after you know it's operating correctly, reconnecting it to the second function. Then, if an error occurs, you have isolated the error to the transfer of data between functions or to the internal operation of the second function.

This specific procedure is an example of the basic rule of testing, which states that each function should be tested only in a program in which all other functions are known to be correct. This rule means one function must first be tested by itself, using stubs if needed for any called functions, and a second tested function should be tested by itself or with a previously tested function, and so on. This testing procedure ensures that each new function is isolated in a test bed of correct functions, with the final program built from tested function code.

---

indicate that the `display()` function takes no parameters and returns an integer. A function with an empty parameter list is called by its name with nothing written inside the required parentheses following the function's name. For example, the statement `display();` correctly calls the `display()` function, whose prototype is shown in the preceding example.

Default Arguments[3]

C++ provides **default arguments** in a function call for added flexibility. The primary use of default arguments is to extend the parameter list of existing functions without requiring any change in the calling argument lists already used in a program.

Default argument values are listed in the function prototype and transmitted automatically to the called function when the corresponding arguments are omitted from the function call. For example, the function prototype

```
void example(int, int = 5, double = 6.78);
```

---

[3]This topic can be omitted on first reading without loss of subject continuity.

provides default values for the last two arguments. If any of these arguments are omitted when the function is actually called, the C++ compiler supplies the default values. Therefore, all the following function calls are valid:

```
example(7, 2, 9.3)  // no defaults used
example(7, 2)       // same as example(7, 2, 6.78)
example(7)          // same as example(7, 5, 6.78)
```

Four rules must be followed when using default arguments:

- Default values should be assigned in the function prototype.[4]
- If any parameter is given a default value in the function prototype, all parameters following it must also be supplied with default values.
- If one argument is omitted in the actual function call, all arguments to its right must also be omitted. The second and third rules make it clear to the C++ compiler which arguments are being omitted and enable the compiler to supply correct default values for the missing arguments, starting with the rightmost argument and working in toward the left.
- The default value used in the function prototype can be an expression consisting of both constants and previously declared variables. If this kind of expression is used, it must pass the compiler's check for validly declared variables, even though the expression's actual value is evaluated and assigned at runtime.

Default arguments are extremely useful when extending an existing function to include more features that require additional arguments. Adding new arguments to the right of the existing arguments and giving each new argument a default value permits all existing function calls to remain as they are. In this way, the effect of the changes is conveniently isolated from existing code in the program.

Reusing Function Names (Overloading)[5]

C++ provides the capability of using the same function name for more than one function, referred to as **function overloading**. The only requirement for creating more than one function with the same name is that the compiler must be able to determine which function to use based on the parameters' data types (not the data type of the return value, if any). For example, take a look at these three functions, all named cdabs():

```
void cdabs(int x) // compute and display absolute value of an integer
{
  if ( x < 0 )
    x = -x;
  cout << "The absolute value of the integer is " << x << endl;
}
```

---

[4]Some compilers accept default assignments in the function definition.
[5]This topic can be omitted on first reading without loss of subject continuity.

```
void cdabs(float x) // compute and display absolute value of a float
{
  if ( x < 0 )
    x = -x;
  cout << "The absolute value of the float is " << x << endl;
}

void cdabs(double x) // compute and display absolute value of a double
{
  if ( x < 0 )
    x = -x;
  cout << "The absolute value of the double is " << x << endl;
}
```

Which of the three cdabs() functions is actually called depends on the argument types supplied at the time of the call. Therefore, the function call cdabs(10); causes the compiler to use the function named cdabs() that expects an integer argument, and the function call cdabs(6.28f); causes the compiler to use the function named cdabs() that expects a double-precision argument.[6]

Notice that overloading a function's name simply means using the same name for more than one function. Each function that uses the name must still be written and exists as a separate entity. The use of the same function name doesn't require code in the functions to be similar, although good programming practice dictates that functions with the same name should perform essentially the same operations. All that's required to use the same function name is ensuring that the compiler can distinguish which function to select, based on the data types of the arguments when the function is called. Clearly, however, if the only difference in the overloaded functions is the argument types, a better programming solution is simply creating a function template, discussed in the next section. Using overloaded functions, however, is extremely useful with constructor functions, explained in Section 10.3.

Function Templates[7]

In most high-level languages, including C++'s immediate predecessor, C, each function must be coded separately, even if function overloading is used to give multiple functions the same name. For example, consider determining and displaying a number's absolute value. If the number passed to the function can be an integer, a single-precision, or a double-precision

---

[6]Selection of the correct function is accomplished by a process called "name mangling." Using this process, the function name the C++ compiler actually generates differs from the function name used in the source code. The compiler appends information to the source code function name, depending on the type of data being passed, and the resulting name is said to be a "mangled" version of the source code name.

[7]This topic can be omitted on first reading without loss of subject continuity.

value, three distinct functions must be written to handle each case correctly. Therefore, if the function name abs() is used, these three functions would have the following prototypes:

```
void abs(int);
void abs(float);
void abs(double);
```

Clearly, each of these functions performs essentially the same operation but on different parameter data types. A much cleaner solution is writing a general function that handles all three parameter data types, but the compiler can set parameters, variables, and even return type based on the data type used when the function is called. You can write this type of function in C++ by using a **function template**, which is a single, complete function that serves as a model for a family of functions. The function from the family that's actually created depends on subsequent function calls. To make this concept more concrete, take a look at a function template that computes and displays the absolute value of a passed argument:

```
template <class T>
void showabs(T number)
{
  if (number < 0)
    number = -number;
  cout << "The absolute value of the number "
       << " is " << number << endl;

  return;
}
```

For the moment, ignore the first line, template <class T>, and look at the second line, consisting of the function header void showabs(T number). Notice that this function header has the same syntax used for all function definitions, except the T where a data type is usually placed. For example, if the function header were void showabs(int number), you should recognize it as a function named showabs() that expects one integer argument to be passed to it and returns no value. Similarly, if the function header were void showabs(double number), you should recognize it as a function that expects one double-precision argument to be passed to it when the function is called.

The advantage of using the T in the function template header is that it represents a general data type that's replaced by an actual data type, such as int, float, double, and so forth, when the compiler encounters an actual function call. For example, if a function call with an integer argument is encountered, the compiler uses the function template to construct a function that expects an integer parameter. Similarly, if a call is made with a double-precision argument, the compiler constructs a function that expects a double-precision parameter. As a specific example, take a look at Program 6.3.

 **Program 6.3**

```cpp
#include <iostream>
using namespace std;

template <class T>
void showabs(T number)
{
  if (number < 0)
    number = -number;
  cout << "The absolute value of the number is "
       << number << endl;

  return;
}

int main()
{
  int num1 = -4;
  float num2 = -4.23F;
  double num3 = -4.23456;

  showabs(num1);
  showabs(num2);
  showabs(num3);

  return 0;
}
```

Notice the three function calls made in the main() function; they call the function showabs() with an integer, float, and double value. Now review the function template for showabs() and look at the first line, template <class T>. This line, called a **template prefix**, is used to inform the compiler that the function immediately following is a template using a data type named T. In the function template, the T is used in the same manner as any other data type, such as int, float, and double. When the compiler encounters an actual function call for showabs(), the data type of the argument passed in the call is substituted for T throughout the function. In effect, the compiler creates a specific function, using the template, that expects the argument type in the call.

Because Program 6.3 makes three calls to showabs(), each with a different argument data type, the compiler creates three separate showabs() functions. The compiler knows which function to use based on the arguments passed at the time of the call. This is the output displayed when Program 6.3 runs:

```
The absolute value of the number is 4
The absolute value of the number is 4.23
The absolute value of the number is 4.23456
```

The letter T in the template prefix template <class T> is simply a placeholder for a data type that's defined when the function is actually called. Any letter or identifier that's not a keyword can be used instead, so the showabs() function template could just as well have been defined as follows:

```
template <class DTYPE>
void showabs(DTYPE number)
{
  if (number < 0)
    number = -number;
  cout << "The absolute value of the number is "
       << number << endl;

  return;
}
```

In this regard, sometimes it's simpler and clearer to read the word *class* in the template prefix as the words *data type*. With this substitution, you can read the template prefix template <class T> as "I'm defining a function template that has a data type named T." Then, in the defined function's header and body, the data type T (or any other letter or identifier defined in the prefix) is used in the same manner as any built-in data type, such as int, float, and double.

EXERCISES 6.1

1. **(Practice)** For the following function headers, determine the number, type, and order (sequence) of the values that must be passed to the function:
   a. void factorial(int n)
   b. void price(int type, double yield, double maturity)
   c. void yield(int type, double price, double maturity)
   d. void interest(char flag, double price, double time)
   e. void total(double amount, double rate)
   f. void roi(int a, int b, char c, char d, double e, double f)
   g. void getVal(int item, int iter, char decflag, char delim)

2. **(Practice) a.** Write a function named `check()` that has three parameters. The first parameter should accept an integer number, and the second and third parameters should accept a double-precision number. The function body should just display the values of data passed to the function when it's called. (*Note:* When tracing errors in functions, having the function display values it has been passed is helpful. Quite often, the error isn't in what the function body does with data, but in the data received and stored.)

   b. Include the function written in Exercise 2a in a working program. Make sure your function is called from `main()`. Test the function by passing various data to it.

3. **(Practice) a.** Write a function named `findAbs()` that accepts a double-precision number passed to it, computes its absolute value, and displays the absolute value. A number's absolute value is the number itself if the number is positive and the negative of the number if the number is negative.

   b. Include the function written in Exercise 3a in a working program. Make sure your function is called from `main()`. Test the function by passing various data to it.

4. **(Practice) a.** Write a function called `mult()` that accepts two double-precision numbers as parameters, multiplies these two numbers, and displays the result.

   b. Include the function written in Exercise 4a in a working program. Make sure your function is called from `main()`. Test the function by passing various data to it.

5. **(Practice) a.** Write a function named `sqrIt()` that computes the square of the value passed to it and displays the result. The function should be capable of squaring numbers with decimal points.

   b. Include the function written in Exercise 5a in a working program. Make sure your function is called from `main()`. Test the function by passing various data to it.

6. **(Practice) a.** Write a function named `powfun()` that raises an integer number passed to it to a positive integer power and displays the result. The positive integer should be the second value passed to the function. Declare the variable used to store the result as a long-integer data type to ensure enough storage for the result.

   b. Include the function written in Exercise 6a in a working program. Make sure your function is called from `main()`. Test the function by passing various data to it.

7. **(Practice) a.** Write a function that produces a table of the numbers from 1 to 10, their squares, and their cubes. The function should produce the same display as Program 5.10.

   b. Include the function written in Exercise 7a in a working program. Make sure your function is called from `main()`. Test the function by passing various data to it.

8. **(Modify) a.** Modify the function written for Exercise 7a to accept the starting value of the table, the number of values to be displayed, and the increment between values. If the increment isn't set explicitly, the function should use a default value of 1. Name your function `selTab()`. A call to `selTab(6,5,2);` should produce a table of five lines, the first line starting with the number 6 and each succeeding number increasing by 2.

   b. Include the function written in Exercise 8a in a working program. Make sure your function is called from `main()`. Test the function by passing various data to it.

9. **(Program) a.** The time in hours, minutes, and seconds is to be passed to a function named `totsec()`. Write `totsec()` to accept these values, determine the total number of seconds in the passed data, and display the calculated value.

   b. Include the `totsec()` function written for Exercise 9a in a working program. The `main()` function should correctly call `totsec()` and display the value the function returns. Use the following test data to verify your program's operation: hours = 10, minutes = 36, and seconds = 54. Make sure to do a hand calculation to verify the result your program displays.

10. **(Program) a.** The volume, *V*, of a sphere is given by this formula, where *r* is the sphere's radius:

$$Volume = \frac{4\pi r^3}{3}$$

   Using this formula, write, compile, and run a C++ function named `spherevol()` that accepts a sphere's radius and then calculates and displays its volume.

   b. Include the function written in Exercise 10a in a working program. Make sure your function is called from `main()`. Test the function by passing various data to it.

11. **(Program) a.** Write and test a C++ function named `makeMilesKmTable()` to display a table of miles converted to kilometers. The arguments to the function should be the starting and stopping values of miles and the increment. The output should be a table of miles and their equivalent kilometer values. Use the relationship that 1 mile = 1.61 kilometers.

   b. Modify the function written for Exercise 12a so that two columns are displayed. For example, if the starting value is 1 mile, the ending value is 20 miles, and the increment is 1, the display should look like the following:

Miles	=	Kilometers	Miles	=	Kilometers
1		1.61	11		17.70
2		3.22	12		19.31
.		.	.		.
.		.	.		.
10		16.09	20		32.18

   (*Hint*: Find *split* = (*start* + *stop*) / 2. Let a loop execute from *miles* = *start* to *split*, and calculate and print across one line the values of miles and kilometers for both *miles* and (*miles* - *start* + *split* + 1).)

12. **(Program) a.** Write a C++ function that accepts an integer argument, determines whether the passed integer is even or odd, and displays the result of this determination. (*Hint*: Use the % operator.)

   b. Include the function written in Exercise 12a in a working program. Make sure your function is called from `main()`. Test the function by passing various data to it.

13. **(Program)** A useful function using no parameters can be constructed to return a value for π that's accurate to the maximum number of decimal places your computer allows. This value is obtained by taking the arcsine of 1.0, which is π / 2, and multiplying the result by 2. In C++, the required expression is `2.0 * asin(1.0)`; the `asin()` function is included in the standard

C++ mathematics library. (Remember to include `cmath` in your preprocessor directives.) Using this expression, write a C++ function named `pi()` that calculates and displays the value of π. (In the next section, you see how to return this value to the calling function.)

14. **(Program) a.** Write a function template named `display()` that displays the value of the single argument passed to it when the function is called.

   b. Include the function template created in Exercise 14a in a complete C++ program that calls the function three times: once with a character argument, once with an integer argument, and once with a double-precision argument.

6.2 Returning a Single Value

Using the method of passing data to a function explained in the previous section, the called function receives only copies of the values contained in arguments at the time of the call. (Review Figure 6.3 if it's unclear to you.) When a value is passed to a called function in this manner, the passed argument is referred to as a **passed by value** and is a distinct advantage of C++.[8] Because the called function doesn't have direct access to the variables used as arguments by the calling function, it can't inadvertently alter the value stored in one of these variables.

The function receiving the passed by value arguments can process the values sent to it in any fashion and return one, and only one, "legitimate" value directly to the calling function (see Figure 6.6). In this section, you see how this value is returned to the calling function. As you might expect, given C++'s flexibility, there's a way of returning more than a single value, but that's the topic of the next section.

A function can receive many values

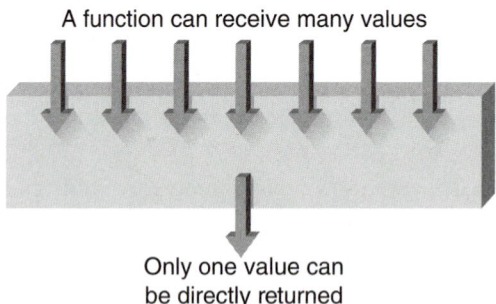

Only one value can
be directly returned

Figure 6.6   A function directly returns at most one value

---

[8]This argument is also referred to as a "call by value." These terms, however, don't refer to the function call as a whole, but to how the calling function passes values to the called function.

As with calling a function, returning a value directly requires handling the interface between the called and calling functions correctly. From its side of the return transaction, the called function must provide the following items:

- The data type of the returned value
- The actual value being returned

A function returning a value must specify, in its header, the data type of the value to be returned. Recall that the function header includes both the function name and a parameter list. For example, the findMax() function written previously determines the maximum value of two numbers passed to it. For convenience, the findMax() code is listed again:

```
void findMax(int x, int y)
{                        // start of function body
  int maxnum;            // variable declaration

  if (x >= y)            // find the maximum number
    maxnum = x;
  else
    maxnum = y;

  cout  << "\nThe maximum of the two numbers is "
        << maxnum << endl;
  return;
}  // end of function body and end of function
```

In this function header, x and y are the names chosen for the function's parameters:

```
void findMax(int x, int y)
```

If findMax() is to return a value, its header must be amended to include the data type of the value being returned. For example, if an integer value is to be returned, this is the correct function header:

```
int findMax(int x, int y)
```

Similarly, if the function is to receive two floating-point values and return a floating-point value, this is the correct function header:

```
float findMax(float x, float y)
```

If the function is to receive two double-precision values and return a double-precision value, the function header should be the following:[9]

```
double findMax(double x, double y)
```

---

[9]The return data type is related to the parameter data types only as much as the returned value is determined by the parameter values. In this case, because the function is used to return the maximum value of its parameters, it would make little sense to return a data type that doesn't match the function's parameter data types.

Now see how to modify the `findMax()` function to return the maximum value of the two numbers passed to it. To do this, you must first determine the data type of the value to be returned and include this data type in the function header. Because the maximum value determined by `findMax()` is stored in the integer variable `maxnum`, the function should return this variable's value. Returning an integer value from `findMax()` requires the following function declaration:

```
int findMax(int x, int y)
```

Observe that it's the same as the original function header for `findMax()`, with the keyword `int` substituted for the keyword `void`.

Having declared the data type that `findMax()` will return, all that remains is including a statement in the function to cause the return of the correct value. To return a value, a function must use a `return` statement, which has this form:[10]

```
return expression;
```

When the `return` statement is encountered, the expression is evaluated first. The value of the expression is then automatically converted to the data type declared in the function header before being sent back to the calling function. After the value is returned, program control reverts to the calling function. Therefore, to return the value stored in `maxnum`, all you need to do is include the statement `return maxnum;` before the closing brace of the `findMax()` function. The complete function code is as follows:

```
These should ──────▶ int findMax(int x, int y)    // function header
be the same          {                            // start of function body
data type               int maxnum;               // variable declaration
                        if (x >= y)
                           maxnum = x;
                        else
                           maxnum = y;

                        return maxnum;             // return statement
                     }
```

In this new code for the `findMax()` function, notice that the data type of the expression in the `return` statement matches the data type in the function header. It's up to the programmer to ensure this match for every function returning a value. Failure to match the return value with the function's declared data type exactly might not result in an error when your program is compiled, but it could lead to undesired results because the return value is always converted to the data type declared in the function declaration. Usually, this is a problem only when the fractional part of a returned floating-point or double-precision number is truncated because the function was declared to return an integer value.

---

[10]Many programmers place the expression in parentheses, as in `return (expression);`. Although either form (with or without parentheses) can be used, choose one and stay with it for consistency.

Having taken care of the sending side of the return transaction, you must now prepare the calling function to receive the value sent by the called function. On the calling (receiving) side, the calling function must

- Be alerted to the type of value to expect back from the called function.
- Use the return value correctly.

Alerting the calling function to the type of return value to expect is taken care of by the function prototype. For example, including the function prototype

```
int findMax(int, int);
```

before the `main()` function is enough to alert `main()` that `findMax()` is a function that returns an integer value.

To actually use a return value, you must provide a variable to store the value or use the value in an expression. To store the return value in a variable, you use a standard assignment statement. For example, the following assignment statement can be used to store the value returned by `findMax()` in the variable `max`:

```
max = findMax(firstnum, secnum);
```

This assignment statement does two things. First, the right side of the assignment statement calls `findMax()`, and then the result returned by `findMax()` is stored in the variable `max`. Because the value returned by `findMax()` is an integer, the variable `max` must also be declared as an integer variable in the calling function's variable declarations.

The value a function returns need not be stored in a variable, but it can be used wherever an expression is valid. For example, the expression `2 * findMax(firstnum, secnum)` multiplies the value returned by `findMax()` by 2, and the following statement displays the return value:

```
cout << findMax(firstnum, secnum);
```

Program 6.4 illustrates including prototype and assignment statements for `main()` to declare, call, and store a return value from `findMax()` correctly. As before, and in keeping with the convention of placing the `main()` function first, the `findMax()` function is placed after `main()`.

 ## Program 6.4

```cpp
#include <iostream>
using namespace std;

int findMax(int, int); // the function prototype

int main()
{
  int firstnum, secnum, max;
```

```
    cout << "\nEnter a number: ";
    cin  >> firstnum;
    cout << "Great! Please enter a second number: ";
    cin  >> secnum;

    max = findMax(firstnum, secnum); // the function is called here

    cout << "\nThe maximum of the two numbers is " << max << endl;

    return 0;
}

int findMax(int x, int y)
{                       // start of function body
    int maxnum;         // variable declaration

    if (x >= y)         // find the maximum number
        maxnum = x;
    else
        maxnum = y;

    return maxnum;      // return statement
}
```

In reviewing Program 6.4, note the four items introduced in this section. First, the function prototype for findMax() is a statement ending with a semicolon, as all declaration statements do; it alerts main() and any subsequent functions using findMax() to the data type that findMax() returns. Second, an assignment statement is used in main() to store the return value from the findMax() call in the variable max. In Program 6.4, max is declared correctly as an integer in main()'s variable declarations so that it matches the return value's data type.

The third and fourth items concern coding the findMax() function: The first line of findMax() declares that the function returns an integer value, and the expression in the return statement evaluates to a matching data type. Therefore, findMax() is internally consistent in sending an integer value back to main(), and main() has been alerted to receive and use the returned integer.

In writing your own functions, always keep these four items in mind. For another example, see whether you can identify these four items in Program 6.5.

Program 6.5

```cpp
#include <iostream>
using namespace std;

double tempvert(double);  // function prototype

int main()
{
  const int CONVERTS = 4;  // number of conversions to be made
  int count;               // start of variable declarations
  double fahren;

  for(count = 1; count <= CONVERTS; count++)
  {
  cout << "\nEnter a Fahrenheit temperature: ";
  cin  >> fahren;
  cout << "The Celsius equivalent is "
       << tempvert(fahren) << endl;
  }

  return 0;
}

// convert fahrenheit to celsius
double tempvert(double inTemp)
{
  return (5.0/9.0) * (inTemp - 32.0);
}
```

In reviewing Program 6.5, first analyze the `tempvert()` function. Its definition begins with the function header and ends with the closing brace after the `return` statement. The function is declared as a `double`, meaning the expression in the function's `return` statement must evaluate to a double-precision number, which it does. Because a function header is not a statement but the start of the code defining the function, it doesn't end with a semicolon.

On the receiving side, `main()` has a prototype for the `tempvert()` function that agrees with `tempvert()`'s function definition. No variable is declared in `main()` to store the returned value from `tempvert()` because the returned value is passed immediately to `cout` for display.

Finally, one purpose of declarations, as you learned in Chapter 2, is to alert the computer to the amount of internal storage reserved for data. The prototype for `tempvert()` performs this task and alerts the compiler to the type of storage needed for the return value. Had the `tempvert()` function definition been placed before `main()`, the function header would serve the same purpose, and the function prototype could be eliminated. Because `main()` is always the first function in a program, however, you must include function prototypes for all functions called by `main()` and any subsequent functions.

Inline Functions[11]

Calling a function places a certain amount of overhead on a computer. This overhead consists of the following steps:

1. Placing argument values in a reserved memory region (called the **stack**) that the function has access to
2. Passing control to the function
3. Providing a reserved memory location for any return value (again, using the stack for this purpose)
4. Returning to the correct point in the calling program

Paying this overhead is justified when a function is called many times because it can reduce a program's size substantially. Instead of the same code being repeated each time it's needed, the code is written once, as a function, and called whenever it's needed.

For small functions that aren't called many times, however, the overhead of passing and returning values might not be warranted. It would still be convenient to group repeating lines of code under a common function name and have the compiler place this code in the program wherever the function is called. **Inline functions** provide this capability.

Telling the C++ compiler that a function is inline causes a copy of the function code to be placed in the program at the point the function is called. For example, because the `tempvert()` function in Program 6.5 is fairly short, it's an ideal candidate to be an inline function. To make it, or any other function, an inline one simply requires placing the reserved keyword `inline` before the function name and defining the function before any calls are made to it. Program 6.6 makes `tempvert()` an inline function.

 **Program 6.6**

```
#include <iostream>
using namespace std;

inline double tempvert(double inTemp)  // an inline function
{
  return (5.0/9.0) * (inTemp - 32.0);
}
```

---

[11]This section is optional and can be omitted on first reading without loss of subject continuity.

```
int main()
{
  const int CONVERTS = 4;  // number of conversions to be made
  int count;               // start of variable declarations
  double fahren;

  for(count = 1; count <= CONVERTS; count++)
  {
    cout << "\nEnter a Fahrenheit temperature: ";
    cin  >> fahren;
    cout << "The Celsius equivalent is "
         << tempvert(fahren) << endl;
  }

  return 0;
}
```

Observe in Program 6.6 that the inline function is placed ahead of any calls to it. This placement is a requirement of all inline functions, so a function prototype isn't needed before subsequent calling functions. Because the function is now inline, its code is expanded into the program wherever it's called.

The advantage of using an inline function is an increase in execution speed. Because the inline function is expanded and included in every expression or statement calling it, no execution time is lost because of the call, return, and stack overhead a non-inline function requires. The disadvantage is the increase in program size when an inline function is called repeatedly. Each time an inline function is referenced, the complete function code is reproduced and stored as an integral part of the program. A non-inline function, however, is stored in memory only once. No matter how many times the function is called, the same code is used. Therefore, inline functions should be used only for small functions that aren't called extensively in a program.

Templates with a Return Value[12]

In Section 6.1, you saw how to construct a function template. Returning a value from a function template is identical to returning a value from a function. For example, take a look at the following function template:

```
template <class T> // template prefix
T abs(T value)     // function header
{
  T absnum;  // variable declaration

  if (value < 0)
    absnum = -value;
```

---

[12]This section is optional and can be omitted on first reading without loss of subject continuity.

```
    else
      absnum = value;

    return absnum;
}
```

In this template definition, the date type T is used to declare three items: the return type of the function, the data type of a single function parameter named `value`, and one variable declared within the function. Program 6.7 shows how this function template could be used in the context of a complete program.

 **Program 6.7**

```cpp
#include <iostream>
using namespace std;

template <class T> // template prefix
T abs(T value)     // function header
{
  T absnum;        // variable declaration

  if (value < 0)
    absnum = -value;
  else
    absnum = value;

  return absnum;
}

int main()
{
  int num1 = -4;
  float num2 = -4.23F;
  double num3 = -4.23456;

  cout << "The absolute value of " << num1
       << " is " << abs(num1) << endl;
  cout << "The absolute value of " << num2
       << " is " << abs(num2) << endl;
  cout << "The absolute value of " << num3
       << " is " << abs(num3) << endl;

  return 0;
}
```

In the first call to abs() made within main(), an integer value is passed as an argument. In this case, the compiler substitutes an int data type for the T data type in the function template and creates the following function:

```
int abs(int value) // function header
{
  int absnum;        // variable declaration

  if (value < 0)
    absnum = -value;
  else
    absnum = value;

  return (absnum);
}
```

Similarly, in the second and third function calls, the compiler creates two more functions: one in which the data type T is replaced by the keyword float and one in which the data type T is replaced by the keyword double. This is the output produced by Program 6.7:

```
The absolute value of -4 is 4
The absolute value of -4.23 is 4.23
The absolute value of -4.23456 is 4.23456
```

The value of using a function template is that one function definition has been used to create three different functions, each of which uses the same logic and operations but operates on different data types.

Finally, although both Programs 6.3 and 6.7 define a function template using a single placeholder data type, function templates with more than one data type can be defined. For example, the following template prefix can be used to create a function template requiring three different data types:

```
template <class DTYPE1, class DTYPE2, class DTYPE3>
```

As before, in the function template's header and body, the data types DTYPE1, DTYPE2, and DTYPE3 are used in the same manner as any built-in data type, such as an int, float, and double. Also, as noted previously, the names DTYPE1, DTYPE2, and DTYPE3 can be any non-keyword identifier. Conventionally, the letter T followed by zero or more digits is used, such as T, T1, T2, T3, and so forth.

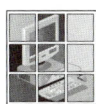

EXERCISES 6.2

1. **(Modify)** Rewrite Program 6.4 so that the findMax() function accepts two double-precision arguments and returns a double-precision value to main(). Make sure to modify main() to pass two double-precision values to findMax() and to accept and store the double-precision value returned by findMax().

2. (**Practice**) Write function headers for the following functions:

   a. A function named check(), which has three parameters. The first parameter should accept an integer number, the second parameter a floating-point number, and the third parameter a double-precision number. The function returns no value.

   b. A function named findAbs() that accepts a double-precision number passed to it and returns that number's absolute value.

   c. A function named mult() that accepts two floating-point numbers as parameters, multiplies these two numbers, and returns the result.

   d. A function named square() that computes and returns the square of the integer value passed to it.

   e. A function named powfun() that raises an integer number passed to it to a positive integer power (also passed as an argument) and returns the result as an integer.

   f. A function named table() that produces a table of numbers from 1 to 10, their squares, and their cubes. No arguments are to be passed to the function, and the function returns no value.

3. (**Program**) a. Write a function named rightTriangle() that accepts the lengths of two sides of a right triangle as the arguments a and b. The subroutine should determine and return the hypotenuse, c, of the triangle. (*Hint*: Use Pythagoras' theorem, $c^2 = a^2 + b^2$.)

   b. Include the function written for Exercise 3a in a working program. The main() function should call rightTriangle() correctly and display the value the function returns. Test the function by passing various data to it and verifying the returned value.

4. (**Program**) a. Write a C++ function named findAbs() that accepts a double-precision number passed to it, computes its absolute value, and returns the absolute value to the calling function. A number's absolute value is the number itself if the number is positive and the negative of the number if the number is negative.

   b. Include the function written in Exercise 4a in a working program. Make sure your function is called from main() and returns a value to main() correctly. Have main() use a cout statement to display the returned value. Test the function by passing various data to it and verifying the returned value.

5. (**Program**) a. The volume, V, of a cylinder is given by the formula

   $$V = \pi r^2 L$$

   where r is the cylinder's radius and L is its length. Using this formula, write a C++ function named cylvol() that accepts a cylinder's radius and length and returns its volume.

   b. Include the function written in Exercise 5a in a working program. Make sure your function is called from main() and returns a value to main() correctly. Have main() use a cout statement to display the returned value. Test the function by passing various data to it and verifying the returned value.

6. (**Program**) a. The surface area, S, of a cylinder is given by the formula

   $$S = 2 \pi r l$$

   where r is the cylinder's radius, and l is the length of the cylinder. Using this formula, write a C++ function named surfarea() that accepts a cylinder's radius and length and returns its surface area.

   b. Include the function written in Exercise 6a in a working program. Make sure your function is called from `main()` and returns a value to `main()` correctly. Have `main()` use a `cout` statement to display the returned value. Test the function by passing various data to it and verifying the returned value.

7. **(Program) a.** Write a function named `totamt()` that uses four parameters named `quarters`, `dimes`, `nickels`, and `pennies`, which represent the number of each of these coins in a piggybank. The function should determine the dollar value of the number of quarters, dimes, nickels, and pennies passed to it and return the calculated value.

   b. Include the function written in Exercise 7a in a working program. Make sure your function is called from `main()` and returns a value to `main()` correctly. Have `main()` use a `cout` statement to display the returned value. Test the function by passing various data to it and verifying the returned value.

8. **(Program) a.** Write a function named `daycount()` that accepts a month, day, and year as its input arguments; calculates an integer representing the total number of days from the turn of the century to the date that's passed; and returns the calculated integer to the calling function. For this problem, assume each year has 365 days and each month has 30 days. Test your function by verifying that the date 1/1/00 returns a day count of 1.

   b. Include the `daycount()` function written for Exercise 8a in a working program. The `main()` function should correctly call `daycount()` and display the integer returned by the function. Test the function by passing various data to it and verifying the returned value.

9. **(Program) a.** A clever and simple method of preparing to sort dates into ascending (increasing) or descending (decreasing) order is to convert a date in the form month/day/year into an integer number with the formula *date = year × 10000 + month × 100 + day*. For example, using this formula, the date 12/6/1999 converts to the integer 19991206, and the date 2/28/2011 converts to the integer 20110228. Sorting the resulting integer numbers puts dates into the correct order automatically. Using this formula, write a function named `convertdays()` that accepts a month, day, and year; converts the passed data into a single date integer; and returns the integer to the calling function.

   b. Include the `convertdays()` function written for Exercise 9a in a working program. The `main()` function should call `convertdays()` correctly and display the integer the function returns. Test the function by passing various data to it and verifying the returned value.

10. **(Program) a.** Write a function named `ReadOneChar()` that reads a key pressed on the keyboard and displays the integer code of the entered character.

   b. Include the `ReadOneChar()` function written for Exercise 10a in a working program. The `main()` function should correctly call `ReadOneChar()` and display the integer the function returns. Test the function by passing various data to it and verifying the returned value.

11. **(Program)** Heron's formula for the area, A, of a triangle with sides of length a, b, and c is

$$A = \sqrt{\left[s(s-a)(s-b)(s-c) \right]}$$

where

$$s = \frac{(a+b+c)}{2}$$

Write, test, and execute a function that accepts the values of a, b, and c as parameters from a calling function, and then calculates the values of s and $[s(s - a)(s - b)(s - c)]$. If this quantity is positive, the function calculates A. If the quantity is negative, a, b, and c do not form a triangle, and the function should set $A = -1$. The value of A should be returned by the function. Test the function by passing various data to it and verifying the returned value.

12. **(Program) a.** Write a function named `whole()` that returns the integer part of any number passed to the function. (*Hint:* Assign the passed argument to an integer variable.)

  b. Include the function written in Exercise 12a in a working program. Make sure your function is called from `main()` and returns a value to `main()` correctly. Have `main()` use a `cout` statement to display the returned value. Test the function by passing various data to it and verifying the returned value.

13. **(Program) a.** Write a C++ function named `fracpart()` that returns the fractional part of any number passed to it. For example, if the number 256.879 is passed to `fracpart()`, the number 0.879 should be returned. Have `fracpart()` call the `whole()` function you wrote in Exercise 12. The number returned can then be determined as the number passed to `fracpart()` less the returned value when the same argument is passed to `whole()`. The completed program should consist of `main()` followed by `fracpart()` followed by `whole()`.

  b. Include the function written in Exercise 13a in a working program. Make sure your function is called from `main()` and returns a value to `main()` correctly. Have `main()` use a `cout` statement to display the returned value. Test the function by passing various data to it and verifying the returned value.

14. **(Program) a.** Years that are evenly divisible by 400 or are evenly divisible by 4 but not by 100 are leap years. For example, because 1600 is evenly divisible by 400, 1600 was a leap year. Similarly, because 1988 is evenly divisible by 4 but not by 100, it was also a leap year. Using this information, write a C++ function that accepts the year as user input and returns a 1 if the passed year is a leap year or a 0 if it isn't.

  b. Include the function written in Exercise 14a in a working program. Make sure your function is called from `main()` and returns a value to `main()` correctly. Have `main()` use a `cout` statement to display the returned value. Test the function by passing various data to it and verifying the returned value.

15. **(Program) a.** A second-degree polynomial in x is given by the expression $ax^2 + bx + c$, where a, b, and c are known numbers and a is not equal to 0. Write a C++ function named `polyTwo` `(a,b,c,x)` that computes and returns the value of a second-degree polynomial for any passed values of a, b, c, and x.

  b. Include the function written in Exercise 15a in a working program. Make sure your function is called from `main()` and returns a value to `main()` correctly. Have `main()` use a `cout` statement to display the returned value. Test the function by passing various data to it and verifying the returned value.

16. **(Program) a.** The following is a useful programming algorithm for rounding a real number to *n* decimal places:

> Step 1: Multiply the number by 10^n.
> Step 2: Add 0.5.
> Step 3: Delete the fractional part of the result.
> Step 4: Divide by 10^n.

For example, using this algorithm to round the number 78.374625 to three decimal places yields:

> Step 1: $78.374625 \times 10^3 = 78374.625$
> Step 2: $78374.625 + 0.5 = 78375.125$
> Step 3: Retaining the integer part = 78375
> Step 4: 78375 divided by $10^3 = 78.375$

Using this algorithm, write a C++ function that accepts a user-entered value and returns the result rounded to two decimal places.

b. Include the function written in Exercise 16a in a working program. Make sure your function is called from `main()` and returns a value to `main()` correctly. Have `main()` use a `cout` statement to display the returned value. Test the function by passing various data to it and verifying the returned value.

6.3 Returning Multiple Values

In a typical function invocation, the called function receives values from its calling function, stores and manipulates the passed values, and directly returns at most one value. When data is passed in this manner, it's referred to as a **pass by value**.

Calling a function and passing arguments by value is a distinct advantage of C++. It allows functions to be written as independent entities that can use any variable or parameter name without concern that other functions might be using the same name. It also alleviates any concern that altering a parameter or variable in one function could inadvertently alter a parameter or variable's value in another function. In this approach, parameters can be considered initialized variables, or variables assigned values when the function is executed. At no time, however, does the called function have direct access to any variable defined in the calling function, even if the variable is used as an argument in the function call.

At times, however, you need to modify this approach by giving a called function direct access to its calling function's variables. This approach allows one function—the called function—to use and change the value of variables that have been defined in the calling function. Doing so requires passing the variable's address to the called function. After the called function has the variable's address, it "knows where the variable lives," so to speak, and can access and change the value stored there.

Passing addresses is referred to as a function **pass by reference**[13] because the called function can reference, or access, the variable whose address has been passed. C++ provides two types of address parameters: references and pointers. The next section describes the method that uses reference parameters.

Passing and Using Reference Parameters

As always, when exchanging data between two functions, you must be concerned with both the sending and receiving sides. From the sending side, calling a function and passing an address as an argument that's accepted as a reference parameter on the receiving side is the same as calling a function and passing a value; the called function is summoned into action by giving its name and a list of arguments. For example, the statement `newval(firstnum, secnum);` calls the function named `newval()` and passes two arguments to it. Whether a value or an address is actually passed depends on the parameter types declared for `newval()`. Now take a look at writing the `newval()` function and prototype so that it receives the addresses rather than the values of the variables `firstnum` and `secnum`, which are assumed to be double-precision variables.

One of the first requirements in writing `newval()` is to declare two reference parameters for accepting passed addresses. In C++, a reference parameter is declared with this syntax:

dataType& referenceName

For example, the reference declaration

```
double& num1;
```

declares that `num1` is a reference parameter used to store the address of a `double`. Similarly, `int& secnum;` declares that `secnum` is a reference to an integer, and `char& key;` declares that `key` is a reference to a character.

The ampersand, `&`, in C++ means "the address of." Additionally, when `&` is used in a declaration, it refers to "the address of" the preceding data type. Using this information, declarations such as `double& num1` and `int& secnum` are sometimes more clearly understood if they're read backward. Reading the declaration `double& num1` in this manner yields the information "num1 is the address of a double-precision value." (This topic is discussed in more detail in Section 8.1.)

Because you need to accept two addresses in the parameter list for `newval()`, the declarations `double& num1` and `double& num2` can be used. Including these declarations in the parameter list for `newval()`, and assuming the function returns no value (void), the function header for `newval()` becomes the following:

```
void newval(double& num1, double& num2)
```

For this function header, the following is a suitable function prototype:

```
void newval(double&, double&);
```

---

[13]It's also referred to as a "call by reference," and again, both terms refer only to the argument whose address has been passed.

This prototype and function header are included in Program 6.8, which uses a `newval()` function body that displays and alters the values stored in these reference variables from within the called function.

 ## Program 6.8

```cpp
#include <iostream>
using namespace std;

void newval(double&, double&);  // prototype with two reference parameters

int main()
{
  double firstnum, secnum;

  cout << "Enter two numbers: ";
  cin  >> firstnum >> secnum;
  cout << "\nThe value in firstnum is: " << firstnum << endl;
  cout << "The value in secnum is: " << secnum << "\n\n";

  newval(firstnum, secnum);     // call the function

  cout << "The value in firstnum is now: " << firstnum << endl;
  cout << "The value in secnum is now: " << secnum << endl;

  return 0;
}

void newval(double& xnum, double& ynum)
{
  cout << "The value in xnum is: " << xnum << endl;
  cout << "The value in ynum is: " << ynum << "\n\n";
  xnum = 89.5;
  ynum = 99.5;

  return;
}
```

In calling the `newval()` function in Program 6.8, you need to understand the connection between the arguments used in the function call, `firstnum` and `secnum`, and the parameters used in the function header, `xnum` and `ynum`. *Both* refer to the same data items. The significance is that the values in the arguments (`firstnum` and `secnum`) can now be altered from within `newval()` by using the parameter names (`xnum` and `ynum`). Therefore, the parameters xnum and ynum don't store copies of the values in firstnum and secnum; instead, they access the locations in memory set aside for these two arguments.

Figure 6.7 shows the equivalence of argument names in Program 6.8, which is the essence of a pass by reference. The argument names and their matching parameter names are simply different names referring to the same memory storage areas. In main(), these memory locations are referenced by the argument names firstnum and secnum, and in newval(), the same locations are referenced by the parameter names xnum and ynum.

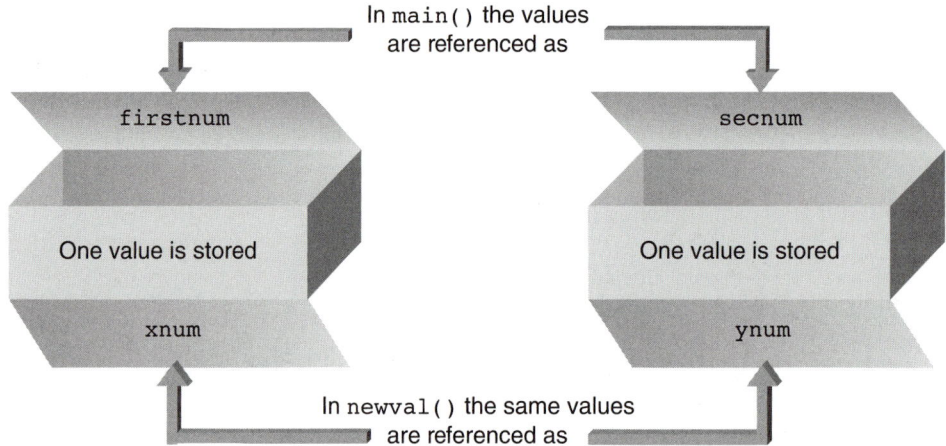

Figure 6.7   The equivalence of arguments and parameters in Program 6.8

The following is a sample run of Program 6.8:

```
Enter two numbers: 22.5 33.0

The value in firstnum is: 22.5
The value in secnum is: 33

The value in xnum is: 22.5
The value in ynum is: 33
The value in firstnum is now: 89.5
The value in secnum is now: 99.5
```

In reviewing this output, notice that the values initially displayed for the parameters xnum and ynum are the same as those displayed for the arguments firstnum and secnum. Because xnum and ynum are reference parameters, however, newval() now has direct access to the arguments firstnum and secnum. Therefore, any change to xnum in newval() alters the value of firstnum in main(), and any change to ynum changes secnum's value. As the final displayed values show, the assignment of values to xnum and ynum in newval() is reflected in main() as the altering of firstnum's and secnum's values.

The equivalence between actual calling arguments and function parameters shown in Program 6.8 provides the basis for returning multiple values from within a function. For example, say you want to write a function to accept three values, compute these values' sum and product, and return these computed results to the calling routine. By naming the function calc() and providing five parameters (three for input data and two references for returned values), the following function can be used:

```
void calc(double n1, double n2, double n3, double& sum, double& product)
{
  sum = n1 + n2 + n3;
  product = n1 * n2 * n3;
  return;
}
```

This function has five parameters named n1, n2, n3, sum, and product. Only the last two are declared as references, so the first three arguments are passed by value and the last two arguments are passed by reference. In this function, only the last two parameters are altered. The value of the fourth parameter, sum, is calculated as the sum of the first three parameters, and the last parameter, product, is computed as the product of the parameters n1, n2, and n3. Program 6.9 includes this function in a complete program.[14]

Program 6.9

```
#include <iostream>
using namespace std;

void calc(double, double, double, double&, double&); // prototype

int main()
{
  double firstnum, secnum, thirdnum, sum, product;

  cout << "Enter three numbers: ";
  cin  >> firstnum >> secnum >> thirdnum;

  calc(firstnum, secnum, thirdnum, sum, product); // function call

  cout << "\nThe sum of the numbers is: " << sum << endl;
  cout << "The product of the numbers is: " << product << endl;

  return 0;
}

void calc(double n1, double n2, double n3, double& sum, double& product)
{
```

---

[14]One of these values could, of course, be returned directly by the function.

```
    sum = n1 + n2 + n3;
    product = n1 * n2 * n3;
    return;
}
```

In main(), the calc() function is called with the five arguments firstnum, secnum, thirdnum, sum, and product. As required, these arguments agree in number and data type with the parameters declared by calc(). Of the five arguments passed, only firstnum, secnum, and thirdnum have been assigned values when the call to calc() is made. The remaining two arguments haven't been initialized and are used to receive values back from calc(). Depending on the compiler used, these arguments initially contain zeros or "garbage" values. Figure 6.8 shows the relationship between actual and parameter names and the values they contain after the return from calc().

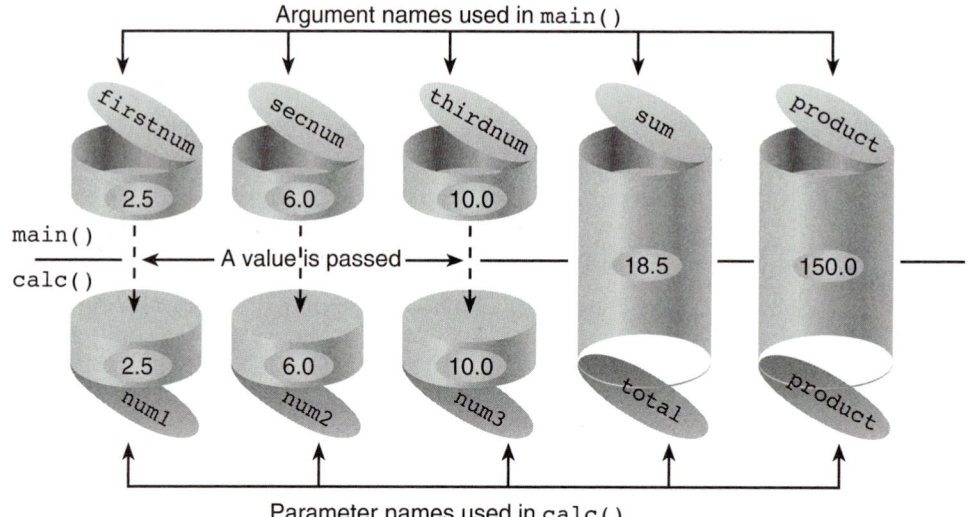

Figure 6.8   The relationship between argument and parameter names

After calc() is called, it uses its first three parameters to calculate values for sum and product and then returns control to main(). Because of the order of its actual calling arguments, main() knows the values calculated by calc() as sum and product, which are then displayed. Following is a sample run of Program 6.9:

```
    Enter three numbers: 2.5 6.0 10.0

    The sum of the entered numbers is: 18.5
    The product of the entered numbers is: 150
```

As a final example of the usefulness of passing references to a called function, take a look at constructing a function named swap() that exchanges the values of two of main()'s double-precision variables. This type of function is useful when sorting a list of numbers.

Because the value of more than one variable is affected, swap() can't be written as a pass by value function that returns a single value. The exchange of main()'s variables by swap() can be accomplished only by giving swap() access to main()'s variables. One way of doing this is using reference parameters.

You have already seen how to pass references to two variables in Program 6.8. Now you see how to construct a function to exchange the values in the passed reference parameters. Exchanging values in two variables is done with this three-step exchange algorithm:

1. Save the first parameter's value in a temporary location (see Figure 6.9a).

Figure 6.9a   Save the first value

2. Store the second parameter's value in the first variable (see Figure 6.9b).

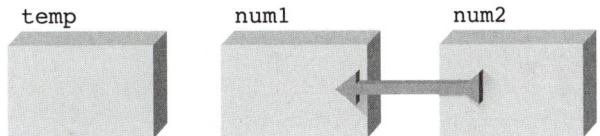

Figure 6.9b   Replace the first value with the second value

3. Store the temporary value in the second parameter (see Figure 6.9c).

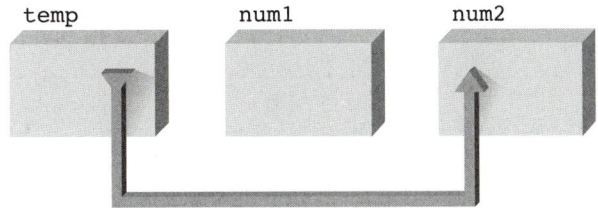

Figure 6.9c   Change the second value

Following is the swap() function written according to these specifications:

```
void swap(double& num1, double& num2)
{
  double temp;

  temp = num1;      // save num1's value
  num1 = num2;      // store num2's value in num1
  num2 = temp;      // change num2's value

  return;
}
```

Notice that the use of references in swap()'s function header gives swap() access to equivalent arguments in the calling function. Therefore, any changes to the two reference parameters in swap() change the values in the calling function's arguments automatically. Program 6.10 contains swap() in a complete program.

 **Program 6.10**

```cpp
#include <iostream>
using namespace std;

void swap(double&, double&);   // function receives two references

int main()
{
  double firstnum = 20.5, secnum = 6.25;

  cout << "The value stored in firstnum is: "
       << firstnum << endl;
  cout << "The value stored in secnum is: "
       << secnum << "\n\n";

  swap(firstnum, secnum);   // call the function with references

  cout << "The value stored in firstnum is now: "
       << firstnum << endl;
  cout << "The value stored in secnum is now: "
       << secnum << endl;

  return 0;
}

void swap(double& num1, double& num2)
{
  double temp;

  temp = num1;       // save num1's value
  num1 = num2;       // store num2's value in num1
  num2 = temp;       // change num2's value

  return;
}
```

The following is a sample run of Program 6.10:

```
The value stored in firstnum is: 20.5
The value stored in secnum is: 6.25

The value stored in firstnum is now: 6.25
The value stored in secnum is now: 20.5
```

As shown by this output, the values stored in `main()`'s variables have been modified from within `swap()`, which was made possible by using reference parameters. If a pass by value had been used instead, the exchange in `swap()` would affect only `swap()`'s parameters and accomplish nothing with `main()`'s variables. A function such as `swap()` can be written only by using a reference or some other means that provides access to `main()`'s variables. (This other means is by pointers, the topic of Chapter 8.)

In using reference parameters, two cautions need to be mentioned. First, reference parameters *must* be variables (that is, they can't be used to change constants). For example, calling `swap()` with two constants, as in the call `swap(20.5, 6.5)`, passes two constants to the function. Although `swap()` can execute, it doesn't change the values of these constants.[15]

Second, a function call gives no indication that the called function will be using reference parameters. The default in C++ is to make passes by value rather than passes by reference, specifically to limit a called function's capability to alter variables in the calling function. This calling procedure should be adhered to whenever possible, which means reference parameters should be used only in restricted situations that require multiple return values, as in the `swap()` function in Program 6.10. The `calc()` function, included in Program 6.9, although useful for illustration purposes, could also be written as two separate functions, each returning a single value.

EXERCISES 6.3

1. **(Practice)** Write parameter declarations for the following:
   a. A parameter named `amount` that will be a reference to a double-precision value
   b. A parameter named `price` that will be a reference to a double-precision number
   c. A parameter named `minutes` that will be a reference to an integer number
   d. A parameter named `key` that will be a reference to a character
   e. A parameter named `yield` that will be a reference to a double-precision number

2. **(Practice)** Three integer arguments are to be used in a call to a function named `time()`. Write a suitable function header for `time()`, assuming that `time()` accepts these variables as the reference parameters `sec`, `min`, and `hours` and returns no value to its calling function.

3. **(Modify) a.** Rewrite the `findMax()` function in Program 6.4 so that the variable `max`, declared in `main()`, is used to store the maximum value of the two passed numbers. The value of `max` should be set from within `findMax()`. (*Hint*: A reference to `max` has to be accepted by `findMax()`.)

---

[15]Most compilers catch this error.

b. Include the function written in Exercise 3a in a working program. Make sure your function is called from `main()` and returns a value to `main()` correctly. Have `main()` use a `cout` statement to display the returned value. Test the function by passing various data to it and verifying the returned value.

4. (**Program**) **a.** Write a function named `change()` that has an integer parameter and six integer reference parameters named `hundreds`, `fifties`, `twenties`, `tens`, `fives`, and `ones`. The function is to consider the passed integer value as a dollar amount and convert the value into the fewest number of equivalent bills. Using the reference parameters, the function should alter the arguments in the calling function.

b. Include the function written in Exercise 4a in a working program. Make sure your function is called from `main()` and returns a value to `main()` correctly. Have `main()` use a `cout` statement to display the returned value. Test the function by passing various data to it and verifying the returned value.

5. (**Program**) Write a function named `time()` that has an integer parameter named `seconds` and three integer reference parameters named `hours`, `mins`, and `secs`. The function is to convert the passed number of seconds into an equivalent number of hours, minutes, and seconds. Using the reference parameters, the function should alter the arguments in the calling function.

6. (**Program**) Write a function named `yearCalc()` that has an integer parameter representing the total number of days from the date 1/1/2000 and reference parameters named `year`, `month`, and `day`. The function is to calculate the current year, month, and day given the number of days passed to it. Using the reference parameters, the function should alter the arguments in the calling function. For this problem, assume each year has 365 days, and each month has 30 days.

7. (**Program**) Write a function named `liquid()` that has an integer number parameter and reference parameters named `gallons`, `quarts`, `pints`, and `cups`. The passed integer represents the total number of cups, and the function is to determine the numbers of gallons, quarts, pints, and cups in the passed value. Using the reference parameters, the function should alter the arguments in the calling function. Use these relationships: 2 cups = 1 pint, 4 cups = 1 quart, and 16 cups = 1 gallon.

8. (**Desk check**) The following program uses the same argument and parameter names in both the calling and called functions. Determine whether doing so causes any problem for the compiler.

```
#include <iostream>
using namespace std;

void time(int&, int&);   // function prototype

int main()
{
  int min, hour;
```

```
   cout << "Enter two numbers :";
   cin  >> min >> hour;
   time(min, hour);

   return 0;
}

void time(int& min, int& hour)    // accept two references
{
   int sec;

   sec = (hour * 60 + min) * 60;
   cout << "The total number of seconds is " << sec << endl;

   return;
```

6.4 Variable Scope

Now that you have begun to write programs containing more than one function, you can look more closely at the variables declared in each function and their relationship to variables in other functions. By their nature, C++ functions are constructed to be independent modules. As you have seen, values are passed to a function by using the function's parameter list, and a single value can be returned from a function by using a return statement. Seen in this light, a function can be thought of as a closed box, with slots at the top to receive values and a single slot at the bottom to return a value (see Figure 6.10).

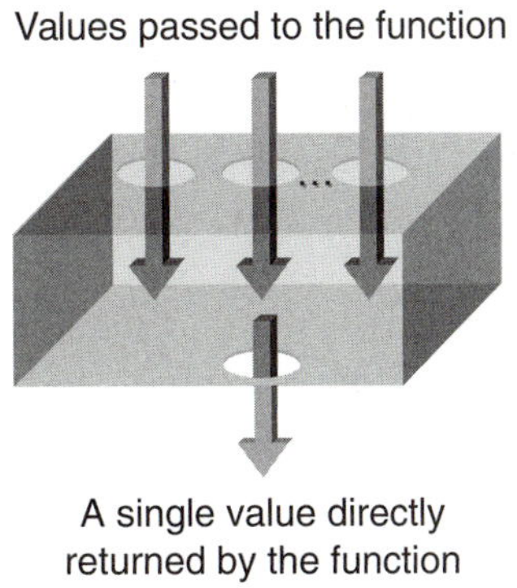

Values passed to the function

A single value directly
returned by the function

Figure 6.10   A function can be considered a closed box

The metaphor of a closed box is useful because it emphasizes that what goes on inside the function (including all variable declarations in the function body) is hidden from the view of all other functions. Because the variables created in a function are conventionally available only to the function, they are said to be local to the function, or **local variables**. This term refers to the scope of an identifier; **scope** is the section of the program where the identifier, such as a variable, is valid or "known." This section of the program is also referred to as where the variable is "visible."

A variable can have a local scope or a global scope. A variable with a **local scope** is simply one with storage locations set aside for it by a declaration statement in a function body. Local variables are meaningful only when used in expressions or statements inside the function that declared them, so the same variable name can be declared and used in more than one function. For each function that declares the variable, a separate and distinct variable is created.

All the variables you have used until now have been local variables, a result of placing declaration statements inside functions and using them as definition statements that cause the computer to reserve storage for the declared variable. As you'll see in the next section, declaration statements can be placed outside functions and need not act as definitions that reserve new storage areas for the declared variable.

A variable with **global scope**, more commonly termed a **global variable**, has storage created for it by a declaration statement located outside any function. These variables can be used by all functions placed after the global variable declaration. Program 6.11 shows using a global variable, and the same variable name has been used on purpose inside both functions in the program.

Program 6.11

```
#include <iostream>
using namespace std;

int firstnum;      // create a global variable named firstnum

void valfun();     // function prototype (declaration)

int main()
{
  int secnum;      // create a local variable named secnum

  firstnum = 10;   // store a value into the global variable
  secnum = 20;     // store a value into the local variable

  cout << "From main(): firstnum = " << firstnum << endl;
  cout << "From main(): secnum = " << secnum << endl;

  valfun();        // call the function valfun

  cout << "\nFrom main() again: firstnum = "
       << firstnum << endl;
  cout << "From main() again: secnum = " << secnum << endl;
```

```
   return 0;
}

void valfun()   // no values are passed to this function
{
   int secnum;   // create a second local variable named secnum

   secnum = 30; // this only affects this local variable's value

   cout << "\nFrom valfun(): firstnum = " << firstnum << endl;
   cout << "From valfun(): secnum = " << secnum << endl;

   firstnum = 40;    // changes firstnum for both functions

   return;
}
```

The variable `firstnum` in Program 6.11 is a global variable because its storage is created by a definition statement located outside a function. Because both `main()` and `valfun()` follow the definition of `firstnum`, both functions can use this global variable with no further declaration needed.

Program 6.11 also contains two separate local variables, both named `secnum`. Storage for the `secnum` variable named in `main()` is created by the definition statement in `main()`. A different storage area for the `secnum` variable in `valfun()` is created by the definition statement in the `valfun()` function. Figure 6.11 shows the three distinct storage areas reserved by the three definition statements in Program 6.11.

Each variable named `secnum` is local to the function in which its storage is created, and each variable can be used only from within its corresponding function. Therefore, when `secnum` is used in `main()`, the storage area `main()` reserves for its `secnum` variable is accessed, and when `secnum` is used in `valfun()`, the storage area `valfun()` reserves for its `secnum` variable is accessed. The following output is produced when Program 6.11 runs:

```
From main(): firstnum = 10
From main(): secnum = 20

From valfun(): firstnum = 10
From valfun(): secnum = 30

From main() again: firstnum = 40
From main() again: secnum = 20
```

Now analyze this output to see how local and global variables work. Because `firstnum` is a global variable, both `main()` and `valfun()` can use and change its value. Initially, both functions print the value of 10 that `main()` stored in `firstnum`. Before returning, `valfun()` changes the value of `firstnum` to 40, which is the value displayed when `firstnum` is next displayed from within `main()`.

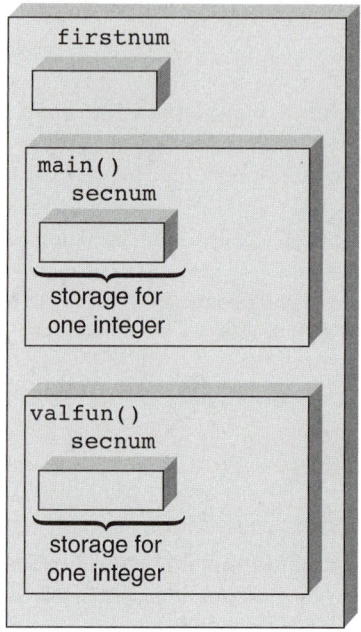

Figure 6.11   The three storage areas reserved by Program 6.11

Because each function "knows" only its own local variables, `main()` can send only the value of its `secnum` to `cout`, and `valfun()` can send only the value of its `secnum` to `cout`. Therefore, whenever `secnum` is obtained from `main()`, the value of 20 is displayed, and whenever `secnum` is obtained from `valfun()`, the value 30 is displayed. C++ doesn't confuse the two `secnum` variables because only one function can execute at a time. While a function is executing, only variables and parameters that are "in scope" for that function (global and local) can be accessed.

The scope of a variable in no way influences or restricts its data type. Just as a local variable can be a character, integer, Boolean, double, or any other data type that's been introduced, global variables can be all these data types, as shown in Figure 6.12. A variable's scope is determined by the placement of the definition statement that reserves storage for it and optionally by a declaration statement that makes it visible, whereas a variable's data type is determined by using a keyword (`char`, `int`, `bool`, `double`, and so on) before the variable's name in a declaration statement.

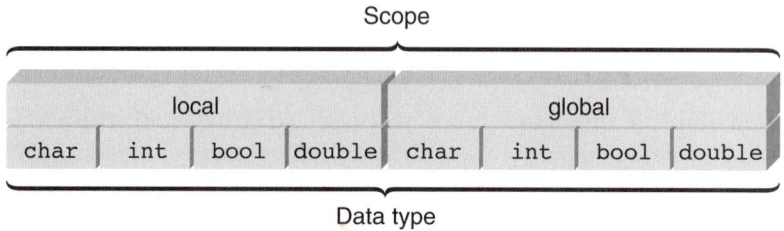

Figure 6.12   Relating the scope and type of a variable

Scope Resolution Operator

When a local variable has the same name as a global variable, all references to the variable name made within the local variable's scope refer to the local variable. This situation is shown in Program 6.12, where the variable name `number` is defined as both a global and local variable.

 **Program 6.12**

```
#include <iostream>
using namespace std;

double number = 42.8;      // a global variable named number

int main()
{
  double number = 26.4;    // a local variable named number

  cout << "The value of number is " << number << endl;

  return 0;
}
```

When Program 6.12 runs, the following output is displayed:

```
The value of number is 26.4
```

As this output shows, the local variable name takes precedence over the global variable. In these cases, you can still access the global variable by using C++'s scope resolution operator, which has the symbol `::`. This operator must be placed immediately before the variable name, as in `::number`. When used in this manner, the `::` tells the compiler to use the global variable. As an example, the scope resolution operator is used in Program 6.12a.

 **Program 6.12a**

```
#include <iostream>
using namespace std;

double number = 42.5;      // a global variable named number

int main()
{
  double number = 26.4;    // a local variable named number

  cout << "The value of number is " << ::number << endl;
```

```
    return 0;
}
```

This is the output produced by Program 6.12a:

```
The value of number is 42.5
```

As this output indicates, the scope resolution operator causes the global, rather than the local, variable to be accessed.

Misuse of Globals

Global variables allow programmers to "jump around" the normal safeguards provided by functions. Instead of passing variables to a function, it's possible to make all variables global. *Do not do this.* By indiscriminately making all variables global, you destroy the safeguards C++ provides to make functions independent and insulated from each other, including designating the type of arguments a function needs, the variables used in the function, and the return value.

Using only global variables can be especially disastrous in large programs with many user-created functions. Because all variables in a function must be declared, creating functions that use global variables requires remembering to write the appropriate global declarations at the top of each program using the function—they no longer come along with the function. More devastating, however, is trying to track down an error in a large program with global variables. Because a global variable can be accessed and changed by any function following the global declaration, locating the origin of an erroneous value is a time-consuming and frustrating task.

Global definitions, however, are sometimes useful in creating symbolic constants that must be shared between many functions. In this case, defining the symbolic constant once as global variable is easier. Doing so also alerts anyone reading the program that many functions use the constant. Most large programs almost always make use of a few global symbolic constants. Smaller programs containing a few functions, however, should almost never use global declarations.

The misuse of globals doesn't apply to function prototypes, which are typically global. All the function prototypes you have used have been of global scope, which declares the prototype to all subsequent functions. Placing a function prototype in a function makes the prototype a local declaration available only to the function it's declared within.

EXERCISES 6.4

1. **(Practice) a.** For the following section of code, determine the data type and scope of all declared variables and symbolic constants on a separate sheet of paper, using the column headings shown in the following chart. (The entries for the first variable have been filled in.)

Variable or Constant Name	Data Type	Scope
PRICE	int	global to `main()`, `roi()`, and `step()`

```
#include <iostream>
using namespace std;

const int PRICE;
const long YEARS;
const double YIELD;
int main()
{
  int bondtype;
  double interest, coupon;

     .

     .

     .

  return 0;
}
double roi(int mat1, int mat2)
{
  int count;
  double effectiveRate;

     .

     .

     .

  return effectiveRate;
}
int step(double first, double last)
{
  int numofyrs;
  double fracpart;

     .

     .

     .

  return(10*numofyrs);
}
```

b. Draw a box around the appropriate section of the preceding code to enclose the scope of each variable or constant.

c. Determine the data type of the arguments that the `roi()` and `step()` functions expect and the data type of the value these functions return.

2. **(Practice) a.** For the following section of code, determine the data type and scope of all declared variables on a separate sheet of paper, using the column headings shown in the following chart. (The entries for the first variable have been filled in.)

Variable Name	Data Type	Scope
key	char	global to `main()`, `func1()`, and `func2()`

```
#include <iostream>
using namespace std;

const char KEY;
const long NUMBER;

int main()
{
  int a,b,c;
  double x,y;

    .

    .

  return 0;
}

double secnum;

int func1(int num1, int num2)
{
  int o,p;
  float q;

    .

    .

  return p;
}

double func2(double first, double last)
{
  int a,b,c,o,p;
  double r;
  double s,t,x;

    .

    .

  return s * t;
}
```

    b. Draw a box around the appropriate section of the preceding code to enclose the scope of each variable or constant.

    c. Determine the data type of the arguments that the func1() and func2() functions expect and the data type of the value these functions return.

3. (Practice) The term "scope" can also apply to a function's parameters. What do you think is the scope of all function parameters?

4. **(Practice)** Define the scope of the parameter p2 and the variables a, b, c, d, e, f, m, n, p, d, q, and r in the following program structure:

```cpp
#include <iostream>
using namespace std;

int a, b;
double One(float);
void Two(void);

int main()
{
  int c, d;
  double e, f;

    .
    .

  return 0;
}

double One(double p2)
{
  char m, n;

    .
    .

}

void Two(void)
{
  int p, d;
  double q, r;

    .
    .

}
```

5. **(Desk check)** Determine the values displayed by each cout statement in the following program:

```cpp
#include <iostream>
using namespace std;

int firstnum = 10;    // declare and initialize a global variable
void display();       // function prototype

int main()
{
  int firstnum = 20;  // declare and initialize a local variable
```

☞

```
    cout << "\nThe value of firstnum is " << firstnum << endl;
    display();

    return 0;
}

void display(void)
{
    cout << "The value of firstnum is now " << firstnum << endl;

    return;
}
```

6.5 Variable Storage Category

The scope of a variable defines the location in a program where that variable can be used. If you draw a box around the section of program code where each variable is valid, the space inside the box represents the variable's scope. From this viewpoint, a variable's scope can be thought of as the space in the program where the variable is valid.

In addition to the space dimension represented by scope, variables have a time dimension that refers to the length of time storage locations are reserved for a variable. This time dimension is referred to as the variable's "lifetime." For example, all variable storage locations are released back to the operating system when a program is finished running. However, while a program is still running, interim variable storage locations are reserved and subsequently released back to the operating system. Where and how long a variable's storage locations are kept before they're released can be determined by the variable's **storage category**.

The four available storage categories are `auto`, `static`, `extern`, and `register`. If one of these category names is used, it must be placed before the variable's data type in a declaration statement. The following are examples of declaration statements that include a storage category designation:

```
auto int num;       // auto storage category and int data type
static int miles;   // static storage category and int data type
register int dist;  // register storage category and int data type
extern int volts;   // extern storage category and int data type
auto float coupon;  // auto storage category and float data type
static double yrs;  // static storage category and double data type
extern float yld;   // extern storage category and float data type
auto char inKey;    // auto storage category and char variable
```

To understand what a variable's storage category means, next you examine local variables (created inside a function) and global variables (created outside a function).

Local Variable Storage Categories

Local variables can be members only of the `auto`, `static`, or `register` storage categories. If no category description is included in the declaration statement, the variable is assigned to the `auto` category automatically, so `auto` is the default category C++ uses. All the local variables you have used have been `auto` variables because the storage category designation was omitted.

The term `auto` is short for "automatic." Storage for `auto` local variables is reserved or created automatically each time a function declaring `auto` variables is called. As long as the function hasn't returned control to its calling function, all `auto` variables local to the function are "alive"—meaning storage for the variables is available. When the function returns control to its calling function, its local `auto` variables "die"—meaning storage for the variables is released back to the operating system. This process repeats each time a function is called. For example, in Program 6.13, the `testauto()` function is called three times from `main()`.

 **Program 6.13**

```cpp
#include <iostream>
using namespace std;

void testauto();   // function prototype

int main()
{
  int count;        // count is a local auto variable

  for(count = 1; count <= 3; count++)
    testauto();

  return 0;
}

void testauto()
{
  int num = 0;     // num is a local auto variable
                   // initialized to zero
  cout << "The value of the automatic variable num is "
       << num << endl;
  num++;

  return;
}
```

This is the output produced by Program 6.13:

```
The value of the automatic variable num is 0
The value of the automatic variable num is 0
The value of the automatic variable num is 0
```

Each time testauto() is called, the auto variable num is created and initialized to 0. When the function returns control to main(), the variable num is destroyed along with any value stored in num. Therefore, the effect of incrementing num in testauto(), before the function's return statement, is lost when control is returned to main().

For most applications, the use of auto variables works just fine and is the reason it's the default storage category. In some cases, however, you want a function to remember values between function calls, which is the purpose of the static storage category. A local variable declared as static causes the program to keep the variable and its latest value even when the function that declared it has finished executing. The following are examples of static variable declarations:

```
static int rate;
static double amount;
static char inKey;
```

A local static variable isn't created and destroyed each time the function declaring it is called. After they're created, local static variables remain in existence for the program's lifetime. This means the last value stored in the variable when the function finishes executing is available to the function the next time it's called.

Because local static variables retain their values, they aren't initialized in a declaration statement in the same way as auto variables. To understand why, consider the auto declaration int num = 0;, which causes the auto variable num to be created and set to 0 each time the declaration is encountered. This procedure is called a **runtime initialization** because initialization occurs each time the declaration statement is encountered. This type of initialization would be disastrous for a static variable because resetting the variable's value to 0 each time the function is called destroys the very value you're trying to save.

Initialization of static variables (both local and global) is done only once, when the program is first compiled. At compile time, the variable is created and any initialization value is placed in it.[16] Thereafter, the value in the variable is kept without further initialization. To see how this process works, examine Program 6.14.

---

[16]Some compilers initialize local static variables the first time the definition statement is executed rather than when the program is compiled.

Program 6.14

```cpp
#include <iostream>
using namespace std;
void teststat();    // function prototype
int main()
{
  int count;          // count is a local auto variable
  for(count = 1; count <= 3; count++)
    teststat();
  return 0;
}

void teststat()
{
  static int num = 0;   // num is a local static variable
  cout << "The value of the static variable num is now "
       << num << endl;
  num++;
  return;
}
```

This is the output produced by Program 6.14:

```
The value of the static variable num is now 0
The value of the static variable num is now 1
The value of the static variable num is now 2
```

As this output shows, the `static` variable `num` is set to 0 only once. The `teststat()` function then increments this variable just before returning control to `main()`. The value that `num` has when leaving the `teststat()` function is retained and displayed when the function is next called.

Unlike `auto` variables that can be initialized by constants or expressions using both constants and previously initialized variables, `static` variables can be initialized only by using constants or constant expressions, such as `3.2 + 8.0`. Also, unlike `auto` variables, all `static` variables are set to 0 when no explicit initialization is given. Therefore, the initialization of `num` to 0 in Program 6.14 isn't required.

The remaining storage category available to local variables, `register`, isn't used as extensively as `auto` or `static` variables. The following are examples of `register` variable declarations:

```cpp
register int time;
register double diffren;
register float coupon;
```

The `register` variables have the same time duration as `auto` variables; that is, a local `register` variable is created when the function declaring it is entered and is destroyed when the function finishes execution. The only difference between `register` and `auto` variables is where storage for the variable is located.

Storage for all variables (local and global), except `register` variables, is reserved in the computer's memory. Most computers also have a few high-speed storage areas, called **registers**, located in the CPU that can also be used for variable storage. Because registers are in the CPU, they can be accessed faster than the normal storage areas in the computer's memory. Also, computer instructions referencing registers typically require less space than instructions referencing memory locations because there are fewer registers than memory locations that can be accessed. When the compiler substitutes a register's location for a variable during program compilation, the instruction needs less space than address memory having millions of locations.

Besides decreasing a compiled C++ program's size, using `register` variables can increase the program's execution speed if your computer supports this data type. Variables declared with the `register` storage category are switched to `auto` automatically if your compiler doesn't support `register` variables or if the declared `register` variables exceed the computer's register capacity. Application programs intended to run on different types of computers shouldn't use `register` variables, however. The only restriction in using the `register` storage category is that a `register` variable's address can't be taken by using the address operator, `&`. This concept is easier to understand when you realize that registers don't have standard memory addresses.

Global Variable Storage Categories

Global variables are created by definition statements external to a function. By their nature, these externally defined variables don't come and go with the calling of a function. After a global variable is created, it exists until the program in which it's declared has finished running. Therefore, global variables can't be declared as `auto` or `register` variables that are created and destroyed as the program is running. Global variables can be declared with the `static` or `extern` storage category (but not both). The following are examples of declaration statements including these two category descriptions:

```
extern int sum;
extern double volts;
static double current;
```

The `static` and `extern` storage categories affect only the scope, not the lifetime, of global variables. As with `static` local variables, all global variables are initialized to 0 at compile time. The purpose of the `extern` storage category is to extend a global variable's scope beyond its normal boundaries. To understand this concept, first note that all the programs written so far have been contained in one file. Therefore, when you have saved or retrieved programs, you have needed to give the computer only a single name for your program. C++ doesn't require doing this, however.

Large programs typically consist of many functions stored in multiple files. For example, Figure 6.13 shows the three functions `main()`, `func1()`, and `func2()` stored in one file and the two functions `func3()` and `func4()` stored in a second file.

Variable Storage Category

file1

```
int volts;
double current;
static double power;
       .
       .
       .
int main()
{
   func1();
   func2();
   func3();
   func4();
}
int func1()
{
       .
       .
       .
}
int func2()
{
       .
       .
       .
}
```

file2

```
double factor;
int func3()
{
       .
       .
       .
}
int func4()
{
       .
       .
       .
}
```

Figure 6.13   A program can extend beyond one file

For the files shown in Figure 6.13, the global variables volts, current, and power declared in file1 can be used only by the functions main(), func1(), and func2() in this file. The single global variable, factor, declared in file2 can be used only by the functions func3() and func4() in file2.

Although the variable volts has been created in file1, you might want to use it in file2. To do this, you place the declaration statement extern int volts; in file2, as shown in Figure 6.14. Putting this statement at the top of file2 extends the scope of volts into file2 so that it can be used by both func3() and func4(). The extern designation simply declares a global variable that's defined in another file. So placing the statement extern double current; in func4() extends the scope of this global variable, created in file1, into func4(). Additionally, the scope of the global variable factor, created in file2, is extended into func1() and func2() by the declaration statement extern double factor; placed before func1(). Notice that factor is not available to main().

file1

file2

```
int volts;                    double factor;
double current;               extern int volts;
static double power;          int func3()
        .                     {
        .                             .
        .                             .
int main()                            .
{                             }
   func1();                   int func4()
   func2();                   {
   func3();                       extern double current;
   func4();                          .
}                                     .
extern double factor;                 .
int func1()                   }
{
        .
        .
        .
}
int func2()
{
        .
        .
        .
}
```

Figure 6.14   Extending the scope of global variables

A declaration statement containing the keyword **extern** is different from other declaration statements, in that it doesn't cause a new variable to be created by reserving new storage for the variable. An **extern** declaration statement simply informs the computer that a global variable already exists and can now be used. The actual storage for the variable must be created somewhere else in the program by using one, and only one, global declaration statement in which the keyword **extern** hasn't been used. The global variable can, of course, be initialized in its original declaration. Initialization in an **extern** declaration statement is not allowed, however, and causes a compilation error.

The existence of the **extern** storage category is the reason for carefully distinguishing between creation and declaration of a variable. Declaration statements containing the keyword **extern** don't create new storage areas; they just extend the scope of existing global variables.

The last global storage category, **static**, is used to prevent extending a global variable into a second file. Global **static** variables are declared in the same way as local **static** variables, except the declaration statement is placed outside any function.

The scope of a global **static** variable can't be extended beyond the file in which it's declared. This rule provides a degree of privacy for global **static** variables. Because they are "known" and can be used only in the file where they're declared, other files can't access or

---

Point of Information

Storage Classes

Variables of type `auto` and `register` are always local variables. Only non-`static` global variables can be declared by using the `extern` keyword. Doing so extends the variable's scope into another file or function.

    Making a global variable `static` makes the variable private to the file in which it's declared. Therefore, `static` variables can't use the `extern` keyword. Except for `static` variables, all variables are initialized each time they come into scope; `static` variables are initialized only once, when they're defined.

---

change their values. Therefore, global `static` variables can't subsequently be extended to a second file by using an `extern` declaration statement. Trying to do so results in a compilation error.

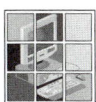

EXERCISES 6.5

1. **(Practice) a.** List the storage categories available to local variables.
   b. List the storage categories available to global variables.

2. **(Practice)** Describe the difference between a local `auto` variable and a local `static` variable.

3. **(Practice)** What's the difference between the following functions?

```cpp
void init1()
{
  static int yrs = 1;

  cout << "The value of yrs is " << yrs << endl;
  yrs = yrs + 2;

  return;
}


void init2()
{
  static int yrs;

  yrs = 1;
  cout << "The value of yrs is " << yrs << endl;
  yrs = yrs + 2;

  return;
}
```

4. **(Practice) a.** Describe the difference between a global `static` variable and a global `extern` variable.

   b. If a variable is declared with an `extern` storage category, what other declaration statement must be present somewhere in the program?

5. **(Practice)** The declaration statement `static double years;` can be used to create a local or global `static` variable. What determines the scope of the variable `years`?

6. **(Practice)** For the function and variable declarations shown in Figure 6.15, place an `extern` declaration to accomplish each of the following:

   a. Extend the scope of the global variable `choice` into `file2`.

   b. Extend the scope of the global variable `flag` into the `average()` function only.

   c. Extend the scope of the global variable `date` into `average()` and `variance()`.

   d. Extend the scope of the global variable `date` into `roi()` only.

   e. Extend the scope of the global variable `coupon` into `roi()` only.

   f. Extend the scope of the global variable `bondtype` into `file1`.

   g. Extend the scope of the global variable `maturity` into both `watts()` and `thrust()`.

file1

```
char choice;
int flag;
long date, time;
int main()
{
     .
     .
     .
}
double factor;
double watts()
{
     .
     .
     .
}
double thrust()
{
     .
     .
     .
}
```

file2

```
char bondtype;
double resistance;
double roi()
{
     .
     .
     .
}
double average()
{
     .
     .
     .
}
double variance()
{
     .
     .
     .
}
```

Figure 6.15 Files for Exercise 6

6.6 Common Programming Errors

The following programming errors are common when constructing and using functions:

1. An extremely common error related to functions is passing incorrect data types. The values passed to a function must correspond to the data types of parameters declared for the function. One way to verify that correct values have been received is to display all passed values in the function body before any calculations are made. After this verification has taken place, you can dispense with the display.[17]

2. Another common error can occur when the same variable is declared locally in both the calling and called functions. Even though the variable name is the same, a change to one local variable *does not* alter the value in the other local variable.

3. A related error is one that can occur when a local variable has the same name as a global variable. Inside the function declaring it, the use of the variable's name affects only the local variable's contents unless the scope resolution operator, : :, is used.

4. Another common error is omitting the called function's prototype before or within the calling function. The called function must be alerted to the type of value to be returned, and the function prototype provides this information. The prototype can be omitted if the called function is placed in a program before its calling function. Although omitting the prototype and return type for functions returning an integer is permitted, doing so is poor documenting practice. The actual value a function returns can be verified by displaying it both before and after it's returned.

5. The last two common errors are terminating a function header with a semicolon and forgetting to include the data type of a function's parameters in the function header.

6.7 Chapter Summary

1. A function is called by giving its name and passing any data to it in the parentheses following the name. If a variable is one of the arguments in a function call, the called function receives a copy of the variable's value.

2. The common form of a user-written function is as follows:

```
returnDataType functionName(parameter list)
{
    Symbolic constants
    Variable declarations

    C++ statements
  return expression;
}
```

The first line of the function is called the function header. The opening and closing braces of the function and all statements between these braces constitute the function body. The parameter list is a comma-separated list of parameter declarations.

---

[17]In practice, a good debugger program should be used.

3. A function's return type is the data type of the value the function returns. If no type is declared, the function is assumed to return an integer value. If the function doesn't return a value, it should be declared as a `void` type.

4. Functions can return at most a single data type value to their calling functions. This value is the value of the expression in the `return` statement.

5. Arguments passed to a function, when it's called, must conform to the parameters specified by the function header in terms of order, number of arguments, and specified data type.

6. Using reference parameters, a variable's address is passed to a function. If a called function is passed an address, it has the capability to access the calling function's variable. Using passed addresses permits a called function to return multiple values.

7. Functions can be declared to all calling functions by means of a function prototype. The prototype provides a declaration for a function that specifies the data type the function returns, the function's name, and the data types of arguments the function expects. As with all declarations, a function prototype is terminated with a semicolon and can be included in local variable declarations or as a global declaration. This is the most common form of a function prototype:

   `dataType functionName(parameter data type list);`

   If the called function is placed above the calling function in the program, no further declaration is required because the function's definition serves as a global declaration to all subsequent functions.

8. Every variable in a program has a scope, which determines where in the program the variable can be used. A variable's scope is local or global and is determined by where the variable's definition statement is placed. A local variable is defined in a function and can be used only in its defining function or block. A global variable is defined outside a function and can be used in any function following the variable's definition. All global variables that aren't specifically initialized by the user are initialized to 0 by the compiler, and global variables not declared as `static` can be shared between files by using the keyword `extern`.

9. Every variable also has a storage category, which determines how long the value in the variable is retained, also known as the variable's lifetime. `auto` variables are local variables that exist only while their defining function is executing; `register` variables are similar to `auto` variables but are stored in a computer's registers rather than in memory; and `static` variables can be global or local and retain their values while the program is running. All `static` variables are set to 0 when they're defined if the user doesn't initialize them explicitly.

6.8 Chapter Supplement: Generating Random Numbers

There are many business and engineering problems in which probability must be considered or statistical sampling techniques must be used. For example, to simulate automobile traffic flow or telephone usage patterns, statistical models are required. In addition, applications such as simple or complex computer games can only be described statistically. All these statistical models require generating **random numbers**—a series of numbers whose order can't be predicted.

In practice, finding truly random numbers is hard. Dice are never perfect, cards are never shuffled completely randomly, and digital computers can handle numbers only in a finite range and with limited precision. The best you can do in most cases is generate **pseudorandom numbers**, which are random enough for the type of applications being programmed.

Some programming languages contain a library function that produces random numbers; others do not. All C++ compilers provide two general-purpose functions for generating random numbers: `rand()` and `srand()`. The `rand()` function produces a series of random numbers in the range $0 \leq$ `rand()` $\leq$ `RAND_MAX`, with the constant `RAND_MAX` defined in the `cstlib` header file. The `srand()` function supplies a starting "seed" value for `rand()`. If `srand()` or another seeding technique isn't used, `rand()` always produces the same series of random numbers.[18]

The following code shows the general procedure for creating a series of *N* random numbers with C++'s library functions:

```
srand(time(NULL)); // generates the first "seed" value

for (int i = 1; i <= N; i++) // generates N random numbers
{
  rvalue = rand();
  cout << rvalue << endl;
}
```

The argument to the `srand()` function is a call to the `time()` function with a `NULL` argument. With this argument, the `time()` function reads the computer's internal clock time in seconds. The `srand()` function then uses this time, converted to an unsigned `int`, to initialize the `rand()` function, which generates random numbers. Program 6.15 uses this code to generate a series of 10 random numbers.

---

[18]Alternatively, many C++ compilers have a `randomize()` routine that's defined by using the `srand()` function. If this routine is available, the call `randomize()` can be used in place of the call `srand(time(NULL))`. In either case, the initializing "seed" routine is called only once, after which `rand()` is used to generate a series of pseudorandom numbers.

Program 6.15

```cpp
#include <iostream>
#include <iomanip>
#include <cstdlib>
#include <ctime>
using namespace std;

// this program generates 10 pseudorandom numbers
// by using C++'s rand() function

int main()
{
  const int NUMBERS = 10;

  double randvalue;
  int i;

  srand(time(NULL));
  for (i = 1; i <= NUMBERS; ++i)
  {
    randvalue = rand();
    cout << setw(20) << randvalue << endl;
  }

  return 0;
}
```

The following is the output produced by one run of Program 6.15:

```
               20203
               21400
               15265
               26935
                8369
               10907
               31299
               15400
                5074
               20663
```

Because of the srand() function call in Program 6.15, the series of 10 random numbers differs each time the program runs. Without this function's randomizing "seeding" effect, the same series of random numbers is always produced. Notice, too, the cstdlib and ctime header files included in this program. The cstdlib header file contains the function prototypes for srand() and rand(), and the ctime header file contains the function prototype for the time() function.

Scaling

In practice, typically you need to make one modification to the random numbers produced by the `rand()` function. The reason is that, in most applications, the random numbers must be double-precision numbers in the range 0.0 to 1.0 or integers in a specified range, such as 1 to 100. The procedure for adjusting the random numbers produced by a random-number generator to fall in a specified range is called **scaling**.

Scaling random numbers to lie in the range 0.0 to 1.0 is easily done by dividing the returned value of `rand()` by `RAND_MAX`. Therefore, the expression `double(rand())/RAND_MAX` produces a double-precision random number between 0.0 and 1.0.

Scaling a random number as an integer value between 0 and N is done with the expression `rand() % (N+1)` or `int(double(rand())/RAND_MAX * N)`. For example, the expression `int(double(rand())/RAND_MAX * 100)` produces a random integer between 0 and 100.

To produce a random integer between 1 and N, you can use the expression `1 + rand() % N`. For example, in simulating the roll of a die, the expression `1 + rand() % 6` produces a random integer between 1 and 6. The more general scaling expression `a + rand() % (b + 1 - a)` can be used to produce a random integer between the numbers a and b.

Chapter

7

Arrays

All the variables you have used so far have a common characteristic: Each variable can be used to store only a single value at a time. For example, although the variables key, count, *and* grade *declared in the statements*

```
char key;
int count;
double grade;
```

are of different data types, each variable can only store one value of the declared data type. These types of variables are called **atomic variables** *(also referred to as* **scalar variables***), which means their values can't be further subdivided or separated into a legitimate data type.*

Often you have a set of values, all the same data type, that form a logical group. For example, the following lists show three groups of items: 1) a list of five integer amounts, 2) a list of four character codes, and 3) a list of six floating-point prices:

Amounts	Codes	Prices
98	x	10.96
87	a	6.43
92	m	2.58
79	n	.86
85		12.27
		6.39

A simple list containing items of the same data type is called a one-dimensional array. This chapter describes how one-dimensional arrays are declared, initialized, stored in a computer, and used. You also explore the use of one-dimensional arrays with sample programs and see the procedures for declaring and using multidimensional arrays.

7.1 One-Dimensional Arrays

A **one-dimensional array**, also referred to as a **single-dimensional array** or a **vector**, is a list of related values with the same data type that's stored with a single group name.[1] In C++, as in other computer languages, the group name is referred to as the **array name**. For example, take another look at the list of amounts shown in the introduction:

```
98
87
92
79
85
```

All the amounts in the list are integer numbers and must be declared as such. However, each item in the list doesn't have to be declared separately. The items in the list can be declared as a single unit and stored under a common variable name called the array name. For example, if amts is chosen as the name for this list, the declaration statement int amts[5]; specifies that amts is to store five integer values. Notice that this declaration statement gives the data type of items in the array, the array (or list) name, and the number of items in the array. It's a specific example of the general syntax of an array declaration statement, as follows:

dataType arrayName[numberOfItems]

---

[1] Lists can be implemented in a variety of ways. An array is simply one list implementation in which all list elements are of the same type, and each element is stored consecutively in a set of contiguous memory locations.

Good programming practice requires defining the number of items in the array as a constant before declaring the array. This constant is useful later for processing all items in the array. So in practice, the previous array declaration for `amts` would be declared with two statements, as in these examples:

```
const int NUMELS = 5; // define a constant for the number of items
int amts[NUMELS];      // declare the array
```

The following are other examples of array declarations using this two-line syntax:

```
const int ARRAYSIZE = 6;
int values[ARRAYSIZE];

const int NUMELS = 4;
char code[NUMELS];

const int SIZE = 100;
double amount[SIZE];
```

In these declaration statements, each array is allocated enough memory to hold the number of data items specified in the declaration statement. For example, the array named `values` has storage reserved for six integers, the array named `code` has storage reserved for four characters, and the array named `amount` has storage reserved for 100 double-precision numbers. The constant identifiers, `ARRAYSIZE`, `NUMELS`, and `SIZE`, are programmer-selected names. Figure 7.1 illustrates the storage reserved for the `values` and `code` arrays, assuming an integer is stored with 4 bytes and a character is stored with 1 byte.

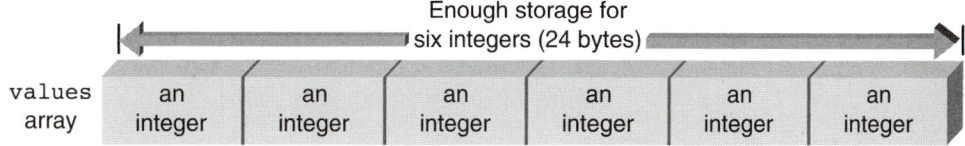

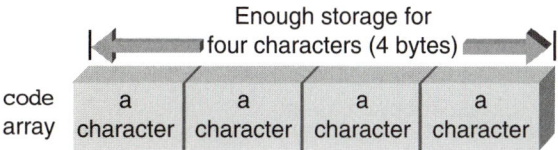

Figure 7.1 The `values` and `code` arrays in memory

Each item in an array is called an **element** or **component** of the array. The elements in the arrays shown in Figure 7.1 are stored sequentially, with the first element stored in the first reserved location, the second element stored in the second reserved location, and so on until the last element is stored in the last reserved location. This contiguous storage allocation is a key feature of arrays because it provides a simple mechanism for locating any element in the list easily.

Because elements in the array are stored sequentially, any single element can be accessed by giving the array's name and the element's position. This position is called the element's **index** or **subscript** value. (The two terms are synonymous.) For a one-dimensional array, the first element has an index of 0, the second element has an index of 1, and so on. In C++, the array name and element index are combined by listing the index in braces after the array name. For example, the declaration `double grade[5];` creates five elements, with the following correspondences:

`grade[0]` refers to the first grade stored in the `grade` array
`grade[1]` refers to the second grade stored in the `grade` array
`grade[2]` refers to the third grade stored in the `grade` array
`grade[3]` refers to the fourth grade stored in the `grade` array
`grade[4]` refers to the fifth grade stored in the `grade` array

Figure 7.2 shows the `grade` array in memory with the correct designation for each array element. Each element is referred to as an **indexed variable** or a **subscripted variable** because both a variable name (the array name, in this case) and an index or a subscript value must be used to reference the element. Remember that the index or subscript value gives the element's *position* in the array.

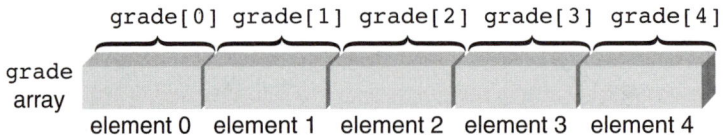

Figure 7.2   Identifying array elements

The subscripted variable, `grade[0]`, is read as "grade sub zero" or "grade zero." It's a shortened way of saying "the `grade` array subscripted by zero." Similarly, `grade[1]` is read as "grade sub one" or "grade one," `grade[2]` as "grade sub two" or "grade two," and so on.

Although referencing the first element with an index of 0 might seem unusual, doing so increases the computer's speed when it accesses array elements. Internally, unseen by the programmer, the computer uses the index as an offset from the array's starting position. As shown in Figure 7.3, the index tells the computer how many elements to skip, starting from the beginning of the array, to get to the correct element.

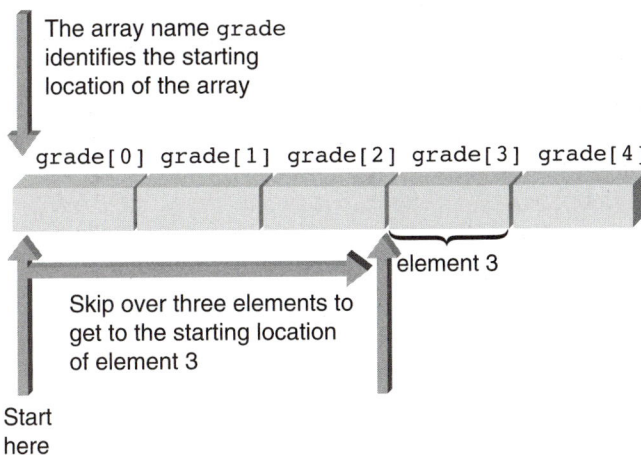

Figure 7.3 Accessing an array element—element 3

Subscripted variables can be used anywhere that scalar (atomic) variables are valid. Here are examples of using the elements of the `grade` array:

```
grade[0] = 95.75;
grade[1] = grade[0] - 11.0;
grade[2] = 5.0 * grade[0];
grade[3] = 79.0;
grade[4] = (grade[1] + grade[2] - 3.1) / 2.2;
sum = grade[0] + grade[1] + grade[2] + grade[3] + grade[4];
```

The subscript in brackets need not be an integer constant; any expression that evaluates to an integer can be used as a subscript.[2] In each case, of course, the value of the expression must be within the valid subscript range defined when the array is declared. For example, assuming i and j are `int` variables, the following subscripted variables are valid:

```
grade[i]
grade[2*i]
grade[j-i]
```

An important advantage of using integer expressions as subscripts is that it allows sequencing through an array by using a loop. This makes statements such as the following unnecessary:

```
sum = grade[0] + grade[1] + grade[2] + grade[3] + grade[4];
```

---

[2]Some compilers permit floating-point variables as subscripts; in these cases, the floating-point value is truncated to an integer value.

The subscript values in this statement can be replaced by a for loop counter to access each element in the array sequentially. For example, the code

```
sum = 0;            // initialize sum to 0
for (i = 0; i < NUMELS; i++)
  sum = sum + grade[i];    // add in a value
```

retrieves each array element sequentially and adds the element to sum. The variable i is used as both the counter in the for loop and a subscript. As i increases by one each time through the loop, the next element in the array is referenced. The procedure for adding array elements in the for loop is similar to the accumulation procedure you have used before.

The advantage of using a for loop to sequence through an array becomes apparent when working with larger arrays. For example, if the grade array contains 100 values rather than just 5, simply setting the symbolic constant NUMELS to 100 is enough to create the larger array and have the for statement sequence through the 100 elements and add each grade to the sum.

As another example of using a for loop to sequence through an array, say you want to locate the maximum value in an array of 1000 elements named prices. The procedure to locate the maximum value is to assume initially that the first element in the array is the largest number. Then, as you sequence through the array, the maximum is compared with each element. When an element with a higher value is located, it becomes the new maximum. The following code does the job:

```
const int NUMELS = 1000;

maximum = prices[0];              // set maximum to element 0
for (int i = 1; i < NUMELS; i++)  // cycle through the rest of the array
  if (prices[i] > maximum)        // compare each element with the maximum
      maximum = prices[i];        // capture the new high value
```

In this code, the for loop consists of one if statement. The search for a new maximum value starts with element 1 of the array and continues through the last element (which is 999 in a 1000-element array). Each element is compared with the current maximum, and when a higher value is encountered, it becomes the new maximum.

Input and Output of Array Values

An array element can be assigned a value interactively by using a cin statement, as shown in these examples of data entry statements:

```
cin >> grade[0];
cin >> grade[1] >> grade[2] >> grade[3];
cin >> grade[4] >> prices[6];
```

In the first statement, a single value is read and stored in the variable grade[0]. The second statement causes three values to be read and stored in the variables grade[1], grade[2], and grade[3]. Finally, the last cin statement is used to read values into the variables grade[4] and prices[6].

Point of Information

Aggregate Data Types

In contrast to atomic types, such as integer and floating-point data, there are aggregate types. An **aggregate type**, also referred to as a "structured type" and a "data structure," is any type with values that can be separated into simpler data types related by some defined structure. Additionally, operations must be available for retrieving and updating values in the data structure.

One-dimensional arrays are examples of a structured type. In a one-dimensional array, such as an array of integers, the array is composed of integer values, with the integers related by their position in the list. Indexed variables provide the means of accessing and modifying values in the array.

Alternatively, a `for` loop can be used to cycle through the array for interactive data input. For example, the following code prompts the user for five grades:

```
const int NUMELS = 5;

for (int i = 0; i < NUMELS; i++)
{
  cout  << "Enter a grade: ";
  cin   >> grade[i];
}
```

The first grade entered is stored in `grade[0]`, the second grade entered is stored in `grade[1]`, and so on until five grades have been entered.

One caution about storing data in an array: Most implementations of C++ don't check the value of the index being used (called a **bounds check**). If an array has been declared as consisting of 10 elements, for example, and you use an index of 12, which is outside the bounds of the array, C++ doesn't notify you of the error when the program is compiled. The program attempts to access element 12 by skipping over the appropriate number of bytes from the start of the array. Usually, this attempt results in a program crash, but not always. If the referenced location contains a value, the program simply accesses the value in the referenced memory location. This leads to more errors, which are troublesome to locate when the variable legitimately assigned to the storage location is retrieved and processed. Using symbolic constants, as done in these examples, helps eliminate this problem.

During output, an array element can be displayed by using a `cout` statement, or complete sections of the array can be displayed by including a `cout` statement in a `for` loop. Examples of both methods of using `cout` to display subscripted variables are shown:

```
cout << prices[5];
```

and

```
cout << "The value of element " << i << " is " << grade[i];
```

and

```
const int NUMELS = 20;

for (int k = 5; k < NUMELS; k++)
  cout << k << " " << amount[k];
```

The first statement displays the value of the subscripted variable `prices[5]`. The second statement displays the values of subscript `i` and `grade[i]`. Before this statement can be executed, `i` must have an assigned value. Finally, the last example includes a `cout` statement in a `for` loop that displays both the value of the index and the value of elements 5 to 19.

Program 7.1 shows these input and output techniques, using an array named `grade` that's defined to store five integer numbers. The program includes two `for` loops. The first `for` loop is used to cycle through each array element and allows the user to input array values. After five values have been entered, the second `for` loop is used to display the stored values.

 **Program 7.1**

```
#include <iostream>
using namespace std;

int main()
{
  const int NUMELS = 5;

  int i, grade[NUMELS];

  for (i = 0; i < NUMELS; i++)    // Enter the grades
  {
    cout << "Enter a grade: ";
    cin  >> grade[i];
  }

  cout << endl;

  for (i = 0; i < NUMELS; i++)    // Print the grades
    cout << "grade [" << i << "] is " << grade[i] << endl;

  return 0;
}
```

A sample run of Program 7.1 follows:

```
Enter a grade: 85
Enter a grade: 90
Enter a grade: 78
```

```
Enter a grade: 75
Enter a grade: 92

grade[0] is 85
grade[1] is 90
grade[2] is 78
grade[3] is 75
grade[4] is 92
```

In reviewing the output of Program 7.1, pay attention to the difference between the subscript value displayed and the numerical value stored in the corresponding array element. The subscript value refers to the element's *location* in the array, and the subscripted variable refers to the *value* stored in the designated location.

In addition to simply displaying the values stored in each array element, elements can also be processed by referencing the desired element. For example, in Program 7.2, the value of each element is accumulated in a total, which is displayed after all array elements have been displayed.

Program 7.2

```cpp
#include <iostream>
using namespace std;
int main()
{
  const int NUMELS = 5;
  int i, grade[NUMELS], total = 0;

  for (i = 0; i < NUMELS; i++)   // Enter the grades
  {
    cout << "Enter a grade: ";
    cin  >> grade[i];
  }

  cout << "\nThe total of the grades";

  for (i = 0; i < NUMELS; i++)   // Display and total the grades
  {
    cout << " " << grade[i];
    total = total + grade[i];
  }

  cout << " is " << total << endl;

  return 0;
}
```

Following is a sample run of Program 7.2:

```
Enter a grade: 85
Enter a grade: 90
Enter a grade: 78
Enter a grade: 75
Enter a grade: 92

The total of the grades 85 90 78 75 92 is 420
```

Note that in Program 7.2, unlike Program 7.1, only the values stored in each array element are displayed. Although the second `for` loop is used to accumulate the total of each element, the accumulation could also have been accomplished in the first `for` loop by placing the statement `total = total + grade[i];` after the `cin` statement used to enter a value. Also, the `cout` statement used to display the total is placed outside the second `for` loop so that the total is displayed only once, after all values have been added to the total. If this `cout` statement were placed inside the `for` loop, five totals would be displayed, with only the last displayed total containing the sum of all array values.

EXERCISES 7.1

1. **(Practice)** Write array declarations for the following:
   a. A list of 100 integer grades
   b. A list of 50 double-precision temperatures
   c. A list of 30 characters, each representing a code
   d. A list of 100 integer years
   e. A list of 32 double-precision velocities
   f. A list of 1000 double-precision distances
   g. A list of 6 integer code numbers

2. **(Practice)** Write correct notation for the first, third, and seventh elements of the following arrays:
   a. `int grades[20]`
   b. `double prices[10]`
   c. `double amounts[16]`
   d. `int dist[15]`
   e. `double velocity[25]`
   f. `double time[100]`

3. **(Practice)** a. Write input statements using `cin` that can be used to enter values in the first, third, and seventh elements of each array declared in Exercise 2.
   b. Write a `for` loop that can be used to enter values for each array declared in Exercise 2.

4. **(Practice) a.** Write output statements using `cout` that can be used to display values from the first, third, and seventh elements of each array declared in Exercise 2.

   b. Write a `for` loop that can be used to display values for each array declared in Exercise 2.

5. **(Desk check)** List the elements displayed by the following sections of code:

   a. `for (m = 1; m <= 5; m++)`
   ```
        cout << a[m] << " ";
   ```
   b. `for (k = 1; k <= 5; k = k + 2)`
   ```
        cout <<   a[k] << " ";
   ```
   c. `for (j = 3; j <= 10; j++)`
   ```
        cout << b[j] << " ";
   ```
   d. `for (k = 3; k <= 12; k = k + 3)`
   ```
        cout << b[k] << " ";
   ```
   e. `for (i = 2; i < 11; i = i + 2)`
   ```
        cout << c[i] << " ";
   ```

6. **(Program) a.** Write, compile, and run a C++ program to input the following values into an array named `prices`: 10.95, 16.32, 12.15, 8.22, 15.98, 26.22, 13.54, 6.45, and 17.59. After the data has been entered, have your program display the values.

   b. Repeat Exercise 6a, but after the data has been entered, have your program display it in the following form:

   ```
   10.95  16.32   12.15
    8.22  15.98   26.22
   13.54   6.45   17.59
   ```

7. **(Program)** Write, compile, and run a C++ program to input eight integer numbers into an array named `grade`. As each number is input, add the numbers to a total. After all numbers are input, display the numbers and their average.

8. **(Program) a.** Write, compile, and run a C++ program to input 10 integer numbers into an array named `fmax` and determine the maximum value entered. Your program should contain only one loop, and the maximum should be determined as array element values are being input. (*Hint:* Set the maximum equal to the first array element, which should be input before the loop used to input the remaining array values.)

   b. Repeat Exercise 8a, keeping track of both the maximum element in the array and the index number for the maximum. After displaying the numbers, display these two messages (replacing the underlines with the correct values):

   ```
   The maximum value is: ____
   This is element number ____ in the list of numbers
   ```

   c. Repeat Exercise 8b, but have your program locate the minimum value of the data entered.

9. **(Program)** Write, compile, and run a C++ program that creates an array of five integer numbers and displays these numbers in reverse order.

10. (**Program**) a. Write, compile, and run a C++ program to input the following integer numbers into an array named `grades`: 89, 95, 72, 83, 99, 54, 86, 75, 92, 73, 79, 75, 82, and 73. As each number is input, add the numbers to a total. After all numbers are input and the total is obtained, calculate the average of the numbers, and use the average to determine the deviation of each value from the average. Store each deviation in an array named `deviation`. Each deviation is obtained as the element value less the average of all the data. Have your program display each deviation with its corresponding element from the `grades` array.

   b. Calculate the variance of the data used in Exercise 10a. The variance is obtained by squaring each deviation and dividing the sum of the squared deviations by the number of deviations.

11. (**Program**) Write, compile, and run a C++ program that specifies three one-dimensional arrays named `price`, `amount`, and `total`. Each array should be capable of holding 10 elements. Using a `for` loop, input values for the `price` and `amount` arrays. The entries in the `total` array should be the product of the corresponding values in the `price` and `amount` arrays (so `total[i] = price[i] * amount[i]`). After all the data has been entered, display the following output, with the corresponding value under each column heading:

```
total     price     amount
-----     -----     ------
```

12. (**Program**) Define an array named `peopleTypes` that can store a maximum of 50 integer values entered at the keyboard. Enter a series of 1s, 2s, 3s, and 4s in the array to represent people at a local school function; 1 represents an infant, 2 represents a child, 3 represents a teenager, and 4 represents an adult. No other integer value should be accepted as valid input, and data entry should stop when a negative value is entered. Your program should count the number of each 1, 2, 3, and 4 in the array and display a list of how many infants, children, teenagers, and adults were at the school function.

13. (**Program**) a. Write, compile, and run a C++ program that reads a list of double-precision grades from the keyboard into an array named `grade`. The grades are to be counted as they're read, and entry is to be terminated when a negative value has been entered. After all grades have been input, your program should find and display the sum and average of the grades. The grades should then be listed with an asterisk (*) placed in front of each grade that's below the average.

   b. Extend the program written for Exercise 13a to display each grade and its letter equivalent, using the following scale:

   Greater than or equal to 90 = A
   Greater than or equal to 80 and less than 90 = B
   Greater than or equal to 70 and less than 80 = C
   Greater than or equal to 60 and less than 70 = D
   Less than 60 = F

14. (**Program**) Using the `srand()` and `rand()` C++ library functions (discussed in Section 6.8), fill an array of 1000 floating-point numbers with random numbers that have been scaled to the range 1 to 100. Then determine and display the number of random numbers having values between 1 and 50 and the number having values greater than 50. What do you expect the output counts to be?

15 (**Program**) **a.** Write, compile, and run a C++ program that inputs 10 double-precision numbers in an array named `raw`. After these numbers are entered in the array, your program should cycle through `raw` 10 times. During each pass through the array, your program should select the lowest value in `raw` and place it in the next available slot in an array named `sorted`. When your program is finished, the sorted array should contain the numbers in `raw` in sorted order from lowest to highest. (*Hint:* Be sure to reset the lowest value selected during each pass to a very high number so that it's not selected again. You need a second `for` loop in the first `for` loop to locate the minimum value for each pass.)

b. The method used in Exercise 15a to sort the values in the array is inefficient. Can you determine why? What might be a better method of sorting the numbers in an array?

7.2 Array Initialization

Array elements can be initialized in their declaration statements in the same manner as scalar variables, except the initializing elements must be included in braces, as shown in these examples:

```
int grade[5] = {98, 87, 92, 79, 85};
char code[6] = {'s', 'a', 'm', 'p', 'l', 'e'};
double width[7] = {10.96, 6.43, 2.58, 0.86, 5.89, 7.56, 8.22};
```

Initializers are applied in the order they're written, with the first value used to initialize element 0, the second value used to initialize element 1, and so on, until all values have been used. For example, in the declaration

```
const NUMELS = 5;
int grade[NUMELS] = {98, 87, 92, 79, 85};
```

`grade[0]` is initialized to 98, `grade[1]` is initialized to 87, `grade[2]` is initialized to 92, `grade[3]` is initialized to 79, and `grade[4]` is initialized to 85.

Because white space is ignored in C++, initializations can be continued across multiple lines. For example, the following declaration for `gallons[]` uses four lines to initialize all the array elements:

```
const int NUMGALS = 20;
int gallons[NUMGALS] = {19, 16, 14, 19, 20, 18,    // initializing values
                        12, 10, 22, 15, 18, 17,    // can extend across
                        16, 14, 23, 19, 15, 18,    // multiple lines
                        21, 5};
```

If the number of initializers is less than the declared number of elements listed in square brackets, the initializers are applied starting with array element 0. Therefore, in the declaration

```
const int ARRAYSIZE = 7;
double length[ARRAYSIZE] = {7.8, 6.4, 4.9, 11.2};
```

only `length[0]`, `length[1]`, `length[2]`, and `length[3]` are initialized with the listed values. The other array elements are initialized to 0.

Unfortunately, there's no method of indicating repetition of an initialization value or of initializing later array elements without first specifying values for earlier elements.

A unique feature of initializers is that the array size can be omitted when initializing values are included in the declaration statement. For example, the following declaration reserves enough storage room for five elements:

```
int gallons[] = {16, 12, 10, 14, 11};
```

Similarly, the following declarations are equivalent:

```
const int NUMCODES = 6;
char codes[6] = {'s', 'a', 'm', 'p', 'l', 'e'};
```

and

```
char codes[] = {'s', 'a', 'm', 'p', 'l', 'e'};
```

Both these declarations set aside six character locations for an array named `codes`. An interesting and useful simplification can also be used when initializing character arrays. For example, the following declaration uses the string `"sample"` to initialize the `codes` array:

```
char codes[] = "sample";    // no braces or commas
```

Recall that a string is any sequence of characters enclosed in double quotation marks. The preceding declaration creates an array named `codes` with seven elements and fills the array with the seven characters shown in Figure 7.4. The first six characters, as expected, consist of the letters s, a, m, p, l, and e. The last character, the escape sequence \0, is called the **null character**. The null character is appended automatically to all strings used to initialize a character array. This character has an internal storage code numerically equal to zero. (The storage code for the 0 character has a numerical value of decimal 48, so the computer can't confuse the two.) The null character is used as a sentinel to mark the end of a string. Strings stored in this manner, as an array of characters terminated with the null character, are known as **C-strings**. All the strings you've encountered so far have been C-strings. In Section 14.1, you see that C++ has another method of storing strings with the `string` data type.

codes[0]   codes[1]   codes[2]   codes[3]   codes[4]   codes[5]   codes[6]

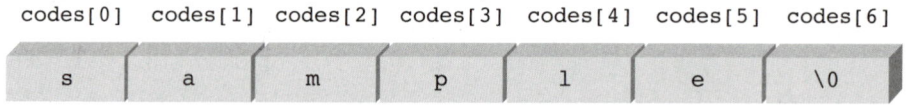

Figure 7.4   Terminating a string with the \0 character

After values have been assigned to array elements, through initialization in the declaration statement or with interactive input, array elements can be processed as described in the previous section. For example, Program 7.3 shows the initialization of array elements in the array declaration statement, and then uses a `for` loop to locate the maximum value stored in the array.

Program 7.3

```cpp
#include <iostream>
using namespace std;

int main()
{
  const int MAXELS = 5;

  int i, max, nums[MAXELS] = {2, 18, 1, 27, 16};

  max = nums[0];

  for (i = 1; i < MAXELS; i++)
    if (max < nums[i])
      max = nums[i];

  cout << "The maximum value is " << max << endl;

  return 0;
}
```

The following output is produced by Program 7.3:

```
The maximum value is 27
```

EXERCISES 7.2

1. **(Practice)** Write array declarations, including initializers, for the following:
   a. A list of 10 integer grades: 89, 75, 82, 93, 78, 95, 81, 88, 77, and 82
   b. A list of five double-precision amounts: 10.62, 13.98, 18.45, 12.68, and 14.76
   c. A list of 100 double-precision interest rates, with the first six rates being 6.29, 6.95, 7.25, 7.35, 7.40, and 7.42
   d. A list of 64 double-precision temperatures, with the first 10 temperatures being 78.2, 69.6, 68.5, 83.9, 55.4, 67.0, 49.8, 58.3, 62.5, and 71.6
   e. A list of 15 character codes, with the first seven codes being f, j, m, q, t, w, and z

2. **(Practice)** Write an array declaration statement that stores the following values in an array named `prices`: 16.24, 18.98, 23.75, 16.29, 19.54, 14.22, 11.13, and 15.39. Include these statements in a program that displays the values in the array.

3. **(Program)** Write, compile, and run a C++ program that uses an array declaration statement to initialize the following numbers in an array named `slopes`: 17.24, 25.63, 5.94, 33.92, 3.71, 32.84, 35.93, 18.24, and 6.92. Your program should locate and display the maximum and minimum values in the array.

4. **(Program)** Write, compile, and run a C++ program that stores the following numbers in an array named `prices`: 9.92, 6.32, 12.63, 5.95, and 10.29. Your program should also create two arrays named `units` and `amounts`, each capable of storing five double-precision numbers. Using a `for` loop and a `cin` statement, have your program accept five user-input numbers in the `units` array when the program is run. Your program should store the product of the corresponding values in the `prices` and `units` array in the `amounts` array. For example, use `amounts[1] = prices[1] * units[1]`. Your program should then display the following output (fill in the chart):

Price	Units	Amount
9.92		
6.32		
12.63		
5.95		
10.29		
Total:		

5. **(Program)** Define an array with a maximum of 20 integer values and fill the array with numbers of your own choosing as intializers. Then write, compile, and run a C++ program that reads the numbers in the array and places all zero and positive numbers in an array named `positive` and all negative numbers in an array named `negative`. Finally, have your program display the values in both the `positive` and `negative` arrays.

6. **(Practice)** The string of characters `"Good Morning"` is to be stored in a character array named `goodstr1`. Write the declaration for this array in three different ways.

7. **(Practice) a.** Write declaration statements to store the string of characters `"Input the Following Data"` in a character array named `message1`, the string `"------------"` in an array named `message2`, the string `"Enter the Date:"` in an array named `message3`, and the string `"Enter the Account Number:"` in an array named `message4`.

   b. Include the array declarations written in Exercise 7a in a program that uses a `cout` statement to display the messages. For example, the statement `cout << message1;` causes the string stored in the `message1` array to be displayed. Your program requires four of these statements to display the four messages. Using a `cout` statement to display a string requires placing the end-of-string marker `\0` in the character array used to store the string.

8. **(Program) a.** Write a declaration to store the string `"This is a test"` in an array named `strtest`. Include the declaration in a program to display the message using the following loop:

```
for (i = 0; i < NUMDISPLAY; i++)
  cout << strtest[i];
```

`NUMDISPLAY` is a named constant for the number 14.
   b. Modify the `for` statement in Exercise 8a to display only the array characters `t`, `e`, `s`, and `t`.
   c. Include the array declaration written in Exercise 8a in a program that uses a `cout` statement to display characters in the array. For example, the statement `cout << strtest;` causes the string stored in the `strtest` array to be displayed. Using this statement requires having the end-of-string marker, `\0`, as the last character in the array.
   d. Repeat Exercise 8a, using a `while` loop. (*Hint:* Stop the loop when the `\0` escape sequence is detected. The expression `while (strtest[i] != '\0')` can be used.)

7.3 Arrays as Arguments

Array elements are passed to a called function in the same manner as scalar variables: They're simply included as subscripted variables when the function call is made. For example, the following function call passes the values of the elements `grades[2]` and `grades[6]` to the function `findMax()`:

```
findMax(grades[2], grades[6]);
```

Passing a complete array of values to a function is, in many respects, easier than passing each element. The called function receives access to the actual array rather than a copy of values in the array. For example, if `grades` is an array, the function call `findMax(grades);` makes the complete `grades` array available to the `findMax()` function. This function call is different from passing a single variable to a function.

Recall that when a single scalar argument is passed to a function (see Section 6.1), the called function receives only a *copy* of the passed value, which is stored in one of the function's parameters. If arrays were passed in this manner, a copy of the complete array would have to be created. For large arrays, making copies for each function call would waste computer storage and frustrate the effort to return multiple-element changes made by the called program. (Remember that a function returns, at most, one value.)

To avoid these problems, the called function is given direct access to the original array.[3] In this way, any changes the called function makes are made directly to the array. For the following examples of function calls, the arrays `nums`, `keys`, `units`, and `grades` are declared as shown:

```
int nums[5];                          // an array of 5 integers
char keys[256];                       // an array of 256 characters
double units[500], grades[500];       // two arrays of 500 doubles
```

---

[3]The called function has access to the original array because the array's starting address is actually passed as an argument. The formal parameter receiving this address argument is a pointer. Section 8.2 explains the close relationship between array names and pointers.

For these arrays, the following function calls can be made; note that in each case, the called function receives direct access to the named array:

```
findMax(nums);
findCharacter(keys);
calcTotal(nums, units, grades);
```

On the receiving side, the called function must be alerted that an array is being made available. For example, the following are suitable function headers for the previous functions:

```
int findMax(int vals[5])
char findCharacter(char inKeys[256])
void calcTotal(int arr1[5], double arr2[500], double arr3[500])
```

In each function header, the programmer chooses the names in the parameter list. However, the parameter names used by the functions still refer to the original array created outside the function, as Program 7.4 makes clear.

 **Program 7.4**

```cpp
#include <iostream>
using namespace std;

const int MAXELS = 5;
int findMax(int [MAXELS]);  // function prototype

int main()
{
  int nums[MAXELS] = {2, 18, 1, 27, 16};

  cout << "The maximum value is " << findMax(nums) << endl;

  return 0;
}

// find the maximum value
int findMax(int vals[MAXELS])
{
  int i, max = vals[0];

  for (i = 1; i < MAXELS; i++)
    if (max < vals[i])
      max = vals[i];

  return max;
}
```

First, note that the symbolic constant MAXELS has been declared globally, not in the main() function. The placement of this declaration means that this symbolic constant can be used in any subsequent declaration or function. Next, notice that the function prototype for findMax() uses this symbolic constant and declares that findMax returns an integer and expects an array of five integers as an argument. It's also important to know that only one array is created in Program 7.4. In main(), this array is known as nums, and in findMax(), the array is known as vals. As illustrated in Figure 7.5, both names refer to the same array, so vals[3] is the same element as nums[3].

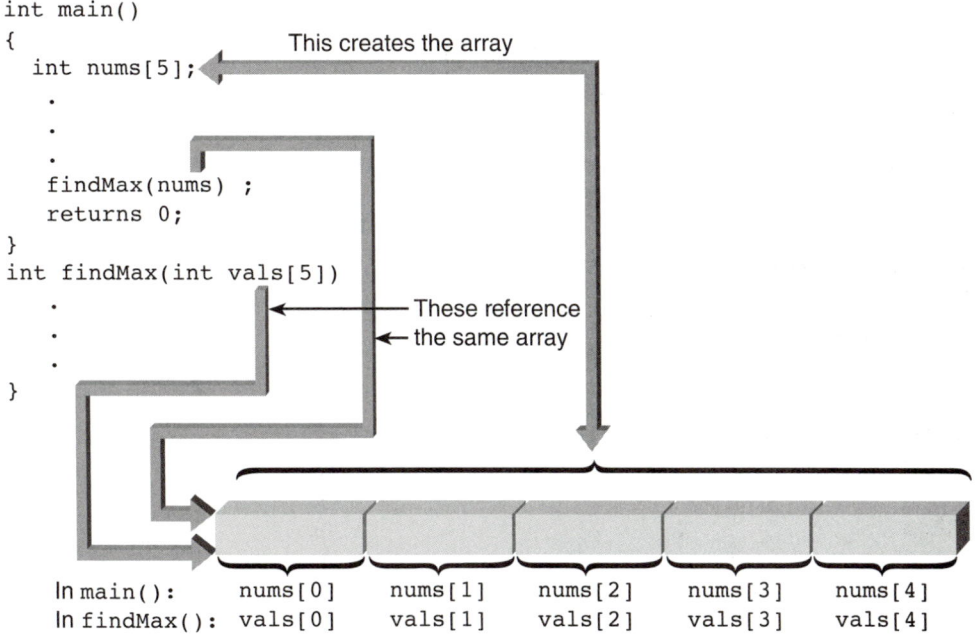

Figure 7.5 Only one array is created

The parameter declaration in the findMax() prototype and function header actually contains extra information not required by the function. All that findMax() must know is that the parameter vals references an array of integers. Because the array has been created in main() and no additional storage space is needed in findMax(), the declaration for vals can omit the array size. Therefore, the following is an alternative function header:

```
int findMax(int vals[])
```

This form of the function header makes more sense when you realize that only one item is actually passed to findMax() when the function is called: the starting address of the nums array, as shown in Figure 7.6.

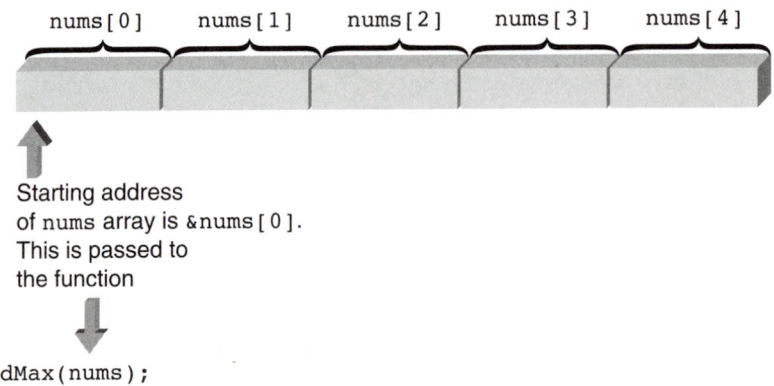

Figure 7.6   The array's starting address is passed

Because only the starting address of vals is passed to findMax(), the number of elements in the array need not be included in the declaration for vals.[4] In fact, generally it's advisable to omit the array size from the function header. For example, this more general form of findMax() can be used to find the maximum value of an integer array of arbitrary size:

```
int findMax(int vals[], int NUMELS)  // find the maximum value
{
  int i, max = vals[0];

  for (i = 1; i < NUMELS; i++)
    if (max < vals[i])
      max = vals[i];

  return max;
}
```

The more general form of findMax() declares that the function returns an integer value. The function expects the starting address of an integer array and the number of elements in the array as arguments. Then, using the number of elements as the boundary for its search, the function's for loop causes each array element to be examined in sequential order to locate the maximum value. Program 7.5 shows using the more general form of findMax() in a complete program.

---

[4]An important consequence of passing the starting address is that findMax() has direct access to the passed array. This access means any change to an element of the vals array is a change to the nums array. This result is much different from the situation with scalar variables, in which the called function doesn't receive direct access to the passed variable.

Program 7.5

```cpp
#include <iostream>
using namespace std;

int findMax(int [], int);   // function prototype

int main()
{
  const int MAXELS = 5;
  int nums[MAXELS] = {2, 18, 1, 27, 16};

  cout << "The maximum value is " << findMax(nums, MAXELS) << endl;

  return 0;
}

// find the maximum value
int findMax(int vals[], int numels)
{
  int i, max = vals[0];

  for (i = 1; i < numels; i++)
    if (max < vals[i]) max = vals[i];

  return max;
}
```

The output displayed by Programs 7.4 and 7.5 is as follows:

```
The maximum value is 27
```

EXERCISES 7.3

1. **(Practice)** The following declarations were used to create the grades array:

```cpp
const int NUMGRADES = 500;
double grades[NUMGRADES];
```

Write two different function headers for a function named sortArray() that accepts the grades array as a parameter named inArray and returns no value.

2. **(Practice)** The following declarations were used to create the keys array:

```cpp
const int NUMKEYS = 256;
char keys[NUMKEYS];
```

Write two different function headers for a function named `findKey()` that accepts the keys array as a parameter named `select` and returns a character.

3. **(Practice)** The following declarations were used to create the `rates` array:

```
const int NUMRATES = 256;
double rates[NUMRATES];
```

Write two different function headers for a function named `prime()` that accepts the `rates` array as an argument named `rates` and returns a double-precision number.

4. **(Modify) a.** Modify the `findMax()` function in Program 7.4 to locate the minimum value of the passed array.

b. Include the function written in Exercise 4a in a complete program and run the program.

5. **(Program)** Write, compile, and run a C++ program that has a declaration in `main()` to store the following numbers in an array named `rates`: 6.5, 7.2, 7.5, 8.3, 8.6, 9.4, 9.6, 9.8, and 10.0. There should be a function call to `show()` that accepts the `rates` array as a parameter named `rates` and then displays the numbers in the array.

6. **(Program) a.** Write, compile, and run a C++ program that has a declaration in `main()` to store the string `"Vacation is near"` in an array named `message`. There should be a function call to `display()` that accepts `message` in a parameter named `strng` and then displays the message.

b. Modify the `display()` function written in Exercise 6a to display the first eight elements of the `message` array.

7. **(Program)** Write, compile, and run a C++ program that declares three one-dimensional arrays named `price`, `quantity`, and `amount`. Each array should be declared in `main()` and be capable of holding 10 double-precision numbers. The numbers to store in `price` are 10.62, 14.89, 13.21, 16.55, 18.62, 9.47, 6.58, 18.32, 12.15, and 3.98. The numbers to store in `quantity` are 4, 8.5, 6, 7.35, 9, 15.3, 3, 5.4, 2.9, and 4.8. Your program should pass these three arrays to a function named `extend()`, which should calculate elements in the `amount` array as the product of the corresponding elements in the `price` and `quantity` arrays (for example, `amount[1] = price[1] * quantity[1]`). After `extend()` has passed values to the `amount` array, the values in the array should be displayed from within `main()`.

8. **(Program)** Write, compile, and run a C++ program that includes two functions named `calcavg()` and `variance()`. The `calcavg()` function should calculate and return the average of values stored in an array named `testvals`. The array should be declared in `main()` and include the values 89, 95, 72, 83, 99, 54, 86, 75, 92, 73, 79, 75, 82, and 73. The `variance()` function should calculate and return the variance of the data. The variance is obtained by subtracting the average from each value in `testvals`, squaring the values obtained, adding them, and dividing by the number of elements in `testvals`. The values returned from `calcavg()` and `variance()` should be displayed by using `cout` statements in `main()`.

7.4 Two-Dimensional Arrays

A **two-dimensional array**, sometimes referred to as a table, consists of both rows and columns of elements. For example, the following array of numbers is called a two-dimensional array of integers:

```
 8    16     9    52
 3    15    27     6
14    25     2    10
```

This array consists of three rows and four columns and is called a 3-by-4 array. To reserve storage for this array, both the number of rows and the number of columns must be included in the array's declaration. Calling the array `val`, the following is the correct specification for this two-dimensional array:

```
int val[3][4];
```

Similarly, the declarations

```
double prices[10][5];
char code[6][26];
```

specify that the `prices` array consists of 10 rows and 5 columns of double-precision numbers, and the `code` array consists of 6 rows and 26 columns, with each element capable of holding one character.

To locate each element in a two-dimensional array, you use its position in the array. As shown in Figure 7.7, the term `val[1][3]` uniquely identifies the element in row 1, column 3. As with one-dimensional array variables, two-dimensional array variables can be used anywhere that scalar variables are valid, as shown in these examples using elements of the `val` array:

```
price = val[2][3];
val[0][0] = 62;
newnum = 4 * (val[1][0] - 5);
sumRow = val[0][0] + val[0][1] + val[0][2] + val[0][3];
```

The last statement causes the values of the four elements in row 0 to be added and the sum to be stored in the scalar variable `sumRow`.

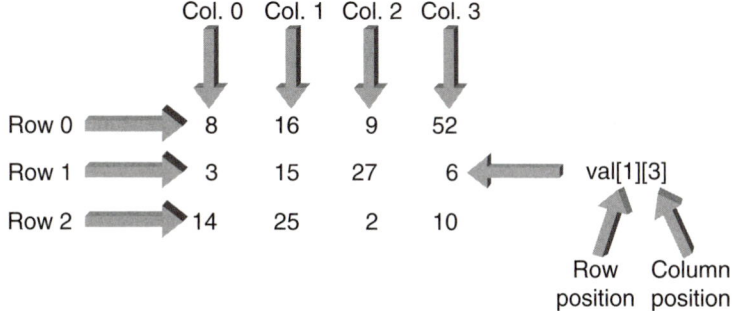

Figure 7.7 Each array element is identified by its row and column position

As with one-dimensional arrays, two-dimensional arrays can be initialized in their declaration statements by listing the initial values inside braces and separating them with commas. Additionally, braces can be used to separate rows. For example, the declaration

```
int val[3][4] = { {8,16,9,52},
                  {3,15,27,6},
                  {14,25,2,10} };
```

declares `val` as an array of integers with three rows and four columns, with the initial values given in the declaration. The first set of braces contains values for row 0 of the array, the second set of braces contains values for row 1, and the third set of braces contains values for row 2.

Although the commas in initialization braces are always required, the inner braces can be omitted. Without them, the initialization for `val` can be written as follows:

```
int val[3][4] = {8,16,9,52,
                 3,15,27,6,
                 14,25,2,10};
```

Separating initial values into rows in the declaration statement isn't necessary because the compiler assigns values beginning with the `[0][0]` element and proceeds row by row to fill in the remaining values. Therefore, the following initialization is equally valid but doesn't clearly indicate to another programmer where one row ends and another begins.

```
int val[3][4] = {8,16,9,52,3,15,27,6,14,25,2,10};
```

As shown in Figure 7.8, a two-dimensional array is initialized in row order. First, the elements of row 0 are initialized, then the elements of row 1 are initialized, and so on, until the initializations are completed. This row ordering is also the same ordering used to store two-dimensional arrays. That is, array element `[0][0]` is stored first, followed by element `[0][1]`, followed by element `[0][2]`, and so on. Following the first row's elements are the second row's elements, and so on for all rows in the array.

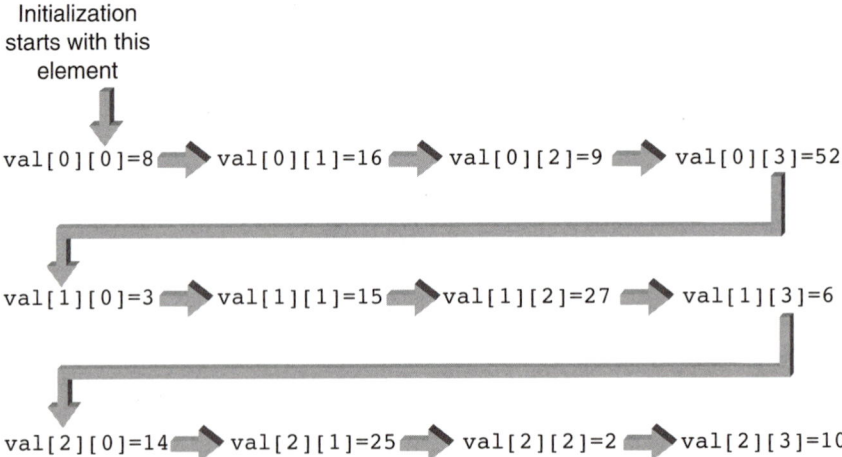

Figure 7.8 Storage and initialization of the `val` array

As with one-dimensional arrays, two-dimensional arrays can be displayed by element nota-tion or by using loops (`while` or `for`). Program 7.6, which displays all elements of a 3-by-4 two-dimensional array, shows using these two techniques. Notice that symbolic constants are used to define the array's rows and columns.

Program 7.6

```cpp
#include <iostream>
#include <iomanip>
using namespace std;

int main()
{
  const int NUMROWS = 3;
  const int NUMCOLS = 4;

  int i, j;
  int val[NUMROWS][NUMCOLS] = {8,16,9,52,3,15,27,6,14,25,2,10};

  cout << "\nDisplay of val array by explicit element"
       << endl << setw(4) << val[0][0] << setw(4) << val[0][1]
       << setw(4) << val[0][2] << setw(4) << val[0][3]
       << endl << setw(4) << val[1][0] << setw(4) << val[1][1]
       << setw(4) << val[1][2] << setw(4) << val[1][3]
       << endl << setw(4) << val[2][0] << setw(4) << val[2][1]
       << setw(4) << val[2][2] << setw(4) << val[2][3];

  cout << "\n\nDisplay of val array using a nested for loop";

  for (i = 0; i < NUMROWS; i++)
  {
    cout << endl;     // print a new line for each row
    for (j = 0; j < NUMCOLS; j++)
      cout << setw(4) << val[i][j];
  }

  cout << endl;

  return 0;
}
```

This is the display produced by Program 7.6:

```
Display of val array by explicit element
    8   16    9   52
    3   15   27    6
   14   25    2   10

Display of val array using a nested for loop
    8   16    9   52
    3   15   27    6
   14   25    2   10
```

The first display of the val array is constructed by designating each array element. The second display of array element values, which is identical to the first, is produced by using a nested for loop. Nested loops are especially useful when dealing with two-dimensional arrays because they allow the programmer to designate and cycle through each element easily. In Program 7.6, the variable i controls the outer loop, and the variable j controls the inner loop. Each pass through the outer loop corresponds to a single row, with the inner loop supplying the column elements. After a complete row is printed, a new line is started for the next row. The result is a display of the array in a row-by-row fashion.

After two-dimensional array elements have been assigned, array processing can begin. Typically, for loops are used to process two-dimensional arrays because, as noted, they allow the programmer to designate and cycle through each array element easily. For example, the nested for loop in Program 7.7 is used to multiply each element in the val array by the scalar number 10 and display the resulting value.

Program 7.7

```cpp
#include <iostream>
#include <iomanip>
using namespace std;

int main()
{
  const int NUMROWS = 3;
  const int NUMCOLS = 4;

  int i, j;
  int val[NUMROWS][NUMCOLS] = {8,16,9,52,
  3,15,27,6,
 14,25,2,10};

  // multiply each element by 10 and display it
  cout << "\nDisplay of multiplied elements";
  for (i = 0; i < NUMROWS; i++)
```

```
{
   cout << endl;    // start each row on a new line
   for (j = 0; j < NUMCOLS; j++)
   {
      val[i][j] = val[i][j] * 10;
      cout << setw(5) << val[i][j];
   }  // end of inner loop
}     // end of outer loop
cout << endl;

return 0;
}
```

Following is the output produced by Program 7.7:

```
Display of multiplied elements
   80   160    90   520
   30   150   270    60
  140   250    20   100
```

Passing two-dimensional arrays to a function is identical to passing one-dimensional arrays. The called function receives access to the entire array. For example, if val is a two-dimensional array, the function call display(val); makes the complete val array available to the function named display(). Consequently, any changes display() makes are made directly to the val array. As further examples, the following two-dimensional arrays named test, code, and stocks are declared as follows:

```
int test[7][9];
char code[26][10];
double stocks[256][52];
```

Then the following function calls are valid:

```
findMax(test);
obtain(code);
price(stocks);
```

On the receiving side, the called function must be alerted that a two-dimensional array is being made available. For example, assuming each of the previous functions returns an integer, the following are suitable function headers:

```
int findMax(int nums[7][9])
int obtain(char key[26][10])
int price(double names[256][52])
```

In these function headers, the parameter names chosen are local to the function (used inside the function body). However, the parameter names still refer to the original array created outside the function. Program 7.8 shows passing a two-dimensional array to a function that displays the array's values.

Program 7.8

```cpp
#include <iostream>
#include <iomanip>
using namespace std;

const int ROWS = 3;
const int COLS = 4;

void display(int [ROWS][COLS]);  // function prototype
int main()
{
  int val[ROWS][COLS] = {8,16,9,52,
                         3,15,27,6,
                         14,25,2,10};

  display(val);

  return 0;
}

void display(int nums[ROWS][COLS])
{
  int rowNum, colNum;
  for (rowNum = 0; rowNum < ROWS; rowNum++)
  {
    for(colNum = 0; colNum < COLS; colNum++)
      cout << setw(4) << nums[rowNum][colNum];
    cout << endl;
  }

  return;
}
```

Only one array is created in Program 7.8. This array is known as `val` in `main()` and as `nums` in `display()`. Therefore, `val[0][2]` refers to the same element as `nums[0][2]`.

Notice the use of the nested `for` loop in Program 7.8 for cycling through each array element. The variable `rowNum` controls the outer loop, and the variable `colNum` controls the inner loop. For each pass through the outer loop, which corresponds to a single row, the inner loop makes one pass through the column elements. After a complete row is printed, a new line is started for the next row. The result is a display of the array in a row-by-row fashion:

```
    8   16    9   52
    3   15   27    6
   14   25    2   10
```

The parameter declaration for `nums` in `display()` contains extra information not required by the function. The declaration for `nums` can omit the row size of the array, so the following is an alternative function prototype:

```
display(int nums[][4]);
```

The reason the column size must be included but the row size is optional becomes obvious when you see how array elements are stored in memory. Starting with element `val[0][0]`, each succeeding element is stored consecutively, row by row, as `val[0][0]`, `val[0][1]`, `val[0][2]`, `val[0][3]`, `val[1][0]`, `val[1][1]`, and so on (see Figure 7.9).

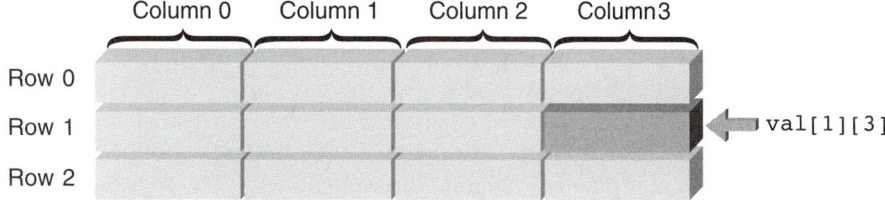

Figure 7.9   Storage of the `val` array

As with all array accesses, a single element of the `val` array is obtained by adding an offset to the array's starting location. For example, element `val[1][3]` of the `val` array in Figure 7.9 is located at an offset of 28 bytes from the start of the array. Internally, the compiler uses the row index, column index, and column size to determine this offset, using the following calculation (assuming 4 bytes for an `int`):

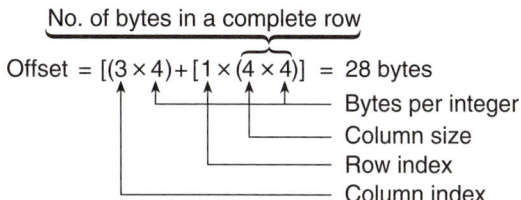

The column size is necessary in the offset calculation so that the compiler can determine the number of positions to skip over to get to the correct row.

Larger Dimensional Arrays

Although arrays with more than two dimensions aren't commonly used, C++ does allow declaring any number of dimensions by listing the maximum size of all dimensions for the array. For example, the declaration `int response [4][10][6];` declares a three-dimensional array. The first element in the array is designated as `response[0][0][0]` and the last element as `response[3][9][5]`.

As shown in Figure 7.10, you can think of a three-dimensional array as a book of data tables. Using this analogy, think of the third subscript value, often called the "rank," as the page number of the selected table, the first subscript value as the row, and the second subscript value as the column.

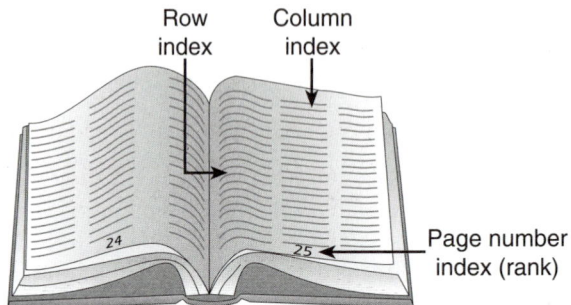

Figure 7.10 Representation of a three-dimensional array

Similarly, arrays of any dimension can be declared. Conceptually, a four-dimensional array can be represented as a shelf of books, with the fourth dimension used to declare a selected book on the shelf, and a five-dimensional array can be viewed as a bookcase filled with books, with the fifth dimension referring to a selected shelf in the bookcase. Using the same analogy, a six-dimensional array can be thought of as a single row of bookcases, with the sixth dimension referring to the selected bookcase in the row; a seven-dimensional array can be thought of as multiple rows of bookcases, with the seventh dimension referring to the selected row, and so on. Alternatively, arrays of three, four, five, six, and so on dimensional arrays can be viewed as mathematical *n*-tuples of order three, four, five, six, and so forth.

EXERCISES 7.4

1. **(Practice)** Write specification statements for the following:
   a. An array of integers with 6 rows and 10 columns
   b. An array of integers with 2 rows and 5 columns
   c. An array of characters with 7 rows and 12 columns
   d. An array of characters with 15 rows and 7 columns
   e. An array of double-precision numbers with 10 rows and 25 columns
   f. An array of double-precision numbers with 16 rows and 8 columns

2. **(Desk check)** Determine the output produced by the following program:

```cpp
#include <iostream>
using namespace std;
int main()
{
   int i, j, val[3][4] = {8,16,9,52,3,15,27,6,14,25,2,10};

   for (i = 0; i < 3; i++)
     for (j = 0; j < 4; j++)
       cout << val[i][j] << " ";

   return 0;
}
```

3. **(Program) a.** Write, compile, and run a C++ program that adds the values of all elements in the `val` array used in Exercise 2 and displays the total.

   b. Modify the program written for Exercise 3a to display the total of each row separately.

4. **(Program)** Write, compile, and run a C++ program that adds equivalent elements of the two-dimensional arrays named `first` and `second`. Both arrays should have two rows and three columns. For example, element `[1][2]` of the resulting array should be the sum of `first[1][2]` and `second[1][2]`. The first and second arrays should be initialized as follows:

   ```
        first                  second
   16    18    23         24    52    77
   54    91    11         16    19    59
   ```

5. **(Program) a.** Write, compile, and run a C++ program that finds and displays the maximum value in a two-dimensional array of integers. The array should be declared as a 4-by-5 array of integers and initialized with the data 16, 22, 99, 4, 18, -258, 4, 101, 5, 98, 105, 6, 15, 2, 45, 33, 88, 72, 16, and 3.

   b. Modify the program written in Exercise 5a so that it also displays the maximum value's row and column subscript values.

6. **(Program)** Write, compile, and run a C++ program that selects the values in a 4-by-5 array of positive integers in increasing order and stores the selected values in a one-dimensional array named `sort`. Use the data given in Exercise 5a to initialize the two-dimensional array.

7. **(Program) a.** A professor has constructed a 3-by-5 two-dimensional array of grades. This array contains the test grades of students in the professor's advanced compiler design class. Write, compile, and run a C++ program that reads 15 array values and then determines the total number of grades in these ranges: less than 60, greater than or equal to 60 and less than 70, greater than or equal to 70 and less than 80, greater than or equal to 80 and less than 90, and greater than or equal to 90.

   b. Entering 15 grades each time you run the program written for Exercise 7a is cumbersome. What method can be used for initializing the array during the testing phase?

   c. How might the program you wrote for Exercise 7a be modified to include the case of no grade being input? That is, what grade could be used to indicate an invalid grade, and how would your program have to be modified to exclude counting an invalid grade?

8. **(Program) a.** Create a two-dimensional list of integer part numbers and quantities of each part in stock, and write a function that displays data in the array in *decreasing* quantity order. No more than 100 different parts are being tracked. Test your program with the following data:

Part No.	Quantity
1001	62
949	85
1050	33
867	125
346	59
1025	105

   b. Modify the function written in Exercise 8a to display the data in part number order.

9. (**Program**) **a.** Your professor has asked you to write a C++ program that determines grades for five students at the end of the semester. For each student, identified by an integer number, four exam grades must be kept, and two final grade averages must be computed. The first grade average is simply the average of all four grades. The second grade average is computed by weighting the four grades as follows: The first grade gets a weight of 0.2, the second grade gets a weight of 0.3, the third grade gets a weight of 0.3, and the fourth grade gets a weight of 0.2. That is, the final grade is computed as follows:

```
0.2 * grade1 0.3 * grade2 0.3 * grade3 0.2 * grade4
```

Using this information, construct a 5-by-6 two-dimensional array, in which the first column is used for the student number, the next four columns for the grades, and the last two columns for the computed final grades. The program's output should be a display of the data in the completed array. For testing purposes, the professor has provided the following data:

Student	Grade 1	Grade2	Grade 3	Grade 4
1	100	100	100	100
2	100	0	100	0
3	82	94	73	86
4	64	74	84	94
5	94	84	74	64

b. What modifications would you need to make to your program so that it can handle 60 students rather than 5?

c. Modify the program written for Exercise 9a by adding an eighth column to the array. The grade in the eighth column should be calculated by computing the average of the top three grades only.

10. (**Program**) The answers to a true-false test are as follows: T T F F T. Given a two-dimensional answer array, in which each row corresponds to the answers provided on one test, write a function that accepts the two-dimensional array and number of tests as parameters and returns a one-dimensional array containing the grades for each test. (Each question is worth 5 points so that the maximum possible grade is 25.) Test your function with the following data:

Test 1:	T	F	T	T	T
Test 2:	T	T	T	T	T
Test 3:	T	T	F	F	T
Test 4:	F	T	F	F	F
Test 5:	F	F	F	F	F
Test 6:	T	T	F	T	F

11. (Modify) Modify the function you wrote for Exercise 10 so that each test is stored in column order rather than row order.

12. (Program) A three-dimensional weather array for the months July and August 2011 has columns labeled by the month numbers 7 and 8. In each column, there are rows numbered 1 through 31, representing the days, and for each day, there are two ranks labeled H and L, representing the day's high and low temperatures. Use this information to write a C++ program that assigns the high and low temperatures for each element of the arrays. Then allow the user to request the following:

- Any day's high and low temperatures
- Average high and low temperatures for a given month
- Month and day with the highest temperature
- Month and day with the lowest temperature

7.5 Common Programming Errors

Four common errors are associated with using arrays:

1. Forgetting to declare the array. This error results in a compiler error message such as "invalid indirection" each time a subscripted variable is encountered in a program.
2. Using a subscript that references a nonexistent array element, such as declaring the array as size 20 and using a subscript value of 25. Most C++ compilers don't detect this error. However, it usually results in a runtime error that causes a program crash or results in a value with no relation to the intended element being accessed from memory. In either case, this error is usually troublesome to locate. The only solution is to make sure, by specific programming statements or by careful coding, that each subscript references a valid array element. Using symbolic constants for an array's size and the maximum subscript value helps eliminate this problem.
3. Not using a large enough counter value in a `for` loop to cycle through all the array elements. This error usually occurs when an array is initially specified as size *n* and there's a `for` loop in the program of the form `for(i = 0; i < n; i++)`. The array size is then expanded, but the programmer forgets to change the interior `for` loop parameters. In practice, this error is eliminated by using the same symbolic constant for the array size declaration and loop parameter.
4. Forgetting to initialize the array. Although many compilers set all elements of integer and real value arrays to 0 automatically and all elements of character arrays to blanks, it's up to the programmer to make sure each array is initialized correctly before processing of array elements begins.

7.6 Chapter Summary

1. A one-dimensional array is a data structure that can be used to store a list of values of the same data type. These arrays must be declared by giving the data type of values stored in the array and the array size. For example, the declaration

```
int num[100];
```

creates an array of 100 integers. A preferable approach is first using a symbolic constant to set the array size, and then using this constant in the array definition, as shown in these examples:

```
const int MAXSIZE = 100;
```

and

```
int num[MAXSIZE];
```

2. Array elements are stored in contiguous locations in memory and referenced by using the array name and a subscript (or index), such as `num[22]`. Any non-negative integer value expression can be used as a subscript, and the subscript 0 always refers to the first element in an array.

3. A two-dimensional array is declared by listing a row and a column size with the data type and array name. For example, the following declarations create a two-dimensional array consisting of five rows and seven columns of integer values:

```
const int ROWS = 5;
const int COLS = 7;
int mat[ROWS][COLS];
```

4. Arrays can be initialized when they're declared. For two-dimensional arrays, you can list the initial values, row by row, inside braces and separate them with commas. For example, the declaration

```
int vals[3][2] = { {1, 2},
                   {3, 4},
                   {5, 6} };
```

produces the following three-row-by-two-column array:

```
1   2
3   4
5   6
```

As C++ uses the convention that initialization proceeds in row order, the inner braces can be omitted. Therefore, the following statement is an equivalent initialization:

```
int vals[3][2] = {1, 2, 3, 4,  5, 6};
```

5. Arrays are passed to a function by passing the array name as an argument. The value actually passed is the address of the first array storage location. Therefore, the called function

receives direct access to the original array, not a copy of the array elements. A parameter must be declared in the called function to receive the passed array name. The declaration of the parameter can omit the array's row size for both one- and two-dimensional arrays.

7.7 Chapter Supplement: Searching and Sorting Methods

Most programmers encounter the need to both sort and search a list of data items at some time in their programming careers. For example, you might have to arrange experiment results in increasing (ascending) or decreasing (descending) order for statistical analysis or sort a list of names in alphabetical order and search this list to find a particular name. Similarly, you might have to arrange a list of dates in ascending or descending order and search this list to locate a certain date. This section introduces the fundamentals of sorting and searching lists. Note that sorting a list before searching it isn't necessary, although much faster searches are possible if the list is in sorted order, as you'll see.

Search Algorithms

A common requirement of many programs is searching a list for a given element. For example, in a list of names and phone numbers, you might search for a specific name so that the corresponding phone number can be printed, or you might need to search the list simply to determine whether a name is there. The two most common methods of performing these searches are the linear and binary search algorithms.

Linear Search   In a **linear search**, also known as a **sequential search**, each item in the list is examined in the order in which it occurs until the desired item is found or the end of the list is reached. This search method is analogous to looking at every name in the phone directory, beginning with Aardvark, Aaron, until you find the one you want or until you reach Zzxgy, Zora. Obviously, it's not the most efficient way to search a long alphabetized list. However, a linear search has these advantages:

- The algorithm is simple.
- The list need not be in any particular order.

In a linear search, the search begins at the first item in the list and continues sequentially, item by item, through the list. The pseudocode for a function performing a linear search is as follows:

> *For all items in the list*
> > *Compare the item with the desired item*
> > *If the item is found*
> > > *Return the index value of the current item*
> > *EndIf*
> *EndFor*
> *Return -1 if the item is not found*

Notice that the function's return value indicates whether the item was found. If the return value is -1, the item isn't in the list; otherwise, the return value in the `for` loop provides the index of where the item is located in the list. The `linearSearch()` function illustrates this procedure as a C++ function:

```cpp
// this function returns the location of key in the list
// a -1 is returned if the value is not found
int linearSearch(int list[], int size, int key)
{
  int i;

  for (i = 0; i < size; i++)
  {
    if (list[i] == key)
      return i;
  }

  return -1;
}
```

In reviewing `linearSearch()`, notice that the `for` loop is simply used to access each element in the list, from first to last, until a match with the desired item is found. If the item is located, the index value of the current item is returned, which causes the loop to terminate; otherwise, the search continues until the end of the list is encountered.

To test this function, a `main()` driver function has been written to call `linearSearch()` and display the results it returns. Program 7.9 shows the complete test program.

 **Program 7.9**

```cpp
#include <iostream>
using namespace std;

int linearSearch(int [], int, int);   // function prototype

int main()
{
  const int NUMEL = 10;
  int nums[NUMEL] = {5,10,22,32,45,67,73,98,99,101};
  int item, location;

  cout << "Enter the item you are searching for: ";
  cin  >> item;

  location = linearSearch(nums, NUMEL, item);
```

```
  if (location > -1)
    cout << "The item was found at index location "
         << location << endl;
  else
    cout << "The item was not found in the list\n";

  return 0;
}


// this function returns the location of key in the list
// a -1 is returned if the value is not found
int linearSearch(int list[], int size, int key)
{
  int i;

  for (i = 0; i < size; i++)
  {
    if (list[i] == key)
      return i;
  }
  return -1;


}
```

The following are sample runs of Program 7.9:

```
Enter the item you are searching for: 101
The item was found at index location 9
```

and

```
Enter the item you are searching for: 65
The item was not found in the list
```

As noted previously, an advantage of linear searches is that the list doesn't have to be in sorted order to perform the search. Another advantage is that if the search item is toward the front of the list, only a small number of comparisons are made. The worst case, of course, occurs when the search item is at the end of the list. On average, however, and assuming the item is equally likely to be anywhere in the list, the number of required comparisons is $n/2$, where n is the list's size. Therefore, for a 10-element list, the average number of comparisons needed for a linear search is 5, and for a 10,000-element list, the average number of comparisons needed is 5000. As you see next, this number can be reduced substantially by using a binary search algorithm.

Binary Search   In a **binary search**, the list must be in sorted order. Starting with an ordered list, the desired item is first compared with the element in the middle of the list. (For lists with an even number of elements, either of the two middle elements can be used.) There are three possibilities after the comparison is made: The desired item might be equal to the middle element, it might be greater than the middle element, or it might be less than the middle element.

In the first case, the search has been successful, and no further searches are required. In the second case, because the desired item is greater than the middle element, it must be in the second half of the list, if it's found at all. This means the first part of the list, consisting of all elements from the first to the midpoint, can be discarded from any further search. In the third case, because the desired item is less than the middle element, it must be in the first part of the list, if it's found at all. For this case, the second half of the list, containing all elements from the midpoint to the last element, can be discarded from any further search.

The algorithm for this search strategy is shown in Figure 7.11 and defined by the following pseudocode:

> **Set the left index to 0**
> **Set the right index to 1 less than the size of the list**
> **Begin with the first item in the list**
>
> **While the left index is less than or equal to the right index**
>   **Set the midpoint index to the integer average of the left and right index values**
>   **Compare the desired item with the midpoint element**
>   **If the desired element equals the midpoint element**
>   **Return the index value of the current item**
>   **Else If the desired element is greater than the midpoint element**
>   **Set the left index value to the midpoint value plus 1**
>   **Else If the desired element is less than the midpoint element**
>   **Set the right index value to the midpoint value less 1**
>   **EndIf**
> **EndWhile**
> **Return -1 if the item is not found**

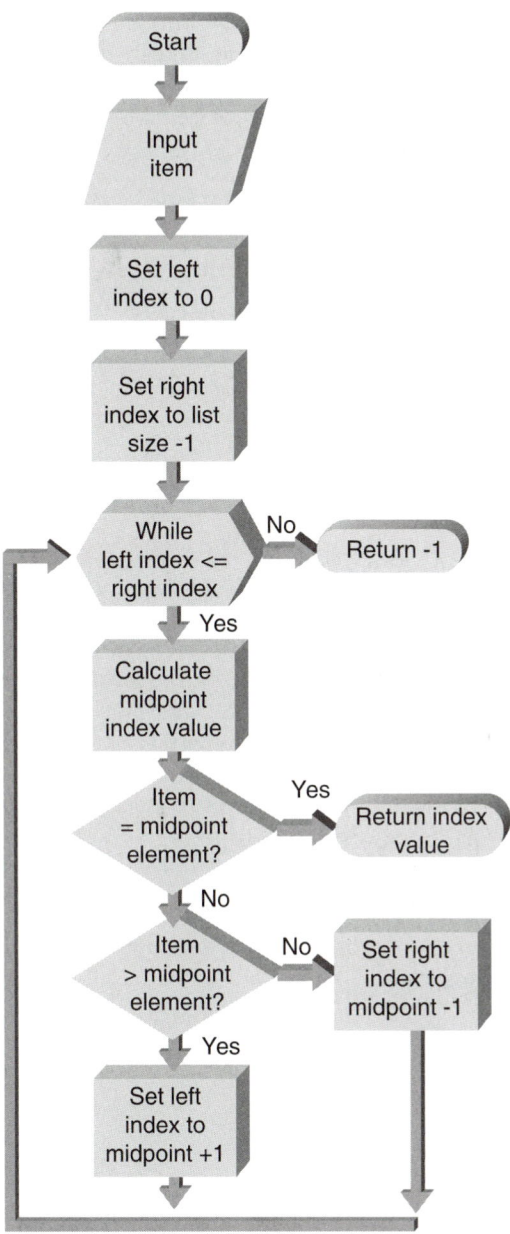

Figure 7.11 The binary search algorithm

In both the pseudocode and Figure 7.11's flowchart, a `while` loop is used to control the search. The initial list is defined by setting the left index value to 0 and the right index value to 1 less than the number of elements in the list. The midpoint element is then taken as the integerized average of the left and right values.

After the comparison with the midpoint element is made, the search is subsequently restricted by moving the left index to one integer value above the midpoint or by moving the right index one integer value below the midpoint. This process continues until the element is found or the left and right index values become equal. The `binarySearch()` function presents the C++ version of this algorithm:

```
// this function returns the location of key in the list
// a -1 is returned if the value is not found
int binarySearch(int list[], int size, int key)
{
  int left, right, midpt;
  left = 0;
  right = size - 1;

  while (left <= right)
  {
    midpt = (int) ((left + right) / 2);
    if (key == list[midpt])
    {
      return midpt;
    }
    else if (key > list[midpt])
      left = midpt + 1;
    else
      right = midpt - 1;
  }

    return -1;
}
```

For purposes of testing this function, Program 7.10 is used. A sample run of Program 7.10 yielded the following:

```
Enter the item you are searching for: 101
The item was found at index location 9
```

Program 7.10

```cpp
#include <iostream>
using namespace std;

int binarySearch(int [], int, int);   // function prototype
int main()
{
  const int NUMEL = 10;
  int nums[NUMEL] = {5,10,22,32,45,67,73,98,99,101};
  int item, location;

  cout << "Enter the item you are searching for: ";
  cin >> item;
  location = binarySearch(nums, NUMEL, item);
  if (location > -1)
    cout << "The item was found at index location "
         << location << endl;
  else
    cout << "The item was not found in the list\n";
  return 0;
}

// this function returns the location of key in the list
// a -1 is returned if the value is not found
int binarySearch(int list[], int size, int key)
{
  int left, right, midpt;
  left = 0;
  right = size - 1;
  while (left <= right)
  {
    midpt = (int) ((left + right) / 2);
    if (key == list[midpt])
    {
      return midpt;
    }
    else if (key > list[midpt])
      left = midpt + 1;
    else
      right = midpt - 1;
  }

  return -1;
}
```

The value of using a binary search algorithm is that the number of elements that must be searched is cut in half each time through the `while` loop. So the first time through the loop, n elements must be searched; the second time through the loop, $n/2$ of the elements has been eliminated and only $n/2$ remain. The third time through the loop, another half of the remaining elements has been eliminated, and so on.

In general, after p passes through the loop, the number of values remaining to be searched is $n/(2^p)$. In the worst case, the search can continue until less than or equal to one element remains to be searched. Mathematically, this procedure can be expressed as $n/(2^p) \le 1$. Alternatively, it can be rephrased as p is the smallest integer so that $2^p > n$. For example, for a 1000-element array, n is 1000 and the maximum number of passes, p, required for a binary search is 10. Table 7.1 compares the number of loop passes needed for a linear and binary search for different list sizes.

Table 7.1   A Comparison of `while` Loop Passes for Linear and Binary Searches

Array size	10	50	500	5000	50,000	500,000	5,000,000	50,000,000
Average linear search passes	5	25	250	2500	25,000	250,000	2,500,000	25,000,000
Maximum linear search passes	10	50	500	5000	50,000	500,000	5,000,000	50,000,000
Maximum binary search passes	4	6	9	13	16	19	23	26

As shown, the maximum number of loop passes for a 50-item list is almost 10 times more for a linear search than for a binary search, and the difference is even more pronounced for larger lists. As a rule of thumb, 50 elements are usually taken as the switch-over point: For lists smaller than 50 elements, linear searches are acceptable; for larger lists, a binary search algorithm should be used.

Big O Notation   On average, over a large number of linear searches with n items in a list, you would expect to examine half ($n/2$) the items before locating the desired item. In a binary search, the maximum number of passes, p, occurs when $n/(2)^p = 1$. This relationship can be manipulated algebraically to $2^p = n$, which yields $p = \log_2 n$, which approximately equals $3.33 \times \log_{10} n$.

For example, finding a particular name in an alphabetical directory with $n = 1000$ names requires an average of 500 ($= n/2$) comparisons with a linear search. With a binary search, only about 10 ($\approx 3.33 \times \log_{10} 1000$) comparisons are required.

A common way to express the number of comparisons required in any search algorithm using a list of n items is to give the order of magnitude of the number of comparisons required, on average, to locate a desired item. Therefore, the linear search is said to be of order n and the binary search of order $\log_2 n$. Notationally, they're expressed as $O(n)$ and $O(\log_2 n)$; the O is read as "the order of."

Sort Algorithms

Two major categories of sorting techniques, called internal and external sorts, are available for sorting data. **Internal sorts** are used when the data list isn't too large and the complete list can be stored in the computer's memory, usually in an array. **External sorts** are used for much larger data sets stored on external storage media and can't be accommodated in the computer's memory as a complete unit. Next, you learn about two internal sort algorithms that can be used when sorting lists with fewer than approximately 50 elements. For larger lists, more sophisticated sorting algorithms are typically used.

Selection Sort   One of the simplest sorting techniques is the **selection sort**, in which the smallest value is selected from the complete list of data and exchanged with the first element in the list. After this first selection and exchange, the next smallest element in the revised list is selected and exchanged with the second element in the list. Because the smallest element is already in the first position in the list, this second pass needs to consider only the second through last elements. For a list consisting of n elements, this process is repeated $n - 1$ times, with each pass through the list requiring one less comparison than the previous pass.

For example, take a look at the list of numbers shown in Figure 7.12. The first pass through the initial list results in the number 32 being selected and exchanged with the first element in the list. The second pass, made on the reordered list, results in the number 155 being selected from the second through fifth elements. This value is then exchanged with the second element in the list. The third pass selects the number 307 from the third through fifth elements in the list and exchanges this value with the third element. Finally, the fourth and last pass through the list selects the remaining minimum value and exchanges it with the fourth list element. Although each pass in this example resulted in an exchange, no exchange would have been made in a pass if the smallest value were already in the correct location.

Initial list	Pass 1	Pass 2	Pass 3	Pass 4
690	32	32	32	32
307	307	155	144	144
32	690	690	307	307
155	155	307	690	426
426	426	426	426	690

Figure 7.12   A sample selection sort

In pseudocode, the selection sort is described as follows:

Set exchange count to 0 (not required, but done to keep track of the exchanges)
For each element in the list from first to next to last

Find the smallest element from the current element being referenced to the last
element by:
  Setting the minimum value equal to the current element
  Saving (storing) the index of the current element
  For each element in the list, from the current element + 1 to the last element in the list
    If element[inner loop index] < minimum value
      Set the minimum value = element[inner loop index]
      Save the index of the newfound minimum value
    EndIf
  EndFor
 Swap the current value with the new minimum value
 Increment the exchange count
EndFor
Return the exchange count

The `selectionSort()` function incorporates this procedure into a C++ function:

```cpp
int selectionSort(int num[], int numel)
{
  int i, j, min, minidx, temp, moves = 0;

  for ( i = 0; i < (numel - 1); i++)
  {
    min = num[i];      // assume minimum is the first array element
    minidx = i;        // index of minimum element
    for(j = i + 1; j < numel; j++)
    {
      if (num[j] < min)       // if you've located a lower value
      {                       // capture it
        min = num[j];
        minidx = j;
      }
    }
    if (min < num[i])     // check whether you have a new minimum
    {                     // and if you do, swap values
      temp = num[i];
      num[i] = min;
      num[minidx] = temp;
      moves++;
    }
  }

  return moves;
}
```

The selectionSort() function expects two arguments: the list to be sorted and the number of elements in the list. As the pseudocode specifies, a nested set of for loops performs the sort. The outer for loop causes one less pass through the list than the total number of items in the list. For each pass, the variable min is initially assigned the value num[i], where i is the outer for loop's counter variable. Because i begins at 0 and ends at 1 less than numel, each element in the list, except the last, is successively designated as the current element.

The inner loop cycles through the elements below the current element and is used to select the next smallest value. Therefore, this loop begins at the index value i + 1 and continues through the end of the list. When a new minimum is found, its value and position in the list are stored in the variables min and minidx. At completion of the inner loop, an exchange is made only if a value less than that in the current position is found.

Program 7.11 was constructed to test selectionSort(). This program implements a selection sort for the same list of 10 numbers used previously to test search algorithms. For later comparison to other sorting algorithms, the number of actual moves the program makes to get data into sorted order is counted and displayed.

 **Program 7.11**

```
#include <iostream>
using namespace std;

int selectionSort(int [], int);
int main()
{
  const int NUMEL = 10;
  int nums[NUMEL] = {22,5,67,98,45,32,101,99,73,10};
  int i, moves;

  moves = selectionSort(nums, NUMEL);

  cout << "The sorted list, in ascending order, is:\n";
  for (i = 0; i < NUMEL; i++)
    cout << "  " << nums[i];

  cout << '\n' << moves << " moves were made to sort this list\n";

  return 0;
}
int selectionSort(int num[], int numel)
{
  int i, j, min, minidx, temp, moves = 0;

  for ( i = 0; i < (numel - 1); i++)
```

```
{
  min = num[i]; // assume minimum is the first array element
  minidx = i;   // index of minimum element
  for(j = i + 1; j < numel; j++)
  {
    if (num[j] < min) // if you've located a lower value
    {                 // capture it
      min = num[j];
      minidx = j;
    }
  }
  if (min < num[i])    // check whether you have a new minimum
  {                    // and if you do, swap values
    temp = num[i];
    num[i] = min;
    num[minidx] = temp;
    moves++;
  }
}

return moves;
}
```

The output Program 7.11 produces is as follows:

```
The sorted list, in ascending order, is:
   5   10   22   32   45   67   73   98   99   101
8 moves were made to sort this list
```

Clearly, the number of moves displayed depends on the initial order of values in the list. An advantage of the selection sort is that the maximum number of moves that must be made is *n* - 1, where *n* is the number of items in the list. Further, each move is a final move that results in an element residing in its final location in the sorted list.

A disadvantage of the selection sort is that $n(n - 1) / 2$ comparisons are always required, regardless of the initial arrangement of data. This number of comparisons is obtained as follows: The last pass always requires one comparison, the next-to-last pass requires two comparisons, and so on up to the first pass, which requires *n* - 1 comparisons. Therefore, the total number of comparisons is the following:

$$1 + 2 + 3 + \ldots + n - 1 = n(n - 1) / 2 = n^2 / 2 - n / 2$$

For large values of *n*, the n^2 dominates, and the order of the selection sort is $O(n^2)$.

Exchange (Bubble) Sort   In an **exchange sort**, adjacent elements of the list are exchanged with one another so that the list becomes sorted. One example of this sequence of exchanges is the **bubble sort**, in which successive values in the list are compared, beginning with the first two elements. If the list is to be sorted in ascending (from smallest to largest) order, the smaller value of the two being compared is always placed before the larger value. For lists sorted in descending (from largest to smallest) order, the smaller of the two values being compared is always placed after the larger value.

For example, a list of values is to be sorted in ascending order. If the first element in the list is larger than the second, the two elements are exchanged. Then the second and third elements are compared. Again, if the second element is larger than the third, these two elements are exchanged. This process continues until the last two elements have been compared and exchanged, if necessary. If no exchanges were made during this initial pass through the data, the data is in the correct order and the process is finished; otherwise, a second pass is made through the data, starting from the first element and stopping at the next-to-last element. The reason for stopping at the next-to-last element on the second pass is that the first pass always results in the most positive value "sinking" to the bottom of the list.

To see a specific example, examine the list of numbers in Figure 7.13. The first comparison results in exchanging the first two element values, 690 and 307. The next comparison, between elements two and three in the revised list, results in exchanging values between the second and third elements, 690 and 32. This comparison and possible switching of adjacent values continues until the last two elements have been compared and possibly exchanged. This process completes the first pass through the data and results in the largest number moving to the bottom of the list. As the largest value sinks to the bottom of the list, the smaller elements slowly rise, or "bubble," to the top of the list. This bubbling effect of the smaller elements is what gave rise to the name "bubble sort" for this sorting algorithm.

690	307	307	307	307
307	690	32	32	32
32	32	690	155	155
155	155	155	690	426
426	426	426	426	690

Figure 7.13   The first pass of an exchange sort

Because the first pass through the list ensures that the largest value always moves to the bottom of the list, the second pass stops at the next-to-last element. This process continues with each pass stopping at one higher element than the previous pass, until $n - 1$ passes through the list have been completed or no exchanges are necessary in any single pass. In both cases, the resulting list is in sorted order. The pseudocode describing this sort is as follows:

> *Set exchange count to 0 (not required, but done to keep track of the exchanges)*
> *For the first element in the list to 1 less than the last element (i index)*
>   *For the second element in the list to the last element (j index)*
>   *If num[j] < num[j - 1]*
>   *{*
>   *Swap num[j] with num[j - 1]*
>   *increment exchange count*
>   *}*

EndFor
EndFor
Return exchange count

This sort algorithm is coded in C++ as the bubbleSort() function, which is included in Program 7.12 for testing purposes. This program tests bubbleSort() with the same list of 10 numbers used in Program 7.11 to test selectionSort(). For comparison with the earlier selection sort, the number of adjacent moves (exchanges) bubbleSort() makes is also counted and displayed.

 **Program 7.12**

```cpp
#include <iostream>
using namespace std;

int bubbleSort(int [], int);   // function prototype

int main()
{
  const int NUMEL = 10;
  int nums[NUMEL] = {22,5,67,98,45,32,101,99,73,10};
  int i, moves;

  moves = bubbleSort(nums, NUMEL);

  cout << "The sorted list, in ascending order, is:\n";
  for (i = 0; i < NUMEL; i++)
    cout << " " << nums[i];

  cout << '\n' << moves << " moves were made to sort this list\n";

  return 0;
}

int bubbleSort(int num[], int numel)
{
  int i, j, temp, moves = 0;

  for ( i = 0; i < (numel - 1); i++)
  {
    for(j = 1; j < numel; j++)
    {
      if (num[j] < num[j-1])
```

```
        {
          temp = num[j];
          num[j] = num[j-1];
          num[j-1] = temp;
          moves++;
        }
      }
    }

    return moves;
}
```

Here's the output produced by Program 7.12:

```
    The sorted list, in ascending order, is:
      5   10   22   32   45   67   73   98   99   101
    18 moves were made to sort this list
```

As with the selection sort, the number of comparisons in a bubble sort is $O(n^2)$, and the number of required moves depends on the initial order of values in the list. In the worst case, when the data is in reverse sorted order, the selection sort performs better than the bubble sort. Both sorts require $n(n - 1)/2$ comparisons, but the selection sort needs only $n - 1$ moves, and the bubble sort needs $n(n - 1)/2$ moves. The additional moves the bubble sort requires result from the intermediate exchanges between adjacent elements to "settle" each element into its final position. In this regard, the selection sort is superior because no intermediate moves are necessary. For random data, such as that used in Programs 7.11 and 7.12, the selection sort generally performs equal to or better than the bubble sort.

Chapter

8

Arrays and Pointers

Programmers often don't consider that memory addresses of variables are used extensively throughout the executable versions of their programs. The computer uses these addresses to keep track of where variables and instructions are physically located in the computer. One of C++'s advantages is that it allows programmers to access these addresses. This access gives programmers a view into a computer's basic storage structure, resulting in capabilities and programming power that aren't available in other high-level languages. This is accomplished by using a feature called pointers. Although other languages provide pointers, C++ extends this feature by providing pointer arithmetic; that is, pointer values can be added, subtracted, and compared.

Fundamentally, pointers are simply variables used to store memory addresses. This chapter discusses the basics of declaring pointers, explains the close relationship of pointers and arrays, and then describes techniques of applying pointer variables in other meaningful ways.

8.1 Introduction to Pointers

In an executable program, every variable has three major items associated with it: the value stored in the variable, the number of bytes reserved for the variable, and where in memory these bytes are located. The memory location of the first byte reserved for a variable is known as the variable's address. Knowing the location of this first byte and how many bytes have been allocated to the variable (which is based on its data type) allows the executable program to access the variable's contents. Figure 8.1 illustrates the relationship between these three items (address, number of bytes, and contents).

One or more bytes in memory

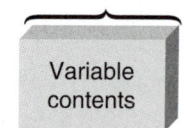

Variable address   Variable contents

Figure 8.1   A typical variable

For most applications, a variable's internal storage is of little or no concern because the variable name is a simple and sufficient means of locating its contents. Therefore, after a variable is declared, programmers are usually concerned only with the name and value assigned to it (its contents) and pay little attention to where this value is stored. For example, take a look at Program 8.1.

 **Program 8.1**

```
#include <iostream>
using namespace std;

int main()
{

  int num;

  num = 22;
  cout << "The value stored in num is " << num << endl;
  cout <<  sizeof(num) << " bytes are used to store this value" << endl;

  return 0;
}
```

This is the output displayed when Program 8.1 is run:

```
The value stored in num is 22
4 bytes are used to store this value
```

Program 8.1 displays both the number 22, which is the value stored in the integer variable num, and the amount of storage used for this integer variable.[1] Figure 8.2 shows the information that Program 8.1 provides.

---

[1]The amount of storage allocated for each data type is compiler dependent. Refer to Section 2.1.

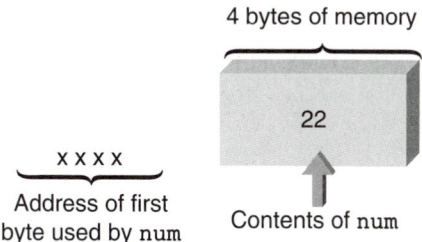

Figure 8.2   The variable num stored somewhere in memory

C++ permits you to go further, however, and display the address corresponding to any variable. The address that's displayed corresponds to the address of the first byte set aside in the computer's memory for the variable.

To determine a variable's address, the address operator, &, must be used. You have seen this symbol before in declaring reference variables. When used to display an address, it means "the address of," and when placed in front of a variable name, it's translated as the address of the variable.[2] For example, &num means "the address of num," &total means "the address of total," and &price means "the address of price." Program 8.2 uses the address operator to display the address of the variable num.

 Program 8.2

```cpp
#include <iostream>
using namespace std;

int main()
{
  int num;

  num = 22;
  cout << "The value stored in num is " << num << endl;
  cout << "The address of num = " << &num << endl;

  return 0;
}
```

This is the output of Program 8.2:

```
The value stored in num is 22
The address of num = 0012FED4
```

---

[2]When used in the declaration of a reference variable (see Section 6.3), the & symbol refers to the data type preceding it. For example, the declaration int &num is read as "num is the address of an int" or, more commonly, "num is a reference to an int."

Figure 8.3 shows the additional address information provided by Program 8.2's output.

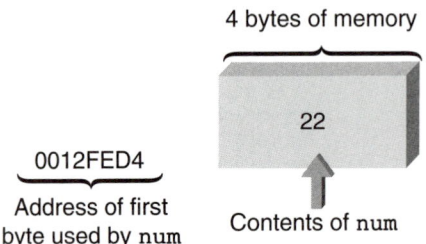

Figure 8.3 A more complete picture of the variable num

Clearly, the address output by Program 8.2 depends on both the computer used to run the program and what other programs or data files are in memory when the program runs. Every time Program 8.2 runs, however, it displays the address of the first memory location used to store num. As Program 8.2's output shows, the address is displayed in hexadecimal notation (see Section 2.6). This display has no effect on how the program uses addresses internally; it merely provides a means of displaying addresses in a more compact representation than the internal binary system used by the computer. As you see in the following sections, however, using addresses (as opposed to just displaying them) gives C++ programmers a powerful programming tool.

Storing Addresses

Besides displaying the address of a variable, as in Program 8.2, you can store addresses in suitably declared variables. For example, the statement

```
numAddr = &num;
```

stores the address corresponding to the variable num in the variable numAddr, as illustrated in Figure 8.4.

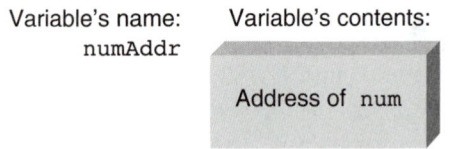

Figure 8.4 Storing num's address in numAddr

Similarly, the statements

```
d = &m;
tabPoint = &list;
chrPoint = &ch;
```

store addresses of the variables m, list, and ch in the variables d, tabPoint, and chrPoint, as shown in Figure 8.5.

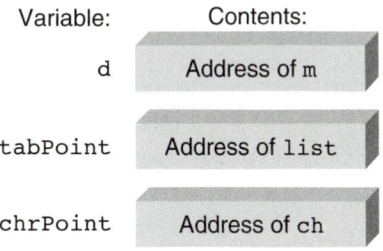

Variable: Contents:

d   Address of m

tabPoint   Address of list

chrPoint   Address of ch

Figure 8.5   Storing more addresses

The variables numAddr, d, tabPoint, and chrPoint are formally called **pointer variables** or **pointers**. Pointers are simply variables used to store the addresses of other variables.

Using Addresses

To use a stored address, C++ provides an **indirection operator**, *. The * symbol, when followed by a pointer (with a space permitted both before and after the *), means "the variable whose address is stored in." Therefore, if numAddr is a pointer (a variable that stores an address), *numAddr means *the variable whose address is stored in* numAddr. Similarly, *tabPoint means *the variable whose address is stored in* tabPoint, and *chrPoint means *the variable whose address is stored in* chrPoint. Figure 8.6 shows the relationship between the address contained in a pointer variable and the variable.

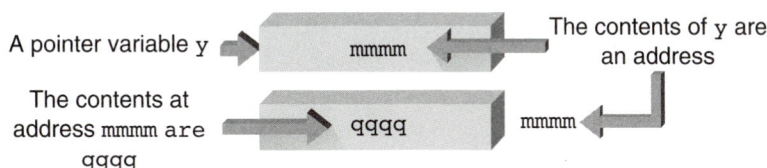

A pointer variable y   mmmm   The contents of y are
                                            an address

The contents at
address mmmm are   qqqq   mmmm
qqqq

Figure 8.6   Using a pointer variable

Although *d means "the variable whose address is stored in d," it's commonly shortened to the statement "the variable pointed to by d." Similarly, referring to Figure 8.6, *y can be read as "the variable pointed to by y." The value that's finally obtained, as shown in this figure, is qqqq.

When using a pointer variable, the value that's finally obtained is always found by first going to the pointer for an address. The address contained in the pointer is then used to get the variable's contents. Certainly, this procedure is a rather indirect way of getting to the final value, so the term **indirect addressing** is used to describe it.

Because using a pointer requires the computer to do a double lookup (retrieving the address first, and then using the address to retrieve the actual data), you might wonder why you'd want to store an address in the first place. The answer lies in the shared relationship between pointers and arrays and the capability of pointers to create and delete variable storage locations dynamically, as a program is running. Both topics are discussed in the next section. For now, however, given that each variable has a memory address associated with it, the idea of storing an address shouldn't seem unusual.

Declaring Pointers

Like all variables, pointers must be declared before they can be used to store an address. When you declare a pointer variable, C++ requires also specifying the type of variable that's pointed to. For example, if the address in the pointer numAddr is the address of an integer, this is the correct declaration for the pointer:

```
int *numAddr;
```

This declaration is read as "the variable pointed to by numAddr (from *numAddr in the declaration) is an integer."[3]

Notice that the declaration int *numAddr; specifies two things: First, the variable pointed to by numAddr is an integer, and second, numAddr must be a pointer (because it's declared with an asterisk, *). Similarly, if the pointer tabPoint points to (contains the address of) a double-precision number and chrPoint points to a character variable, the required declarations for these pointers are as follows:

```
double *tabPoint;
char *chrPoint;
```

These two declarations can be read as "the variable pointed to by tabPoint is a double" and "the variable pointed to by chrPoint is a char." Because all addresses appear the same, the compiler needs this additional information to know how many storage locations to access when it uses the address stored in the pointer.

Here are other examples of pointer declarations:

```
char *inkey;
int *numPt;
double *nm1Ptr
```

To understand pointer declarations, reading them backward is helpful, starting with the asterisk, *, and translating it as "the variable whose address is stored in" or "the variable pointed to by." Applying this method to pointer declarations, the declaration char *inkey;, for example, can be read as "the variable whose address is stored in inkey is a char" or "the variable pointed to by inkey is a char." Both these statements are often shortened to the simpler "inkey points to a char." All three interpretations of the declaration statement are correct, so you can select and use the description that makes the most sense to you. Program 8.3 puts this information together to construct a program using pointers.

---

[3]Pointer declarations can also be written in the form *dataType* *pointerName*, with a space between the indirection operator and the pointer name. This form, however, is error prone when multiple pointers are declared in the same declaration statement and the asterisk is inadvertently omitted after declaring the first pointer name. For example, the declaration int* num1, num2; declares num1 as a pointer variable and num2 as an integer variable. To accommodate multiple pointers in the same declaration and clearly mark a variable as a pointer, the examples in this book adhere to the convention of placing an asterisk in front of each pointer name. This potential error rarely occurs with reference declarations because references are used almost exclusively as formal parameters, and single declarations of parameters are mandatory.

 **Program 8.3**

```cpp
#include <iostream>
using namespace std;

int main()
{
  int *numAddr;        // declare a pointer to an int
  int miles, dist;     // declare two integer variables

  dist = 158;          // store the number 158 in dist
  miles = 22;          // store the number 22 in miles
  numAddr = &miles;    // store the "address of miles" in numAddr

  cout << "The address stored in numAddr is " << numAddr << endl;
  cout << "The value pointed to by numAddr is " << *numAddr << "\n\n";

  numAddr = &dist;  // now store the address of dist in numAddr
  cout << "The address now stored in numAddr is " << numAddr << endl;
  cout << "The value now pointed to by numAddr is " << *numAddr << endl;

  return 0;
}
```

The output of Program 8.3 is as follows:

```
The address stored in numAddr is 0012FEC8
The value pointed to by numAddr is 22

The address now stored in numAddr is 0012FEBC
The value now pointed to by numAddr is 158
```

The only use for Program 8.3 is to help you understand what gets stored where, so review the program to see how the output was produced. The declaration statement int *numAddr; declares numAddr to be a pointer used to store the address of an integer variable. The statement numAddr = &miles; stores the address of the variable miles in the pointer numAddr. The first cout statement causes this address to be displayed. The second cout statement uses the indirection operator (*) to retrieve and display the value pointed to by numAddr, which is, of course, the value stored in miles.

Because numAddr has been declared as a pointer to an integer variable, you can use this pointer to store the address of any integer variable. The statement numAddr = &dist illustrates this use by storing the address of the variable dist in numAddr. The last two cout statements verify the change in numAddr's value and confirm that the new stored address points to the variable dist. As shown in Program 8.3, only addresses should be stored in pointers.

It certainly would have been much simpler if the pointer used in Program 8.3 could have been declared as `pointer numAddr;`. This declaration, however, conveys no information about the storage used by the variable whose address is stored in `numAddr`. This information is essential when the pointer is used with the indirection operator, as in the second `cout` statement in Program 8.3. For example, if an integer's address is stored in `numAddr`, typically only 4 bytes of storage are retrieved when the address is used. If a character's address is stored in `numAddr`, only 1 byte of storage is retrieved, and a `double` typically requires retrieving 8 bytes of storage. The declaration of a pointer must, therefore, include the data type of the variable being pointed to, as shown in Figure 8.7.

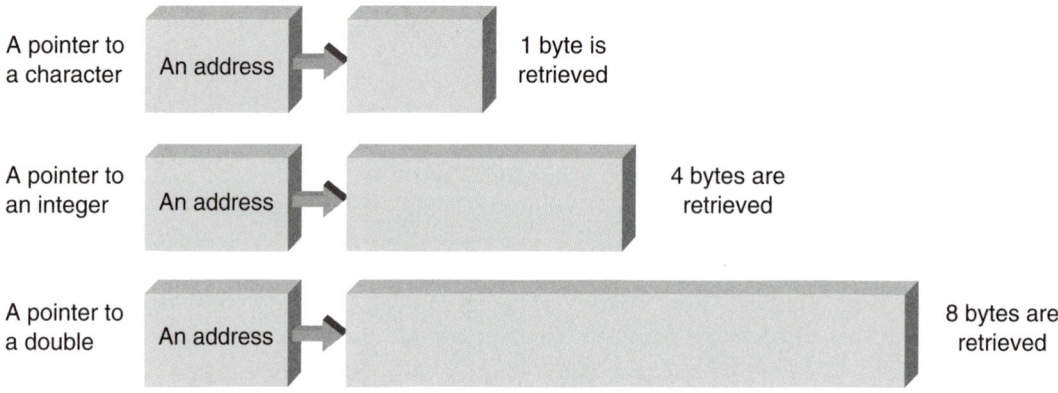

Figure 8.7   Addressing different data types by using pointers

References and Pointers

At this point, you might be asking what the difference is between a pointer and a reference. Essentially, a **reference** is a named constant for an address; therefore, the address named as a reference can't be altered after the address has been assigned. Clearly, for a reference parameter (see Section 6.3), a new reference is created and assigned an address each time the function is called. The address in a pointer, used as a variable or function parameter (discussed in Section 8.4), can be changed after its initial assignment.

In passing an address to a function, beginning programmers tend to prefer using references, as described in Section 6.3. The reason is the simpler notation for reference parameters, which eliminates the address operator (`&`) and indirection operator (`*`) required for pointers. Technically, references are said to be **automatically dereferenced** or **implicitly dereferenced** (the two terms are used synonymously). In contrast, pointers must be explicitly dereferenced by using the indirection operator. In other situations, such as dynamically allocating new sections of memory for additional variables as a program is running and as an alternative to accessing array elements (both discussed in Section 8.2), pointers are required.

Reference Variables[4]   Although references are used almost exclusively as function parameters and return types, they can also be declared as variables. For completeness, this use of references is explained in this section.

After a variable has been declared, it can be given an additional name by using a **reference declaration**, which has this form:

dataType& newName = existingName;

For example, the reference declaration

`double& sum = total;`

equates the name `sum` to the name `total`. Both now refer to the same variable, as shown in Figure 8.8.

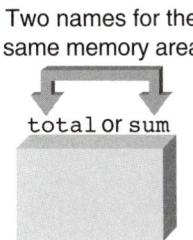

Two names for the
same memory area

total or sum

Figure 8.8   sum is an alternative name for total

After establishing another name for a variable by using a reference declaration, the new name, referred to as an **alias**, can be used in place of the original name. For example, take a look at Program 8.4.

Program 8.4

```
#include <iostream>
using namespace std;

int main()
{
  double total = 20.5;    // declare and initialize total
  double& sum = total;    // declare another name for total

  cout << "sum = " << sum << endl;
  sum = 18.6;                // this changes the value in total
  cout << "total = " << total << endl;

  return 0;
}
```

---

[4]This section can be omitted with no loss of subject continuity.

The following output is produced by Program 8.4:

```
sum = 20.5
total = 18.6
```

Because the variable `sum` is simply another reference to the variable `total`, the first `cout` statement in Program 8.4 displays the value stored in `total`. Changing the value in `sum` then changes the value in `total`, which the second `cout` statement in this program displays.

When constructing reference variables, keep two points in mind. First, the reference variable should be of the same data type as the variable it refers to. For example, this sequence of declarations

```
int num = 5;
double& numref = num;   // INVALID - CAUSES A COMPILER ERROR
```

doesn't equate `numref` to `num`; rather, it causes a compiler error because the two variables are of different data types.

Second, a compiler error is produced when an attempt is made to equate a reference variable to a constant. For example, the following declaration is invalid:

```
int& val = 5;  // INVALID - CAUSES A COMPILER ERROR
```

After a reference name has been equated to one variable name correctly, the reference *can't* be changed to refer to another variable.

As with all declaration statements, multiple references can be declared in a single statement, as long as each reference name is preceded by an ampersand. Therefore, the following declaration creates two reference variables named `sum` and `average`:[5]

```
double& sum = total, & average;
```

Another way of looking at references is to consider them pointers with restricted capabilities that hide a lot of the dereferencing required with pointers. For example, take a look at these statements:

```
int b;      // b is an integer variable
int& a = b; // a is a reference variable that stores b's address
a = 10;     // this changes b's value to 10
```

Here, `a` is declared as a reference variable that's effectively a named constant for the address of the `b` variable. Because the compiler knows from the declaration that `a` is a reference variable, it automatically assigns `b`'s address (rather than `b`'s contents) to `a` in the declaration statement. Finally, in the statement `a = 10;`, the compiler uses the address stored in `a` to change the value stored in `b` to 10. The advantage of using the reference is that it accesses `b`'s value automatically without having to use the indirection operator, `*`. As noted previously, this type of access is referred to as an "automatic dereference."

---

[5]Reference declarations can also be written in the form *dataType &newName = existingName*, with a space between the ampersand and the data type. This form isn't used much, however, because it can be confused easily with the notation used to assign addresses to pointer variables.

The following sequence of instructions makes use of this same correspondence between a and b by using pointers:

```
int b;       // b is an integer variable
int *a = &b; // a is a pointer - store b's address in a
*a = 10;     // this changes b's value to 10 by explicit
             // dereference of the address in a
```

Here, a is defined as a pointer initialized to store the address of b. Therefore, *a (which can be read as "the variable whose address is in a" or "the variable pointed to by a") is b, and the expression *a = 10 changes b's value to 10. Notice that with pointers, the stored address can be altered to point to another variable; with references, the reference variable can't be altered to refer to any variable except the one it's initialized to. Also, notice that to dereference a, you must use the indirection operator, *. As you might expect, the * is also called the **dereferencing operator**.

EXERCISES 8.1

1. **(Review)** What are the three items associated with the variable named `total`?

2. **(Review)** If `average` is a variable, what does `&average` mean?

3. **(Practice)** For the variables and addresses in Figure 8.9, determine the addresses corresponding to the expressions `&temp`, `&dist`, `&date`, and `&miles`.

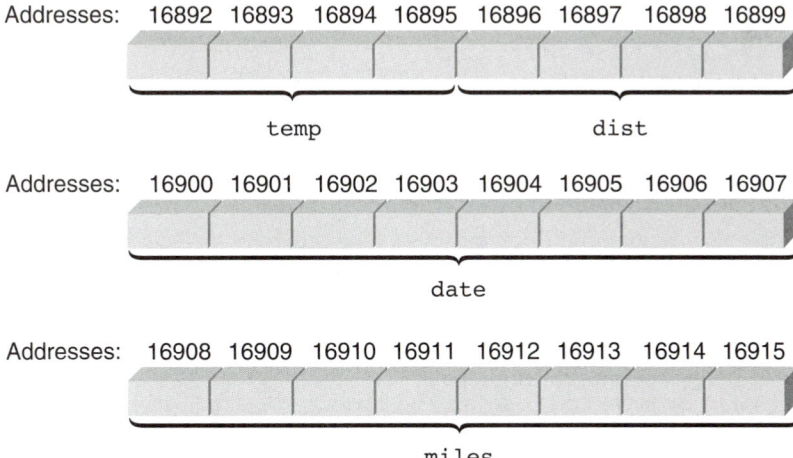

Figure 8.9 Memory bytes for Exercise 3

4. (**Practice**) **a.** Write a C++ program that includes the following declaration statements. Have the program use the address operator and a cout statement to display the addresses corresponding to each variable.

```
int num, count;
long date;
float slope;
double yield;
```

   b. After running the program written for Exercise 4a, draw a diagram of how your computer has set aside storage for the variables in the program. On your diagram, fill in the addresses the program displays.

   c. Modify the program written in Exercise 4a (using the sizeof() operator discussed in Section 2.1) to display the amount of storage your computer reserves for each data type. With this information and the address information provided in Exercise 4b, determine whether your computer set aside storage for the variables in the order in which they were declared.

5. (**Review**) If a variable is declared as a pointer, what must be stored in the variable?

6. (**Practice**) Using the indirection operator, write expressions for the following:
   a. The variable pointed to by xAddr
   b. The variable whose address is in yAddr
   c. The variable pointed to by ptYld
   d. The variable pointed to by ptMiles
   e. The variable pointed to by mptr
   f. The variable whose address is in pdate
   g. The variable pointed to by distPtr
   h. The variable pointed to by tabPt
   i. The variable whose address is in hoursPt

7. (**Practice**) Write declaration statements for the following:
   a. The variable pointed to by yAddr is an integer.
   b. The variable pointed to by chAddr is a character.
   c. The variable pointed to by ptYr is a long integer.
   d. The variable pointed to by amt is a double-precision variable.
   e. The variable pointed to by z is an integer.
   f. The variable pointed to by qp is a single-precision variable.
   g. datePt is a pointer to an integer.
   h. yldAddr is a pointer to a double-precision variable.
   i. amtPt is a pointer to a single-precision variable.
   j. ptChr is a pointer to a character variable.

8. (**Review**) **a.** What are the variables yAddr, chAddr, ptYr, amt, z, qp, datePt, yldAddr, amtPt, and ptChr used in Exercise 7 called?

   b. Why are the variable names amt, z, and qp used in Exercise 7 not good choices for pointer names?

9. (**Practice**) Write English sentences that describe what's contained in the following declared variables:

a. char *keyAddr;

b. int *m;

c. double *yldAddr;

d. long *yPtr;

e. double *pCou;

f. int *ptDate;

10. (**Practice**) Which of the following is a declaration for a pointer?

a. long a;

b. char b;

c. char *c;

d. int x;

e. int *p;

f. double w;

g. float *k;

h. float l;

i. double *z;

11. (**Practice**) For the following declarations,

```
int *xPt, *yAddr;
long *dtAddr, *ptAddr;
double *ptZ;
int a;
long b;
double c;
```

determine which of the following statements is valid:

a. yAddr = &a;	b. yAddr = &b;	c. yAddr = &c;
d. yAddr = a;	e. yAddr = b;	f. yAddr = c;
g. dtAddr = &a;	h. dtAddr = &b;	i. dtAddr = &c;
j. dtAddr = a;	k. dtAddr = b;	l. dtAddr = c;
m. ptZ = &a;	n. ptAddr = &b;	o. ptAddr = &c;
p. ptAddr = a;	q. ptAddr = b;	r. ptAddr = c;
s. yAddr = xPt;	t. yAddr = dtAddr;	u. yAddr = ptAddr;

12. (**Practice**) For the variables and addresses in Figure 8.10, fill in the data determined by the following statements:

a. ptNum = &m;

b. amtAddr = &amt;

c. *zAddr = 25;

d. k = *numAddr;

e. ptDay = zAddr;

f. *ptYr = 2011;

g. *amtAddr = *numAddr;

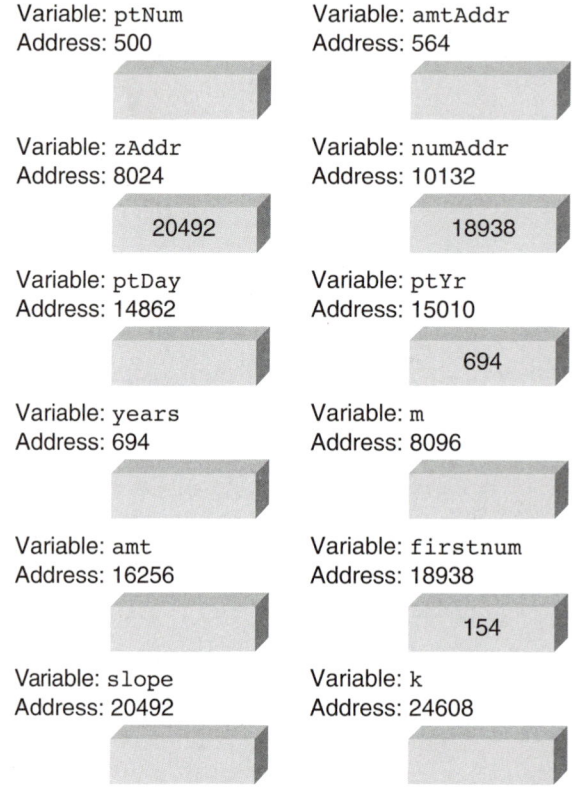

Figure 8.10   Memory locations for Exercise 12

8.2 Array Names as Pointers

Although pointers are simply, by definition, variables used to store addresses, there's also a direct and close relationship between array names and pointers. This section describes this relationship in detail. Figure 8.11 illustrates the storage of a one-dimensional array named `grade`, which contains five integers. Each integer requires 4 bytes of storage.

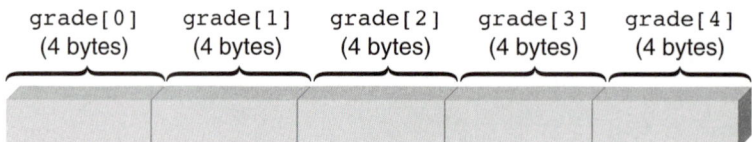

Figure 8.11   The `grade` array in storage

Using subscripts, the fourth element in the `grade` array is referred to as `grade[3]`. The use of a subscript, however, conceals the computer's extensive use of addresses. Internally, the computer immediately uses the subscript to calculate the array element's address, based on both the array's starting address and the amount of storage each element uses. Calling the fourth element `grade[3]` forces the compiler to make this address computation:

```
&grade[3] = &grade[0] + (3 * sizeof(int))
```

Remembering that the address operator (`&`) means "the address of," this statement is read as "the address of `grade[3]` equals the address of `grade[0]` plus 3 times the size of an integer (which is 12 bytes)." Figure 8.12 shows the address computation used to locate `grade[3]`.

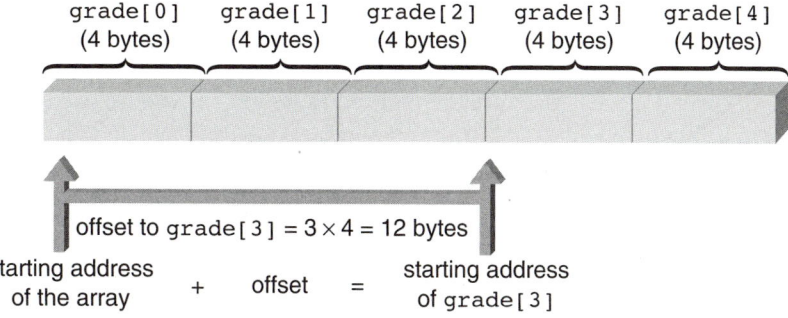

Figure 8.12   Using a subscript to obtain an address

Because a pointer is a variable used to store an address, you can create a pointer to store the address of the first element of an array. Doing so allows you to mimic the computer's operation in accessing array elements. Before you do this, take a look at Program 8.5.

 ## Program 8.5

```cpp
#include <iostream>
using namespace std;

int main()
{
  const int ARRAYSIZE = 5;

  int i, grade[ARRAYSIZE] = {98, 87, 92, 79, 85};

  for (i = 0; i < ARRAYSIZE; i++)
    cout << "\nElement " << i << " is " << grade[i];

  cout << endl;

  return 0;
}
```

When Program 8.5 runs, it produces the following display:

```
Element 0 is 98
Element 1 is 87
Element 2 is 92
Element 3 is 79
Element 4 is 85
```

Program 8.5 displays the values of the `grade` array by using standard subscript notation. By storing the address of array element 0 in a pointer first, you can use the address in the pointer to access each array element. For example, if you store the address of `grade[0]` in a pointer named `gPtr` by using the assignment statement `gPtr = &grade[0];`, the expression `*gPtr` (which means "the variable pointed to by `gPtr`") can be used to access `grade[0]`, as shown in Figure 8.13.

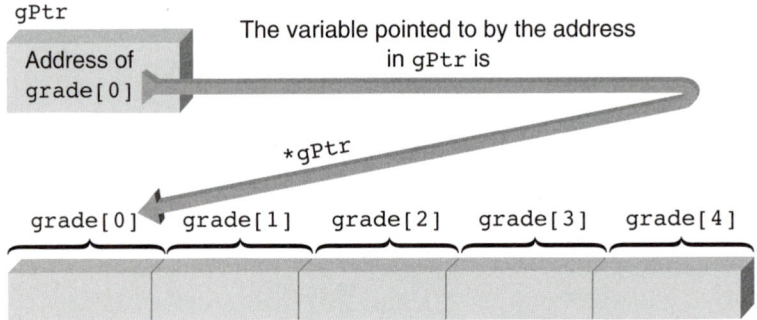

Figure 8.13   The variable pointed to by `*gPtr` is `grade[0]`

One unique feature of pointers is that offsets can be included in expressions using pointers. For example, the 1 in the expression `*(gPtr + 1)` is an **offset**. The complete expression references the integer that's one beyond the variable pointed to by `gPtr`. Similarly, as illustrated in Figure 8.14, the expression `*(gPtr + 3)` references the variable that's three integers beyond the variable pointed to by `gPtr`: the variable `grade[3]`.

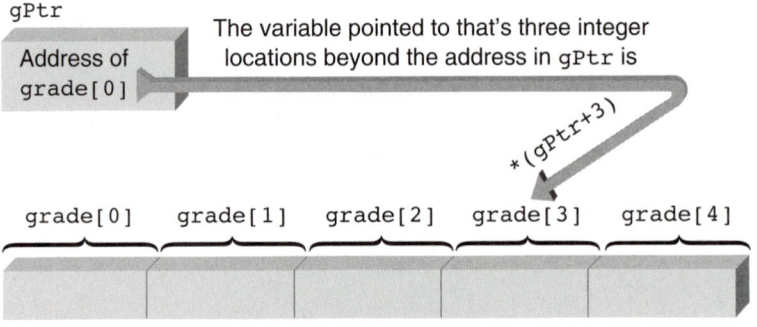

Figure 8.14   An offset of 3 from the address in `gPtr`

Table 8.1 shows the correspondence between elements referenced by subscripts and by pointers and offsets. Figure 8.15 illustrates the relationships listed in this table.

Table 8.1 Array Elements Can Be Referenced in Two Ways

Array Element	Subscript Notation	Pointer Notation
Element 0	grade[0]	*gPtr or (gPtr + 0)
Element 1	grade[1]	*(gPtr + 1)
Element 2	grade[2]	*(gPtr + 2)
Element 3	grade[3]	*(gPtr + 3)
Element 4	grade[4]	*(gPtr + 4)

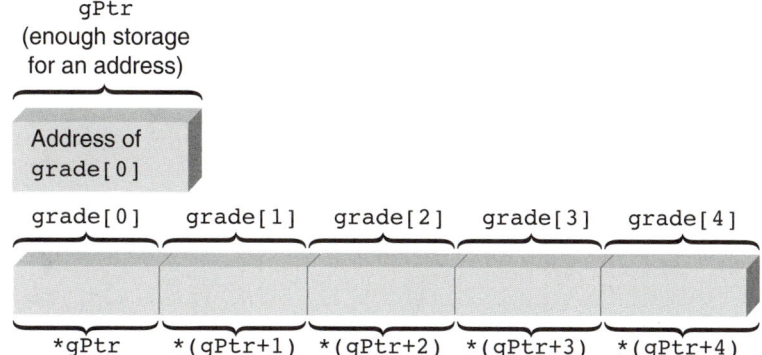

Figure 8.15 The relationship between array elements and pointers

Using the correspondence between pointers and subscripts shown in Figure 8.15, the array elements accessed in Program 8.5 with subscripts can now be accessed with pointers, which is done in Program 8.6.

The following display is produced when Program 8.6 runs:

```
Element 0 is 98
Element 1 is 87
Element 2 is 92
Element 3 is 79
Element 4 is 85
```

Program 8.6

```cpp
#include <iostream>
using namespace std;

int main()
{

   const int ARRAYSIZE = 5;

   int *gPtr;              // declare a pointer to an int
   int i, grade[ARRAYSIZE] = {98, 87, 92, 79, 85};

   gPtr = &grade[0];       // store the starting array address
   for (i = 0; i < ARRAYSIZE; i++)
     cout << "\nElement " << i << " is " << *(gPtr + i);

   cout << endl;

   return 0;
}
```

Notice that this display is the same as Program 8.5's display. The method used in Program 8.6 to access array elements simulates how the compiler references array elements internally. The compiler automatically converts any subscript a programmer uses to an equivalent pointer expression. In this case, because the declaration of gPtr includes the information that integers are pointed to, any offset added to the address in gPtr is scaled automatically by the size of an integer. Therefore, *(gPtr + 3), for example, refers to the address of grade[0] plus an offset of 12 bytes (3 * 4), assuming sizeof(int) = 4. This result is the address of grade[3] shown in Figure 8.15.

The parentheses in the expression *(gPtr + 3) are necessary to reference an array element correctly. Omitting the parentheses results in the expression *gPtr + 3. Because of operator precedence, this expression adds 3 to "the variable pointed to by gPtr." Because gPtr points to grade[0], this expression adds the value of grade[0] and 3 together. Note also that the expression *(gPtr + 3) doesn't change the address stored in gPtr. After the computer uses the offset to locate the correct variable from the starting address in gPtr, the offset is discarded and the address in gPtr remains unchanged.

Although the pointer gPtr used in Program 8.6 was created specifically to store the grade array's starting address, doing so is unnecessary. When an array is created, the compiler creates an internal pointer constant for it automatically and stores the array's starting address in this pointer. In almost all respects, a pointer constant is identical to a programmer-created pointer variable, but as you'll see, there are some differences.

For each array created, the array name becomes the name of the pointer constant the compiler creates for the array, and the starting address of the first location reserved for the array is stored in this pointer. Therefore, declaring the `grade` array in Programs 8.4 and 8.5 actually reserves enough storage for five integers, creates an internal pointer named `grade`, and stores the address of `grade[0]` in the pointer, as shown in Figure 8.16.

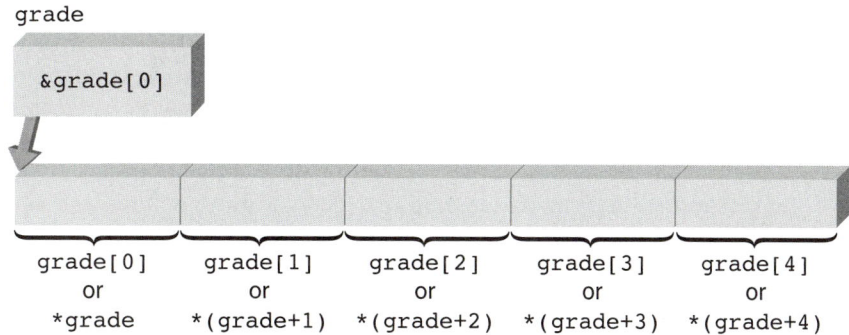

Figure 8.16 Creating an array also creates a pointer

The implication is that every access to `grade` made with a subscript can be replaced by an access using the array name, `grade`, as a pointer. Therefore, wherever the expression `grade[i]` is used, the expression `*(grade + i)` can also be used. This equivalence is shown in Program 8.7, where `grade` is used as a pointer to access all its elements. It produces the same output as Programs 8.5 and 8.6. However, using `grade` as a pointer makes it unnecessary to declare and initialize the pointer `gPtr` used in Program 8.6.

Program 8.7

```
#include <iostream>
using namespace std;

int main()
{
  const int ARRAYSIZE = 5;

  int i, grade[ARRAYSIZE] = {98, 87, 92, 79, 85};

  for (i = 0; i < ARRAYSIZE; i++)
    cout << "\nElement " << i << " is " << *(grade + i);
  cout << endl;

  return 0;
}
```

In most respects, an array name and a pointer can be used interchangeably. A true pointer, however, is a variable, and the address stored in it *can* be changed. An *array name is a pointer constant*, and the address stored in the pointer *can't* be changed by an assignment statement. Therefore, a statement such as grade = &grade[2]; is invalid. This should come as no surprise. Because the purpose of an array name is to locate the beginning of the array correctly, allowing a programmer to change the address stored in the array name defeats this purpose and leads to havoc when array elements are accessed. Also, expressions taking the address of an array name are invalid because the pointer the compiler creates is internal to the computer, not stored in memory, as pointer variables are. Therefore, trying to store the address of grade by using the expression &grade results in a compiler error.

An interesting sidelight of accessing array elements with pointers is that any pointer access can always be replaced with a subscript reference, even if the pointer "points to" a scalar variable. For example, if numPtr is declared as a pointer variable, the expression *(numPtr + i) can also be written as numPtr[i], even though numPtr isn't created as an array. As before, when the compiler encounters the subscript notation, it replaces it internally with the equivalent pointer notation.

Dynamic Array Allocation[6]

As each variable is defined in a program, it's assigned sufficient storage from a pool of computer memory locations made available to the compiler. After memory locations have been reserved for a variable, these locations are fixed for the life of that variable, whether they're used or not. For example, if a function requests storage for an array of 500 integers, the storage is allocated and fixed from the point of the array's definition. If the application requires fewer than 500 integers, the unused allocated storage isn't released back to the system until the array goes out of existence. If, on the other hand, the application requires more than 500 integers, the integer array's size must be increased and the function defining the array must be recompiled.

An alternative to this fixed or static allocation of memory storage locations is **dynamic allocation** of memory. Under a dynamic allocation scheme, the amount of storage to be allocated is determined and adjusted at runtime rather than compile time. Dynamic allocation of memory is useful when dealing with lists because it allows expanding the list as new items are added and contracting the list as items are deleted. For example, in constructing a list of grades, you don't need to know the exact number of grades. Instead of creating a fixed array to store grades, having a mechanism for enlarging and shrinking the array as needed is useful. Table 8.2 describes two C++ operators, new and delete, that provide this capability. (These operators require the new header file.)

---

[6]This topic can be omitted on first reading with no loss of subject continuity.

Table 8.2 The `new` and `delete` Operators (Require the `new` Header File)

Operator Name	Description
`new`	Reserves the number of bytes requested by the declaration. Returns the address of the first reserved location or `NULL` if not enough memory is available.
`delete`	Releases a block of bytes reserved previously. The address of the first reserved location must be passed as an argument to the operator.

Dynamic storage requests for scalar variables or arrays are made as part of a declaration or an assignment statement.[7] For example, the declaration statement `int *num = new int;` reserves an area large enough to hold one integer and places this storage area's address in the pointer num. This same dynamic allocation can be made by first declaring the pointer with the declaration statement `int *num;` and then assigning the pointer an address with the assignment statement `num = new int;`. In either case, the allocated storage comes from the computer's free storage area.[8]

Dynamic allocation of arrays is similar but more useful. For example, the declaration

```
int *grades = new int[200];
```

reserves an area large enough to store 200 integers and places the first integer's address in the pointer grades. Although the constant 200 has been used in this declaration, a variable dimension can be used. For example, take a look at this sequence of instructions:

```
cout << "Enter the number of grades to be processed: ";
cin  >> numgrades;
int *grades = new int[numgrades];
```

In this sequence, the actual size of the array that's created depends on the number the user inputs. Because pointer and array names are related, each value in the newly created storage area can be accessed by using standard array notation, such as `grades[i]`, instead of the pointer notation `*(grades + i)`. Program 8.8 shows this sequence of code in the context of a complete program.

---

[7]Note that the compiler provides dynamic allocation and deallocation from the stack for all `auto` variables automatically.

[8]A computer's free storage area is formally called the **heap**. It consists of unallocated memory that can be allocated to a program, as requested, while the program is running.

Program 8.8

```cpp
#include <iostream>
#include <new>
using namespace std;

int main()
{
  int numgrades, i;

  cout << "Enter the number of grades to be processed: ";
  cin  >> numgrades;

  int *grades = new int[numgrades];  // create the array

  for(i = 0; i < numgrades; i++)
  {
    cout << "  Enter a grade: ";
    cin  >> grades[i];
  }
  cout << "\nAn array was created for " << numgrades << " integers\n";
  cout << " The values stored in the array are:";
  for (i = 0; i < numgrades; i++)
    cout << "\n    " << grades[i];
  cout << endl;

  delete[] grades;    // return the storage to the heap
                      // the [] is required for array deletions
  return 0;
}
```

Notice in Program 8.8 that the `delete` operator is used with braces where the new operator was used previously to create an array. The `delete[]` statement restores the allocated block of storage back to the free storage area (the heap) while the program is running.[9] The only address `delete` requires is the starting address of the dynamically allocated storage block. Therefore, any address returned by `new` can be used subsequently by `delete` to restore reserved memory back to the computer. The `delete` operator doesn't alter the address passed

---

[9]The operating system should return allocated storage to the heap automatically when the program has finished running. Because this return doesn't always happen, however, it's crucial to restore dynamically allocated memory explicitly to the heap when the storage is no longer needed. The term **memory leak** is used to describe the condition that occurs when dynamically allocated memory isn't returned explicitly by using the `delete` operator and the operating system doesn't reclaim previously allocated memory.

to it, but simply removes the storage the address references. Following is a sample run of Program 8.8:

```
Enter the number of grades to be processed: 4
   Enter a grade: 85
   Enter a grade: 96
   Enter a grade: 77
   Enter a grade: 92

An array was created for 4 integers
 The values stored in the array are:
   85
   96
   77
   92
```

EXERCISES 8.2

1. **(Practice)** Replace each of the following references to a subscripted variable with a pointer reference:

   a. prices[5]   **b.** grades[2]   **c.** yield[10]
   d. dist[9]   **e.** mile[0]   **f.** temp[20]
   g. celsius[16]   **h.** num[50]   **i.** time[12]

2. **(Practice)** Replace each of the following pointer references with a subscript reference:

   a. *(message + 6)   **b.** *amount   **c.** *(yrs + 10)
   d. *(stocks + 2)   **e.** *(rates + 15) **f.** *(codes + 19)

3. **(Practice) a.** List three things the declaration statement double prices[5]; causes the compiler to do.

   b. If each double-precision number uses 8 bytes of storage, how much storage is set aside for the prices array?

   c. Draw a diagram similar to Figure 8.16 for the prices array.

   d. Determine the byte offset in relation to the start of the prices array, corresponding to the offset in the expression *(prices + 3).

4. **(Practice) a.** Write a declaration to store the string "This is a sample" in an array named samtest. Include the declaration in a program that displays the values in samtest by using a for loop that uses a pointer access to each element in the array.

   b. Modify the program written in Exercise 4a to display only array elements 10 through 15 (the letters s, a, m, p, l, and e).

5. **(Practice)** Write a declaration to store the following values in an array named `rates`: 12.9, 18.6, 11.4, 13.7, 9.5, 15.2, and 17.6. Include the declaration in a program that displays the values in the array by using pointer notation.

6. **(Modify) a.** Repeat Exercise 6a in Section 7.1, but use pointer references to access all array elements.

   b. Repeat Exercise 6b in Section 7.1, but use pointer references to access all array elements.

7. **(Modify)** Repeat Exercise 7 in Section 7.1, but use pointer references to access all array elements.

8. **(Modify)** As described in Table 8.2, the `new` operator returns the address of the first new storage area allocated or returns `NULL` if there's insufficient storage. Modify Program 8.8 to check that a valid address has been returned before attempting to place values in the `grades` array. Display an appropriate message if not enough storage is available.

8.3 Pointer Arithmetic

Pointer variables, like all variables, contain values. The value stored in a pointer is, of course, an address. Therefore, by adding and subtracting numbers to pointers, you can obtain different addresses. Additionally, the addresses in pointers can be compared by using any of the relational operators (`==`, `!=`, `<`, `>`, and so forth) that are valid for comparing other variables. When performing arithmetic on pointers, you must be careful to produce addresses that point to something meaningful. In comparing pointers, you must also make comparisons that make sense. Take a look at these declarations:

```
int nums[100];
int *nPt;
```

To set the address of `nums[0]` in `nPt`, either of these assignment statements can be used:

```
nPt = &nums[0];
nPt = nums;
```

Both assignment statements produce the same result because `nums` is a pointer constant containing the address of the first location in the array: the address of `nums[0]`. Figure 8.17 illustrates the memory allocation resulting from the previous declaration and assignment statements, assuming each integer requires 4 bytes of memory, and the location of the beginning of the `nums` array is address 18934.

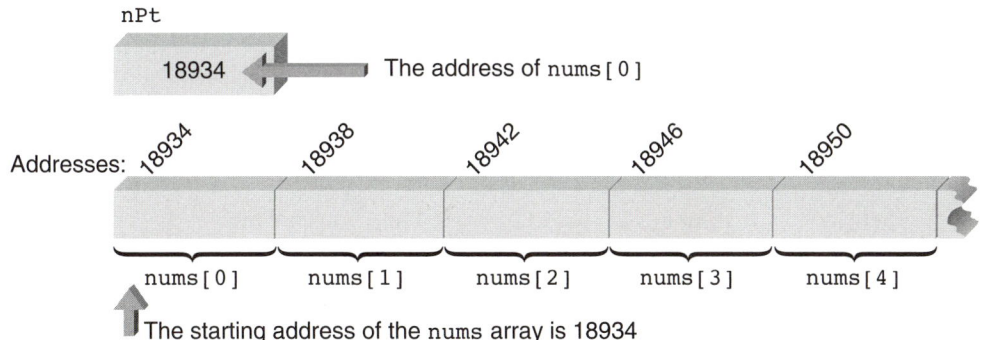

nPt

18934 ◄ ───── The address of nums[0]

Addresses: 18934   18938   18942   18946   18950

nums[0]   nums[1]   nums[2]   nums[3]   nums[4]

↑ The starting address of the nums array is 18934

Figure 8.17   The nums array in memory

After nPt contains a valid address, values can be added and subtracted from the address to produce new addresses. When adding or subtracting numbers to pointers, the computer adjusts the number automatically to ensure that the result still "points to" a value of the correct type. For example, the statement nPt = nPt + 4; forces the computer to scale the 4 by the correct number to make sure the resulting address is the address of an integer. Assuming each integer requires 4 bytes of storage, as shown in Figure 8.17, the computer multiplies the 4 by 4 and adds 16 to the address in nPt. The resulting address is 18950, which is the correct address of nums[4].

The computer's automatic scaling ensures that the expression nPt + i, where i is any positive integer, points to the ith element beyond the one currently pointed to by nPt. Therefore, if nPt initially contains the address of nums[0], nPt + 4 is the address of nums[4], nPt + 50 is the address of nums[50], and nPt + i is the address of nums[i]. Although actual addresses are used in Figure 8.17 to illustrate the scaling process, programmers don't need to be concerned with the actual addresses the computer uses. Manipulating addresses with pointers generally doesn't require knowledge of the actual addresses.

Addresses can also be incremented or decremented with the prefix and postfix increment and decrement operators. Adding 1 to a pointer causes the pointer to point to the next element of the type being pointed to. Decrementing a pointer causes the pointer to point to the previous element. For example, if the pointer variable p is a pointer to an integer, the expression p++ increments the address in the pointer to point to the next integer, as shown in Figure 8.18.

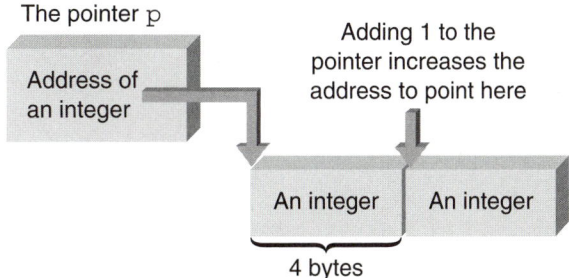

The pointer p   Adding 1 to the
                                       pointer increases the
Address of   address to point here
an integer

                        An integer   An integer

                              4 bytes

Figure 8.18   Increments are scaled when used with pointers

In reviewing Figure 8.18, notice that the increment added to the pointer is scaled to account for the fact that the pointer is used to point to integers. It is, of course, up to the programmer to make sure the correct type of data is stored in the new address contained in the pointer.

The increment and decrement operators can be applied as both prefix and postfix pointer operators. All the following combinations using pointers are valid:

```
*ptNum++    // use the pointer and then increment it
*++ptNum    // increment the pointer before using it
*ptNum--    // use the pointer and then decrement it
*--ptNum    // decrement the pointer before using it
```

Of these four possible forms, the most commonly used is *ptNum++ because it allows accessing each array element as the address is "marched along" from the array's starting address to the address of the last array element. Program 8.9 shows this use of the increment operator. In this program, each element in the nums array is retrieved by successively incrementing the address in nPt.

Program 8.9

```cpp
#include <iostream>
using namespace std;

int main()
{
  const int VALUES = 5;

  int nums[VALUES] = {16, 54, 7, 43, -5};
  int i, total = 0, *nPt;

  nPt = nums;     // store address of nums[0] in nPt
  for (i = 0; i < VALUES; i++)
    total = total + *nPt++;

  cout << "The total of the array elements is " << total << endl;

  return 0;
}
```

Program 8.9 produces the following output:

```
The total of the array elements is 115
```

The expression total = total + *nPt++ in Program 8.9 accumulates the values pointed to by the nPt pointer. In this expression, the *nPt part causes the computer to retrieve the integer pointed to by nPt. Next, the postfix increment, ++, adds 1 to the address in nPt so that nPt then contains the address of the next array element. The computer, of course, scales the increment so that the actual address in nPt is the correct address of the next element.

Pointers can also be compared, which is particularly useful when dealing with pointers that point to elements in the same array. For example, instead of using a counter in a for loop to access each array element, the address in a pointer can be compared to the array's starting and ending addresses. The expression

```
nPt <= &nums[4]
```

is true (non-zero) as long as the address in nPt is less than or equal to the address of nums[4]. Because nums is a pointer constant containing the address of nums[0], the term &nums[4] can be replaced by the equivalent term nums + 4. Using either form, Program 8.9 can be rewritten in Program 8.10 to continue adding array elements while the address in nPt is less than or equal to the address of the last array element.

Program 8.10

```cpp
#include <iostream>
using namespace std;

int main()
{
  const int VALUES = 5;

  int nums[VALUES] = {16, 54, 7, 43, -5};
  int total = 0, *nPt;

  nPt = nums;     // store address of nums[0] in nPt
  while (nPt < nums + VALUES)
    total += *nPt++;

  cout << "The total of the array elements is " << total << endl;

  return 0;
}
```

In Program 8.10, the compact form of the accumulating expression total += *nPt++ was used in place of the longer form, total = total + *nPt++. Also, the expression nums + 4 doesn't change the address in nums. Because nums is an array name, not a pointer variable, its value can't be changed. The expression nums + 4 first retrieves the address in nums, adds 4 to this address (scaled appropriately), and uses the result for comparison purposes. Expressions such as *nums++, which attempt to change the address, are invalid. Expressions such as *nums or *(nums + i), which use the address without attempting to alter it, are valid.

Pointer Initialization

Like all variables, pointers can be initialized when they're declared. When initializing pointers, however, you must be careful to set an address in the pointer. For example, an initialization such as

```
int *ptNum = &miles;
```

is valid only if `miles` is declared as an integer variable before `ptNum` is. This statement creates a pointer to an integer and sets the address in the pointer to the address of an integer variable. If the variable `miles` is declared after `ptNum` is declared, as follows, an error occurs:

```
int *ptNum = &miles;
int miles;
```

The error occurs because the address of `miles` is used before `miles` has even been defined. Because the storage area reserved for `miles` hasn't been allocated when `ptNum` is declared, the address of `miles` doesn't exist yet.

Pointers to arrays can also be initialized in their declaration statements. For example, if `prices` has been declared as an array of double-precision numbers, either of the following declarations can be used to initialize the pointer `zing` to the address of the first element in `prices`:

```
double *zing = &prices[0];
double *zing = prices;
```

The last initialization is correct because `prices` is a pointer constant containing an address of the correct type. (The variable name `zing` was selected in this example to reinforce the idea that any variable name can be selected for a pointer.)

EXERCISES 8.3

1. **(Modify)** Replace the `while` statement in Program 8.10 with a `for` statement.

2. **(Program) a.** Write a program that stores the following numbers in an array named `rates`: 6.25, 6.50, 6.8, 7.2, 7.35, 7.5, 7.65, 7.8, 8.2, 8.4, 8.6, 8.8, and 9.0. Display the values in the array by changing the address in a pointer called `dispPt`. Use a `for` statement in your program.
   b. Modify the program written in Exercise 2a to use a `while` statement.

3. **(Program) a.** Write a program that stores the string `Hooray for All of Us` in an array named `strng`. Use the declaration `strng[] = "Hooray for All of Us";`, which ensures that the end-of-string escape sequence `\0` is included in the array. Display the characters in the array by changing the address in a pointer called `messPt`. Use a `for` statement in your program.
   b. Modify the program written in Exercise 3a to use the `while` statement while (`*messPt++ != '\0'`).
   c. Modify the program written in Exercise 3a to start the display with the word `All`.

4. **(Program)** Write a program that stores the following numbers in the array named `miles`: 15, 22, 16, 18, 27, 23, and 20. Have your program copy the data stored in `miles` to another array named `dist`, and then display the values in the `dist` array. Your program should use pointer notation when copying and displaying array elements.

5. **(Program)** Write a C++ program that stores the following letters in the array named `message`: `This is a test`. Have your program copy the data stored in `message` to another array named `mess2` and then display the letters in the `mess2` array.

6. **(Program)** Write a program that declares three one-dimensional arrays named `miles`, `gallons`, and `mpg`. Each array should be capable of holding 10 elements. In the `miles` array, store the numbers 240.5, 300.0, 189.6, 310.6, 280.7, 216.9, 199.4, 160.3, 177.4, and 192.3. In the `gallons` array, store the numbers 10.3, 15.6, 8.7, 14, 16.3, 15.7, 14.9, 10.7, 8.3, and 8.4. Each element of the `mpg` array should be calculated as the corresponding element of the `miles` array divided by the equivalent element of the `gallons` array: for example, `mpg[0] = miles[0] / gallons[0]`. Use pointers when calculating and displaying the elements of the `mpg` array.

8.4 Passing Addresses

In Section 6.3, you saw one method of passing addresses to a function: using reference parameters. Passing a reference to a function is an implied use of an address because the reference does provides the function with an address. Unfortunately, the actual call statement doesn't reveal what's being passed—it could be an address or a value. For example, the function call `swap(num1,num2);` doesn't reveal whether `num1` or `num2` is a reference (an address) or a value. Only by looking at the declarations for the variables `num1` and `num2`, or by examining the function header for `swap()`, can you determine the data types of `num1` and `num2`. If they have been defined as reference variables, an address is passed; otherwise, the value stored in the variables is passed.

In contrast to passing addresses implicitly with references, addresses can be passed explicitly with pointers. To pass an address to a function explicitly, all you need to do is place the address operator, `&`, in front of the variable being passed. For example, this function call

```
swap(&firstnum, &secnum);
```

passes the addresses of the variables `firstnum` and `secnum` to `swap()`, as shown in Figure 8.19. This function call also clearly indicates that addresses are being passed to the function.

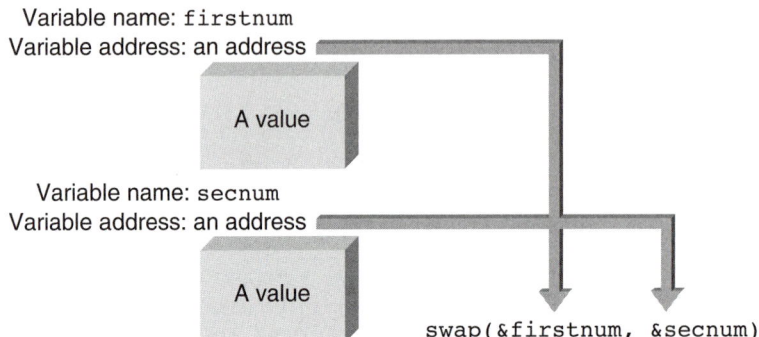

Figure 8.19   Explicitly passing addresses to swap()

Passing an address with a reference parameter or the address operator is referred to as a **pass by reference** because the called function can reference, or access, variables in the calling function by using the passed addresses. As you saw in Section 6.3, pass by references can be made with reference parameters. In this section, you see how addresses passed with the address operator are used. Specifically, you use the addresses of the variables firstnum and secnum passed to swap() to exchange their values—a procedure done previously in Program 6.8 with reference parameters.

One of the first requirements in writing swap() is to construct a function header that receives and stores the passed values, which in this case are two addresses. As you saw in Section 8.1, addresses are stored in pointers, which means the parameters of swap() must be declared as pointers.

Assuming firstnum and secnum are double-precision variables and swap() returns no value, a suitable function header for swap() is as follows:

```
void swap(double *nm1Addr, double *nm2Addr);
```

The choice of the parameter names nm1Addr and nm2Addr is, as with all parameter names, up to the programmer. The declaration double *nm1Addr, however, states that the parameter named nm1Addr is used to store the address of a double-precision value. Similarly, the declaration double *nm2Addr specifies that nm2Addr also stores the address of a double-precision value.

Before writing the body of swap() to exchange the values in firstnum and secnum, it's useful to verify that the values accessed by using the addresses in nm1Addr and nm2Addr are correct. Program 8.11 performs this check.

The output displayed when Program 8.11 runs is as follows:

```
The number whose address is in nm1Addr is 20.5
The number whose address is in nm2Addr is 6.25
```

 **Program 8.11**

```cpp
#include <iostream>
using namespace std;

void swap(double *, double *);    // function prototype
int main()
{
  double firstnum = 20.5, secnum = 6.25;

  swap(&firstnum, &secnum);     // call swap
  return 0;
}

// this function illustrates passing pointer arguments
void swap(double *nm1Addr, double *nm2Addr)
{

  cout << "The number whose address is in nm1Addr is "
       << *nm1Addr << endl;
  cout << "The number whose address is in nm2Addr is "
       << *nm2Addr << endl;
  return;
}
```

In reviewing Program 8.11, note two things. First, the function prototype for `swap()`

```cpp
void swap(double *, double *)
```

declares that `swap()` returns no value directly, and its parameters are two pointers that "point to" double-precision values. When the function is called, it requires that two addresses be passed, and each address is the address of a double-precision value.

Second, the indirection operator is used in `swap()` to access the values stored in `firstnum` and `secnum`. The `swap()` function has no knowledge of these variable names, but it does have the address of `firstnum` stored in `nm1Addr` and the address of `secnum` stored in `nm2Addr`. The expression `*nm1Addr` in the first `cout` statement means "the variable whose address is in `nm1Addr`." It is, of course, the `firstnum` variable. Similarly, the second `cout` statement obtains the value stored in `secnum` as "the variable whose address is in `nm2Addr`." As the output shows, pointers have been used successfully to allow `swap()` to access variables in `main()`. Figure 8.20 illustrates storing addresses in parameters.

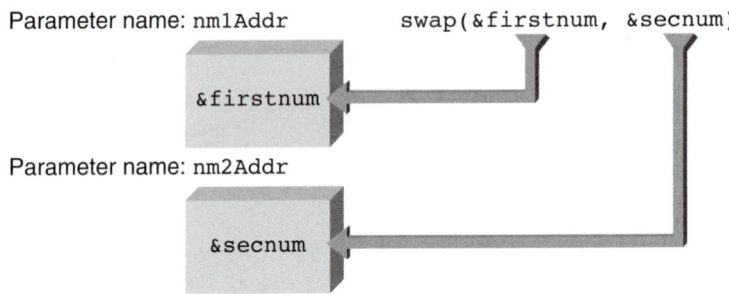

Figure 8.20   Storing addresses in parameters

Having verified that `swap()` can access `main()`'s local variables `firstnum` and `secnum`, you can now expand `swap()` to exchange the values in these variables. The values in `main()`'s variables `firstnum` and `secnum` can be interchanged from within `swap()` by using the three-step interchange algorithm described in Section 6.3:

1. Store `firstnum`'s value in a temporary location.
2. Store `secnum`'s value in `firstnum`.
3. Store the temporary value in `secnum`.

Using pointers in `swap()`, this algorithm takes the following form:

1. Store the value of the variable that `nm1Addr` points to in a temporary location by using the statement `temp = *nm1Addr;` (see Figure 8.21).

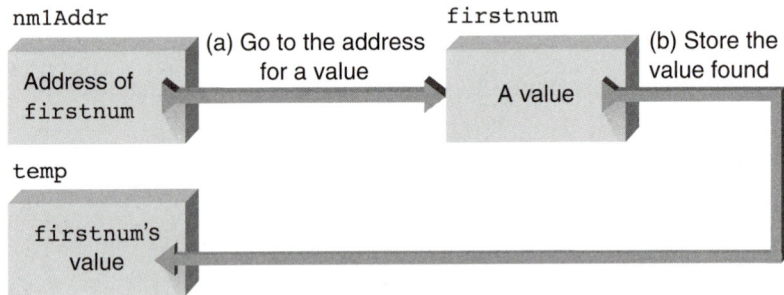

Figure 8.21   Indirectly storing `firstnum`'s value

2. Store the value of the variable whose address is in `nm2Addr` in the variable whose address is in `nm1Addr` with the statement `*nm1Addr = *nm2Addr;` (see Figure 8.22).

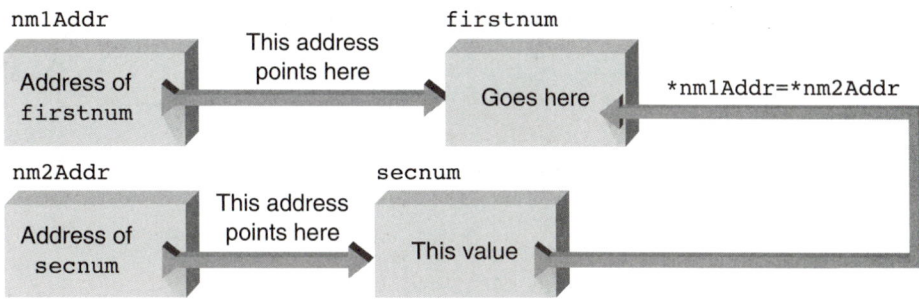

Figure 8.22 Indirectly changing `firstnum`'s value

3. Move the value in the temporary location into the variable whose address is in nm2Addr by using the statement `*nm2Addr = temp;` (see Figure 8.23).

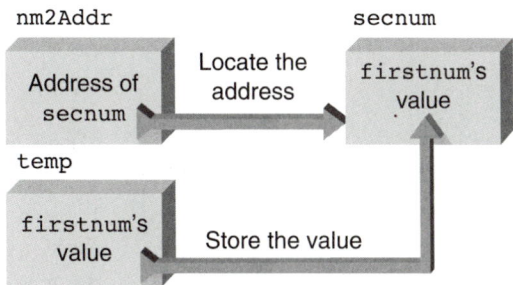

Figure 8.23 Indirectly changing `secnum`'s value

Program 8.12 contains the final form of `swap()`, written according to this description. A sample run of Program 8.12 produced this output:

```
The value stored in firstnum is: 20.5
The value stored in secnum is: 6.25

The value stored in firstnum is now: 6.25
The value stored in secnum is now: 20.5
```

Program 8.12

```cpp
#include <iostream>
using namespace std;

void swap(double *, double *);    // function prototype
int main()
{
  double firstnum = 20.5, secnum = 6.25;

  cout << "The value stored in firstnum is: " << firstnum << endl;
  cout << "The value stored in secnum is: " << secnum << "\n\n";

  swap(&firstnum, &secnum);          // call swap

  cout << "The value stored in firstnum is now: "
       << firstnum <<  endl;
  cout << "The value stored in secnum is now: "
       << secnum << endl;
  return 0;
}

// this function swaps the values in its two arguments
void swap(double *nm1Addr, double *nm2Addr)
{
  double temp;

  temp = *nm1Addr;       // save firstnum's value
  *nm1Addr = *nm2Addr;   // move secnum's value into firstnum
  *nm2Addr = temp;       // change secnum's value
  return;
}
```

As the program output shows, the values stored in main()'s variables have been modified in swap(), which was made possible by using pointers. To make sure you understand, you could compare this version of swap() with the version using references in Program 6.10. The advantage of using pointers rather than references is that the function call specifies that addresses are being used, which is an alert that the function will most likely alter variables of the calling function. The advantage of using references is that the notation is much simpler. Generally, for functions such as swap(), ease of notation wins out, and references are used. In passing arrays to functions, however, which is the next topic, the compiler passes an address automatically, which dictates using pointers to store the address.

Passing Arrays

When an array is passed to a function, its address is the only item actually passed. "Address" means the address of the first location used to store the array, as shown in Figure 8.24. Because the first location reserved for an array corresponds to element 0 of the array, the "address of the array" is also the address of element 0.

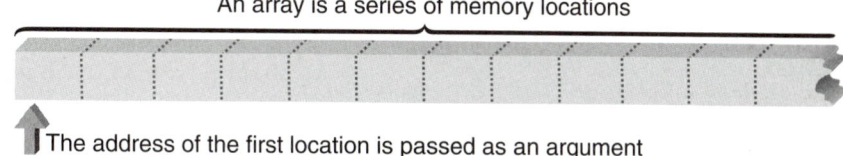

An array is a series of memory locations

The address of the first location is passed as an argument

Figure 8.24 An array's address is the address of the first location reserved for the array

For a specific example of passing an array to a function, examine Program 8.13. In this program, the nums array is passed to the `findMax()` function, using conventional array notation.

Program 8.13

```
#include <iostream>
using namespace std;

int findMax(int [], int);    // function prototype
int main()
{
  const int NUMPTS = 5;

  int nums[NUMPTS] = {2, 18, 1, 27, 16};

  cout << "\nThe maximum value is "
       << findMax(nums,NUMPTS) << endl;
  return 0;
}

// this function returns the maximum value in an array of ints
int findMax(int vals[], int numels)
{
  int i, max = vals[0];

  for (i = 1; i < numels; i++)
   if (max < vals[i])
     max = vals[i];
  return max;
}
```

The following output is displayed when Program 8.13 runs:

```
The maximum value is 27
```

The parameter named `vals` in the function header declaration for `findMax()` actually receives the address of the nums array. Therefore, `vals` is really a pointer because pointers are variables (or parameters) used to store addresses. Because the address passed to `findMax()` is the address of an integer, the following function header for `findMax()` is also suitable:

```
int findMax(int *vals, int numels) // vals is declared as
                                   // a pointer to an integer
```

The declaration `int *vals` in the function header declares that `vals` is used to store an address of an integer. The address stored is, of course, the location of the beginning of an array. The following is a rewritten version of the `findMax()` function that uses the new pointer declaration for `vals` but retains the use of subscripts to refer to array elements:

```
int findMax(int *vals, int numels)   // find the maximum value
{
  int i, max = vals[0];

  for (i = 1; i < numels; i++)
   if (max < vals[i])
     max = vals[i];
  return max;
}
```

Regardless of how `vals` is declared in the function header or how it's used in the function body, it's truly a pointer variable. Therefore, the address in `vals` can be modified. This isn't true for the name nums, however. Because nums is the name of the originally created array, it's a pointer constant. As described in Section 8.2, this means the address in nums can't be changed, and the address of nums can't be taken. No such restrictions, however, apply to the pointer variable `vals`. Therefore, all the pointer arithmetic you learned in Section 8.3 can be applied to `vals`.

Following are two more versions of `findMax()`, both using pointers instead of subscripts. In the first version, you simply substitute pointer notation for subscript notation. In the second version, you use pointer arithmetic to change the address in the pointer. As stated, access to an array element with the subscript notation *arrayName*[i] can always be replaced by the pointer notation *(*arrayName* + i).

In the first modification to `findMax()`, you make use of this correspondence by simply replacing all references to `vals[i]` with the expression `*(vals + i)`:

```
int findMax(int *vals, int numels)    // find the maximum value
{
  int i, max = *vals;

  for (i = 1; i < numels; i++)
   if (max < *(vals + i) )
     max = *(vals + i);
  return max;
}
```

The second modification of `findMax()` makes use of being able to change the address stored in `vals`. After each array element is retrieved by using the address in `vals`, the address is incremented by 1 in the altering list of the `for` statement. The expression `max = *vals` previously used to set `max` to the value of `vals[0]` is replaced by the expression `max = *vals++`, which adjusts the address in `vals` to point to the second array element. The element this expression assigns to `max` is the array element `vals` points to before it's incremented. The postfix increment, ++, doesn't change the address in `vals` until after the address has been used to retrieve the first array element.

```
int findMax(int *vals, int numels)    // find the maximum value
{
  int i, max = *vals++;    // get the first element and increment it
  for (i = 1; i < numels; i++, vals++)
  {
    if (max < *vals)
      max = *vals;
  }
  return max;
}
```

Review this version of `findMax()`. Initially, the maximum value is set to "the thing pointed to by `vals`." Because `vals` initially contains the address of the first array element passed to `findMax()`, the value of this first element is stored in `max`. The address in `vals` is then incremented by 1. The 1 added to `vals` is scaled automatically by the number of bytes used to store integers. Therefore, after the increment, the address stored in `vals` is the address of the next array element, as shown in Figure 8.25. The value of this next element is compared with the maximum, and the address is again incremented, this time in the altering list of the `for` statement. This process continues until all array elements have been examined.

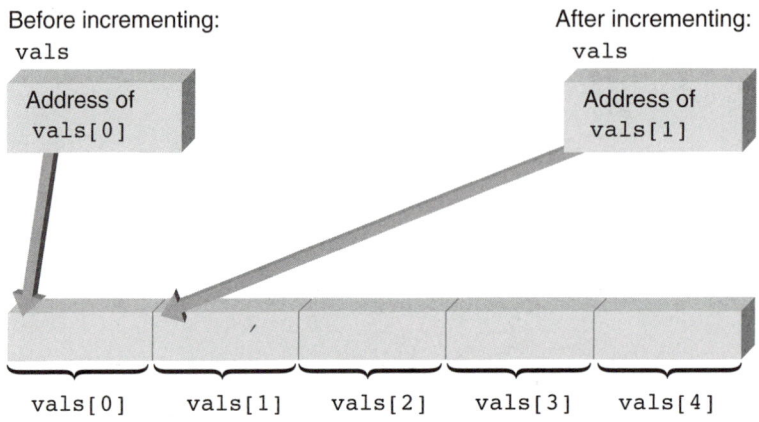

Figure 8.25 Pointing to different elements

The version of `findMax()` you choose is a matter of personal style. Generally, beginning programmers feel more at ease using subscripts rather than pointers. Also, if the program uses an array as the natural storage structure for the application and data, an array access using subscripts is more appropriate to indicate the program's intent clearly. However, as you learn more about data structures, pointers become an increasingly useful and powerful tool. In more complex data structures, there's no simple or easy equivalence for subscripts.

There's one more neat trick you can glean from this discussion. Because passing an array to a function actually involves passing an address, you can pass any valid address. For example, the function call `findMax(&nums[2],3)` passes the address of `nums[2]` to `findMax()`. In `findMax()`, the pointer `vals` stores the address, and the function starts the search for a maximum at the element corresponding to this address. Therefore, from `findMax()`'s perspective, it has received an address and proceeds appropriately.

Advanced Pointer Notation[10]

You can also access multidimensional arrays by using pointer notation, although the notation becomes more cryptic as the array dimensions increase. Pointer notation is especially useful with two-dimensional character arrays, and this section discusses pointer notation for two-dimensional numeric arrays. For example, examine this declaration:

```
int nums[2][3] = { {16,18,20},
                   {25,26,27} };
```

This declaration creates an array of elements and a set of pointer constants named `nums`, `nums[0]`, and `nums[1]`. Figure 8.26 shows the relationship between these pointer constants and the elements of the `nums` array.

---

[10]This topic can be omitted without loss of subject continuity.

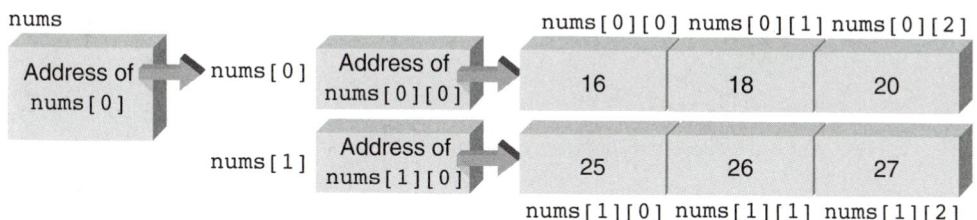

Figure 8.26   Storage of the `nums` array and associated pointer constants

The availability of the pointer constants associated with a two-dimensional array enables you to access array elements in a variety of ways. One way is to view a two-dimensional array as an array of rows, with each row as an array of three elements. From this viewpoint, the address of the first element in the first row is provided by `nums[0]`, and the address of the first element in the second row is provided by `nums[1]`. Therefore, the variable pointed to by `nums[0]` is `nums[0][0]`, and the variable pointed to by `nums[1]` is `nums[1][0]`. Each element in the array can be accessed by applying an offset to the correct pointer. Therefore, the following notations are equivalent:

Pointer Notation	Subscript Notation	Value
`*nums[0]`	`nums[0][0]`	16
`*(nums[0] + 1)`	`nums[0][1]`	18
`*(nums[0] + 2)`	`nums[0][2]`	20
`*nums[1]`	`nums[1][0]`	25
`*(nums[1] + 1)`	`nums[1][1]`	26
`*(nums[1] + 2)`	`nums[1][2]`	27

You can now go further and replace `nums[0]` and `nums[1]` with their pointer notations, using the address of `nums`. As shown in Figure 8.26, the variable pointed to by `nums` is `nums[0]`. That is, `*nums` is `nums[0]`. Similarly, `*(nums + 1)` is `nums[1]`. Using these relationships leads to the following equivalences:

Pointer Notation	Subscript Notation	Value
`*(*nums)`	`nums[0][0]`	16
`*(*nums + 1)`	`nums[0][1]`	18
`*(*nums + 2)`	`nums[0][2]`	20
`*(*(nums + 1))`	`nums[1][0]`	25
`*(*(nums + 1) + 1)`	`nums[1][1]`	26
`*(*(nums + 1) + 2)`	`nums[1][2]`	27

The same notation applies when a two-dimensional array is passed to a function. For example, the two-dimensional array `nums` is passed to the `calc()` function by using the call `calc(nums);`. As with all array passes, an address is passed. A suitable function header for the `calc()` function is as follows:

`void calc(int pt[2][3])`

As you have seen, the parameter declaration for `pt` can also be the following:

`void calc(int pt[][3])`

Using pointer notation, the following is another suitable declaration:

`void calc(int (*pt)[3])`

In this declaration, the inner parentheses are required to create a single pointer to arrays of three integers. Each array is, of course, equivalent to a single row of the `nums` array. By offsetting the pointer, each element in the array can be accessed. Notice that without the parentheses, the declaration becomes

`int *pt[3]`

which creates an array of three pointers, each one pointing to a single integer. After the correct declaration for `pt` is made (any of the three valid declarations can be used), all the following notations in the `calc()` function are equivalent:

Pointer Notation	Subscript Notation	Value
`*(*pt)`	`pt[0][0]`	16
`*(*pt+1)`	`pt[0][1]`	18
`*(*pt+2)`	`pt[0][2]`	20
`*(*(pt+1))`	`pt[1][0]`	25
`*(*(pt+1)+1)`	`pt[1][1]`	26
`*(*(pt+1)+2)`	`pt[1][2]`	27

The last two notations using pointers are seen in more advanced C++ programs. The first occurs because functions can return any valid C++ scalar data type, including pointers to any of these data types. If a function returns a pointer, the data type being pointed to must be declared in the function's declaration. For example, the declaration

`int *calc()`

declares that `calc()` returns a pointer to an integer value, which means the address of an integer variable is returned. Similarly, the declaration

`double *taxes()`

declares that `taxes()` returns a pointer to a double-precision value, which means the address of a double-precision variable is returned.

In addition to declaring pointers to integers, double-precision numbers, and C++'s other data types, you can declare pointers that point to (contain the address of) a function. Pointers to functions are possible because function names, like array names, are pointer constants. For example, the declaration

```
int (*calc)()
```

declares `calc` to be a pointer to a function that returns an integer. This means `calc` contains the address of a function, and the function whose address is in the variable `calc` returns an integer value. If, for example, the function `sum()` returns an integer, the assignment `calc = sum;` is valid.

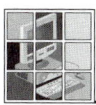

EXERCISES 8.4

1. **(Practice)** The following declaration was used to create the `prices` array:
   ```
   double prices[500];
   ```

   Write three different headers for a function named `sortArray()` that accepts the `prices` array as a parameter named `inArray` and returns no value.

2. **(Practice)** The following declaration was used to create the `keys` array:
   ```
   char keys[256];
   ```

   Write three different headers for a function named `findKey()` that accepts the `keys` array as a parameter named `select` and returns no value.

3. **(Practice)** The following declaration was used to create the `rates` array:
   ```
   double rates[256];
   ```

   Write three different headers for a function named `maximum()` that accepts the `rates` array as a parameter named `speed` and returns a double-precision value.

4. **(Modify)** Modify the `findMax()` function to locate the minimum value of the passed array. Write the function using only pointers.

5. **(Debug)** In the second version of `findMax()`, `vals` was incremented in the altering list of the `for` statement. Instead, you do the incrementing in the condition expression of the `if` statement, as follows:

```
int findMax(int *vals, int numels)     // incorrect version
{
  int i, max = *vals++;    // get the first element and increment

  for (i = 1; i < numels; i++)
    if (max < *vals++)
      max = *vals;
  return (max);
}
```

Determine why this version produces an incorrect result.

6. (**Program**) a. Write a program that has a declaration in `main()` to store the following numbers in an array named `rates`: 6.5, 7.2, 7.5, 8.3, 8.6, 9.4, 9.6, 9.8, and 10.0. Include a function call to `show()` that accepts `rates` in a parameter named `rates` and then displays the numbers by using the pointer notation `*(rates + i)`.

   b. Modify the `show()` function written in Exercise 6a to alter the address in `rates`. Always use the expression `*rates` rather than `*(rates + i)` to retrieve the correct element.

7. (**Program**) a. Write a program that has a declaration in `main()` to store the string `Vacation is near` in an array named `message`. Include a function call to `display()` that accepts `message` in an argument named `strng` and then displays the contents of `message` by using the pointer notation `*(strng + i)`.

   b. Modify the `display()` function written in Exercise 7a to use the expression `*strng` rather than `*(strng + i)` to retrieve the correct element.

8. (**Program**) Write a program that declares three one-dimensional arrays named `price`, `quantity`, and `amount`. Each array should be declared in `main()` and be capable of holding 10 double-precision numbers. The numbers to be stored in `price` are 10.62, 14.89, 13.21, 16.55, 18.62, 9.47, 6.58, 18.32, 12.15, and 3.98. The numbers to be stored in `quantity` are 4, 8.5, 6, 7.35, 9, 15.3, 3, 5.4, 2.9, and 4.8. Have your program pass these three arrays to a function called `extend()`, which calculates the elements in the `amount` array as the product of the equivalent elements in the `price` and `quantity` arrays: for example, `amount[1] = price[1] * quantity[1]`.

   After `extend()` has put values in the `amount` array, display the values in the array from within `main()`. Write the `extend()` function by using pointers.

9. (**Program**) Write a function named `trimfrnt()` that deletes all leading blanks from a string. Write the function using pointers with the return type `void`.

10. (**Program**) Write a function named `trimrear()` that deletes all trailing blanks from a string. Write the function using pointers with the return type `void`.

11. (**Program**) Write a C++ program that asks for two lowercase characters. Pass the two entered characters, using pointers, to a function named `capit()`. The `capit()` function should capitalize the two letters and return the capitalized values to the calling function through its pointer arguments. The calling function should then display all four letters.

12. (**Desk check**) a. Determine the output of the following program:

```
#include <iostream>
using namespace std;
void arr(int [] [3]); // equivalent to void arr(int (*) [3]);

int main()
{
  const int ROWS = 2;
  const int COLS = 3;
```

```
      int nums[ROWS][COLS] = { {33,16,29},
                               {54,67,99}};
      arr(nums);
      return 0;
   }

   void arr(int (*val) [3])
   {
      cout << endl << *(*val);
      cout << endl << *(*val + 1);
      cout << endl << *(*(val + 1) + 2);
      cout << endl << *(*val) + 1;
      return;
   }
```

b. Given the declaration for `val` in the `arr()` function, is the notation `val[1][2]` valid in the function?

8.5 Common Programming Errors

In using the material in this chapter, be aware of the following possible errors:

1. Attempting to store an address in a variable that hasn't been declared as a pointer.
2. Using a pointer to access nonexistent array elements. For example, if `nums` is an array of 10 integers, the expression `*(nums + 15)` points to a location six integer locations beyond the last array element. Because C++ doesn't do bounds checking on array accesses, the compiler doesn't catch this type of error. It's the same error, disguised in pointer notation form, that occurs when using a subscript to access an out-of-bounds array element.
3. Forgetting to use the brackets, `[ ]`, after the `delete` operator when dynamically deallocating memory that was allocated dynamically as a array.
4. Incorrectly applying address and indirection operators. For example, if `pt` is a pointer variable, both expressions

```
   pt = &45
   pt = &(miles + 10)
```

are invalid because they attempt to take the address of a value. Notice that the expression `pt = &miles + 10`, however, is valid. This expression adds 10 to the address of `miles`. It's the programmer's responsibility to ensure that the final address points to a valid data element.

5. Taking addresses of pointer constants. For example, given the declarations

```
int nums[25];
int *pt;
```

the assignment

```
pt = &nums;
```

is invalid. The constant `nums` is a pointer constant that's equivalent to an address. The correct assignment is `pt = nums`.

6. Taking addresses of a reference argument, reference variable, or register variable. The reason is that reference arguments and variables are essentially the same as pointer constants, in that they're named address values. Similarly, the address of a register variable can't be taken. Therefore, for the declarations

```
register int total;
int *ptTot;
```

the assignment

```
ptTot = &total;   // INVALID
```

is invalid. The reason is that register variables are stored in a computer's internal registers, and these storage areas don't have standard memory addresses.

7. Initializing pointer variables incorrectly. For example, the following initialization is invalid:

```
int *pt = 5;
```

Because `pt` is a pointer to an integer, it must be initialized with a valid address.

8. Becoming confused about whether a variable *contains* an address or *is* an address. Pointer variables and pointer arguments contain addresses. Although a pointer constant is synonymous with an address, it's useful to treat pointer constants as pointer variables with two restrictions:

- The address of a pointer constant can't be taken.
- The address "contained in" the pointer constant can't be altered.

Except for these two restrictions, pointer constants and pointer variables can be used almost interchangeably. Therefore, when an address is required, any of the following can be used:

- A pointer variable name
- A pointer argument name
- A pointer constant name
- A non-pointer variable name preceded by the address operator (for example, `&variable`)
- A non-pointer argument name preceded by the address operator (for example, `&argument`)

Some confusion surrounding pointers is caused by careless use of the word *pointer*. For example, the phrase "a function requires a pointer argument" is more clearly understood when you realize it actually means "a function requires an address as an argument." Similarly, the phrase "a function returns a pointer" actually means "a function returns an address."

If you're ever in doubt as to what's contained in a variable or how it should be treated, use a cout statement to display the variable's contents, the "thing pointed to," or "the address of the variable." Seeing what's actually displayed often helps sort out what the variable contains.

8.6 Chapter Summary

1. Every variable has an address. In C++, you can obtain the address of a variable by using the address operator, &.

2. A pointer is a variable used to store the address of another variable. Pointers, like all C++ variables, must be declared. An asterisk, *, is used both to declare a pointer variable and to access the variable whose address is stored in a pointer.

3. An array name is a pointer constant. The value of the pointer constant is the address of the first element in the array. Therefore, if val is the name of an array, val and &val[0] can be used interchangeably.

4. Any access to an array element with subscript notation can always be replaced with pointer notation. That is, the notation a[i] can always be replaced by the notation *(a + i). This is true whether a was initially declared as an array or a pointer.

5. Arrays can be created dynamically as a program is running. For example, the following sequence of statements creates an array named grades of size num:

```
cout   << "Enter the array size: ";
cin    >> num;
int    *grades = new int[num];
```

The area allocated for the array can be destroyed dynamically by using the delete[] operator. For example, the statement delete[] grades; returns the allocated area for the grades array back to the computer.

6. Arrays are passed to functions as addresses. The called function always receives direct access to the originally declared array elements.

7. When a one-dimensional array is passed to a function, the function's parameter declaration can be an array declaration or a pointer declaration. Therefore, the following parameter declarations are equivalent:

```
double a[];
double *a;
```

8. Pointers can be incremented, decremented, compared, and assigned. Numbers added to or subtracted from a pointer are scaled automatically. The scale factor used is the number of bytes required to store the data type originally pointed to.

Chapter

9

I/O Streams and Data Files

The data for the programs you have used so far has been assigned internally in the programs or entered by the user during program execution. Therefore, the data used in these programs is stored in the computer's main memory and ceases to exist after the program using it has finished executing. This type of data entry is fine for small amounts of data. However, imagine a company having to pay someone to type in the names and addresses of hundreds or thousands of customers every month when bills are prepared and sent.

As you learn in this chapter, storing large amounts of data outside a program on a convenient storage medium is more sensible. Data stored together under a common name on a storage medium other than the computer's main memory is called a data file. Typically, data files are stored on disks, USB drives, or CD/DVDs. Besides providing permanent storage for data, data files can be shared between programs, so the data one program outputs can be input in another program. In this chapter, you learn how data files are created and maintained in C++.

9.1 I/O File Stream Objects and Methods

To store and retrieve data outside a C++ program, you need two things:

- A file
- A file stream object

Files

A **file** is a collection of data stored together under a common name, usually on a disk, USB drive, or CD/DVD. For example, the C++ programs you store on disk are examples of files. The stored data in a program file is the code that becomes input data to the C++ compiler. In the context of data processing, however, stored programs aren't usually considered data files; the term "data file" typically refers only to files containing the data used in a C++ program.

Each stored data file has a unique filename, referred to as the file's **external name**. The external name is how the operating system (OS) knows the file. When you review the contents of a directory or folder (for example, in Windows Explorer), you see files listed by their external names. Each computer OS has its own specification for the maximum number of characters permitted for an external filename. Table 9.1 lists these specifications for common current and past OSs.

Table 9.1   Maximum Allowable Filename Characters

OS	Maximum Filename Length
DOS	8 characters plus an optional period and 3-character extension
Windows 98, 2000, XP, Vista	255 characters
Windows 7	255 characters

UNIX
  Early versions
  Current versions
	
	14 characters
	255 characters

For current OSs, you should take advantage of the increased length specification to create descriptive filenames, but avoid using extremely long filenames because they take more time to type and can result in typing errors. A manageable length for a filename is 12 to 14 characters, with a maximum of 25 characters.

For all the OSs listed in Table 9.1, the following are valid data filenames:

```
prices.dat      records       info.txt
exper1.dat      mvRecord      math.mem
```

Choose filenames that indicate the type of data in the file and the application for which it's used. Typically, the first 8 to 10 characters describe the data, and an optional extension (a period and three or four characters) describes the application used to create the file. For example,

Point of Information

Functions and Methods

C++ programmers can make full use of the many functions C++ classes provide without knowing the internal details of how the function is constructed or even how to construct a class. Functions provided as part of a class are formally referred to as **class methods** (or **methods**, for short). Although a method is often referred to as a function, the term "method" tells you it's not just a stand-alone function, as discussed in Chapter 6, but is available as part of a class. Typically, a class contains other methods of a similar type. More important, almost all class methods are invoked in a different manner from functions. Chapters 10 and 11 in Part II explain classes and their construction in detail. As you'll see, a class is constructed from C++ code that includes both data and methods.

Excel adds the `.xls` or `.xlsx` extension automatically to all spreadsheet files (x refers to the version number), Microsoft Word stores files with the extension `.doc` or `.docx`, and C++ compilers require a program file with the extension `.cpp`. When creating your own filenames, you should adhere to this practice of using descriptive filenames. For example, the name `exper1.dat` is suitable for describing a file of data corresponding to experiment number 1.

Two basic types of files exist: **text files**, also known as **character-based files**, and **binary-based files**. Both file types store data by using a binary code; the difference is in what the codes represent. Briefly, text files store each character, such as a letter, digit, dollar sign, decimal point, and so on, by using a character code (typically ASCII or Unicode). With a character code, a word-processing program or text editor can read and display these files. Additionally, because text files are easy to create, most programmers use them more often. Text files are the default file type in C++ and the file type discussed in this chapter.

Binary-based files use the same code the C++ compiler uses for primitive data types. This means numbers appear in their true binary form and can't be read by word-processing programs and text editors. The advantage of binary-based files is compactness; storing numbers with their binary code usually takes less space than with character values.

File Stream Objects

A **file stream** is a one-way transmission path used to connect a file to a program. Each file stream has its own mode that determines the direction of data on the transmission path—that is, whether the path moves data from a file to a program *or* from a program to a file. A file stream used to transfer data from a file to a program is an **input file stream**. A file stream that sends data from a program to a file is an **output file stream**. The direction, or mode, is defined in relation to the program, not the file; data going into a program is considered **input data**, and data sent out from a program is considered **output data**. Figure 9.1 illustrates the data flow from and to a file, using input and output file streams.

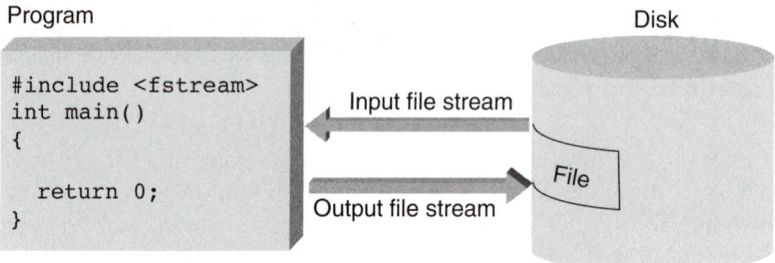

Figure 9.1   Input and output file streams

For each file your program uses, regardless of the file's type (text or binary), a distinct file stream object must be created. If you want your program to read from and write to a file, both input and output file stream objects are required. Input file stream objects are declared to be of type `ifstream`, and output file stream objects are declared to be of type `ofstream`. For example, the following declaration statement declares an input file stream object named inFile to be an object of the `ifstream` class:

```
ifstream inFile;
```

Similarly, the following declaration statement declares an output file stream object named outFile to be an object of the `ofstream` class:

```
ofstream outFile;
```

In a C++ program, a file stream is accessed by its stream object name: one name for reading the file and one name for writing to the file. Object names, such as `inFile` and `outFile`, can be any programmer-selected name that conforms to C++'s identifier rules.

File Stream Methods

Each file stream object has access to the methods defined for its `ifstream` or `ofstream` class. These methods include connecting a stream object name to an external filename (called **opening a file**), determining whether a successful connection has been made, closing a connection (called **closing a file**), getting the next data item into the program from an input stream, putting a new data item from the program onto an output stream, and detecting when the end of a file has been reached.

Opening a file connects a file stream object to a specific external filename by using a file stream's `open()` method, which accomplishes two purposes. First, opening a file establishes the physical connecting link between a program and a file. Because details of this link are handled by the computer's OS, not by the program, normally the programmer doesn't need to consider them.

From a coding perspective, the second purpose of opening a file is more relevant. Besides establishing the actual physical connection between a program and a data file, opening a file connects the file's external OS name to the file stream object name the program uses internally. The method that performs this task, `open()`, is provided by the `ifstream` and `ofstream` classes.

Point of Information

Input and Output Streams

A **stream** is a one-way transmission path between a source and a destination. In data transmission, a stream of bytes is sent down this transmission path, similar to a stream of water providing a one-way path for water to travel from a source to a destination.

Stream objects are created from stream classes. You have already used two stream objects extensively: the input stream object named `cin` and the output stream object named `cout`. The `cin` object, created from the `istream` class, provides a transmission path from keyboard to program, and the `cout` object, created from the `ostream` class, provides a transmission path from program to screen. The `istream` and `ostream` classes are used to construct a class named `iostream`. When the `iostream` header file is included in a program with the `#include <iostream>` directive, the `cin` and `cout` stream objects are declared automatically and opened by the C++ compiler.

File stream objects provide the same capabilities as the `cin` and `cout` objects, except they connect a program to a file rather than the keyboard or screen. File stream objects must be created and declared in a similar manner as variables. Instead of being declared as `int` or `char`, however, file stream objects are declared as being of the `ifstream` class (for input) or of the `ofstream` class (for output). These two classes are made available by including the `fstream` header file with the `#include <fstream>` directive.

In using the `open()` method to connect the file's external name to its internal object stream name, only one argument is required: the external filename. For example, the following statement connects the external text file named `prices.dat` to the internal file stream object named `inFile`:

```
inFile.open("prices.dat");
```

This statement assumes, of course, that `inFile` has been declared as an `ifstream` or `ofstream` object. If a file has been opened with the preceding statement, the program accesses the file by using the internal object name `inFile`, and the OS accesses the file under the external name `prices.dat`. The external filename argument passed to `open()` is a string enclosed in double quotation marks. The `prices.dat` file exists or is created (depending on whether it's designated as an input or output file) in the same folder as the program. More generally, data files are stored in separate folders, and the data file's full pathname can be specified as in this example:

```
inFile.open("c:\\datafiles\\prices.dat");
```

Notice that two slashes separate folder names and filenames, which is required when providing a full pathname. Also, in these two examples, the `open()` method is called by giving the object name (`inFile`) first, followed by a period, and then the method name (`open`). With a few notable exceptions, this is how all class methods are called.

When an existing file is connecting to an input file stream, the file's data is made available for input, starting at the first data item in the file. Similarly, a file connected to an output file stream creates a new file, said to be in **output mode**, and makes the file available for output. If a file exists with the same name as a file opened in output mode, the old file is erased (over-written) and all its data is lost.

When opening a file for input or output, good programming practice requires checking that the connection has been established before attempting to use the file. You can do this with the `fail()` method, which returns a true value if the file was opened unsuccessfully (that is, it's true the open failed) or a false value if the open succeeded. Typically, the `fail()` method is used in code similar to the following, which attempts to open the `prices.dat` file for input, checks that a valid connection was made, and reports an error message if the file wasn't opened for input successfully:

```
ifstream inFile;  // any object name can be used here
inFile.open("prices.dat");  // open the file

// check that the connection was opened successfully
if (inFile.fail())
{
  cout << "\nThe file was not successfully opened"
       << "\n Please check that the file currently exists."
       << endl;
  exit(1);
}
```

If the `fail()` method returns a true, indicating that the open failed, this code displays an error message. In addition, the `exit()` function, which is a request to the OS to end program execution immediately, is called. The `cstdlib` header function must be included in any program using `exit()`, and `exit()`'s single-integer argument is passed directly to the OS for any further program action or user inspection. Throughout the remainder of the book, this type of error checking is included whenever a file is opened. (Section 14.4 shows how to use exception handling for the same type of error checking.) In addition to the `fail()` method, C++ provides three other methods, listed in Table 9.2, for detecting a file's status.

Table 9.2 File Status Methods

Prototype	Description
`fail()`	Returns a Boolean `true` if the file hasn't been opened successfully; otherwise, returns a Boolean `false` value.
`eof()`	Returns a Boolean `true` if a read has been attempted past the end of file; otherwise, returns a Boolean `false`. The value becomes `true` only when the first character after the last valid file character is read.

Table 9.2   File Status Methods (*continued*)

Prototype	Description
good()	Returns a Boolean **true** while the file is available for program use. Returns a Boolean **false** if a read has been attempted past the end of file. The value becomes **false** only when the first character after the last valid file character is read.
bad()	Returns a Boolean **true** if a read has been attempted past the end of file; otherwise, returns a **false**. The value becomes **true** only when the first character after the last valid file character is read.

Program 9.1 shows the statements required to open a file for input, including an error-checking routine to ensure that the open was successful. A file opened for input is said to be in **read mode** or **input mode**. (These two terms are synonymous.)

Program 9.1

```
#include <iostream>
#include <fstream>
#include <cstdlib>    // needed for exit()
using namespace std;
int main()
{
  ifstream inFile;
  inFile.open("prices.dat");  // open the file with the
                              // external name prices.dat
  if (inFile.fail())  // check for a successful open
  {
    cout << "\nThe file was not successfully opened"
         << "\n Please check that the file currently exists."
         << endl;
    exit(1);
  }
  cout << "\nThe file has been successfully opened for reading."
       << endl;
    // statements to read data from the file are placed here
  return 0;
}
```

A sample run of Program 9.1 produces the following output:

```
The file has been successfully opened for reading.
```

A different check is required for output files (files that are written to) because if a file exists with the same name as the file to be opened in output mode, the existing file is erased and all its data is lost. To avoid this situation, the file is first opened in input mode to see whether it exists. If it does, the user is given the choice of permitting it to be overwritten when it's opened later in output mode. The code to perform this check is shaded in Program 9.2.

 **Program 9.2**

```cpp
#include <iostream>
#include <fstream>
#include <cstdlib>    // needed for exit()
using namespace std;

int main()
{
  ifstream inFile;
  ofstream outFile;
  char response;
  inFile.open("prices.dat");   // attempt to open the file for input

  if (!inFile.fail())  // if it doesn't fail, the file exists
  {
    cout << "A file by the name prices.dat exists.\n"
         << "Do you want to continue and overwrite it\n"
         << " with the new data (y or n): ";
    cin  >> response;
    if (tolower(response) == 'n')
    {
      cout << "The existing file will not be overwritten." << endl;
      exit(1);  //terminate program execution
    }
  }

  outFile.open("prices.dat"); // now open the file for writing
```

```
if (inFile.fail())  // check for a successful open
{
  cout << "\nThe file was not successfully opened" << endl;
  exit(1);
}

cout << "The file has been successfully opened for output." << endl;

// statements to write to the file would be placed here

return 0;
}
```

The following two runs were made with Program 9.2:

```
A file by the name prices.dat exists.
Do you want to continue and overwrite it
  with the new data (y or n): n
The existing file will not be overwritten.
```

and

```
A file by the name prices.dat exists.
Do you want to continue and overwrite it
  with the new data (y or n): y
The file has been successfully opened for output.
```

Although Programs 9.1 and 9.2 can be used to open an existing file for reading and writing, both programs lack statements to perform a read or write and close the file. These topics are discussed shortly. Before moving on, however, note that it's possible to combine the declaration of an ifstream or ofstream object and its associated open() statement into one statement. For example, examine these two statements in Program 9.1:

```
ifstream inFile;
inFile.open("prices.dat");
```

They can be combined into a single statement:

```
ifstream inFile("prices.dat");
```

Embedded and Interactive Filenames   Programs 9.1 and 9.2 have two problems:

- The external filename is embedded in the program code.
- There's no provision for a user to enter the filename while the program is running.

As both programs are written, if the filename is to change, a programmer must modify the external filename embedded in the call to open() and recompile the program. Both these problems can be avoided by assigning the filename to a string variable.

Point of Information

Using C-Strings as Filenames

If you use a C-string (which is simply a one-dimensional array of characters) to store an external filename, you must specify the C-string's maximum length in brackets immediately after it's declared. For example, examine the following declaration:

```
char filename[21] = "prices.dat";
```

The number in brackets (21) is one more than the maximum number of characters that can be assigned to the variable `filename` because the compiler adds an end-of-string character to terminate the string. Therefore, the string value `"prices.dat"`, which consists of 10 characters, is actually stored as 11 characters. In this example, the maximum value that can be assigned to the string variable `filename` is a string value consisting of 20 characters.

In declaring and initializing a string variable for use in an `open()` method, the variable must represent a C-string, a one-dimensional array of characters terminated with a null character. (See the Point of Information "Using C-Strings as Filenames" for precautions when using a C-string.) A safer alternative, as it doesn't require specifying a character count—and one used throughout this book—is to use an object created from the `string` class. To do this, add an `#include <string>` directive, declare an object to be of this class, and convert the object to a C-string in the `open()` method call by using the `string` class method `c_str()`.

After a string variable is declared to store a filename, it can be used in one of two ways. First, as shown in Program 9.3a, it can be used to avoid embedding a filename in the `open()` method by placing the declaration statement at the top of a program. This method also clearly identifies the file's name up front.

Program 9.3a

```cpp
#include <iostream>
#include <fstream>
#include <cstdlib>  // needed for exit()
#include <string>   // needed for the string class
using namespace std;

int main()
{
  string filename = "prices.dat"; // create and initialize a string object
                                  // with the filename at the top of the
                                  // main() function

  ifstream inFile;
```

```
   inFile.open(filename.c_str());  // open the file

   if (inFile.fail())  // check for successful open
   {
      cout << "\nThe file named " << filename
           << " was not successfully opened"
           << "\n Please check that the file currently exists."
           << endl;
      exit(1);
   }


   cout << "\nThe file has been successfully opened for reading.\n";

   return 0;
}
```

In Program 9.3a, the string object is declared and initialized with the name `filename`.[1] This name is placed at the top of `main()` for easy file identification and modification. When a string object is used, as opposed to a string literal, the object name isn't enclosed in double quotation marks in the `open()` method call. However, because `open()` requires a C-string (the `string` class doesn't use C-strings), the string object must be converted to a C-string in the `open()` call, which is done by using the `c_str()` method in the expression `filename.c_str()`.

Finally, in the `fail()` method, the file's external name is displayed by inserting the string object's name in the `cout` output stream. External names of files are identified in this manner in this book.

Another useful role string objects play is to permit users to enter the filename as the program is running. For example, the code

```
string filename;

cout << "Please enter the name of the file you wish to open: ";
cin  >> filename;
```

allows a user to enter a file's external name at runtime. The only restriction in this code is that the user must not enclose the entered string value in double quotation marks, and the entered string value can't contain any blanks. The reason no blanks can be included is that when `cin` is used, the compiler terminates the string when it encounters a blank. Program 9.3b uses this code in the context of a complete program.

---

[1] If the file were located in the `datafiles` folder on the C drive, specifying the full pathname would require the statement `string filename = "C:\\datafiles\\prices.dat";`.

Program 9.3b

```cpp
#include <iostream>
#include <fstream>
#include <cstdlib>    // needed for exit()
#include <string>     // needed for the string class
using namespace std;

int main()
{
  string filename; // declare a string object with no initialization
  ifstream inFile;

  cout << "Please enter the name of the file you wish to open: ";
  cin  >> filename;

  inFile.open(filename.c_str());  // open the file
  if (inFile.fail())  // check for successful open
  {
    cout << "\nThe file named " << filename
         << " was not successfully opened"
         << "\n Please check that the file currently exists."
         << endl;
    exit(1);
  }
  cout << "\nThe file has been successfully opened for reading.\n";

  return 0;
}
```

The following is a sample output of Program 9.3b:

```
Please enter the name of the file you wish to open: foobar

The file named foobar was not successfully opened
  Please check that the file currently exists.
```

Point of Information

A Way to Identify a File's Name and Location

During program development, test files are usually placed in the same directory or folder as the program. Therefore, a method call such as `inFile.open("exper.dat")` causes no problems to the OS. In production systems, however, it's not uncommon for data files to reside in one folder and program files to reside in another. For this reason, including the full pathname of any file that's opened is always a good idea.

For example, if the `exper.dat` file resides in the `C:\test\files` directory, the `open()` call should include the full pathname: `inFile.open("C:\\test\\files\\exper.dat")`. Then, no matter where the program is run from, the OS knows where to locate the file. Note the use of double backslashes, which is required.

Another important convention is to list all filenames at the top of a program instead of embedding the names deep in the code. You can do this easily by declaring each filename as a string object (or a one-dimensional array of characters). For example, placing the following statement at the top of a program file clearly lists both the name of the file and its location:

```
string filename = "c:\\test\\files\\exper.dat";
```

If some other file is to be tested, all that's required is a simple change to the string literal in this easy-to-find statement. Remember that using the `string` class requires adding the `#include <string>` directive in your program.

Closing a File   A file is closed by using the `close()` method. This method breaks the connection between the file's external name and the file stream object, which can be used for another file. Examine the following statement, which closes the `inFile` stream's connection to its current file:

```
inFile.close();
```

As indicated, the `close()` method takes no argument.

Because all computers have a limit on the maximum number of files that can be open at one time, closing files that are no longer needed makes good sense. Any open files existing at the end of normal program execution are closed automatically by the OS.

Point of Information

Using `fstream` Objects

In using `ifstream` and `ofstream` objects, the input or output mode is indicated by the object. Therefore, `ifstream` objects must be used for input, and `ofstream` objects must be used for output. Another means of creating file streams is with `fstream` objects that can be used for input or output, but this method requires an explicit mode designation. An `fstream` object is declared by using the following syntax:

        fstream *objectName*;

When using the `fstream` class's `open()` method, two arguments are required: a file's external name and a mode indicator. Here are the permissible mode indicators; except for the first two, they can also be used when opening `ifstream` and `ofstream` objects:

Indicator	Description
`ios::in`	Open a text file in input mode (not used for `ifstream` objects)
`ios::out`	Open a text file in output mode (not used for `ofstream` objects)
`ios::app`	Open a text file in append mode
`ios::ate`	Go to the end of the opened file
`ios::binary`	Open a binary file in input mode (default is text file)
`ios::trunc`	Delete file contents if it exists
`ios::nocreate`	If file doesn't exist, open fails
`ios::noreplace`	If file exists, open for output fails

As with `ofstream` objects, an `fstream` object in output mode creates a new file and makes the file available for writing. If a file exists with the same name as a file opened for output, the old file is erased. For example, the following statement declares `file1` as an object of type `fstream`:

        fstream file1;

The following statement attempts to open the text file `prices.dat` for output:

        file1.open("prices.dat",ios::out);

After this file has been opened, the program accesses the file by using the internal object name `file1`, and the computer saves the file under the external name `prices.dat`.

An `fstream` file object opened in **append mode** means an existing file is available for data to be added to the end of the file. If the file opened for appending doesn't exist, a new file with the designated name is created and made available to receive output from the program. For example, the following statement declares `file1` as an `fstream` object and attempts to open a text file named `prices.dat` and make it available for data to be added to the end of the file:

        file1.open("prices.dat",ios::app);

continued

Point of Information

Using `fstream` Objects (*continued*)

Finally, an `fstream` object opened in input mode means an existing external file has been connected and its data is available as input. For example, the following statement declares `file1` to be of type `fstream` and attempts to open a text file named `prices.dat` for input:

```
file1.open("prices.dat",ios::in);
```

Mode indicators can be combined by the bitwise OR operator, | (see Appendix C, available online). For example, the following statement opens the `file1` stream, which can be an `fstream` or `ifstream` object, as an input binary stream:

```
file1.open("prices.dat", ios::in | ios::binary)
```

If the mode indicator is omitted as the second argument for an `ifstream` object, the stream is opened as a text input file by default; if the mode indicator is omitted for an `ofstream` object, the stream is opened as a text output file by default.

EXERCISES 9.1

1. **(Practice)** Write declaration and open statements that link the following external filenames to their corresponding internal filenames. All files are text-based.

External Filename	Internal Filename	Mode
coba.mem	memo	output
book.let	letter	output
coupons.bnd	coups	append
yield.bnd	yield	append
prices.dat	priFile	input
rates.dat	rates	input

2. **(Practice) a.** Write a set of two statements that declares the following objects as `ifstream` objects and then opens them as text input files: `inData.txt, prices.txt, coupons.dat,` and `exper.dat`.

   b. Rewrite the two statements for Exercise 2a, using a single statement.

3. **(Practice) a.** Write a set of two statements declaring the following objects as `ofstream` objects and then opening them as text output files: `outDate.txt, rates.txt, distance.txt,` and `file2.txt`.

   b. Rewrite the two statements for Exercise 3a, using a single statement.

Point of Information

Checking for a Successful Connection

You should always check that the `open()` method established a connection between a file stream and an external file successfully because the `open()` call is a request to the OS that can fail for various reasons. Chief among these reasons is a request to open an existing file for reading that the OS can't locate or a request to open a file for output in a nonexistent folder. If the OS can't satisfy the open request, you need to know about it and terminate your program. Failure to do so can result in abnormal program behavior or a program crash.

The most common method for checking that a fail didn't occur when attempting to use a file for input is the one coded in Program 9.1, which uses separate calls to the `open()` and `fail()` methods. Similarly, the check made in Program 9.2 is typically included when a file is being opened in output mode.

Alternatively, you might encounter programs that use `fstream` objects in place of `ifstream` and `ofstream` objects (see the previous Point of Information box). Except for the `open()` method (which requires two arguments: a file's external name and a mode indicator), the `fail()` method is called the same as in Program 9.1 or Program 9.2.

In all these cases, you can substitute the expression `!inFile` for the conditional expression `inFile.fail()`.

4. **(Practice)** Enter and run Program 9.1 on your computer.

5. **(Practice)** Enter and run Program 9.2 on your computer.

6. **(Practice) a.** Enter and run Program 9.3a on your computer.
   b. Add a `close()` method to Program 9.3a, and then run the program.

7. **(Practice) a.** Enter and run Program 9.3b on your computer.
   b. Add a `close()` method to Program 9.3b, and then run the program.

8. **(Practice)** Using the reference manuals provided with your computer's OS, determine the following:
   a. The maximum number of characters the computer can use to name a file for storage
   b. The maximum number of data files that can be open at the same time

9. **(Practice)** Is calling a saved C++ program a file appropriate? Why or why not?

10. **(Practice) a.** Write declaration and open statements to link the following external filenames to their corresponding internal filenames. Use only `ifstream` and `ofstream` objects.

External Filename	Internal Filename	Mode
`coba.mem`	`memo`	binary and output
`coupons.bnd`	`coups`	binary and append
`prices.dat`	`priFile`	binary and input

b. Redo Exercise 10a, using only `fstream` objects.

c. Write `close()` statements for each file opened in Exercise 10a.

9.2 Reading and Writing Text Files

Reading or writing text files involves almost the identical operations for reading input from the keyboard and writing data to the screen. For writing to a file, the `cout` object is replaced by the `ofstream` object name declared in the program. For example, if `outFile` is declared as an object of type `ofstream`, the following output statements are valid:

```
outFile << 'a';
outFile << "Hello World!";
outFile << descrip << ' ' << price;
```

The filename in each of these statements, in place of `cout`, directs the output stream to a specific file instead of to the screen. Program 9.4 shows using the insertion operator, `<<`, to write a list of descriptions and prices to a file.

When Program 9.4 runs, the, `prices.dat` file is created and saved by the computer as a text file (the default file type) in the same folder where the program is located. It's a sequential file consisting of the following data:

```
Mats 39.95
Bulbs 3.22
Fuses 1.08
```

The actual storage of characters in the file depends on the character codes the computer uses. Although only 30 characters appear to be stored in the file—corresponding to the descriptions, blanks, and prices written to the file—the file contains 36 characters.

 **Program 9.4**

```cpp
#include <iostream>
#include <fstream>
#include <cstdlib>    // needed for exit()
#include <string>     // needed for the string class
#include <iomanip>    // needed for formatting
using namespace std;

int main()
{
  string filename = "prices.dat";  // put the filename up front
  ofstream outFile;

  outFile.open(filename.c_str());

  if (outFile.fail())
  {
    cout << "The file was not successfully opened" << endl;
    exit(1);
  }

  // set the output file stream formats
  outFile << setiosflags(ios::fixed)
          << setiosflags(ios::showpoint)
          << setprecision(2);

  // send data to the file
  outFile << "Mats "  << 39.95 << endl
          << "Bulbs " << 3.22 << endl
          << "Fuses " << 1.08 << endl;

  outFile.close();
  cout << "The file " << filename
       << " has been successfully written." << endl;

  return 0;
}
```

The extra characters consist of the newline escape sequence at the end of each line created by the endl manipulator, which is created as a carriage return character (cr) and linefeed (lf). Assuming characters are stored with the ASCII code, the prices.dat file is physically stored as shown in Figure 9.2. For convenience, the character corresponding to each hexadecimal code is listed below the code. A code of 20 represents the blank character. Additionally,

Point of Information

Formatting Text File Output Stream Data

Output file streams can be formatted in the same manner as the `cout` standard output stream. For example, if an output stream named `fileOut` has been declared, the following statement formats all data inserted in the `fileOut` stream in the same way these manipulators work for the `cout` stream:

```
fileOut << setiosflags(ios::fixed)
        << setiosflags(ios::showpoint)
        << setprecision(2);
```

The first manipulator parameter, `ios::fixed`, causes the stream to output all numbers as though they were floating-point values. The next parameter, `ios::showpoint`, tells the stream to always provide a decimal point. Therefore, a value such as 1.0 appears as 1.0, not as 1, which doesn't contain a decimal point. Finally, the `setprecision()` manipulator tells the stream to display two decimal values after the decimal point. Therefore, the number 1.0, for example, appears as 1.00.

Instead of using manipulators, you can use the stream methods `setf()` and `precision()`. For example, the previous formatting can be accomplished with the following code:

```
fileOut.setf(ios::fixed);
fileOut.setf(ios::showpoint);
fileOut.precision(2);
```

The style you select is a matter of preference. In both cases, the formats need be specified only once and remain in effect for every number subsequently inserted in the file stream.

C and C++ append the low-value hexadecimal byte 0x00 as the end-of-file (EOF) sentinel when the file is closed. This EOF sentinel is never counted as part of the file.

```
4D 61 74 73 20 33 39 2E 39 35 0D 0A 42 75 6C 62 73 20

 M  a  t  s     3  9  .  9  5 cr lf  B  u  l  b  s


33 2E 32 32 0D 0A 46 75 73 65 73 20 31 2E 30 38 0D 0A

 3  .  2  2 cr lf  F  u  s  e  s     1  .  0  8 cr lf
```

Figure 9.2   The `prices.dat` file as stored by the computer

Point of Information

Writing One Character at a Time with the `put()` Method

All output streams have access to the `fstream` class's `put()` method, which permits character-by-character output to a stream. This method works in the same manner as the character insertion operator, `<<`. The syntax of this method call is the following:

```
ofstreamName.put(characterExpression);
```

The *characterExpression* can be a character variable or literal value. For example, the following code can be used to output an `'a'` to the screen:

```
cin.put('a');
```

In a similar manner, if `outFile` is an `ofstream` object file that has been opened, the following code outputs the character value in the character variable named `keycode` to the `outFile` stream:

```
char keycode;
    .
    .
outFile.put(keycode);
```

Reading from a Text File

Reading data from a text file is almost identical to reading data from a standard keyboard, except the `cin` object is replaced by the `ifstream` object declared in the program. For example, if `inFile` is declared as an object of type `ifstream` that's opened for input, the following statement reads the next two items in the file and stores them in the variables `descrip` and `price`:

```
inFile >> descrip >> price;
```

The file stream name in this statement, in place of `cin`, directs the input to come from the file stream rather than the keyboard. Table 9.3 lists other methods that can be used for stream input. When called, these methods must be preceded by a stream object name.

Table 9.3 `fstream` Methods

Method Name	Description
`get()`	Returns the next character extracted from the input stream as an `int`.
`get(charVar)`	Overloaded version of `get()` that extracts the next character from the input stream and assigns it to the specified character variable, `charVar`.
`getline(strObj, termChar)`	Extracts characters from the specified input stream, `strObj`, until the terminating character, `termChar`, is encountered. Assigns the characters to the specified `string` class object, `strObj`.
`peek()`	Returns the next character in the input stream without extracting it from the stream.
`ignore(int n)`	Skips over the next *n* characters. If *n* is omitted, the default is to skip over the next single character.

Program 9.5 shows how the `prices.dat` file created in Program 9.4 can be read. This program illustrates one way of detecting the EOF marker by using the `good()` method (see Table 9.2). Because this method returns a Boolean `true` value before the EOF marker has been read or passed over, it can be used to verify that the data read is valid file data. Only after the EOF marker has been read or passed over does this method return a Boolean `false`. Therefore, the notation `while(inFile.good())` used in Program 9.5 ensures that data is from the file before the EOF has been read.

Program 9.5

```cpp
#include <iostream>
#include <fstream>
#include <cstdlib>   // needed for exit()
#include <string>    // needed for the string class
using namespace std;

int main()
{
  string filename = "prices.dat";  // put the filename up front
  string descrip;
  double price;

  ifstream inFile;

  inFile.open(filename.c_str());

  if (inFile.fail())  // check for successful open
  {
    cout << "\nThe file was not successfully opened"
         << "\n Please check that the file currently exists."
         << endl;
    exit(1);
  }

  // read and display the file's contents
  inFile >> descrip >> price;
  while (inFile.good()) // check next character
  {
    cout << descrip << ' ' << price << endl;
    inFile >> descrip >> price;
  }

  inFile.close();

  return 0;
}
```

Program 9.5 produces the following display:

```
Mats 39.95
Bulbs 3.22
Fuses 1.08
```

Examine the expression `inFile.good()` used in the `while` statement. This expression is true as long as the EOF marker hasn't been read. Therefore, as long as the last character read is good (that is, the EOF marker hasn't been passed), the loop continues to read the file. Inside the loop, the items just read are displayed, and then a new string and a double-precision number are input to the program. When the EOF has been detected, the expression returns a Boolean value of `false` and the loop terminates. This termination ensures that data is read and displayed up to, but not including, the EOF marker.

A replacement for the expression `while(inFile.good())` is the expression `while(!inFile.eof())`, which is read as "while the end of file has *not* been reached." This replacement works because the `eof()` method returns a `true` only after the EOF marker has been read or passed over. In effect, the relational expression checks that the EOF *hasn't* been read—hence, the use of the NOT operator, `!`.

Another means of detecting the EOF is to use the fact that the extraction operator, `>>`, returns a Boolean value of `true` if data is extracted from a stream; otherwise, it returns a Boolean `false` value. Using this return value, the following code can be used in Program 9.5 to read the file:

```
// read and display the file's contents
while (inFile >> descrip >> price) // check next character
  cout << descrip << ' ' << price << endl;
```

Although this code seems a bit cryptic at first glance, it makes perfect sense when you understand that the expression being tested extracts data from the file and returns a Boolean value to indicate whether the extraction was successful.

Finally, in the previous `while` statement or in Program 9.5, the expression `inFile >> descrip >> price` can be replaced by a `getline()` method (see Table 9.3). For file input, this method has the following syntax:

```
getline(fileObject, strObj, terminatingChar)
```

fileObject is the name of the `ifstream` file, *strObj* is a `string` class object , and *terminatingChar* is an optional character constant or variable specifying the terminating character. If this optional third argument is omitted, the default terminating character is the newline (`'\n'`) character. Program 9.6 shows using `getline()` in the context of a complete program.

Program 9.6

```cpp
#include <iostream>
#include <fstream>
#include <cstdlib>    // needed for exit()
#include <string>     // needed for the string class
using namespace std;

int main()
{
  string filename = "prices.dat";  // put the filename up front
  string line;
  ifstream inFile;

  inFile.open(filename.c_str());

  if (inFile.fail())  // check for successful open
  {
    cout << "\nThe file was not successfully opened"
         << "\n Please check that the file currently exists."
         << endl;
    exit(1);
  }

  // read and display the file's contents
  while (getline(inFile,line))
    cout << line << endl;

  inFile.close();

  return 0;
}
```

Program 9.6 is a line-by-line text-copying program, which reads a line of text from the file and then displays it on the screen. This program's output is the following:

```
Mats 39.95
Bulbs 3.22
Fuses 1.08
```

If obtaining the description and price as separate variables is necessary, either Program 9.5 should be used, or the string returned by getline() in Program 9.6 must be processed further to extract the separate data items. (See Section 9.7 for parsing procedures.)

Point of Information

The get() and putback() Methods

All input streams have access to the `fstream` class's `get()` method, used for character-by-character input from an input stream. This method works similarly to character extraction, using the `>>` operator, with two important differences: If a newline character, `'\n'`, or a blank character, `'  '`, is encountered, these characters are read in the same manner as any other alphanumeric character. The syntax of this method call is the following:

```
istreamName.get(characterVariable);
```

For example, the following code can be used to read the next character from the standard input stream and store the character in the variable `ch`:

```
char ch;
cin.get(ch);
```

Similarly, if `inFile` is an `ifstream` object that has been opened to a file, the following code reads the next character in the stream and assigns it to the character variable `keycode`:

```
char keycode;
inFile.get(keycode);
```

In addition to the `get()` method, all input streams have a `putback()` method for putting the last character read from an input stream back on the stream. This method has the following syntax (with *characterExpression* representing any character variable or character value):

```
ifstreamName.putback(characterExpression);
```

The `putback()` method provides output capability to an input stream. The putback character need not be the last character read; it can be any character. All putback characters, however, have no effect on the data file. They affect only the open input stream. Therefore, the data file characters remain unchanged, although the characters subsequently read from the input stream can change.

Standard Device Files

The file stream objects you have seen so far have been logical file objects. A **logical file object** is a stream that connects a file of logically related data, such as a data file, to a program. In addition, C++ supports a **physical file object**, which is a stream that connects to a hardware device, such as a keyboard, screen, or printer.

The actual physical device assigned to your program for data entry is formally called the **standard input file**. Usually, it's the keyboard. When a `cin` object method call is encountered in a C++ program, it's a request to the OS to go to this standard input file for the expected input. Similarly, when a `cout` object method call is encountered, the output is automatically displayed or "written to" a device that has been assigned as the **standard output file**. For most systems, it's a computer screen, although it can also be a printer.

When a program including the `iostream` header file is executed, the standard input stream `cin` is connected to the standard input device. Similarly, the standard output stream `cout` is connected to the standard output device. These two object streams are available for programmer use, as are the standard error stream, `cerr`, and the standard log stream, `clog`. Both these streams connect to the screen.

Other Devices

The keyboard, display, error, and log streams are connected automatically to the stream objects `cin`, `cout`, `cerr`, and `clog` when the `iostream` header file is included in a program. Other devices can be used for input or output if the name the system assigns is known. For example, most PCs assign the name `prn` to the printer connected to the computer. For these computers, a statement such as `outFile.open("prn")` connects the printer to the `ofstream` object named `outFile`. A subsequent statement, such as `outFile << "Hello World!";`, would cause the string `Hello World!` to be output directly to the printer. As the name of an actual file, `prn` must be enclosed in double quotation marks in the `open()` method call.

EXERCISES 9.2

1. **(Practice and Modify) a.** Enter and run Program 9.5.
   b. Modify Program 9.5 to use the expression `!inFile.eof()` in place of the expression `inFile.good()`, and run the program to see whether it operates correctly.

2. **(Practice and Modify) a.** Enter and run Program 9.6.
   b. Modify Program 9.6 by replacing `cout` with `cerr`, and verify that the output for the standard error file stream is the screen.
   c. Modify Program 9.6 by replacing `cout` with `clog`, and verify that the output for the standard log stream is the screen.

3. **(Practice and Modify) a.** Write a C++ program that accepts lines of text from the keyboard and writes each line to a file named `text.dat` until an empty line is entered. An empty line is a line with no text that's created by pressing the Enter (or Return) key.
   b. Modify Program 9.6 to read and display the data stored in the `text.dat` file created in Exercise 3a.

4. **(Practice)** Determine the OS command or procedure your computer provides to display the contents of a saved file.

5. **(Program) a.** Create a text file named `employee.dat` containing the following data:

Anthony	A	10031	11.82	12/18/2010
Burrows	W	10067	12.14	6/9/2011
Fain	B	10083	10.79	5/18/2011
Janney	P	10095	12.57	9/28/2008
Smith	G	10105	9.50	12/20/2006

b. Write a C++ program to read the `employee.dat` file created in Exercise 5a and produce a duplicate copy of the file named `employee.bak`.

c. Modify the program written in Exercise 5b to accept the names of the original and duplicate files as user input.

d. The program written for Exercise 5c always copies data from an original file to a duplicate file. What's a better method of accepting the original and duplicate filenames, other than prompting the user for them each time the program runs?

6. **(Program) a.** Write a C++ program that opens a file and displays its contents with line numbers. That is, the program should print the number 1 before displaying the first line, print the number 2 before displaying the second line, and so on for each line in the file.

   b. Modify the program written in Exercise 6a to list the file's contents on the printer assigned to your computer.

7. **(Program) a.** Create a text file named `info.dat` containing the following data (without the headings):

Name	Social Security Number	Hourly Rate	Hours Worked
B Caldwell	555-88-2222	10.50	37
D Memcheck	555-77-4444	12.80	40
R Potter	555-77-6666	16.54	40
W Rosen	555-99-8888	11.80	35

   b. Write a C++ program that reads the data file created in Exercise 7a and computes and displays a payroll schedule. The output should list the Social Security number, name, and gross pay for each person, calculating gross pay as *Hourly Rate × Hours Worked*.

8. **(Program) a.** Create a text file named `car.dat` containing the following data (without the headings):

Car Number	Miles Driven	Gallons of Gas Used
54	250	19
62	525	38
71	123	6
85	1322	86
97	235	14

   b. Write a C++ program that reads the data in the file created in Exercise 8a and displays the car number, miles driven, gallons of gas used, and miles per gallon (mpg) for each car. The output should contain the total miles driven, total gallons of gas used, and average mpg for all cars. These totals should be displayed at the end of the output report.

9. (**Program**) **a.** Create a text file named `parts.dat` with the following data (without the headings):

Part Number	Initial Amount	Quantity Sold	Minimum Amount
QA310	95	47	50
CM145	320	162	200
MS514	34	20	25
EN212	163	150	160

b. Write a C++ program to create an inventory report based on the data in the file created in Exercise 9a. The display should consist of the part number, current balance, and the amount needed to bring the inventory to the minimum level. The current balance is the initial amount minus the quantity sold.

10. (**Program**) **a.** Create a text file named `pay.dat` containing the following data (without the headings):

Name	Rate	Hours
Callaway, G.	16.00	40
Hanson, P.	15.00	48
Lasard, D.	16.50	35
Stillman, W.	12.00	50

b. Write a C++ program that uses the information in the file created in Exercise 10a to produce the following pay report for each employee:

```
Name    Pay Rate    Hours    Regular Pay    Overtime Pay    Gross Pay
```

Compute regular pay as any hours worked up to and including 40 hours multiplied by the pay rate. Compute overtime pay as any hours worked above 40 hours at a pay rate of 1.5 multiplied by the regular rate. The gross pay is the sum of regular and overtime pay. At the end of the report, the program should display the totals of the regular, overtime, and gross pay columns.

11. (**Program**) **a.** Store the following data in a file named `numbers.dat`:

5 96 87 78 93 21 4 92 82 85 87 6 72 69 85 75 81 73

b. Write a C++ program to calculate and display the average of each group of numbers in the file created in Exercise 11a. The data is arranged in the file so that each group of numbers is preceded by the number of data items in the group. Therefore, the first number in the file, 5, indicates that the next five numbers should be grouped together. The number 4 indicates that the following four numbers are a group, and the 6 indicates that the last six numbers are a group. (*Hint*: Use a nested loop. The outer loop should terminate when the end of file has been encountered.)

12. **(Program)** Write a C++ program that allows users to enter the following information from the keyboard for each student in a class (up to 20 students) and stores the data in a text file named `grade.dat`:

    Name   Exam 1 Grade   Exam 2 Grade   Homework Grade   Final Exam Grade

    For each student, your program should first calculate a final grade, using this formula:

    Final Grade = 0.20 × Exam 1 + 0.20 × Exam 2 + 0.35 × Homework + 0.25 × Final Exam

    Then assign a letter grade on the basis of 90–100 = A, 80–89 = B, 70–79 = C, 60–69 = D, and less than 60 = F. All the information, including the final grade and the letter grade, should then be displayed and written to a file.

13. **(Program)** A bank's customer records are to be stored in a file and read into a set of arrays so that a customer's record can be accessed randomly by account number. Create the file by entering five customer records, with each record consisting of an integer account number (starting with account number 1000), a first name (maximum of 10 characters), a last name (maximum of 15 characters), and a double-precision number for the account balance.

    After the file is created, write a C++ program that requests a user-input account number and displays the corresponding name and account balance from the file. (*Hint:* Read the data in the file into an array, and then search the array for the account number.)

14. **(Program)** Create a text file with the following data or use the `shipped.dat` file provided on this book's Web site. The headings aren't part of the file; they simply indicate what the data represents.

Shipped Date	Tracking Number	Part Number	First Name	Last Name	Company
04/12/11	D50625	74444	James	Lehoff	Rotech
04/12/11	D60752	75255	Janet	Lezar	Rotech
04/12/11	D40295	74477	Bill	McHenry	Rotech
04/12/11	D23745	74470	Diane	Kaiser	Rotech
04/12/11	D50892	75155	Helen	Richardson	NapTime

The format of each line in the file is identical, with fixed-length fields defined as follows:

Field Position	Field Name	Starting Col. No.	Ending Col. No.	Field Length
1	Shipped Date	1	8	8
2	Tracking Number	12	17	6
3	Part Number	22	26	5
4	First Name	31	35	5
5	Last Name	39	48	10
6	Company	51	64	14

Using this data file, write a C++ program that reads the file and produces a report listing the shipped date, part number, first name, last name, and company name.

9.3 Random File Access

The term **file access** refers to the process of retrieving data from a file. There are two types of file access: sequential access and random access. To understand file access types, first you need to understand how data is organized in a file.

The term **file organization** refers to the way data is stored in a file. The files you have used, and will continue to use, have a **sequential organization**, meaning characters in the file are stored in a sequential manner. In addition, each open file has been read in a sequential manner, meaning characters are accessed one after another, which is called **sequential access**. Although characters are stored sequentially, they don't have to be accessed the same way. In fact, you can skip over characters and read a sequentially organized file in a nonsequential manner.

In **random access**, any character in the opened file can be read without having to sequentially read all characters stored ahead of it first. To provide random access to files, each `ifstream` object creates a file position marker automatically that keeps track of where the next character is to be read from or written to. Table 9.4 lists the methods used to access and change the file position marker. The suffixes g and p in these method names denote `get` and `put`; `get` refers to an input (get from) file, and `put` refers to an output (put to) file.

Table 9.4   File Position Marker Methods

Name	Description
`seekg(offset, mode)`	For input files, move to the offset position indicated by the mode.
`seekp(offset, mode)`	For output files, move to the offset position indicated by the mode.
`tellg(void)`	For input files, return the current value of the file position marker.
`tellp(void)`	For output files, return the current value of the file position marker.

To understand these methods, you must know how data is referenced in the file by using the file position marker and how an offset can be used to alter the file position marker's value. Each character in a data file is located by its position in the file. The first character in the file is located at position 0, the next character at position 1, and so forth. The file position marker contains the positional value, starting from the first character in the file, of where the next character is to be read from or written. Therefore, if the first character is accessed (read from or written to), the file position marker is 0; if the second character is to be accessed, the file position marker is 1, and so on, for each character in the file. By adjusting the file position marker's value, the `seek()` methods enable the programmer to move to any position in the file. This adjustment is specified by an **offset value**.

The seek() methods require two arguments: an offset value, as a long integer, and what position in the file the offset is to be applied to, determined by the mode. The three available modes are ios::beg, ios::cur, and ios::end, which denote the beginning of the file, current position, and end of the file. Therefore, the mode ios::beg means the offset is relative to the position of the first character in the file. The mode ios::cur means the offset is relative to the current position in the file, and the mode ios::end means the offset is relative to the last character in the file. From a practical standpoint, a positive offset means move forward in the file from the designated starting position, and a negative offset means move backward from this position.

Examples of seek() method calls are shown in the following code. In these examples, inFile has been opened as an input file and outFile as an output file. The offset passed to seekg() and seekp() must be a long integer, hence the uppercase L appended to each number in the method calls.

```
inFile.seekg(4L,ios::beg);     // go to the fifth character in the input
                               // file
outFile.seekp(4L,ios::beg);    // go to the fifth character in the output
                               // file
inFile.seekg(4L,ios::cur);     // move ahead five characters in the input
                               // file
outFile.seekp(4L,ios::cur);    // move ahead five characters in the output
                               // file
inFile.seekg(-4L,ios::cur);    // move back five characters in the input
                               // file
outFile.seekp(-4L,ios::cur);   // move back five characters in the output
                               // file
inFile.seekg(0L,ios::beg);     // go to start of the input file
outfile.seekp(0L,ios::beg);    // go to start of the output file
inFile.seekg(0L,ios::end);     // go to end of the input file
outFile.seekp(0L,ios::end);    // go to end of the output file
inFile.seekg(-10L,ios::end);   // go to 10 characters before the input
                               // file's end
outFile.seekp(-10L,ios::end);  // go to 10 characters before the output
                               // file's end
```

As opposed to seek() methods that move the file position marker, the tell() methods return the file position marker's offset value. For example, if 10 characters have been read from an input file named inFile, the method call returns the long integer 10:

```
inFile.tellg();
```

This method call means the next character to be read is offset 10 byte positions from the start of the file and is the 11th character in the file.

Program 9.7 shows using seekg() and tellg() to read a file in reverse order, from the last character to the first. As each character is read, it's also displayed.

Program 9.7

```cpp
#include <iostream>
#include <fstream>
#include <string>
#include <cstdlib>
using namespace std;

int main()
{
  string filename = "test.dat";
  char ch;
  long offset, last;

  ifstream inFile(filename.c_str());

  if (inFile.fail())   // check for successful open
  {
    cout << "\nThe file was not successfully opened"
         << "\n Please check that the file currently exists"
         << endl;
    exit(1);
  }

  inFile.seekg(0L,ios::end);   // move to the end of the file
  last = inFile.tellg();       // save the offset of the last character

  for(offset = 1L; offset <= last; offset++)
  {
    inFile.seekg(-offset, ios::end);
    ch = inFile.get();
    cout << ch << " : ";
  }

  inFile.close();

  cout << endl;

  return 0;
}
```

Assume the test.dat file contains the following characters:

    The grade was 92.5

The output of Program 9.7 is the following:

```
5 : . : 2 : 9 :    : s : a : w :    : e : d : a : r : g :    : e : h : T :
```

Program 9.7 initially goes to the last character in the file. The offset of this character, the EOF character, is saved in the variable `last`. Because `tellg()` returns a long integer, `last` has been declared as a long integer.

Starting from the end of the file, `seekg()` is used to position the next character to be read, referenced from the end of the file. As each character is read, it's displayed, and the offset is adjusted to access the next character. The first offset used is -1, which represents the character immediately preceding the EOF marker.

EXERCISES 9.3

1. **(Practice) a.** Create a file named `test.dat` containing the data in the `test.dat` file used in Program 9.7. (You can use a text editor or copy the `test.dat` file from this book's Web site.)
   b. Enter and run Program 9.7 on your computer.

2. **(Modify)** Rewrite Program 9.7 so that the origin for the `seekg()` method used in the `for` loop is the start of the file rather than the end.

3. **(Modify)** Modify Program 9.7 to display an error message if `seekg()` attempts to reference a position beyond the end of file.

4. **(Practice)** Write a program that reads and displays every second character in a file named `test.dat`.

5. **(Practice)** Using the `seek()` and `tell()` methods, write a function named `fileChars()` that returns the total number of characters in a file.

6. **(Practice) a.** Write a function named `readBytes()` that reads and displays *n* characters starting from any position in a file. The function should accept three arguments: a file object name, the offset of the first character to be read, and the number of characters to be read. (*Note*: The prototype for `readBytes()` should be `void readBytes(fstream&, long, int)`.)
   b. Modify the `readBytes()` function written in Exercise 6a to store the characters read into a string or an array. The function should accept the storage address as a fourth argument.

9.4 File Streams as Function Arguments

A file stream object can be used as a function argument. The only requirement is that the function's formal parameter be a reference (see Section 6.3) to the correct stream: `ifstream&` or `ofstream&`. For example, in Program 9.8, an `ofstream` object named `outFile` is opened in `main()`, and this stream object is passed to the `inOut()` function. The function prototype and header for `inOut()` declare the formal parameter as a reference to an `ostream` object type. The `inOut()` function is then used to write five lines of user-entered text to the file.

 Program 9.8

```cpp
#include <iostream>
#include <fstream>
#include <cstdlib>
#include <string>
using namespace std;

int main()
{
  string fname = "list.dat";   // here is the file you are working with
  void inOut(ofstream&);       // function prototype
  ofstream outFile;

  outFile.open(fname.c_str());

  if (outFile.fail())    // check for a successful open
  {
    cout << "\nThe output file " << fname << " was not successfully opened"
         << endl;
    exit(1);
  }

  inOut(outFile);  // call the function

  return 0;
}

void inOut(ofstream& fileOut)
{
  const int NUMLINES = 5;  // number of lines of text
  string line;
  int count;

  cout << "Please enter five lines of text:" << endl;
  for (count = 0; count < NUMLINES; count++)
  {
    getline(cin,line);
    fileOut << line << endl;
  }

  cout << "\nThe file has been successfully written." << endl;

  return;
}
```

In main(), the file is an ostream object named outFile. This object is passed to the inOut() function and accepted as the formal parameter fileOut, which is declared as a reference to an ostream object type. The inOut() function then uses its reference parameter outFile as an output file stream name in the same manner that main() would use the fileOut stream object. Program 9.8 uses the getline() method introduced in Section 9.2 (see Table 9.3).

Program 9.9 expands on Program 9.8 by adding a getOpen() function to perform the open. Like inOut(), getOpen() accepts a reference argument to an ofstream object. After getOpen() finishes executing, this reference is passed to inOut(), as in Program 9.8. Although you might be tempted to write getOpen() to return a reference to an ofstream, it won't work because it results in an attempt to assign a returned reference to an existing one.

Program 9.9

```cpp
#include <iostream>
#include <fstream>
#include <cstdlib>
#include <string>
using namespace std;

int getOpen(ofstream&);   // function prototype - pass a
                          // reference to an fstream
void inOut(ofstream&);    // function prototype - pass a
                          // reference to an fstream

int main()
{
  ofstream outFile;     // filename is an fstream object

  getOpen(outFile);     // open the file
  inOut(outFile);       // write to it

  return 0;
}

int getOpen(ofstream& fileOut)
{
  string name;

  cout << "\nEnter a filename: ";
  getline(cin,name);

  fileOut.open(name.c_str());        // open the file
```

```
  if (fileOut.fail())      // check for successful open
  {
    cout << "Cannot open the file" << endl;
    exit(1);
  }
  else
    return 1;
}

void inOut(ofstream& fileOut)
{
  const int NUMLINES = 5;   // number of lines
  int count;
  string line;

  cout << "Please enter five lines of text:" << endl;
  for (count = 0; count < NUMLINES; ++count)
  {
    getline(cin,line);
    fileOut << line << endl;
  }
  cout << "\nThe file has been successfully written.";

  return;
}
```

Program 9.9 allows the user to enter a filename from the standard input device and then opens the ofstream connection to the external file. If an existing data file's name is entered, the file is destroyed when it's opened for output. A useful trick for preventing this mishap is shown in the shaded code in Program 9.2.

EXERCISES 9.4

1. **(Practice)** A function named pFile() is to receive a filename as a reference to an ifstream object. What declarations are required to pass a filename to pFile()?

2. **(Practice)** Write a function named fcheck() that checks whether a file exists. The function should accept an ifstream object as a formal reference parameter. If the file exists, the function should return a value of 1; otherwise, the function should return a value of 0.

3. **(Practice)** A data file consisting of a group of lines has been created. Write a function named printLine() that reads and displays any line of the file. For example, the function called printLine(fstream& fName,5); should display the fifth line of the passed object stream.

4. **(Modify)** Rewrite the `getOpen()` function used in Program 9.9 to incorporate the file-checking procedures described in this section. Specifically, if the entered filename exists, an appropriate message should be displayed. The user should be given the option of entering a new filename or allowing the program to overwrite the existing file. Use the function written for Exercise 2 in your program.

9.5 Common Programming Errors

The common programming errors with files are as follows:

1. Forgetting to open a file before attempting to read from it or write to it.
2. Using a file's external name in place of the internal file stream object name when accessing the file. The only stream method that uses the data file's external name is the `open()` method. As always, all stream methods discussed in this chapter must be preceded by a stream object name followed by a period (the dot operator).
3. Opening a file for output without first checking that a file with the same name already exists. If it does and you didn't check for a preexisting filename, the file is overwritten.
4. Not understanding that the end of a file is detected only after the EOF marker has been read or passed over.
5. Attempting to detect the end of a file by using character variables for the EOF marker. Any variable used to accept the EOF must be declared as an integer variable. For example, if ch is declared as a character variable, the following expression produces an infinite loop:[2]

```
while ( (ch = in.file.peek()) != EOF )
```

This problem occurs because a character variable can never take on an EOF code. EOF is an integer value (usually -1) with no character representation, which ensures that the EOF code can't be confused with a legitimate character encountered as normal data in the file. To terminate the loop created by the preceding expression, the variable ch must be declared as an integer variable.

6. Using an integer argument with the `seekg()` and `seekp()` functions. This offset must be a long integer constant or variable. Any other value passed to these functions can have unpredictable results.

9.6 Chapter Summary

1. A data file is any collection of data stored together in an external storage medium under a common name.

2. A data file is connected to a file stream by using a file stream object.

---

[2]This infinite loop doesn't occur on UNIX systems, where characters are stored as signed integers.

3. File stream objects are created from the ifstream, ofstream, or fstream classes. File stream objects declared as ifstream objects are created as input streams, and file streams declared as ofstream objects are created as output streams. File stream objects declared as fstream objects must indicate the type of stream explicitly. To do this, use declaration statements similar to the following (inFile and outFile are user-selected object names):

   ```
   ifstream inFile; or fstream(inFile, ios::in)
   ofstream outFile; or fstream(outFile, ios::out)
   ```

4. After a file stream object is created, it's connected to a file by using an open() method. This method connects a file's external name with an internal stream object name. After the file is opened, all subsequent accesses to it require the internal stream object name.

5. An opened output file stream creates a new data file or erases the data in an existing opened file. An opened input file stream makes an existing file's data available for input. An error condition results if the file doesn't exist and can be detected by using the fail() method.

6. In addition to any files opened in a function, the standard stream objects cin, cout, and cerr are declared and opened automatically when a program runs. cin is an input file stream object used for data entry (usually from the keyboard), cout is an output file stream object used for data display (usually onscreen), and cerr is an output file stream object used for displaying system error messages (usually onscreen).

7. Data files can be accessed randomly by using the seekg(), seekp(), tellg(), and tellp() methods. The g versions of these methods are used to alter and query the file position marker for input file streams, and the p versions do the same for output file streams.

8. Table 9.5 lists class-supplied methods for file manipulation. The getline() method is defined in the string class, and all other methods are defined in the fstream class. These methods can be used by all ifstream and ofstream files.

Table 9.5   File Manipulation Methods

Method Name	Description
get()	Extract the next character from the input stream and return it as an int.
get(chrVar)	Extract the next character from the input stream and assign it to chrVar.
getline(fileObj, string, termChar)	Extract the next string of characters from the input file stream object and assign them to string until the specified terminating character is detected. If omitted, the default terminating character is a newline.

Table 9.5 File Manipulation Methods (*continued*)

Method Name	Description
`getline(C-stringVar,int n,'\n')`	Extract and return characters from the input stream until `n-1` characters are read or a newline is encountered (terminates the input with a `'\0'`).
`peek()`	Return the next character in the input stream without extracting it from the stream.
`put(chrExp)`	Put the character specified by `chrExp` on the output stream.
`putback(chrExp)`	Push the character specified by `chrExp` back onto the input stream. Does not alter the data in the file.
`ignore(int n)`	Skip over the next *n* characters; if *n* is omitted, the default is to skip over the next single character.
`eof()`	Returns a Boolean `true` if a read has been attempted past the end of file; otherwise, it returns a Boolean `false`. The value becomes `true` only when the first character after the last valid file character is read.
`good()`	Returns a Boolean `true` while the file is available for program use. Returns a Boolean `false` if a read has been attempted past the end of file. The value becomes `false` only when the first character after the last valid file character is read.
`bad()`	Returns a Boolean `true` if a read has been attempted past the end of file; otherwise, it returns a `false`. The value becomes `true` only when the first character after the last valid file character is read.
`fail()`	Returns a Boolean `true` if the file hasn't been opened successfully; otherwise, it returns a Boolean `false`.

9.7 Chapter Supplement: The `iostream` Class Library

As you have seen, the classes in the `iostream` class library access files by using entities called streams. For most systems, the data bytes transferred on a stream represent ASCII characters or binary numbers. The mechanism for reading a byte stream from a file or writing a byte stream to a file is hidden when using a high-level language, such as C++. Nevertheless, understanding this mechanism is useful so that you can place the services provided by the `iostream` class library in context.

File Stream Transfer Mechanism

Figure 9.3 illustrates the mechanism for transferring data between a program and a file. As shown, this transfer involves an intermediate file buffer contained in the computer's memory. Each opened file is assigned its own file buffer, which is a storage area used by the data transferred between the program and the file.

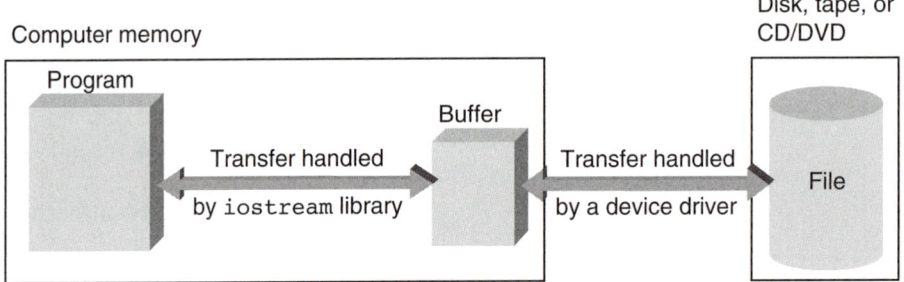

Figure 9.3   The data transfer mechanism

The program either writes a set of data bytes to the file buffer or reads a set of data bytes from the file buffer by using a stream object. The data transfer between the device storing the data file (usually a disk or CD/DVD) and the file buffer is handled by special OS programs. These programs, called device drivers, aren't stand-alone programs; they're an integral part of the OS. A **device driver** is a section of OS code that accesses a hardware device, such as a disk, and handles the data transfer between the device and the computer's memory. Because the computer's internal data transfer rate is generally much faster than any device connected to it, the device driver must correctly synchronize the data transfer speed between the computer and the device sending or receiving data.

Typically, a disk device driver transfers data between the disk and file buffer only in fixed sizes, such as 1024 bytes at a time. Therefore, the file buffer is a convenient means of permitting a device driver to transfer data in blocks of one size, and the program can access them by using a different size (typically, as separate characters or as a fixed number of characters per line).

Components of the `iostream` Class Library

The `iostream` class library consists of two primary base classes: `streambuf` and `ios`. The `streambuf` class provides the file buffer, shown in Figure 9.3, and general routines for transferring binary data. The `ios` class contains a pointer to the file buffers provided by the streambuf class and general routines for transferring text data. From these two base classes, several other classes are derived and included in the iostream class library.

Figure 9.4 is an inheritance diagram for the ios family of classes as it relates to the ifstream, ofstream, and fstream classes. Figure 9.5 is an inheritance diagram for the streambuf family of classes. In these diagrams, the arrows point from a derived class to a base class, so they're actually easier to read from top to bottom. For example, Figure 9.4 indicates that all the stream objects shown are derived from the ios class, and the ifstream class is derived from both the fstream and istream classes. In all cases, a derived class has full access to all methods of its base class.

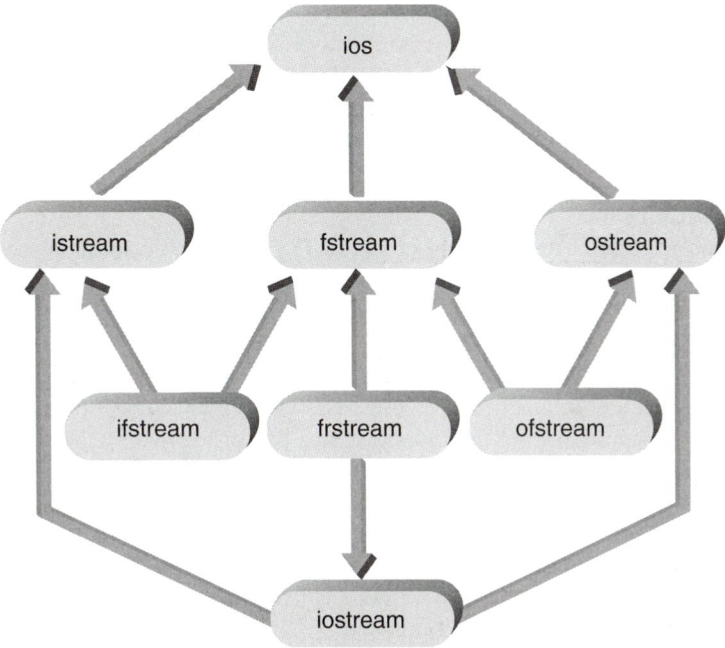

Figure 9.4   The base class ios and its derived classes

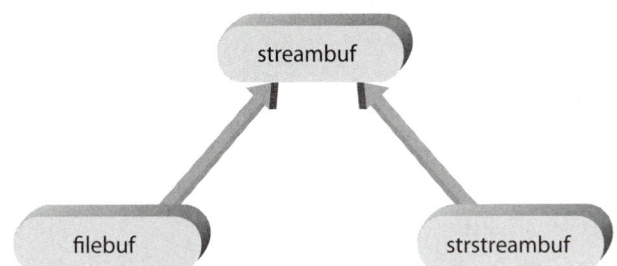

Figure 9.5   The base class streambuf and its derived classes

Table 9.6 lists the correspondence between the classes shown in Figures 9.4 and 9.5, including the header files defining these classes.

Table 9.6 Correspondence Between Classes in Figures 9.4 and 9.5

`ios` **Class**	`streambuf` **Class**	**Header File**

`istream`
`ostream`
`iostream`
	`streambuf`	`iostream or fstream`

`ifstream`
`ofstream`
`fstream`
	`filebuf`	`fstream`

Therefore, the `ifstream`, `ofstream`, and `fstream` classes you have used for file access use a buffer provided by the `filebuf` class and defined in the `fstream` header file. Similarly, the `cin`, `cout`, `cerr`, and `clog iostream` objects use a buffer provided by the `streambuf` class and defined in the `iostream` header file.

In-Memory Formatting

In addition to the classes shown in Figure 9.5, a class named `strstream` is derived from the `ios` class. This class uses the `strstreambuf` class shown in Figure 9.5, requires the `strstream` header file, and provides capabilities for writing and reading strings to and from in-memory defined streams.

When created as an output stream, in-memory streams are typically used to "assemble" a string from smaller pieces until a complete line of characters is ready to be written to `cout` or to a file. Attaching a `strstream` object to a buffer for this purpose is similar to attaching an `fstream` object to an output file. For example, the statement

```
strstream inmem(buf, 72, ios::out);
```

creates a `strstream` object named `buf` to have a capacity of 72 bytes in output mode. Program 9.10 shows how this statement is used in the context of a complete program.

Program 9.10 produces the following output:

```
|No. of units =  10  Price per unit = $  36.85|
```

This output illustrates that the character buffer has been filled in correctly by insertions to the `inmem` stream. (Note that the end-of-string NULL, `'\0'`, which is the last insertion to the stream, is required to close off the C-string correctly.) After the character array has been filled, it's written to a file as a single string.

Program 9.10

```cpp
#include <iostream>
#include <strstream>
#include <iomanip>
using namespace std;

int main()
{
  const int MAXCHARS = 81;   // one more than the maximum characters in a line
  int units = 10;
  double price = 36.85;
  char buf[MAXCHARS];

  strstream inmem(buf, MAXCHARS, ios::out);   // open an in-memory stream

  // write to the buffer through the stream
  inmem << "No. of units = "
        << setw(3) << units
        << "  Price per unit = $"
        << setw(6) << setprecision(2) << fixed << price << '\0';

  cout << '|' << buf << '|';

  cout << endl;

  return 0;
}
```

In a similar manner, a strstream object can be opened in input mode. Input in-memory streams are used as a working storage area, or buffer, for accepting and storing a complete line of text read from a file or standard input. After the buffer has been filled, the extraction operator would be used to "disassemble" the string into component parts and convert each data item into its designated data type. Doing this allows inputting data from a file on a line-by-line basis before assigning data items to their respective variables.

Part Two

Object-Oriented Programming

Chapter 10

Introduction to Classes

Besides being an improved version of C, the distinguishing characteristic of C++ is its support of object-oriented programming. Central to this object orientation is the concept of a class, which is a programmer-defined data type. Objects are created from classes.

This chapter explores the implications of allowing programmers to define their own data types by using classes. Additionally, you see how to construct classes and create objects from them. As you'll see, the construction of a class is based on variables and methods. What C++ provides is a unique way of combining these two elements into a self-contained, cohesive unit from which objects can be created.

10.1 Object-Based Programming

As you learned in Chapter 1, a procedural program is simply an algorithm written in a programming language. The reasons for this emphasis on procedural programming are mostly historical. When computers were developed in the 1940s, mathematicians used them for military purposes. These early computers computed bomb trajectories and decoded enemy orders and diplomatic transmissions. Until well into the 1970s, computers were still used mainly for mathematical and scientific as well as accounting and payroll applications. The common factor in all these applications is that they use well-defined algorithms and equations. This use was reflected in the name of the first commercial high-level language, introduced in 1957: Formula Translation (FORTRAN).[1] In the 1960s, nearly all computer courses were taught in engineering or mathematics departments. The term **computer science** wasn't yet in common use, and computer science departments were just being formed.

This situation has changed dramatically, mainly for two reasons. One reason was the failure of procedural programs to adequately contain software costs for larger programming projects. These costs included both initial program development and subsequent program maintenance costs. As Figure 10.1 shows, the major cost of most large computer projects, whether technical or commercial, is software. Software costs contribute so heavily to total project costs because they're related to human productivity and are labor-intensive, whereas equipment costs are related to manufacturing technologies.

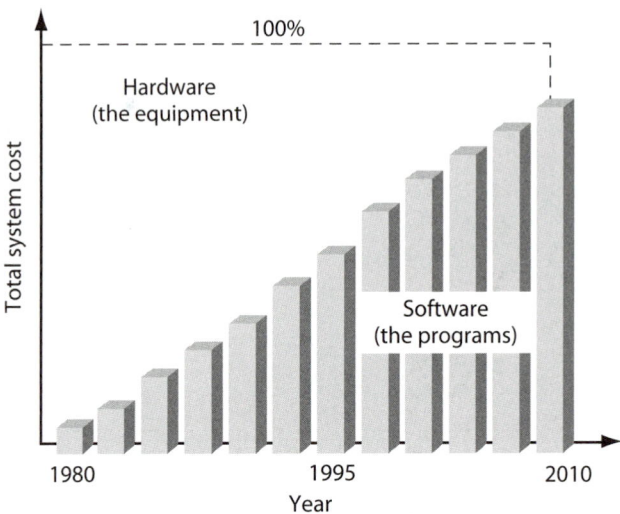

Figure 10.1   Software is the major cost of most computer projects

Increasing manufacturing productivity a thousandfold, with the resulting decrease in hardware costs, is far easier than for programmers to double the quantity or quality of the code they produce. For example, microchips that cost more than $500 10 years ago can now be purchased for less than $1. Similarly, the processing power of computers that cost more than a million dollars in the 1960s is now exceeded by laptop computers costing only hundreds of dollars. Consequently, as hardware costs have plummeted, software productivity and its associated costs have remained fairly constant. Therefore, the ratio of software costs to total system costs (hardware plus software) has increased substantially. One way to increase programmer productivity is to create code that can be reused easily without extensive revising, retesting, and revalidating. Procedural code didn't provide this reusability, which has led to the search for better software approaches.

---

[1]Business-oriented applications, such as accounting and payroll, were usually coded in Common Business-Oriented Language (COBOL).

Point of Information

Procedural, Hybrid, and Pure Object-Oriented Languages

Most high-level programming languages can be categorized as procedural, object-oriented, or hybrid. FORTRAN, the first commercial high-level programming language, is procedural. This makes sense because FORTRAN was designed to perform mathematical calculations that used standard algebraic formulas. These formulas were described as algorithms, and then the algorithms were coded by using function and subroutine procedures. Subsequent procedural languages included BASIC, COBOL, and Pascal.

The first requirement of a pure object-oriented language, such as Smalltalk and Eiffel, is that it must contain three specific features: classes, inheritance, and polymorphism (described in this chapter and Chapter 12). In addition, however, a "pure" object-oriented language must always use classes. In a pure object-oriented language, all data types are constructed as classes, all data values are objects, all operators can be overloaded, and every data operation can be executed only by using a class member method. In a pure object-oriented language, it's impossible *not* to use object-oriented features in a program. This isn't the case in a hybrid language.

In a hybrid language, such as C++, it's impossible *not* to use procedural elements in a program because the use of any non-class data type or operation, such as adding two integers, violates pure object-oriented requirements. Although a hybrid language must be able to define classes, its distinguishing feature is that it's possible to write a complete program with only procedural code. Additionally, hybrid languages need not provide inheritance and polymorphism—but they must provide classes. Languages that use classes but don't provide inheritance and polymorphism are referred to as object-*based* languages rather than object-*oriented* languages. All versions of Visual Basic before version 4 are examples of object-based hybrid languages.

A second reason for disenchantment with traditional procedural programming was the emergence of graphical screens and windowed applications. Programming multiple windows on the same graphical screen is almost impossible with standard procedural programming techniques. The solution to producing cost-effective and reusable graphical programs was found in artificial intelligence–based and simulation programming techniques. Artificial intelligence programming contained extensive research on object recognition, and simulation programming required considerable background on representing items as objects, with well-defined interactions between them. This object-based paradigm was well suited for graphical windowed environments, in which each window can be specified as a self-contained object. Items then placed in a window can also be represented as objects.

Objects are also well suited to a programming representation because an object can be specified by two basic characteristics: a current **state**, which defines how the object appears at the moment, and a **behavior**, which defines how the object reacts to external inputs. Both characteristics can be coded easily by using an object-based approach.

To understand this point, consider a physical object, such as an elevator. Like all objects, an elevator can be modeled in terms of a state and a behavior. Its state might be given in terms of its size, location, interior decoration, or any number of attributes, and its behavior might be specified in terms of its reaction when one of its buttons is pushed. Constructing a model of an elevator, however, requires selecting the attributes and behaviors that are of interest. For purposes of a simulation, for example, you might be concerned only with the elevator's current floor position and how to simulate movement between floors. Other attributes and behaviors might be left out of the model because they don't affect the aspects of the elevator you're interested in studying. In Section 10.4, you see how to create an elevator object in C++ and then simulate its movement from floor to floor.

A Class Is a Plan

In creating C++'s objects, you must first create a structure, or plan, for a class of objects from which individual objects are created. For example, before attempting to assemble a bicycle or a backyard basketball hoop, you would want to know that all the parts are available and have a set of assembly instructions. In preparing a dinner, you might consult a recipe that specifies a list of ingredients and procedures for combining them correctly. In all these examples, even if written instructions aren't available, they have to at least exist in the mind of the builder, the chef, or whoever is in charge of the project. In C++, the plans from which objects are created and used are referred to as classes.

From a programming perspective, a class can be considered a construction plan for objects and how they can be used. This plan lists the required data items and supplies instructions for using the data. After one or more objects from this plan, or class, have been constructed, they can then be operated on only in ways defined by the class. Although many objects can be created from the same class, each different object type requires its own class, which is similar to producing many Chevrolet Camaros from one set of plans and Chevrolet Malibus from another.

To understand how a C++ class is actually constructed, a recipe is a useful analogy. The difference is that a C++ class is a recipe for assembling data rather than food items. Other than that, the relationship between a C++ class and a somewhat modified recipe is almost one to one and is extremely informative.

Take a look at the recipe shown in Figure 10.2. Most recipes contain similar types of components, but what's surprising is that almost exactly the same elements are required in constructing a C++ class. Notice that the recipe shown in this figure isn't the final spread; it merely provides a plan for creating a sardine spread. The recipe can be used many times, and each time it's used, a particular batch of sardine spread is produced.

From Recipe to Class

Now you can make the connection between the recipe in Figure 10.2 and a C++ class. As mentioned, a class can be considered the plan or recipe from which programming objects are created. Like its recipe counterpart, a class typically contains sections for ingredients and methods.

Recipe Name: Gary's Sardine Spread

Ingredients:

Measure	*Contents*
1 can	Boneless and skinless sardines
2 stalks	Celery
1/4 medium	Red onion
1 tablespoon	Mayonnaise
1/4 cup	Parsley
dash	Olive oil
splash	Red wine vinegar
dash	Salt
dash	Pepper

Method of Preparation:

Finely shred the sardines using two forks

Finely dice the celery and onion and mix well with sardines

Add olive oil and mix well

Add mayonnaise and mix well

Add red wine vinegar and mix well

Finely dice the parsley and mix well

Salt and pepper to taste

Figure 10.2   Recipe for Gary's sardine spread

In the ingredients section, instead of recipe measures such as a teaspoon or cup, C++ deals with measures for holding integers, double-precision numbers, strings, and other types of suitable data "ingredients." Besides a measure, each data item has a specific value, such as 5, and a name, such as `firstIntegerNumber`. Therefore, the list of data items used in a C++ class is, like the list of ingredients in a recipe, contained in a specific section. As an example, suppose you're creating a C++ program to calculate the average of two numbers. The following programming plan for determining an average shows the data elements and methods for constructing a class for this application, which will form the basis of an object-oriented solution:

```
// Class declaration section
Class Name: AverageofTwoNumbers
    // A list of data items to use (the parts list)
    Type      Name
    double    firstNumber
    double    secondNumber
    // A list of necessary methods (prototypes)
    double assignValues(double, double);
    double calculateAndDisplay(double, double);
// Class implementation section (the instructions)
    Code for the two methods listed previously
```

Notice that this programming plan contains the same two basic sections shown in Figure 10.2: a list of ingredients (in this case, the ingredients are data items) and an assembly section containing the actual instructions, as methods, for using the ingredients listed.

There are, however, three notable differences in the ingredients section. First, the Measure column in Figure 10.2 is relabeled as Type in the programming plan. Second, the Contents column in Figure 10.2 is missing in the programming plan. The actual values, or contents, can be assigned as default method parameters or, more typically, provided as user-entered values requested by the listed methods. Finally, the class declaration section provides not only a list of data "ingredients," but also a list of method names and data types (the proto-types). Using this basic structure, you're ready to learn how to develop C++ classes in the next section for constructing working object-oriented programs.

EXERCISES 10.1

1. **(Practice)** Figure 10.3 is a simplified diagram for assembling a birdhouse. Referring to this diagram, create a parts list and instructions for constructing it.

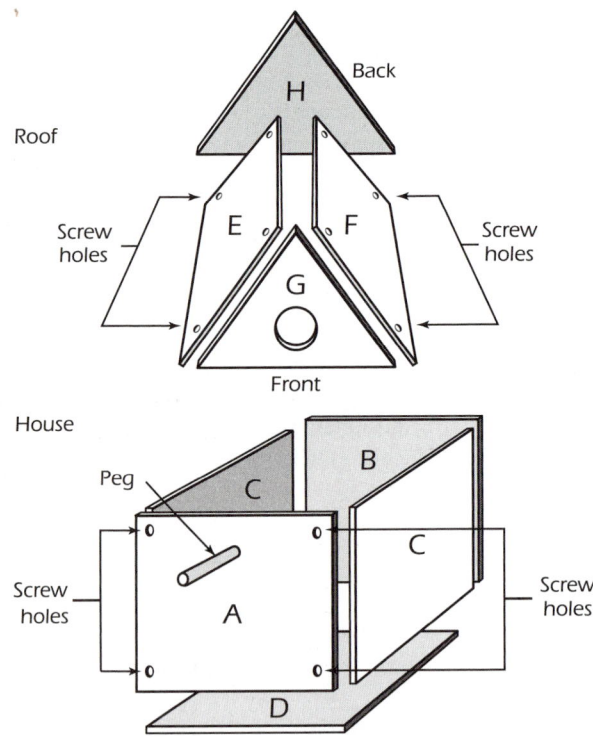

Figure 10.3   Building a birdhouse

2. **(Practice) a.** List the items you need to build a staircase with five steps.
   b. Write instructions for assembling the items listed in Exercise 2a.

3. **(Practice) a.** List the ingredients you need to create 10 peanut butter and jelly sandwiches.
   b. Write instructions for assembling the items listed in Exercise 3a.

4. **(Practice)** Find assembly instructions from a recent item you have built (for example, a bicycle or a bookcase with one shelf). Identify the major elements in the assembly instructions that correspond to the Ingredients and Method of Preparation sections shown in Figure 10.2.

5. **(Practice)** Determine the data items and methods that would be useful for a class used for simulating tossing a single die. Choose your own class name and data item names.

6. **(Practice)** Determine the data items and methods that would be useful for a class used for calculating the floor space of a rectangular room. Choose your own class name and data item names.

10.2 Creating Your Own Classes

In computer terminology, the combination of data and associated operations is defined as a **class**. That is, a class defines *both* the types of data and the types of operations that can be performed on the data. Seen in this light, the built-in data types in C++ can also be considered classes, in that they provide types of data and operations that can be performed on the data. Because of this correspondence, C++ classes are sometimes referred to as programmer-defined data types or **abstract data types**. In a simplified form, this relationship can be described as follows:

class = allowable data values + operational capabilities

Before seeing how to construct your own classes, take a moment to review a list of the operational capabilities supplied with C++'s built-in data types. The reason for this review is that you have to provide some of these capabilities as part of the classes you create. Although you probably don't think of these capabilities when you use them, the designers of C++ clearly had to when they created the C++ compiler. Table 10.1 lists the minimum set of these capabilities.

Table 10.1   Operational Capabilities of C++'s Built-In Data Types

Capability	Example
Define one or more variables of the class	`int a, b;`
Initialize a variable at definition	`int a = 5;`
Assign a value to a variable	`a = 10;`
Assign one variable's value to another variable	`a = b;`
Perform mathematical operations	`a + b;`
Convert from one data type to another	`a = int (7.2);`

Constructing a class is easy, and you already have all the necessary tools in variables and functions. In C++, variables provide the means of defining new data types, and functions provide the means of defining operational capabilities. Using this information, you can extend the previous definition of a class to its C++ representation:

C++ class = data + functions

In other words, a C++ class provides a mechanism for packaging data and functions together in a self-contained unit. This chapter explains how classes are constructed and how objects are created from them, including initialization and assignment of values to objects. The mathematical and conversion capabilities listed in Table 10.1, as they apply to classes, are discussed in Chapter 11.

Class Construction

A class defines both data and functions. This definition is usually accomplished by constructing a class in two parts: a declaration section and an implementation section. As shown in the following code example, the **declaration section** declares both the data types and functions for the class. The **implementation section** then defines the functions whose prototypes have been declared in the declaration section.[2]

```
// class declaration section
class className
{
  data declarations
  function prototypes
};


// class implementation section
function definitions
```

Both the variables and functions listed in the class declaration section are collectively referred to as **class members**. Separately, the variables are referred to as both **data members** and **instance variables** (the terms are synonymous), and the functions are referred to as **member functions** and **methods**. (The term "class methods" is also used.) A method can't have the same name as a data member.

As a specific example of a class, take a look at the following definition of a class named Date. This type of class is important in applications where equipment delivery dates and schedules depend on exact date determinations. To accomplish this task, a number of methods for determining whether a date falls on a weekend or holiday, for example, would still have to be added to this class:

```
//class declaration section
class Date
{
  private:            // notice the colon after the word private
      int month;      // a data member
      int day;        // a data member
      int year;       // a data member
```

---

[2]This separation into two parts isn't mandatory, as the implementation can be included in the declaration statement.

```
   public:         // again, notice the colon here
      Date(int = 7, int = 4, int = 2012); // a member method
      void setDate(int, int, int);        // a member method
      void showDate();                    // a member method
}; // this is a declaration - don't forget the semicolon

// class implementation section
// this is where methods are defined
Date::Date(int mm, int dd, int yyyy)
{
   month = mm;
   day = dd;
   year = yyyy;
}

void Date::setDate(int mm, int dd, int yyyy)
{
   month = mm; day = dd; year = yyyy;
   return;
}

void Date::showDate()
{
   cout << "The date is ";
   cout << setfill('0')
        << setw(2) << month << '/'
        << setw(2) << day << '/'
        << setw(2) << year % 100; // extract the last 2 year digits
   cout << endl;
   return;
}
```

Because this definition might look overwhelming, first notice that it does consist of two sections—a declaration section and an implementation section. The declaration section begins with the keyword class followed by a class name. Following the class name are the class's variable declarations and method prototypes, enclosed in a brace pair terminated with a semicolon. The general structure of this form is as follows:[3]

```
//class declaration section
class Name
{
```

---

[3]Other forms are possible. However, this form is commonly used and easy to understand, so it serves as the standard model in this book.

```
    private:
      a list of variable declarations
    public:
      a list of method prototypes
};
```

Notice that the Date class follows this format. For convenience, it's listed again with no internal comments:

```
// class declaration section
class Date
{
  private:
      int month;
      int day;
      int year;
  public:
      Date(int = 7, int = 4, int = 2012);
      void setDate(int, int, int);
      void showDate();
};
```

The name of this class is Date. Although the initial uppercase letter isn't required, it's used by convention to designate a class. The body of the class declaration section, enclosed in braces, consists of variable and method declarations. In this case, the data members month, day, and year are declared as integers, and three methods named Date(), setDate(), and showDate() are declared via prototypes. The keywords private and public are **access specifiers** that define access rights.

The private keyword specifies that the class members following it—in this case, month, day, and year—can be accessed only by using the class methods (or friend functions, as discussed in Section 11.1).[4] The private designation is meant to enforce data security by requiring that all access to private data members be made through the provided member methods. This type of access, which prevents a user from seeing how data is actually stored, is referred to as **data hiding**. After a class category such as private is designated, it remains in force until a new category is listed.

In this Date class, a date is stored by using three integers for the month, day, and year. In addition, the year will always be stored as a four-digit number. For example, the year 1998 is stored as 1998, not as 98. Making sure to store all years with their century designation eliminates a multitude of problems that can crop up if only the last two digits are stored. For example, the number of years between 2012 and 1999 can be calculated quickly as 2012 - 1999 = 13 years, but getting this same answer isn't as easy with the year values 12 and 99. Additionally, with four digits, it's clear what the year 2012 refers to, but the two-digit value 12 could refer to 1912 or 2012.

---

[4]Note that the default membership category in a class is private, which means this keyword can be omitted. In this book, the private designation is used to reinforce the idea of access restrictions in class memberships.

Following the `private` class data members, the method prototypes listed in the `Date` class have been declared as `public`. This means these class methods *can* be called by any objects and functions not in the class (from outside the class, in other words). In general, all class methods should be `public` so that they provide capabilities to manipulate class variables from outside the class.

The `Date` class provides three methods named `Date()`, `setDate()`, and `showDate()`. Notice that one of these member methods has the same name, `Date`, as the class name. It's referred to as a **constructor method**, and it has a special purpose: It can be used to initialize class data members with values. The default values used for this method are the numbers 7, 4, and 2012, which, as you see shortly, are used as the default `month`, `day`, and `year` values. Note that the default year is represented as a four-digit integer to retain the century designation. Also, notice that the constructor method has no return type, which is a requirement for this special method. The two remaining methods declared in the `Date` class, `setDate()` and `showDate()`, have been declared as returning no value (`void`).

The class implementation section is where the member methods declared in the declaration section are written to permit the initialization, assignment, and display capabilities implied by their names.[5] The following example shows the general form of methods written in the implementation section. This format is correct for all methods except the constructor, which, as stated previously, has no return type:

```
returnType className::methodName(parameter list)
{
    method body
}
```

As this example shows, member methods defined in the class implementation section have the same format as all user-written C++ functions, with the addition of the class name and scope resolution operator, `::`, that identifies the method as a member of a particular class. Now take another look at the implementation section of the `Date` class, which is repeated for convenience:

```
// class implementation section
Date::Date(int mm, int dd, int yyyy)
{
  month = mm;
  day = dd;
  year = yyyy;
}
```

---

[5]You can also define these methods in the declaration section by declaring and writing them as inline functions. Section 10.3 includes examples of inline member functions.

```
void Date::setDate(int mm, int dd, int yyyy)
{
  month = mm;
  day = dd;
  year = yyyy;
  return;
}

void Date::showDate()
{
  cout << "The Date is ";
  cout << setfill('0')
       << setw(2) << month << '/'
       << setw(2) << day << '/'
       << setw(2) << year % 100; // extract the last 2 year digits
  cout << endl;
  return;
}
```

Notice that the first method in this implementation section has the same name as the class, which makes it a constructor method. Therefore, it has no return type. The `Date::` at the beginning of the header identifies this method as a member of the `Date` class. The rest of the header

```
Date(int mm, int dd, int yyyy)
```

defines the method as having three integer parameters. The body of this method simply assigns the data members `month`, `day`, and `year` with the values of the parameters `mm`, `dd`, and `yyyy`.

The next header

```
void Date::setDate(int mm, int dd, int yyyy)
```

defines `setDate()` as belonging to the `Date` class (`Date::`). This method returns no value (void) and expects three integer parameters: `mm`, `dd`, and `yyyy`. In a manner similar to the `Date()` method, the body of this method assigns the data members `month`, `day`, and `year` the values of its parameters.

Finally, the last header in the class implementation section

```
void Date::showDate()
```

defines a method named `showDate()`. This method has no parameters, returns no value, and is a member of the `Date` class. The body of this method, however, needs a little more explanation.

Although all years have been stored as four-digit values to retain century information, users are accustomed to seeing dates with the year represented as a two-digit value, such as 12/15/12. To display the last two digits of the `year` value, the expression `year % 100` can be used. For example, if the year is 1999, the expression `1999 % 100` yields the value 99, and if the year is 2012, the expression `2012 % 100` yields the value 12.

If you had used an assignment statement such as `year = year % 100;`, however, you would actually be altering the stored value of `year` to correspond to the last two digits of the year. Because you want to retain the year as a four-digit number, you must be careful to manipulate only the *displayed* value by using the expression `year % 100` in the `cout` statement. The `setfill` and `setw` manipulators are used to make sure the displayed values correspond to conventionally accepted dates. For example, the date March 9, 2008, should appear as 3/9/08 or 03/09/08. The `setw` manipulator forces each value to be displayed in a field width of 2. Because this manipulator remains in effect only for the next insertion, it's used before the display of each date value. Because the `setfill` manipulator remains in effect until the fill character is changed, however, it must be included only once. The `setfill` manipulator has been used to change the fill character from the default of a blank space to the character 0. Doing this ensures that a date such as December 9, 2009 appears as `12/09/09`, not as `12/ 9/ 9`.

To see how the `Date` class can be used in the context of a complete program, take a look at Program 10.1. To make the program easier to read, the shaded area contains the class declaration and implementation sections. The unshaded area contains the header and `main()` function. This shading is used in the remainder of the book for all programs using classes.[6]

Program 10.1

```cpp
#include <iostream>
#include <iomanip>
using namespace std;

// class declaration section
class Date
{
  private:
    int month;
    int day;
    int year;
  public:
    Date(int = 7, int = 4, int = 2012); // constructor
    void setDate(int, int, int);   // member method to copy a date
    void showDate();               // member method to display a date
};
// class implementation section
Date::Date(int mm, int dd, int yyyy)
{
  month = mm;
  day = dd;
  year = yyyy;
}
```

---

[6]This shading isn't accidental. In practice, the shaded area containing the class definition is placed in a separate file. A single `#include` statement is then used to include this class declaration in the program. The final program would consist of the unshaded areas in Program 10.1, with the addition of another `#include` statement.

```
void Date::setDate(int mm, int dd, int yyyy)
{
  month = mm;
  day = dd;
  year = yyyy;
  return;
}
void Date::showDate()
{
    cout << "The date is ";
    cout << setfill('0')
        << setw(2) << month << '/'
        << setw(2) << day << '/'
        << setw(2) << year % 100; // extract the last 2 year digits
    cout << endl;

  return;
}
```

```
int main()
{
  Date a, b, c(4,1,2000);   // declare 3 objects

  b.setDate(12,25,2009);   // assign values to b's data members
  a.showDate();            // display object a's values
  b.showDate();            // display object b's values
  c.showDate();            // display object c's values

  return 0;
}
```

The class declaration and implementation sections in the shaded area of Program 10.1 should look familiar to you. Notice, however, that this area only declares the class; it doesn't create any variables of this class type. This is true of all C++ types, including the built-in types, such as integers and doubles. Just as a variable of an integer type must be defined, variables of a user-declared class must also be defined. Variables defined to be of a user-declared class are referred to as **objects**.

Using this new terminology, the first statement in Program 10.1's main() function defines three objects—named a, b, and c—to be of the class type Date. In C++, when a new object is defined, memory is allocated for the object, and its data members are initialized automatically by a call to the class constructor method. For example, examine the definition Date a, b, c(4,1,2000); in main(). When the object named a is defined, the constructor method `Date()` is called automatically. Because no parameters have been assigned to a, the constructor method's default values are used, resulting in this initialization:

```
a.month = 7
a.day = 4
a.year = 2012
```

Notice the notation used here: an object name and an attribute name separated by a period. This is the standard syntax for referring to an object's attribute:

objectName.attributeName

The *objectName* is the name of a specific object, and *attributeName* is the name of a data member defined for the object's class. Therefore, the notation a.month = 7 indicates that object a's month data member has been set to the value 7. Similarly, the notations a.day = 4 and a.year = 2012 indicate that a's day and year data members have been set to the values 4 and 2012.

In the same manner, when the object named b is defined, the same default parameters are used, resulting in the initialization of b's data members as follows:

```
b.month = 7
b.day = 4
b.year = 2012
```

The object named c, however, is defined with the arguments 4, 1, and 2000. These three arguments are passed to the constructor method when the object is defined, resulting in the following initialization of c's data members:

```
c.month = 4
c.day = 1
c.year = 2000
```

The next statement in main(), b.setDate(12,25,2009), calls b's setDate() method, which assigns the argument values 12, 25, and 2009 to b's data members, resulting in this assignment:

```
b.month = 12
b.day = 25
b.year = 2009
```

Notice the syntax for referring to an object's method:

objectName.methodName(parameters)

The *objectName* is the name of a specific object, and *methodName* is the name of a method defined for the object's class. Because all class methods have been defined as public, a statement such as b.setDate(12,25,2009) is valid inside the main() function and is a call to the class's setDate() method. This statement tells the setDate() method to operate on the b object with the arguments 12, 25, and 2009. It's important to understand that because all class data members have been specified as private, a statement such as b.month = 12 would be invalid inside main(). Therefore, you're forced to rely on member methods to access data member values.

The last three statements in `main()` call the `showDate()` method to operate on the a, b, and c objects. The first call results in the display of a's data values, the second call in the display of b's data values, and the third call in the display of c's data values. Therefore, the output of Program 10.1 is the following:

```
The date is 07/04/12
The date is 12/25/09
The date is 04/01/00
```

Notice that a statement such as `cout << a;` is invalid inside `main()` because `cout` doesn't know how to handle an object of class `Date`. Therefore, the `Date` class is supplied with a method that can be used to access and display an object's internal values.

Terminology

As there's sometimes confusion about the terms classes, objects, and other object-oriented programming terminology, taking a moment to clarify and review the terminology is helpful.

A **class** is a programmer-defined data type from which objects can be created. **Objects** are created from classes; they have the same relationship to classes as variables do to C++'s built-in data types. For example, in the declaration

```
int a;
```

a is said to be a variable, and in the Program 10.1 declaration

```
Date a;
```

a is said to be an object. If it helps you to think of an object as a variable, do so.

Objects are also referred to as **instances** of a class, and the process of creating a new object is often referred to as an **instantiation** of the object. Each time a new object is instantiated (created), a new set of data members belonging to the object is created.[7] The values contained in these data members determine the object's **state**.

Seen in this way, a class can be thought of as a blueprint for creating particular instances (objects). Each instance (object) of a class has its own set of values for the set of data members specified in the class declaration section.

In addition to the data types allowed for an object, a class also defines **behavior**—that is, the operations permitted to be performed on an object's data members. Users of the object need to know *what* these methods can do and how to activate them through method calls but generally don't need to know *how* the operation is done. The actual implementation details of an object's operations are in the class implementation, which can (and should) be hidden from the user. Other names for the operations defined in a class implementation section are procedures, functions, services, and methods. These terms are used interchangeably throughout the remainder of the book.

EXERCISES 10.2

1. **(Review)** Define the following terms:
   a. Class
   b. Object
   c. Declaration section
   d. Implementation section
   e. Instance variable
   f. Member method
   g. Data member
   h. Constructor
   i. Class instance
   j. Services
   k. Methods
   l. Interface

2. **(Practice)** Write a class declaration section for each of the following specifications. In each case, include a prototype for a constructor and a member method named `showData()` that can be used to display data member values.
   a. A class named `Time` that has integer data members named `secs`, `mins`, and `hours`
   b. A class named `Complex` that has double-precision data members named `real` and `imaginary`
   c. A class named `Circle` that has integer data members named `xcenter` and `ycenter` and a double-precision data member named `radius`
   d. A class named `System` that has character data members named `computer`, `printer`, and `screen`, each capable of holding 30 characters (including the end-of-string `NULL`), and double-precision data members named `compPrice`, `printPrice`, and `scrnPrice`

---

[7]Note that only one set of class methods is created. These methods are shared between objects.

3. **(Practice) a.** Construct a class implementation section for the constructor and `showData()` member methods corresponding to the class declaration created for Exercise 2a.

   b. Construct a class implementation section for the constructor and `showData()` methods corresponding to the class declaration created for Exercise 2b.

   c. Construct a class implementation section for the constructor and `showData()` methods corresponding to the class declaration created for Exercise 2c.

   d. Construct a class implementation section for the constructor and `showData()` methods corresponding to the class declaration created for Exercise 2d.

4. **(Program) a.** Include the class declaration and implementation sections prepared for Exercises 2a and 3a in a complete working program.

   b. Include the class declaration and implementation sections prepared for Exercises 2b and 3b in a complete working program.

   c. Include the class declaration and implementation sections prepared for Exercises 2c and 3c in a complete working program.

   d. Include the class declaration and implementation sections prepared for Exercises 2d and 3d in a complete working program.

5. **(Desk check)** Determine the errors in the following class declaration section:

```
class Employee
{
public:
    int empnum;
    char code;
private:
    class(int = 0);
    void showemp(int, char);
};
```

6. **(Modify) a.** Add another member method named `convert()` to Program 10.1 that does the following: The method should access the `month`, `year`, and `day` data members and display and then return an integer calculated as *year* × *10000* + *month* × *100* + *day*. For example, if the date is 4/1/2014, the returned value is 20140401. (Dates in this form are useful when performing sorts because placing the numbers in numerical order automatically places the corresponding dates in chronological order.)

   b. Include the modified `Date` class constructed for Exercise 6a in a complete C++ program.

7. **(Modify) a.** Add to Program 10.1's class definition an additional member method named `leapyr()` that returns a `true` if the year is a leap year and a `false` if it's not a leap year. A leap year is any year that's evenly divisible by 4 but not by 100, with the exception that all years evenly divisible by 400 are leap years. For example, the year 1996 is a leap year because it's evenly divisible by 4 and not evenly divisible by 100. The year 2000 is a leap year because it's evenly divisible by 400.

   b. Include the class definition constructed for Exercise 7a in a complete C++ program. The `main()` function should display the message `The year is a leap year` or the message `The year is not a leap year` (depending on the `Date` object's year value).

8. **(Modify) a.** Add a member method named `dayOfWeek()` to Program 10.1's class definition that determines the day of the week for any `Date` object. An algorithm for determining the day of the week, known as Zeller's algorithm, is the following:

> *If mm is less than 3*
>   *mm = mm + 12 and yyyy = yyyy - 1*
> *Endif*
> *Set century = int(yyyy/100)*
> *Set year = yyyy % 100*
> *Set T = dd + int(26 * (mm + 1)/10) + year + int(year / 4)*
>   *int(century / 4) - 2 * century*
> *Set DayOfWeek = T % 7*
> *If DayOfWeek is less than 0*
>   *DayOfWeek = DayOfWeek + 7*
> *Endif*

Using this algorithm, the variable `DayOfWeek` has a value of 0 if the date is a Saturday, 1 if a Sunday, and so forth.

b. Include the class definition constructed for Exercise 8a in a complete C++ program. The `main()` function should display the name of the day (Sun, Mon, Tue, and so on) for the `Date` object being tested.

9. **(Program) a.** Construct a class named `Rectangle` that has double-precision data members named `length` and `width`. The class should have member methods named `perimeter()` and `area()` to calculate a rectangle's perimeter and area, a member method named `setData()` to set a rectangle's length and width, and a member method named `showData()` that displays a rectangle's length, width, perimeter, and area.

b. Include the `Rectangle` class constructed in Exercise 9a in a working C++ program.

10. **(Modify) a.** Modify the `Date` class defined in Program 10.1 to include a `nextDay()` method that increments a date by one day. Test your method to ensure that it increments days into a new month and into a new year correctly.

b. Modify the `Date` class defined in Program 10.1 to include a `priorDay()` method that decrements a date by one day. Test your method to ensure that it decrements days into a prior month and into a prior year correctly.

11. **(Modify)** Modify the `Date` class in Program 10.1 to contain a method that compares two `Date` objects and returns the larger of the two. The method should be written according to the following algorithm:

> *Accept two* `Date` *values as parameters*
> *Determine the later date by using the following procedure:*
>   *Convert each date into an integer value having the form yyyymmdd*
>   *(This can be accomplished with the formula year * 10000 + month * 100 + day)*
>   *Compare the corresponding integers for each date*
>   *The larger integer corresponds to the later date*
> *Return the later date*

10.3 Constructors

As you learned in Section 10.2, a constructor method is any method with the same name as its class. Multiple constructors can be defined for each class, as long as they can be distinguished by the number and types of their parameters.

A constructor's intended purpose is to initialize a new object's data members. Depending on the number and types of supplied arguments, one constructor method is called automatically each time an object is created. If no constructor method is written, the compiler supplies a default constructor. In addition to its initialization role, a constructor method can perform other tasks when it's called and be written in a variety of ways. This section explains possible variations of constructor methods and introduces another method, the destructor, which is called automatically whenever an object goes out of existence.

The following code example shows the general format of a constructor method:

```
className::className(parameter list)
{
  // method body
}
```

As this format shows, a constructor must have the following:

- The same name as the class to which it belongs
- No return type (not even `void`)

If you don't include a constructor in your class definition, the compiler supplies a do-nothing default one for you. For example, examine the following class declaration:

```
// class declaration section
class Date
{
  private:
    int month, day, year;
  public:
    void setDate(int, int, int);
    void showDate(void);
};
```

Because no user-defined constructor has been declared, the compiler creates a default constructor. For the `Date` class, this default constructor is equivalent to `Date::Date(void){}`—that is, the compiler-supplied default constructor expects no parameters and has an empty body. Clearly, this default constructor isn't very useful, but it does exist if no other constructor is declared.

The term **default constructor** is used often in C++ and refers to any constructor that doesn't require arguments when it's called. The reason it doesn't require arguments is that no arguments are declared, as with the compiler-supplied default, or all arguments have been given default values. For example, `Date(int mm = 7, int dd = 4, int yyyy = 2012)` is a valid prototype for a default constructor. Each argument has been given a default value, and an object can be declared as type `Date` without supplying any further arguments. Using this

Point of Information

Constructors

A constructor is any method with the same name as its class. Its main purpose is to initialize an object's member variables when an object is created, so a constructor is called automatically when an object is declared.

A class can have multiple constructors if each constructor can be distinguished by having a different formal parameter list. A compiler error results when unique identification of a constructor isn't possible. If no constructor is provided, the compiler supplies a do-nothing default constructor.

Every constructor method must be declared with *no return type* (not even `void`). Because they're methods, constructors can also be called in nondeclaration statements. When used in this manner, the method call requires parentheses following the constructor name, even if no parameters are used. However, when used in a declaration, parentheses *must not* be included for a constructor. For example, the declaration `Date a();` is incorrect. The correct declaration is `Date a;`. When parameters are used, however, they must be enclosed in parentheses in both declaration and nondeclaration statements. Default parameter values should be included in the constructor's prototype.

default constructor, the declaration `Date a;` initializes the a object with the default values 7, 4, and 2012.

To verify that a constructor method is called automatically when a new object is created, examine Program 10.2. Notice that in the implementation section, the constructor uses `cout` to display the message `Created a new date object with data values`. Therefore, whenever the constructor is called, this message is displayed. Because the `main()` function creates three objects, the constructor is called three times, and the message is displayed three times.

The following output is produced when Program 10.2 runs:

```
Created a new date object with data values 7, 4, 2012
Created a new date object with data values 7, 4, 2012
Created a new date object with data values 4, 1, 2009
```

Although any legitimate C++ statement can be used in a constructor method, such as the `cout` statement in Program 10.2, it's best to keep constructors simple and use them only for initializing purposes. One further point needs to be made about the constructor in Program 10.2. According to C++ rules, object members are initialized in the order they're declared in the class declaration section, *not* in the order they might appear in the method's definition in the implementation section. Usually, this order isn't an issue, unless one data member is initialized by using another data member's value.

Program 10.2

```cpp
#include <iostream>
using namespace std;

// class declaration section
class Date
{
  private:
    int month;
    int day;
    int year;
  public:
    Date(int = 7, int = 4, int = 2012);    // constructor
};

// class implementation section
Date::Date(int mm, int dd, int yyyy)
{
  month = mm;
  day = dd;
  year = yyyy;
  cout << "Created a new date object with data values "
       << month << ", " << day << ", " << year << endl;
}

int main()
{
  Date a;              // declare an object
  Date b;              // declare an object
  Date c(4,1,2009);    // declare an object
  return 0;
}
```

Calling Constructors

As you have seen, constructors are called whenever an object is created. The actual declaration, however, can be made in a variety of ways. For example, the declaration

```cpp
Date c(4,1,2009);
```

used in Program 10.2 could also have been written as

```cpp
Date c = Date(4,1,2009);
```

This second form declares c as being of type Date and then makes a direct call to the constructor with the arguments 4, 1, and 2009. This second form can be simplified when only one argument is passed to the constructor. For example, if only the month data member of the c object needs to be initialized with the value 8 and the day and year members can use the default values, the object can be created by using this declaration:

```
Date c = 8;
```

Because the form using an equal sign resembles declarations in C, it's referred to as the **C style of initialization**. The declaration form in Program 10.2, referred to as the **C++ style of initialization**, is the form used predominantly in the remainder of this book.

Regardless of which initialization form you use, an object should never be declared with empty parentheses. For example, the declaration Date a(); is not the same as the declaration Date a;. The second declaration uses the default constructor values, and the first declaration results in no object being created.

Overloaded and Inline Constructors

The main difference between a constructor and other user-written methods is how the constructor is called: Constructors are called automatically each time an object is created, and other methods must be called explicitly by name.[8] As a method, however, a constructor must still follow all the rules for user-written functions discussed in Chapter 6. Therefore, constructors can have default arguments (as in Program 10.1), can be overloaded, and can be written as inline functions.

Recall from Section 6.1 that function overloading permits using the same function name with different argument lists. Based on the supplied argument types, the compiler determines which function to use when the call is encountered. To see how overloading can be applied to the Date class, take another look at the class declaration repeated here:

```
// class declaration section
class Date
{
  private:
    int month;
    int day;
    int year;
  public:
    Date(int = 7, int = 4, int = 2012);     // constructor
};
```

The constructor prototype specifies three integer parameters, which are used to initialize the month, day, and year data members.

Another method of specifying a date is using a long integer in the form year * 10000 + month * 100 + day. With this form, the date 12/24/1998 is 19981224, and the date 2/5/2009 is 20090205.[9] A suitable prototype for a constructor that uses dates in this form is shown here:

```
Date(long);     // an overloaded constructor
```

---

[8]This rule is true for all methods except destructors, described later in this section. A destructor method is called automatically each time an object is destroyed.

[9]The reason for specifying dates in this manner is that only one number needs to be used per date, and sorting the numbers puts the corresponding dates into chronological order automatically.

The constructor is declared as receiving one long integer argument. The code for this new Date() method must, of course, convert its single argument into a month, day, and year and is included in the class implementation section. The actual code for this constructor is as follows:

```
Date::Date(long yyyymmdd)    // a second constructor
{
  // extract the year
  year = int(yyyymmdd/10000.0);
  // extract the month
  month = int( (yyyymmdd - year * 10000.0) / 100.00 );
  // extract the day
  day = int(yyyymmdd - year * 10000.0 - month * 100.0);
}
```

Don't be overly concerned with the conversion code used in the method body. The important point is the concept of overloading the Date() method to provide two constructors. Program 10.3 contains the complete class definition in the context of a working program.

Program 10.3

```
#include <iostream>
#include <iomanip>
using namespace std;
```

```
// class declaration section
class Date
{
  private:
    int month;
    int day;
    int year;
  public:
    Date(int = 7, int = 4, int = 2012);   // constructor
    Date(long);            // another constructor
    void showDate();       // member method to display a date
};

// class implementation section
Date::Date(int mm, int dd, int yyyy)
{
  month = mm;
  day = dd;
  year = yyyy;
}
```

☞

```
Date::Date(long yyyymmdd)
{
  year = int(yyyymmdd/10000.0);    // extract the year
  month = int( (yyyymmdd - year * 10000.0)/100.00 ); // extract the month
  day = int(yyyymmdd - year * 10000.0 - month * 100.0); // extract the day
}
void Date::showDate()
{
  cout << "The date is ";
  cout << setfill('0')
       << setw(2) << month << '/'
       << setw(2) << day << '/'
       << setw(2) << year % 100; // extract the last 2 year digits
  cout << endl;
  return;
}
```

```
int main()
{
  Date a, b(4,1,1998), c(20090515L); // declare three objects
  a.showDate();            // display object a's values
  b.showDate();            // display object b's values
  c.showDate();            // display object c's values

  return 0;
}
```

The output of Program 10.3 is as follows:

```
The date is 07/04/12
The date is 04/01/98
The date is 05/15/09
```

Three objects are created in Program 10.3's main() function. The first object, a, is initialized with the default constructor, using its default arguments. Object b is also initialized with the default constructor but uses the arguments 4, 1, and 1998. Finally, object c, which is initialized with a long integer, uses the second constructor in the class implementation section. The compiler knows to use this second constructor because the specified argument, 20090515L, is designated as a long integer by the uppercase L. It's worth pointing out that a compiler error would occur if both Date constructors had default values. For example, a declaration such as Date d; would be ambiguous to the compiler because it couldn't determine which constructor to use. Therefore, in each implementation section, only one constructor can be written as the default.

As mentioned, constructors can also be written as inline functions. Doing so simply means defining the function in the class declaration section. For example, the following declaration section makes both constructors in Program 10.3 inline:

```cpp
// class declaration section
class Date
{
  private:
    int month;
    int day;
    int year;
  public:
    Date(int mm = 7, int dd = 4, int yyyy = 2012)
    {
      month = mm;
      day = dd;
      year = yyyy;
    }
    Date(long yyyymmdd)    // here is the overloaded constructor
    {
      year = int(yyyymmdd/10000.0);    // extract the year
      // extract the month
      month = int( (yyyymmdd - year * 10000.0)/100.00 );
      // extract the day
      day = int(yyyymmdd - year * 10000.0 - month * 100.0);
    }
};
```

The keyword `inline` isn't required in this declaration because member methods defined in the class declaration are inline by default.

Generally, only methods that can be coded on a single line are good candidates for inline functions. This guideline reinforces the convention that inline functions should be small. Therefore, the first constructor is more conventionally written as follows:

```cpp
Date(int mm = 7, int dd = 4, int yyyy = 2012)
  { month = mm; day = dd; year = yyyy; }
```

The second constructor, which extends over three lines, should not be written as an inline function.

Destructors

The counterpart to constructor methods are **destructor methods**. Destructors are methods with the same class name as constructors but are preceded with a tilde (~). Therefore, for the Date class, the destructor name is ~Date(). Like constructors, the C++ compiler provides a default do-nothing destructor in the absence of an explicit destructor. Unlike constructors, however, there can be only one destructor method per class because destructors take no parameters and return no values.

Point of Information

Accessor Methods

An **accessor method** is any non-constructor member method that accesses a class's private data members. For example, the `showDate()` method in the `Date` class is an accessor method. These methods are extremely important because they provide a means of displaying private data members' stored values.

When you construct a class, make sure to provide a complete set of accessor methods. Each accessor method doesn't have to return a data member's exact value, but it should return a useful representation of the value. For example, if the date 12/25/2012 is stored as a long integer member variable in the form 20122512, an accessor method could display this value. A more useful representation, however, is 12/25/12 or December 25, 2012.

Destructors are called automatically when an object goes out of existence and are meant to "clean up" any undesirable effects the object might leave. Generally, these effects occur only when an object contains a pointer member.

Arrays of Objects[10]

The importance of default constructors becomes evident when arrays of objects are created. Because a constructor is called each time an object is created, the default constructor provides an efficient way of initializing all objects to the same state.

Declaring an array of objects is the same as declaring an array of any built-in type. For example, the following declaration creates five objects named `theDate[0]` through `theDate[4]`:

```
Date theDate[5];
```

Member methods for each of these objects are called by listing the object name followed by a dot (.) and the method. Program 10.4 shows using an array of objects, which includes `cout` statements in both the constructor and destructor. As this program's output shows, the constructor is called for each declared object, followed by five member method calls to `showDate()`, followed by five destructor calls. The destructor is called when the objects go out of scope. In this case, the destructor is called when the `main()` function stops execution.

---

[10]This topic can be omitted with no loss of subject continuity.

Point of Information

Mutator Methods

A **mutator method**, more commonly called a "mutator," is any nonconstructor class method that changes an object's data values. Mutators are used to alter an object's data values after a constructor method has created and initialized the object automatically. A class can contain multiple mutators, as long as each one has a unique name or parameter list. For example, in the Date class, you could have a mutator for changing a Date object's month, day, and year values. Constructors, which have the main purpose of initializing an object's member variables when the object is created, aren't considered mutators.

 **Program 10.4**

```cpp
#include <iostream>
#include <iomanip>
using namespace std;
```

```cpp
// class declaration section
class Date
{
  private:
    int month;
    int day;
    int year;
  public:
    Date();    // constructor
    ~Date();   // destructor
    void showDate();
};
// class implementation section
Date::Date()    // user-defined default constructor
{
  cout << "*** A Date object is being initialized ***\n";
  month = 1;
  day = 1;
  year = 2015;
}
Date::~Date()   // user-defined default destructor
{
  cout << "*** A Date object is going out of existence ***\n";
}
```

☞

```
void Date::showDate()
{
  cout << "         The date is " << setfill('0')
       << setw(2) << month << '/'
       << setw(2) << day << '/'
       << setw(2) << year % 100; // extract the last 2 year digits
  return;
}
int main()
{
  const int NUMDATES = 5;
  Date thedate[NUMDATES];
  for(int i = 0; i < NUMDATES; i++)
  {
    thedate[i].showDate();
    cout << endl;
  }
  return 0;
}
```

Program 10.4 produces the following output:

```
*** A Date object is being initialized ***
*** A Date object is being initialized ***
*** A Date object is being initialized ***
*** A Date object is being initialized ***
*** A Date object is being initialized ***
          The date is 01/01/2015
          The date is 01/01/2015
          The date is 01/01/2015
          The date is 01/01/2015
          The date is 01/01/2015
*** A Date object is going out of existence ***
*** A Date object is going out of existence ***
*** A Date object is going out of existence ***
*** A Date object is going out of existence ***
*** A Date object is going out of existence ***
```

EXERCISES 10.3

1. (Review) Determine whether the following statements are true or false:

   a. A constructor method must have the same name as its class.

   b. A class can have only one constructor method.

   c. A class can have only one default constructor method.

d. A default constructor can be supplied only by the compiler.

e. A default constructor can have no parameters or all parameters must have default values.

f. A constructor must be declared for each class.

g. A constructor must be declared with a return type.

h. A constructor is called automatically each time an object is created.

i. A class can have only one destructor method.

j. A destructor must have the same name as its class, preceded by a tilde (~).

k. A destructor can have default arguments.

l. A destructor must be declared for each class.

m. A destructor must be declared with a return type.

n. A destructor is called automatically each time an object goes out of existence.

o. Destructors aren't useful when the class contains a pointer data member.

2. **(Desk check)** For Program 10.3, what date is initialized for object c if the declaration `Date c(15);` is used instead of the declaration `Date c(20090515L);`?

3. **(Modify)** Modify Program 10.3 so that the only data member of the class is a long integer named `yyyymmdd`. Do this by substituting the declaration `long yyyymmdd;` for these existing declarations:

```
int month;
int day;
int year;
```

Using the same constructor prototypes currently declared in the class declaration section, rewrite them so that the `Date(long)` method becomes the default constructor, and the `Date(int, int, int)` method converts a month, day, and year into the correct form for the class data members.

4. **(Program) a.** Construct a `Time` class containing integer data members `seconds`, `minutes`, and `hours`. Have the class contain two constructors: The first should be a default constructor having the prototype `Time(int, int, int)`, which uses default values of 0 for each data member. The second constructor should accept a long integer representing a total number of seconds and disassemble the long integer into `hours`, `minutes`, and `seconds`. The final member method should display the class data members.

   b. Include the class written for Exercise 4a in the context of a complete program.

5. **(Program) a.** Construct a class named `Student` consisting of an integer student ID number, an array of five double-precision grades, and an integer representing the total number of grades entered. The constructor for this class should initialize all `Student` data members to 0. Included in the class should be member methods to 1) enter a student ID number, 2) enter a single test grade and update the total number of grades entered, and 3) compute an average grade and display the student ID followed by the average grade.

   b. Include the class constructed in Exercise 5a in the context of a complete program. Your program should declare two objects of type `Student` and accept and display data for the two objects to verify operation of the member methods.

6. **(Modify) a.** In Exercise 4, you were asked to construct a `Time` class. For this class, include a `tick()` method that increments the time by one second. Test your method to ensure that it increments time into a new minute and a new hour correctly.

   b. Modify the `Time` class written for Exercise 6a to include a `detick()` method that decrements the time by one second. Test your method to ensure that it decrements time into a prior hour and into a prior minute correctly.

7. **(Program) a.** Construct a class named `Coord` containing two double-precision data members named `xval` and `yval`, used to store a point's x and y values in Cartesian coordinates. The member methods should include constructor and display methods and a method named `convToCartesian()`. The `convToCartesian()` method should accept two double-precision numbers named `r` and `theta` representing a point in polar coordinates and convert them into Cartesian coordinates. For conversion from polar to Cartesian coordinates, use these formulas:

   $x = r \cos (theta)$

   $y = r \sin (theta)$

   b. Include the program written for Exercise 7a in a working C++ program.

10.4 Examples

Now that you have an understanding of how classes are constructed and the terminology for describing them, you can apply this knowledge to creating two examples with an object-oriented approach. In the first example, you develop a class for determining the floor area of a rectangular room. In the second example, you construct a single elevator object. Assume the elevator can travel between the 1st and 15th floors of a building, and the elevator's location must be known at all times.

Example 1: Constructing a Room Object

In this example, you create a class from which room objects can be constructed and their floor area calculated. For modeling purposes, assume that every room is rectangular, so the floor area can be calculated as the room's length times its width.

Solution   In this application, you have one type of object, which is a rectangular room, so its floor can be designated by the room's length and width. After these values have been assigned to a room, its floor area can be calculated easily as the room's length times its width. Therefore, a room can be represented by double-precision variables named `length` and `width`. Additionally, you need a constructor that enables you to specify values for `length` and `width` when a room object is instantiated.

   In addition to the constructor, the services required are an accessor to display a room's `length` and `width` values, a mutator to change these values, and a method to calculate a room's floor area from its `length` and `width` values. To accomplish this, the following is a suitable class declaration:

```
// class declaration section
class RoomType
{
  private:
    double length;   // declare length as a double variable
    double width;    // declare width as a double variable
  public:
    RoomType(double = 0.0, double = 0.0); // constructor
    void showRoomValues();      // an accessor method
    void setNewRoomValues();    // a mutator method
    double calculateRoomArea(); // a calculation method
};
```

This code declares two data members, length and width, and four class methods. The data members length and width store a room's length and width. As private class data members, they can be accessed only through the class's member methods. These member methods are used to define the external services available to each RoomType object. Specifically, the RoomType() method, which has the same name as its class, becomes a constructor that's called automatically when an object of type RoomType is created. You use this method to initialize a room's length and width values. The showRoomValues() method is written as an accessor method to display a room object's length and width values, the setNewRoomValues() method is written as a mutator method to change a room's length and width values, and the calculateRoomArea() method is written to calculate and display a room's floor area.

To perform these services, the following class implementation section is suitable:

```
// class implementation section
RoomType::RoomType(double l, double w)  // this is a constructor
{
  length = l;
  width = w;
  cout << "Created a new room object using the default constructor.\n\n";
}
void RoomType::showRoomValues()    // this is an accessor
{
  cout << "  length = " << length
       << "\n   width = " << width << endl;
}
void RoomType::setNewRoomValues(double l, double w)  // this is a mutator
{
  length = l;
  width = w;
}
double RoomType::calculateRoomArea()  // this performs a calculation
{
  return (length * width);
}
```

These methods are straightforward. When a room object is declared, it's initialized with a `length` and `width` of 0, unless specific values are provided in the declaration. The accessor method displays the values stored in `length` and `width`, and the mutator method allows reassigning values after a room object has been created. Finally, the calculation method displays a room's area by multiplying its length by its width. Program 10.5 includes this class in a working program.

 **Program 10.5**

```cpp
#include <iostream>
using namespace std;
```

```cpp
// class declaration section
class RoomType
{
  private:
    double length; // declare length as a double variable
    double width;  // declare width as a double variable

  public:
    RoomType(double = 0.0, double = 0.0); // the constructor's declaration
    void showRoomValues();
    void setNewRoomValues(double, double);
    double calculateRoomArea();
};

// class implementation section
RoomType::RoomType(double l, double w)  // this is a constructor
{
  length = l;
  width = w;
  cout << "Created a new room object using the default constructor.\n\n";
}
void RoomType::showRoomValues()  // this is an accessor
{
  cout << "  length = " << length
       << "\n  width = " << width << endl;
}

void RoomType::setNewRoomValues(double l, double w)  // this is a mutator
{
  length = l;
  width = w;
}
```

```
double RoomType::calculateRoomArea()   // this performs a calculation
{
  return (length * width);
}
```

```
int main()
{
  RoomType roomOne(12.5, 18.2);   // declare a variable of type RoomType

  cout << "The values for this room are:\n";
  roomOne.showRoomValues();       // use a class method on this object
  cout << "\nThe floor area of this room is: ";
  roomOne.calculateRoomArea();    // use another class method on this object

  roomOne.setNewRoomValues(5.5, 9.3);   // call the mutator

  cout << "\n\nThe values for this room have been changed to:\n";
  roomOne.showRoomValues();
  cout << "\nThe floor area of this room is: ";
  roomOne.calculateRoomArea();

  cout << endl;

  return 0;
}
```

The shaded portion of Program 10.5 defines the class. To see how this class is used, concentrate on the unshaded section containing the `main()` function. This function creates one room object with a `length` of 12.5 and a `width` of 18.2. These room dimensions are displayed by using the `showRoomValues()` method, and the area is calculated and displayed by using the `calculateRoomArea()` method. The room's dimensions are reset and displayed, and the room's area is recalculated. Program 10.5 produces the following output:

```
Created a new room object using the default constructor.

The values for this room are:
   length = 12.5
    width = 18.2

The floor area of this room is: 227.5

The values for this room have been changed to:
   length = 5.5
    width = 9.3

The floor area of this room is: 51.15
```

The basic requirements of object-oriented programming are evident even in as simple a program as Program 10.5. Before the `main()` function can be written, a useful class must be constructed, which is typical of programs using objects. For these programs, the design process is front-loaded with the requirement to give careful consideration to the class—its declaration and implementation. Code in the implementation section effectively removes code that would otherwise be part of `main()`'s responsibility. Therefore, any program using the object doesn't have to repeat the implementation details in its `main()` function. Instead, the `main()` function and any function called by `main()` are concerned only with calling class methods to activate them correctly. How the object responds to the messages and how the object's state is retained are not `main()`'s concern—these details are hidden in the class construction.

Example 2: Constructing an Elevator Object

In this example, you see how to simulate an elevator's operation. The required output describes the current floor on which the elevator is stationed or passing by. Additionally, you should provide an internal elevator button that's pushed as a request to move to another floor. The elevator is to be identified by a number, such as Elevator Number 1 (to allow placing additional elevators into operation, if needed), and it can travel between the 1st and 15th floor of the building in which it's situated.

Solution   For this application, the object under consideration is an elevator. The three attributes of interest are the elevator's number, its current location, and the highest floor it can reach. The single requested service is the ability to request a change in the elevator's position (its state). Additionally, you must be able to establish the initial floor position when a new elevator is put into service.

The elevator's location, which corresponds to its current floor position, can be represented by an integer member variable with a value ranging between 1 and the highest floor it can reach. The value of this variable, named `currentFloor`, represents the elevator's current state. The services for changing the elevator's state are a constructor to set the initial floor position and the highest floor when a new elevator is put in service and a request method to change the elevator's position (state) to a new floor. Putting an elevator into service is accomplished by declaring a single class instance (declaring an object of type `Elevator`), and requesting a new floor position is equivalent to pushing an elevator button. To perform these services, the following class declaration is suitable:

```
// class declaration section
class Elevator
{
  private:
    int elNum;
    int currentFloor;
    int highestFloor;
  public:
    Elevator(int = 1, int = 1, int = 15);   // constructor
    void request(int);
};
```

This code declares three data members (`elNum`, `currentFloor`, and `highestFloor`) and two class methods. The first data member, `elNum`, is used to store the elevator's number. The second data member, `currentFloor`, is used to store the elevator's current floor position, and the last data member, `highestFloor`, is used to store the highest floor the elevator can reach. As private data members, they can be accessed only through member methods. The two declared public member methods, `Elevator()` and `request()`, are used to define the external services each `Elevator` object provides. The `Elevator()` method, which has the same name as its class, becomes a constructor method that's called automatically when an object of type `Elevator` is created. You use this method to initialize the elevator's number, starting floor position, and highest floor. The `request()` method is used to alter the elevator's position. To perform these services, the following class implementation section is suitable:

```cpp
// class implementation section
Elevator::Elevator(int idnum, int cfloor, int maxfloor)   // constructor
{
  int elNum = idnum;
  currentFloor = cfloor;
  highestFloor = maxfloor;
}

void Elevator::request(int newfloor)   // accessor
{
  if (newfloor < 1||newfloor > highestFloor||newfloor == currentFloor)
    ; // do nothing
  else if (newfloor > currentFloor)  // move elevator up
  {
    cout << "\nStarting at floor " << currentFloor << endl;
    while (newfloor > currentFloor)
    {
      currentFloor++;   // add one to current floor
      cout << " Going Up - now at floor " << currentFloor << endl;
    }
    cout << "Stopping at floor " << currentFloor << endl;
  }
  else // move elevator down
  {
    cout << "\nStarting at floor " << currentFloor << endl;
    while (newfloor < currentFloor)
    {
      currentFloor--;   // subtract one from current floor
      cout << " Going Down - now at floor " << currentFloor << endl;
    }
    cout << "Stopping at floor " << currentFloor << endl;
  }

  return;
}
```

The constructor is straightforward. When an `Elevator` object is created, its elevator number can be set, it can be initialized to a specified floor, and its highest floor can be specified; if no values are supplied, it's given a default elevator number of 1, its initial floor is set as the first floor, and the highest floor is set to 15. For example, the declaration

```
Elevator a;
```

uses all three default argument values provided by the constructor. The variable `a.elNum` is set to 1, the variable `a.currentFloor` is set to 1, and the variable `a.highestFloor` is set to 15. The declaration

```
Elevator a(2, 4, 20);
```

initializes an elevator to have the number 2, starts the elevator at the 4th floor, and designates that the highest floor this elevator can reach is the 20th floor.

The `request()` method defined in the implementation section is more complicated and provides the class's primary service. Essentially, it consists of an `if-else` statement with three parts: If an incorrect floor is requested, no action is taken; if a floor above the current position is selected, the elevator is moved up; and if a floor below the current position is selected, the elevator is moved down. For movement up or down, the method uses a `while` loop to increment the position one floor at a time and reports the elevator's movement by using a `cout` statement. Program 10.6 includes this class in a working program. To see how this class is used, concentrate on the `main()` function.

 ## Program 10.6

```cpp
#include <iostream>
using namespace std;

// class declaration section
class Elevator
{
  private:
    int elNum;
    int currentFloor;
    int highestFloor;
  public:
    Elevator(int = 1, int = 1, int = 15);  // constructor
    void request(int);
};

// class implementation section
Elevator::Elevator(int idnum, int cfloor, int maxfloor)
```

☞

```
{
  elNum = idnum;
  currentFloor = cfloor;
  highestFloor = maxfloor;
}
void Elevator::request(int newfloor)
{

  if (newfloor < 1 || newfloor > highestFloor || newfloor == currentFloor)
    ;  // do nothing
  else if (newfloor > currentFloor) // move elevator up
  {
    cout << "\nElevator " << elNum
         << " starting at floor " << currentFloor << endl;
    while (newfloor > currentFloor)
    {
      currentFloor++; // add one to current floor
      cout << " Going Up - now at floor " << currentFloor << endl;
    }
    cout << "Elevator " << elNum
         << " stopping at floor " << currentFloor << endl;
  }
  else // move elevator down
  {
    cout << "\nElevator " << elNum
         << " starting at floor " << currentFloor << endl;
    while (newfloor < currentFloor)
    {
      currentFloor--;   // subtract one from current floor
      cout << " Going Down - now at floor " << currentFloor << endl;
    }
    cout << "Elevator "<< elNum
         << " Stopping at floor " << currentFloor << endl;
  }
  return;
}
```

```
int main()
{
  Elevator a;    // declare 1 object of type Elevator

  a.request(6);
  a.request(3);

  return 0;
}
```

Point of Information

Encapsulation

The term **encapsulation** refers to packaging a number of items into a single unit. For example, a function is used to encapsulate the details of an algorithm. Similarly, a class encapsulates variables and methods together in a single package. Although "encapsulation" is sometimes used to refer to the process of data hiding, this usage isn't technically accurate. The terms "information hiding" refers to encapsulating *and* hiding all implementation details.

Three class method calls are included in the `main()` function. The first statement creates an object named a of type `Elevator`. Because no floor has been given, the constructor's default arguments are used. This means the elevator is designated as elevator number 1, it begins operation at floor 1, and can go up to only the 15th floor. A request is then made to move the elevator to floor 6, which is followed by a request to move to floor 3. Program 10.6 produces the following output:

```
Elevator 1 starting at floor 1
   Going Up - now at floor 2
   Going Up - now at floor 3
   Going Up - now at floor 4
   Going Up - now at floor 5
   Going Up - now at floor 6
Elevator 1 stopping at floor 6

Elevator 1 starting at floor 6
   Going Down - now at floor 5
   Going Down - now at floor 4
   Going Down - now at floor 3
Elevator 1 stopping at floor 3
```

In Program 10.6, notice the control the `main()` function provides. This sequential control, with two calls made to the same object operation and using different argument values, is suitable for testing purposes. However, by incorporating calls to `request()` inside a `while` loop and using the random number function `rand()` to generate random floor requests, a continuous simulation of the elevator's operation is possible (see Exercise 6).

EXERCISES 10.4

1. **(Practice)** Enter and run Program 10.5 on your computer.

2. **(Modify)** Modify the `main()` function in Program 10.5 to create a second room with a length of 9 and a width of 12. Have the program calculate this new room's area.

3. **(Modify) a.** Modify the `main()` function in Program 10.5 to create four rooms: hall, kitchen, dining room, and living room. The dimensions for these rooms are as follows:

Hall: length = 12.40, width = 3.5
Kitchen: length = 14, width = 14
Living room: length = 12.4, width = 20
Dining room: length = 14, width = 10.5.

Your program should display the area of each room and the total area of all four rooms combined.

4. **(Practice)** Enter and run Program 10.6 on your computer.

5. **(Modify) a.** Modify the `main()` function in Program 10.6 to put a second elevator in service starting at the 5th floor and have a maximum floor of 20. Have this second elevator move to the 1st floor and then move to the 12th floor.
   b. Verify that the constructor is called by adding a message in it that's displayed each time a new object is created. Run your program to verify its operation.

6. **(Modify)** Modify the `main()` function in Program 10.6 to use a `while` loop that calls the `Elevator`'s `request()` method with a random number between 1 and 15. If the random number is the same as the elevator's current floor, generate another request. The `while` loop should terminate after five valid requests have been made and be satisfied by movement of the elevator. (*Hint*: Review Section 6.8 about the use of random numbers.)

7. **(Program)** Construct a class named `Light` that simulates a traffic light. The class's `color` attribute should change from `Green` to `Yellow` to `Red` and then back to `Green` by using the class's `change()` method. When a new `Light` object is created, its initial color should be `Red`.

8. **(Program) a.** Construct a class definition to represent an employee of a company. Each employee is defined by an integer ID number, a double-precision pay rate, and the maximum number of hours the employee should work each week. The class should provide these services: the capability to enter data for a new employee, the capability to change data for a new employee, and the capability to display existing data for a new employee.
   b. Include the class definition created for Exercise 8a in a working C++ program that asks the user to enter data for three employees and then displays the entered data.
   c. Modify the program written for Exercise 8b to include a menu that offers the user the following choices:

   1. Add an employee
   2. Modify employee data
   3. Delete an employee
   4. Exit this menu

   In response to the user's choice, the program should initiate an action to implement the choice.

9. **(Program) a.** Construct a class definition to represent types of food. A type of food is classified as basic or prepared. Basic foods are further classified as `Dairy`, `Meat`, `Fruit`, `Vegetable`, or `Grain`. The class should provide these services: the capability to enter data for a new food, the capability to change data for a new food, and the capability to display existing data for a new food.

b. Include the class definition created for Exercise 9a in a working C++ program that asks the user to enter data for four food items and then displays the entered data.

c. Modify the program written for Exercise 9b to include a menu that offers the user the following choices:

1. Add a food item
2. Modify a food item
3. Delete a food item
4. Exit this menu

In response to the user's choice, the program should initiate an action to implement the choice.

10.5 Class Scope and Duration Categories

As you learned in Section 6.4, the scope of an identifier defines the portion of a program where the identifier is valid. There are two categories of scope: local and global. In addition, each identifier has a duration, which refers to the length of time storage locations are reserved for the variable or method the identifier names (see Section 6.5).

Just as a variable is local to the method that declares it, class data members are local to the class in which they're declared. This means class data members are known only within the class, which includes the class methods. Similarly, just as a method's local variable always takes precedence over a global variable having the same name, a class data member takes precedence over a global variable of the same name. Additionally, class method names are local to the class they're declared in and can be used only by objects declared for the class. Figure 10.4 illustrates these scope rules for the following declarations:

```
double rate;    // global scope
// class declaration section
class Test
{
  private:
    double amount, price, total;    // class scope
  public:
    double extend(double, double);  // class scope
};
```

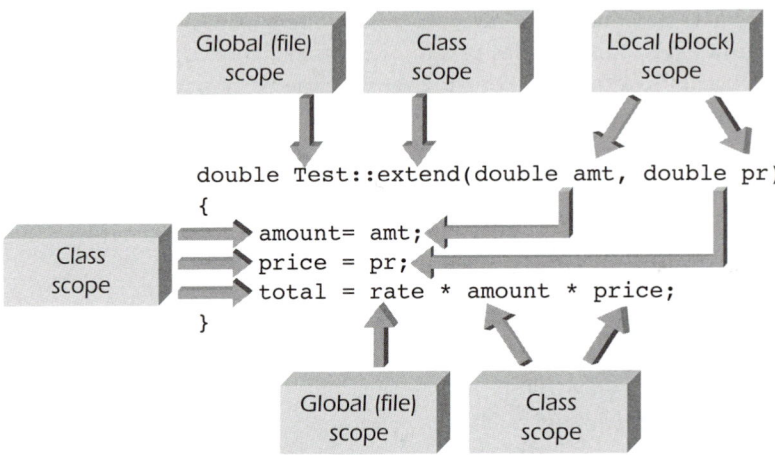

Figure 10.4   Examples of scopes

Static Class Members

As each class object is created, it gets its own block of memory for its data members. In some cases, however, it's convenient for every created object to share the same memory location for a specific variable. For example, in a class consisting of employee payment information, each employee is subject to the same social security tax rate. Clearly, you could make the tax rate a global variable, but this method isn't very safe. As a global variable, the data could be modified anywhere in the program or could conflict with an identical variable name of local scope, and making it a global variable also violates C++'s principle of data hiding.

C++ handles this situation by declaring a class variable to be static. Static class variables share the same storage space for all class objects; in this way, they act as global variables for the class and provide a means of communication between objects. C++ requires declaring static class variables in the class declaration section. Memory allocation for these variables is then allocated (that is, the variables are actually created) outside the class declaration section. For example, take a look at this class declaration, in which a static variable named `taxRate` is declared:

```
//class declaration section
class Employee
{
  private:
    static double taxRate;
    int idNum;
  public:
    Employee(int);    //constructor
    void display();   // accessor method
};
```

Having been declared in the class declaration section, the static variable `taxRate` must then be defined (that is, created) outside the declaration section. A statement such as the following can be used to define `taxRate`:

```
double Employee::taxRate = 0.07;  // defines and initializes taxRate
```

In this statement, the scope resolution operator, `::`, is used to identify `taxRate` as a data member of the class `Employee`, and the `static` keyword isn't included. In addition, the initialization of `taxRate` in this definition statement isn't required. Assigning a value to `taxRate` can be done anywhere after its definition statement. Program 10.7 uses this definition in the context of a complete program.

 **Program 10.7**

```cpp
#include <iostream>
using namespace std;

// class declaration section
class Employee
{
  private:
    static double taxRate;
    int idNum;
  public:
    Employee(int = 0);    // constructor
    void display();       // accessor method
};
// static member definition
double Employee::taxRate = 0.07;   // defines and initializes taxRate
// class implementation section
Employee::Employee(int num)
{
  idNum = num;
}
void Employee::display()
{
  cout << "Employee number " << idNum
       << " has a tax rate of " << taxRate << endl;
  return;
}

int main()
{
  Employee emp1(11122), emp2(11133);

  emp1.display();
  emp2.display();

  return 0;
}
```

The output produced by Program 10.7 is as follows:

```
Employee number 11122 has a tax rate of 0.07
Employee number 11133 has a tax rate of 0.07
```

After the definition for `taxRate` is made, any other definition results in an error. Therefore, the actual definition of a static data member remains the responsibility of the class creator, and a compiler error occurs if this definition is omitted.

Figure 10.5 illustrates the storage sharing produced by the static data member and the objects created in Program 10.7.

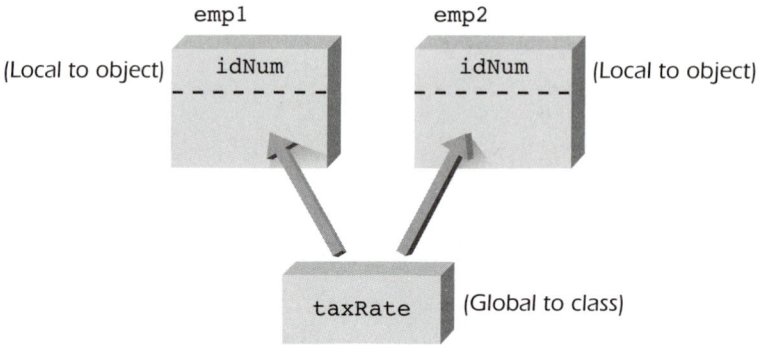

Figure 10.5   Sharing the static data member `taxRate`

In addition to static data members, static member methods can be created. These methods apply to a class as a whole instead of to specific objects. Therefore, they're not called by an object and can access only static data members and other static member methods of the class. Program 10.8 includes an example of a static member method. Notice that the call to the static member method `dispRate()` in `main()` is preceded by its class name, not an object name.

Program 10.8

```cpp
#include <iostream>
using namespace std;

// class declaration section
class Employee
{
  private:
    static double taxRate;
    int idNum;
```

```
  public:
    Employee(int = 0);        // constructor
    void display();           // accessor method
    static void dispRate();   // static member method
};
// static member definition
double Employee::taxRate = 0.07;
// class implementation section
Employee::Employee(int num)
{
  idNum = num;
}
void Employee::display()
{
  cout << "Employee number " << idNum
       << " has a tax rate of " << taxRate << endl;
  return;
}
void Employee::dispRate()
{
  cout << "The static tax rate is " << taxRate << endl;
  return;
}
```

```
int main()
{
  Employee emp1(11122), emp2(11133);

  Employee::dispRate();    // call the static member methods
  emp1.display();
  emp2.display();

  return 0;
}
```

Program 10.8 produces the following output:

```
The static tax rate is 0.07
Employee number 11122 has a tax rate of 0.07
Employee number 11133 has a tax rate of 0.07
```

Friend Functions

The only method you currently have for accessing and manipulating a class's private variables is through the class member methods. You can view this arrangement as illustrated in Figure 10.6a. At times, however, providing access to selected nonmember methods is useful.

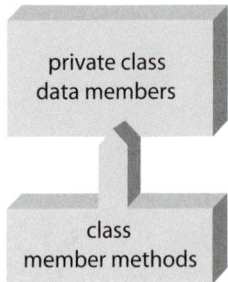

Figure 10.6a   Direct access provided to member methods

The procedure for providing this external access is simple: The class maintains an approved list of nonmember methods that are granted the same privileges as its member methods. The nonmember methods in the list are called **friend functions**, and the list is referred to as a **friends list**.

Figure 10.6b shows using a friends list for nonmember access. Any method attempting access to an object's private variables is first checked against the friends list: If the method is on the list, access is approved; otherwise, access is denied.

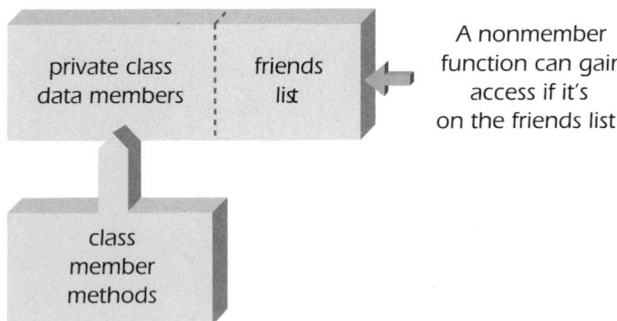

Figure 10.6b   Access provided to nonmember methods

From a coding standpoint, the friends list is simply a series of method prototype declarations preceded with the keyword `friend` and included in the class declaration section. For example, if the `addreal()` and `addimag()` methods are to be allowed access to private members of the `Complex` class, the following prototypes must be included in `Complex`'s class declaration section:

```
friend double addreal(Complex&, Complex&);
friend double addimag(Complex&, Complex&);
```

This friends list consists of two declarations. The prototypes indicate that each method returns a floating-point number and expects two references to objects of type `Complex` as arguments. Program 10.9 includes these two friend declarations in a complete program.

 ## Program 10.9

```cpp
#include <iostream>
#include <cmath>
using namespace std;
```

```cpp
// class declaration section
class Complex
{
  // friends list
  friend double addreal(Complex&, Complex&);
  friend double addimag(Complex&, Complex&);
  private:
    double real;
    double imag;
  public:
    Complex(double = 0, double = 0);  // constructor
    void display();
};

// class implementation section
Complex::Complex(double rl, double im)
{
  real = rl;
  imag = im;
}
void Complex::display()
{
  char sign = '+';
  if(imag < 0) sign = '-';
  cout << real << sign << abs(imag) << 'i';
  return;
}

// friend implementations
double addreal(Complex &a, Complex &b)
{
  return(a.real + b.real);
}
```

```
double addimag(Complex &a, Complex &b)
{
  return(a.imag + b.imag);
}
```

```
int main()
{
  Complex a(3.2, 5.6), b(1.1, -8.4);
  double re, im;

  cout << "\nThe first complex number is ";
  a.display();
  cout << "\nThe second complex number is ";
  b.display();

  re = addreal(a,b);
  im = addimag(a,b);
  Complex c(re,im);  // create a new Complex object
  cout << "\n\nThe sum of these two complex numbers is ";
  c.display();

  return 0;
}
```

Program 10.9 produces the following output:

```
The first complex number is 3.2+5.6i
The second complex number is 1.1-8.4i
The sum of these two complex numbers is 4.3-2.8i
```

In reviewing Program 10.9, notice these four points:

- Because friends are not class members, they aren't affected by the access section in which they're declared—they can be declared *anywhere in the declaration section*. The convention Program 10.9 follows is to include all friend declarations immediately after the class header.
- The keyword `friend` (like the keyword `static`) is used only in the class declaration, not in the actual function definition.
- Because a friend function is intended to have access to an object's private variables, at least one of the friend's arguments should be a reference to an object of the class that made it a friend.
- As Program 10.9 shows, it's the class that grants friend status to a method, not the other way around. A method can never confer friend status on itself because doing so violates the concepts of data hiding and access provided by a class.

EXERCISES 10.5

1. **(Modify) a.** Rewrite Program 10.8 to include an integer static variable named `numemps`. This variable should act as a counter that's initialized to 0 and incremented by the class constructor each time a new object is declared. Rewrite the static method `dispRate()` to display this counter's value.

   b. Test the program written for Exercise 1a. Have the `main()` function call `dispRate()` after each `Employee` object is created.

2. **(Program) a.** Construct a class named `Circle` containing two integer variables named `xCenter` and `yCenter` and a double-precision variable named `radius`. Additionally, the class should contain a static data member named `scaleFactor`. The `xCenter` and `yCenter` values represent a circle's center point, `radius` represents the circle's actual radius, and `scaleFactor` represents a scale factor used to scale the circle to fit on a variety of display devices.

   b. Include the class written for Exercise 2a in a working C++ program.

3. **(Debug) a.** State whether the following three statements in Program 10.9

   ```
   re = addreal(a,b);
   im = addimag(a,b);
   Complex c(re,im);  // create a new Complex object
   ```

   could be replaced by this single statement:

   ```
   Complex c(addreal(a,b), addimag(a,b));
   ```

   b. Verify your answer to Exercise 3a by running Program 10.9 with the suggested replacement statement.

4. **(Modify) a.** Rewrite the program written for Exercise 2a, but include a friend function that multiples an object's radius by a static `scaleFactor` and then displays the actual radius value and the scaled value.

   b. Test the program written for Exercise 4a.

5. **(Modify)** Rewrite Program 10.9 to have only one friend function named `addComplex()`. This function should accept two `Complex` objects and return a `Complex` object. The real and imaginary parts of the returned object should be the sum of the real and imaginary parts of the two objects passed to `addComplex()`.

6. **(Program) a.** Construct a class named `Coord` containing two double-precision variables named `xval` and `yval`, used to store the x and y values of a point in rectangular coordinates. The class methods should include constructor and display methods and a friend function named `convPol()`. The `convPol()` function should accept two double-precision numbers, `r` and `theta`, representing a point in polar coordinates and convert them into rectangular coordinates. For conversion from polar to rectangular coordinates, use these formulas:

   $x = r \cos(theta)$
   $y = r \sin(theta)$

   b. Include the class written for Exercise 6a in a working C++ program.

10.6 Common Programming Errors

The common programming errors associated with constructing classes are as follows:

1. Failing to terminate the class declaration section with a semicolon.
2. Including a return type with the constructor's prototype or failing to include a return type with the other methods' prototypes.
3. Using the same name for a data member as for a member method.
4. Defining more than one default constructor for a class.
5. Forgetting to include the class name and scope operator, `::`, in the header of all member methods defined in the class implementation section.
6. Using the `static` keyword when defining a static data member or member method. It should be used only in the class declaration section.
7. Using the `friend` keyword when defining a friend function. It should be used only in the class declaration section.
8. Failing to instantiate static data members before creating class objects that must access these data members.

10.7 Chapter Summary

1. A class is a programmer-defined data type. Objects of a class can be defined and have the same relationship to their class as variables do to C++'s built-in data types.

2. A class definition consists of declaration and implementation sections. The most common form of a class definition is as follows:

```
// class declaration section
class name
{
  private:
    // a list of variable declarations;
  public:
    // a list of method prototypes;
};
// class implementation section
    // class method definitions
```

The variables and methods declared in the class declaration section are collectively called class members. The variables are referred to as class data members, and the methods are referred to as class member methods. The keywords `private` and `public` are access specifiers. After an access specifier is listed, it remains in force until another access specifier is given. The `private` keyword specifies that class members following it are private to the class and can be accessed only by member methods. The `public` keyword specifies that the class members following it can be accessed from outside the class. Generally, all data members should be specified as `private` and all member methods as `public`.

3. Class methods listed in the declaration section can be written inline, or their definitions can be included in the class implementation section. Except for constructor and destructor methods, all class methods defined in the class implementation section use this form for the header:

```
returnType className::methodName(parameter list);
```

Except for the addition of the class name and scope operator, `::`, which are required to identify the method name with the class, this header is identical to the one for any user-written function.

4. A constructor is a special method that's called automatically each time an object is declared. It must have the same name as its class and can't have any return type. Its purpose is to initialize each declared object.

5. If no constructor is declared for a class, the compiler supplies a default constructor. It's a do-nothing method with the definition `className::className(void){}`.

6. The term "default constructor" refers to any constructor that doesn't require arguments when it's called. The reason it doesn't require arguments is that no parameters are declared (as with the compiler-supplied default constructor) or all arguments have been given default values.

7. Each class can only have one default constructor. If a user-defined constructor is defined, the compiler doesn't create a default constructor.

8. Objects are created by using a C++ or C style of declaration. The C++ style of declaration has the form

```
className list-of-objectNames(list of initializers);
```

where the `list of initializers` is optional. An example of the C++ style, including initializers, for a class named `Date` is as follows:

```
Date a, b, c(12,25,2012);
```

The objects `a` and `b` are declared to be of type `Date` and are initialized by using the default constructor; the object `c` is initialized with the values 12, 25, and 2012.

The equivalent C style of declaration, including the optional list of initializers, has this form:

```
className objectName = className(list of initializers);
```

An example of the C style for a class named `Date` is as follows:

```
Date c = Date(12,25,2012)
```

The object `c` is created and initialized with the values 12, 25, and 2012.

9. Constructors can be overloaded in the same manner as any other user-written C++ method.

10. If a constructor is defined for a class, a user-defined default constructor should also be written, as the compiler doesn't supply it.

11. A destructor is called each time an object goes out of scope. Destructors must have the same name as their class but are preceded with a tilde (~). There can be only one destructor per class.

12. A destructor takes no arguments and returns no value. If a user-defined destructor isn't included in a class, the compiler provides a do-nothing destructor.

13. Each class has an associated class scope, which is defined by the brace pair, { }, containing the class declaration. Data members and member methods are local to the scope of their class and can be used only by objects declared for the class. If a global variable name is reused in a class, the global variable is hidden by the class variable. Within the scope of the class variable, the global variable can be accessed by using the scope resolution operator, : :.

14. For each class object, a separate set of memory locations is reserved for all data members, except those declared as static. A static data member is shared by all class objects and provides a means of communication between objects. Static data members must be declared in the class declaration section and are defined outside the declaration section.

15. Static member methods apply to the class as a whole rather than to separate objects. Therefore, a static member method can access only static data members and other static member methods. Any static member methods must be declared in the class declaration section and are defined outside the declaration section.

16. A nonmember method can access a class's private data members if it's granted friend status by the class. This is done by declaring it as a friend in the class's declaration section. Therefore, the class always determines which nonmember methods are friends; a method can never confer friend status on itself.

10.8 Chapter Supplement: Thinking in Terms of Objects

When solving any problem, often it's helpful to start by creating a diagram or map or devising a theoretical analogy for the problem you're trying to solve. In other words, you need to create some kind of model. Creating a model helps you see all parts of the problem and helps you understand what you need to do to solve it.

The first step in constructing an object-based program is developing an object-based model of the problem. Each class then becomes a description of the model written in C++. For example, if you're writing an object-oriented program to calculate the area of a room, the first step is thinking about a room as an object. This step probably isn't difficult, and assigning attributes of length, width, and height to a room correspond to physical characteristics you're familiar with. To become a good object-oriented programmer, however, you need to be able to analyze more complex situations so that you can think of and organize programming problems as the interaction of different objects. In this section, you explore this object-based concept in more detail. You also learn how to develop programs systematically by using object-based models. Figure 10.7 illustrates the concepts discussed in this section.

Chapter Supplement: Thinking in Terms of
Objects

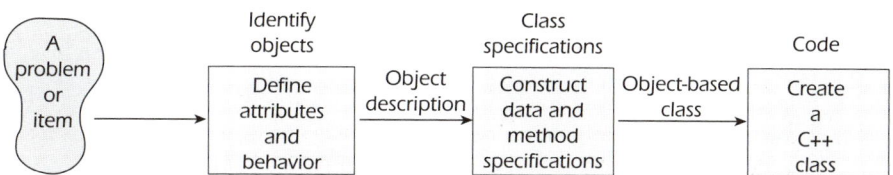

Figure 10.7   A class is a programming-language description of a model

Representing Problems with Models

Formally, a **model** is a representation of a problem. The first step in creating an object-based model is to begin "thinking in objects." For example, if you want to know the result of tossing a coin 100 times, you can certainly do so by tossing a real coin. However, if a coin could be modeled accurately, you could find the result by writing a program to simulate a coin toss. Similarly, a game of solitaire could be simulated if a realistic model of a deck of cards could be created and if methods such as shuffling the deck could be coded.

Objects, such as coins, cards, and more complicated graphical objects, are well suited to a programming representation because they can be modeled by two basic characteristics: attributes and behaviors. **Attributes** define the properties of interest, and **behaviors** define how the object reacts to its environment. When designing and developing an object-oriented program, you need to follow these two steps:

1. Identify the required objects.
2. For each object:
   a. Identify the attributes of interest.
   b. Identify the behaviors (operations) of interest.

To make this process more tangible, think about a coin-tossing experiment. Step 1 tells you to identify the required objects. For this experiment, the object is a coin. Step 2 tells you to identify the relevant attributes and behaviors. In terms of attributes, a coin has a denomination, size, weight, color, condition (tarnished, worn, proof), country of origin, and side (head or tail). If you're purchasing a coin for collectible purposes, you're interested in all these attributes but the side. For a coin toss, however, the only attribute that's of interest is the side; it doesn't matter whether the coin is a penny or a quarter, copper or silver, or tarnished or not. In terms of modeling a coin for a coin-tossing experiment, the only attribute you must consider is what side is visible when the coin is tossed. It's important to understand the significance of the choice of attributes. Very few models include every aspect of the objects they represent; a model should include only attributes that are relevant to the problem.

Having determined the attributes to use in modeling a coin, the next step requires identifying the behavior this object should exhibit. In this case, you must have a means of simulating a toss and determining the side that faces up when the toss is completed.

Figure 10.8 summarizes the initial results of the two steps in developing the object-oriented coin toss program: It identifies the required object and lists its relevant attributes and behaviors. This diagram is called an **object description**. It doesn't tell you everything there is to know about a coin, only what you need to know to create a coin toss program. For programming purposes, this description must be translated into a programming language, whether it's C++ or another object-oriented language.

Object: A coin
Attributes: Side (head or tail)
Behavior: Landing with heads up or tails up

Figure 10.8   An initial coin object description

As you expand your design for a program, often you have to refine and expand the object description. Refinement, or improving and modifying the model, is almost always required for all but extremely simple problems. In Section 12.6, you learn about a more structured approach to modeling, based on a methodology known as the Unified Modeling Language (UML). This methodology, like all object-oriented design and development techniques, requires identifying the necessary objects and then identifying the objects' attributes and behaviors. After you build a model, you must then translate it into C++. The main point of this book is to teach you how to do just that. Your job as a programmer, however, will be much easier if you take the time first to master the techniques for modeling a program.

Modeling Classes

Identifying the objects to be used in a program is only the first step in the modeling process. Attributes and behaviors actually define a category or type of object, out of which many objects can then be designated. For example, suppose you want to display a geometric object, such as a rectangle, onscreen. In its simplest representation, a rectangle has a shape and location, which can be represented by the object description in Figure 10.9.

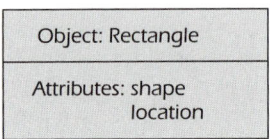

Figure 10.9   An initial rectangle object description

Now you can refine this model to define more accurately what's meant by shape and location. A rectangle's `shape` attribute can actually be broken down into two more specific attributes: `length` and `width`. As for the behavior listed in Figure 10.9 (`location`), you can also break it down into more specific behaviors. For example, one approach might be listing the position of the rectangle's upper-left corner in relation to the screen's upper-left corner, and then do the same for the rectangle's upper-right corner. These two positions, along with the rectangle's length and width, are enough information to allow the program to generate a rectangle. However, simply specifying one location for the rectangle might not be enough. For example, you might want to give the rectangle the capability to move its position and change its length or width. Figure 10.10 shows a refined object description that takes this additional behavior into account.

Chapter Supplement: Thinking in Terms of
Objects

Object: Rectangle

Attributes: length
     width
     top-left corner
     opposite corner

Behavior: move
     change length
     change width

Figure 10.10 A refined rectangle object description

As you've seen, in object-based programming, the category of objects defined by a set of attributes and behaviors is called a class. For example, the `length` and `width` attributes can define a general type of shape, or class, called a rectangle. Only when specific values have been assigned to these attributes have you represented a specific rectangle. This distinction carries over into C++. The attributes and behaviors in an object description are used to define a general class, or type, of object. An object comes into existence only when you assign specific values to attributes. The term "state" is then used to refer to how the created object appears at any one moment.

In practice, an object's state is defined by the values assigned to its attributes. For example, you can specify a rectangle's state by saying that its width is 1 inch, its length is 2 inches, its upper-left corner is positioned 4 inches from the top of the screen and 5 inches from the screen's left side, and its opposite corner is positioned 5 inches from the top of the screen and 7 inches from the screen's left side. Figure 10.11 shows a rectangle with this state.

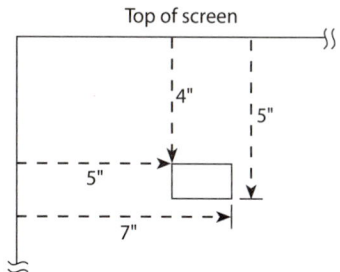

Figure 10.11 Defining a rectangle's state

Finally, when each object is created, it must be given an identity—a name by which it can be uniquely identified in a program. This is similar to giving each car a vehicle identification number (VIN) when it's assembled or giving a different name to each person in a family. Objects are given names by declaration statements, which also create the object.

The fundamental difference between object-oriented and procedural programs is the model on which they're based, and as you program, you should be aware of this difference. The essence of object-oriented design is constructing and testing classes that can be used by any other class or program to create as many objects as needed and provide the methods that allow manipulating these objects in a useful manner. Therefore, in object-oriented programming, the emphasis is on the attributes and behavior of objects. In procedure-oriented programming, no objects are created or named. The emphasis is always on the operations to be performed, such as add, multiply, and divide, and in creating methods to perform calculations by using these operations.

Because procedural programs can be helpful when learning how to use C++ statements, methods, or streams, such as `cout`, you use and create procedural programs in this book. In fact, you have already used these programs—all the program listings in chapters are procedural programs. You might also find these programs useful for constructing output quickly for simple programming problems in your professional work. However, be aware that relying on procedural programming too much can be detrimental for serious programmers, who eventually must address more complex programming situations. So even when creating a procedural program is convenient, at least contemplate how you might construct a programming solution with objects.

EXERCISES 10.8

1. **(Review)** Define the following terms:
   - **a.** Attribute
   - **b.** Behavior
   - **c.** Class
   - **d.** Identity
   - **e.** Model
   - **f.** Object
   - **g.** Object description
   - **h.** State
   - **i.** Value
   - **j.** Operation

2. **(Practice)** Classify each of the following as classes or objects:
   - **a.** Maple trees
   - **b.** Ford cars
   - **c.** My collie dog
   - **d.** The oak tree in your neighbor's yard
   - **e.** Boeing 767 planes
   - **f.** Your Ford Taurus
   - **g.** Kitchen tables
   - **h.** Student desks
   - **i.** The chair you're sitting on

3. **(Practice) a.** For each of the following, determine what attributes might be of interest to someone buying the item:
   - **i.** A book
   - **ii.** A can of soda
   - **iii.** A pen
   - **iv.** An elevator
   - **v.** A car

   b. Do the attributes you used in Exercise 4a model an object or a class of objects?

4. (Practice) For each of the following, determine what behavior might be of interest to someone buying the item.

   a. A car

   b. An elevator

5. (Practice) a. List five attributes for a character in a video game.

   b. List five behaviors that a character in a video game should have.

   [**Add** the following as the last exercise:]

6. (Practice) a. List the attributes and behaviors of interest in a program that simulates dealing
a hand of playing cards. For this exercise, use any card game you're familiar with.

   b. What attributes of cards wouldn't be of interest for purposes of the simulation?

Chapter

11 **Adding Functionality to Your Classes**

Creating a class requires providing the capabilities to declare, initialize, assign, manipulate, and display data members. In Chapter 10, you learned about declaring, initializing, and displaying objects. In this chapter, you see how to create operator and conversion capabilities similar to those inherent in C++'s built-in types. With these additions, your classes will have all the functionality of built-in types.

11.1 Creating Class Operators

C+ provides operators for its built-in data types, such as +, −, ==, >=, and so on, and you can make these operators available to your constructed classes. To do this, you have to select a suitable operator symbol, and then alter it to work with objects defined by your class. You must select an operator symbol for class use from the built-in symbols listed in Table 11.1. These symbols can be adopted for class use with no limitation in their meaning by creating a class method or a friend function; both are discussed in this section.

Table 11.1 Operators Available for Class Use

Operator	Description
( )	Function call (see Section 11.4)
[ ]	Array element (see Section 11.4)
->	Structure member pointer reference
new	Dynamic allocation of memory
delete	Dynamic deallocation of memory
++	Increment
--	Decrement
-	Unary minus
!	Logical negation
~	Ones complement
*	Indirection
*	Multiplication
/	Division
%	Modulus (remainder)
+	Addition
-	Subtraction
<<	Left shift
>>	Right shift
<	Less than
<=	Less than or equal to
>	Greater than
>=	Greater than or equal to
==	Equal to
!=	Not equal to
&&	Logical AND
||	Logical OR
&	Bit-by-bit AND
^	Bit-by-bit exclusive OR
|	Bit-by-bit inclusive OR
= += -= *= /= %= &= ^= |= <<= >>=	Assignment
,	Comma

The first step in providing a class with operators from Table 11.1 is to decide which operations make sense for the class and how they should be defined. As an example, you'll continue building on the Date class introduced in Chapter 10.

Clearly, the addition of two dates isn't meaningful. The addition of a date and an integer, however, does make sense if the integer is taken as the number of days to be added to the date. Likewise, subtracting an integer from a date makes sense. Also, the subtraction of two dates is meaningful if you define the difference to mean the number of days between the two dates. Similarly, it makes sense to compare two dates and determine whether the dates are equal or one date occurs before or after another date. Now see how two of these operators, == and +, can be adapted for use with the Date class.

Operations on class objects that use C++'s built-in operator symbols are referred to as **operator functions**. Operator functions are declared and implemented in the same manner as all member functions, with one exception: The function name must use the form *operator<symbol>*, where *<symbol>* is an operator symbol in Table 11.1. For example, the function name operator+ is the name of a class addition function, and the function name operator== is the name of a class comparison function. It's important to understand that an operator function can be redefined to perform *any* operation. Good programming practice, however, dictates writing a function to actually perform the operation implied by the function's name.

After the function name is selected, the process of writing the function simply amounts to having it accept inputs and produce the correct returned value. For example, to compare two Date objects for equality, you select C++'s equality operator (==), and the function name becomes operator==. For the Date class, this comparison operation should accept two Date objects, compare them, and return a Boolean value indicating the result of the comparison: true for equality and false for inequality. A suitable prototype for this operator function is as follows:

```
bool operator==(const Date&);  //pass a reference to a Date object
```

This prototype indicates the function is named operator==, it returns a Boolean value, and it accepts a reference to a Date object.[1] The use of a reference parameter isn't accidental. One of the main reasons for references in C++ is to facilitate the construction of overloaded operators. The reason is that references make notation in the function more natural than when using pointers. Including the const keyword ensures that the passed reference can't be altered by the function. This prototype must be included in the Date class's declaration section.

Now see how to write the function definition for the operator to include in the class implementation section. For the Date class, the following definition is suitable:

```
bool Date::operator==(const Date& date2)
{
  if(day == date2.day && month == date2.month && year == date2.year)
    return true;
  else
    return false;
}
```

---

[1]The prototype bool operator==(Date) works, too. Passing a reference, however, is preferable to passing an object because it reduces the function call's overhead by giving the function access to the object whose address is passed. Overhead is reduced because passing an address means a copy of the object isn't made for the called function.

After this function has been defined, it can be called by using the relational expressions a == b or a.operator==(b), assuming both a and b are Date objects. More typically, it's used in a conditional expression, such as if (a == b). Program 11.1 includes this if statement and the operator function in the context of a complete program. The shaded lines indicate statements pertaining to the operator function.

 **Program 11.1**

```cpp
#include <iostream>
using namespace std;

// class declaration section
class Date
{
  private:
    int month;
    int day;
    int year;
  public:
    Date(int = 7, int = 4, int = 2012);  // constructor
    bool operator==(Date&);  // prototype for the operator== function
};

// class implementation section
Date::Date(int mm, int dd, int yyyy)
{
  month = mm;
  day = dd;
  year = yyyy;
}

bool Date::operator==(Date& date2)
{
  if(day == date2.day && month == date2.month && year == date2.year)
    return true;
  else
    return false;
}

int main()
{
  Date a(4,1,2012), b(12,18,2010), c(4,1,2012); // declare 3 objects
```

```
  if (a == b)
    cout << "Dates a and b are the same." << endl;
  else
    cout << "Dates a and b are not the same." << endl;
  if (a == c)
    cout << "Dates a and c are the same." << endl;
  else
    cout << "Dates a and c are not the same." << endl;
  return 0;
}
```

The following output is produced by Program 11.1:

```
Dates a and b are not the same.
Dates a and c are the same.
```

The first new feature shown in Program 11.1 is the declaration and implementation of the `operator==` function. Except for its name, this operator function is constructed in the same manner as any other class method: It's declared in the class declaration section and defined in the class implementation section.

The second new feature is how the function is called. Operator functions can be called by using their associated symbols. Because operator functions are true functions, however, the traditional method of calling them can also be used—specifying the function name and including appropriate arguments. Therefore, instead of being called by the expression `a == b` in Program 11.1, the call `a.operator==(b)` could have been used.

Now see how to create another operator for the `Date` class—an addition operator. As before, creating this operator requires specifying three items:

- The name of the operator function
- The processing the function is to perform
- The data type, if any, the function is to return

Clearly, for addition you would use the addition symbol with the operator function name: `operator+`. Having selected the function's name, you must then determine what you want this function to do with `Date` objects. As noted, adding two dates makes no sense. Adding an integer to a date is meaningful, however, when the integer represents the number of days before or after a given date. The sum of an integer and a `Date` object is simply another `Date` object, which should be returned by the addition operation. Therefore, the following prototype is suitable for the addition function:

```
Date operator+(int);
```

This prototype, included in the class declaration section, specifies adding an integer to a class object and returning a `Date` object. Therefore, if `a` is a `Date` object, the function call `a.operator+(284)`, or its more common alternative, `a + 284`, should cause the number 284 to be added to a's date value correctly.

Next, you must construct the function to accomplish this task, which requires selecting a calendar convention first. For simplicity, adopt the financial date convention of each month consisting of 30 days and each year consisting of 360 days. Using this convention, the function adds an integer number of days to the `Date` object's `day` value, and then adjusts the resulting `day` value to fall in the range 1 to 30 and the `month` value to fall in the range 1 to 12. The following function accomplishes these tasks:

```
Date Date::operator+(int days)
{
  Date temp;   // a temporary Date to store the result

  temp.day = day + days;    // add the days
  temp.month = month;
  temp.year = year;

  while (temp.day > 30)    // adjust the months
  {
    temp.month++;
    temp.day -= 30;
  }
  while (temp.month > 12)  // adjust the years
  {
    temp.year++;
    temp.month -= 12;
  }

  return temp;     // the values in temp are returned
}
```

The important feature to notice is the use of the `temp` object. Its purpose is to ensure that the function doesn't alter the object on the right side of the assignment statement. To understand this point, consider a statement such as `newDate = oldDate + 284;` that uses this operator function; `newDate` and `oldDate` are `Date` objects. This statement should never modify `oldDate`'s value, which the function has access to.[2] Rather, the expression `oldDate + 284` should yield a new date value that's then assigned to `newDate`. This new `Date` object is named `temp` in the operator function and becomes the `Date` object returned by the `operator+()` function, which is then assigned to `newDate`. Program 11.2 uses this function in the context of a complete program. Statements relating to the operator function have been shaded.

---

[2]Another way of looking at this is that the expression `oldDate + 284` is the same as the expression `oldDate.operator+(284)`. Therefore, the `day`, `month`, and `year` variables in the operator function are `oldDate`'s data members. Any changes to these variables are changes to `oldDate`.

 Program 11.2

```cpp
#include <iostream>
#include <iomanip>
using namespace std;

// class declaration section
class Date
{
  private:
    int month;
    int day;
    int year;
  public:
    Date(int = 7, int = 4, int = 2012);      // constructor
    Date operator+(int); // prototype for the + operator function
    void showDate();       // member function to display a date
};

// class implementation section
Date::Date(int mm, int dd, int yyyy)
{
  month = mm;
  day = dd;
  year = yyyy;
}

Date Date::operator+(int days)
{
  Date temp;  // a temporary date to store the result

  temp.day = day + days;    // add the days
  temp.month = month;
  temp.year = year;

  while (temp.day > 30)     // adjust the months
  {
    temp.month++;
    temp.day -= 30;
  }
  while (temp.month > 12)  // adjust the years
```

```
    {
        temp.year++;
        temp.month -= 12;
    }
    return temp;        // the values in temp are returned
}
```

```
void Date::showDate()
{
    cout << setfill('0')
         << setw(2) << month << '/'
         << setw(2) << day << '/'
         << setw(2) << year % 100;
    return;
}

int main()
{
    Date oldDate(4,1,2011), newDate; // declare two objects

    cout << "The initial date is ";
    oldDate.showDate();
    cout << endl;
    newDate = oldDate + 284;     // add in 284 days = 9 months and 14 days
    cout << "The new date is ";
    newDate.showDate();
    cout << endl;

    return 0;
}
```

Program 11.2 produces the following output:

```
The initial date is 04/01/11
The new date is 01/15/12
```

In constructing your own operator functions, the only restrictions on selecting and using the operator symbols in Table 11.1 are the following:[3]

- An operator's syntax can't be changed, so a binary operator must remain binary, and a unary operator must remain unary.
- Symbols not in Table 11.1 can't be used. For example, the ., ::, and ?: symbols can't be used as operator functions.

---

[3]Note that an operator symbol can be used to produce any operation, whether or not the operation is consistent with the symbol's accepted use. For example, you could redefine the addition symbol to provide multiplication. Clearly, this redefinition violates the intent of making these symbols available, so care must be taken to redefine each symbol in a manner consistent with its accepted use.

- New operator symbols can't be created. For example, because %% is not an operator in C++, it can't be defined as a class operator.
- Neither the precedence nor the associativity of C++'s operators can be modified. Therefore, you can't give the addition operator a higher precedence than the multiplication operator.
- Operators can't be redefined for C++'s built-in types.
- The operator must be a class member or friend function and must be defined to take at least one class member as an operand.

Assignment Operator

The **assignment operator**, =, is the one operator that works with all classes without requiring an operator function. For example, if a and b are objects constructed from the Date class, the statement a = b; sets a's data members equal to their equivalent b members. Therefore, if b's month, day, and year members are 12, 25, 2014, the expression a = b sets a's month variable to 12, its day variable to 25, and its year variable to 2014. This type of assignment is referred to as **memberwise assignment**.

In the absence of a user-written assignment operator, the C++ compiler builds a memberwise assignment operator as the default assignment operator for each class, which is generally adequate for most classes. However, if the class contains any pointer data members, this default assignment operator usually has to be created explicitly (see Section 12.4). Creating an assignment function is the same as creating any other operator function, such as == and +: declaring it in the class declaration section and then defining it in the class implementation section. A simple assignment operator declaration has this form:

```
void operator=(const ClassName&);
```

As in all functions, the keyword void indicates that the assignment operator returns no value. The class name and ampersand in parentheses indicate that the argument passed to the operator is a class reference, and the const keyword ensures that the function can't change the reference.

The following definition in the class implementation section creates an explicit assignment that corresponds to this operator's prototype. It mimics the operation of the default assignment operator:

```
void Date::operator=(Date& olddate)
{
  day = olddate.day;       // assign the day
  month = olddate.month;   // assign the month
  year = olddate.year;     // assign the year
}
```

In this definition, olddate is defined as a reference to a Date class and refers to the object passed to the function when it's called. The call can be made by using an expression such as a.operator=(b) or a = b, with a and b replaced by the names of the Date objects you're using. In the called function, the day, month, and year data members referenced internally by olddate (which correspond to b's data members) are assigned to the equivalent data members in a. (You can see that b is the reference argument passed to olddate in the function call a.operator=(b);, where b is the argument inside the function's parentheses.)

One useful modification concerns the operation's return value. As constructed, your simple assignment operator returns no value, which precludes you from using it in multiple assignments, such as a = b = c. The reason is that operator functions retain the same precedence and associativity as their built-in counterparts. Therefore, an expression such as a = b = c is evaluated in the order a = (b = c). Because of the way assignment has been defined by the operator function, unfortunately, the expression b = c returns no value, making subsequent assignment to a an error because it results in the invalid expression a = void. To allow multiple assignments, a more complete assignment operation would return a Date type. Returning the correct date requires a special class pointer, which is discussed in Section 11.2.

Copy Constructors[4]

Although assignment looks similar to initialization, they're entirely different operations. In C++, an initialization occurs every time a new object is created. In an assignment, no new object is created—the value of an existing object is simply changed. Figure 11.1 shows this difference.

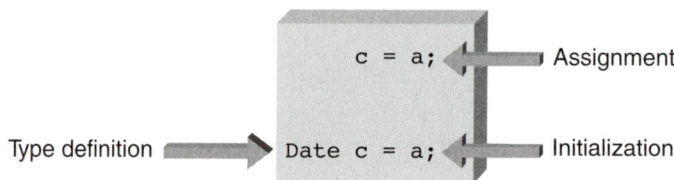

Figure 11.1   Initialization and assignment

One type of initialization that closely resembles assignment occurs in C++ when one object is initialized by using another object of the same class. For example, in the declaration

Date b = a;

or its equivalent form

Date b(a);

the b object is initialized to the previously declared a object. The constructor performing this type of initialization is called a **copy constructor**, and if you don't declare one, the compiler creates it for you. The compiler's default copy constructor performs similarly to the default assignment operator by doing a memberwise assignment between objects. Therefore, for the declaration Date b = a;, the default copy constructor sets b's month, day, and year values to their counterparts in a.

As with default assignment operators, default copy constructors work just fine unless the class contains pointer data members. Before considering the possible complications with pointer data members and how to handle them, seeing how to construct your own copy constructor is helpful.

---

[4]The material in this section is included for completeness and can be omitted without loss of subject continuity.

Copy constructors, like all operator functions, are declared in the class declaration section and defined in the class implementation section. The declaration of a copy constructor has this syntax:

```
ClassName(const ClassName&);
```

As with all constructors, the function name *must* be the class name. Also, the argument is a reference to the class, which is a characteristic of all copy constructors.[5] To ensure that the argument isn't altered inadvertently, it's always specified as a constant. Applying this general form to the Date class, a copy constructor can be declared as follows:

```
Date(const Date&);
```

The actual implementation of this constructor, if it were to perform the same memberwise assignment as the default copy constructor, would take this form:

```
Date:: Date(const Date& olddate)
{
  month = olddate.month;
  day = olddate.day;
  year = olddate.year;
}
```

A comparison of this copy constructor with the assignment operator defined previously shows them to be the same function. The difference is that the copy constructor, like all constructors, creates an object's data members before using assignment to specify member values. Therefore, the copy constructor doesn't perform a true initialization, but a creation followed by assignment. Program 11.3 contains this copy constructor in the context of a complete program.

Program 11.3

```
#include <iostream>
#include <iomanip>
using namespace std;

// class declaration section
class Date
{
  private:
    int month;
    int day;
    int year;
```

[5]A copy constructor is often defined as a constructor whose first argument is a reference to its class type, with any additional arguments being defaults.

```
   public:
      Date(int = 7, int = 4, int = 2012);    // constructor
      Date(const Date&);     // copy constructor
      void showDate();     // member function to display a date
};
// class implementation section
Date::Date(int mm, int dd, int yyyy)
{
   month = mm;
   day = dd;
   year = yyyy;
}

Date::Date(const Date& olddate)
{
   month = olddate.month;
   day = olddate.day;
   year = olddate.year;
}
void Date::showDate()
{
   cout << setfill('0')
        << setw(2) << month << '/'
        << setw(2) << day << '/'
        << setw(2) << year % 100;
   return;
}

int main()
{
   Date a(4,1,2011), b(12,18,2012); // use the constructor
   Date c(a);    // use the copy constructor
   Date d = b;   // use the copy constructor

   cout << "\nThe date stored in a is ";
   a.showDate();
   cout << "\nThe date stored in b is ";
   b.showDate();
   cout << "\nThe date stored in c is ";
   c.showDate();
   cout << "\nThe date stored in d is ";
   d.showDate();
   cout << endl;
   return 0;
}
```

Program 11.3 produces the following output:

```
The date stored in a is 04/01/11
The date stored in b is 12/18/12
The date stored in c is 04/01/11
The date stored in d is 12/18/12
```

As this output shows, the copy constructor has initialized c's and d's data members to a's and b's values. Although the copy constructor in Program 11.3 adds nothing to the functionality of the compiler's default copy constructor, it does give you the fundamentals of defining your own copy constructors.

Base/Member Initialization[6]

A true initialization has no reliance on assignment and is possible in C++ by using a **base/member initialization list**. This list can be applied only to constructor functions and can be written in two ways. The first way is inside a class's declaration section in this form:

ClassName(argument list):list of data members(initializing values) {}

Here's an example of a default constructor performing true initialization in this form:

```
// class declaration section
public:
  Date(int mo=4, int da=1, int yr=2012):month(mo), day(da), year(yr) {}
```

The second way is to declare a function prototype with defaults in the class declaration section followed by the initialization list in the class implementation section. For the Date constructor, it takes this form:

```
// class declaration section
public:
  Date(int = 4, int = 1, int = 2012);   // prototype with defaults


// class implementation section
Date::Date(int mo, int da, int yr) : month(mo), day(da), year(yr) {}
```

Notice that in both forms, the body of the constructor function is empty. This isn't a requirement, and the body can include any subsequent operations you want the constructor to perform. The interesting feature of this type of constructor is that it clearly differentiates between the initialization tasks performed in the member initialization list (between the colon and the braces) and any subsequent assignments in the function's body. Although you won't be using this type of initialization in this book, it's required whenever a const class instance variable is used.

---

[6]The material in this section is included for completeness and can be omitted without loss of subject continuity.

Point of Information

Values and Identities

Apart from object behaviors, a characteristic feature that objects share with variables is they always have a unique identity. An object's identity is what permits distinguishing one object from another. This feature isn't true of a value, such as the number 5, because all occurrences of 5 are indistinguishable from one another. Therefore, values aren't considered objects in object-oriented programming languages, such as C++.

Another difference between an object and a value is that a value can never be a container whose value can change, but an object clearly can. A value is simply an entity that stands for itself.

Now consider a string such as `"Chicago"`. As a string, it's a value. However, because `Chicago` could also be a specific and identifiable object of the class `city`, the context in which the name is used is important.

Operator Functions as Friends[7]

The operator functions shown previously have been constructed as class functions. An interesting feature of operator functions is that except for the operator functions =, (), [ ], and ->, they can also be written as friend functions. For example, if the `operator+()` function used in Program 11.2 is written as a friend, the following is a suitable class declaration section prototype:

```
friend Date operator+(Date& , int);
```

Notice that the friend version contains a reference to a `Date` object that isn't in the member function version. In all cases, the friend version of a member operator function *must* contain an additional class reference that the member function doesn't require.[8] Table 11.2 lists this equivalence for both unary and binary operators.

Table 11.2 Operator Function Argument Requirements

Operator	Member Function	Friend Function
Unary	1 implicit	1 explicit
Binary	1 implicit and 1 explicit	2 explicit

---

[7]The material in this section is included for completeness and can be omitted without loss of subject continuity.
[8]The extra argument is needed to identify the correct object. This argument isn't necessary with a member function because the member function "knows" which object it's operating on. The mechanism of this "knowing" is supplied by an implied member function argument, explained in Section 11.2.

Program 11.2's `operator+()` function, written as a friend function, is as follows:

```
Date operator+(Date& op1, int days)
{
  Date temp;   // a temporary Date to store the result

  temp.day = op1.day + days;   // add the days
  temp.month = op1.month;
  temp.year = op1.year;
  while (temp.day > 30)     // adjust the months
  {
    temp.month++;
    temp.day -= 30;
  }
  while (temp.month > 12)   // adjust the years
  {
    temp.year++;
    temp.month -= 12;
  }
  return temp;      // the values in temp are returned
}
```

The only difference between this version and the member function version is the explicit use of a `Date` argument named `op1` (an arbitrary name choice) in the friend version. Therefore, in the friend function's body, the first three assignment statements reference `op1`'s data members as `op1.day`, `op1.month`, and `op1.year`, whereas the member function simply refers to its arguments as `day`, `month`, and `year`.

In determining whether to overload a binary operator as a friend or member operator function, follow this guideline: Friend functions are more appropriate for binary functions that don't modify either of their operands (such as ==, +, –, and so forth), and member functions are more appropriate for binary functions that modify operands (such as =, +=, and –=, and so forth).

EXERCISES 11.1

1. **(Practice)** Enter and run Program 11.1 on your computer.

2. **(Program) a.** Define a *greater than* relational operator function named `operator>()` that can be used with the `Date` class declared in Program 11.1.

   b. Define a *less than* relational operator function named `operator<()` that can be used with the `Date` class declared in Program 11.1.

   c. Include the operator function written for Exercises 2a and 2b in a working C++ program.

3. **(Debug) a.** Determine whether the following addition operator function produces the same result as the function in Program 11.2:

```
Date Date::operator+(int days)    // return a Date object
{
  Date temp;

  temp.day = day + days;    // add the days in
  temp.month = month + int(day/30);         // determine total months
  temp.day = temp.day % 30;                 // determine actual day
  temp.year = year + int(temp.month/12);    // determine total years
  temp.month = temp.month % 12;             // determine actual month
  return temp;
}
```

b. Verify your answer to Exercise 3a by including the function in a working C++ program.

4. **(Program) a.** Construct a class named `Cartesian` containing two double-precision data members named x and y, used to store a point's x and y values in rectangular coordinates. The member functions should include a constructor that initializes an object's x and y values to 0 and functions to input and display an object's x and y values. Additionally, include an assignment function that performs a memberwise assignment between two `Cartesian` objects.

b. Include the class written for Exercise 4a in a working C++ program that creates and displays the values of two `Cartesian` objects; the second object is assigned the values of the first object.

5. **(Program) a.** Construct a class named `Time` containing three integer data members named `hrs`, `mins`, and `secs` used to store hours, minutes, and seconds. The member functions should include a constructor that provides default values of 0 for each data member, a display function that prints an object's data values, and an assignment operator that performs a memberwise assignment between two `Time` objects.

b. Include the `Time` class developed in Exercise 5a in a working C++ program that creates and displays two `Time` objects; the second object is assigned the values of the first object.

6. **(Program) a.** Construct a class named `Complex` containing two double-precision data members named `real` and `imag`, used to store the real and imaginary parts of a complex number. The member functions should include a constructor that provides default values of 0 for each data member, a display function that prints an object's data values, and an assignment operator that performs a memberwise assignment between two `Complex` objects.

b. Include the class written for Exercise 6a in a working C++ program that creates and displays the values of two `Complex` objects; the second object is assigned the values of the first object.

7. **(Program) a.** Construct a class named `Car` containing these three data members: a double-precision variable named `engineSize`, a character variable named `bodyStyle`, and an integer variable named `colorCode`. The member functions should include a constructor that provides default values of 0 for each numeric data member and an X for each character variable; a display function that prints the engine size, body style, and color code; and an assignment operator that performs a memberwise assignment between two `Car` objects for each instance variable.

b. Include the class written for Exercise 7a in a working C++ program that creates and displays two Car objects; the second object is assigned the values of the first object.

8. **(Program) a.** Create a class named String and include an addition operator function that concatenates two strings. The function should return a string.

b. Include the overloaded operator written for Exercise 8a in a working C++ program.

9. **(Program) a.** Define a subtraction operator function that can be used with the Date class declared in Program 11.1. The subtraction should accept a long integer argument representing the number of days to be subtracted from an object's date and return a Date. In doing the subtraction, assume all months consist of 30 days and all years consist of 360 days. Additionally, an end-of-month adjustment should be made, if necessary, that converts any resulting day of 31 to a day of 30, unless the month is February. If the resulting month is February and the day is 29, 30, or 31, it should be changed to 28.

b. Define another subtraction operator function named operator-() that can be used with the Date class defined in Program 11.1. The subtraction should yield a long integer representing the difference in days between two dates. In calculating the day difference, use the financial assumption that all months have 30 days and all years have 360 days.

c. Include the overloaded operators written for Exercise 9a and 9b in a working C++ program.

10. **(Modify) a.** Rewrite the addition operator function in Program 11.2 to account for the actual days in a month, omitting leap years. (*Note*: This function requires an array to store the days in each month.)

b. Verify the operation of the operator function written for Exercise 10a by including it in a working C++ program.

11. **(Program) a.** Construct a class named Fractions containing two integer data members named num and denom, used to store the numerator and denominator of a fraction having the form num/denom. Your class should include a default constructor that initializes num and denom to 1 and four operator functions for adding, subtracting, multiplying, and dividing the two fractions, as follows:

```
Addition: a/b + c/d = (a * d + b * c) / (b * d)
Subtraction: a/b - c/d = (a * d - b * c) / (b * d)
Multiplication: a/b * c/d = (a* c) / (b * d)
Division: (a/b) / (c/d) = (a * d) / (b * c)
```

Your class should have input and output functions for entering and displaying a fraction.

b. Include the class written for Exercise 11a by including it in a working C++ program that can be used to test each of the class's member methods.

12. **(Modify) a.** Rewrite the comparison operator function in Program 11.1 as a friend function.

b. Verify the operation of the friend operator function written for Exercise 12a by including it in a working C++ program.

11.2 How Methods Are Shared

Each time an object is created from a class, a distinct area of memory is set aside for its data members. For example, if two objects named a and b are created from the Date class you've been using in this chapter, the memory storage for these objects is as shown in Figure 11.2. Note that each set of data members has its own starting address in memory, which corresponds to the address of the object's first data member.

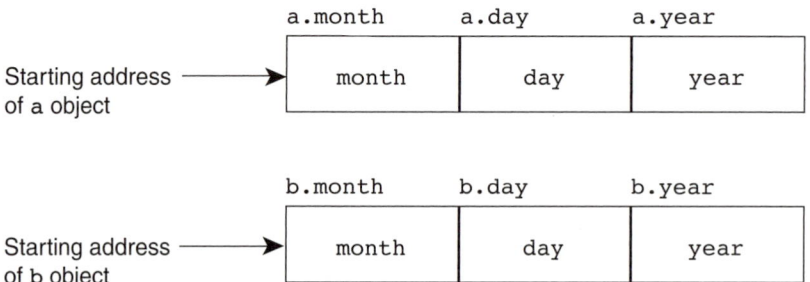

Figure 11.2   Storing two Date objects in memory

This replication of data storage isn't implemented for member methods. In fact, for each class, *only one copy* of the member methods is retained in memory, and each object uses these same methods.

Sharing member methods requires providing a means of identifying which specific object a member method should be operating on. This is accomplished by the name of the object preceding the method call, as shown in Figure 11.3.

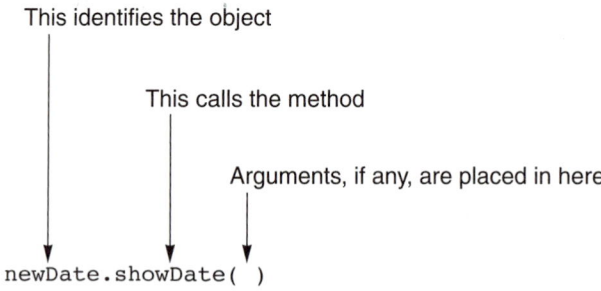

Figure 11.3   Calling a class method

In reviewing Figure 11.3, note that the actual method call and passing data to the method are made in the same manner as all C++ function calls—by providing the method name and placing all passed data in the parentheses following the method's name. The called method receives a copy of any arguments passed to it through the parentheses. However, the method gets direct access to the object used in calling it. This is accomplished as follows: The object name preceding the method's name sends its address to the method. This address tells the method where in memory the object it's to operate on is located. In this way, it enables the method to access the object and its data members directly. For example, the statement `oldDate.showDate()` passes the `oldDate` object's address to the `showDate()` member method.

Two questions at this point are as follows:

- How is this address passed to `showDate()`?
- Where is this address stored?

The answer to the first question is that the address is passed to the called function as a hidden argument. Therefore, the call `oldDate.showDate()` passes `&oldDate` to `showDate()`. Recall from Section 8.1 that placing the address operator, `&`, in front of an identifier means "the address of," so the expression `&oldDate` should be read as "the address of `oldDate`." In effect, then, the call `oldDate.showDate()` corresponds to `showDate(&oldDate)`. Although this call is invalid because it violates the syntax rules for calling a member method, it clearly illustrates that an address is passed. The question then is how is the passed address saved and accessed by `showDate()`?

It's saved in the same manner as any passed address must be saved—by using a pointer. This special pointer is created automatically as a hidden argument for each nonstatic class method, when the method is defined. The name of this special pointer is `this`, described next.

The `this` Pointer

The `this` pointer is added automatically to each nonstatic class method as a hidden argument. When a method is called, the calling object's address is passed to it and stored in the method's `this` pointer. Therefore, each member method actually receives an extra argument that's the address of an object.

Although it's not usually necessary to do so, the address in the `this` pointer can be used explicitly in the called method. For example, when `showDate()` is called by the expression `oldDate.showDate()`, the `this` pointer in `showDate()` can be used to access any data member in the `oldDate` object by using the following syntax:

```
(*this).month accesses oldDate's month member.
(*this).day accesses oldDate's day member.
(*this).year accesses oldDate's year member.
```

These relationships are shown in Figure 11.4. As shown, the starting address of the `oldDate` object is also the address of the object's first data member. Except for the dot notation to locate the correct member item, it's the same technique for passing addresses that you saw in Section 8.4.

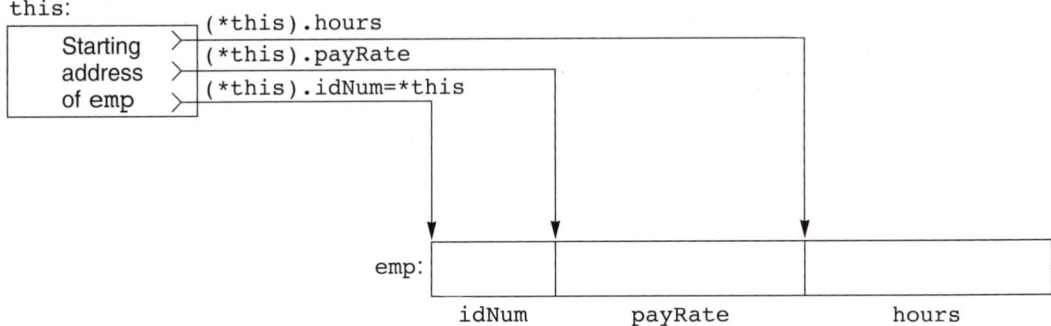

Figure 11.4 A pointer can be used to access object members

The parentheses around the *this shown in Figure 11.4 are necessary to initially access "the object whose address is in the this pointer." The dot operator, ., is then followed by the data member's name. The parentheses are needed to override the dot operator's precedence over the indirection operator, *.

Without the parentheses, the expression becomes *this.hours, which is equivalent to *(this.hours). In both expressions, the dot operator is applied before the * operator, and both expressions refer to "the data member whose address is in the this.hours variable." This reference clearly makes no sense because there's no object named this, and hours doesn't contain an address.

The use of pointers in this manner is so common that a special notation exists for it. The general expression (*pointer).member can always be replaced with the notation pointer->member. The -> operator is constructed with a hyphen followed by the greater-than symbol. Either notation can be used to locate a data member. Therefore, the following expressions are equivalent:

(*this).day can be replaced by this->day
(*this).month can be replaced by this->month
(*this).year can be replaced by this->year

For example, by using the this pointer, the Date class's showDate() method, repeated here for convenience,

```
void Date::showDate()
{
  cout << setfill('0')
       << setw(2) << month << '/'
       << setw(2) << day << '/'
       << setw(2) << year % 100;
  return;
}
```

Point of Information

Pointers Versus References

The distinguishing characteristic of a pointer, as a formal parameter or variable, is that every pointer contains a value that's an address. Whereas a pointer is a variable or argument with an address as its content, a reference *is* an address. Therefore, a reference can be thought of as a named constant, with the constant being a valid memory address.

From an advanced programming viewpoint, pointers are more flexible than references because a pointer's contents can be manipulated in much the same manner as any other variable's value. The disadvantage of pointers is that their flexibility makes them more complicated to understand and use than references. Because references (as both variables and arguments) can be used only as named addresses, they're easier to use. Therefore, when the compiler encounters a reference, it dereferences the address automatically to obtain the contents of the address. This isn't the case with pointers. If you use a pointer's name, as noted previously, you access the pointer's contents. To dereference the address stored in a pointer correctly, you must use C++'s indirection operator, *, in front of the pointer name. This operator informs the compiler that what you want is the item whose address stored in the pointer variable.

---

can be written as follows:

```cpp
void Date::showDate()
{
  cout << setfill('0')
       << setw(2) << this->month << '/'
       << setw(2) << this->day << '/'
       << setw(2) << this->year % 100;
  return;
}
```

Clearly, using the `this` pointer in this manner is unnecessary and simply clutters up `showDate()`'s code. At times, however, an object must be returned from a method. In many of these situations, one of which is discussed in the next section, the address stored in the `this` pointer must be used.

The Assignment Operator Revisited

Section 11.1 showed a simple assignment operator method that has the following prototype:

```cpp
void operator=(const Date &);
```

The drawback of the method this prototype declares is that it returns no value. Consequently, multiple assignments, such as a = b = c, aren't possible. The reason is that the right-to-left association of the = operator causes the assignment b = c to be made first. This assignment results in a `void` being returned from this expression. Attempting to assign this data type to the `Date` object a results in an error.

To fix this problem, you need the method to return a Date object that has the same data members as those assigned to b. A suitable prototype for this method is as follows:

```
Date operator=(const Date&);
```

Returning the assigned Date object is now possible by using the this pointer. Following is a suitable method definition, with the return statement shaded to indicate the this pointer:

```
Date Date::operator=(const Date &newdate)
{
  day = newdate.day;        // assign the day
  month = newdate.month;    // assign the month
  year = newdate.year;      // assign the year
  return *this;
}
```

Because a Date object is now returned by this method, an assignment such as a = b = c or its equivalent form, a.operator(b.operator=(c)), can be made. In both expressions, the assignment method first alters b's member values. It then returns the object pointed to by this, which is the b object. This Date object is then assigned to a. Program 11.4 shows using this method in the context of a complete program.

Program 11.4

```
#include <iostream>
#include <iomanip>
using namespace std;

// class declaration section
class Date
{
  private:
    int month;
    int day;
    int year;
  public:
    Date(int = 7, int = 4, int = 2012);    // constructor
    Date operator=(const Date &);  // assignment operator prototype
    void showDate();            // member method to display a date
};

// class implementation section
Date::Date(int mm, int dd, int yyyy)
{
```

☞

```
  month = mm;
  day = dd;
  year = yyyy;
}
```

```
//The new assignment operator returns an object of type Date
Date Date::operator=(const Date& newdate)
{
  day = newdate.day;        // assign the day
  month = newdate.month;    // assign the month
  year = newdate.year;      // assign the year
  return *this;
}
```

```
void Date::showDate()
{
  cout << setfill('0')
       << setw(2) << month << '/'
       << setw(2) << day << '/'
       << setw(2) << year % 100;
  return;
}
```

```
int main()
{
  Date a(4,1,1999), b(14,18,2012), c(1,1,2014); // declare three objects

  cout << "Before assignment a's date value is ";
  a.showDate();
  cout << "\nBefore assignment b's date value is ";
  b.showDate();
  cout << "\nBefore assignment c's date value is ";
  c.showDate();
```

```
  a = b = c;     // multiple assignment
```

```
  cout << "\n\nAfter assignment a's date value is ";
  a.showDate();
  cout << "\nAfter assignment b's date value is ";
  b.showDate();
  cout << "\nAfter assignment c's date value is ";
  c.showDate();
  cout << endl;
  return 0;
}
```

This is the output produced by Program 11.4, which verifies that the multiple assignment was successful:

```
Before assignment a's date value is 04/01/99
Before assignment b's date value is 14/18/12
Before assignment c's date value is 01/01/14

After assignment a's date value is 01/01/14
After assignment b's date value is 01/01/14
After assignment c's date value is 01/01/14
```

The only restriction on the assignment operator method is that it must be a member method. It can't be overloaded as a friend.

Objects as Arguments

As you have seen, an object's address is passed implicitly to a called member method and stored in its `this` pointer. An object identifies itself to the called method by this means. For completeness, this section shows how an object can be passed to a member method explicitly. Specifically, there are three different ways of providing a method with an object argument: by name, as a reference, or with a pointer. Table 11.3 shows an example of each way; both `newDate` and `oldDate` have been declared as `Date` objects.

Table 11.3 Examples of Object Arguments

	Passing an Object	**Passing a Reference**	**Passing an Address**
Method call	`newDate.swap(oldDate)`	`newDate.swap(oldDate)`	`newDate.swap(&oldDate)`
Method prototype	`void swap(Date)`	`void swap(Date&)`	`void swap(Date *)`
Method header	`void swap(Date temp)`	`void swap(Date& temp)`	`void swap(Date *temp)`
Comments	A copy of `oldDate` is passed; `temp` is an object, and `newDate` is passed to the `this` pointer.	The address of `oldDate` is passed; `temp` is a reference, and `newDate` is passed to the `this` pointer.	The address of `oldDate` is passed; `temp` is a pointer, and `newDate` is passed to the `this` pointer.

When an object is passed to a method, the method receives a copy of it. This means any changes made to the object in the method are lost after the method has finished operating. Passing a reference or an address, however, permits the called method to make changes directly to the addressed object. These changes are retained after the called method has completed its operation.

Notation

In using a reference or pointer, you must pay attention to using the passed address correctly. For pointers, the notation is the same as that used for the `this` pointer. For example, if the call `newDate.swap(&oldDate)` is made, and the passed address is stored in a pointer named `temp` (see the last column in Table 11.3), the correct notations are as follows:

Both `(*temp).month` and `temp->day` access `oldDate`'s month member.
Both `(*temp).day` and `temp->month` access `oldDate`'s day member.
Both `(*temp).year` and `temp->year` access `oldDate`'s year member.

Program 11.5 shows passing an object's address and using a pointer to access and swap two objects' data members. The name of the pointer parameter declared in Program 11.5 is, of course, selected by the programmer. When `swap()` is called, `oldDate`'s starting address is passed to the method. Using this address as a starting point, object members are accessed by including their names with the correct pointer notation.

Program 11.5

```cpp
#include <iostream>
#include <iomanip>
using namespace std;

// class declaration section
class Date
{
  private:
    int month;
    int day;
    int year;
  public:
    Date(int = 7, int = 4, int = 2012);   // constructor
    void showDate();        // method to display a date
    void swap(Date *);      // method to swap two dates
};

// class implementation section
Date::Date(int mm, int dd, int yyyy)
{
  month = mm;
  day = dd;
  year = yyyy;
}
```

☞

```cpp
void Date::showDate()
{
  cout << setfill('0')
       << setw(2) << month << '/'
       << setw(2) << day << '/'
       << setw(2) << year % 100;
  return;
}
```

```cpp
void Date::swap(Date *temp) // method to swap two dates
{
  int tempstore;

  // swap the day member
  tempstore = temp->day;
  temp->day = day;
  day = tempstore;

  // swap the month member
  tempstore = temp->month;
  temp->month = month;
  month = tempstore;

  // swap the year member
  tempstore = temp->year;
  temp->year = year;
  year = tempstore;

  return;
}
```

```cpp
int main()
{
  Date oldDate(4,3,1999);
  Date newDate(12,18,2012);

  cout << "The date stored in oldDate is ";
  oldDate.showDate();
  cout << "\nThe date stored in newDate is ";
  newDate.showDate();

  newDate.swap(&oldDate);  // swap dates by passing an address

  cout << "\n\nAfter the swap:\n" <<endl;
```

```
  cout << "The date stored in oldDate is ";
  oldDate.showDate();
  cout << "\nThe date stored in newDate is ";
  newDate.showDate();
  cout << endl;

  return 0;
}
```

As this output of Program 11.5 shows, date values have been swapped successfully:

```
    The date stored in oldDate is 04/03/99
    The date stored in newDate is 12/18/12

    After the swap:

    The date stored in oldDate is 12/18/12
    The date stored in newDate is 04/03/99
```

This same output is produced by the following swap() method, which uses a reference argument instead of a pointer:

```
void Date::swap(Date& temp) // method to swap two dates
{
  int tempstore;

  // swap the day member
  tempstore = temp.day;
  temp.day = day;
  day = tempstore;

  // swap the month member
  tempstore = temp.month;
  temp.month = month;
  month = tempstore;

  // swap the year member
  tempstore = temp.year;
  temp.year = year;
  year = tempstore;

  return;
}
```

Clearly, the reference version of swap() is easier to read than the pointer version. In fact, one of the main reasons for including references in C++ is for their use as function arguments. However, in some applications, pointers must be used.

One application requiring pointers was discussed previously: returning a `Date` object by using the `this` pointer. Another application is dynamically creating arrays (see Section 8.2) and objects (see Section 12.3). Professional programmers are quite at ease using pointers and often prefer them over references. The reason is that pointers indicate clearly that an address is being used, and references appear the same as nonreference variables. Also, pointers are more flexible than references because addresses can be manipulated in a pointer. For these reasons, as you develop as a programmer, you should strive to understand pointer notation and become comfortable using it.

EXERCISES 11.2

1. **(Practice)** Enter and run Program 11.4.

2. **(Modify) a.** Modify all the member methods in Program 11.4 to use the `this` pointer. For example, the expression `month = mm` should be replaced by `this->month = mm`.
   b. Run the program written for Exercise 2a to verify that your modified program produces the same output as Program 11.4.

3. **(Practice)** Enter and run Program 11.5.

4. **(Modify) a.** Modify Program 11.5 to use the last version of `swap()` shown in this section. Make sure to modify the method prototype for `swap()` and the call statement.
   b. Run the program written for Exercise 4a to verify that the `swap()` method using a reference argument produces the same result as Program 11.5.

5. **(Desk check)** In place of the prototype and method header for `swap()` used in Program 11.5, a student used the following:

```
void swap(Date);    // method prototype
void Date::swap(Date temp)  // method header
```
   a. Determine what Program 11.5 will produce if these two changes are made.
   b. Verify your answer to Exercise 5a by making the changes and running the modified program.

6. **(Desk check) a.** Determine what the following method does when called by the statement `newDate.addSixMonths(&oldDate);`:

```
void Date::addSixMonths(Date *pt)   //method to add 6 months
{
  pt->month = pt->month + 6;        // add 6 months to the date

  //adjust the "pointed to" date's month and year
  if(pt->month > 12) // adjust the month and year
  {
    pt->month = pt->month - 12;
    pt->year++;  //add 1 to the year
  }
```

```
    day = pt->day;
    month=pt->month;
    year = pt->year;

    return;
}
```

    b. Include the `addSixMonths()` method given in Exercise 6a in Program 11.5 and verify your answer to Exercise 6a.

7. **(Modify) a.** Modify the `addSixMonths()` method given in Exercise 6a to use a reference argument rather than a pointer.

    b. Include the `addSixMonths()` method written for Exercise 7a in Program 11.5 and verify that this method works as expected.

8. **(Modify) a.** Modify the `addSixMonths()` method given in Exercise 6a so that it doesn't alter the data values in the passed object. Do this by passing a copy of `oldDate` (rather than a pointer or a reference) to the method.

    b. Include the `addSixMonths()` method written for Exercise 8a in Program 11.5 and verify that this method works as expected.

11.3 Data Type Conversions

You have already seen the conversion from one built-in data type to another (see Sections 3.1 and 3.3). With the introduction of classes, there are now three new conversion possibilities:

- Conversion from a class type to a built-in type
- Conversion from a built-in type to a class type
- Conversion from a class type to a class type

    Clearly, a conversion makes sense only when there's a meaningful relationship between data types. The `Date` class is used in this section to explain these conversions because a useful relationship does exist between a `Date` object consisting of `day`, `month`, and `year` variables and an integer in the form `yyyymmdd`. For example, a date such as 9/15/2012 can be represented by the integer 20120915. Dates represented in this manner, as integers, are useful for sorting and comparing dates. Because integers representing dates can exceed the size of a normal integer, long integers are used, as shown in Figure 11.5.

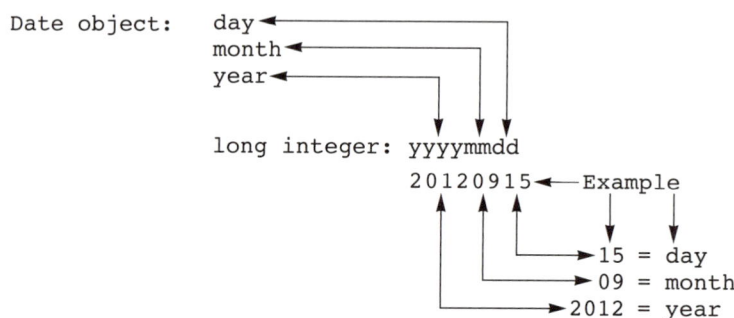

Figure 11.5 Two date representations

Conversions between a class and a built-in data type and between a class and a class can be made with methods almost identical in form to the operator functions shown in Section 11.1. A conversion from a built-in data type to a class is made by using constructor methods. All three new conversion possibilities are shown by using the `Date` class and the long integer relationship shown in Figure 11.5. For completeness, the conversion from a built-in data type to a built-in data type is included.

Built-in to Built-in Conversion

A built-in to built-in conversion is handled by C++'s implicit conversion rules or its explicit cast operator. To review briefly, this type of conversion is implicit or explicit. An implicit conversion can occur by assignment. For example, when a floating-point value is assigned to an integer variable, only the integer portion of the value is stored. Implied conversions are performed automatically by the compiler.

An explicit conversion occurs when a cast is used. In C++, two cast notations exist. The older C notation has the form `(dataType)expression`, and the newer C++ notation has the function-like form `dataType(expression)`. For example, both the expressions `(int)24.32` and `int(24.32)` cause the double-precision value 24.32 to be truncated to the integer value 24.

Class to Built-in Conversion

Conversion from a user-defined data type to a built-in data type is accomplished by using a **conversion operator function**. These conversions are also referred to as "casts." Creating a conversion operator or cast is identical to creating an operator function (discussed in Section 11.1) with one exception: A built-in data type name is used instead of a built-in symbol in the function's header. Therefore, a conversion operator function for casting a `Date` object to a long integer must be named `operator long()`. Program 11.6 defines this function and uses it to convert a `Date` object to a long integer. The function's prototype, definition, and call are shaded in the program.

 **Program 11.6**

```cpp
#include <iostream>
#include <iomanip>
using namespace std;

// class declaration section
class Date
{
  private:
    int month, day, year;
  public:
    Date(int = 7, int = 4, int = 2012);    // constructor
    operator long();        // conversion operator prototype
    void showDate();
};

// class implementation section
Date::Date(int mm, int dd, int yyyy) // constructor
{
  month = mm;
  day = dd;
  year = yyyy;
}

// conversion operator definition for converting a Date to a long int
Date::operator long()    // must return a long, as its name implies
{
  long yyyymmdd;
  yyyymmdd = year * 10000 + month * 100 + day;
  return(yyyymmdd);
}

// member function to display a date
void Date::showDate()
{
   cout << setfill('0')
        << setw(2) << month << '/'
        << setw(2) << day << '/'
        << setw(2) << year % 100;
   return;
}
```

```
int main()
{
  Date a(4,1,2012);   // declare and initialize one object of type Date
  long b;             // declare an object of type long

  b = long(a);         // call the conversion function

  cout << "a's date is ";
  a.showDate();
  cout << "\nThis date, as a long integer, is " << b << endl;

  return 0;
}
```

Program 11.6 produces the following output:

```
a's date is 04/01/12
This date, as a long integer, is 20120401
```

As this output shows, the change in a's date value to a long integer is produced by the assignment expression b = long(a). This assignment could also have been written as b = a. In this case, the conversion to long is implicit. Because the explicit conversion statement in Program 11.6 clearly documents what conversion is taking place, its use is preferable.

Notice that the conversion operator was declared with no explicit argument or return type, which is true of all conversion operators. This is because the data type of the object being converted is an implied argument that must be an object of the declared class, and the return type is provided by the function's name.

Built-in to Class Conversion

A user-defined function for converting a built-in type to a class type is created as a constructor function. For converting a long integer date to a date stored as a month, day, and year, the following is a suitable constructor:

```
// constructor for converting from long to Date
Date::Date(long findate)
{
  year = int(findate/10000.0);
  month = int((findate - year * 10000.0)/100.0);
  day = int(findate - year * 10000.0 - month * 100.0);
}
```

Program 11.7 uses this constructor in two ways. First, it's used as a constructor to initialize a Date object when it's declared. Second, it's used to cast a long integer to a Date object explicitly. All statements pertaining to the conversion function are shaded in the program.

Program 11.7

```cpp
#include <iostream>
#include <iomanip>
using namespace std;

// class declaration section
class Date
{
  private:
    int month, day, year;
  public:
    Date(int = 7, int = 4, int = 2012);  // constructor
    // constructor for converting from long to Date
    Date(long);
    void showDate();
};
// class implementation section
Date::Date(int mm, int dd, int yyyy)  // constructor
{
  month = mm;
  day = dd;
  year = yyyy;
}

// constructor for converting from long to Date
Date::Date(long findate)
{
  year = int(findate/10000.0);
  month = int((findate - year * 10000.0)/100.0);
  day = int(findate - year * 10000.0 - month * 100.0);
}

// member function to display a date
void Date::showDate()
{
  cout << setfill('0')
       << setw(2) << month << '/'
       << setw(2) << day << '/'
       << setw(2) << year % 100;
  return;
}
```

☞

```
int main()
{
  Date a;    // initialized by the default constructor
  Date b(20061225L);  // initialize with a long integer
  Date c(4,1,2007);   // initialize with the specified values

  cout << "Dates a, b, and c are ";
  a.showDate();
  cout << ", ";
  b.showDate();
  cout << ", and ";
  c.showDate();
  cout << ".\n";


  a = Date(20150103L);   // convert a long to a Date

  cout << "Date a is now ";
  a.showDate();
  cout << ".\n";

  return 0;
}
```

Program 11.7 produces the following output:

```
Dates a, b, and c are 07/04/12, 12/25/06, and 04/01/07.
Date a is now 01/03/15.
```

In reviewing Program 11.7, notice that the constructor function for converting changes b's long integer value to conform to the structure of a Date object. The conversion is made by the constructor function when b is declared. (For clarity, each object was declared separately.) Subsequently, a's date value is changed by calling the constructor function explicitly in the assignment statement a = Date(20080103L);.

Formally, the constructor function defined in Program 11.7 is known as a **type conversion constructor**. This name is given to any constructor whose first argument is *not* a member of its class and whose remaining arguments, if any, have default values. If the first argument's data type is a built-in data type, as in Program 11.7, the constructor can be used to convert this built-in data type to a class object. In this case, because the first argument's data type is long, the constructor is used to convert a long to a Date object when the object is declared.

Additionally, because a constructor function can be called explicitly after all objects have been declared, it can be used as a cast independent of its initialization purpose. It's used in this manner in the following statement:

```
a = Date(20150103L);   // convert a long to a Date
```

Class to Class Conversion

Converting from a class data type to a class data type is done in the same manner as a conversion from a class to a built-in data type—by using a conversion operator function. In this case, however, the operator function uses the class name being converted to instead of a built-in data name. For example, if you have two classes named `Date` and `Intdate`, the operator function `operator Intdate()` can be placed in the `Date` class to convert from a `Date` object to an `Intdate` object. Similarly, the operator function `Date()` can be placed in the `Intdate` class to convert from an `Intdate` to a `Date`. Notice that as before, in converting from a class data type to a built-in data type, the operator function's name determines the result of the conversion; the class containing the operator function determines the data type being converted from.

Before seeing an example of a class to class conversion, you should note one additional point. Converting between classes clearly implies having two classes: One is always defined first, and one is defined second. Having a conversion operator function in the second class with the same name as the first class poses no problem because the compiler knows of the first class's existence. However, including a conversion operator function with the second class's name in the first class *does* pose a problem because the second class hasn't been defined yet. To remedy this problem, a declaration for the second class must be made *before* the first class's definition. This declaration, formally called a **forward declaration**, is shown in Program 11.8, which also includes conversion operators between the two defined classes. The relevant statements for this conversion have been shaded.

Program 11.8

```
#include <iostream>
#include <iomanip>
using namespace std;

// forward declaration of class Intdate
class Intdate;

// class declaration section for Date
class Date
{
  private:
    int month, day, year;
  public:
    Date(int = 7, int = 4, int = 2012);  // constructor
    operator Intdate();  // conversion operator from Date to Intdate
    void showDate();
};

// class declaration section for Intdate
class Intdate
```

```
{
  private:
    long yyyymmdd;
  public:
    Intdate(long = 0);    // constructor
    operator Date();  // conversion operator from Intdate to Date
    void showint();
};

// class implementation section for Date
Date::Date(int mm, int dd, int yyyy)  // constructor
{
  month = mm;
  day = dd;
  year = yyyy;
}

// conversion operator function converting from Date to Intdate class
Date::operator Intdate()   // must return an Intdate object
{
  long temp;
  temp = year * 10000 + month * 100 + day;
  return(Intdate(temp));
}

// member function to display a Date
void Date::showDate()
{
  cout << setfill('0')
       << setw(2) << month << '/'
       << setw(2) << day << '/'
       << setw(2) << year % 100;
  return;
}

// class implementation section for Intdate
Intdate::Intdate(long ymd)  // constructor
{
  yyyymmdd = ymd;
}

// conversion operator function converting from Intdate to Date class
Intdate::operator Date()    // must return a Date object
```

```
{
  int mo, da, yr;
  yr = int(yyyymmdd/10000.0);
  mo = int((yyyymmdd - yr * 10000.0)/100.0);
  da = int(yyyymmdd - yr * 10000.0 - mo * 100.0);
  return(Date(mo,da,yr));
}

// member function to display an Intdate
void Intdate::showint()
{
  cout << yyyymmdd;
  return;
}

int main()
{
  Date a(4,1,2011), b;        // declare two Date objects
  Intdate c(20121215L), d;    // declare two Intdate objects
  b = Date(c);         // cast c into a Date object
  d = Intdate(a);      // cast a into an Intdate object

  cout << " a's date is ";
  a.showDate();
  cout << "\n    as an Intdate object this date is ";
  d.showint();

  cout << "\n c's date is ";
  c.showint();
  cout << "\n    as a Date object this date is ";
  b.showDate();
  cout << endl;

  return 0;
}
```

Program 11.8 produces the following output:

```
a's date is 04/01/11
    as an Intdate object this date is 20110401
c's date is 20121215
    as a Date object this date is 12/15/12
```

As Program 11.8 shows, the cast from Date to Intdate is produced by the assignment b = Date(c), and the cast from Intdate to Date is produced by the assignment d = Intdate(a). Alternatively, the assignments b = c and d = a would produce the same results. Notice, too, the forward declaration of the `Intdate` class before the `Date` class's declaration. It's required so that the `Date` class can reference `Intdate` in its conversion operator function.

EXERCISES 11.3

1. **(For review) a.** Define the three new data type conversions introduced in this section and the method of performing each conversion.

   b. Define the terms "type conversion constructor" and "conversion operator function" and describe how they're used in user-defined conversions.

2. **(Program)** Write a C++ program that declares a class named `Time` having integer data members named `hours`, `minutes`, and `seconds`. Include a type conversion constructor that converts a long integer, representing the elapsed seconds from midnight, into an equivalent representation as *hours:minutes:seconds*. For example, the long integer 30336 should convert to the time 8:25:36. Use military time—for example, 2:30 p.m. is represented as 14:30:00. The relationship between time representations is as follows:

   elapsed seconds = hours × 3600 + minutes × 60 + seconds

3. **(Program)** A Julian date is represented as the number of days from a known base date. The following pseudocode shows one algorithm for converting from a Gregorian date, in the form *month/day/year*, to a Julian date with a base date of 00/00/0000. All calculations in this algorithm use integer arithmetic, which means the fractional part of all divisions must be discarded. In this algorithm, M = month, D = day, and Y = year.

   > **If M is less than or equal to 2**
   >   **Set the variable MP = 0 and YP = Y - 1**
   > **Else**
   >   **Set MP = int(0.4 × M + 2.3) and YP = Y**
   > **EndIf**
   > **T = int(YP / 4) - int(YP / 100) + int(YP / 400)**
   > **Julian date = 365 × Y + 31 × (M - 1) + D + T - MP**

   Using this algorithm, modify Program 11.7 to cast from a Gregorian `Date` object to its corresponding Julian representation as a long integer. Test your program by using the Gregorian dates 1/31/2011 and 3/16/2012, which correspond to the Julian dates 734533 and 734943.

4. **(Modify)** Modify the program written for Exercise 2 to include a conversion operator function that converts an object of type `Time` into a long integer representing the number of seconds from midnight.

5. **(Program)** Write a C++ program that has a `Date` class and a `Julian` class. The `Date` class should be the same `Date` class used in Program 11.6, and the `Julian` class should represent a date as a long integer. For this program, include a conversion operator function in the `Date` class that converts a `Date` object to a `Julian` object, using the algorithm shown in Exercise 3.

Test your program by converting 1/31/2011 and 3/16/2012, which correspond to the Julian dates 734533 and 734943.

6. **(Program)** Write a C++ program that has a Time class and an Ltime class. The Time class should have integer data members named hours, minutes, and seconds, and the Ltime class should have a long integer data member named elsecs, which represents the number of elapsed seconds since midnight. For the Time class, include a conversion operator function named Ltime() that converts a Time object to an Ltime object. For the Ltime class, include a conversion operator function named Time() that converts an Ltime object to a Time object.

11.4 Two Useful Alternatives: operator() and operator[]

At times, it's convenient to define an operation having more than two arguments, which is the limit imposed on all binary operator functions. For example, each Date object contains three integer data members: month, day, and year. For this object, you might want to add an integer value to one of the other members instead of just the day member, as was done in Program 11.2. C++ makes this possible by supplying the parentheses operator function, operator(), which has no limits on the number of arguments that can be passed to it.

Additionally, the case used in Program 11.2—in which only a single non-object argument is required—occurs so frequently that C++ provides an alternative means of achieving it: For this case, C++ supplies the subscript operator function, operator[], which permits a maximum of one argument. The only restriction C++ imposes on the operator() and operator[] functions is that they must be defined as member (not friend) functions.

For simplicity, the operator[] function is discussed first. It's declared and defined in the same manner as any other operator function, but it's called differently from the normal function and operator call. For example, if you want to use the operator[] function to accept an integer argument and return a Date object, the following prototype is valid:

```
Date operator[](int);  // declare the subscript operator
```

Except for the operator function's name, it's similar in construction to any other operator function prototype. Assuming you want this function to add its integer argument to a Date object, a suitable function implementation is as follows:

```
Date Date::operator[](int days)
{
  Date temp;     // a temporary Date to store the result

  temp.day = day + days;    // add the days
  temp.month = month;
  temp.year = year;
```

```
      while (temp.day > 30)    // now adjust the months
      {
        temp.month++;
        temp.day -= 30;
      }
      while (temp.month > 12)  // adjust the years
      {
        temp.year++;
        temp.month -= 12;
      }
      return temp;    // the values in temp are returned
    }
```

Again, except for the function header, it's similar in construction to the operator function definitions covered in Section 11.1. After the function is created, however, it can be called only by passing the required argument through the subscript brackets. For example, if oldDate is a Date object, the function call oldDate[284] calls the subscript operator function and causes the function to operate on the a object with the integer value 284. This function's prototype, definition, and call are shaded in Program 11.9.

 ## Program 11.9

```cpp
#include <iostream>
#include <iomanip>
using namespace std;

// class declaration section
class Date
{
  private:
    int month;
    int day;
    int year;
  public:
    Date(int = 7, int = 4, int = 2012);    // constructor
    Date operator[](int);    // function prototype
    void showDate();            // member function to display a Date
};

// class implementation section
Date::Date(int mm, int dd, int yyyy)
{
  month = mm;
  day = dd;
  year = yyyy;
}
```

```
Date Date::operator[](int days)
{
  Date temp;    // a temporary Date to store the result

  temp.day = day + days;    // add the days
  temp.month = month;
  temp.year = year;
  while (temp.day > 30)     // now adjust the months
  {
    temp.month++;
    temp.day -= 30;
  }
  while (temp.month > 12)    // adjust the years
  {
    temp.year++;
    temp.month -= 12;
  }
  return temp;    // the values in temp are returned
}
```

```
void Date::showDate()
{
  cout << setfill('0')
       << setw(2) << month << '/'
       << setw(2) << day << '/'
       << setw(2) << year % 100;
  return;
}

int main()
{
  Date oldDate(7,4,2011), newDate; // declare two objects

  cout << "The initial Date is ";
  oldDate.showDate();

  newDate = oldDate[284]; // add in 284 days = 9 months and 14 days

  cout << "\nThe new Date is ";
  newDate.showDate();
  cout << endl;

  return 0;
}
```

Program 11.9 is almost identical to Program 11.2, except that a subscript operator function is used in place of an overloaded addition operator function. Both programs produce the same output. In general, the overloaded operator used in Program 11.2 is preferable because the operator's name documents what operation is being performed. Although Program 11.9 shows how a subscript operator is created, in practice these operators are used for more complicated operations that other operator functions don't handle suitably. Therefore, subscript operators must be commented carefully to indicate their intended purpose.

Although the expression `oldDate[284]` used in Program 11.9 appears to indicate that `oldDate` is an array, it's not. It's simply the notation required to call an overloaded subscript function.

The parentheses operator function, `operator()`, is almost identical in construction and calling to the subscript function, `operator[]`, with the substitution of parentheses, `()`, for brackets, `[]`. The difference between these two operator functions is in the number of allowable arguments. The subscript operator function permits passing zero or one argument, but the parentheses operator function has no limit on the number of its arguments. For example, a suitable parentheses operator function prototype to add an integer number of months, days, or years to a `Date` object is as follows:

```
Date operator()(int, int, int);
```

After this function is implemented (which you do in Exercises 11.4), a call such as `a(2,3,4)` can be used to add 2 months, 4 days, and 3 years to the `Date` object named a.

These two extra functions offer a lot of programming flexibility. When only one argument is needed, they permit writing two different functions, both with the same argument type. For example, you could use `operator[]` to add an integer number of days to a `Date` object and `operator()` to add an integer number of months. Because both functions have the same argument type, one function name can't be overloaded for both cases. These two functions also give you the flexibility to restrict all other operator functions to class member arguments and then use these two functions for operations using nonclass arguments.

EXERCISES 11.4

1. **(Modify) a.** Replace the `operator[]` function in Program 11.9 with the `operator()` function.
   b. Include the `operator()` function written for Exercise 1a in a working C++ program and verify its operation.

2. **(Modify) a.** Replace the `operator[]` function in Program 11.9 with a member `operator()` function that accepts an integer month, day, and year count. Have the function add the input days, months, and years to the object's date and return the resulting date. For example, if the input is 3, 2, 1 and the object's date is 7/16/2011, the function should return the date 10/18/2012. Make sure your function correctly handles an input such as 37 days and 15 months and adjusts the calculated day to be within the range 1 to 30 and the month to be within the range 1 to 12. Therefore, if the input is 37, 15, 1 and the object's date is 7/16/2011, the function should return the date 9/1/2015.
   b. Include the `operator()` function written for Exercise 2a in a working C++ program and verify its operation.

3. **(Program) a.** Construct a class named `Student` consisting of these private data members: an integer ID number, an integer count, and an array of four double-precision grades. The constructor for this class should set all data member values to 0. The class should also include a member function that displays all valid member grades, as determined by the grade count, and calculates and displays the average of the grades. Include the class in a working C++ program that declares three class objects named `a`, `b`, and `c`.

   b. Modify the class constructed for Exercise 3a to include a member `operator[]` function that has a double-precision grade count argument. The function should check the grade count data member and, if fewer than four grades have been entered, store its argument in the grade array, using the count as an index value. If four grades have already been entered, the function should return an error message indicating that the new grade can't be accepted. Additionally, a new grade should force an increment to the count data member.

   c. Modify the class constructed for Exercise 3a to include a member `operator()` function that has a grade index and grade value as arguments. The function should force a change to the grade corresponding to the index value and update the count, if necessary. For example, an argument list of 4, 98.5 should change the fourth test grade value to 98.5.

4. **(Modify) a.** Modify Program 10.9 to include a member `operator[]` function that multiplies an object's complex number (both the real and the imaginary parts) by a real number and returns a complex number. For example, if the real number is 2 and the complex number is 3 + 4i, the result is 6 + 8i.

   b. Verify the operation of the `operator[]` function written for Exercise 4a by including it in a working C++ program.

11.5 Common Programming Errors

1. Attempting to redefine an operator's meaning as it applies to C++'s built-in data types.
2. Redefining an overloaded operator to perform a function not indicated by its conventional meaning. Although this method works, it's an example of bad programming practices.
3. Using a user-defined assignment operator in a multiple assignment expression when the operator hasn't been defined to return an object.
4. Attempting to make a conversion operator function a friend rather than a member function.
5. Attempting to specify a return type for a conversion operator function.
6. Forgetting that `this` is a pointer that must be dereferenced by using `*this` or `this->`.

11.6 Chapter Summary

1. User-defined operators can be constructed for classes by using operator functions. An operator function has the form *operator<symbol>*, where *<symbol>* is one of the following:

```
()   []   ->   new   delete   ++   --   !   ~   *   /   %   +   -
<<   >>   <   <=   >   >=   ++  !=   &&  ||   &   ^   |   =   +=
-=   *=   /=   %=   &=   ^=   |=   <<=  >>=   ,
```

For example, the function prototype `Date operator+(int);` declares that the addition operator is defined to accept an integer and return a `Date` object.

2. User-defined operators can be called in one of two ways—as a conventional function with arguments or as an operator function. For example, for an operator function having the function header

```
Date Date::operator+(int)
```

if `dte` is an object of type `Date`, these two calls produce the same effect:

```
dte.operator+(284)
dte + 284
```

3. Operator functions can also be written as friend functions. The friend version of an operator function always contains an additional class reference that isn't required by the member function.

4. With the introduction of classes, three new categories of data type conversions exist (in addition to the built-in to built-in data type conversion):

   - Built-in types to class types
   - Class types to built-in types
   - Class types to class types

   Built-in to class type conversions are done by using type constructor functions. Conversions from class types to built-in types or from class types to class types are done by using conversion operator functions.

5. A type conversion constructor is a constructor whose first argument is *not* a member of its class and whose remaining arguments, if any, have default values.

6. A conversion operator function is a member operator function having the name of a class. It has no explicit arguments or return type; rather, the return type is the name of the function.

7. An object can be used as a method's argument, in which case the called method receives a copy of the object.

8. The address of an object can also be passed as an argument, either as a reference or as a pointer, which gives the called method direct access to the object's members.

9. For each class object, a separate set of memory locations is reserved for all data members, except those declared as static.

10. For each class, only one copy of the member methods is retained in memory, and each object uses the same function. The address of the object's data members is provided to the member method by passing a hidden argument, corresponding to the selected object's memory address, to the member method. The address is passed in a special pointer argument named `this`. The `this` pointer can be used explicitly by a member method to access a data member.

11. The subscript operator function, `operator[ ]`, permits a maximum of one nonclass argument. This function can be defined only as a member function.

12. The parentheses operator function, `operator( )`, has no limits on the number of arguments. This function can be defined only as a member function.

11.7 Chapter Supplement: Insides and Outsides

Just as the concept of an algorithm is central to procedures, the concept of encapsulation is central to objects. This section explains the encapsulation concept by using an inside-outside analogy, which should help you understand what object-oriented programming is all about.

In programming terms, an object's attributes are described by data, such as the length and width of a rectangle, and operations that can be applied to the attributes are described by methods. As a practical example, say you're writing a program that can deal a hand of cards. From an object-oriented approach, one object you must model is a deck of cards. For this program, the attributes of interest for the card deck is that it contains 52 cards divided into 4 suits (hearts, diamonds, spades, and clubs), with each suit consisting of 13 values (ace to ten, jack, queen, and king).

The behavior of the deck of cards consists of operations that can be applied to the deck. At a minimum, you want the ability to shuffle the deck and to deal single cards. Take a look at how this simple example illustrates encapsulation by using an inside-outside analogy. A useful visualization is comparing an object with a boiled egg (see Figure 11.6). The egg consists of three parts: a very inside yolk, a less inside white surrounding the yolk, and an outside shell, which is the only part of the egg visible to the outside world.

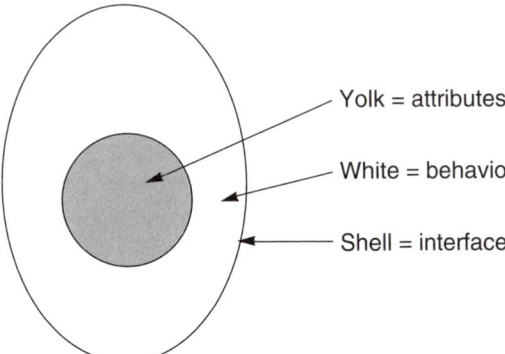

Yolk = attributes

White = behavior

Shell = interface

Figure 11.6 The boiled egg object model

In the boiled egg model, an object's attributes correspond to the yolk (the egg's innermost protected area), and its behavior corresponds to the white. In other words, surrounding the data attributes, much as an egg's white surrounds its yolk, are the operations you choose to incorporate in an object. Finally, the shell represents the interface to the outside world—the means by which a user calls the object's internal methods.

The boiled egg model, with its egg shell interface separating the egg's inside from the outside, is useful because it clearly depicts the separation between what should be contained in an object and what should be seen from the outside. This separation is an essential element in object-oriented programming. From an inside-outside perspective, an object's data attributes, the selected algorithms for the object's operations, and how these algorithms are actually implemented are always "inside" issues hidden from the user's view. How a user or another object can actually activate an inside procedure is an "outside" issue.

Now apply this concept to the deck of cards. First, think about attributes you might use to represent cards in the deck. You could use any of the following attributes (and others are possible):

- Two integer variables, one representing a suit (a number from 1 to 4) and one representing a value (a number from 1 to 13)
- One character variable representing a card's suit, and one integer variable representing a card's value
- One integer variable having a value from 0 to 51; the expression `int(number / 13 + 1)` provides a number from 1 to 4 to represent the suit, and the expression `(number % 13 + 1)` represents a card value from 1 to 13

Which attributes you select, however, isn't relevant to the outside. The way you choose to represent a card is an inside issue for the object designer to decide. From the outside, the only concern is having access to a deck consisting of 52 cards that have the necessary suits and values.

The same is true for operations you decide to provide as part of the card deck object. Start with the shuffling operation. A number of algorithms can be used to produce a shuffled deck. For example, you could use C++'s random number function, `rand()`, or create your own random number generator. Again, the selection of an algorithm is an inside issue for the class designer to determine. The algorithm that's selected and how it's applied to the attributes you have chosen for cards aren't relevant from the object's outside. For this example's purposes, assume you decide to use C++'s `rand()` function to produce a randomly shuffled deck.

If you use the first attribute set (two integer variables), each card in a shuffled deck is produced by using `rand()` at least twice: once to create a random number from 1 to 4 for the suit and again to create a random number from 1 to 13 for the card's value. This sequence must be carried out to construct 52 different attribute sets, with no duplicates allowed.

If you use the second attribute set (one character variable and one integer variable), a shuffled deck can be produced in the same fashion, with one modification: The first random number (from 1 to 4) must be changed into a character to represent the suit.

Finally, if you use the third attribute set, you need to use `rand()` once for each card to produce 52 random numbers from 0 to 51, with no duplicates allowed.

The important point is that selecting an algorithm and deciding how it's applied to an object's attributes are implementation issues, and implementation issues are *always* inside issues. A user of the card deck, who is outside, doesn't need to know how the shuffling is done. All the user must know is how to produce a shuffled deck. In practice, this means the user is supplied with enough information to call the shuffle function correctly. This information corresponds to the interface, or the egg's outer shell.

Abstraction and Encapsulation

The distinction between insides and outsides is related to the concepts of abstraction and encapsulation. **Abstraction** means concentrating on what an object is and does before making any decisions about how to implement the object. Therefore, you define a deck and the operations you want to provide abstractly. (Remember that if your abstraction is to be useful, it should capture the attributes and operations of a real-world deck.) After deciding on the attributes and operations, you can actually implement—that is, code—them.

Encapsulation generally means separating the implementation details of the abstract attributes and behavior and hiding them from the object's outside users. An object's external side should give users only the interface needed to activate internal procedures. Imposing a strict inside-outside discipline when creating classes is really another way of saying that the class encapsulates all implementation details. In the card deck example, encapsulation means users never need to know how you have modeled the deck internally or how an operation, such as shuffling, is performed; they just need to know how to activate an operation.

Code Extensibility

An advantage of the inside-outside object approach is that it encourages extending existing code without needing to completely rewrite it. This advantage is possible because all interactions between objects are centered on the outside interface and all implementation details are hidden in the object's inside. For example, in Figure 11.7, the object's two operations can be activated by calling the circle or square on the outside, which in practice is simply a method call. The circle and square emphasize that two methods are provided for outside use. In the card deck example, activating one method might produce a shuffled deck, and activating another method might result in a card suit and value being returned from the object.

Now say you want to alter the implementation of an existing operation or add more functionality to the class. *As long as the existing outside interface is maintained*, the internal implementation of any operations can be changed without the user being aware that a change took place. This is a result of encapsulating the attribute data and operations in the class from which an object is created.

The interface

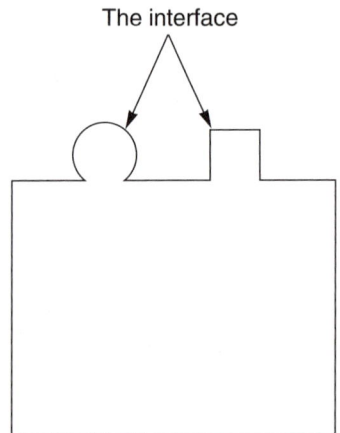

Figure 11.7   Using an object's interface

Furthermore, as long as the interface to existing operations isn't changed, new operations can be added as needed. Essentially, from the outside world's perspective, all that's being added is another method call that accesses the inside attributes and modifies them in a new way.

Chapter

12

Extending Your Classes

The ability to create new classes from existing ones is the underlying motivation and power behind class- and object-oriented programming techniques. Doing so makes it possible to reuse existing code in new ways without the need for retesting and validation. With this ability, designers of a class can make it available to other programmers without relinquishing control over existing class features yet allow other programmers to make additions and extensions.

For a programming language to be classified as an object-oriented language, it must include the features of classes, inheritance, and polymorphism. In this chapter, you learn about the central object-oriented capabilities of inheritance and polymorphism. Additionally, you learn how to create and delete objects dynamically—that is, while a program is running.

12.1 Class Inheritance

Constructing one class from another is accomplished by using **inheritance**, which is the capability of deriving one class from another class. An equally important and related feature called **polymorphism** allows redefining how member functions of the same name operate, based on an object's class. This section describes C++'s inheritance features, and polymorphism is discussed in Section 12.2.

The class used as the basis for a derived class is referred to as the **base class**, **parent class**, or **superclass**. The **derived class**, also referred to as the **child class** or **subclass**, is a new class incorporating all data members and member functions of its base class. However, it can, and usually does, add its own new data members and member functions and can override any base class function.

As an example of inheritance, consider three geometric shapes: a circle, a cylinder, and a sphere. All these shapes share a common characteristic—a radius. Therefore, you can make the circle a base type for the other two shapes, as shown in Figure 12.1. By convention, arrows always point from the derived class to the base class. In this example, the circle is the base class, and the cylinder and sphere are the derived classes.

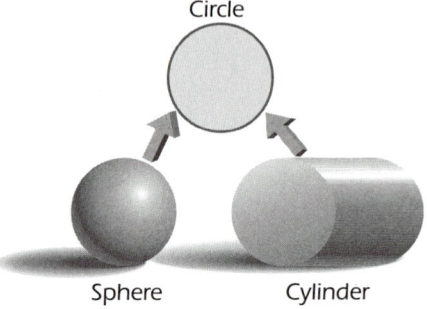

Figure 12.1   Relating object types

The relationships shown in Figure 12.1 are examples of **simple inheritance**, in which each derived type has only one base type. The complement to simple inheritance is **multiple inheritance**, in which a derived type has two or more base types. Figure 12.2 shows an example of multiple inheritance, but only simple inheritance is discussed in this section.

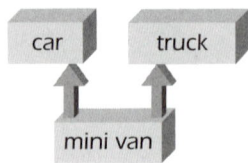

Figure 12.2   An example of multiple inheritance

Point of Information

Object-Based Versus Object-Oriented Languages

In an **object-based** language, data and operations can be incorporated in such a way that data values can be isolated and accessed through the specified class functions. The capability to bind data members with operations in a single unit is referred to as "encapsulation." In C++, encapsulation is provided by the class capability.

For a language to be classified as **object-oriented**, it must also include inheritance and polymorphism. As discussed, inheritance is the capability to derive one class from another. A derived class incorporates all data members and member functions of the parent class and can add its own data and function members. The class used as the basis for the derived class is the base or parent class, and the derived class is also called the subclass or child class. Polymorphism allows using the same function name to use one operation in a parent class's objects and a different operation in a derived class's objects.

The class derivations in Figures 12.1 and 12.2 are formally called **class hierarchies** because they illustrate the hierarchy, or order, in which one class is derived from another. With this information as background, now you can see how to derive one class from another.

A derived class has the same form as any other class: It consists of both declaration and implementations. The only difference is in the first line of the declaration section. For a derived class, this line is extended to include an access specifier and a base class name in this form:

class derivedClassName : classAccess baseClassName

For example, if `Circle` is the name of an existing class, a new class named `Cylinder` can be derived as follows:

```
class Cylinder : public Circle
{
    // place any additional data members and
    // member functions in here
};  // end of Cylinder class declaration
```

Except for the class access specifier after the colon and the base class's name, there's nothing new or complicated about constructing the `Cylinder` class. Before providing a description of the `Circle` class and adding data and function members to the derived `Cylinder` class, you need to reexamine access specifiers and how they relate to derived classes.

Access Specifications

Until now, you have used only private and public access specifiers in a class. Giving all data members private status ensures that they can be accessed only by class member functions or friends. This restricted access prevents access by any nonclass functions (except friends) but also precludes access by any derived class functions. This restriction is sensible because without it, anyone could bypass the private restriction by simply deriving a class.

To retain restricted access across derived classes, C++ provides a third access specification—protected. **Protected access** behaves the same as private access, in that it permits access only to member or friend functions, but it allows any derived class to inherit this restriction. The derived class then defines the type of inheritance it's willing to take on, subject to the base class's access restrictions. This definition is done by the class access specifier, which is listed after the colon at the start of the class declaration section. Table 12.1 lists the derived class member access resulting from the base class's member specifications and the derived class access specifier.

The shaded rows in Table 12.1 show that if the base class member has a protected access and the derived class access specifier is public, the derived class member is protected to its class. Similarly, if the base class has a public access and the derived class access specifier is public, the derived class member is public. These specifications for base class data members and member functions are the most commonly used, so they're the ones used in this section. So for all classes intended for use as a base class, a protected data member access is used instead of a private designation.

Table 12.1   Inherited Access Restrictions

Base Class Member	Derived Class Access Specifier	Derived Class Member
private	: private	inaccessible
protected	: private	private
public	: private	private
private	: public	inaccessible
protected	: public	protected
public	: public	public
private	: protected	inaccessible
protected	: protected	protected
public	: protected	protected

An Example   To understand how to derive one class from another, examine the process of deriving the `Cylinder` class from the base class `Circle`. The definition of the `Circle` class is as follows:

```
// class declaration section
class Circle
{
  protected:
    double radius;
  public:
    Circle(double = 1.0);  // constructor
    double calcval();
};
```

```
// class implementation section
Circle::Circle(double r)   // constructor
{
  radius = r;
}


// calculate the area of a circle
double Circle::calcval()
{
  return(PI * radius * radius);
}
```

Except for substituting the access specifier `protected` in place of the usual `private` specifier for the data member, this code is a standard class definition. The only variable not defined is `PI`, which is used in the `calcval()` function. It's defined as follows:

```
const double PI = 2.0 * asin(1.0);
```

This definition is simply a "trick" that forces the computer to return the value of `PI` accurate to as many decimal places as your computer allows. This value is obtained by taking the arcsine of 1.0, which is $\pi/2$, and multiplying the result by 2.

Having defined the base class, you can now extend it to a derived class, which has this definition:

```
// class declaration section where Cylinder is derived from Circle
class Cylinder : public Circle
{
  protected:
    double length;   // add one data member and
  public:            // two member functions
  Cylinder(double r = 1.0, double l = 1.0) : Circle(r), length(l) {}
  double calcval();
};


// class implementation section
double Cylinder::calcval()   // calculates a volume
{
  return (length * Circle::calcval()); // note the base function call
}
```

This definition encompasses several important concepts related to derived classes. First, as a derived class, `Cylinder` contains all the data members and member functions of its base class, `Circle`, plus any of its own members it might add. In this case, the `Cylinder` class consists of a `radius` data member, inherited from the `Circle` class, plus a `length` data member. Therefore, each `Cylinder` object contains two data members, as shown in Figure 12.3.

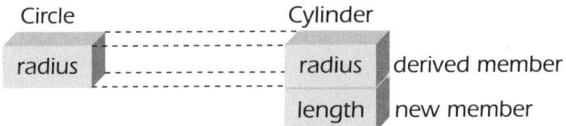

Figure 12.3   Relationship between `Circle` and `Cylinder` data members

In addition, the `Cylinder` class inherits `Circle`'s member functions. This inheritance is shown in the `Cylinder` constructor, which uses a base/member initialization list (see Section 11.1) that calls the `Circle` constructor. It's also shown in `Cylinder`'s `calcval()` function, which makes a call to `Circle::calcval()`.

In both classes, the same function name, `calcval()`, has been used to illustrate overriding a base function with a derived function. When a `Cylinder` object calls `calcval()`, it's a request to use the `Cylinder` version of the function; a `Circle` object call to `calcval()` is a request to use the `Circle` version. In this case, the `Cylinder` class can access only the class version of `calcval()` by using the scope resolution operator, as in the call `Circle::calcval()`. Program 12.1 uses these two classes in the context of a complete program.

Program 12.1

```cpp
#include <iostream>
#include <cmath>
using namespace std;

const double PI = 2.0 * asin(1.0);

// class declaration section
class Circle
{
  protected:
    double radius;
  public:
    Circle(double = 1.0);  // constructor
    double calcval();
};

// class implementation section for Circle
Circle::Circle(double r)  // constructor
{
  radius = r;
}
```

```
// calculate the area of a Circle
double Circle::calcval()
{
  return(PI * radius * radius);
}

// class declaration section where Cylinder is derived from Circle
class Cylinder : public Circle
{
  protected:
    double length;   // add one data member and
  public:            // two member functions
    Cylinder(double r = 1.0, double l = 1.0) : Circle(r), length(l) {}
    double calcval();
};

// class implementation section for Cylinder
double Cylinder::calcval()   // calculates a volume
{
  return (length * Circle::calcval()); // note the base function call
}
```

```
int main()
{
  Circle Circle_1, Circle_2(2);  // create two Circle objects
  Cylinder Cylinder_1(3,4);      // create one Cylinder object

  cout << "The area of Circle_1 is " << Circle_1.calcval() << endl;
  cout << "The area of Circle_2 is " << Circle_2.calcval() << endl;
  cout << "The volume of Cylinder_1 is " << Cylinder_1.calcval() << endl;

  Circle_1 = Cylinder_1;  // assign a Cylinder to a Circle

  cout << "\nThe area of Circle_1 is now " << Circle_1.calcval() << endl;
  return 0;
}
```

Program 12.1 produces the following output:

```
The area of Circle_1 is 3.14159
The area of Circle_2 is 12.5664
The volume of Cylinder_1 is 113.097

The area of Circle_1 is now 28.2743
```

The first three output lines are straightforward and are produced by the first three cout statements in the program. As the output shows, a call to calcval() with a Circle object activates the Circle version of this function, and a call to calcval() with a Cylinder object activates the Cylinder version.

The assignment statement Circle_1 = Cylinder_1; introduces another important relationship between a base and derived class: *A derived class object can be assigned to a base class object.* This relationship shouldn't be surprising because base and derived classes share a common set of data member types. In this type of assignment, only this set of data members, which consists of all the base class data members, is assigned. Therefore, as shown in Figure 12.4, the Cylinder to Circle assignment results in the following memberwise assignment:

```
Circle_1.radius = Cylinder_1.radius;
```

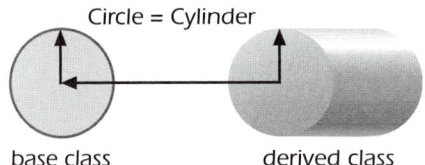

Figure 12.4   An assignment from derived to base class

The length data member of the Cylinder object isn't used in the assignment because it has no equivalent variable in the Circle class. The reverse cast, from base to derived class, isn't as simple and requires a constructor to initialize the derived class members that aren't in the base class.

Before leaving Program 12.1, one other point should be made. Although the Circle constructor was called explicitly by using a base/member initialization list for the Cylinder constructor, an implicit call could have been made. In the absence of an explicit derived class constructor, the compiler automatically calls the default base class constructor first, before the derived class constructor is called. This order of calling works because the derived class contains all the base class's data members. In a similar fashion, destructor methods are called in the reverse order—first derived class and then base class.

EXERCISES 12.1

1. **(Review)** Define the following terms:
   - **a.** inheritance
   - **b.** base class
   - **c.** derived class
   - **d.** simple inheritance
   - **e.** multiple inheritance
   - **f.** class hierarchy

2. **(Review)** Describe the difference between private and protected class members.

3. **(Review)** What three features must a programming language include to be classified as an object-oriented language?

4. **(Modify) a.** Modify Program 12.1 to include a derived class named Sphere from the base Circle class. The only additional class members of Sphere should be a constructor and a calcval() function that returns the sphere's volume. (*Note: Volume = 4 / 3 πr^3.*)

   b. Include the class constructed for Exercise 4a in a working C++ program. Have your program call all the member functions in the Sphere class.

5. **(Program) a.** Create a base class named Point consisting of x and y data members representing point coordinates. From this class, derive a class named Circle with another data member named radius. For this derived class, the x and y data members represent a circle's center coordinates. The member functions of the Point class should consist of a constructor, an area() function that returns 0, and a distance() function that returns the distance between two points, (x_1, y_1) and (x_2, y_2), where

   $$distance = \sqrt{\left(x_2 - x_1\right)^2 + \left(y_2 - y_1\right)^2}$$

   Additionally, the derived class should have a constructor and an override function named area() that returns a circle's area.

   b. Include the classes constructed for Exercise 5a in a working C++ program. Have your program call all the member functions in each class. In addition, call the base class's distance() function with two Circle objects and explain the result this function returns.

6. **(Modify) a.** Using the classes constructed for Exercise 5a, derive a class named Cylinder from the Circle class. The Cylinder class should have a constructor and a member function named area() that determines a cylinder's surface area. For this function, use the algorithm *surface area = 2 π r(l + r)*, where r is the radius of the cylinder and l is the length.

   b. Include the classes constructed for Exercise 6a in a working C++ program. Have your program call all the member functions in the Cylinder class.

   c. What do you think the result might be if the Point (base) class's distance() function is called with two Cylinder objects?

7. **(Program) a.** Create a base class named Rectangle containing length and width data members. From this class, derive a class named Box with another data member named depth. The member functions of the base Rectangle class should consist of a constructor and an area() function. The derived Box class should have a constructor, a volume() function, and an override function named area() that returns the surface area of the box.

   b. Include the classes constructed for Exercise 7a in a working C++ program. Have your program call all the member functions in each class, and verify the results manually.

12.2 Polymorphism

As defined previously, polymorphism allows using the same function name to invoke one response in a base class's objects and another response in a derived class's objects. Overriding a base member function by using an overloaded derived member function, as shown with the calcval() function in Program 12.1, is an example of polymorphism. In some situations, however, this method of overriding doesn't work the way you might want. To understand why, take a look at Program 12.2.

Program 12.2

```cpp
#include <iostream>
#include <cmath>
using namespace std;

// class declaration section for the base class
class One
{
  protected:
    double a;
  public:
    One(double = 2.0);    // constructor
    double f1(double);    // a member function
    double f2(double);    // another member function
};

// class implementation section for One
One::One(double val)    // constructor
{
  a = val;
}

double One::f1(double num)   // a member function
{
  return(num/2);
}

double One::f2(double num)   // another member function
{
  return( pow(f1(num),2) );  // square the result of f1()
}

// class declaration section for the derived class
class Two : public One
{
  public:
    double f1(double);      // this overrides class One's f1()
};

// class implementation section for Two
double Two::f1(double num)
{
  return(num/3);
}
```

```
int main()
{
  One object_1;   // object_1 is an object of the base class
  Two object_2;   // object_2 is an object of the derived class

  // call f2() using a base class object call
  cout << "The computed value using a base class object call is "
       << object_1.f2(12) << endl;

  // call f2() using a derived class object call
  cout << "The computed value using a derived class object call is "
       << object_2.f2(12) << endl;

  return 0;
}
```

The following output is produced by Program 12.2:

```
The computed value using a base class object call is 36
The computed value using a derived class object call is 36
```

As this output shows, the same result is obtained, no matter which object type calls the f2() function, because the derived class doesn't have an override of the base class's f2() function. Therefore, both calls to f2() result in the base class's f2() function being called.

After the base class's f2() function is called, it always calls the base class's version of f1() rather than the derived class's override version. This behavior is caused by a process referred to as **function binding**. In normal function calls, **static binding** is used, meaning the determination of which function is called is made at compile time. Therefore, when the compiler first encounters the f1() function in the base class, it makes the determination that whenever f2() is called, from either a base or derived class object, it subsequently calls the base class's f1() function.

In place of static binding, say you want to use a binding method capable of determining which function should be called at runtime, based on the object type making the call. This type of binding, referred to as **dynamic binding**, is achieved in C++ with virtual functions. A **virtual function** tells the compiler to create a pointer to a function, but not fill in the pointer's value until the function is actually called. Then at runtime, *based on the object making the call*, the appropriate function address is used.

Creating a virtual function is easy—simply place the keyword virtual before the function's return type in the class declaration section. For example, examine Program 12.3, which is identical to Program 12.2, except for the virtual declaration of the f1() function.

Program 12.3

```cpp
#include <iostream>
#include <cmath>
using namespace std;

// class declaration section for the base class
class One
{
  protected:
    double a;
    public:
    One(double = 2.0);          // constructor
    virtual double f1(double);  // a member function
    double f2(double);          // another member function
};

// class implementation section for One
One::One(double val)    // constructor
{
  a = val;
}

double One::f1(double num)    // a member function
{
  return(num/2);
}

double One::f2(double num)    // another member function
{
  return( pow(f1(num),2) );  // square the result of f1()
}

// class declaration section for the derived class
class Two : public One
{
  public:
    virtual double f1(double);    // overrides class One's f1()
};

// class implementation section for Two
double Two::f1(double num)
{
  return(num/3);
}
```

☞

```
int main()
{
  One object_1;   // object_1 is an object of the base class
  Two object_2;   // object_2 is an object of the derived class

  // call f2() using a base class object call
  cout << "The computed value using a base class object call is "
       << object_1.f2(12) << endl;

  // call f2() using a derived class object call
  cout << "The computed value using a derived class object call is "
       << object_2.f2(12) << endl;

  return 0;
}
```

Program 12.3 produces the following output:

```
The computed value using a base class object call is 36
The computed value using a derived class object call is 16
```

As this output shows, the f2() function now calls different versions of the overloaded f1() function based on the object type making the call. Basing the selection on the object making the call is the classic definition of polymorphic behavior and is caused by the dynamic binding imposed on f1() because it's a virtual function.

After a function is declared as virtual, it remains virtual for the next derived class, with or without a virtual declaration in the derived class. Therefore, the second virtual declaration in the derived class isn't strictly necessary but should be included for clarity and to make sure any subsequently derived classes inherit the function correctly.

In the inheritance diagram in Figure 12.5, class C is derived from class B and class B is derived from class A.[1] In this situation, if the f1() function is virtual in class A but not declared in class B, it isn't virtual in class C. The only other requirement is that after a function has been declared as virtual, the return type and parameter list of all subsequent derived class override versions *must* be the same.

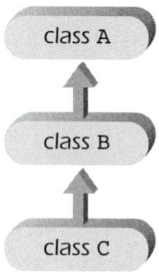

Figure 12.5   An inheritance diagram

---

[1]By convention, as noted in Section 12.1, arrows always point from the derived class to the base class.

EXERCISES 12.2

1. **(Practice)** Enter and run Programs 12.2 and 12.3 so that you understand the relationship between function calls in each program.

2. **(Review)** Describe the difference between static binding and dynamic binding.

3. **(Review)** Describe the difference between a virtual function and a nonvirtual function.

4. **(Review)** Explain what polymorphism is and give an example of polymorphic behavior.

5. **(Review)** Describe the two methods C++ provides for implementing polymorphism.

6. **(Review)** Explain whether the multiplication operator provided for integer and double-precision built-in types is an example of overloading or polymorphism.

12.3 Dynamic Object Creation and Deletion

As each object is defined in a program, the compiler designates enough storage for it; this storage is subsequently assigned from a pool of computer memory locations before the program runs. After memory locations have been assigned, they remain fixed for the object's lifetime or until the program finishes running. For example, if a `main()` function declares three `Date` objects, the storage for these objects remains fixed from the point of their definition until `main()` completes execution.

An alternative to this fixed allocation of memory storage locations is **dynamic allocation** of memory, in which the amount of storage to be allocated is assigned, as requested, at runtime instead of being fixed at compile time. Dynamic allocation of memory is useful when dealing with lists and objects because it allows expanding the list as new items are added and contracting the list as items are deleted. For object-oriented programs, it allows creating and destroying new objects as required.

As an example of dynamic object creation, say you're creating a program designed to track the flow of customers at a large outlet chain's self-checkout registers. You don't know in advance the number of transactions taking place at each register. However, by using dynamic allocation, the program can create an object as each checkout transaction occurs for tracking customer use of the checkout process. This object might consist of the number of items checked out and the arrival time of each customer at the register. Although the class's do-nothing methods are completed later, the following class adequately defines the information this object needs. In reviewing this class, notice the shaded constructor and destructor methods:

```
// class declaration section
class Checkout
{
  private:
    int numItems;
    double arrivalTime;
```

```
  public:
    Checkout();    // constructor
    // the following is an inline destructor
    ~Checkout()
     {cout << "!!!! This Customer object has been deleted !!!!\n";}
    void showObject();
    void getItems(){return;}   // inline do-nothing methods
    void getTime() {return;}   // will be used in Program 12.5
};

// class implementation section
Checkout::Checkout() // constructor
{
  cout << "\n**** A new Customer object has been created ****\n";
  numItems = 5;
  arrivalTime = 2.5;
}
```

```
void Checkout::showObject()
{
   cout << "     For this object:\n";
   cout << "     numItems = " << numItems
        << "     arrivalTime = " << arrivalTime << endl;
   return;
}
```

The constructor method causes the following display whenever an object is created:

```
**** A new Customer object has been created ****
```

Similarly, the destructor method, which is called automatically when an object is destroyed, causes the following message to be displayed:

```
!!!! This Customer object has been deleted !!!!
```

These messages are included to help you monitor creation and deletion of an object by using dynamic allocation. Table 12.2 describes two C++ operators, new and delete, that provide this capability. (These operators require the new header file.)

Table 12.2   Dynamic Allocation and Deallocation Operators

Operator Name	Description
new	Reserves the correct number of bytes for the variable or object type requested by the declaration. Returns the address of the first reserved location or a NULL value if not enough memory is available.
delete	Releases previously reserved memory. The address of the first reserved location must be passed as an argument to the operator.

After an object has been dynamically created, it can be accessed only by using the address the new operator returns. So like the `this` pointer, the newly created object's address must be stored in a pointer variable. The mechanism for doing this is rather simple. For example, the statement

```
Checkout *anotherTrans = new Checkout;
```

declares `anotherTrans` as a pointer to a `Checkout` object, reserves memory for the object, and places this newly created object's address in the `anotherTrans` pointer.

This dynamic creation of a `Checkout` object can also be made in two steps. The first step is to declare a pointer variable with a declaration statement. Then, when an object is actually required, a request can be made to create the object. When the object is created, its address is assigned to the previously declared pointer. Following are the two required statements:

```
Checkout *anotherTrans;      // declares anotherTrans as a pointer
                             // that can store the address
                             // of a Checkout object

anotherTrans = new Checkout; // creates a new Checkout object and
                             // stores this object's address in
                             // the pointer named anotherTrans
```

The expression new `Checkout` on the right of the equals sign creates a new `Checkout` object. The address returned by the new operator is then assigned to the pointer variable on the left of the equals sign. These two statements are the first two shaded statements in Program 12.4's `main()` function.

Program 12.4

```cpp
#include <iostream>
using namespace std;

// class declaration section
class Checkout
{
  private:
    int numItems;
    double arrivalTime;

  public:
    Checkout();     // the constructor
    // the following is an inline destructor
    ~Checkout()
    {cout << "!!!! This Customer object has been deleted !!!!\n";}};
```

```
     void showObject();
     void getItems(){return;};  // inline do-nothing methods
     void getTime() {return;};  // will be used in Program 12.5
};

// class implementation section
Checkout::Checkout() // constructor
{
  cout << "\n**** A new Customer object has been created ****\n";
  numItems = 5;
  arrivalTime = 2.5;
}

void Checkout::showObject()
{
   cout << "     For this object:\n";
   cout << "     numItems = " << numItems
        << "     arrivalTime = " << arrivalTime << endl;
   return;
}

int main()
{
  Checkout *anotherTrans;  // pointer to a Checkout object
  int i, howMany;

  cout << "Enter the number of transactions to be created: ";
  cin >> howMany;

  for(i = 1; i <= howMany; i++)
  {
    anotherTrans = new Checkout; // create a new Checkout object

    // display the address of the created object
    cout << "The memory address of this object is: " << anotherTrans << endl;
    anotherTrans->showObject();  // display contents of this object
    delete anotherTrans;  // delete the object
  }

  return 0;
}
```

Following is a sample output produced by Program 12.4:

```
Enter the number of transactions to be created: 1

**** A new Customer object has been created ****
The memory address of this object is: 003B65A0
      For this object:
         numItems = 5    arrivalTime = 2.5
!!!! This Customer object has been deleted !!!!
```

Take a look at how this output was produced. The first shaded statement in main()—Checkout *anotherTrans;—defines a pointer to a Checkout object. The user is then prompted to enter the number of dynamic objects to be created, which in this case is one.

The next shaded statement—anotherTrans = new Checkout;—creates a new Checkout object and stores its address in the anotherTrans variable. This stored address is then displayed by inserting the pointer's name in a cout stream (the third shaded statement). Because the content of a pointer variable is a value, this value, even though it happens to be an address, can be displayed in this manner. Figure 12.6 shows the allocation of memory corresponding to this address.

1st allocation at 003B65A0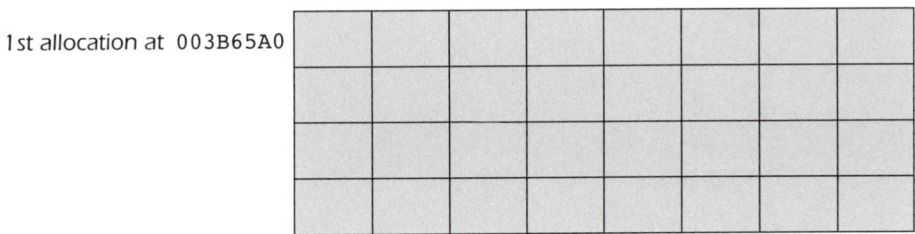

Figure 12.6   The memory allocation produced by a sample run of Program 12.4

Now notice the fourth shaded statement, which shows the notation used to apply a member method to a newly created object. The statement anotherTrans->showObject(); applies the showObject() method to the object whose address resides in the pointer variable anotherTrans. Because dynamically created objects don't have symbolic names, they can be accessed only by using the address information in the pointer variable. However, as explained in Section 11.2, the notation anotherTrans->showObject(); can be replaced by (*anotherTrans).showObject();.

Finally, the last shaded statement in the main() function deletes the object and returns the memory previously assigned to it to the computer's operating system.[2] Deleting dynamically created objects when their usefulness ends is crucial. Otherwise, as new objects are created, the computer starts to "eat up" available memory space, especially if the same pointer is used in creating a new object before the old object is deleted. The reason is that after an existing object's address is overwritten with a new object's address, there's no way for the system to reclaim the memory. This condition is referred to as **memory leak**. In the worst case,

---

[2]The allocated storage is returned automatically to the heap (a computer's free storage area) when the program has finished running. It is, however, a good practice to restore allocated storage back to the heap by using delete when the memory is no longer needed, especially for large programs that make numerous requests for additional storage areas.

as available memory is lost because of a memory leak, system operation can slow down, applications can fail, and the computer can crash.

Next, a modified version of the Checkout class defined in Program 12.4 is used in Program 12.5, which shows the basic elements of a simulation to predict the flow of customers to express self-checkout counters. The assumption is that a customer arrives randomly during an interval of between 0 and 5 minutes and has a maximum of 15 items to check out.

Except for using random numbers and coding the constructor as an inline function, the Checkout class in this program is essentially the same one used in Program 12.4. There are no class members in the class, however, because in practice, the data the simulation generates would be written to a file for later analysis.

 **Program 12.5**

```
#include <iostream>
#include <ctime>
#include <cmath>
using namespace std;

// Checkout class
// precondition:
//    srand() must be called once before any member method
// post-conditions:
//    getItems() returns an integer random no. of items between 1 and 20
//    getTime() returns an arrival time between 0.0 and 3.0

// class declaration section
class Checkout
{
  private:
    // no class variables
  public:
    Checkout() {cout << "\n**** A new Customer has arrived ****\n";};
    ~Checkout()
     {cout << "!!!! This Customer object has been deleted !!!!\n";};
    int getItems(){return(1 + rand() % 15);};
    double getTime(){return((double(rand())/RAND_MAX)*3);};
};

int main()
{
  Checkout *anotherTrans;  // declare a pointer to a Checkout object
  int i, howMany;
```

```
cout << "Enter the number of simulations to be created: ";
cin >> howMany;

srand(time(NULL));
for(i = 1; i <= howMany; i++)
{
  // create a new Checkout object
  anotherTrans = new Checkout;

  // use the pointer to access the member methods
  cout << "The arrival time is " << anotherTrans->getTime() << endl;
  cout << "The number of items is "<< anotherTrans->getItems() << endl;

  // delete the object
  delete anotherTrans;
}

  return 0;
}
```

Following is a sample output produced by Program 12.5. The main difference between this output and that of Program 12.4 is that the arrival of customers to the checkout counter and the number of items to be checked out are determined randomly.

```
Enter the number of simulations to be created: 4

**** A new Customer has arrived ****
The arrival time is 2.23121
The number of items is 7
!!!! This Customer object has been deleted !!!!

**** A new Customer has arrived ****
The arrival time is 4.78301
The number of items is 14
!!!! This Customer object has been deleted !!!!

**** A new Customer has arrived ****
The arrival time is 2.94565
The number of items is 9
!!!! This Customer object has been deleted !!!!

**** A new Customer has arrived ****
The arrival time is 1.3329
The number of items is 3
!!!! This Customer object has been deleted !!!!
```

EXERCISES 12.3

1. **(Review) a.** Explain how dynamic allocation of memory works.

   b. Describe the process of creating a dynamically allocated object. Specifically, discuss the roles of a pointer variable and the new operator in creating a dynamically allocated object.

   c. Discuss the importance of deleting dynamically allocated objects, and explain what can happen if these objects aren't deleted.

2. **(Review) a.** Explain what a pointer is.

   b. For each of the following pointer declarations, identify the pointer variable's name and the data type of the object to be accessed when the address in the pointer variable is dereferenced:

   i.   `Checkout *a;`

   ii. `Pump *pointer1;`

   iii. `Pump *addr_of_aPump;`

   iv. `int *addr_of_int;`

   v.   `double *b;`

   c. If the asterisks were removed from the declarations in Exercise 2b, what would the names before the semicolon represent?

3. **(Practice) a.** Enter and run Program 12.4, but specify the number of objects to be created as four. Explain why your program outputs the same memory addresses.

   b. Remove the statement `delete anotherTrans;` or convert it to a comment (called "commenting out"), and rerun Program 12.4. Again, make sure to have the program create four new objects. Explain why the memory addresses now differ for each new object.

   c. Using the results of Exercise 3b, why is it no longer possible to access any of the first three created objects after the fourth object has been dynamically created? What does this imply about the previously allocated memory, and why is it a serious flaw in the program?

4. **(Practice)** Enter and run Program 12.5.

5. **(Desk check)** For the following class, determine what the two member methods accomplish:

```
#include <iostream>
#include <ctime>
#include <cmath>
using namespace std;

// Coin class
// precondition:
//     srand() must be called once before the flip()method is called
```

```
// class declaration section
class Coin
{
  private:
    static int totalHeads;
    static int totalTails;
  public:
    Coin() {cout << "\n**** A new Coin object has been created ****";};
    ~Coin() {cout << "\n!!!! This Coin object has been deleted !!!!\n";};
    void flip();
    static void percentages();
};

// static member definition
int Coin::totalHeads = 0;
int Coin::totalTails = 0;

// class implementation section
void Coin::flip()
{
  if( double(rand())/RAND_MAX < 0.5)
  {
    ++totalTails;
    cout << "\nThe coin flip came up tails";
  }
   else
  {
    ++totalHeads;
    cout << "\nThe coin flip came up heads";
  }
  return;
}

void Coin::percentages() // this calculates the percentages of
{                        // heads and tails and displays the result
  int tosses = totalHeads + totalTails;

  cout << "\nNumber of coin tosses: " << tosses;
  cout << "\n   " << totalHeads << " Heads      "
       << totalTails << " Tails\n";

  cout << "\nHeads came up " << 100.0 * double(totalHeads)/tosses
       << " percent of the time.";
  cout << "\nTails came up " << 100.0 * double(totalTails)/tosses
       << " percent of the time.";
  return;
}
```

6. **(Program) a.** Compile a program that uses the following `main()` function with the `Coin` class given in Exercise 5:

```
int main()
{
  Coin *anewCoin;   // declare a pointer to a Coin object
  int i, howMany;

  cout << "Enter the number of flips: ";
  cin >> howMany;

  srand(time(NULL));

  for(i = 1; i <= howMany; i++)
  {
    anewCoin = new Coin; // create a new Coin object
    anewCoin->flip();      // flip the coin
    delete anewCoin;       // delete the object
  }

  Coin::percentages();    // call the static member method

  return 0;
}
```

   b. Run the program written for Exercise 6a so that it produces four flips of the coin.

7. **(Modify) a.** Remove all the `cout` statements from the constructor, destructor, and `flip()` methods in the `Coin` class given in Exercise 5. Then combine the modified class with the `main()` function given in Exercise 6a to produce an executable program.

   b. Run the program written for Exercise 7a three times. On the first run, have your program simulate flipping the coin 10 times; the second run, 100 times; and the third run, 1000 times. Make sure each created object is deleted in the `while` loop.

   c. What problem can occur if each created object isn't deleted in your program? Do you think this problem is serious?

8. **(Modify) a.** Modify the program written for Exercise 6a or 7a to contain a single dynamically allocated `Coin` object. It should be created before the `for` loop is entered and deleted after the loop completes its execution.

   b. Discuss the advantages and disadvantages of using multiple `Coin` objects compared with creating a single `Coin` object.

   c. Is using a dynamically created object for the program written for Exercise 7a necessary?

9. **(Program) a.** Write a program that simulates a customer's arrival at a gas station and the amount of gas requested. Each customer should arrive randomly between 1 and 15 minutes and request between 3 and 15 gallons of gas. The name of your class should be `Customer`.

   b. Include the class written for Exercise 9a in a program that simulates the arrival of 10 customers (using a `while` loop). The arrival time and number of gallons of gas each customer requests should be displayed. After the last customer, your program should display the total number of gallons requested.

10. (Modify) a. Modify the class written for Exercise 9a to include the grade of gas. Assume there are three grades of gas: 87 octane, 93 octane, and 97 octane.

    b. Include the class written for Exercise 10a in a program that simulates the arrival of 10 customers (using a `while` loop). The arrival time, number of gallons of gas each customer requests, and octane rating of the gas should be displayed. After the last customer, your program should display the total number of gallons requested for each grade of gas.

    c. What does your simulation assume about the comparative desirability of each grade of gas? Is this assumption realistic?

    d. Based on your answer to Exercise 10c, what are the implications of using the simulation to determine how much of each grade of gas to supply to a gas station?

12.4 Pointers as Class Members

As you learned in Section 10.2, a class can contain any C++ data type, so including a pointer variable in a class shouldn't seem surprising. As an example of the usefulness of a pointer instance variable, say you need to store a list of book titles. Instead of using a fixed-length character array with a data member to hold each title, you could include a pointer member to a character array and then allocate an array of the correct size for each book title as it's needed. Figure 12.7 shows this arrangement of two objects, `book1` and `book2`, each consisting of a single pointer data member. As shown, object `book1`'s pointer contains the address of ("points to") a character array containing the characters `Windows Primer`, and object `book2`'s pointer contains the address of a character array containing the characters `A Brief History of Western Civilization`.

Object book1's data member:

Object book2's data member:

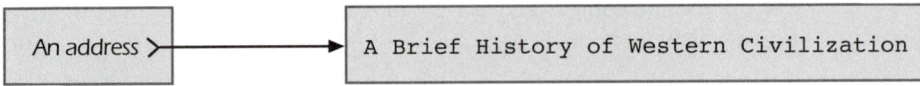

Figure 12.7   Two objects containing pointer data members

The following is a suitable class declaration section for the list of book titles to be accessed, as shown in Figure 12.7:

```
//class declaration section
class Book
{
  private:
    char *title;       // a pointer to a book title
  public:
    Book(char * = '\0');       // constructor
    void showtitle(void);      // display the title
};
```

The constructor, `Book()`, and the display function, `showtitle()`, are defined in the class implementation section:

```
// class implementation section
Book::Book(char *name)
{
  title = new char[strlen(name)+1];  // allocate memory
  strcpy(title,name);                // store the string
}

void Book::showtitle(void)
{
  cout << title << endl;
}
```

The body of the `Book()` constructor contains two statements. The first statement, `title = new char[strlen(name)+1];`, performs two tasks. First, the right side of the statement allocates enough storage for the length of the name parameter plus 1 to accommodate the end-of-string null character, `'\0'`, and returns the address of the first allocated character position. Because of the assignment operator, `=`, this address is then assigned to the pointer variable `title`. Figure 12.8 shows these operations. The second statement in the constructor copies the characters in the name argument to the newly created memory allocation. If no argument is passed to the constructor, `title` is set to `NULL`. Program 12.6 uses this class definition in the context of a complete program.

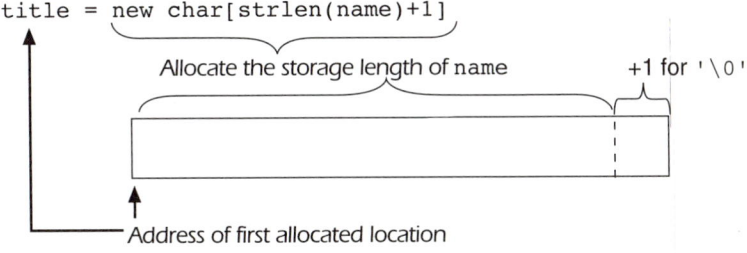

Figure 12.8 Allocating memory for `title = new char[strlen(name)+1)]`

Program 12.6

```cpp
#include <iostream>
#include <string>
using namespace std;

// class declaration section
class Book
{
  private:
    char *title;    // a pointer to a book title
  public:
    Book(char * = '\0');    // constructor
    void showtitle(void);   // display the title
};

// class implementation section
Book::Book(char *strng)
{
  title = new char[strlen(strng)+1];   // allocate memory
  strcpy(title,strng);                 // store the string
}

void Book::showtitle(void)
{
  cout << title << endl;

  return;
}

int main()
{
  Book book1("Windows Primer");       // create 1st title
  Book book2("A Brief History of Western Civilization");  // 2nd title

  book1.showtitle();  // display book1's title
  book2.showtitle();  // display book2's title

  return 0;
}
```

This is the output produced by Program 12.6:

```
Windows Primer
A Brief History of Western Civilization
```

Assignment Operators and Copy Constructors Reconsidered[3]

When a class contains no pointer data members, the compiler-supplied defaults for the assignment operator and copy constructor perform their intended tasks adequately. Both these defaults provide a member-by-member operation that produces no adverse side effects. However, this isn't the case when a pointer member is included in the class declaration. The following discussion explains why.

Figure 12.9a shows the arrangement of pointers and allocated memory that Program 12.6 produces just before it finishes running. Now assume that you insert the assignment statement `book2 = book1;` before the closing brace of the `main()` function. Because you haven't defined an assignment operation, the compiler's default assignment is used. As you know, this assignment produces a memberwise copy (that is, `book2.title = book1.title`) and means the address in `book1`'s pointer is copied into `book2`'s pointer. Therefore, both pointers now "point to" the character array containing the characters `Windows Primer`, and the address of `A Brief History of Western Civilization` has been lost. This situation is shown in Figure 12.9b.

book1's pointer

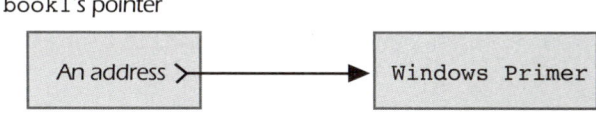

book2's pointer

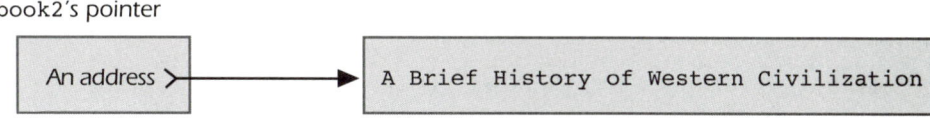

Figure 12.9a   Before the assignment `book2 = book1;`

---

[3]The material in this section explains the problems that occur when the default assignment, copy constructor, and destructor methods are used with classes containing pointer members and discusses how to overcome these problems. On first reading, this section can be omitted without loss of subject continuity.

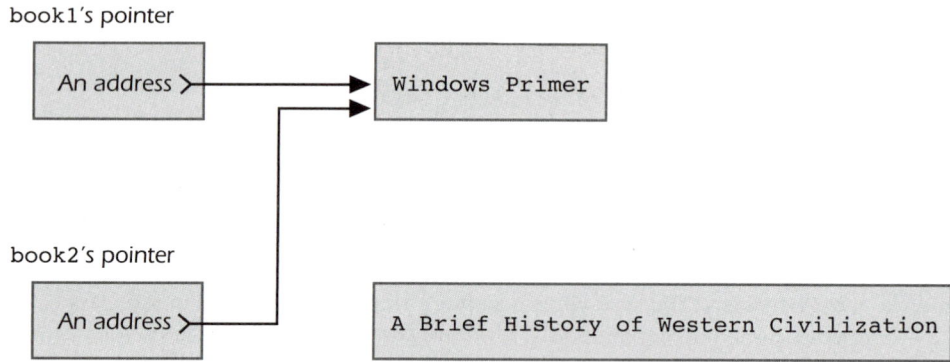

book1's pointer

book2's pointer

Figure 12.9b   The effect of default assignment

Because the memberwise assignment shown in Figure 12.9b results in losing the address of A Brief History of Western Civilization, there's no way for the program to release this memory storage. (The operating system cleans it up when the program terminates.) Worse, however, is a destructor method attempting to release the memory. After the memory pointed to by book2 is released (again, referring to Figure 12.9b), book1 points to an undefined memory location. If this memory area is subsequently reallocated before book1 is deleted, the deletion releases memory that another object is using. The results can wreak havoc on a program.

Typically, what you want is to have the book titles copied, as shown in Figure 12.9c, and leave the pointers alone. This situation also removes the side effects of a subsequent deletion of any Book object.

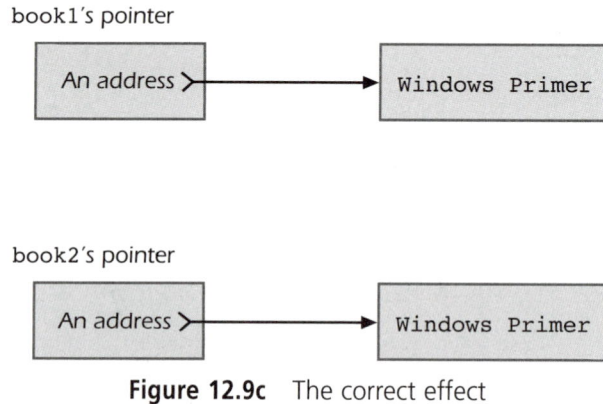

book1's pointer

book2's pointer

Figure 12.9c   The correct effect

To achieve the assignment you want, you must write your own assignment operator. A suitable definition for this operator is as follows:

```
void Book::operator=(Book& oldbook)
{
  if(oldbook.title != NULL)  // check that it exists
    delete(title);           // release existing memory
  title = new char[strlen(oldbook.title) + 1];  // allocate new memory
  strcpy(title, oldbook.title);                 // copy the title
}
```

This definition cleanly releases the memory previously allocated for the object and then allocates enough memory to store the copied title.

The problems associated with the default assignment operator also exist with the default copy constructor because it performs a memberwise copy, too. As with the default assignment operator, you can avoid these problems by writing your own copy constructor. For the `Book` class, this constructor is as follows:

```
Book::Book(Book& oldbook)
{

  title = new char[strlen(oldbook.title)+1];  // allocate new memory
  strcpy(title, oldbook.title);               // copy the title
}
```

Comparing the body of this copy constructor with the assignment operator's function body reveals they're identical except for the deallocation of memory the assignment operator performs. This is because the copy constructor doesn't have to release the existing array before allocating a new one; none exists when the constructor is called.

EXERCISES 12.4

1. **(Program)** Include the copy constructor and assignment operator explained in this section in Program 12.6, and run the program to verify their operation.

2. **(Program)** Write a suitable destructor method for Program 12.6.

3. **(Program)** a. Construct a class named `Car` containing these four data members: a double-precision variable named `engineSize`, a character variable named `bodyStyle`, an integer variable named `colorCode`, and a character pointer named `vinPtr` to a vehicle ID code. The member functions should include a constructor that provides default values of 0 for each numeric data member, an `X` for each character variable, and a `NULL` for each pointer; a display function that prints the engine size, body style, color code, and vehicle ID code; and an assignment operator that performs a memberwise assignment between two `Car` objects and handles the pointer member correctly.

   b. Include the class written for Exercise 3a in a working C++ program that creates two `Car` objects; the second object should be assigned the values of the first object.

4. **(Modify)** Modify Program 12.6 to include the assignment statement b = a, and then run the modified program to assess any error messages that occur.

5. **(Modify)** Using Program 12.6 as a start, write a program that creates five Book objects. The program should allow the user to enter the five book titles interactively and then display the titles entered.

6. **(Modify)** Modify the program written in Exercise 5 so that the program sorts the entered book titles in alphabetical order before it displays them. (*Hint*: You have to define a sort routine for the titles; refer back to Section 7.7.)

12.5 Common Programming Errors

1. Attempting to override a virtual function without using the same type and number of arguments as the original function.

2. Using the keyword `virtual` in the class implementation section. Functions are declared as virtual only in the class declaration section.

3. Forgetting to delete dynamically created objects.

4. Attempting to use memberwise assignment between objects containing a pointer member.

12.6 Chapter Summary

1. Inheritance is the capability of deriving one class from another class. The class used as the basis for the derived class is referred to as the base class, parent class, or superclass. The derived class is also referred to as the child class or subclass.

2. Base class functions can be overridden by derived class functions with the same name. The override function is simply an overloaded version of the base member function defined in the derived class.

3. Polymorphism is the capability of having the same function name invoke different responses, based on the object used in making the function call. It can be accomplished with override functions or virtual functions.

4. In static binding, the determination of which function is called is made at compile time. In dynamic binding, the determination is made at runtime.

5. A virtual function designates that dynamic binding should take place. The specification is made in the function's prototype by placing the keyword `virtual` before the function's return type. After a function has been declared as `virtual`, it remains so for all derived classes, as long as there's a continuous trail of function declarations through the derived chain of classes.

6. Pointers can be included as class data members. A pointer member adheres to the same rules as a pointer variable.

7. The default copy constructor and assignment operators typically aren't useful with classes containing pointer members. The reason is that these default functions perform a member-wise copy, in which the address in the source pointer is copied to the destination pointer, resulting in both pointers "pointing to" the same memory area. For these situations, you must define your own copy constructor and assignment operator.

12.7 Chapter Supplement: UML Class and Object Diagrams

For all but extremely simple programs, you should start by creating an explicit design; after you finish the design, you can begin coding. This process is equivalent to designing a house with blueprints and physical models before beginning construction. Formally, the process of designing an application is referred to as **program modeling**. This section introduces the **Unified Modeling Language (UML)**, which is widely accepted as a technique for developing object-oriented programs. UML isn't a programming language, nor is it part of C++. It's a separate language with its own rules and notations for creating an object-oriented design. If used correctly, a UML design can help you understand and clarify a program's requirements. The finished design can serve as a set of detailed specifications (which can be coded easily in an object-oriented programming language, such as C++) and as documentation for the final program.

UML uses diagrams and techniques that are easy to understand, and it supports all the features required to implement an object-oriented design. Additionally, UML is the predominant object-oriented design procedure that professional programmers use. At the most fundamental level, designing an object-oriented application requires understanding and specifying the following:

- The objects in the system
- What can happen to these objects
- When something can happen to these objects

In a UML analysis, each item is addressed by separate views and diagrams. This procedure is similar to the plan for a house, which contains several diagrams required for the final construction. For example, there must be blueprints for the physical outlay as well as diagrams for electrical wiring, plumbing, heating and cooling ducts, and landscape and elevation views. Each diagram presents a different view of the completed house and provides different information, but all the information is required for the finished product.

The same is true for the diagrams in a UML analysis. UML has nine diagram types: class, object, state, sequence, activity, use case, component, deployment, and collaboration. Not all these diagram types are required for every analysis; some provide specific details that are needed only in more advanced situations. This book covers the two basic UML diagrams you should be familiar with—class and object diagrams—and the rules for creating them. After you understand these rules, you'll be able to read almost any UML diagram you encounter.

Class and object diagrams are similar in structure, and both include attributes and operations for classes or objects and the relationship between classes or objects. For many systems, the descriptions that class and object diagrams provide are more than enough for designing and creating an object-oriented program.

Class and Object Diagrams

Class diagrams are used to describe classes and their relationships, and **object diagrams** are used to describe objects and their relationships. As you know, a class refers to a type of object, from which many specific objects can be created, and an object refers to a specific single item created from a class. For example, a class of books might be described as fiction or nonfiction, of which many specific instances, or objects, exist. The book *A History of England* is a specific object of the nonfiction class, and *Pride and Prejudice* is a specific object of the fiction class. Therefore, the class is always the basic plan, or recipe, from which real objects are created. It describes the properties and operations each object must have to be a member of the class.

An attribute, as described in Section 10.7, is simply a characteristic each object in the class must have. For example, title and author are attributes of `Book` objects; name, age, sex, weight, and height are attributes of `Person` objects. After data values are assigned to attributes, a unique object is created. Every object created from a class must also have an identity to distinguish it from another object of the same class. This rule isn't true of a pure data value, such as the number 5; all occurrences of this number are indistinguishable from one another.

Both classes and objects are represented with a diagram consisting of a box. In class diagrams, the class name is in bold text and centered at the top of the box. In object diagrams, the object's name is also centered at the top of box, but it's underlined. Figure 12.10 shows the representation of a `Person` class along with a `Person` object named Janet Smith.

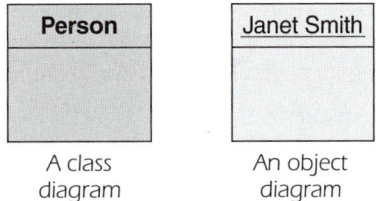

| A class
diagram | An object
diagram |

Figure 12.10   Class and object representations

Including the class name in object diagrams is optional, but if you do, underline it and precede the class name with an object name, using a colon to separate the two names. For example, in Figure 12.10's object diagram, you could use the name <u>Janet Smith:Person</u>. Figure 12.11 shows the basic symbols and notations for constructing class and object diagrams.

After class attributes have been identified, they're listed in a box below the class name, separated by a line. Objects are shown in a similar manner, with data values included for all attributes. For example, Figure 12.12 shows the attributes associated with the `Country` class and the values of these attributes for the `U.S.A.` and `Spain` objects. As you might expect, the attributes listed in a class diagram become, in C++, the variables declared in the class declaration section.

Chapter Supplement: UML Class and Object
Diagrams

Class:

ClassName

`attribute`
`attribute:data-type`
`attribute:data-type=init-value`
`...`

`operation`
`operation (arg-list):return-type`
`...`

Object:

Object Name
`attribute-name = value` . . .

Figure 12.11   Basic UML symbols and notation

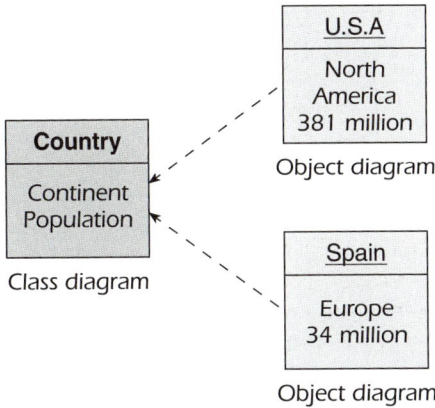

Figure 12.12   Including attributes in UML class and object diagrams

Attributes have two qualities: type and visibility. An attribute's **type** is either a primitive data type—such as integer, double, Boolean, or character—or a class data type, such as a string. Type is required in a class diagram and is indicated after an attribute name with a colon followed by the data type.

Visibility defines where an attribute can be seen—that is, whether the attribute can be used in other classes or is restricted to the class defining it. The following list explains the types of visibility and the UML notation for indicating visibility:

- *Private*—An attribute with private visibility can be used only in its defining class and can't be accessed by other classes directly. A minus sign (-) in front of the attribute name designates the attribute as private.
- *Public*—An attribute with public visibility can be used in any other class. Public visibility is indicated with a plus sign (+) in front of the attribute name.
- *Protected*—An attribute with protected visibility can be passed along to a derived class; neither a plus sign nor a minus sign is used to indicate protected visibility.

In a class diagram, an attribute's name and type are required; all other information is optional. Figure 12.13 shows the class diagram for a class named `RoomType` containing two private attributes: `length` and `width`. Notice that it includes the default values the class is expected to provide to its attributes.

```
          RoomType

    -length : double = 25.0
    -width  : double = 12.0
```

Figure 12.13   A class with attributes

Just as attributes are designated in a class diagram, so are operations. **Operations** are transformations that can be applied to attributes and are coded as C++ functions. Operation names are listed below attributes and separated from them by a line. Figure 12.14 shows two class diagrams that include operations.

```
          Person

    name:string
    street address:string
    city:string
    state:string
    zip:string
    age:double

    setName()
    setAddress()
    setAge()
    changeName()
    changeAddress()
    changeAge()
```

```
          Gas Pump

    gallonsInTank:double
    costPerGallon:double

    enablePump()
    disablePump()
    setPricePerGallon()
```

Figure 12.14   Including operations in class diagrams

Chapter

13

The Standard Template Library

A driving force behind the development of object-oriented programming was the need to create easily reusable source code. For example, re-creating source code each time an array or a list is needed wastes both time and programming effort. In addition, time is spent testing and reverifying code that might have been modified only minimally.

Suppose, for example, that a program uses three arrays: an array of characters, an array of integers, and an array of double-precision numbers. Rather than code three different arrays, it makes more sense to implement each list from a single, fully tested, generic array class. This class would have a complete set of methods for processing the array, including methods for sorting, inserting, finding maximum and minimum values, locating values, copying the list, comparing lists, and dynamically expanding and contracting the list, as needed. This generic list structure, referred to as a container, forms the basis of the Standard Template Library (STL).

This chapter is intended as an introduction to the STL. Currently, it provides seven different types of lists, each supported by its own class. The STL capabilities discussed in this chapter represent an extremely small subset of what's available in the STL. Typically, an advanced course in a computer science curriculum is devoted to covering the advanced applications that are programmed with the STL or similarly constructed classes.

13.1 The Standard Template Library

You've already worked with one kind of list, an array, which is the list of choice for a fixed-length set of related data. Many programming applications, however, require expanding and contracting lists as list items are added and removed. Although expanding and contracting an array can be accomplished by creating, copying, and deleting arrays, this solution is costly in terms of programming, maintenance, and testing time.

In all but the simplest situations, it's usually more efficient to use the **Standard Template Library (STL)** to create and manipulate lists. Among other uses, one purpose of the STL is to provide a tested and generic set of easily used lists that can be maintained in various configurations. This is done by calling prewritten class methods or using generalized algorithms applicable to all STL-created list types. The STL gives you a broad range of generic capabilities for constructing and manipulating lists of objects rapidly—objects consisting of built-in variables or other objects. These capabilities enable you to maintain lists and perform operations on them, such as sorting and searching, without having to fully understand or program the advanced and often complicated underlying algorithms.

Table 13.1 summarizes the seven types of lists available in the STL. Each list type is derived from its own class.

Table 13.1   STL Lists

List Type	Classification	Use
Vector	Sequence	Dynamic arrays
List	Sequence	Linked lists
Deque	Sequence	Stacks and queues
Set	Associative	Binary trees without duplicate objects
Multiset	Associative	Binary trees that might have duplicate objects
Map	Associative	Binary trees with a unique key that doesn't permit duplicate objects
Multimap	Associative	Binary trees with a unique key that permits duplicate objects

As shown in the Classification column, each list type is categorized as sequence or associative. In a **sequence list**, a list object is determined solely by its position in the list—that is, by where the object was placed in the list and how it might have been moved subsequently. For example, arrays are sequence lists, and an object's position in the list is determined by the exact order in which it was added to the array or moved subsequently. An **associative list** is maintained automatically in a sorted order. An object's position in an associative list depends on its value and a selected sorting criterion. For example, an alphabetical list of names depends on the name and a sorting rule rather than the exact order in which names were entered into the list. In this chapter, you're concerned only with STL's sequence types.

Before you begin working with lists and the STL, it's helpful to understand the difference between lists in the STL and arrays. An array is a built-in list type. By contrast, lists provided by the STL are class types. Although arrays are used most often to store built-in numerical data

Point of Information

Homogeneous and Heterogeneous Data Structures

Both lists and objects are data structures. A **data structure** is a container of data organized in a way that facilitates inserting, retrieving, and deleting data. The difference between these two data structures is the types of objects they contain. A list is a **homogeneous** data structure, which means all its components must be of the same data type. An object is a **heterogeneous** data structure, which means its components can be of different data types.

For example, an object could contain a name stored as a string data type, a pay rate stored as a double-precision data type, and an ID number stored as an integer data type. Because an object can be composed of different data types, it's a heterogeneous data structure. However, the list holding all the objects is a homogeneous data structure, in which each object has the same heterogeneous structure.

types, they still retain general characteristics common to more advanced STL list types. For example, like an array, an STL list can be empty, meaning it currently holds no items. As it applies to both arrays and STL lists, a **list** is considered a container that can hold a collection of zero or more items of the same type. For this reason, STL lists and arrays are referred to as both **containers** and **collections**, and these terms are used interchangeably. A list must also provide a means for accessing each object. When a list provides this data location capability, the list becomes a data structure. In an array, this location capability is provided by the position of each object in the array; the position is designated by using an integer index value.

Although STL lists can also store built-in data types, they're more commonly used to store and maintain objects. In commercial applications, these objects are usually referred to as "records." To make the concept of a record more tangible, take a look at the data items typically used in preparing mailing labels:

Name:
Street Address:
City:
State:
Zip:

Each data item in this list is a separate entity referred to as a **data field**. Taken together, the data fields form a single unit referred to as a **record**. Although there could be thousands of names and addresses in a mailing list, all the mailing labels are identical in form. The general form of the record is described as a class's data members, and each record is represented as an object to be stored in a list.

After an object's structure has been defined, some means for collecting all the objects into a single list is required. Additionally, a means is needed to locate, display, print, and update objects in the list. The STL provides these capabilities.

Before describing specific types of applications in detail, however, it's worth emphasizing that only objects—not a class's methods—are stored in a list. The methods, which apply to the class as a whole, simply provide ways to initialize each object before it's placed in the list and report and modify an object before it's inserted in the list or after it's extracted from the list. Figure 13.1 shows the process of creating and using objects and lists.

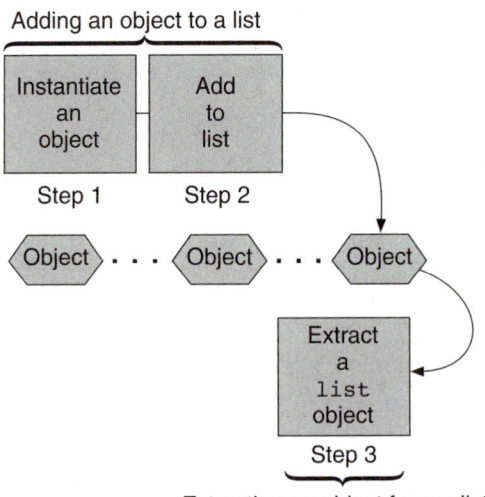

Figure 13.1   The list creation process

Each STL class provides its own set of methods for list maintenance. Additionally, the STL provides a general set of methods (called algorithms) that can be applied to any range of objects stored in any STL-created list. Table 13.2 lists these algorithms.

Table 13.2   Commonly Used STL Algorithms

Algorithm Name	Description
accumulate	Returns the sum of the numbers in a specified range.
binary_search	Returns a Boolean value of **true** if the specified value exists within the specified range; otherwise, returns **false**. Can be used only on a sorted set of values.
copy	Copies objects from a source range to a destination range.
copy_backward	Copies objects from a source range to a destination range in a reverse direction.
count	Returns the number of objects in a specified range that match a specified value.
equal	Compares the objects in one range of objects, object by object, to the objects in a second range.
fill	Assigns every object in a specified range to a specified value.

Table 13.2 Commonly Used STL Algorithms (*continued*)

Algorithm Name	Description
find	Returns the position of an object's first occurrence in a specified range having a specified value if the value exists. Performs a linear search, starting with the first object in a specified range, and proceeds one object at a time until the complete range has been searched or the specified object has been found.
max_object	Returns the maximum value of objects in the specified range.
min_object	Returns the minimum value of objects in the specified range.
random_shuffle	Randomly shuffles object values in a specified range.
remove	Removes a specified value in a specified range without changing the order of the remaining objects.
replace	Replaces each object in a specified range having a specified value with a newly specified value.
reverse	Reverses objects in a specified range.
search	Finds the first occurrence of a specified value or sequence of values within a specified range.
sort	Sorts objects in a specified range into ascending order.
swap	Exchanges object values between two objects.
unique	Removes duplicate adjacent objects in a specified range.

Finally, the STL provides additional components referred to as **iterators**, used to specify the means of accessing list objects, in much the same way as an index does for an array.

To create and use STL lists, you must do the following:

1. Select a suitable STL class to construct the container type.
2. Store objects in the list.
3. Apply the STL class's methods or the more general STL algorithms to the stored objects.

You put these steps into practice in the following sections when you construct three commonly used lists: linked lists, stacks, and queues.

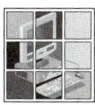

EXERCISES 13.1

1. **(Review)** Define the following terms:
   a. Container
   b. Collection
   c. Data structure
   d. Iterator
   e. List
   f. Standard Template Library

2. **(Review)** What sequential container types are supported in the STL?

3. **(Review)** What associative container types are supported in the STL?

4. **(Practice)** For each of the following, define a class containing only a class declaration section that can be used to create the following objects:

   a. An object (known as a student record) containing a student ID number, the number of credits completed, and a cumulative grade point average

   b. An object (known as a student record) capable of holding a student's name, date of birth, number of credits completed, and cumulative grade point average

   c. A mailing list containing a title field, last name field, first name field, two street address fields, a city field, a state field, and a zip code field

   d. A stock object containing the stock's name, the purchase price, and the date of purchase

   e. An inventory object containing an integer part number, a string part description, an integer number of parts in inventory, and an integer reorder value

5. **(Practice)** For each class declared in Exercise 4, add a suitable constructor and accessor method. Test each method to initialize and display the following data:

   a. ID Number: 4672
      Number of Credits Completed: 68
      Grade Point Average: 3.01

   b. Name: Rhona Karp
      Date of Birth: 8/4/60
      Number of Credits Completed: 96
      Grade Point Average: 3.89

   c. Title: Dr.
      Last Name: Kingsley
      First Name: Kay
      Address 1: Apt. 2B
      Address 2: 614 Freeman Street
      City: Indianapolis
      State: IN
      Zip Code: 07030

   d. Stock: IBM
      Purchase Price: 134.5
      Date Purchased: 10/1/2010

   e. Part Number: 16879
      Description: Battery
      Number in Stock: 10
      Reorder Number: 3

6. **(Program) a.** Write a C++ program that prompts a user to input the current month, day, and year. Store the data entered in a suitably defined object and display the date in an appropriate manner.

   b. Modify the program written in Exercise 6a to use an object that accepts the current time in hours, minutes, and seconds.

7. **(Program)** Define a class capable of creating objects that can store a business's name, description of its product or services, address, number of employees, and annual revenue.

8. **(Practice)** Define a class capable of creating objects for different screw types held in inventory. Each object should contain a field for an integer inventory number, a double-precision screw length, a double-precision diameter, the kind of head (Phillips or standard slot), the material (steel, brass, other), and the cost.

9. **(Program)** Write a C++ program that defines a class capable of creating objects for storing the name of a stock, its estimated earnings per share, and its estimated price-to-earnings ratio. Have the program prompt the user to enter these items for five different stocks. When data has been entered for a particular stock, have the program compute and display the anticipated stock price based on the entered earnings and price-per-earnings values. For example, if a user enters the data `XYZ 1.56 12`, the anticipated price for a share of XYZ stock is `(1.56)*(12)` `= $18.72`.

13.2 Linked Lists

A classic data-handling problem is making additions or deletions to existing objects that are maintained in a specific order. (Recall that objects in a list are also referred to as "records.") This problem is best illustrated by the alphabetical telephone list shown here:

Acme, Sam
(555) 898-2392
Dolan, Edith
(555) 682-3104
Lanfrank, John
(555) 718-4581
Mening, Stephen
(555) 382-7070
Zemann, Harold
(555) 219-9912

Starting with this list of names and phone numbers, you want to add new objects to the list in such a way that alphabetic ordering is maintained. Although ordered objects can be inserted or deleted by using an array, it's not an efficient representation for adding or deleting objects in the list. Arrays are fixed and have a specified size. Therefore, deleting an object from an array creates an empty slot that requires shifting up all objects below the deleted object to close the empty slot.

Similarly, adding an object to an array requires shifting all objects below the addition down to make room for the new entry. Therefore, adding or deleting objects in an array generally requires restructuring objects in the container—a cumbersome, time-consuming, and inefficient practice.

A linked list is a convenient method for maintaining a constantly changing list without needing to reorder and restructure the entire list. In a **linked list**, each object contains one variable specifying the location of the next object in the list. Instead of requiring each object to be physically stored in the correct order, each new object is physically added wherever the computer has free storage space. If an object is added to the list, only the variables for objects immediately before and after the new object must be updated with new location information. Therefore, from a programming standpoint, information is always contained in one object that allows locating the next object, no matter where it's actually stored.

Figure 13.2 illustrates the concept of a linked list. Each object consists of a name and phone number plus a variable for storing the address of the next object in the list. Although the actual data for the `Lanfrank` object in the figure can be physically stored anywhere in the computer, the variable at the end of the `Dolan` object maintains the correct alphabetical order. This variable is a pointer variable that provides the starting address of the location where the `Lanfrank` object is stored. All you need to know at this point, however, is that each object in a linked list must contain information to locate the next object.

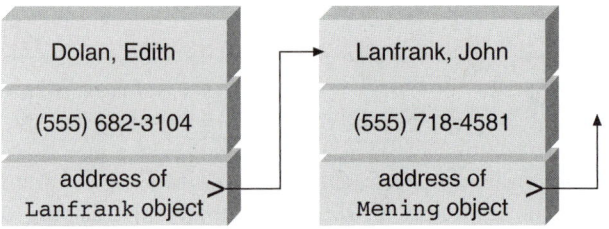

Figure 13.2   Using pointer variables to link objects

To illustrate the usefulness of a pointer variable in the `Dolan` object, Figure 13.3 shows adding a phone number for June Hagar to the alphabetical list. The data for June Hagar is stored in an object, using the same data type as for existing objects. To make sure the phone number for Hagar is displayed correctly after the Dolan phone number, the pointer variable in the `Dolan` object must be altered to locate the `Hagar` object, and the pointer variable in the `Hagar` object must be set to locate the `Lanfrank` object. As Figure 13.3 shows, the pointer variable in each object simply locates the next object in the list, even if this object isn't physically stored in the correct order.

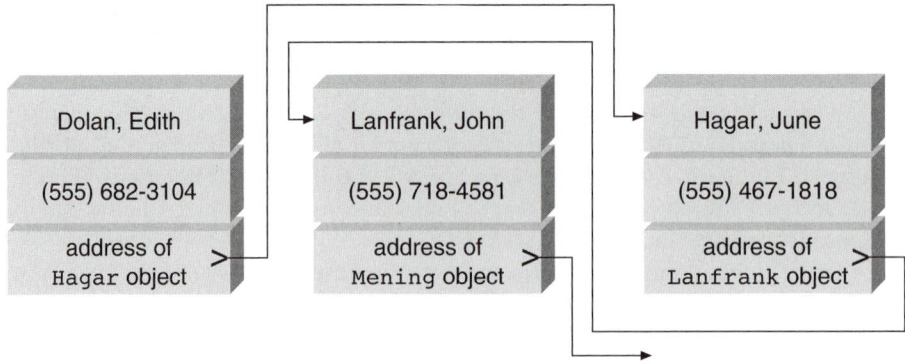

Figure 13.3   Adjusting pointer variables to point to the correct objects

Removing an object from a linked list is the reverse of adding an object. The actual object is logically removed from the list simply by changing the pointer variable's value in the object preceding it to the location of the object immediately after the deleted object.

There are two different approaches to constructing a linked list. The first is using the STL `list` class; the second is "making your own," in which the programmer defines a class that includes an object's declaration and the code for creating and maintaining the list.

The usefulness of the STL `list` class is that the linked list, as shown in Figure 13.3, can be constructed without the programmer having to understand or code the internal details of pointer variables. The programmer doesn't even have to understand the details of how an STL list is created and maintained. This is, of course, the major benefit of object-oriented programming with existing classes. Therefore, except for highly specialized cases, you should almost always use the STL `list` class, which is described next.

Using the STL `list` Class

Figure 13.4 shows the internal structure the STL `list` class uses to maintain a list of linked objects. The important point to notice is that access through the list occurs only via **link variables** in each object that contain location information for an object. This structure makes it possible to insert a new object into the list simply by storing it in any available memory location and adjusting the location information in at most two link variables. Unlike an array, storing list objects in contiguous memory locations isn't necessary. Similarly, an object can be removed by adjusting the link information in two link variables. As explained earlier, this means expanding and contracting the list are more efficient operations than in an array.

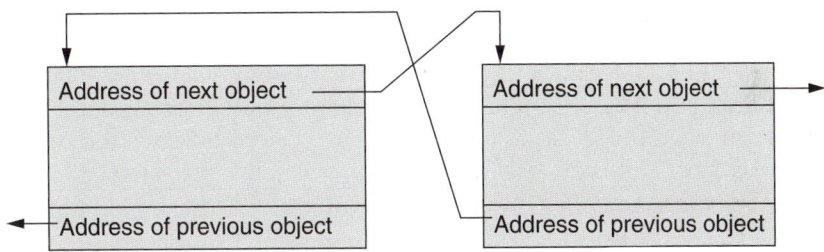

Figure 13.4   A class with four link variables

Table 13.3 lists the methods available in the STL `list` class. These methods deal with adding, removing, and locating objects from the front or back of the list. Note that linked lists provide no random access methods. To get to any internal object, the list must be traversed sequentially, object by object, starting at the front or back of the list.

Table 13.3   Summary of STL `list` Class Methods and Operations

Methods and Operations	Type	Description
`list<DataType> name`	constructor	Creates an empty list named `name` with a compiler-dependent initial size
`list<DataType> name(source)`	constructor	Creates a copy of the `source` list
`list<DataType> name(n)`	constructor	Creates a list of size n
`list<DataType> name(n, object)`	constructor	Creates a list of size n with each object initialized as `object`
`list<DataType> name(src.beg,src.end)`	constructor	Creates a list initialized with objects from a source container, beginning at `src.beg` and ending at `src.end`
`~list<DataType>()`	destructor	Destroys the list and all objects it contains
`name.front()`	accessor	Returns the object at the front of the list (the first object) with no check for the existence of a first object
`name.pop_front()`	mutator	Removes but does not return the object at the front of the list
`name.push_front(object)`	mutator	Inserts object at the front of the list
`name.back()`	accessor	Returns the object at the back of the list with no check for the existence of a last object
`name.pop_back()`	mutator	Removes but does not return the object at the back of the list (the last object)
`name.push_back(object)`	mutator	Inserts object at the back of the list
`name.insert(itr, object)`	mutator	Inserts object at the iterator position `itr`
`name.insert(itr, src.beg, src.end)`	mutator	Inserts copies of objects from a source container, beginning at `src.beg` and ending at `src.end`, at iterator position `itr`
`name.insert(itr, n, object)`	mutator	Inserts n copies of object at iterator position `itr`
`name.assign(n, object)`	mutator	Assigns n copies of object
`name.(src.begin, src.end)`	mutator	Assigns the objects of the `src` container (need not be a list), between the range `src.begin` and `src.end`, to the named list

Table 13.3 Summary of STL `list` Class Methods and Operations (*continued*)

Methods and Operations	Type	Description
`name.erase(pos)`	mutator	Removes the object at the specified position `pos`
`name.erase(begin, end)`	mutator	Removes objects within the specified range
`name.resize(value)`	mutator	Resizes the list larger with new objects instantiated by using the default constructor
`name.resize(value, object)`	mutator	Resizes the list larger with new objects instantiated as `object`
`name.clear()`	mutator	Removes all objects from the list
`nameA.swap(nameB)`	mutator	Swaps the objects of `nameA` and `nameB` lists; can be performed with the `swap()` algorithm
`name.begin()`	accessor	Returns an iterator to the first object in the list
`name.end()`	accessor	Returns an iterator to the position after the last object in the list
`name.rbegin()`	accessor	Returns a reverse iterator to the first object in the list
`name.rend()`	accessor	Returns a reverse iterator to the position after the last object in the list
`name.unique()`	mutator	Removes consecutive duplicate objects
`name.merge(nameB)`	mutator	Merges sorted objects of `nameB` into sorted objects of `name`, creating a final sorted list
`name.reverse()`	mutator	Reverses objects in the list
`name.splice(itr, nameB)`	mutator	Inserts `nameB` objects into `name` at position `itr`
`name.splice(itr, nameB, beg, end)`	mutator	Inserts `nameB` objects in the position range from `beg` to `end` into `name` at position `itr`
`name.sort()`	mutator	Sorts objects in the list
`nameA == nameB`	relational	Returns a Boolean `true` if all `nameA` objects equal `nameB` objects; otherwise, returns `false`
`nameA != nameB`	relational	Returns a Boolean `false` if all `nameA` objects equal `nameB` objects; otherwise, returns `true`; same as `!(nameA == nameB)`

Table 13.3   Summary of STL `list` Class Methods and Operations (*continued*)

Methods and Operations	Type	Description
nameA < nameB	relational	Returns a Boolean `true` if `nameA` is less than `nameB`; otherwise, returns `false`
nameA > nameB	relational	Returns a Boolean `true` if `nameA` is greater than `nameB`; otherwise, returns `false`; same as `nameB < nameA`
nameA <= nameB	relational	Returns a Boolean `true` if `nameA` is less than or equal to `nameB`
nameA >= nameB	relational	Returns a Boolean `true` if `nameA` is greater than or equal to `nameB`
name.size()	capacity	Returns the number of objects in the list as an integer
name.empty()	capacity	Returns a Boolean `true` if list is empty; otherwise, returns `false`
name.max_size()	capacity	Returns the maximum possible objects as an integer
name.capacity()	capacity	Returns the maximum possible objects as an integer without relocating the list

The `list` class has no method for returning any object except the first and last objects. Instead, to access an internal object, the list must be traversed from one end, and all objects before the one you're accessing must be removed from the list. Technically, when an item is removed in this fashion, it's referred to as "popping" the object from the list. Generally, to make sure removed objects aren't lost, a copy of the list is made, either as a complete list or an object-by-object list as each object is removed, or popped.

In the next two programs, Program 13.1 creates and displays a single linked list of names, stored as strings, and Program 13.2 shows how to store and retrieve user-created objects. Because of the STL's structure, the two applications are virtually the same.

Program 13.1

```cpp
#include <iostream>
#include <list>
#include <algorithm>
#include <string>
using namespace std;

int main()
{
  list<string> names, addnames;
  string n;

  // add names to the original list
  names.push_front("Dolan, Edith");
  names.push_back("Lanfrank, John");

  // create a new list
  addnames.push_front("Acme, Sam");
  addnames.push_front("Mening, Stephen");
  addnames.push_front("Zemann, Frank");

  names.sort();
  addnames.sort();

  // merge the second list into the first
  names.merge(addnames);
  cout << "The final list size is: " <<  names.size() << endl;
  cout << "This list contains the names:\n";

  while (!names.empty())
  {
    cout << names.front() << endl;
    names.pop_front();  // remove the object
  }
  return 0;
}
```

Point of Information

List Application Considerations

Vectors are the preferred list type when you need random access to objects but don't need many insertions or deletions. The reason is that an index value can be used to go directly to the object being accessed. Insertions and deletions require modifying the underlying array supporting the vector and can be costly in terms of the overhead needed to perform these operations when many insertions and deletions are required.

Because the only way to get to an object in the middle of a list is by traversing all the objects before it or by traversing objects from the back of the list toward the object in the middle, attempts at random access tend to be costly in terms of access time. Therefore, a list is the preferred list type when many object insertions and deletions need to be made and object access tends to be sequential.

Finally, if you need to store only primitive data types, such as integers or double-precision values, a simple array should be your first choice.

The output Program 13.1 produces is as follows:

```
The final list size is: 5
This list contains the names:
Acme, Sam
Dolan, Edith
Lanfrank, John
Mening, Stephen
Zemann, Frank
```

Using User-Defined Objects

In practice, most real-life applications using linked lists require a user-defined object consisting of a combination of data types. For example, consider the problem of creating a linked list for the simplified telephone directory object class shown in Figure 13.5.

```
                    Class Name: NameTele


  Attributes
     name: string
     phoneNum: string


  Methods
     NameTele(name, phoneNum)            //constructor
     string getName(): return name       // input name
     string getPhone(): return phoneNum // input phone number
```

Figure 13.5   A class description for a telephone directory object

The following class definition corresponds to Figure 13.5:

```
// class declaration section
class NameTele
{
  private:
    string name;
    string phoneNum;

// class implementation section
  public:
    NameTele(string nn, string phone)  // constructor
    {
      name = nn;
      phoneNum = phone;
    }
    // inline method definitions
    string getName(){return name;}
    string getPhone(){return phoneNum;}
};
```

This class permits constructing objects consisting of `name` and `phoneNum` instance variables by using a constructor and accessor methods for setting and retrieving these variables. Program 13.2 instantiates four objects of this class and stores them in a linked list. After it's created, the complete list is displayed.

Program 13.2

```cpp
#include <iostream>
#include <list>
#include <string>
using namespace std;

// class declaration section
class NameTele
{
  private:
    string name;
    string phoneNum;

// class implementation section
  public:
    NameTele(string nn, string phone)    // constructor
    {
      name = nn;
      phoneNum = phone;
    }
    // inline method definitions
    string getName(){return name;}
    string getPhone(){return phoneNum;}
};

  int main()
  {
    list<NameTele> employee;   // instantiate and initialize the list
                               // using objects in the array

    employee.push_front(NameTele("Acme, Sam", "(555) 898-2392"));
    employee.push_back(NameTele("Dolan, Edith", "(555) 682-3104"));
    employee.push_back(NameTele("Lanfrank, John", "(555) 718-4581"));
    employee.push_back(NameTele("Mening, Stephen", "(555) 382-7070"));
    employee.push_back(NameTele("Zemann, Harold", "(555) 219-9912"));

    // retrieve all list objects
    // use accessor methods to extract the name and pay rate
    cout <<"The size of the list is " << employee.size() << endl;
    cout <<"\n      Name                Telephone";
    cout <<"\n--------------        --------------\n";
```

```
    while (!employee.empty())
    {
      cout << employee.front().getName()
           << "\t    " << employee.front().getPhone() << endl;
      employee.pop_front();  // remove the object
    }
  return 0;
}
```

Program 13.2 produces the following output:

```
The size of the list is 5
       Name                Telephone
   ---------------     ---------------
   Acme, Sam           (555) 898-2392
   Dolan, Edith        (555) 682-3104
   Lanfrank, John      (555) 718-4581
   Mening, Stephen     (555) 382-7070
   Zemann, Harold      (555) 219-9912
```

Notice that after each object is retrieved from the list, the underlying class's accessor methods extract name and phoneNum values. Because the dot operator has a left-to-right associativity, an expression such as employee.front().getName() is interpreted as (employee.front()).getName(). Therefore, the STL list class's front() method is used to return the front object from the list, which is then further processed by the NameTele class's getName() method.

EXERCISES 13.2

1. **(Practice)** Enter and run Program 13.1.

2. **(Practice)** Enter and run Program 13.2.

3. **(Modify)** Modify Program 13.2 to prompt the user for a name. Have the program search the existing list for the entered name. If the name is in the list, display the corresponding phone number; otherwise, display this message: The name is not in the current phone list.

4. **(Practice)** Write a C++ program containing a linked list of 10 integer numbers. Have the program display the numbers in the list.

5. **(Practice)** Using the linked list of objects shown in Figure 13.3, write the sequence of steps for deleting the object for John Lanfrank from the list.

6. **(Practice)** Generalize the description in Exercise 5 to describe the sequence of steps for removing the nth object from a list of linked objects. The nth object is preceded by the $(n - 1)$st object and followed by the $(n + 1)$st object. Make sure to store all pointer values correctly.

7. **(Desk check)** Determine the output of this program:

```cpp
#include <iostream>
#include <list>
using namespace std;
int main()
{
  int intValue;
  double sum = 0.0;
  double average;

   int nums[] = {1, 2, 3, 4, 5 };  // create array of integer values

   list<int> x(nums, nums + 4); // instantiate a list of ints using
                                // a constructor that initializes
                                // the list with values from array

   cout <<"\nThe list x initially has a size of " << x.size()
        << ",\n and contains the objects: ";

   while (!x.empty())
   {
     cout << x.front() << "   ";
     x.pop_front();
   }

   cout << endl;
}
```

13.3 Stacks

A **stack** is a special type of list in which objects can be added and removed only from the top of the list. Therefore, it's a **last-in, first-out (LIFO) list**—that is, a LIFO list in which the last item added to the list is the first item that can be removed. An example of this type of operation is a stack of dishes in a cafeteria; the last dish placed on top of the stack is the first dish removed. Another example is the inbox on a desk, where the last paper placed in the inbox is typically the first one removed. In programming, stacks are used in all function calls to store and retrieve data to and from the function. As a stack example, Figure 13.6 shows an existing list of three last names. The top name on this list is Barney.

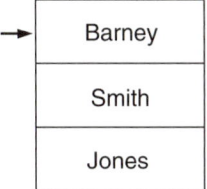

Figure 13.6 A list of names

If you restrict access to the list so that names can be added and removed only from the top of the list, the list becomes a stack, so you must designate which end of the list is the top and which is the bottom. Because the name Barney is physically placed above the other names, it's considered the top of the list. The arrow in the figure is used to indicate the top of the list.

Figure 13.7 (which consists of six parts, labeled a through f) illustrates how the stack expands and contracts as names are added and deleted. For example, in part b, the name Ventura has been added to the list. By part c, a total of two new names have been added, and the top of the list has changed accordingly. By removing the top name, Lanfrank, from the list in part c, the stack then shrinks to what's shown in part d, where Ventura is now at the top of the stack. As names continue to be removed from the list (parts e and f), the stack continues to contract.

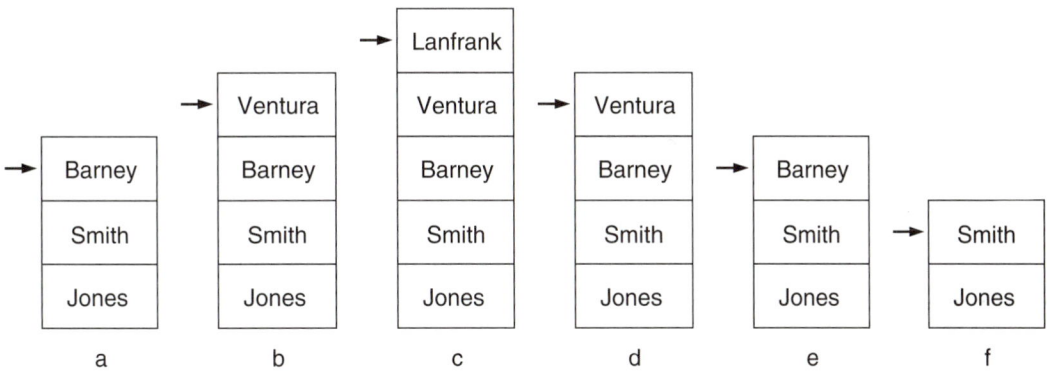

Figure 13.7 An expanding and contracting list of names

> ## Point of Information
>
> ### Dr. Lukasiewicz and RPN
>
> Dr. Jan Lukasiewicz, born in 1878, studied and taught mathematics at the University of Lvov in Poland before becoming a respected professor at the University of Warsaw. He was appointed to the post of Minister of Education in Poland in 1919 and, with Stanislaw Lesniewski, founded the Warsaw School of Logic. After World War II, Dr. Lukasiewicz and his wife, Regina, were exiled in Belgium. When he was offered a professorship at the Royal Academy in Dublin, they moved to Ireland, where they remained until his death in 1956.
>
> In 1951, Dr. Lukasiewicz developed a new set of postfix algebraic notation, which was critical in the design of early microprocessors in the 1960s and 1970s. The actual implementation of postfix algebra was done by using stack arithmetic, in which data was pushed on a stack and popped off when an operation needed to be performed. These stack-handling instructions required no address operands and made it possible for very small computers to handle large tasks effectively.
>
> Stack arithmetic, which is based on Dr. Lukasiewicz's work, reverses the more commonly known prefix algebra and became known as Reverse Polish Notation (RPN). Early pocket calculators developed by Hewlett-Packard Corporation were especially notable for their use of RPN and made stack arithmetic the favorite of many scientists and engineers.

Although Figure 13.7 is an accurate representation of a list of names, it contains additional information that a true stack object doesn't provide. When names are added to or removed from a stack, no count is kept of how many names have been added or deleted or of how many items the stack contains at any time. For example, by examining each part of Figure 13.7, you can determine how many names are on the list. In a true stack, the only item that can be seen and accessed is the top one on the list. Finding out how many items the list contains would require removing the top item continually until no more items exist.

Stack Implementation with the deque Class

Creating a stack requires the following four components:

- A container for holding items in the list
- A method of designating the current top stack item
- An operation for placing a new item on the stack
- An operation for removing an item from the stack

By convention, the operation of placing a new item on the top of a stack is called a **push**, and the operation of removing an item from a stack is called a **pop**. How these operations are implemented depends on the container type used to represent a stack. In C++, a stack can be created easily with STL's deque class. This class creates a double-ended list, where objects can be pushed and popped from either end. To create a stack, only the front end of the deque is used. Table 13.4 summarizes the deque class's methods and operations.

Table 13.4 Summary of `deque` Class Methods and Operations

Methods and Operations	Type	Description
`deque<DataType> name`	constructor	Creates an empty deque named `name` with a compiler-dependent initial size
`deque<DataType> name(source)`	constructor	Creates a copy of the source deque
`deque<DataType> name(n)`	constructor	Creates a deque of size n
`deque<DataType> name(n, object)`	constructor	Creates a deque of size n with each object initialized as `object`
`deque<DataType> name(src.beg,src.end)`	constructor	Creates a deque initialized with objects from a source container beginning at `src.beg` and ending at `src.end`
`~deque(DataType>()`	destructor	Destroys the deque and all objects it contains
`name.at(index)`	accessor	Returns the object at `index` and throws an exception if the index is out of bounds
`name.front()`	accessor	Returns the first object at the front of the deque with no check for the existence of a first object
`name.pop_front()`	mutator	Removes but does not return the first object at the front of the deque
`name.push_front(object)`	mutator	Inserts object at the front of the deque
`name.back()`	accessor	Returns the object at the back of the deque with no check for the existence of a last object
`name.pop_back()`	mutator	Removes but does not return the last object at the back of the deque
`name.push_back(object)`	mutator	Inserts object at the back of the deque
`name.insert(itr, object)`	mutator	Inserts object at iterator position `itr`
`name.insert(itr, src.beg, src.end)`	mutator	Inserts object at iterator position `itr`

Table 13.4 Summary of `deque` Class Methods and Operations (*continued*)

Methods and Operations	Type	Description
`name.insert(itr, n, object)`	mutator	Inserts *n* copies of object at iterator position `itr`
`name2.assign(n, object)`	mutator	Assigns *n* copies of object
`name2.(src.begin, src.end)`	mutator	Assigns objects of the `src` container (need not be a deque) between the range `src.begin` and `src.end` to `name2`
`name.erase(pos)`	mutator	Removes the object at the specified position `pos`
`name.erase(begin, end)`	mutator	Removes objects within the specified range
`name.resize(value)`	mutator	Resizes the deque larger with new objects instantiated by using the default constructor
`name.resize(value, object)`	mutator	Resizes the deque larger with new objects instantiated as `object`
`name.clear()`	mutator	Removes all objects from the deque
`name.swap(nameB)`	mutator	Swaps objects of `name` and `nameB` deques; can be performed by using the `swap()` algorithm
`name.begin()`	accessor	Returns an iterator to the first object in the deque
`name.end()`	accessor	Returns an iterator to the position after the last object in the deque
`name.rbegin()`	accessor	Returns a reverse iterator to the first object in the deque
`name.rend()`	accessor	Returns a reverse iterator to the position after the last object in the deque
`nameA == nameB`	relational	Returns a Boolean `true` if all `nameA` objects equal `nameB` objects; otherwise, `returns false`

Table 13.4 Summary of deque Class Methods and Operations (*continued*)

Methods and Operations	Type	Description
`nameA != nameB`	relational	Returns a Boolean `false` if all `nameA` objects equal `nameB` objects; otherwise, returns `true`; same as `!(nameA == nameB)`
`nameA < nameB`	relational	Returns a Boolean `true` if `nameA` is less than `nameB`; otherwise, returns `false`
`nameA > nameB`	relational	Returns a Boolean `true` if `nameA` is greater than `nameB`; otherwise, returns `false`; same as `nameB < nameA`
`nameA <= nameB`	relational	Returns a Boolean `true` if `nameA` is less than or equal to `nameB`
`nameA >= nameB`	relational	Returns a Boolean `true` if `nameA` is greater than or equal to `nameB`
`name.size()`	capacity	Returns number of objects in the deque as an integer
`name.empty()`	capacity	Returns a Boolean `true` if deque is empty; otherwise, returns `false`
`name.max_size()`	capacity	Returns the maximum possible objects as an integer
`name.capacity()`	capacity	Returns the maximum possible objects as an integer without relocating the deque

Program 13.3 uses the `deque` class to implement a stack. This program is straightforward in that only one stack is instantiated, and user-entered names are pushed to the front of the deque until the sentinel value of x is entered. At detection of this sentinel string value, names are popped from the front of the deque as long as the deque isn't empty.

Point of Information

Stacking the Deque

Stacks and queues are two special forms of a more general data object called a **deque** (stands for "double-ended queue" and is pronounced "deck"). In a deque object, data can be handled in one of four ways:

1. Insert at the beginning and remove from the beginning, which is a last-in, first-out (LIFO) stack.
2. Insert at the beginning and remove from the end, which is a first-in, first-out (FIFO) queue.
3. Insert at the end and remove from the end, which represents an inverted LIFO technique.
4. Insert at the end and remove from the beginning, which represents an inverted FIFO queue.

Implementation 1 (a stack object) is discussed in this section, and implementation 2 (a queue object) is covered in the next section. Implementations 3 and 4 are sometimes used for keeping track of memory addresses, as when programming is done in machine language or when objects are handled in a file. When a high-level language, such as C++, manages the data area automatically, users might not be aware of where data is being stored or which type of deque is being applied.

Program 13.3

```cpp
#include <iostream>
#include <deque>
#include <string>
#include <cctype>
using namespace std;

int main()
{
  string name;
  deque<string> stack;

  cout << "Enter as many names as you want, one per line" << endl;
  cout << "To stop enter a single x" << endl;
  while(true)
  {
    cout << "Enter a name (or x to stop): ";
    getline(cin, name);
    if (tolower(name.at(0)) == 'x') break;
    stack.push_front(name);
  }
```

```
cout << "\nThe names in the stack are:\n";

// pop names from the stack
while(!stack.empty())
{
   name = stack.front();   // retrieve the name
   stack.pop_front();      // pop name from the stack
   cout << name << endl;
}
return 0;
}
```

Following is a sample run of Program 13.3:

```
Enter as many names as you want, one per line
 To stop enter a single x
Enter a name (or x to stop): Jane Jones
Enter a name (or x to stop): Bill Smith
Enter a name (or x to stop): Jim Robinson
Enter a name (or x to stop): x

The names in the stack are:
Jim Robinson
Bill Smith
Jane Jones
```

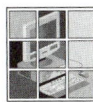

EXERCISES 13.3

1. **(Review)** State whether a stack is appropriate for each of the following tasks, and indicate why or why not:

   a. A word-processing program must remember a line of up to 80 characters. Pressing the Backspace key deletes the previous character, and pressing Ctrl+Backspace deletes the entire line. Users must be able to undo deletion operations.

   b. Customers must wait one to three months for delivery of their new cars. The dealer creates a list to determine the "fair" order in which customers should get their cars; the list is prepared in the order in which customers placed their requests for a new car.

   c. You're required to search downward in a pile of magazines to locate the issue for last January. Each magazine was placed on the pile as soon as it was received.

   d. A programming team accepts jobs and prioritizes them on the basis of urgency.

   e. A line forms at a bus stop.

2. **(Practice)** Enter and run Program 13.3.

3. **(Modify)** Modify Program 13.3 to implement a stack of integers rather than a stack of strings.

4. **(Modify)** Modify Program 13.3 to instantiate three stacks of digits named `digits1`, `digits2`, and `digits3`. Initialize `digits1` to contain the digits 9, 8, 5, and 2, which is the number 2589 in reverse order. Similarly, the `digits2` stack should be initialized to contain the digits 3, 1, 5, and 7, which is the number 7513 in reverse order. Calculate and place the sum of these two numbers in the `digits3` stack. This sum should be obtained by popping objects from `digits1` and `digits2` and adding them together with a variable named `carry`, which is initialized to 0. If the sum of the two popped objects and `carry` doesn't exceed 10, the sum should be pushed onto `digits3` and `carry` should be set to 0; otherwise, `carry` should be set to 1, and the units digit of the sum should be pushed onto the `digits3` stack.

5. **(Program)** Write a C++ program that allows a user to enter a maximum of 100 integers in a stack object. Then have the program do the following:
   a. Reverse the stack's contents into a second stack of integers.
   b. Using two additional stacks, reverse the contents in the original stack. For example, if the original stack contains the integers 1, 2, 3, and 4, it should contain the integers 4, 3, 2, and 1 at the end of the program.

6. **(Program)** Write a C++ program that allows a user to enter a maximum of 50 characters in a stack object. Then have the program sort the stack contents in increasing order. For example, if the stack's contents are initially D, E, A, and B, its final contents are A, B, D, and E.

13.4 Queues

A **queue** (pronounced "cue") is a list in which items are added to one end of the list, called the top, and removed from the other end of the list, called the bottom. This arrangement ensures that items are removed from the list in the exact order in which they were entered. This means the first item placed on the list is the first item to be removed, the second item placed on the list is the second item to be removed, and so on. Therefore, a queue is a **first-in, first-out (FIFO) list**—a list in which the first item added to the list is the first item that can be removed.

As an example of a queue, think of a list of people waiting to purchase season tickets to a professional football team. The first person on the list should be called when the first set of tickets becomes available, the second person should be called for the second available set, and so on. Figure 13.8 shows the names of people currently on the list.

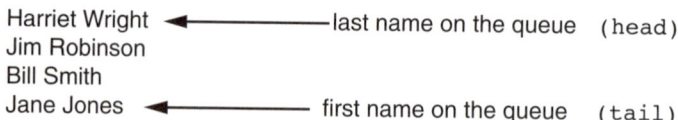

Figure 13.8   A queue with its pointers

The names have been added in the same fashion as on a stack: As new names are added to the list, they're stacked on top of existing names. The difference in a queue relates to how the names are popped off the list. Clearly, the people on this list expect to be serviced in the order they were placed on the list—that is, first in, first out. Therefore, unlike a stack, the name added to the list most recently is *not* the first name removed. Rather, the oldest name still on the list is always the first name removed.

Point of Information

Artificial Intelligence

A major step toward creating programs that "learn" as they work is the development of dynamic data objects. In 1950, Alan Turing proposed a test in which an expert enters questions at an isolated terminal. Presumably, artificial intelligence (AI) is achieved when the expert can't discern whether the answers displayed onscreen have been produced by a human or a machine. Although there are problems with the Turing test, its concepts have spawned numerous research efforts.

By the mid-1960s, many AI researchers believed the efforts to create "thinking machines" were futile. Today, however, much lively research and development focus on topics such as dynamic problem solving, computer vision, parallel processing, natural language processing, and speech and pattern recognition—all of which are encompassed in the field of AI.

Techniques that allow machines to emulate humans have proliferated in recent years, concurrent with smaller, faster, more powerful, and cheaper computers. Most people agree that computers could never replace all human decision making. There's also general agreement that society must remain alert and in control of important decisions that require human compassion, ethics, and understanding.

To keep the list in the correct order, with new names added to one end of the list and old names removed from the other end, using two link variables is convenient: one that locates the front of the list for the next person to be serviced and one that locates the end of the list where new people will be added. The link variable that locates the front of the list where the next name is to be removed is referred to as the **tail pointer** (or tail, for short). The second link variable, which locates the last person in the list and indicates where the next person entering the list is to be placed, is called the **head pointer** (or head, for short). For the list in Figure 13.8, the tail points to Jane Jones, and the head points to Harriet Wright. If Jane Jones were removed from the list and Lou Hazlet and Teresa Filer were added, the queue and its associated position indicators would look like Figure 13.9.

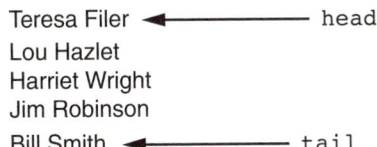

Figure 13.9   The updated queue pointers

Queue Implementation with the deque Class

A queue can be derived easily by using the STL deque class. The operation of placing a new item on a queue is formally referred to as **enqueuing** and casually called a "push operation," and removing an item from a queue is formally referred to as **serving** and casually called a "pop operation." Operationally, enqueuing is similar to pushing on one end of a stack, and serving is similar to popping from the other end of a stack. How these operations are implemented depends on the list used to represent a queue. Because you're using the deque class as the base class, you can easily create push and pop operations by using the deque class's push_front() and pop_back() methods (see Table 13.4).

Program 13.4 shows using the deque class to construct a queue in the context of a complete program, where names are pushed onto the front of the deque and popped from the back. This process creates the FIFO ordering that characterizes a queue.

Program 13.4

```
#include <iostream>
#include <deque>
#include <string>
#include <cctype>
using namespace std;
int main()
{
  string name;
  deque<string> queue;

  cout << "Enter as many names as you want, one per line" << endl;
  cout << " To stop enter a single x" << endl;

  // push names onto the queue
  while(true)
  {
     cout << "Enter a name (or x to stop): ";
     getline(cin, name);
     if (tolower(name.at(0)) == 'x') break;
     queue.push_front(name);
  }

  cout << "\nThe names in the queue are:\n";

  // pop names from the queue
  while(!queue.empty())
  {
    name = queue.back();  // retrieve the name
    queue.pop_back();     // pop a name from the queue
    cout << name << endl;
  }
  return 0;
}
```

A sample run of Program 13.4 produced the following:

```
Enter as many names as you want, one per line
 To stop enter a single x
Enter a name (or x to stop): Jane Jones
Enter a name (or x to stop): Bill Smith
Enter a name (or x to stop): Jim Robinson
Enter a name (or x to stop): x

The names in the queue are:
Jane Jones
Bill Smith
Jim Robinson
```

EXERCISES 13.4

1. **(Review)** State whether a queue, a stack, or neither object is appropriate for each of the following tasks, and indicate why or why not:
   a. A list of customers waiting to be seated in a restaurant
   b. A group of student tests waiting to be graded
   c. An address book listing names and phone numbers in alphabetical order
   d. Patients waiting for examinations in a doctor's office

2. **(Practice)** Enter and run Program 13.4.

3. **(Modify)** Modify Program 13.4 to use a queue of integers rather than a queue of strings.

4. **(Program)** Write a C++ program that allows a user to enter a maximum of 20 characters in a queue. Then have the program sort the queue contents in increasing order. For example, if the queue's contents are initially D, E, A, and B, its final contents are A, B, D, and E.

5. **(Program)** Write a queue program that accepts an object consisting of an integer ID number and a double-precision hourly pay rate.

6. **(Modify)** Add a menu method to Program 13.4 that gives the user a choice of adding a name to the queue, removing a name from the queue, or listing the queue's contents without removing any objects from it.

7. **(Program)** A group of people have arrived at a bus stop and are lined up in this order:

1. Chaplin	4. Laurel	7. Oliver	10. Garland
2. West	5. Smith	8. Hardy	11. Wayne
3. Taylor	6. Grisby	9. Burton	12. Stewart

   Read the names from an input file into a queue and display the order in which passengers board the bus.

13.5 Common Programming Errors

There are two common programming errors related to using STL's `list` and `deque` classes:

1. Inserting objects instantiated from different classes into the same list
2. Attempting to use indexes rather than iterators when using STL class methods and algorithms

The five most common programming errors related to linked lists, stacks, and queues that occur when programmers attempt to construct their own lists are as follows:

1. Not checking the pointer provided by the `new` operator when constructing a non-STL list. If this operator returns a `NULL` value, the user should be notified that the allocation didn't take place, and normal program operation must be altered appropriately. You simply can't assume that all calls to `new` will result in the requested allocation of memory space being successful.
2. Not updating all relevant pointer addresses correctly when adding or removing records from dynamically created stacks and queues. Unless extreme care is taken in updating all addresses, these dynamic data structures can become corrupted quickly.
3. Forgetting to free previously allocated memory space when the space is no longer needed. This error is typically a problem only in a large application program that's expected to run continuously and can make many requests for allocated space based on user demand.
4. Not preserving the integrity of addresses in the top-of-stack pointer when dealing with a stack and the queue-in and queue-out pointers when dealing with a queue. As these pointers locate a starting position in their data structures, the complete list will be lost if the starting addresses are incorrect.
5. Not updating internal record pointers correctly when inserting and removing records from a stack or queue. After an internal pointer in these lists contains an incorrect address, it's almost impossible to locate and reestablish the missing set of objects.

13.6 Chapter Summary

1. An object allows storing data items under a common variable name. These objects can then be stored together in a list.

2. A linked list is a list of objects in which each object contains a pointer variable that locates the next object in the list. Each linked list must have a pointer to locate the first object in the list. The last object's pointer variable is set to `NULL` to indicate the end of the list.

3. Linked lists can be constructed automatically by using the STL's `list` class.

4. A stack is a list consisting of objects that can be added and removed only from the top of the list. This object is a LIFO (last-in, first-out) list, which means the last object added to the list is the first object removed. Stacks can be implemented with STL's `deque` class.

5. A queue is a list consisting of objects that are added to the top of the list and removed from the bottom of the list. This object is a FIFO (first-in, first-out) list, which means objects are removed in the order in which they were added. Queues can be implemented with STL's `deque` class.

Part Three

Additional Topics

Chapter

14

The string Class and Exception Handling

Manipulating strings stored as a one-dimensional array of characters terminated with the null character (referred to as C-strings), as done in Section 7.2, can be time consuming. This is especially true for applications requiring numerous string operations, such as inserting, searching, and/or deleting characters in an existing string. The reason is that each time a string is lengthened by adding characters, a new and larger array must be created, and removing characters requires shifting characters to fill the empty spaces left by deleted characters, with adjustment of the end-of-string null character. Searching for specific characters in a string requires nested loops.

To circumvent the coding required for these types of operations, C++ provides the `string` class as part of the standard C++ library. This class provides an expanded set of class functions, including easy insertion and removal of characters from a string, automatic string expansion when a string's original capacity is exceeded, string contraction when characters are removed from a string, and range checking to detect invalid character positions. In many ways, the strings created from the `string` class can also be manipulated by using the array techniques suitable for C-strings. The main difference is that `string` class strings aren't terminated with a null character, and the `string` class provides many useful functions for operating on strings.

Exception handling is a means of error detection and processing that has gained increasing acceptance in programming technology. It permits detecting an error at the point in the code where the error has *occurred and provides a means of processing the error and returning control to the line that generated the error. As you also see, although error detection and code correction are possible by using if statements and functions, exception handling is one more useful programming tool for validating user input. Both the string class and exception handling are discussed in this chapter.*

14.1 The string Class

The programs in this book have used the istream class's cout object extensively for displaying output, but you haven't investigated this class in detail or learned how the cout object is created. An advantage of object-oriented programming languages, however, is that you can use thoroughly tested classes without knowing how the class is constructed. In this section, you use another class provided by C++'s standard library: the string class. However, you're going to create objects from the class before using them instead of using an existing object, such as cout.

As discussed in Chapter 10, a class is a user-created data type. Like built-in data types, a class defines a valid set of data values and a set of operations that can be used on them. The difference between a user-created class and a built-in data type is how the class is constructed. A built-in data type is provided as an integral part of the compiler, and a class is constructed by a programmer using a programming language's code. Other than that and the terminology used, the two data types are used in much the same manner. The key difference in terminology is that storage areas for built-in data types are referred to as variables, whereas storage areas declared for a class are referred to as objects.

The values the string class permits are referred to as string literals. As you've seen, a **string literal** is any sequence of characters enclosed in quotation marks. It's also referred to as a string value, a string constant, and, more conventionally, a string. Examples of strings are "This is a string", "Hello World!", and "xyz 123 *!#@&". The quotation marks indicate the beginning and ending points of the string and are never stored with the string. As you learned in Section 7.2, when a string literal is used to initialize a character array, the null character, '\0', is appended to the string; this isn't the case with string objects created from the string class. However, string objects can be accessed by using array notation, although there's rarely any need to do so because of the extensive set of string operations available with the string class.

Figure 14.1 shows the programming representation of the string Hello when this string is created as an object of the string class. By convention, the first character in a string is always designated as position 0. This position value is also referred to as the character's **index value** or its **offset value**.

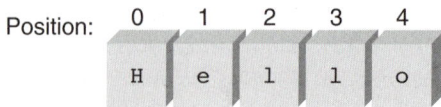

Figure 14.1   Storing a string as a sequence of characters

`string` Class Functions

The `string` class provides a number of functions for declaring, creating, and initializing a string. In C++, the process of creating a new object is referred to as **instantiating an object**, which in this case becomes instantiating a string object, or creating a string, for short. Table 14.1 lists the functions the `string` class provides for creating and initializing a string object. In class terminology, functions are formally referred to as methods, and the methods that perform the tasks of creating and initializing are called **constructor methods**, or just **constructors**.

Table 14.1 `string` Class Constructors (Require the Header File `string`)

Constructor	Description	Examples

`string objectName = value`	Creates and initializes a string object to a value that can be a string literal, a previously declared string object, or an expression containing string literals and string objects	`string str1 = "Good Morning";`
		`string str2 = str1;`
		`string str3 = str1 + str2;`

`string objectName(stringValue)`	Produces the same initialization as the preceding item	`string str1("Hot");` `string str1(str1 + " Dog");`
`string objectName(str, n)`	Creates and initializes a string object with a substring of string object `str`, starting at index position `n` of `str`	`string str1(str2, 5);` If `str2` contains the string Good Morning, `str1` becomes the string Morning
`string objectName(str, n, p)`	Creates and initializes a string object with a substring of string object `str`, starting at index position `n` of `str` and containing `p` characters	`string str1(str2, 5,2);` If `str2` contains the string Good Morning, `str1` becomes the string Mo
`string objectName(n, char)`	Creates and initializes a string object with `n` copies of `char`	`string str1(5,'*');` This makes `str1` = "*****"
`string objectName`	Creates and initializes a string object to represent an empty character sequence (same as `string objectName = "";`, so the string's length is 0)	`string message;`

Program 14.1 shows examples of each constructor the `string` class provides.

Program 14.1

```cpp
#include <iostream>
#include <string>
using namespace std;

int main()
{
  // Seven ways to instantiate (create) a string object
  string str1; // create an empty string named str1
  string str2("Good Morning");
  string str3 = "Hot Dog";
  string str4(str3);
  string str5(str4, 4);
  string str6 = "linear";
  string str7(str6, 3, 3);

  cout << "str1 is: " << str1 << endl;
  cout << "str2 is: " << str2 << endl;
  cout << "str3 is: " << str3 << endl;
  cout << "str4 is: " << str4 << endl;
  cout << "str5 is: " << str5 << endl;
  cout << "str6 is: " << str6 << endl;
  cout << "str7 is: " << str7 << endl;

  return 0;
}
```

In reviewing Program 14.1, notice that the `string` library is included with the `#include <string>` statement. Inside `main()`, objects are created in a similar manner as declaring variables, but instead of using built-in data types, such as `int` or `double`, the keyword `string` is used. Each string, except the first one (`str1`), has also been initialized explicitly. Because no explicit string is used to initialize `str1`, it's initialized automatically with no characters at all. These strings are referred to as "empty strings." Here's the output created by Program 14.1:

```
str1 is:
str2 is: Good Morning
str3 is: Hot Dog
str4 is: Hot Dog
str5 is: Dog
str6 is: linear
str7 is: ear
```

This output is straightforward; str1 is an empty string consisting of no characters, and the other strings display the characters they were initialized with. Because the first character in a string is designated as position 0, not 1, the character position of D in the string Hot Dog, for example, is position 4, as shown in Figure 14.2.

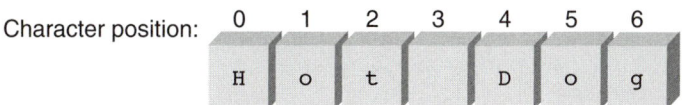

Figure 14.2 The character positions of the string Hot Dog

String Input and Output

In addition to a string being initialized with the constructors listed in Table 14.1, strings can be input from the keyboard and displayed onscreen. Table 14.2 lists the basic methods and objects for input and output of string values.

Table 14.2 string Class Input and Output

C++ Object or Method	Description
cout	General-purpose screen output object
cin	General-purpose keyboard input object that stops reading string input when white space is encountered
getline(cin, strObj)	General-purpose keyboard input method that inputs all characters entered, stores them in the string strObj, and stops accepting characters when it receives a newline character (\n)

In addition to the standard cout and cin streams you have been using throughout this book, the string class provides the getline() method for string input. For example, the expression getline(cin, message) continuously accepts and stores characters typed at the keyboard until the Enter key is pressed. Pressing the Enter key generates a newline character, '\n', which getline() interprets as the end-of-line entry. All the characters encountered by getline(), except the newline character, are stored in the string message, as shown in Figure 14.3.

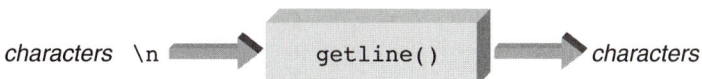

Figure 14.3 Inputting a string with getline()

Program 14.2 shows using the getline() method and cout stream to input and output a string that's entered at the user's keyboard. Although cout is used in this program for string output, cin generally can't be used in place of getline() for string input because cin reads a set of characters up to a blank space or a newline character. Therefore, attempting to enter the characters This is a string by using the statement cin >> message; results in only the word This being assigned to message. Because a blank space terminates a cin extraction operation, cin's usefulness for entering string data is restricted; therefore, getline() is used.

Program 14.2

```
#include <iostream>
#include <string>
using namespace std;

int main()
{
  string message;     // declare a string object

  cout << "Enter a string:\n";

  getline(cin, message);

  cout << "The string just entered is:\n"
       << message << endl;

  return 0;
}
```

The following is a sample run of Program 14.2:

```
Enter a string:
This is a test input of a string of characters.
The string just entered is:
This is a test input of a string of characters.
```

In its most general form, the getline() method has the following syntax:

getline(cin, *strObj*, *terminatingChar*)

In this syntax, *strObj* is a string object name and *terminatingChar* is an optional character constant, or variable, specifying the terminating character. For example, the expression getline(cin, message, '!') accepts all characters entered at the keyboard, including a newline character, until an exclamation point is entered. The exclamation point isn't stored as part of the string.

If the optional third argument, *terminatingChar*, is omitted when getline() is called, the default terminating character is the newline ('\n') character. Therefore, the statement getline(cin,message,'\n'); can be used in place of the statement getline (cin, message);. Both these statements stop reading characters when the Enter key is pressed. In all the programs used from this point on, input is terminated by pressing the Enter key, which generates a newline character. For this reason, the optional third argument passed to getline(), which is the terminating character, is omitted.

Caution: The Phantom Newline Character   Seemingly strange results can happen when the cin input stream and getline() method are used together to accept data or when cin is used by itself to accept characters. To see how this result can occur, take a look at Program 14.3, which uses cin to accept an integer entered at the keyboard. The integer is then stored in the variable value, and a getline() method call follows.

Program 14.3

```
#include <iostream>
#include <string>
using namespace std;

int main()
{
  int value;
  string message;

  cout << "Enter a number: ";
  cin  >> value;
  cout << "The number entered is:\n"
       << value << endl;

  cout << "Enter text:\n";
  getline(cin, message);
  cout << "The text entered is:\n"
       << message << endl;
  cout << int(message.length());

  return 0;
}
```

When Program 14.3 runs, the number entered in response to the prompt Enter a number: is stored in the variable value. At this point, everything seems to be working fine. Notice, however, that in entering a number, you type the number and press the Enter key. On almost all computer systems, this entered data is stored in a temporary holding area called a **buffer** immediately after the characters are entered, as shown in Figure 14.4.

Point of Information

The string and char Data Types

A string can consist of zero, one, or more characters. When the string has no characters, it's said to be an **empty string** with a length of 0. A string with a single character, such as "a", is a string of length 1 and is stored differently from a char data type, such as 'a'. However, for many practical purposes, a string of length 1 and a char respond in the same manner; for example, both cout >> "\n" and cout >> '\n' produce a new line onscreen. It's important to understand that they're different data types. For example, both these declarations

```
string sl = 'a';   // INVALID INITIALIZATION
char key = "\n";   // INVALID INITIALIZATION
```

produce a compiler error because they attempt to initialize one data type with literal values of another type.

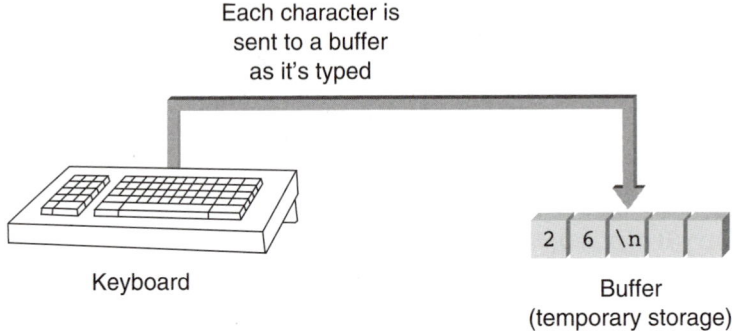

Figure 14.4 Typed characters are first stored in a buffer

The cin input stream in Program 14.3 accepts the number entered but leaves the '\n' in the buffer. The next input statement, which is a call to getline(), picks up the code for the Enter key as the next character and terminates any further input. Following is a sample run of Program 14.3:

```
Enter a number: 26
The number entered is 26
Enter text:
The text entered is
```

In this output, no text is accepted in response to the prompt Enter text:. No text is accepted because after the program accepts the number 26, the code for the Enter key, which is a newline escape sequence, remains in the buffer and is picked up and interpreted by getline() as the end of its input. This result occurs whether an integer (as in Program 14.3), a string, or any other input is accepted by cin and then followed by a getline() method call. There are three solutions to this "phantom" Enter key problem:

- Don't mix cin with getline() inputs in the same program.
- Follow the cin input with the call to cin.ignore().
- Accept the Enter key in a character variable and then ignore it.

The first solution is preferred. All solutions, however, center on the fact that the Enter key is a legitimate character input and must be recognized as such. You encounter this problem again when you learn about accepting char data types in Section 14.2.

String Processing

Strings can be manipulated by using string class functions or the character-at-a-time functions described in Section 14.2. Table 14.3 lists the most commonly used string class methods plus the standard arithmetic and comparison operators that can also be used with strings. In the examples, class methods are called by giving the object's name first, followed by a period, and then the method's name. With a few notable exceptions, all class methods are called in this way.

Table 14.3 The string Class Processing Methods (Require #include <string>)

Method/Operation	Description	Example
int length()	Returns the length of the string	string.length()
int size()	Same as the preceding item	string.size()
at(index)	Returns the character at the specified index and throws an exception if the index is nonexistent	string.at(4)
int compare(str)	Compares the given string with str; returns a negative value if the given string is less than str, a 0 if they're equal, and a positive value if the given string is greater than str	string1.compare(string2)
c_str()	Returns the string as a NULL-terminated C-string	string1.c_str()
bool empty	Returns true if the string is empty; otherwise, returns false	string1.empty()
erase(ind,n);	Removes n characters from the string, starting at index ind	string1.erase(2,3)
erase(ind)	Removes all characters from the string, starting from index ind until the end of the string, and the length of the remaining string becomes ind	string1.erase(4)

Table 14.3 The string Class Processing Methods (Require #include <string>) (continued)

`int find(str)`	Returns the index of the first occurrence of str in the string	`string1.find("the")`
`int find(str, ind)`	Returns the index of the first occurrence of str in the string, with the search beginning at index ind	`string1.find("the",5)`
`int find_first_of (str, ind)`	Returns the index of the first occurrence of any character in str in the string, with the search starting at index ind	`string1.find_first_of ("lt",6)`
`int find_first_not_ of(str, ind)`	Returns the index of the first occurrence of any character *not* in str in the string, with the search starting at index ind	`string1.find_first_not_of("lt",6)`
`void insert (ind, str)`	Inserts the string str into the string, starting at index ind	`string.insert(4, "there")`
`void replace(ind, n, str)`	Removes *n* characters in the string object, starting at index position ind, and inserts the string str at index position ind	`string1.replace(2,4, "okay")`
`string substr(ind,n)`	Returns a string consisting of *n* characters extracted from the string, starting at index ind; if *n* is greater than the remaining number of characters, the rest of the string is used	`string2 = string1.substr(0,10)`
`void swap(str)`	Swaps characters in str with those in the first string	`string1.swap(string2)`
`string[ind]` (*Note*: This is standard array notation.)	Returns the character at index ind, without checking whether ind is a valid index	`string1[5]`
`=`	Assignment (also converts a C-string to a string)	`string1 = string`
`+`	Concatenates two strings	`string1 + string2`
`+=`	Concatenation and assignment	`string2 += string1`

`== !=`
 `< <=`
 `> >=`
	Relational operators Return true if the relation is satisfied; otherwise, return false	`string1 == string2`
		 `string1 <= string2`
		 `string1 > string2`

One of the most commonly used methods in Table 14.3 is `length()`. It returns the number of characters in the string, which is referred to as the string's length. For example, the value returned by the method call `"Hello World!".length()` is 12. As always, the quotation marks surrounding a string value aren't considered part of the string. Similarly, if the string referenced by `string1` contains the value `"Have a good day."`, the value returned by the call `string1.length()` is 16.

Two string expressions can be compared for equality by using the standard relational operators. Each character in a string is stored in binary with the ASCII or Unicode code. Although these codes are different, they have some characteristics in common. In both, a blank precedes (is less than) all letters and numbers, letters of the alphabet are stored in order from A to Z, and digits are stored in order from 0 to 9. In addition, digits come before (that is, are less than) uppercase characters, which are followed by lowercase characters. Therefore, uppercase characters are mathematically less than lowercase characters.

When two strings are compared, their characters are compared a pair at a time (both first characters, then both second characters, and so on). If no differences are found, the strings are equal; if a difference is found, the string with the first lower character is considered the smaller string, as shown in these examples:

- `"Hello"` is greater than `"Good Bye"` because the H in `Hello` is greater than the G in `Good Bye`.
- `"Hello"` is less than `"hello"` because the H in `Hello` is less than the h in `hello`.
- `"SMITH"` is greater than `"JONES"` because the S in `SMITH` is greater than the J in `JONES`.
- `"123"` is greater than `"1227"` because the third character in `123`, the 3, is greater than the third character in `1227`, the 2.
- `"Behop"` is greater than `"Beehive"` because the third character in `Behop`, the h, is greater than the third character in `Beehive`, the e.

Program 14.4 uses `length()` and several relational expressions in the context of a complete program.

Program 14.4

```
#include <iostream>
#include <string>
using namespace std;

int main()
{
  string string1 = "Hello";
  string string2 = "Hello there";

  cout << "string1 is the string: " <<  string1 << endl;
  cout << "The number of characters in string1 is "
```

```
              <<  int(string1.length()) << endl << endl;
    cout << "string2 is the string: " <<  string2 << endl;
    cout << "The number of characters in string2 is "
              << int(string2.length()) << endl << endl;
    if (string1 < string2)
       cout << string1 <<  " is less than " <<  string2 << endl << endl;
    else if (string1 == string2)
       cout << string1 <<  " is equal to " <<  string2 << endl << endl;
    else
       cout << string1 <<  " is greater than " <<  string2 << endl << endl;

    string1 = string1 + " there world!";
    cout << "After concatenation, string1 contains the characters: "
              << string1 << endl;
    cout << "The length of this string is " <<  int(string1.length()) << endl;

    return 0;
}
```

Following is a sample output produced by Program 14.4:

```
string1 is the string: Hello
The number of characters in string1 is 5

string2 is the string: Hello there
The number of characters in string2 is 11

Hello is less than Hello there

After concatenation, string1 contains the characters: Hello there world!
The length of this string is 18
```

When reviewing this output, refer to Figure 14.5, which shows how the characters in string1 and string2 are stored in memory. The length of each string refers to the total number of characters in the string, and the first character in each string is located at index position 0. Therefore, the length of a string is always 1 more than the index number of the last character's position in the string.

Although you use the concatenation operator and length() method most often, at times you'll find the other string methods described in Table 14.3 useful. One of the most useful is the at() method, which enables you to retrieve separate characters in a string. Program 14.5 uses this method to select one character at a time from the string, starting at string position 0 and ending at the index of the last character in the string. This last index value is always 1 less than the number of characters (that is, the string's length) in the string.

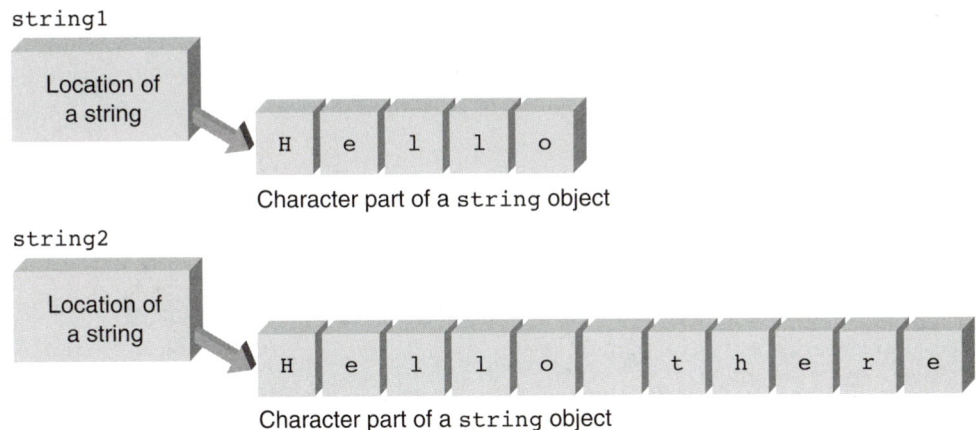

string1

Location of a string

H　e　l　l　o

Character part of a `string` object

string2

Location of a string

H　e　l　l　o　t　h　e　r　e

Character part of a `string` object

Figure 14.5　The initial strings used in Program 14.4

Program 14.5

```cpp
#include <iostream>
#include <string>
using namespace std;

int main()
{
  string str = "Counting the number of vowels";
  int i, numChars;
  int vowelCount = 0;

  cout << "The string: " <<  str << endl;
  numChars = int(str.length());
  for (i = 0; i < numChars; i++)
  {
    switch(str.at(i))    // here's where a character is retrieved
    {
      case 'a':
      case 'e':
      case 'i':
      case 'o':
      case 'u':
        vowelCount++;
    }
  }
  cout << "has " <<  vowelCount <<  " vowels." << endl;
  return 0;
}
```

The expression `str.at(i)` in the `switch` statement retrieves the character at position `i` in the string. This character is then compared with five different character values. The `switch` statement uses the fact that selected cases "drop through" in the absence of `break` statements. Therefore, all selected cases result in an increment to `vowelCount`. Program 14.5 displays the following output:

```
The string: Counting the number of vowels
has 9 vowels.
```

As an example of inserting and replacing characters in a string with the methods listed in Table 14.3, assume you start with a string created by the following statement:

```
string str = "This cannot be";
```

Figure 14.6 illustrates how this string is stored in the buffer created for it. As indicated, the length of the string is 14 characters.

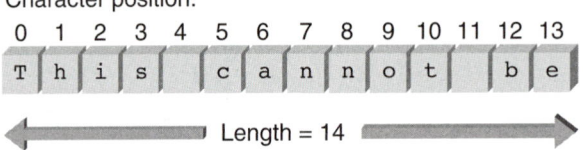

Figure 14.6   Initial storage of a `string` object

Now assume the following statement is executed:

```
str.insert(4," I know");
```

This statement inserts the designated seven characters in `" I know"`, beginning with a blank, into the existing string (`"This cannot be"`) starting at index position 4. Figure 14.7 shows the string after the insertion.

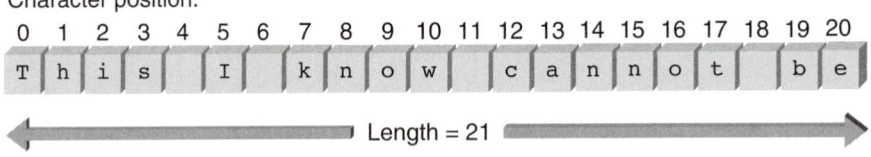

Figure 14.7   The string after the insertion

If the statement `str.replace(12, 6, "to");` is executed next, the existing characters in index positions 12 through 17 are deleted, and the two characters contained in `to` are inserted starting at index position 12. Figure 14.8 shows the net effect of this replacement. The number of replacement characters (in this case, two) can be fewer than, equal to, or greater than the number of characters being replaced, which in this case is six.

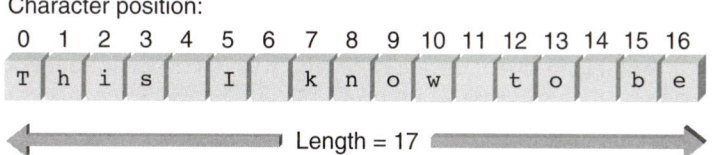

Figure 14.8 The string after the replacement

Finally, if you append the string `"correct"` to the string shown in Figure 14.8 by using the concatenation operator, +, you get the string shown in Figure 14.9.

Character position:

0 1 2 3 4 5 6 7 8 9 10 11 12 13 14 15 16 17 18 19 20 21 22 23 24

| T | h | i | s | | I | | k | n | o | w | | t | o | | b | e | | c | o | r | r | e | c | t |

Length = 25

Figure 14.9 The string after the append

Program 14.6 uses these statements in a complete program.

Program 14.6

```cpp
#include <iostream>
#include <string>
using namespace std;

int main()
{
  string str = "This cannot be";

  cout << "The original string is: " << str << endl
       << "   and has " << int(str.length()) << " characters." << endl;

  // insert characters
  str.insert(4," I know");
  cout << "The string, after insertion, is: " << str << endl
       << "   and has " << int(str.length()) << " characters." << endl;
```

☞

```
  // replace characters
  str.replace(12, 6, "to");
  cout << "The string, after replacement, is: " << str << endl
       << "  and has " << int(str.length()) << " characters." << endl;

  // append characters
  str = str + " correct";
  cout << "The string, after appending, is: " << str << endl
       << "  and has " << int(str.length()) << " characters." << endl;

  return 0;
}
```

The following output produced by Program 14.6 matches the strings shown in Figures 14.6 to 14.9:

```
     The original string is: This cannot be
       and has 14 characters.
     The string, after insertion, is: This I know cannot be
       and has 21 characters.
     The string, after replacement, is: This I know to be
       and has 17 characters.
     The string, after appending, is: This I know to be correct
       and has 25 characters.
```

Of the remaining string methods in Table 14.3, the most commonly used are those that locate specific characters in a string and create substrings. A **substring** is any sequence of characters contained in the original string. Program 14.7 shows how some of these other methods are used.

 Program 14.7

```
#include <iostream>
#include <string>
using namespace std;

int main()
{

  string string1 = "LINEAR PROGRAMMING THEORY";
  string s1, s2, s3;
  int j, k;

  cout << "The original string is " <<  string1 << endl;
```

```
j = int(string1.find('I'));
cout << "  The first position of an 'I' is " <<  j << endl;


k = int(string1.find('I', (j+1)));
cout << "  The next position of an 'I' is " <<  k << endl;

j = int(string1.find("THEORY"));
cout << "  The first location of \"THEORY\" is " <<  j << endl;

k = int(string1.find("ING"));
cout << "  The first index of \"ING\" is " <<  k << endl;

// now extract three substrings
s1 = string1.substr(2,5);
s2 = string1.substr(19,3);
s3 = string1.substr(6,8);

cout << "The substrings extracted are:" << endl
     << "  " << s1 + s2 + s3 << endl;

return 0;
}
```

Here's the output produced by Program 14.7:

```
The original string is LINEAR PROGRAMMING THEORY
  The first position of an 'I' is 1
  The next position of an 'I' is 15
  The first location of "THEORY" is 19
  The first index of "ING" is 15
 The substrings extracted are:
  NEAR THE PROGRAM
```

The main point shown in Program 14.7 is that characters and sequences of characters can be located and extracted from a string with string class methods.

EXERCISES 14.1

1. **(Practice)** Enter and run Program 14.2.

2. **(Practice)** Determine the value of text.at(0), text.at(3), and text.at(10), assuming for each one that text is each of the following strings:
   a. Now is the time
   b. Rocky raccoon welcomes you
   c. Happy Holidays
   d. The good ship

3. **(Practice)** Enter and run Program 14.5.

4. **(Modify)** Modify Program 14.5 to count and display the numbers of each vowel contained in the string.

5. **(Modify)** Modify Program 14.5 to display the number of vowels in a user-entered string.

6. **(Program)** Using the at() method, write a C++ program that reads in a string by using getline(), stores the string in a string object named message, and then displays the string in reverse order. (*Hint*: After the string has been entered and saved, retrieve and display characters, starting from the end of the string. The last character is located at the position message.length() - 1.)

7. **(Program)** Write a C++ program that accepts both a string and a single character from the user. The program should determine how many times the character is contained in the string. (*Hint*: Search the string by using the find(str, ind) method. This method should be used in a loop that starts the index value at 0 and then changes the index value to 1 past the index of where the char was last found.)

8. **(Practice)** Enter and run Program 14.6.

9. **(Practice)** Enter and run Program 14.7.

14.2 Character Manipulation Methods

In addition to the string methods from the string class, C++ provides several useful character class methods, listed in Table 14.4. The header files string and cctype must be included in any program using these methods.

Table 14.4   Character Library Methods (Require the Header Files string and cctype)

Method Prototype	Description	Example
int isalpha (charExp)	Returns a true (non-zero integer) if charExp evaluates to a letter; otherwise, it returns a false (zero integer)	isalpha('a')
int isalnum (charExp)	Returns a true (non-zero integer) if charExp evaluates to a letter or a digit; otherwise, it returns a false (zero integer)	isalnum(key)
int isupper (charExp)	Returns a true (non-zero integer) if charExp evaluates to an uppercase letter; otherwise, it returns a false (zero integer)	isupper('a')
int islower (charExp)	Returns a true (non-zero integer) if charExp evaluates to a lowercase letter; otherwise, it returns a false (zero integer)	islower('a')
int isdigit (charExp)	Returns a true (non-zero integer) if charExp evaluates to a digit (0 through 9); otherwise, it returns a false (zero integer)	isdigit('a')

Table 14.4   Character Library Methods (Require the Header Files `string` and `cctype`) (*continued*)

`int isascii (charExp)`	Returns a `true` (non-zero integer) if `charExp` evaluates to an ASCII character; otherwise, returns a `false` (zero integer)	`isascii('a')`
`int isspace (charExp)`	Returns a `true` (non-zero integer) if `charExp` evaluates to a space; otherwise, returns a `false` (zero integer)	`isspace(' ')`
`int isprint (charExp)`	Returns a `true` (non-zero integer) if `charExp` evaluates to a printable character; otherwise, returns a `false` (zero integer)	`isprint('a')`
`int isctrl (charExp)`	Returns a `true` (non-zero integer) if `charExp` evaluates to a control character; otherwise, it returns a `false` (zero integer)	`isctrl('a')`
`int ispunct (charExp)`	Returns a `true` (non-zero integer) if `charExp` evaluates to a punctuation character; otherwise, returns a `false` (zero integer)	`ispunct('!')`
`int isgraph (charExp)`	Returns a `true` (non-zero integer) if `charExp` evaluates to a printable character other than white space; otherwise, returns a `false` (zero integer)	`isgraph(' ')`
`int toupper (charExp)`	Returns the uppercase equivalent if `charExp` evaluates to a lowercase character; otherwise, returns the character code without modification	`toupper('a')`
`int tolower (charExp)`	Returns the lowercase equivalent if `charExp` evaluates to an uppercase character; otherwise, returns the character code without modification	`tolower('A')`

Because all the `istype()` methods listed in Table 14.4 return a non-zero integer (interpreted as a Boolean `true` value) when the character meets the condition and a zero integer (interpreted as a Boolean `false` value) when the condition isn't met, these methods are typically used in an `if` statement. For example, the following code segment assumes `ch` is a character variable:

```
if(isdigit(ch))
  cout << "The character just entered is a digit" << endl;
else if(ispunct(ch))
  cout << "The character just entered is a punctuation mark" << endl;
```

In this example, if ch contains a digit character, the first cout statement is executed; if the character is a letter, the second cout statement is executed. In both cases, however, the character to be checked is included as an argument to the method. Program 14.8 shows this type of code in a program that counts the number of letters, digits, and other characters in a string. The characters to be checked are obtained by using the string class's at() method. In this program, this method is used in a for loop that cycles through the string from the first character to the last.

 **Program 14.8**

```cpp
#include <iostream>
#include <string>
#include <cctype>
using namespace std;

int main()
{
    string str = "This -123/ is 567 A ?<6245> Test!";
    char nextChar;
    int i;
    int numLetters = 0, numDigits = 0, numOthers = 0;
    cout << "The original string is: " <<  str
         << "\nThis string contains " <<  int(str.length())
         <<  " characters," <<  " which consist of" << endl;

    // check each character in the string
    for (i = 0; i < int(str.length()); i++)
    {
      nextChar = str.at(i);   // get a character
      if (isalpha(nextChar))
        numLetters++;
      else if (isdigit(nextChar))
        numDigits++;
      else
        numOthers++;
    }

    cout << "     " <<  numLetters <<  " letters" << endl;
    cout << "     " <<  numDigits <<  " digits" << endl;
    cout << "     " <<  numOthers <<  " other characters." << endl;

    cin.ignore();
    return 0;
}
```

Program 14.8 produces the following output:

```
The original string is: This -123/ is 567 A ?<6245> Test!
This string contains 33 characters, which consist of
        11 letters
        10 digits
        12 other characters.
```

As indicated by this output, each of the 33 characters in the string has been categorized correctly as a letter, a digit, or other character.

Typically, as in Program 14.8, the methods in Table 14.4 are used in a character-by-character manner on each character in a string. You see this again in Program 14.9, where each lowercase string character is converted to its uppercase equivalent by using the `toupper()` method. This method converts only lowercase letters, leaving all other characters unaffected.

 **Program 14.9**

```cpp
#include <iostream>
#include <string>
using namespace std;

int main()
{
    int i;
    string str;

    cout << "Type in any sequence of characters: ";
    getline(cin,str);

    // cycle through all elements of the string
    for (i = 0; i < int(str.length()); i++)
        str[i] = toupper(str[i]);

    cout << "The characters just entered, in uppercase, are: "
        << str << endl;

    return 0;
}
```

Point of Information

Why the char Data Type Uses Integer Values

In C++, a character is stored as an integer value, which is sometimes confusing to beginning programmers. The reason is that in addition to standard English letters and characters, a program needs to store special characters that have no printable equivalents. One is the end-of-file (EOF) sentinel that all computer systems use to designate the end of a data file. The EOF sentinel can be transmitted from the keyboard. For example, on UNIX-based systems, it's generated by holding down the Ctrl key and pressing D; on Windows-based systems, it's generated by holding down Ctrl and pressing Z. On both systems, the EOF sentinel is stored as the integer number -1, which has no equivalent character value. You can check this by displaying the integer value of each entered character (see Program 14.10) and pressing Ctrl+D or Ctrl+Z, depending on the system you're using.

By using a 16-bit integer value, more than 64,000 different characters can be represented. This number of characters provides enough storage for multiple character sets, including Arabic, Chinese, Hebrew, Japanese, and Russian, and almost all known language symbols. Therefore, storing a character as an integer value has a practical value.

An important consequence of using integer codes for string characters is that characters can be compared easily for alphabetical ordering. For example, as long as each subsequent letter in an alphabet has a higher value than its preceding letter, the comparison of character values is reduced to the comparison of numeric values. Because characters are stored in sequential numerical order, adding 1 to a letter produces the next letter in the alphabet.

A sample run of Program 14.9 produced the following output:

```
Type in any sequence of characters: this is a test of 12345.
The characters just entered, in uppercase, are: THIS IS A TEST OF 12345.
```

In this program, pay particular attention to the statement used to cycle through each character in the string: for (i = 0; i < int(str.length()); i++). Typically, cycling through the string one character at a time is how each element in a string is accessed, using the length() method to determine when the end of the string has been reached. (Review Program 14.8 to see that it's used in the same way.) The only real difference is that in Program 14.9, each element is accessed by using the array subscript notation str[i]; in Program 14.8, the at() method is used. Although these two notations are interchangeable—and which one you use is a matter of choice—for consistency, the two notations shouldn't be mixed in the same program.

Character I/O

Although you have used `cin` and `getline()` to accept data entered from the keyboard in a more or less "cookbook" manner, understanding what data is being sent to the program and how the program must react to process the data is useful. At a fundamental level, all input (as well as output) is done on a character-by-character basis, as shown in Figure 14.10.

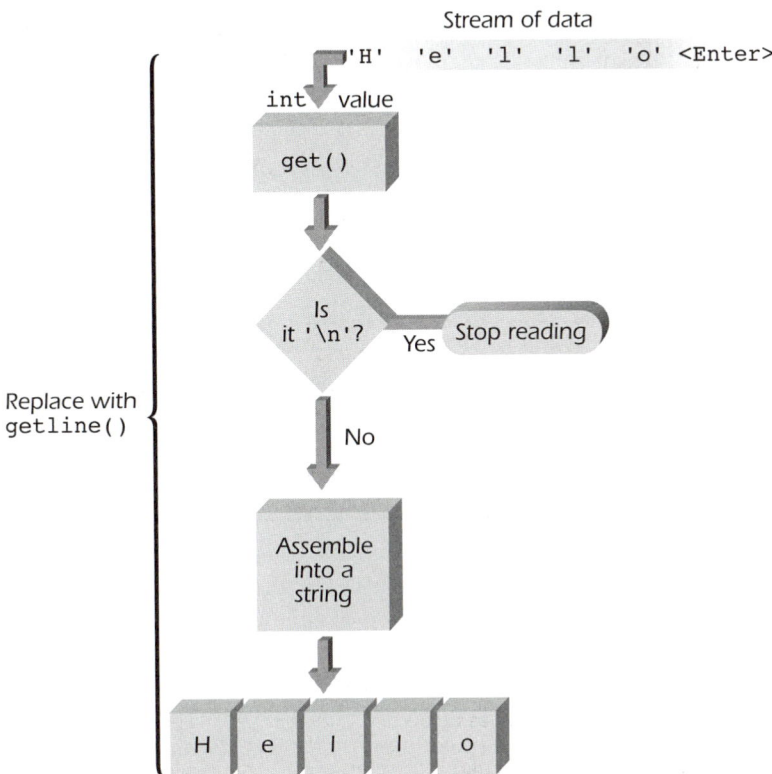

Figure 14.10 Accepting keyboard-entered characters

As this figure shows, the entry of every piece of data, whether it's a string or a number, consists of typing characters. For example, entry of the string `Hello` consists of pressing and releasing the five character keys H, e, l, l, o, and the Enter key. Similarly, output of the number 26.95 consists of displaying the five characters 2, 6, ., 9, and 5. Although programmers usually don't think of data in this manner, programs are restricted to this character-by-character I/O, and all of C++'s higher-level I/O methods and stream objects are based on lower-level character I/O methods. These more basic character methods, which can be used by a programmer, are listed in Table 14.5.

Table 14.5 Basic Character I/O Methods (Require the Header File `iostream`)

Method	Description	Example
`cout.put(charExp)`	Places the character value of `charExp` on the output stream	`cout.put('A');`
`cin.get(charVar)`	Extracts the next character from the input stream and assigns it to the variable `charVar`	`cin.get(key);`
`cin.peek(charVar)`	Assigns the next character from the input stream to the variable `charVar` *without* extracting the character from the stream	`cin.peek(nextKey);`
`cin.putback(charExp)`	Pushes a character value of `charExp` back onto the input stream	`cin.putback(cKey);`
`cin.ignore(n, char)`	Ignores a maximum of the next *n* input characters, up to and including the detection of `char`; if no arguments are specified, ignores the next single character on the input stream	`cin.ignore(80,'\n');` `cin.ignore();`

The `get()` method reads the next character in the input stream and assigns it to the method's character variable. For example, examine this statement:

`cin.get(nextChar);`

It causes the next character entered at the keyboard to be stored in the character variable `nextChar`. This method is useful for inputting and checking characters before they're assigned to a complete string, character, or numeric variable.

The character output method corresponding to `get()` is `put()`. This method expects a single-character argument and displays onscreen the character passed to it. For example, the statement `cout.put('A')` causes the letter A to be displayed onscreen.

Of the last three methods listed in Table 14.5, `cin.ignore()` is the most useful. This method permits skipping over input until a designated character, such as `'\n'`, is encountered. For example, the statement `cin.ignore(80, '\n')` skips up to a maximum of the next 80 characters or stops the skipping if the newline character is encountered. This statement can be useful for skipping all further input on a line, up to a maximum of 80 characters, or until the end of the current line is encountered. Input would begin with the next line.

The `peek()` method in Table 14.5 returns the next character on the stream but doesn't remove it from the stream's buffer. For example, the expression `cin.peek(nextChar)` returns the next character input at the keyboard but leaves it in the buffer. This action is sometimes useful for peeking ahead and seeing what the next character is but leaving it in place for the next input.

Point of Information

A Notational Inconsistency

All the `character` class methods in Table 14.5 use the standard object-oriented notation of preceding the method's name with an object name and a period, as in `cin.get()`. However, the `string` class `getline()` method uses the notation `getline(cin, strVar)`. In this notation, the object (`cin`) appears as an argument inside the parentheses, which is how procedural-based functions pass variables. For consistency, you would expect `getline()` to be called as `cin.getline()`. Unfortunately, this notation was already in use for a `getline()` function created for C-style strings (which are simply one-dimensional arrays of characters, as discussed in Section 7.2) before the class methods in Table 14.5 were included in the C++ library. Keeping the original invocation syntax meant that a notational inconsistency was created.

Finally, the `putback()` method places a character back on the stream so that it's the next character read. The argument passed to `putback()` can be any character expression that evaluates to a legitimate character value; it doesn't have to be the last input character.

The Phantom Newline Character Revisited As you saw in Section 14.1, sometimes you get seemingly strange results when a `cin` input stream is followed by a `getline()` method call. This same result can occur when characters are inputted by using the `get()` character method. To see how it can occur, take a look at Program 14.10, which uses the `get()` method to accept the next character entered at the keyboard, and then stores the character in the variable `fkey`.

Program 14.10

```
#include <iostream>
using namespace std;

int main()
{
  char fkey;

  cout << "Type in a character: ";
  cin.get(fkey);
  cout << "The key just accepted is " << int(fkey) << endl;

  return 0;
}
```

When Program 14.10 is run, the character entered in response to the prompt `Type in a character:` is stored in the character variable `fkey`, and the decimal code for the character is displayed by explicitly casting the character into an integer to force its display as an integer value. The following sample run illustrates this technique:

```
Type in a character: m
The key just accepted is 109
```

At this point, everything seems to be working, although you might be wondering why the decimal value of m is displayed instead of the character. As you'll see in Program 14.11, in typing m, two keys are usually pressed: the m key and the Enter key. As explained in Section 14.1, these two characters are stored in a buffer after they're pressed (refer back to Figure 14.2). The first key pressed—m, in this case—is taken from the buffer and stored in `fkey`, but the code for the Enter key is still in the buffer. Therefore, a subsequent call to `get()` for a character input picks up the code for the Enter key as the next character automatically. To see an example, take a look at Program 14.11.

 ## Program 14.11

```cpp
#include <iostream>
using namespace std;

int main()
{
  char fkey, skey;

  cout << "Type in a character: ";
  cin.get(fkey);
  cout << "The key just accepted is " << int(fkey) << endl;

  cout << "Type in another character: ";
  cin.get(skey);
  cout << "The key just accepted is " << int(skey) << endl;

  return 0;
}
```

The following is a sample run of Program 14.11:

```
Type in a character: m
The key just accepted is 109
Type in another character: The key just accepted is 10
```

To review what happened in this program, after entering the letter m in response to the first prompt, the Enter key is also pressed. From a character standpoint, this input represents the entry of two distinct characters. The first character is m, which is coded and stored as the integer 109. The second character also gets stored in the buffer with the numerical code for the Enter key. The second call to get() picks up this code immediately, without waiting for another key to be pressed. The last cout stream displays the code for this key. The reason for displaying the numerical code rather than the character is that the Enter key has no printable character associated with it that can be displayed.

Remember that every key has a numerical code, including Enter, the spacebar, Escape, and Ctrl. These keys generally have no effect when entering numbers because the input methods ignore them as leading or trailing input with numerical data. These keys also don't affect the entry of a single character requested as the first user data to be inputted, as in Program 14.10. Only when a character is requested after the user has already input other data, as in Program 14.11, does the usually invisible Enter key become noticeable.

In Section 14.5, you learn other ways to prevent the Enter key from being accepted as a legitimate character input when the getline() method is used. However, when the get() method is used in a program, you can use the following ways:

- Follow the cin.get() input with the call cin.ignore().
- Accept the Enter key in a character variable, and then don't use it again.

Program 14.12 applies the first solution to Program 14.11. Ignoring the Enter key after the first character is read and displayed clears the buffer of the Enter key, which gets it ready to store the next valid input character as its first character.

 **Program 14.12**

```cpp
#include <iostream>
using namespace std;

int main()
{
  char fkey, skey;

  cout << "Type in a character: ";
  cin.get(fkey);
  cout << "The key just accepted is " << int(fkey) << endl;
  cin.ignore();

  cout << "Type in another character: ";
  cin.get(skey);
  cout << "The key just accepted is " << int(skey) << endl;

  return 0;
}
```

In this program, observe that when the user types the letter m and presses the Enter key, the m is assigned to `fkey` and the code for the Enter key is ignored. The next call to `get()` stores the code for the next key pressed in the variable `skey`. From the user's standpoint, the Enter key has no effect, except to signal the end of each character input. The following is a sample run of Program 14.12:

```
Type in a character: m
The key just accepted is 109
Type in another character: b
The key just accepted is 98
```

A Second Look at User-Input Validation

As mentioned in the first look at user-input validation (in Section 3.4), programs that respond effectively to unexpected user input are formally referred to as robust programs and informally as "bulletproof" programs. Code that validates user input and ensures that a program doesn't produce unintended results caused by unexpected input is a sign of a well-constructed, robust program. One of your jobs as a programmer is to produce robust programs. To see how unintended results can occur, examine the following two code examples. First, assume your program contains the following statements:

```
int value;
cout << "Enter an integer: ";
cin  >> value;
```

By mistake, a user enters the characters e4. In earlier versions of C++, this input would cause the program to terminate unexpectedly, or **crash**. Although a crash can still occur for other reasons, it doesn't in this case. Instead, a meaningless integer value is assigned to the variable `value`. This assignment, of course, invalidates any results obtained by using this variable.

As a second example, take a look at the following code, which causes an infinite loop if the user enters a non-numeric value. (The program can be halted by holding down Ctrl and pressing C.)

```
double value;
  do
  {
    cout << "Enter a number (enter 0 to exit): ";
    cin  >> value;

    cout << "The square root of this number is: " << sqrt(value) << endl;
  } while (value !=0);
```

The basic technique for handling invalid data input and preventing seemingly innocuous code from producing unintended results, as in these two examples, is called **user-input validation**. This term means validating the entered data during or after data entry and giving the user a way of reentering invalid data. User-input validation is an essential part of any commercially viable program, and if done correctly, it protects a program from attempting to process data types that can cause a program to crash, create infinite loops, or produce more invalid results.

The central element in user-input validation is checking each entered character to verify that it qualifies as a legitimate character for the expected data type. For example, if an integer is required, the only acceptable characters are a leading plus (+) or minus (-) sign and the digits 0 through 9. These characters can be checked as they're being typed, which means the `get()` method is used to input a character at a time, or after all the characters can be accepted in a string, and then each string character is checked for validity. After all the entered characters have been validated, the entered string can be converted into the correct data type.

Two basic techniques can be used to verify the validity of entered characters: character-by-character checking and exception processing, both discussed in Section 14.5.

EXERCISES 14.2

1. **(Practice)** Enter and run Program 14.8.

2. **(Practice)** Enter and run Program 14.9.

3. **(Program)** Write a C++ program that counts the number of words in a string. A word is encountered whenever a transition from a blank space to a nonblank character is encountered. The string contains only words separated by blank spaces.

4. **(Practice)** Generate 10 random numbers in the range 0 to 129. (If necessary, review Section 6.8 for how to do this.) If the number represents a printable character, print the character with a message that indicates the following:

   The character is a lowercase letter.
   The character is an uppercase letter.
   The character is a digit.
   The character is a space.
   If the character is none of these, display its value in integer format.

5. **(Practice) a.** Write a function named `reverse()` that returns a string in reverse order without using the `string` class's `length()` method.
   b. Write a simple `main()` function to test the `reverse()` function written for Exercise 5a.

6. **(Practice) a.** Write a function named `countlets()` that returns the number of letters in a string passed as an argument. Digits, spaces, punctuation, tabs, and newline characters shouldn't be included in the returned count.
   b. Include the `countlets()` function written for Exercise 6a in an executable C++ program, and use the program to test the function.

7. **(Program)** Write a program that accepts a string from the console and displays the hexadecimal equivalent of each character in the string.

8. **(Program)** Write a C++ program that accepts a string from the keyboard and displays the string one word per line.

9. **(Debug)** In response to the following code, suppose a user enters the data `12e4`:

```
cout << "Enter an integer: ";
cin  >> value;
```

What value will be stored in the integer variable `value`?

10. **(Useful utility) a.** Write a C++ function that accepts a string and two character values. The function should return the string with each occurrence of the first character replaced by the second character.

   b. Test the function written for Exercise 10a by writing a program that accepts a string from the user, calls the function written for Exercise 10a to replace all occurrences of the letter e with the letter x from the user-entered string, and then displays the changed string.

11. **(Useful utility)** Modify the function written for Exercise 10a to search for all occurrences of a user-entered sequence of characters, and then replace this sequence, when it's found in the string, with a second user-entered sequence. For example, if the entered string is `Figure 4-4 illustrates the output of Program 4-2` and the user specifies that `4-` is to be replaced by `3-`, the resulting string is `Figure 3-4 illustrates the output of Program 3-2`. (All occurrences of the searched-for sequence have been changed.)

12. **(Program) a.** Write a C++ program that stops reading a line of text when a period is entered and displays the sentence with correct spacing and capitalization. For this program, correct spacing means only one space should be used between words, and all letters should be lowercase, except the first letter. For example, if the user enters the text `i  am        going    to      Go  TO THe moVies.`, the displayed sentence should be `I am going to go to the movies.`

   b. Determine what characters, if any, aren't displayed correctly by the program you created for Exercise 12a.

14.3 Exception Handling

The traditional C++ approach to error handling uses a function to return a specific value to indicate specific operations. Typically, a return value of 0 or 1 is used to indicate successful completion of the function's task, whereas a negative value indicates an error condition. For example, with a function used to divide two numbers, a return value of -1 could indicate that the denominator is 0, and the division can't be performed. When multiple error conditions can occur, different return values can be used to indicate specific errors.

   Although this approach is still available and often used, a number of problems can occur. First, the programmer must check the return value to detect whether an error did occur. Next, the error-handling code that checks the return value frequently becomes intermixed with normal processing code, so sometimes it's difficult to determine which part of the code is handling errors, as opposed to normal program processing. Finally, returning an error condition from a function means the condition must be the same data type as a valid returned value; hence, the error code must be a specially identified value that can be identified as an error alert. This means the error code is embedded as one of the possible nonerror values the function might require and is available only at the point where the function returns a value. A function returning a Boolean value has no additional values for reporting an error condition, except `true` and `false`.

None of these problems is insurmountable, and many times this approach is simple and effective. However, another technique is available that's designed for error detection and handling: **exception handling**. With this technique, when an error occurs while a function is executing, the function creates an exception. An **exception** is a value, a variable, or an object containing information about the error at the point the error occurs. This exception is immediately passed, at the point it's generated, to code called the **exception handler**, which is designed to deal with the exception. The process of generating and passing an exception is referred to as **throwing an exception**. The exception is thrown from within the function while it's still executing, which permits handling the error and then returning control back to the function so that it can complete its assigned task.

In general, two fundamental types of errors can cause C++ exceptions: those resulting from a program's inability to obtain a required resource and those resulting from flawed data. Examples of the first error type are attempts to obtain a system resource, such as locating and finding a file for input. These errors are the result of external resources over which the programmer has no control.

The second type of error can occur when a program prompts the user to enter an integer, and the user enters a string, such as e234, that can't be converted to a numerical value. Another example is the attempt to divide two numbers when the denominator has a 0 value, a condition referred to as a "division by zero error." These errors can always be checked and handled in a manner that doesn't result in a program crash. Before seeing how to use exception handling, review Table 14.6 to familiarize yourself with the terminology used with processing exceptions.

Table 14.6 Exception-Handling Terminology

Terminology	Description
Exception	A value, a variable, or an object that identifies a specific error that has occurred while a program is running
Throw an exception	Send the exception to a section of code that processes the detected error
Catch or handle an exception	Receive a thrown exception and process it
Catch clause	The section of code that processes the error
Exception handler	The code that throws and catches an exception

The general syntax of the code required to throw and catch an exception is as follows:

```
try
{
  // one or more statements,
  // at least one of which should
  // be capable of throwing an exception
}
catch(exceptionDataType parameterName)
{
  // one or more statements
}
```

This example uses two new keywords: `try` and `catch`. The `try` keyword identifies the start of an exception-handling block of code. At least one of the statements inside the braces defining this block of code should be capable of throwing an exception. As an example, examine the `try` block in the following section of code:

```
try
{
  cout << "Enter the numerator (whole numbers only): ";
  cin  >> numerator;
  cout << "Enter the denominator (whole numbers only):";
  cin  >> denominator;
  result = numerator/denominator;
}
```

The `try` block contains five statements, three of which might result in an error you want to catch. In particular, a professionally written program would make sure valid integers are entered in response to both prompts and the second entered value isn't a 0. For this example, you see how to ensure that the second value entered isn't 0.

Therefore, for the purposes of this example, only the value of the second number matters. The `try` block is altered to say "Try all the statements in me to see whether an exception, which in this case is a 0 second value, occurs." To check that the second value isn't 0, you add a `throw` statement in the `try` block, as follows:

```
try
{
  cout << "Enter the numerator: (whole number only): ";
  cin  >> numerator;
  cout << "Enter the denominator: (whole number only): ";
  cin  >> denominator;
  if (denominator == 0)
    throw denominator;
  else
    result = numerator/denominator;
}
```

In this `try` block, the thrown item is an integer value. A string literal, a variable, or an object could have been used, but only one of these items can be thrown by any single `throw` statement. The first four statements in the `try` block don't have to be included in the code; however, doing so keeps all the relevant statements together. Keeping related statements together makes it easier to add `throw` statements in the same `try` block to ensure that both input values are integer values.

A `try` block must be followed by one or more `catch` blocks, which serve as exception handlers for any exceptions thrown by statements in the `try` block. Here's a `catch` block that handles the thrown exception, which is an integer:

```
catch(int e)
{
  cout << "A denominator value of " << e << " is invalid." << endl;
  exit (1);
}
```

The exception handling this `catch` block provides is an output statement that identifies the caught exception and then terminates program execution. Notice the parentheses following the `catch` keyword. Inside the parentheses are the data type of the exception that's thrown and a parameter named e used to receive the exception. This parameter, which is a programmer-selected identifier but conventionally uses the letter e for exception, is used to hold the exception value generated when an exception is thrown.

Multiple `catch` blocks can be used as long as each block catches a unique data type. The only requirement is providing at least one `catch` block for each `try` block. The more exceptions that can be caught with the same `try` block, the better. Program 14.13 is a complete program that includes a `try` block and a `catch` block to detect a division-by-zero error.

 **Program 14.13**

```
#include <iostream>
using namespace std;

int main()
{
  int numerator, denominator;

  try
  {
    cout << "Enter the numerator (whole number only): ";
    cin  >> numerator;
    cout << "Enter the denominator(whole number only): ";
    cin  >> denominator;

    if (denominator == 0)
        throw denominator;  // an integer value is thrown
```

```
    else
        cout << numerator <<'/' << denominator
                << " = " << double(numerator)/ double(denominator) << endl;
  }
  catch(int e)
  {
    cout << "A denominator value of " << e << " is invalid." << endl;
    exit (1);
  }

  return 0;
}
```

Following are two sample runs of Program 14.13. Note that the second output indicates that an attempt to divide by a zero denominator has been detected successfully before the operation is performed.

```
Enter the numerator (whole number only): 12
Enter the denominator(whole number only): 3
12/3 = 4
```

and

```
Enter the numerator (whole number only): 12
Enter the denominator(whole number only): 0
A denominator value of 0 is invalid.
```

Instead of terminating program execution when a zero denominator is detected, a more robust program can give the user the opportunity to reenter a non-zero value. To do this, the try block is included in a while statement, and then the catch block returns program control to the while statement after informing the user that a zero value has been entered. Program 14.14 accomplishes this.

 **Program 14.14**

```
#include <iostream>
using namespace std;

int main()
{
  int numerator, denominator;
  bool needDenominator = true;

  cout << "Enter a numerator (whole number only): ";
  cin  >> numerator;
```

```
cout << "Enter a denominator (whole number only): ";

while(needDenominator)
{
  cin  >> denominator;
  try
  {
    if (denominator == 0)
      throw denominator;  // an integer value is thrown
  }
  catch(int e)
  {
    cout << "A denominator value of " << e << " is invalid." << endl;
    cout << "Please reenter the denominator (whole number only): ";
    continue;  // send control back to the while statement
  }
  cout << numerator <<'/' << denominator
       << " = " << double(numerator)/ double(denominator) << endl;
    needDenominator = false;
}

  return 0;
}
```

In reviewing this code, notice that it's the `continue` statement in the `catch` block that returns control to the top of the `while` statement. (See Section 5.2 for a review of the `continue` statement.) Following is a sample run of Program 14.14:

```
Enter a numerator (whole number only): 12
Enter a denominator (whole number only): 0
A denominator value of 0 is invalid.
Please reenter the denominator (whole number only): 5
12/5 = 2.4
```

When throwing string literals as opposed to numeric values, one caution should be mentioned. When a string literal is thrown, it's a C-string, not a `string` class object, that's thrown. This means the `catch` statement must declare the received argument as a C-string (which is a character array) rather than as a string. As an example, take a look at using the following statement instead of throwing the value of the `denominator` variable in Programs 14.3 and 14.4:

```
throw "***Invalid input - A zero denominator value is not permitted***";
```

Here's a correct `catch` statement for the preceding `throw` statement:

```
catch(char e[])
```

An attempt to declare the exception as a `string` class variable results in a compiler error.

EXERCISES 14.3

1. **(Practice)** Define the following terms:
   a. Exception
   b. `try` block
   c. `catch` block
   d. Exception handler
   e. Throw an exception
   f. Catch an exception

2. **(Practice)** Enter and run Program 14.14.

3. **(Modify)** Replace the following statement in Program 14.14
   ```
   cout << numerator <<'/' << denominator
       << " = " << double (numerator)/ double (denominator) << endl;
   ```
   with the statement
   ```
   cout << numerator <<'/' << denominator
       << " = " << numerator/denominator << endl;
   ```
   and run the modified program. Enter the values 12 and 5, and explain why the result is incorrect from the user's viewpoint.

4. **(Modify)** Modify Program 14.14 so that it throws and catches the message `***Invalid input -A denominator value of zero is not permitted***`. (*Hint*: Review the caution at the end of this section.)

5. **(Modify)** Modify Program 14.14 so that the `try` and `catch` blocks are included in a `while` statement. The `while` statement should provide code that continuously requests the user to enter a denominator until a non-zero number is entered. (*Hint*: The prompt to enter a new denominator should be made in the `catch` block immediately after the message informing the user an invalid denominator has been entered.)

6. **(Modify)** Modify Program 14.14 so that it continues to divide two numbers until the user enters the number 999 (as a numerator or denominator) to terminate program execution.

14.4 Exceptions and File Checking

Error detection and processing with exception handling are used extensively in C++ programs that require one or more files. For example, if a user deletes or renames a file by using an OS command, this action causes a C++ program to fail when an `open()` function call attempts to open the file with its original name.

Recall from Section 14.3 that the code for general exception handling looks like this:

```
try
{
  // one or more statements,
  // at least one of which should
  // throw an exception
}
catch(exceptionDataType parameterName)
{
  // one or more statements
}
```

In this code, the `try` block statements are executed. If no error occurs, the `catch` block statements are omitted, and processing continues with the statement following the `catch` block. However, if any statement in the `try` block throws an exception, the `catch` block with the exception data type matching the exception is executed. If no `catch` block is defined for a `try` block, a compiler error occurs. If no `catch` block exists that catches a thrown data type, a program crash occurs if the exception is thrown. The simplest approach is to have the `catch` block display an error message and terminate processing with a call to the `exit()` function. Program 14.15 shows the statements required to open a file in read mode and includes exception handling.

Program 14.15

```
#include <iostream>
#include <fstream>
#include <cstdlib>    // needed for exit()
#include <string>
using namespace std;

int main()
{
  string filename = "prices.dat";  // put the filename up front
  string descrip;
  double price;

  ifstream inFile;

  try  // tries to open the file, read it, and display file's data
  {
    inFile.open(filename.c_str());

    if (inFile.fail()) throw filename; // exception being checked
```

```
    // read and display the file's contents
    inFile >> descrip >> price;
    while (inFile.good()) // check next character
    {
      cout << descrip << ' ' << price << endl;
      inFile >> descrip >> price;
    }
    inFile.close();

    return 0;
  }
  catch (string e)
  {
    cout << "\nThe file "<< e << " was not successfully opened."
         << "\n Please check that the file currently exists."
         << endl;
    exit(1);
  }
}
```

This is the exception message Program 14.15 displays when the `prices.dat` file isn't found:

```
The file prices.dat was not successfully opened.
 Please check that the file currently exists.
```

Although the exception-handling code in this program can be used to check for a successful file open for input and output, a more rigorous check is usually required for an output file because a file opened for output is almost guaranteed to be found. If it exists, the file will be found; if it doesn't exist, the operating system creates it (unless append mode is specified and the file exists). Knowing that the file has been found and opened, however, isn't enough for output purposes when an existing output file must not be overwritten. In these cases, the file can be opened for input, and if the file is found, a further check can be made to ensure that the user explicitly approves overwriting it. The shaded code in Program 14.16 shows how to make this check.

 ## Program 14.16

```
#include <iostream>
#include <fstream>
#include <cstdlib>   // needed for exit()
#include <string>
#include <iomanip>   // needed for formatting
using namespace std;
```

```
int main()
{
  char response;
  string filename = "prices.dat";   // put the filename up front
  ifstream inFile;
  ofstream outFile;

  try // open a basic input stream to check whether the file exists
  {
    inFile.open(filename.c_str());

    if (inFile.fail()) throw 1; // this means the file doesn't exist
      // only get here if the file is found;
      // otherwise, the catch block takes control
    cout << "A file by the name " << filename << " currently exists.\n"
         << "Do you want to overwrite it with the new data (y or n): ";
    cin >> response;

    if (tolower(response) == 'n')
    {
      inFile.close();
      cout << "The existing file has not been overwritten." << endl;
      exit(1);
    }
  }
  catch(int e) {};   // a do-nothing block that permits
                     // processing to continue
  try
  {
    // open the file in write mode and continue with file writes
    outFile.open(filename.c_str());

    if (outFile.fail()) throw filename;
    // set the output file stream formats
    outFile << setiosflags(ios::fixed)
            << setiosflags(ios::showpoint)
            << setprecision(2);
    // write the data to the file
    outFile << "Mats " << 39.95 << endl
            << "Bulbs "  << 3.22 << endl
            << "Fuses " << 1.08 << endl;
    outFile.close();
    cout << "The file " << filename
         << " has been successfully written." << endl;
    return 0;
```

☞

```
    }
    catch(string e)
    {
      cout << "The file " << filename
          << " was not opened for output and has not been written."
          << endl;
    }
}
```

In Program 14.16, the `try` blocks are separate. Because a `catch` block is affiliated with the closest previous `try` block, there's no ambiguity about unmatched `try` and `catch` blocks.

Opening Multiple Files

To understand how to apply exception handling to opening two files at the same time, assume you want to read data from a character-based file named `info.txt`, one character at a time, and write this data to a file named `info.bak`. Essentially, this application is a file-copying program that reads data from one file in a character-by-character manner and writes the data to a second file. Figure 14.11 shows the characters stored in the input file.

```
Now is the time for all good people
    to come to the aid of their party.
Please call (555) 888-6666 for
    further information.
```

Figure 14.11   The data stored in the `info.txt` file

Figure 14.12 illustrates the structure of the streams needed to produce the file copy. In this figure, an input stream object referenced by the variable `inFile` reads data from the `info.txt` file, and an output stream object referenced by the variable `outFile` writes data to the `info.bak` file.

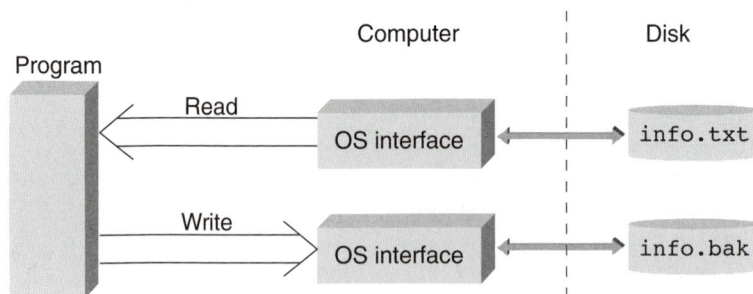

Figure 14.12   The file copy stream structure

Now examine Program 14.17, which creates the `info.bak` file as a duplicate of the `info.txt` file, using the procedure shown in Figure 14.12.

Point of Information

Checking That a File Was Opened Successfully

When using exception handling, the most common method for checking that the operating system located the designated file is the one coded in Program 14.15. The key coding points are repeated here for convenience:

```cpp
try // tries to open the file, read it,
    // and display file's data
{
  // open the file, throwing an exception if the open fails
  // perform all required file processing
  // close the file
}
catch (string e)
{
  cout << "\nThe file "<< e << " was not successfully opened."
       << "\n Please check that the file currently exists."
       << endl;
  exit(1);
}
```

Program 14.17

```cpp
#include <iostream>
#include <fstream>
#include <cstdlib>   // needed for exit()
#include <string>
using namespace std;

int main()
{
  string fileOne = "info.txt";  // put the filename up front
  string fileTwo = "info.bak";
  char ch;
  ifstream inFile;
  ofstream outFile;

  try  //this block tries to open the input file
  {
    // open a basic input stream
    inFile.open(fileOne.c_str());
    if (inFile.fail()) throw fileOne;
```

```
} // end of outer try block
catch (string in)  // catch for outer try block
{
  cout << "The input file " << in
       << " was not successfully opened." << endl
       << " No backup was made." << endl;
  exit(1);
}

try  // this block tries to open the output file and
{    // perform all file processing
  outFile.open(fileTwo.c_str());

  if (outFile.fail())throw fileTwo;

  while ((ch = inFile.get())!= EOF)
     outFile.put(ch);

  inFile.close();
  outFile.close();
}
catch (string out)  // catch for inner try block
{
  cout << "The backup file " << out
       << " was not successfully opened." << endl;
  exit(1);
}

  cout << "A successful backup of " << fileOne
       << " named " << fileTwo << " was made." << endl;

  return 0;
}
```

For simplicity, Program 14.17 attempts to open the input and output files in separate and unnested `try` blocks. More generally, the second file is opened in a nested inner `try` block, so the attempt to open this second file wouldn't be made if opening the first file threw an exception. (The next Point of Information box explains how to nest `try` blocks.)

In reviewing this program, pay particular attention to this statement:

```
while((ch = inFile.get())!= EOF)
```

This statement reads a value from the input stream continuously until the EOF value is detected. As long as the returned value doesn't equal the EOF value, the value is written to the output object stream. The parentheses surrounding the expression (ch = inFile.get())

Point of Information

Nesting `try` Blocks

When more than one file stream is involved, opening each file stream in its own `try` block permits isolating and identifying exactly which file caused an exception, if one occurs. The `try` blocks can be nested, however. For example, Program 14.17 has been rewritten with nested `try` blocks. Notice that the `catch` block for the inner `try` block must be nested in the same block scope as the `try` block:

```cpp
#include <iostream>
#include <fstream>
#include <cstdlib>    // needed for exit()
#include <string>
using namespace std;

int main()
{
  string fileOne = "info.txt";   // put the filename up front
  string fileTwo = "info.bak";
  char ch;
  ifstream inFile;
  ofstream outFile;

  try  //this block tries to open the input file
  {
    // open a basic input stream
    inFile.open(fileOne.c_str());
    if (inFile.fail()) throw fileOne;
    try  // this block tries to open the output file and
    {    // perform all file processing
         // open a basic output stream
      outFile.open(fileTwo.c_str());
      if (outFile.fail())throw fileTwo;
      while ((ch = inFile.get()) != EOF)
        outFile.put(ch);

      inFile.close();
      outFile.close();
    } // end of inner try block
    catch (string out)  // catch for inner try block
    {
      cout << "The backup file " << out
           << " was not successfully opened." << endl;
      exit(1);
    }
```

Point of Information

Nesting try Blocks (*continued*)

```
      }   // end of outer try block
      catch (string in)   // catch for outer try block
      {
        cout << "The input file " << in
             << " was not successfully opened." << endl
             << " No backup was made." << endl;
        exit(1);
      }

      cout << "A successful backup of " << fileOne
           << " named " << fileTwo << "was made." << endl;

      return 0;
}
```

The important point to notice is nesting the `try` blocks. If the two `try` blocks aren't nested and the input stream declaration, `ifstream inFile;`, is placed in the first block, it can't be used in the second `try` block without producing a compiler error. The reason is that all variables declared in a block of code (defined by an opening and closing brace pair) are local to the block in which they're declared.

---

are necessary to make sure a value is read and then assigned to the variable ch before the retrieved value is compared with the EOF value. Without parentheses, the complete expression would be ch = inFile.get()!= EOF. Given the precedence of operations, the relational expression inFile.get()!= EOF would be executed first. Because it's a relational expression, its result is a Boolean true or false value based on the data the get() method retrieves. Attempting to assign this Boolean result to the character variable ch is an invalid conversion across an assignment operator.

EXERCISES 14.4

1. **(Practice)** List two conditions that cause a fail condition when a file is opened for input.

2. **(Practice)** List two conditions that cause a fail condition when a file is opened for output.

3. **(Practice)** If an existing file is opened for output in write mode, what happens to the data currently in the file?

4. **(Modify)** Modify Program 14.15 to use an identifier of your choice, in place of the letter e, for the catch block's exception parameter name.

5. **(Practice)** Enter and run Program 14.16.

6. **(Debug)** Determine why the two unnested `try` blocks in Program 14.16 cause no problems in compilation or execution. (*Hint*: Place the declaration for the filename in the first `try` block and compile the program.)

7. **(Debug) a.** If the nested `try` blocks in the preceding Point of Information are separated into unnested blocks, the program won't compile. Determine why this is so.

   b. What additional changes have to be made to the program in Exercise 7a to allow it to be written with unnested blocks? (*Hint*: See Exercise 6.)

8. **(Program)** Enter the data for the `info.txt` file in Figure 14.11 or download it from this book's Web site (see this book's introduction for the URL). Then enter and run Program 14.17 and verify that the backup file was written.

9. **(Modify)** Modify Program 14.17 to use a `getline()` method in place of the `get()` method currently in the program.

14.5 Input Data Validation

One of the major uses of strings in programs is for user-input validation. Validating user input is essential: Even though a program prompts the user to enter a specific type of data, such as an integer, the prompt doesn't ensure that the user will comply. What a user enters is, in fact, totally out of the programmer's control. What *is* in your control is how you deal with the entered data.

It certainly does no good to tell a frustrated user that "The program clearly tells you to enter an integer, and you entered a date." Successful programs anticipate invalid data and prevent it from being accepted and processed. Typically, this is accomplished by first validating that input data is of the correct type. If it is, the data is accepted; otherwise, the user is prompted to reenter the data, with an explanation of why the entered data was invalid.

A common method of validating numerical input data is accepting all numbers as strings. Each character in the string can then be checked to make sure it complies with the requested data type. After this check is made and data is verified to be the correct type, the string is converted to an integer or double-precision value by using the conversion functions listed in Table 14.7. (For data accepted with `string` class objects, the `c_str()` method must be applied to the string before the conversion function is called.)

As an example, consider inputting an integer number. To be valid, the data entered must adhere to the following conditions:

- The data must contain at least one character.
- If the first character is a + or - sign, the data must contain at least one digit.
- Only digits from 0 to 9 are acceptable following the first character.

Table 14.7 C-String Conversion Functions

Function	Description	Example
`int atoi(stringExp)`	Converts `stringExp` to an integer. Conversion stops at the first non-integer character.	`atoi("1234")`
`double atof(stringExp)`	Converts `stringExp` to a double-precision number. Conversion stops at the first character that can't be interpreted as a `double`.	`atof("12.34")`
`char[] itoa(integerExp)`	Converts `integerExp` to a character array. The space allocated for the returned characters must be large enough for the converted value.	`itoa(1234)`

The following function, `isvalidInt()`, can be used to check that an entered string complies with these conditions. This function returns the Boolean value `true` if the conditions are satisfied; otherwise, it returns a Boolean `false` value.

```
bool isvalidInt(string str)
{
  int start = 0;
  int i;
  bool valid = true;   // assume a valid
  bool sign = false;   // assume no sign


  // check for an empty string
  if (int(str.length()) == 0)  valid = false;

  // check for a leading sign
  if (str.at(0) == '-'|| str.at(0) == '+')
  {
    sign = true;
    start = 1;   // start checking for digits after the sign
  }

  // check that there is at least one character after the sign
  if (sign && int(str.length() == 1)) valid = false;

  // now check the string, which you know has at least one non-sign char
  i = start;
  while(valid && i < int(str.length()))
```

```
  {
    if(!isdigit(str.at(i))) valid = false; //found a non-digit character
    i++;  // move to next character
  }
  return valid;
}
```

In the code for this function, pay attention to the conditions being checked. They are commented in the code and consist of the following:

- The string is not empty.
- A valid sign (+ or -) is present.
- If a sign is present, at least one digit follows it.
- All remaining characters in the string are digits.

Only if all these conditions are met does the function return a Boolean `true` value. After this value is returned, the string can be converted into an integer safely with the assurance that no unexpected value will result to hamper further data processing. Program 14.18 uses this function in the context of a complete program.

Program 14.18

```cpp
#include <iostream>
#include <string>
using namespace std;

bool isvalidInt(string);  // function prototype (declaration)
int main()
{
  string value;
  int number;

  cout << "Enter an integer: ";
  getline(cin, value);

  if (!isvalidInt(value))
    cout << "The number you entered is not a valid integer.";
  else
  {
    number = atoi(value.c_str());
    cout << "The integer you entered is " << number;
  }

  return 0;
}
```

```
bool isvalidInt(string str)
{
  int start = 0;
  int i;
  bool valid = true;   // assume a valid
  bool sign = false;   // assume no sign


  // check for an empty string
  if (int(str.length()) == 0)  valid = false;

  // check for a leading sign
  if (str.at(0) == '-'|| str.at(0) == '+')
  {
    sign = true;
    start = 1;  // start checking for digits after the sign
  }

  // check that there is at least one character after the sign
  if (sign && int(str.length()) == 1) valid = false;

  // now check the string, which you know has at least one non-sign char
  i = start;
  while(valid && i < int(str.length()))
  {
    if(!isdigit(str.at(i))) valid = false; //found a non-digit character
    i++;   // move to next character
  }
  return valid;
}
```

Two sample runs of Program 14.18 produced the following output:

```
Enter an integer: 12e45
The number you entered is not a valid integer.
```

and

```
Enter an integer: -12345
The integer you entered is -12345
```

As this output shows, the program determines that an invalid character was entered in the first run.

A second line of defense is to use exception-handling code, which typically allows the user to correct a problem, such as invalid data entry, by reentering new data until a valid value is supplied or an entry is made that ends the program. Using exception handling and the `isvalidInt()`

function in Program 14.18, you can develop a more comprehensive function named `getanInt()` that accepts user input continuously until a string corresponding to a valid integer is detected. After the string is entered, `getanInt()` converts it to an integer and returns the integer value. This technique ensures that a program requesting an integer actually receives an integer and prevents any undesirable effects, such as a program crash caused by an invalid data type being entered. The algorithm used to perform this task is as follows:

> **Set a Boolean variable named notanint to true**
> **while (notanint is true)**
>   **try**
>   **Accept a string value**
>   **If the string value doesn't correspond to an integer, throw an exception**
>   **catch the exception**
>   **Display the error message "Invalid integer - Please reenter: "**
>   **Send control back to the while statement**
>   **Set notanint to false (causes the loop to terminate)**
>   **End while**
>   **Return the integer corresponding to the entered string**

The code corresponding to this algorithm is shaded in Program 14.19.

Program 14.19

```cpp
#include <iostream>
#include <string>
using namespace std;

int getanInt();  // function prototype)
int main()
{
  int value;

  cout << "Enter an integer value: ";
  value = getanInt();
  cout << "The integer entered is: " << value << endl;

  return 0;
}

int getanInt()
{
  bool isvalidInt(string);  // function prototype
  bool notanint = true;
  string svalue;
```

```
    while (notanint)
    {
      try
      {
        cin >> svalue;  // accept a string input
        if (!isvalidInt(svalue)) throw svalue;
      }
      catch (string e)
      {
        cout << "Invalid integer - Please reenter: ";
          continue; // send control to the while statement
      }
      notanint = false;
    }
    return atoi(svalue.c_str());  // convert to an integer
}

  bool isvalidInt(string str)
  {
    int start = 0;
    int i;
    bool valid = true;  // assume a valid
    bool sign = false;  // assume no sign

    // check for an empty string
    if (int(str.length()) == 0)  valid = false;

    // check for a leading sign
    if (str.at(0) == '-'|| str.at(0) == '+')
    {
      sign = true;
      start = 1;  // start checking for digits after the sign
    }

    // check that there is at least one character after the sign
    if (sign && int(str.length()) == 1) valid = false;

    // now check the string, which you know has at least one non-sign char
    i = start;
    while(valid && i < int(str.length()))
    {
      if(!isdigit(str.at(i))) valid = false; //found a non-digit character
      i++;  // move to next character
    }
    return valid;
  }
```

Following is a sample output produced by Program 14.19:

```
Enter an integer value: abc
Invalid integer - Please reenter: 12.
Invalid integer - Please reenter: 12e
Invalid integer - Please reenter: 120
The integer entered is: 120
```

As this output shows, the `getanInt()` function works correctly. It requests input continuously until a valid integer is entered.

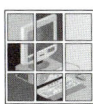

EXERCISES 14.5

1. **(Practice)** Write a C++ program that prompts the user to enter an integer. Have your program use `cin` to accept the number as an integer and use `cout` to display the value your program actually accepted from the data entered. Run your program four times. The first time you run the program, enter a valid integer number; the second time, enter a double-precision number; the third time, enter a character; and the fourth time, enter the value 12e34.

2. **(Modify)** Modify the program you wrote for Exercise 1 to prompt for and accept a double-precision number. Run the program four times: First, enter an integer; second, enter a decimal number; third, enter a decimal number with an "f" as the last character entered; and fourth, enter a character. Using the output display, keep track of the number your program actually accepted from the data you entered. What happened, if anything, and why?

3. **(For thought) a.** Why do you think successful application programs contain extensive data input validity checks? (*Hint*: Review Exercises 1 and 2.)
   b. What do you think the difference is between a data-type check and a data-reasonableness check?
   c. A program requests that the user enter a month, day, and year. What are some reasonable checks that could be made on the data entered?

4. **(Practice) a.** Enter and run Program 14.18.
   b. Run Program 14.18 four times, using the data listed in Exercise 1 for each run.

5. **(Modify)** Modify Program 14.18 to display any invalid characters that were entered.

6. **(Modify)** Modify Program 14.18 to request an integer continuously until a valid number is entered.

7. **(Modify)** Modify Program 14.18 to remove all leading and trailing spaces from the entered string before it's checked for validity.

8. **(Useful utility)** Write a function that checks each digit as it's entered, instead of checking the completed string, as in Program 14.18.

9. **(Practice)** Enter and run Program 14.19.

10. **(For thought)** Discuss whether the `isvalidInt()` function used in Program 14.19 should be modified to accept a string that ends in a decimal point. For example, should the input 12. be accepted and converted to the integer number 12 or simply be rejected as noninteger input?

11. **(Useful utility) a.** Write a C++ function named `isvalidReal()` that checks for a valid double-precision number. This kind of number can have an optional + or - sign, at most one decimal point (which can be the first character), and at least one digit between 0 and 9. The function should return the Boolean value `true` if the entered number is a real number; otherwise, it should return the Boolean value `false`.

   b. Modify the `isvalidReal()` function written for Exercise 11a to remove all leading and trailing blank spaces from its string argument before determining whether the string corresponds to a valid real number.

12. **(Useful utility)** Write and test a C++ function named `getaReal()` that uses exception handling to accept an input string continuously until a string that can be converted to a real number is entered. This function should return a `double` value corresponding to the string value the user enters.

14.6 Common Programming Errors

Here are the common errors associated with defining and processing strings:

1. Forgetting to include the `string` header file when using `string` class objects.
2. Forgetting that the newline character, `'\n'`, is a valid data input character.
3. Forgetting to convert a `string` class object by using `c_str()` when converting `string` class objects to numerical data types.
4. Not defining a `catch` block with the correct parameter data type for each thrown exception.
5. Attempting to declare an exception parameter in a `catch` block as a `string` class variable.

14.7 Chapter Summary

1. A string literal is any sequence of characters enclosed in quotation marks. It's referred to as a string value, a string constant, and, more conventionally, a string.

2. A string can be constructed as an object of the `string` class.

3. The `string` class is commonly used for constructing strings for input and output purposes, as for prompts and displayed messages. Because of its capabilities, this class is used when strings need to be compared or searched or specific characters in a string need to be examined or extracted as a substring. It's also used in more advanced situations when characters in a string need to be replaced, inserted, or deleted regularly.

4. Strings can be manipulated by using the functions of the class they're objects of or by using the general-purpose string and character methods.

5. The `cin` object, by itself, tends to be of limited usefulness for string input because it terminates input when a blank is encountered.

6. For `string` class data input, use the `getline()` method.

7. The `cout` object can be used to display `string` class strings.

8. In exception handling, information about the error that caused the exception is sent to an exception handler.

9. The process of generating and passing an exception at the point the error is detected is referred to as throwing an exception.

10. The general syntax of the code for throwing and catching an exception is as follows:

```
try
{
  // one or more statements,
  // at least one of which should
  // throw an exception
}
catch(exceptionDataType parameterName)
{
  // one or more statements
}
```

11. The `catch` block is the exception handler that identifies a thrown exception by its data type. The exception's data type must match the parameter data type inside the parentheses of the `catch` statement.

12. Multiple `catch` blocks can be used as long as each block catches a unique data type. The only requirement is providing at least one `catch` block for each `try` block.

14.8 Chapter Supplement: Namespaces and Creating a Personal Library

Until the introduction of PCs in the early 1980s, with their extensive use of integrated circuits and microprocessors, computer speed and available memory were severely restricted. For example, the most advanced computers had speeds measured in milliseconds (one-thousandth of a second); current computers have speeds measured in nanoseconds (one-billionth of a second) and higher. Similarly, the memory capacity of early desktop computers consisted of 4000 bytes, but today's computer memories are in the gigabit range and even higher.

With these early hardware restrictions, programmers had to use every possible trick to save memory space and make programs run more efficiently. Almost every program was hand-crafted and included what was called "clever code" to minimize runtime and maximize use of memory storage. Unfortunately, this individualized code became a liability. New programmers had to spend considerable time to understand existing code; even the original programmer had trouble figuring out code written only months before. This complexity in code made modifications time consuming and costly and precluded cost-effective reuse of existing code for new installations.

The inability to reuse code efficiently, combined with expanded hardware capabilities, prompted the discovery of more efficient programming. This discovery began with structured programming concepts incorporated into procedural languages, such as C and Pascal, and led to the object-oriented techniques that form the basis of C++. Although an early criticism of C++ was that it didn't have a comprehensive library of classes, this is no longer the case.

No matter how many useful classes and functions the standard library provides, however, each major type of programming application, such as engineering, commercial, and financial, has its own specialized requirements. For example, the ctime header file in C++ provides good date and time functions. However, for specialized needs, such as scheduling problems, these functions must be expanded to include finding the number of working days between two dates, taking into account weekends and holidays, and implementing previous-day and next-day algorithms to account for leap years and the actual days in each month.

To meet these specialized needs, programmers create and share their own libraries of classes and functions with other programmers working on the same or similar projects. After the classes and functions have been tested, they can be incorporated into any program without further coding time.

At this stage in your programming career, you can begin building your own library of specialized functions and classes. Section 14.5 described how to do this with the input validation functions, isvalidInt() and getanInt(), which are reproduced here for convenience:

```cpp
bool isvalidInt(string str)
{
    int start = 0;
    int i;
    bool valid = true;   // assume a valid
    bool sign = false;   // assume no sign

    // check for an empty string
    if (int(str.length()) == 0)  valid = false;

    // check for a leading sign
    if (str.at(0) == '-'|| str.at(0) == '+')
    {
        sign = true;
        start = 1;  // start checking for digits after the sign
    }

    // check that there's at least one character after the sign
    if (sign && int(str.length()) == 1) valid = false;

    // check the string, which has at least one non-sign char
    i = start;
    while(valid && i < int(str.length()))
```

```
    {
      if(!isdigit(str.at(i))) valid = false; //found a nondigit character
      i++;  // move to next character
    }
    return valid;
}

int getanInt()
{
  bool isvalidInt(string);  // function prototype
  bool notanint = true;
  string svalue;

  while (notanint)
  {
    try
    {
      cin >> svalue;  // accept a string input
      if (!isvalidInt(svalue)) throw svalue;
    }
    catch (string e)
    {
      cout << "Invalid integer - Please reenter: ";
        continue; // send control to the while statement
    }
    notanint = false;
  }
  return atoi(svalue.c_str());  // convert to an integer
}
```

The first step in creating a library is to encapsulate all the specialized functions and classes into one or more namespaces and then store the complete code in one or more files. For example, you can create one namespace, dataChecks, and save it in a file named dataChecks.cpp. Note that the namespace's filename need not be the same as the namespace name used in the code.

The following is the syntax for creating a namespace:

```
namespace name
{
    // functions and/or classes in here
}  // end of namespace
```

The following code includes the two functions isvalidInt() and getanInt() in the namespace dataChecks and adds the #include and using statements the new namespace needs. The syntax required to create the namespace has been shaded:

```
#include <iostream>
#include <string>
```

```cpp
using namespace std;

namespace dataChecks
{
  bool isvalidInt(string str)
  {
    int start = 0;
    int i;
    bool valid = true;   // assume a valid
    bool sign = false;   // assume no sign

    // check for an empty string
    if (int(str.length()) == 0)  valid = false;

    // check for a leading sign
    if (str.at(0) == '-'|| str.at(0) == '+')
    {
      sign = true;
      start = 1;  // start checking for digits after the sign
    }

    // check that there's at least one character after the sign
    if (sign && int(str.length()) == 1) valid = false;

    // check the string, which has at least one non-sign char
    i = start;
    while(valid && i < int(str.length()))
    {
    if(!isdigit(str.at(i))) valid = false; //found a nondigit
    // character
      i++;   // move to next character
    }
    return valid;
  }

  int getanInt()
  {
    bool isvalidInt(string);   // function prototype
    bool notanint = true;
    string svalue;

    while (notanint)
    {
      try
      {
        cin >> svalue;  // accept a string input
```

```
        if (!isvalidInt(svalue)) throw svalue;
      }
      catch (string e)
      {
        cout << "Invalid integer - Please reenter: ";
        continue; // send control to the while statement
      }
      notanint = false;
    }
    return atoi(svalue.c_str());   // convert to an integer
  }
} // end of dataChecks namespace
```

After the namespace has been created and stored in a file, it can be included in another file by supplying a preprocessor directive to inform the compiler where the namespace file is found and by adding an #include statement and a using directive that tell the compiler which namespace in the file to use. For the dataChecks namespace, which is stored in a file named dataChecks.cpp, the following statements perform these tasks:

```
#include <c:\\mylibrary\\dataChecks>
using namespace dataChecks;
```

The first statement provides the full pathname for the source code file. Notice that two backslashes are used to separate items in pathnames. The double backslashes are required when providing a relative or full pathname. The only time backslashes aren't required is when the library code is in the same folder as the program being executed. As indicated, the dataChecks source file is saved in the mylibrary folder. The second statement tells the compiler to use the dataChecks namespace in the designated file. Program 14.20 includes these two statements in an executable program.

 **Program 14.20**

```
#include <c:\\mylibrary\\dataChecks.cpp>
using namespace dataChecks;

int main()
{
  int value;

  cout << "Enter an integer value: ";
  value = getanInt();
  cout << "The integer entered is: " << value << endl;

  return 0;
}
```

The only requirement for the #include statement in Program 14.20 is that the filename and location must correspond to an existing file with the same name in the designated path; otherwise, a compiler error occurs. If you want to name the source code file with a file extension, any extension can be used as long as these rules are followed:

- The filename under which the code is stored includes the extension.
- The same filename, including extension, is used in the #include statement.

Therefore, if the filename used to store the functions is dataLib.cpp, the #include statement in Program 14.20 would be the following:

```
#include <c::\\mylibrary\\dataLib.cpp>
```

Note that a namespace isn't required in the file. Using a namespace enables you to isolate specific code in one named area and add more namespaces to the file as needed. Designating a namespace in the using statement tells the compiler to include only the code in the specified namespace rather than all the code in the file. In Program 14.20, if the data-checking functions weren't enclosed in a namespace, the using statement for the dataChecks namespace would have to be omitted.

Including the previously written and tested data-checking functions in Program 14.20 as a separate file allows you to focus on the code using these functions for the task being programmed instead of being concerned with the namespace's code. In Program 14.20, the main() function exercises the data-checking functions and produces the same output as Program 14.19. In creating the dataChecks namespace, you have included source code for the two functions. Including this code isn't required, and a compiled version of the source code can be saved instead. Finally, one namespace can access another by the same technique of adding #include and using statements.

EXERCISES 14.8

1. **(Practice)** Enter and compile Program 14.20. (*Hint*: The namespace file dataChecks and the program file are available with the source code provided on this book's Web site. See this book's introduction for the URL.)

2. **(For thought) a.** What is an advantage of namespaces?
   b. What is a possible disadvantage of namespaces?

3. **(For thought)** What types of classes and functions would you include in a personal library? Why?

4. **(For thought)** Why would a programmer supply a namespace file in its compiled form rather than as source code?

5. **(Useful utility) a.** Write a C++ function named whole() that returns the integer part of any number passed to the function. (*Hint*: Assign the passed argument to an integer variable.)
   b. Include the function written in Exercise 5a in a working program. Make sure your function is called from main() and correctly returns a value to main(). Have main() use a cout statement to display the returned value. Test the function by passing various data to it.

    c. When you're confident that the `whole()` function written for Exercise 5a works correctly, save it in a namespace and a personal library of your choice.

6. **(Useful utility) a.** Write a C++ function named `fracpart()` that returns the fractional part of any number passed to the function. For example, if the number 256.879 is passed to `fracpart()`, the number .879 should be returned. Have the `fracpart()` function call the `whole()` function you wrote in Exercise 5a. The number returned can then be determined as the number passed to `fracpart()` less the returned value when the same argument is passed to `whole()`.

    b. Include the function written in Exercise 6a in a working program. Make sure the function is called from `main()` and correctly returns a value to `main()`. Have `main()` use a `cout` statement to display the returned value. Test the function by passing various data to it.

    c. When you're confident the `fracpart()` function written for Exercise 6a works correctly, save it in the same namespace and personal library selected for Exercise 5c.

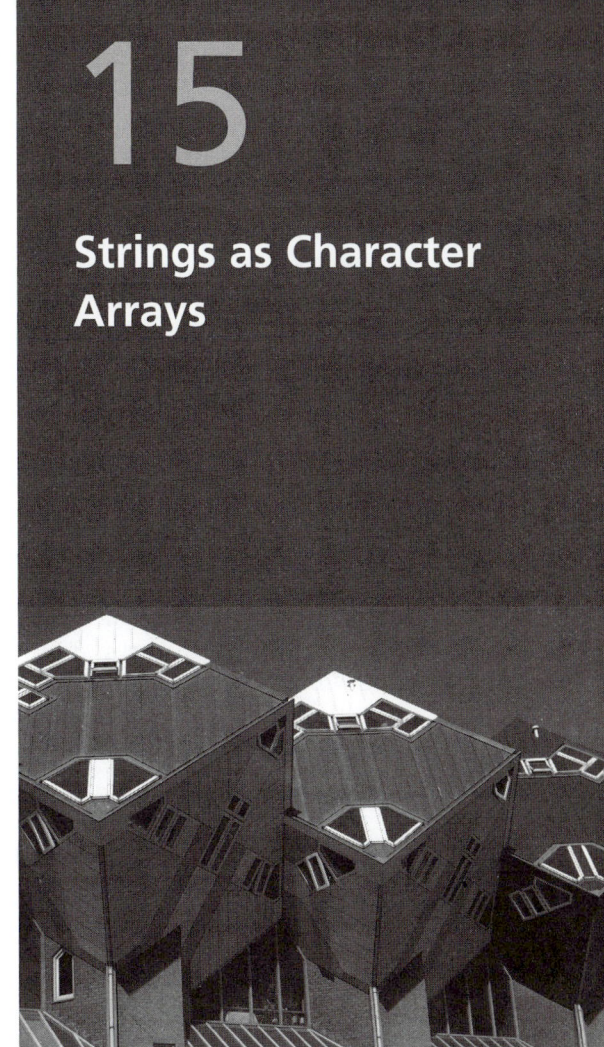

Chapter

15

Strings as Character Arrays

C++ has two different ways of storing and manipulating strings. The newer way, using the string *class, was explained in Chapter 14. The original procedure for storing a string, and the one described in this chapter, is as an array of characters terminated by a sentinel value, which is the escape sequence* '\0'. *This representation allows manipulating strings with standard element-by-element array-processing techniques. Strings stored in this manner are now referred to as character strings—or C-strings, for short. Additionally, the character-based methods previously discussed in Chapter 14, which can also be used to process elements of C-strings, are summarized in this chapter.*

15.1 C-String Fundamentals

A **C-string**, which is short for "character string," is an array of characters terminated by a special end-of-string marker called the NULL character.[1] The NULL character, represented by the escape sequence '\0', is the sentinel marking the end of the string.

C-strings can be created in a number of ways. For example, each of the following declarations creates the same C-string.

```
char test[5] = "abcd";
char test[] = "abcd";
char test[5] = {'a', 'b', 'c', 'd', '\0'};
char test[] = {'a', 'b', 'c', 'd', '\0'};
```

Each declaration creates storage for an array of exactly five characters and initializes this storage with the characters 'a', 'b', 'c', 'd', and '\0'. When a string literal is used for initialization, as in the first two declarations, the compiler automatically supplies the end-of-string NULL character. Figure 15.1 shows how the string created by each of these declarations is stored in memory.

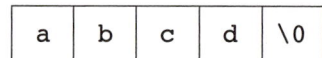

Figure 15.1   Storing a string in memory

As shown in Figure 15.1, this string uses five storage locations, and the last character in the string is the end-of-string marker '\0'. As indicated, the quotation marks surrounding the string in the first two declarations aren't stored as part of the string. Because it's an array, characters can be input, manipulated, or output by using standard array-handling techniques, including subscript and pointer notation.

C-String Input and Output

Inputting a C-string from the keyboard and displaying it require using a standard library function or class method. In addition to the standard input and output streams, cin and cout, library functions for both character-by-character and complete C-string input/output are available. Table 15.1 lists commonly used methods, which require the iostream header file.

---

[1]This method of storing a string is derived from the C language, in which a string could be stored only as a character array.

Point of Information

Should You Use a C-String or a `string` Class Object?

The reasons for using a C-string are as follows:
- The programmer has control over how the C-string is stored and manipulated.
- Many useful functions are available for entering, examining, and processing C-strings.
- C-strings are an excellent way to explore advanced programming techniques with pointers (see Section 15.2).
- You'll encounter them throughout your programming career, as they're embedded in almost all existing C++ code.
- They're fun to program.

The reasons for using a `string` class object are as follows:
- The `string` class does an automatic bounds check on every index used to access string elements. This isn't true for C-strings, and using an invalid C-string subscript can result in a system crash.
- The `string` class automatically expands and contracts storage as needed. C-strings are fixed in length and subject to overrunning the allocated storage space.
- The `string` class provides extensive methods for operating on a string. C-strings almost always require a subsidiary set of functions.
- When necessary, it's easy to convert to a C-string with the `string` class's `c_str()` method. Conversely, a C-string can be converted to a `string` class object easily by simply assigning it to a `string` object.

Table 15.1   String and Character I/O Methods (Require the Header File `iostream`)

C++ Method	Description	Example
`cin.getline(str,n,ch)`	Inputs a C-string (`str`) from the keyboard, up to a maximum of *n* characters, that's terminated by the character `ch` (typically the newline character, `'\n'`)	`cin.getline(str, 81, '\n');`
`cin.get()`	Extracts the next character from the input stream	`nextKey = cin.get();`
`cin.peek()`	Returns the next character from the input stream *without* extracting the character from the stream	`nextKey = cin.peek();`
`cout.put(charExp)`	Places the character value of `charExp` on the output stream	`cout.put('A');`

Table 15.1   String and Character I/O Methods (Require the Header File `iostream`) *(continued)*

C++ Method	Description	Example
`cin.putback(charExp)`	Pushes the character value of `charExp` back onto the input stream	`cin.putback(cKey);`
`cin.ignore(n, char)`	Ignores a maximum of the next *n* input characters, up to and including the detection of `char`; if no arguments are specified, ignores the next single character on the input stream	`cin.ignore(80,'\n');cin.ignore();`

The methods `cin.getline()`, `cin.get()`, and `cin.peek()` listed in Table 15.1 are provided for input. (They aren't the same as the methods with the same names defined for the `string` class.) The character output functions `put()` and `putback()`, however, are the same as those for the `string` class.

Program 15.1 shows using `cin.getline()` and `cout` to input and output a string entered at the user's keyboard.

Program 15.1

```cpp
#include <iostream>
using namespace std;

int main ()
{
  const int MAXCHARS  =  81;
  char message [MAXCHARS]; // an array of characters with
                           // enough storage for a complete line
  cout << "Enter a string:\n";
  cin.getline(message,MAXCHARS, '\n');
  cout << "The string just entered is:\n"
       << message << endl;

  return 0;
}
```

The following is a sample run of Program 15.1:

```
Enter a string:
This is a test input of a string of characters.
The string just entered is:
This is a test input of a string of characters.
```

The cin.getline() method used in Program 15.1 continuously accepts and stores characters typed at the keyboard into the character array named message until 80 characters are entered (the 81st character is then used to store the end-of string NULL character, '\0'), or the Enter key is detected. Pressing the Enter key generates a newline character, '\n', which cin.getline() interprets as the end-of-line entry. All the characters cin.getline() encounters, except the newline character, are stored in the message array. Before returning, cin.getline() appends a NULL character, '\0', to the stored set of characters, as shown in Figure 15.2. The cout object is then used to display the C-string.

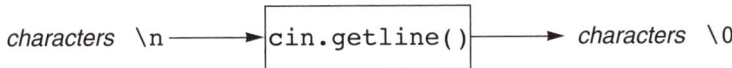

characters \n ──────▶ cin.getline() ─────▶ *characters* \0

cin.getline() substitutes \0 for the entered \n

Figure 15.2   Inputting a C-string with cin.getline()

Although the cout object is used in Program 15.1 for C-string output, the cin object can't be used in place of cin.getline() for C-string input because it stops reading characters when it encounters a blank space or a newline character. The cin.getline() method has this syntax:

cin.getline(*str*, *terminatingLength*, *terminatingChar*)

str is a C-string or a pointer to a character (discussed in Chapter 8), *terminatingLength* is an integer constant or variable indicating the maximum number of characters that can be input, and *terminatingChar* is an optional character constant or variable specifying the terminating character. If this optional third argument is omitted, the default terminating character is the newline ('\n') character. Therefore, the statement

cin.getline(message, MAXCHARS);

can be used in place of this longer statement:

cin.getline(message, MAXCHARS, '\n');

Both method calls stop reading characters when the Enter key is pressed or until MAXCHARS characters have been read, whichever comes first. Because cin.getline() permits specifying any terminating character for the input stream, a statement such as cin.getline (`message`, `MAXCHARS`, `'x'`); is also valid. This statement stops accepting characters when the x key is pressed. In all future programs, assume that input is terminated by pressing Enter, which generates a newline character. So the optional third argument passed to `getline()`, which is the terminating character, is omitted.

C-String Processing

C-strings can be manipulated with standard library functions or as subscripted array variables. (Pointers can also be used, as discussed in Section 15.2.) For now, concentrate on processing a C-string in a character-by-character fashion with subscripts. (The library functions typically available for use are also discussed in Section 15.2.)

For a specific example, look at the `strcopy()` function that copies the contents of `string2` to `string1`:

```
// copy string2 to string1
void strcopy(char string1[], char string2[])
{
  int i = 0;                    // i is used as a subscript

  while ( string2[i] != '\0')   // check for end of string
  {
    string1[i] = string2[i];    // copy the element to string1
    i++;
  }
  string1[i] = '\0';            // terminate the first string
  return;
}
```

The `strcopy()` function is used to copy the characters from one character array to another, one character at a time. As written, the subscript `i` in the function is used to access each character in the `string2` array by "marching along" the string one character at a time. As each character is accessed from the `string2` array, it's copied to the `string1` array. Although this function can be shortened considerably and written more compactly, which is done in Section 15.2, it does illustrate the main features of C-string manipulation:

- Accessing array elements by using subscripts (pointers can also be used)
- Using the end-of-string `NULL` character to determine when to stop processing

In reviewing `strcopy()`, note that the two C-strings are passed to the function as arrays. Each element of `string2` is then assigned to the equivalent element of `string1` until the end-of-string marker is encountered. The detection of the `NULL` character forces the termination of the `while` loop that controls the copying of elements. Because the `NULL` character isn't copied from `string2` to `string1`, the last statement in `strcopy()` appends an end-of-string character to `string1`. In using `strcopy()`, you must ensure that enough space has been allocated for the `string1` array to be able to store the `string2` array's elements.

Program 15.2 includes the `strcopy()` function in a complete program. Note that its function prototype declares that it expects to receive two character arrays.

Program 15.2

```cpp
#include <iostream>
using namespace std;

void strcopy(char [], char []);  // function prototype

int main()
{
  const int MAXCHARS = 81;
  char message[MAXCHARS];        // enough storage for a complete line
  char newMessage[MAXCHARS];     // enough storage for a copy of message
  int i;

  cout << "Enter a sentence: ";
  cin.getline(message,MAXCHARS);    // get the string
  strcopy(newMessage,message);      // pass two array addresses
  cout << newMessage << endl;

  return 0;
}

void strcopy(char string1[], char string2[])  // copy string2 to string1
{
  int i = 0;                         // i is used as a subscript

  while (string2[i] != '\0')       // check for end of string
  {
    string1[i] = string2[i];       // copy the element to string1
    i++;
  }
  string1[i] = '\0';               // terminate the first string

  return;
}
```

The following is a sample run of Program 15.2:

Enter a sentence: **How much wood could a woodchuck chuck.**
How much wood could a woodchuck chuck.

Character-by-Character Input Just as C-strings can be processed by using character-by-character techniques, they can also be entered and displayed in this manner. For example, take a look at Program 15.3, which uses the character input function `cin.get()` to accept a string one character at a time. The shaded portion of Program 15.3 essentially replaces the `cin.getline()` function used in Program 15.1.

Program 15.3

```
#include <iostream>
using namespace std;

int main()
{
  const int MAXCHARS = 81;
  char message[MAXCHARS], c;

  cout << "Enter a sentence:\n";

  int i = 0;
  while(i < MAXCHARS && (c = cin.get()) != '\n')
  {
    message[i] = c;        // store the character entered
    i++;
  }
  message[i] = '\0';       // terminate the string

  cout << "The sentence just entered is:\n";
  cout << message << endl;

  return 0;
}
```

The following is a sample run of Program 15.3:

```
Enter a sentence:
This is a test input of a string of characters.
The sentence just entered is:
This is a test input of a string of characters.
```

The while statement in Program 15.3 causes characters to be read and assigned to the variable c. Each entered character is stored correctly in the message array, provided the number of characters entered is less than 81 and the character returned by cin.get() isn't the newline character. The parentheses surrounding the expression c = cin.get() are necessary to assign the character returned by cin.get() to the variable c before comparing it with the newline escape sequence. Without the parentheses, the comparison operator, !=, which takes precedence over the assignment operator, causes the entire expression to be equivalent to the following, which is an invalid application of cin.get():[2]

```
(c = (cin.get() != '\n'))
```

[2]The equivalent statement in C is c = (getchar() != '\n'), which is a valid expression that produces an unexpected result for most beginning programmers. The reason is that the character returned by cin.get() is compared with '\n', and the value of the comparison is 0 or 1, depending on whether cin.get() received the newline character. This value (0 or 1) is then assigned to c.

Program 15.3 also shows a useful technique for developing functions. The shaded statements constitute a self-contained unit for entering a complete line of characters from the keyboard. These statements can be removed from `main()` and placed together as a new function.

In Program 15.4, the shaded statements from Program 15.3 are placed in a separate function named `getaline()`. Notice that in the process, the `MAXCHARS` constant has been placed above the `main()` function. This placement gives the constant a global scope, which makes it available to both the `main()` and `getaline()` functions.

 Program 15.4

```
#include <iostream>
using namespace std;

const int MAXCHARS = 81;   // global symbolic constant
void getaline(char []);    // function prototype

int main()
{
  char message[MAXCHARS];  // enough storage for a complete line

  cout << "Enter a sentence:\n";
  getaline(message);
  cout << "The sentence just entered is:\n";
  cout << message << endl;
}

void getaline(char strng[])
{
  int i = 0;
  char c;
  while(i < MAXCHARS && (c = cin.get()) != '\n')
  {
    strng[i] = c;     // store the character entered
    i++;
  }
  strng[i] = '\0';    // terminate the string

  return;
}
```

EXERCISES 15.1

1. **(Program) a.** The following function can be used to select and display all vowels in a user-entered string:

```
void vowels(char strng[])
{
  int i = 0;
  char c;
  while ((c = strng[i++]) != '\0')
    switch(c)
    {
      case 'a':
      case 'e':
      case 'i':
      case 'o':
      case 'u':
        cout << c;
    } // end of switch
  cout << endl;
  return;
}
```

Note that the `switch` statement in `vowels()` uses the fact that selected cases "drop through" in the absence of `break` statements. Therefore, all selected cases result in a `cout` object call. Include `vowels()` in a working program that accepts a user-entered string and then displays all vowels in the string. In response to the input `How much is the little worth worth?`, your program should display `ouieieoo`.

   b. Modify `vowels()` to count and display the total number of vowels in the string passed to it.

2. **(Modify)** Modify the `vowels()` function in Exercise 1a to count and display the numbers of each vowel in the string.

3. **(Program) a.** Write a C++ function to count the total number of characters, including blanks, in a string. Don't include the end-of-string marker in the count.

   b. Include the function written for Exercise 3a in a complete working program.

4. **(Program)** Write a program that accepts a string of characters from the keyboard and displays the hexadecimal equivalent of each character.

5. **(Program)** Write a C++ program that accepts a string of characters from the keyboard and displays the string with one word per line.

6. **(Program)** Write a function that reverses the characters in a string. (*Hint*: It can be considered a string copy, starting from the back end of the first string.)

7. **(Program)** Write a function called `delChar()` that can be used to delete characters from a string. The function should take three arguments: the string name, the number of characters to delete, and the starting position in the string where characters should be deleted. For example, the call `delChar(strng,13,5)`, when applied to the string `all enthusiastic people`, should result in the string `all people`.

8. **(Program)** Write a function called `addChar()` to insert one string of characters into another string. The function should take three arguments: the string to be inserted, the original string, and the position in the original string where the insertion should begin. For example, the call `addChar("for all",message,6)` should insert the characters `for all` in `message`, starting at `message[5]`.

9. **(Program) a.** Write a C++ function named `toUpper()` that converts lowercase letters to uppercase letters. The expression `c - 'a' + 'A'` can be used to make the conversion for any lowercase character stored in `c`.
   b. Add a data input check to the function written in Exercise 9a to verify that a valid lowercase letter is passed to the function. A character in ASCII is lowercase if it's greater than or equal to `a` and less than or equal to `z`. If the character isn't a valid lowercase letter, have the `toUpper()` function return the passed character unaltered.
   c. Write a C++ program that accepts a string from the keyboard and converts all lowercase letters in the string to uppercase letters.

10. **(Program)** Write a C++ program that accepts a string from the keyboard and converts all uppercase letters in the string to lowercase letters.

11. **(Program)** Write a C++ program that counts the number of words in a string. A word is encountered whenever there's a transition from a blank space to a nonblank character. Assume the string contains only words separated by blank spaces.

15.2 Pointers and C-String Library Functions

Pointers are exceptionally useful in constructing functions that manipulate C-strings. When pointer notation is used in place of subscripts to access characters in a C-string, the resulting statements are more compact and more efficient. This section describes the equivalence between subscripts and pointers when accessing characters in a C-string.

Take another look at the `strcopy()` function introduced in Section 15.1. It was used to copy the characters of one C-string to a second C-string. For convenience, this function is repeated here:

```
// a function to copy string2 to string1
void strcopy(char string1[], char string2[])
{
  int i = 0;

  while (string2[i] != '\0')      // check for end of string
  {
    string1[i] = string2[i];      // copy the element to string1
    i++;
  }
  string1[i] = '\0';              // terminate the first string

  return;
}
```

Before you see how to write a pointer version of `strcopy()`, two modifications should be made to the function to make it more efficient. The first modification has to do with the expression in the function's `while` statement. As written, it tests each character to ensure that the end of the C-string hasn't been reached. Like all relational expressions, the tested expression, `string2[i] != '\0'`, is true or false. Take the string `this is a string` shown in Figure 15.3 as an example. As long as `string2[i]` doesn't access the end-of-C-string character, the expression's value is non-zero and considered to be true. The expression is false only when the expression's value is zero, which occurs when the last element in the C-string is accessed.

Recall that C++ defines false as zero and true as anything else. Therefore, the expression `string2[i] != '\0'` becomes zero (false) when the end of the string is reached. It's non-zero (true) everywhere else. The NULL character has an internal value of zero, so the comparison with `'\0'` isn't necessary. When `string2[i]` accesses the end-of-C-string character, the value of `string2[i]` is zero. When `string2[i]` accesses any other character, the value of `string2[i]` is the value of the code used to store the character and is non-zero. Figure 15.4 lists the ASCII codes for the string `this is a string`. As the figure shows, each element has a non-zero value except the NULL character.

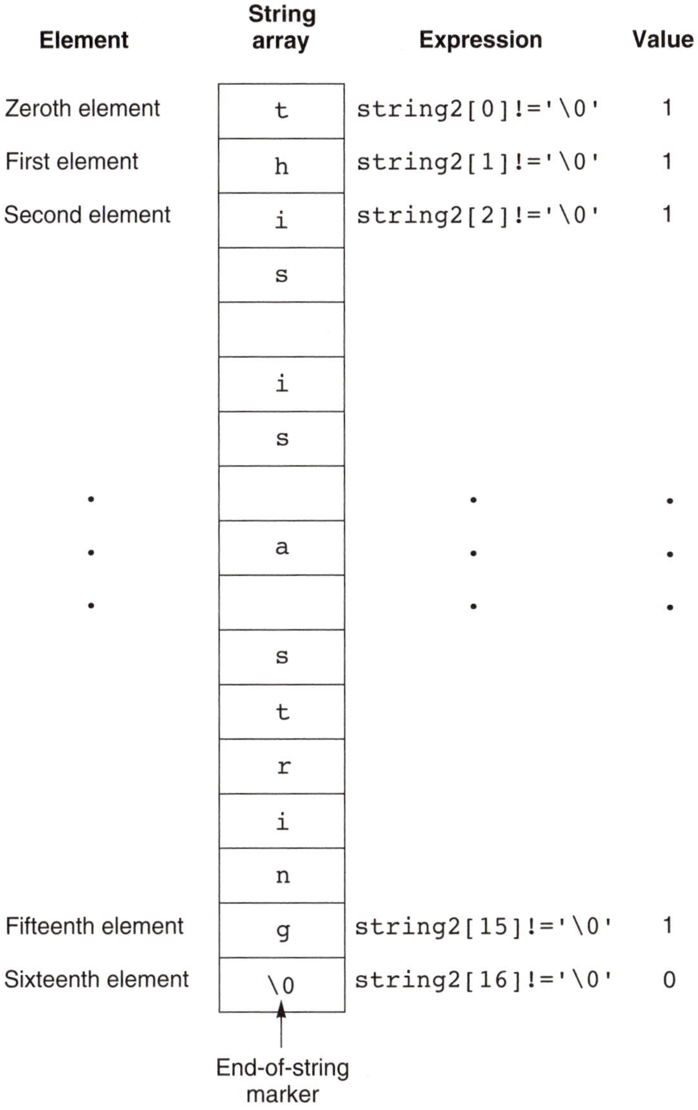

Element	String array	Expression	Value
Zeroth element	t	`string2[0]!='\0'`	1
First element	h	`string2[1]!='\0'`	1
Second element	i	`string2[2]!='\0'`	1
	s		
	i		
	s		
.		.	.
.	a	.	.
.		.	.
	s		
	t		
	r		
	i		
	n		
Fifteenth element	g	`string2[15]!='\0'`	1
Sixteenth element	\0	`string2[16]!='\0'`	0

End-of-string
marker

Figure 15.3 The while test becomes false at the end of the string

String array	Stored codes	Expression	Value
t	116	string2[0]	116
h	104	string2[1]	104
i	105	string2[2]	105
s	115		
	32		
i	105		
s	115		
	32	.	.
a	97	.	.
	32	.	.
s	115		
t	116		
r	114		
i	105		
n	110		
g	103	string2[15]	103
\0	0	string2[16]	0

Figure 15.4   The ASCII codes used to store this is a string

Because the expression string2[i] is zero only at the end of a C-string and non-zero for every other character, the expression while (string2[i] != '\0') can be replaced by the simpler expression while(string2[i]). Although it might seem confusing at first, the revised test expression is certainly more compact than the longer version. Advanced C++ programmers often write end-of-C-string tests in this shorter form, so being familiar with this expression is worthwhile. Including this expression in strcopy() results in the following version:

```
// a function to copy string2 to string1
void strcopy(char string1[], char string2[])
{
   int i = 0;
```

```
  while (string2[i])
  {
    string1[i] = string2[i];   // copy the element to string1
    i++;
  }

  string1[i] = '\0';           // terminate the first string

  return;
}
```

The second modification that can be made to this C-string copy function is to include the assignment inside the test portion of the `while` statement. The new version of `strcopy()` is as follows:

```
// a function to copy string2 to string1
void strcopy(char string1[], char string2[])
{
  int i = 0;

  while (string1[i] = string2[i])
     i++;

  return;
}
```

Note that including the assignment statement in the test part of the `while` statement eliminates the necessity of terminating the copied string separately with the NULL character. The assignment in parentheses ensures that the NULL character is copied from `string2` to `string1`. The value of the assignment expression becomes zero only after the NULL character is assigned to `string1`, at which point the `while` loop is terminated.

Converting `strcopy()` from subscript notation to pointer notation is now straightforward. Although each subscript version of `strcopy()` can be rewritten with pointer notation, the following is the equivalent of the previous subscript version:

```
// a function to copy string2 to string1
void strcopy(char *string1, char *string2)
{
  while (*string1 = *string2)
  {
    string1++;
    string2++;
  }

  return;
}
```

In both subscript and pointer versions of `strcopy()`, the function receives the name of the array being passed. Recall that passing an array name to a function actually passes the address of the array's first location. In the pointer version of `strcopy()`, the two passed addresses are stored in the pointer parameters `string1` and `string2`.

The declarations `char *string1;` and `char *string2;` used in the pointer version of `strcopy()` indicate that `string1` and `string2` are pointers containing the address of a character. This notation emphasizes that two addresses are actually being passed. (Remember that an array name is a pointer constant.) These declarations are equivalent to the declarations `char string1[];` and `char string2[];`.

Inside `strcopy()`, the pointer expression `*string1`, which refers to "the element whose address is in `string1`," replaces the equivalent subscript expression `string1[i]`. Similarly, the pointer expression `*string2` replaces the equivalent subscript expression `string2[i]`. The expression `*string1 = *string2` causes the element pointed to by `string2` to be assigned to the element pointed to by `string1`. Because the starting addresses of both C-strings are passed to `strcopy()` and stored in `string1` and `string2`, the expression `*string1` initially refers to `string1[0]`, and the expression `*string2` initially refers to `string2[0]`.

Consecutively incrementing both pointers in `strcopy()` with the expressions `string1++` and `string2++` simply causes each pointer to "point to" the next consecutive character in the C-string. As with the subscript version, the pointer version of `strcopy()` steps along, copying element by element, until the end of the string is copied. One final change to the C-string copy function can be made by including the pointer increments as postfix operators in the test part of the `while` statement. The final form of this function is as follows:

```
// a function to copy string2 to string1
void strcopy(char *string1, char *string2)
{
  while (*string1++ = *string2++)
    ;
 return;
}
```

There's no ambiguity in the expression `*string1++ = *string2++`, even though the indirection operator, `*`, and increment operator, `++`, have the same precedence. Here the character pointed to is accessed before the pointer is incremented. It's not until the assignment `*string1 = *string2` is completed that the pointers are incremented to point correctly to the next characters in the respective C-strings.

The C-string copy function included in the standard library supplied with C++ compilers is typically written exactly like the pointer version of `strcopy()`.

Point of Information

Processing C-Strings

C-string variables can't be assigned values after being declared. For example, if `test` has been declared as a C-string with the declaration statement

```
char test[] = "abcd";
```

a subsequent assignment, such as `test = "efgh";`, is invalid.

In place of an assignment, you can use the `strcpy()` function, such as `strcpy(test, "efgh")`. The only restriction on using `strcpy()` is that the size of the declared array (five elements, in this case) can't be exceeded. Attempting to copy a larger C-string value into `test` causes the copy to overflow the destination array, beginning with the memory area immediately after the last array element. This memory overflow overwrites whatever was in these memory locations and typically causes a runtime crash when the overwritten areas are accessed via their legitimate identifier names.

The same problem can happen when using the `strcat()` function. It's your responsibility to ensure that the concatenated C-string fits into the original string.

An interesting situation arises when C-string variables are defined with pointers (see the Point of Information in Section 15.3). In these situations, assignments can be made after the declaration statement.

Library Functions

Because a C-string is an array and C++ doesn't provide built-in operations for arrays, such as array assignment and relational comparisons, these operations aren't provided for C-strings. Extensive collections of C-string-handling functions, however, are included with all C++ compilers. They effectively supply C-string assignment, comparison, and other useful C-string operations. Table 15.2 lists the more common C-string library functions, which are called in the same manner as all C++ functions. The declarations for these functions are in the standard header file `cstring` and must be included in your program before the function is called.

Table 15.2 C-String Library Functions (Require the Header File `cstring`)

Name	Description	Example
`strcpy(stringVar, stringExp)`	Copies `stringExp` to `stringVar`, including the `'\0'`.	`strcpy(test, "efgh")`
`strcat(stringVar, stringExp)`	Appends `stringExp` to the end of the string value contained in `stringVar`.	`strcat(test, "there")`
`strlen(stringExp)`	Returns the length of the string. Does not include the `'\0'` in the length count.	`strlen("Hello World!")`

Table 15.2 C-String Library Functions (Require the Header File `cstring`) (*continued*)

Name	Description	Example
`strcmp(stringExp1,stringExp2)`	Compares `stringExp1` with `stringExp2`. Returns a negative integer if `stringExp1 < stringExp2`, 0 if `stringExp1 == stringExp2`, and a positive integer if `stringExp1 > stringExp2`.	`strcmp("Bebop","Beehive")`
`strncpy(stringVar,stringExp,n)`	Copies at most *n* characters of `stringExp` to `stringVar`. If `stringExp` has fewer than *n* characters, it pads `stringVar` with '\0's.	`strncpy(str1, str2, 5)`
`strncmp(stringExp1,stringExp2, n)`	Compares at most *n* characters of `stringExp1` with `stringExp2`. Returns the same values as `strcmp()` based on the number of characters compared.	`strncmp("Bebop",Beehive",2)`
`strchr(stringExp, character)`	Locates the first occurrence of the character in the string. Returns the address of the character.	`strchr("Hello", 'l')`
`strtok(string1, character)`	Parses `string1` into tokens. Returns the next sequence of characters contained in `string1`, up to but not including the delimiter character `character`.	`strtok("Hello there World!",'')`

The first four functions listed in Table 15.2 are used most often. The `strcpy()` function copies a source C-string expression, which consists of a string literal or the contents of a C-string variable, into a destination C-string variable. For example, in the function call `strcpy(string1, "Hello World!")`, the source string literal `"Hello World!"` is copied into the destination C-string variable `string1`. Similarly, if the source string is a C-string variable named `src_string`, the function call `strcpy(string1, src_string)` copies the contents of `src_string` into `string1`. In both cases, it's the programmer's responsibility to ensure that `string1` is large enough to contain the source C-string (see the previous Point of Information).

The `strcat()` function appends a string expression to the end of a C-string variable. For example, if the contents of a C-string variable named `dest_string` is `"Hello"`, the function call `strcat(dest_string, " there World!")` results in assigning the string value

"Hello there World!" to dest_string. As with the strcpy() function, it's the programmer's responsibility to ensure that the destination C-string is defined as large enough to hold the additional concatenated characters.

The strlen() function returns the number of characters in its C-string parameter but doesn't include the terminating NULL character in the count. For example, the value returned by the function call strlen("Hello World!") is 12.

Finally, two string expressions can be compared for equality by using the strcmp() function. This comparison is done character by character in the same manner described in Section 14.1 for string class objects. Program 15.5 uses these C-string functions in the context of a complete program.

Program 15.5

```cpp
#include <iostream>
#include <cstring>  // required for the string function library
using namespace std;
int main()
{
  const int MAXELS = 50;
  char string1[MAXELS] = "Hello";
  char string2[MAXELS] = "Hello there";
  int n;

  n = strcmp(string1, string2);

  if (n < 0)
    cout << string1 << " is less than " << string2 << endl;
  else if (n == 0)
    cout << string1 << " is equal to " << string2 << endl;
  else
    cout << string1 << " is greater than " << string2 << endl;

  cout << "\nThe length of string1 is " << strlen(string1)
       << " characters" << endl;
  cout << "The length of string2 is " << strlen(string2)
       << " characters" << endl;

  strcat(string1," there World!");

  cout << "\nAfter concatenation, string1 contains "
       << "the string value\n" << string1
       << "\nThe length of this string is "
       << strlen(string1) << " characters" << endl;
```

```
cout << "\nType in a sequence of characters for string2: ";
cin.getline(string2, MAXELS);

strcpy(string1, string2);

cout << "After copying string2 to string1, "
     << "the string value in string1 is:\n" << string2
     << "\nThe length of this string is "
     << strlen(string1) << " characters" << endl;

return 0;
}
```

Following is a sample output produced by Program 15.5:

```
Hello is less than Hello there

The length of string1 is 5 characters
The length of string2 is 11 characters

After concatenation, string1 contains the string value
Hello there World!
The length of this string is 18 characters

Type in a sequence of characters for string2: It's a wonderful day
After copying string2 to string1, the string value in string1 is:
It's a wonderful day
The length of this string is 20 characters
```

Character-Handling Functions

In addition to C-string manipulation functions, all C++ compilers include the character-handling functions covered previously in Section 14.2 and repeated in Table 15.3 for convenience. The prototypes for these functions are in the header file cctype, which should be included in any program using these functions.

Table 15.3   Character Library Functions (Require the Header Files string and cctype)

Function Prototype	Description	Example
int isalpha(charExp)	Returns a true (non-zero integer) if charExp evaluates to a letter; otherwise, it returns a false (zero integer)	isalpha('a')

Table 15.3 Character Library Functions (Require the Header Files `string` and `cctype`) (*continued*)

Function Prototype	Description	Example
`int isalnum(charExp)`	Returns a `true` (non-zero integer) if `charExp` evaluates to a letter or a digit; otherwise, it returns a `false` (zero integer)	`isalnum(key);`
`int isupper(charExp)`	Returns a `true` (non-zero integer) if `charExp` evaluates to an uppercase letter; otherwise, it returns a `false` (zero integer)	`isupper('a')`
`int islower(charExp)`	Returns a `true` (non-zero integer) if `charExp` evaluates to a lowercase letter; otherwise, it returns a `false` (zero integer)	`islower('a')`
`int isdigit(charExp)`	Returns a `true` (non-zero integer) if `charExp` evaluates to a digit (0 through 9); otherwise, it returns a `false` (zero integer)	`isdigit('5')`
`int isascii(charExp)`	Returns a `true` (non-zero integer) if `charExp` evaluates to an ASCII character; otherwise, returns a `false` (zero integer)	`isascii('a')`
`int isspace(charExp)`	Returns a `true` (non-zero integer) if `charExp` evaluates to a space; otherwise, returns a `false` (zero integer)	`isspace(' ')`
`int isprint(charExp)`	Returns a `true` (non-zero integer) if `charExp` evaluates to a printable character; otherwise, returns a `false` (zero integer)	`isprint('a')`

Table 15.3   Character Library Functions (Require the Header Files `string` and `cctype`) (*continued*)

Function Prototype	Description	Example
`int isctrl(charExp)`	Returns a `true` (non-zero integer) if `charExp` evaluates to a control character; otherwise, it returns a `false` (zero integer)	`isctrl('a')`
`int ispunct(charExp)`	Returns a `true` (non-zero integer) if `charExp` evaluates to a punctuation character; otherwise, returns a `false` (zero integer)	`ispunct('!')`
`int isgraph(charExp)`	Returns a `true` (non-zero integer) if `charExp` evaluates to a printable character other than white space; otherwise, returns a `false` (zero integer)	`isgraph(' ')`
`int toupper(charExp)`	Returns the uppercase equivalent if `charExp` evaluates to a lowercase character; otherwise, returns the character code without modification	`toupper('a')`
`int tolower(charExp)`	Returns the lowercase equivalent if `charExp` evaluates to an uppercase character; otherwise, returns the character code without modification	`tolower('A')`

Because all the `istype()` functions listed in Table 15.3 return a non-zero integer (interpreted as a Boolean `true` value) when the character meets the condition and return a zero integer (interpreted as a Boolean `false` value) when the condition isn't met, these functions can be used in an `if` statement. For example, take a look at the following code segment:

```
char ch;
ch = cin.get();   // get a character from the keyboard

if(isdigit(ch))
  cout << "The character just entered is a digit" << endl;
else if(ispunct(ch))
  cout << "The character just entered is a punctuation mark" << endl;
```

Note that the character function is included as a condition in the `if` statement. This is possible because the function returns a Boolean `true` (non-zero) or `false` (zero) value.

Program 15.6 shows using the `toupper()` function in the `ConvertToUpper()` function, which converts all lowercase string characters to their uppercase form.

Program 15.6

```
#include <iostream>
using namespace std;

void ConvertToUpper(char []);   // function prototype

int main()
{
  const int MAXCHARS = 100;
  char message[MAXCHARS];

  cout << "\nType in any sequence of characters: ";
  cin.getline(message,MAXCHARS);

  ConvertToUpper(message);

  cout << "The characters just entered in uppercase are: "
       << message << endl;

  return 0;
}

// this function converts all lowercase characters to uppercase
void ConvertToUpper(char message[])
{
  for(int i = 0; message[i] != '\0'; i++)
    message[i] = toupper(message[i]);

  return;
}
```

The output produced when Program 15.6 runs is as follows:

```
Type in any sequence of characters: this is a test OF 12345.
The characters just entered in uppercase are: THIS IS A TEST OF 12345.
```

Note that the `toupper()` library function converts only lowercase letters; all other characters are unaffected.

Conversion Functions

The last group of standard string library functions, listed in Table 15.4, is used to convert C-strings to and from integer and double-precision data types. The prototypes for these functions are in the header file `cstdlib`, which must be included in any program using these functions. Program 15.7 shows using the `atoi()` and `atof()` functions.

Table 15.4   String Conversion Functions (Require the Header File `cstdlib`)

Function Prototype	Description	Example
`int atoi(stringExp)`	Converts `stringExp` (an ASCII string) to an integer. Conversion stops at the first non-integer character.	`atoi("1234")`
`double atof(stringExp)`	Converts `stringExp` (an ASCII string) to a double-precision number. Conversion stops at the first character that can't be interpreted as a `double`.	`atof("12.34")`
`char[] itoa(integerExp)`	Converts `integerExp` (an integer) to a character array. The space allocated for the returned characters must be large enough for the converted value.	`itoa(1234)`

Program 15.7 produces the following output:

```
The string "12345" as an integer number is: 12345
This number divided by 3 is: 4115
The string "12345.96" as a double number is: 12345.96
This number divided by 3 is: 4115.32
```

As this output shows, after a string has been converted to an integer or a double-precision value, mathematical operations on the numerical value are valid.

Program 15.7

```cpp
#include <iostream>
#include <cstring>
#include <cstdlib>
#include <iomanip>
using namespace std;

int main()
{
  const int MAXELS = 20;
  char string[MAXELS] = "12345";
  int num;
  double dnum;

  num = atoi(string);

  cout << "The string \"" << string << "\" as an integer number is: "
       << num;
  cout << "\nThis number divided by 3 is: " << num / 3 << endl;

  strcat(string, ".96");

  dnum = atof(string);

  cout << "The string \"" << string << "\" as a double number is: "
       << fixed << setprecision(2) << dnum;
  cout << "\nThis number divided by 3 is: " << dnum / 3 << endl;

  return 0;
}
```

EXERCISES 15.2

1. **(Practice)** Determine the value of *text, *(text + 3), and *(text + 10), assuming text is an array of characters and the following has been stored in the array:
   a. Be of good purpose
   b. Harry Houdini was a magician
   c. What a great movie
   d. Oops, my bad!

2. **(Program) a.** The following function, `convert()`, "marches along" the C-string passed to it and sends each character in the string one at a time to the `ToUpper()` function until the NULL character is encountered:

```
// convert a string to uppercase letters
void convert(char strng[])
{
  int i = 0;
  while (strng[i] != '\0')
  {
    strng[i] = ToUpper(strng[i]);
    i++;
  }

  return;
}
```

```
char ToUpper(char letter) // convert a character to uppercase
{
  if( (letter >= 'a') && (letter <= 'z') )
    return (letter - 'a' + 'A');
  else
    return (letter);
}
```

The `ToUpper()` function takes each character passed to it and examines it to determine whether the character is a lowercase letter (any character from a to z). Assuming that characters are stored with the standard ASCII character codes, the expression `letter - 'a' + 'A'` converts a lowercase letter to its uppercase equivalent. Rewrite the `convert()` function with pointers.

   b. Include the `convert()` and `ToUpper()` functions in a working program. The program should prompt the user for a string and display the string in uppercase letters.

3. **(Program)** Using pointers, repeat Exercise 1 from Section 15.1.

4. **(Program)** Using pointers, repeat Exercise 2 from Section 15.1.

5. **(Program)** Using pointers, repeat Exercise 3 from Section 15.1.

6. **(Program)** Write a function named `remove()` that returns nothing and deletes all occurrences of a character from a C-string. The function should take two arguments: the string name and the character to remove. For example, if `message` contains the string `Happy Holidays`, the function call `remove(message,'H')` should place the string `appy olidays` in `message`.

7. **(Program)** Using pointers, repeat Exercise 6 from Section 15.1.

8. **(Program)** Write a program using the `cin.get()` and `toupper()` library functions, along with a `cout` stream object to display each entered letter in its uppercase form. The program should terminate when the 1 key (the digit) is pressed.

9. **(Program)** Write a function that uses pointers to add a single character at the end of an existing C-string. The function should replace the existing `'\0'` character with the new character and add a new \0 at the end of the string. The function returns nothing.

10. **(Program)** Write a function that uses pointers to delete a single character from the end of a C-string, which is achieved by moving the `'\0'` character one position closer to the start of the string. The function returns nothing.

11. **(Program)** Write a function named `trimfrnt()` that deletes all leading blanks from a C-string and returns nothing. Write the function by using pointers.

12. **(Program)** Write a function named `trimrear()` that deletes all trailing blanks from a C-string and returns nothing. Write the function using pointers.

13. **(Program)** Write a function named `strlen()` that returns the number of characters in a C-string. Don't include the \0 character in the returned count.

15.3 C-String Definitions and Pointer Arrays

The definition of a C-string automatically involves a pointer. For example, the definition `char message1[80];` reserves storage for 80 characters and automatically creates a pointer constant, `message1`, containing the address of `message1[0]`. As a pointer constant, the address associated with the pointer can't be changed; it must always "point to" the beginning of the created array.

Instead of creating a C-string as an array, creating a C-string with a pointer is also possible. For example, the definition `char *message2;` creates a pointer to a character. In this case, `message2` is a true pointer variable. After a pointer to a character is defined, assignment statements, such as `message2 = "this is a string";`, can be made. In this assignment, `message2`, which is a pointer, receives the address of the first character in the string.

The main difference in the definitions of `message1` as an array and `message2` as a pointer is the way the pointer is created. Defining `message1` with the declaration `char message1[80];` explicitly calls for a fixed amount of storage for the array, which causes the compiler to create a pointer constant. Defining `message2` with the declaration `char *message2;` explicitly creates a pointer variable first. This pointer is then used to hold the address of a C-string when the C-string is actually specified. This difference in definitions has both storage and programming consequences.

From a programming perspective, defining `message2` as a pointer to a character allows making C-string assignments, such as `message2 = "this is a string";`, in a program. Similar assignments aren't allowed for C-strings defined as arrays, so the statement `message1 = "this is a string";` isn't valid. Both definitions, however, allow initializations to be made with a string literal. For example, both the following initializations are valid:

```
char message1[80] = "this is a string";
char *message2 = "this is a string";
```

From a storage perspective, the allocation of space for `message1` is quite different from that for `message2`. As shown in Figure 15.5, both initializations cause the computer to store the same C-string but in different locations. In the case of message1, a specific set of 80 storage locations is reserved, and the first 17 locations are initialized. Different C-strings can be stored, but each string overwrites the previously stored characters. The same isn't true for message2.

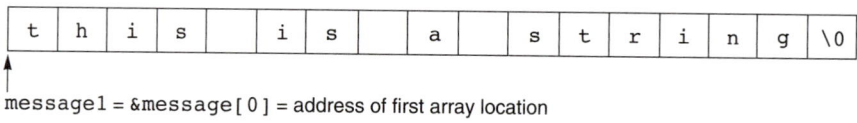

message1 = &message[0] = address of first array location

a. Storage allocation for a C-string defined as an array

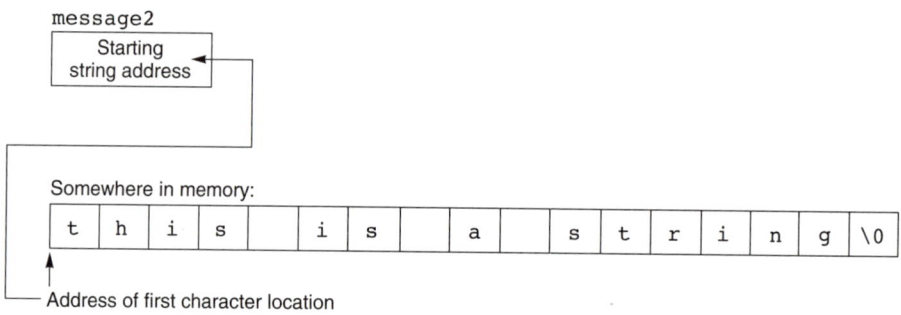

b. Storage of a C-string using a pointer

Figure 15.5   C-string storage allocation

The definition of message2 reserves enough storage for one pointer. The initialization then causes the string literal to be stored in memory and the address of the string's first character—in this case, t's address—to be loaded into the pointer. If a later assignment is made to message2, the initial C-string remains in memory, and new storage locations are allocated to the new C-string. For example, take a look at this sequence of instructions:

```
char *message2 = "this is a string";
message2 = "A new message";
```

The first statement defines message2 as a pointer variable, stores the initialization string in memory, and loads the starting address of the string (the address of the t in this) into message2. The next assignment statement causes the computer to store the second string and change the address in message2 to point to the starting location of this new string.

It's important to realize that the second string assigned to message2 doesn't overwrite the first string but simply changes the address in message2 to point to the new string. As Figure 15.6 shows, both strings are stored in the computer. Any additional string assignment to message2 would result in additional storage of the new string and a corresponding change in the address stored in message2. Doing so also means you no longer have access to the original C-string memory location.

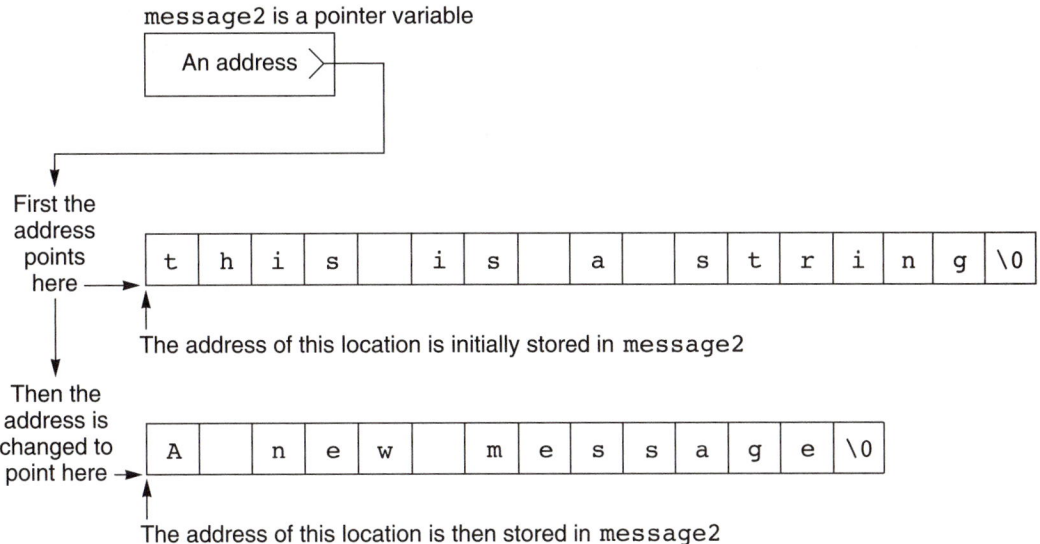

Figure 15.6 Storage allocation for Figure 15.5

Pointer Arrays

The declaration of an array of character pointers is a useful extension to single string pointer declarations. For example, the following declaration creates an array of four elements, in which each element is a pointer to a character:

```
char *seasons[4];
```

Each pointer can be assigned to point to a string by using string assignment statements. Therefore, the following statements set appropriate addresses in the pointers:

```
seasons[0] = "Winter";
seasons[1] = "Spring";
seasons[2] = "Summer";
seasons[3] = "Fall";  // string lengths can differ
```

Figure 15.7 shows the addresses loaded into the pointers for these assignments. As shown, the `seasons` array doesn't contain the actual strings assigned to the pointers. These strings are stored in the normal data area allocated to the program, elsewhere in the computer. The array of pointers contains only the addresses of the starting location for each string.

Point of Information

Allocating Space for a String

Although both the following declarations

```
char test[5] = "abcd";
char *test = "abcd";
```

create storage for the characters `'a'`, `'b'`, `'c'`, `'d'`, and `'\0'`, there's a subtle difference between the two declarations and in how values can be assigned to `test`. An array declaration, such as `char test[5];`, precludes subsequent use of an assignment expression, such as `test = "efgh"`, to assign values to the array. Using the `strcpy()` function, as in `strcpy(test,"efgh")`, however, is valid. The only restriction on `strcpy()` is the array size, which in this case is five elements. This situation is reversed when a pointer is created. A pointer declaration, such as `char *test;`, precludes using `strcpy()` to initialize the memory locations pointed to by the pointer, but it does allow assignments. For example, the following sequence of statements is valid:

```
char *test;
test = "abcd";
test = "here is a longer string";
```

The difference in use is explained by the fact that the compiler automatically allocates enough new memory space for any C-string pointed to by a pointer variable but doesn't do so for an array of characters. The array size is fixed by the definition statement.

Formally, any expression yielding a value that can be used on the left side of an assignment expression is said to be an **lvalue**. (Similarly, any expression yielding a value that can be used on the right side of an assignment statement is said to be an **rvalue**.) Therefore, a pointer variable can be an **lvalue**, but an array name can't.

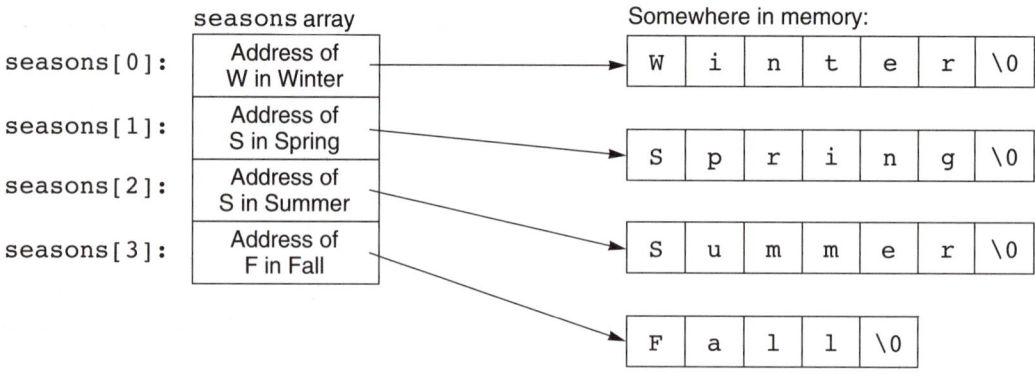

Figure 15.7 The addresses in the `seasons[]` pointers

The initialization of the **seasons** array can also be incorporated into the definition of the array, as follows:

```
char *seasons[4] = {"Winter",
                    "Spring",
                    "Summer",
                    "Fall"};
```

This declaration both creates an array of pointers and initializes the pointers with appropriate addresses. After addresses have been assigned to the pointers, each pointer can be used to access its corresponding string. Program 15.8 uses the **seasons** array to display each season by using a **for** loop.

Program 15.8

```
#include <iostream>
using namespace std;
int main()
{
  const int NUMSEASONS = 4;
  int n;
  char *seasons[] = {"Winter",
                     "Spring",
                     "Summer",
                     "Fall"};

  for( n = 0; n < NUMSEASONS; n++)
  cout << "\nThe season is " << seasons[n];

  return 0;
}
```

The output of Program 15.8 is as follows:

```
The season is Winter
The season is Spring
The season is Summer
The season is Fall
```

The advantage of using a list of pointers is that logical groups of data headings can be collected and accessed with one array name. For example, the months in a year can be grouped in one array called **months**, and the days in a week can be grouped in an array called **days**. The grouping of like headings enables the programmer to access and print a corresponding heading simply by specifying the heading's correct position in the array. Program 15.9 uses the **seasons** array to identify and display the season corresponding to a user-entered month.

Program 15.9

```
#include <iostream>
using namespace std;
int main()
{
  int n;
  char *seasons[] = {"Winter",
                     "Spring",
                     "Summer",
                     "Fall"};

  cout << "\nEnter a month (use 1 for Jan., 2 for Feb., etc.): ";
  cin  >> n;
  n = (n % 12) / 3;  // create the correct subscript
  cout << "The month entered is a "<< seasons[n] << " month.";

  return 0;
}
```

Except for the expression n = (n % 12) / 3, Program 15.9 is rather straightforward. The program requests the user to enter a month and accepts the number corresponding to the month, using a cin object to display the selected month. The expression n = (n % 12) / 3 uses a common programming "trick" to scale a set of numbers into a more useful set. Using subscripts, the four elements of the seasons array must be accessed via a subscript from 0 through 3. Therefore, the months of the year, which correspond to the numbers 1 through 12, must be adjusted to correspond to the correct season subscript by using the expression n = (n % 12) / 3. The expression n % 12 adjusts the user-entered month to lie in the range 0 through 11, with 0 corresponding to December, 1 to January, and so on. Dividing by 3 causes the resulting number to range between 0 and 3, corresponding to the possible seasons elements. The result of the division by 3 is assigned to the integer variable n. The months 0, 1, and 2, when divided by 3, are set to 0; the months 3, 4, and 5 are set to 1; the months 6, 7, and 8 are set to 2; and the months 9, 10, and 11 are set to 3. It's equivalent to the following assignments:

Months	Season
December, January, February	Winter
March, April, May	Spring
June, July, August	Summer
September, October, November	Fall

The following is a sample output from Program 15.9:

```
Enter a month (use 1 for Jan., 2 for Feb., etc.): 12
The month entered is a Winter month.
```

EXERCISES 15.3

1. **(Practice)** Write two declaration statements that can be used in place of the declaration `char text[] = "Hooray!";`.

2. **(Desk check)** Determine the value of `*text`, `*(text + 3)`, and `*(text + 7)` for each of the following sections of code:

   a. `char *text;`
   `char message[] = "the check is in the mail";`
   `text = message;`

   b. `char *text;`
   `char formal[] = {'T','h','i','s',' ','i','s',' ','a','n',' ',`
                      `'i','n','v','i','t','a','t','i','o','n','\0'};`
   `text = &formal[0];`

   c. `char *text;`
   `char more[] = "Happy Holidays";`
   `text = &more[4];`

   d. `char *text, *second;`
   `char blip[] = "The good ship";`
   `second = blip;`
   `text = ++second;`

3. **(Debug)** Determine the error in the following program:

```
#include <iostream>
using namespace std;
int main()
{
  int i = 0;
  char message[] = {'H','e','l','l','o','\0'};

  for( ; i < 5; i++)
  {
    cout << *message;
    message++;
  }

  return 0;
}
```

4. **(Program) a.** Write a C++ function that displays the day of the week corresponding to a user-entered number between 1 and 7. That is, in response to the input 2, the program displays the name Monday. Use an array of pointers in the function.

   b. Include the function written for Exercise 4a in a complete working program.

5. **(Modify)** Modify the function written in Exercise 4a so that it returns the address of the character string containing the correct day to be displayed.

6. **(Program)** Write a function that accepts 10 lines of user-entered text and stores them as 10 C-strings. Use a pointer array in your function.

15.4 Common Programming Errors

The following errors are frequently made when pointers to C-strings are used:

1. Using the pointer to "point to" a nonexistent data element. This error is, of course, the same error you have already seen when using subscripts. C++ compilers don't perform bounds checking on arrays, so it's the programmer's responsibility to ensure that the address in the pointer is the address of a valid data element.

2. Not providing enough space for the C-string to be stored. A simple variation of this error is not providing space for the end-of-string NULL character when a C-string is defined as an array of characters and not including the '\0' character when the array is initialized. A more complicated variation of this error is declaring a character pointer, such as char *p, and then attempting to copy a C-string with a statement such as strcpy(p,"Hello");. Because no space has been allocated for the C-string, the C-string overwrites the memory area pointed to by p.

3. Misunderstanding the terminology. For example, if message is defined as

   ```
   char *message;
   ```

   the variable message is sometimes referred to as a string. Therefore, you might see wording such as "Store the characters Hooray for the Hoosiers in the string named message." Strictly speaking, calling message a string or a C-string variable is incorrect. It's a pointer containing the address of the first character in a C-string. Nevertheless, referring to a character pointer as a C-string occurs often enough that you should be aware of it.

15.5 Chapter Summary

1. A C-string is an array of characters terminated by the NULL character, '\0'.

2. C-strings can always be processed with standard array-processing techniques. Entering and displaying a C-string, however, always require relying on standard library functions.

3. The cin object and the cin.get() and cin.getline() functions can be used to input a C-string. The cin object tends to be of limited usefulness for C-string input because it terminates input when encountering a blank.

4. The cout object can be used to display C-strings.

5. In place of subscripts, pointer notation and pointer arithmetic are especially useful for manipulating C-string elements.

6. Many standard library functions are available for processing C-strings as a complete unit. Internally, these functions manipulate C-strings in a character-by-character manner, generally using pointers.

7. C-string storage can be created by declaring an array of characters and by declaring and initializing a pointer to a character.

8. Arrays can be initialized by using a string literal assignment in this form:

```
char *arr_name[ ] = "text";
```

This initialization is equivalent to the following:

```
char *arr_name[ ] = {'t','e','x','t','\0'};
```

9. A pointer to a character can be assigned a string literal. String literal assignment to an array of characters is invalid except for initialization in a declaration statement.

Chapter

16

Data Structures

A structure is a historical holdover from C. From a programmer's perspective, a structure is equivalent to a class having all public instance variables and no methods. In commercial applications, a structure is referred to, and is the same thing as, a record. In C++, a structure provides a way to store values of different data types, such as an integer part number, a character description, and a double-precision price.

For example, a store maintains a record of items in inventory, with the following data items maintained for each inventory item:

Part Number:
Description:
Quantity in Stock:
Price:

*Each data item is a separate entity referred to as a **data field**. Taken together, the data fields form a single unit referred to as a **record**, which in C++ is called a **structure**.*

Although the store could keep track of hundreds of inventory items, the form of each item's structure is identical. In dealing with structures, distinguishing between a structure's form and its contents is important. A structure's form consists of the symbolic names, data types, and arrangement of data fields in the structure. The structure's contents refer to the actual data stored in the symbolic names. The following list shows acceptable contents for the structure form shown previously:

```
Part Number: 23421
Description: Stapler
Quantity in Stock: 3
Price: $5.98
```

This chapter describes the C++ statements required to create, fill, and manipulate structures.

16.1 Single Structures

Creating and using a structure involves the same two steps for creating and using any variable. First, the structure must be declared. Second, specific values can be assigned to the structure elements. Declaring a structure requires listing the data types, data names, and arrangement of data items. For example, the definition

```
struct
{
  int month;
  int day;
  int year;
} birth;
```

gives the form of a structure called `birth` and reserves storage for the data items listed in the structure. The `birth` structure consists of three data items or fields, which are called **structure members**.

Assigning actual data values to structure members is referred to as **populating the structure**, which is a straightforward procedure. Each structure member is accessed by giving the structure name and data item name, separated by a period. For example, `birth.month` refers to the first member of the `birth` structure, `birth.day` refers to the second member of the structure, and `birth.year` refers to the third member. The period in these names is called the **member access operator** or **dot operator**. (Both terms are used.) Program 16.1 shows assigning values to members of the `birth` structure.

Program 16.1

```cpp
// a program that defines and populates a structure
#include <iostream>
using namespace std;
int main()
{
  struct
  {
    int month;
    int day;
    int year;
  } birth;

  birth.month = 12;
  birth.day = 28;
  birth.year = 1992;

  cout << "My birth date is "
       << birth.month << '/'
       << birth.day   << '/'
       << birth.year  << endl;

  return 0;
}
```

Program 16.1 produces the following output:

```
My birth date is 12/28/1992
```

As in most C++ statements, the spacing of a structure definition isn't rigid. For example, the birth structure could just as well have been defined as the following:

```cpp
struct {int month; int day; int year;} birth;
```

Also, as with all C++ definition statements, multiple variables can be defined in the same statement. For example, the following definition statement creates two structure variables having the same form:

```cpp
struct
{
  int month;
  int day;
  int year;
} birth, current;
```

The members of the first structure are referenced by the names `birth.month`, `birth.day`, and `birth.year`, and the members of the second structure are referenced by the names `current.month`, `current.day`, and `current.year`. Notice that the form of this structure definition statement is identical to the form for defining any program variable: The data type is followed by a list of variable names.

The most commonly used modification for defining structure types is listing the structure's form with no variable names following. In this case, however, the list of structure members must be preceded by a user-selected data type name. For example, in the declaration

```
struct Date
{
  int month;
  int day;
  int year;
};
```

the term `Date` is a structure type name: It defines a new data type that's a data structure of the declared form.[1] By convention, the first letter of a user-selected data type name is uppercase, as in the name `Date`, which helps identify it when it's used in subsequent definition statements. This declaration for the `Date` structure creates a new data type without actually reserving any storage locations.[2] Therefore, it's not a definition statement. It simply declares a `Date` structure type and describes how data items are arranged in the structure. Actual storage for the structure members is reserved only when variable names are assigned. For example, the definition statement

```
Date birth, current;
```

reserves storage for two `Date` structure variables named `birth` and `current`. Each structure has the form declared previously for the `Date` structure.[3]

The declaration of structure data types, like all declarations, can be global or local. Program 16.2 shows the global declaration of a `Date` data type. In `main()`, the variable `birth` is defined as a local variable of `Date` type. The output Program 16.2 produces is identical to the output of Program 16.1.

---

[1]For completeness, it should be mentioned that a C++ structure can also be declared as a class with no member methods and all public data members. Similarly, a C++ class can be declared as a structure having all private data members and all public member methods. Therefore, C++ provides two syntaxes for structures and classes. The convention, however, is to not mix notations; in other words, always use structures for creating record types, and use classes for providing true information and implementation hiding.
[2]The `struct` declaration is equivalent to the class declaration section.
[3]The declaration `Date birth, current;` is equivalent to creating two objects.

 **Program 16.2**

```cpp
#include <iostream>
using namespace std;
struct Date      // this is a global declaration
{
   int month;
   int day;
   int year;
};

int main()
{
   Date birth;

   birth.month = 12;
   birth.day = 28;
   birth.year = 1992;

   cout << "My birth date is "
        << birth.month    << '/'
        << birth.day      << '/'
        << birth.year     << endl;

   return 0;
}
```

The initialization of structures follows the same rules as the initialization of arrays does: Global and local structures can be initialized by following the definition with a list of initializers. For example, the definition statement

```cpp
Date birth = {12, 28, 1992};
```

can be used to replace the first four statements in main() in Program 16.2. Notice that the initializers are separated by commas, not semicolons.

Structure members aren't restricted to integer data types, as in the Date structure. Any valid C++ data type can be used. For example, an employee record consists of the following data items:

```
Name:
Identification Number:
Regular Pay Rate:
Overtime Pay Rate:
```

The following is a suitable declaration for these data items:

```
struct PayRecord
{
    string name;
    int idNum;
    double regRate;
    double otRate;
};
```

After the `PayRecord` data type is declared, a structure variable using this type can be defined and initialized. For example, the definition

```
PayRecord employee = {"H. Price",12387,15.89,25.50};
```

creates a structure named `employee` of the `PayRecord` data type. The members of `employee` are initialized with the data listed between braces in the definition statement.

Notice that a single structure is simply a convenient method for combining and storing related items under a common name. Although a single structure is useful in identifying the relationship among its members, the members could be defined as separate variables. One of the real advantages of using structures is realized only when the same data type is used in a list many times over. Creating lists with the same data type is discussed in Section 16.2.

Before leaving single structures, it's worth noting that structure members can be any valid C++ data type, including both arrays and structures. Accessing an element of a member array requires giving the structure's name, followed by a period and the array designation.

Including a structure inside a structure follows the same rules for including any data type in a structure. For example, a structure is to consist of a name and a birth date, and a `Date` structure has been declared as follows:

```
struct Date
{
    int month;
    int date;
    int year;
};
```

A suitable definition of a structure that includes a name and a `Date` structure is as follows:

```
struct
{
    string name;
    Date birth;
} person;
```

Notice that in declaring the `Date` structure, the term `Date` is a data type name, so it appears before the braces in the declaration statement. In defining the `person` structure variable, `person` is a variable name, so it's the name of a specific structure. The same is true of the variable `birth`; it's the name of a specific `Date` structure. Members in the `person` structure are accessed by using the structure name, followed by a period and the structure member. For example, `person.birth.month` refers to the `month` variable in the `birth` structure contained in the `person` structure.

Point of Information

Homogeneous and Heterogeneous Data Structures

Both arrays and records are structured data types. The difference between these two data structures is the types of elements they contain. An array is a **homogeneous** data structure, which means all its components must be of the same data type. A record is a **heterogeneous** data structure, which means its components can be of different data types. Therefore, an array of records is a homogeneous data structure with elements of the same heterogeneous type.

EXERCISES 16.1

1. **(Practice)** Declare a structure data type named `stemp` for each of the following records:
   a. A student record consisting of a student identification number, number of credits completed, and cumulative grade point average
   b. A student record consisting of a student's name, birth date, number of credits completed, and cumulative grade point average
   c. A mailing list consisting of last name, first name, street address, city, state, and zip code
   d. A stock record consisting of the stock's name, the stock's price, and the date of purchase
   e. An inventory record consisting of an integer part number, a part description, the number of parts in inventory, and an integer reorder number

2. **(Practice)** For the data types declared in Exercise 1, define a suitable structure variable name, and initialize each structure with the following data:
   a. Identification Number: 4672
      Number of Credits Completed: 68
      Grade Point Average: 3.01

   b. Name: Rhona Karp
      Birth Date: 8/4/1980
      Number of Credits Completed: 96
      Grade Point Average: 3.89

   c. Name: Kay Kingsley
      Street Address: 614 Freeman Street
      City: Indianapolis
      State: IN
      Zip Code: 07030

    d. Stock Name: IBM
        Stock Price: 134.5
        Date Purchased: 10/1/2010

    e. Part Number: 16879
        Part Description: Battery
        Number in Stock: 10
        Reorder Number: 3

3. **(Program) a.** Write a C++ program that prompts a user to enter the current month, day, and year. Store the entered data in a suitably defined record and display the date in an appropriate manner.

    b. Modify the program written in Exercise 3a to use a record that accepts the current time in hours, minutes, and seconds.

4. **(Program)** Write a C++ program that uses a structure for storing a stock name, its estimated earnings per share, and its estimated price-to-earnings ratio. Have the program prompt the user to enter these items for five different stocks, each time using the same structure to store the entered data. When data has been entered for a particular stock, have the program compute and display the anticipated stock price based on the entered earnings and price-per-earnings values. For example, if a user enters the data XYZ 1.56 12, the anticipated price for a share of XYZ stock is (1.56) × (12) = $18.72.

5. **(Program)** Write a C++ program that accepts a user-entered time in hours and minutes. Have the program calculate and display the time 1 minute later.

6. **(Program) a.** Write a C++ program that accepts a user-entered date. Have the program calculate and display the date of the next day. For the purposes of this exercise, assume all months consist of 30 days.

    b. Modify the program written in Exercise 6a to account for the actual number of days in each month.

16.2 Arrays of Structures

The real power of structures is realized when the same structure is used for lists of data. For example, the data shown in Figure 16.1 must be processed. Clearly, the employee numbers can be stored together in an array of integers, the names in an array of strings, and the pay rates in an array of double-precision numbers. In organizing the data in this fashion, each column in Figure 16.1 is considered a separate list stored in its own array. The correspondence between data items for each employee is maintained by storing an employee's data in the same array position in each array.

Employee Number	Employee Name	Employee Pay Rate
32479	Abrams, B.	16.72
33623	Bohm, P.	17.54
34145	Donaldson, S.	15.56
35987	Ernst, T.	15.43
36203	Gwodz, K.	18.72
36417	Hanson, H.	17.64
37634	Monroe, G.	15.29
38321	Price, S.	19.67
39435	Robbins, L.	18.50
39567	Williams, B.	17.20

Figure 16.1   A list of employee data

The separation of the list into three arrays is unfortunate because all the items relating to a single employee constitute a single record. Using a structure, you can make the program maintain and reflect the integrity of the data as a record. With this approach, the list in Figure 16.2 can be processed as a single array of 10 structures.

	Employee Number	Employee Name	Employee Pay Rate
1st structure ⟶	32479	Abrams, B.	16.72
2nd structure ⟶	33623	Bohm, P.	17.54
3rd structure ⟶	34145	Donaldson, S.	15.56
4th structure ⟶	35987	Ernst, T.	15.43
5th structure ⟶	36203	Gwodz, K.	18.72
6th structure ⟶	36417	Hanson, H.	17.64
7th structure ⟶	37634	Monroe, G.	15.29
8th structure ⟶	38321	Price, S.	19.67
9th structure ⟶	39435	Robbins, L.	18.50
10th structure ⟶	39567	Williams, B.	17.20

Figure 16.2   A list of structures

Declaring an array of structures is the same as declaring an array of any other variable type. For example, if the data type `PayRecord` is declared as

```
struct PayRecord
{
  int idnum;
  string name;
  double rate;
};
```

then an array of 10 such structures can be defined as follows:

```
PayRecord employee[10];
```

This definition statement constructs an array of 10 elements, and each element is a structure of the data type `PayRecord`. Notice that creating an array of 10 structures has the same form as creating any other array. For example, creating an array of 10 integers named `employee` requires the following declaration:

```
int employee[10];
```

In this declaration, the data type is integer; in the previous declaration for `employee`, the data type is `PayRecord`.

After an array of structures is declared, a data item is referenced by giving the position of the structure in the array, followed by a period and the structure member. For example, the variable `employee[0].rate` references the `rate` member of the first `employee` structure in the `employee` array. Including structures as elements of an array makes it possible to process a list of structures by using standard array programming techniques. Program 16.3 displays the first five employee records in Figure 16.2.

 Program 16.3

```cpp
#include <iostream>
#include <iomanip>
#include <string>
using namespace std;

struct PayRecord        // this is a global declaration
{
  int id;
  string name;
  double rate;
};

int main()
{

const int NUMRECS = 5;   // maximum number of records

  int i;
  PayRecord employee[NUMRECS] = {
                      { 32479, "Abrams, B.", 16.72},
                      { 33623, "Bohm, P.", 17.54},
                      { 34145, "Donaldson, S.", 15.56},
                      { 35987, "Ernst, T.", 15.43},
                      { 36203, "Gwodz, K.", 18.72}
                      };
```

```
cout << endl;   // start on a new line
cout << setiosflags(ios::left);  // left-justify the output
for (i = 0; i < NUMRECS; i++)
  cout << setw(7)  << employee[i].id
       << setw(15) << employee[i].name
       << setw(6)  << employee[i].rate << endl;

return 0;
}
```

Program 16.3 displays the following output:

```
32479  Abrams, B.     16.72
33623  Bohm, P.       17.54
34145  Donaldson, S.  15.56
35987  Ernst, T.      15.43
36203  Gwodz, K.      18.72
```

In reviewing Program 16.3, notice the initialization of the array of structures. Although the initializers for each structure have been enclosed in inner braces, they aren't strictly necessary because all members have been initialized. As with all external and static variables, in the absence of explicit initializers, the numeric elements of static and external arrays or structures are initialized to 0, and their character elements are initialized to NULLs. The setiosflags(ios::left) manipulator included in the cout object stream forces each name to be displayed left-justified in its designated field width.

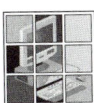

EXERCISES 16.2

1. **(Practice)** Define arrays of 100 structures for each of the data types described in Exercise 1 of Section 16.1.

2. **(Program) a.** Using the data type

```
struct DaysInMonth
{
  string name;
  int days;
};
```

define an array of 12 structures of type DaysInMonth. Name the array convert[ ], and initialize the array with the names of the 12 months in a year and the number of days in each month.

   b. Include the array created in Exercise 2a in a program that displays the names of months and number of days in each month.

3. **(Program)** Using the data type declared in Exercise 2a, write a C++ program that accepts a month from a user in numerical form and displays the name of the month and the number of days in the month. For example, in response to an input of 3, the program would display March has 31 days.

4. **(Program) a.** Declare a single structure data type suitable for an `employee` structure of the type shown in the following chart:

Number	Name	Rate	Hours
3462	Jones	9.62	40
6793	Robbins	8.83	38
6985	Smith	8.22	45
7834	Swain	9.89	40
8867	Timmins	8.43	35
9002	Williams	9.75	42

b. Using the data type declared in Exercise 4a, write a C++ program that interactively accepts the chart's data in an array of six structures. After the data has been entered, the program should create a payroll report listing each employee's name, number, and gross pay. Include the total gross pay of all employees at the end of the report.

5. **(Program) a.** Declare a single structure data type suitable for a `car` structure of the type shown in the following chart:

Car Number	Miles Driven	Gallons Used
25	1450	62
36	3240	136
44	1792	76
52	2360	105
68	2114	67

b. Using the data type declared for Exercise 5a, write a C++ program that interactively accepts the chart's data in an array of five structures. After the data has been entered, the program should create a report listing each car number and the car's miles per gallon. At the end of the report, include the average miles per gallon for the entire fleet of cars.

16.3 Structures as Function Arguments

Structure members can be passed to a function in the same manner as any scalar variable. For example, given the structure definition

```
struct
{
  int idNum;
  double payRate;
  double hours;
} emp;
```

the following statement passes a copy of the structure member `emp.idNum` to a function named `display()`:

```
display(emp.idNum);
```

Similarly, the statement

```
calcPay(emp.payRate,emp.hours);
```

passes copies of the values stored in structure members `emp.payRate` and `emp.hours` to the `calcPay()` function. Both functions, `display()` and `calcPay()`, must declare the correct data types for their parameters.

Copies of all structure members can also be passed to a function by including the name of the structure as an argument to the called function. For example, this function call passes a copy of the `emp` structure to `calcNet()`:

```
calcNet(emp);
```

Inside `calcNet()`, a declaration must be made to receive the structure. Program 16.4 declares a global data type for an `employee` structure. The `main()` and `calcNet()` functions then use this data type to define structures with the names `emp` and `temp`, respectively.

Program 16.4

```cpp
#include <iostream>
#include <iomanip>
using namespace std;
struct Employee     // declare a global data type
{
  int idNum;
  double payRate;
  double hours;
};

double calcNet(Employee);     // function prototype

int main()
{
  Employee emp = {6782, 8.93, 40.5};
  double netPay;

  netPay = calcNet(emp);     // pass copies of the values in emp
```

```
    // set output formats
  cout << setw(10)
       << setiosflags(ios::fixed)
       << setiosflags(ios::showpoint)
       << setprecision(2);

  cout << "The net pay for employee " << emp.idNum
       << " is $" << netPay << endl;

  return 0;
}


double calcNet(Employee temp)   // temp is of data type Employee
{
  return (temp.payRate * temp.hours);
}
```

The output produced by Program 16.4 is as follows:

```
The net pay for employee 6782 is $361.66
```

In reviewing Program 16.4, observe that both `main()` and `calcNet()` use the same data type to define their structure variables. The structure variable defined in `main()` and the structure variable defined in `calcNet()` are two different structures. Any changes made to the local `temp` variable in `calcNet()` aren't reflected in the `emp` variable of `main()`. In fact, because both structure variables are local to their functions, the same structure variable name could have been used in both functions with no ambiguity.

When `calcNet()` is called by `main()`, copies of `emp`'s structure values are passed to the `temp` structure. `calcNet()` then uses two of the passed member values to calculate a number, which is returned to `main()`. An alternative to the pass-by-value function call in Program 16.4, in which the called function receives a copy of a structure, is a pass by reference that passes a reference to a structure. Doing so allows the called function to access and alter values directly in the calling function's structure variable. For example, in Program 16.4, the prototype of `calcNet()` can be modified to the following:

```
double calcNet(Employee &);
```

If this function prototype is used and the `calcNet()` function is rewritten to conform to it, the `main()` function in Program 16.4 can be used as is. Program 16.4a shows these changes in the context of a complete program, with the two changed statements shaded.

Program 16.4a

```cpp
#include <iostream>
#include <iomanip>
using namespace std;
struct Employee     // declare a global data type
{
  int idNum;
  double payRate;
  double hours;
};

double calcNet(Employee&);      // function prototype

int main()
{
  Employee emp = {6782, 8.93, 40.5};
  double netPay;

  netPay = calcNet(emp);      // pass a reference

    // set output formats
  cout << setw(10)
       << setiosflags(ios::fixed)
       << setiosflags(ios::showpoint)
       << setprecision(2);

  cout << "The net pay for employee " << emp.idNum
       << " is $" << netPay << endl;

  return 0;
}

double calcNet(Employee& temp)    // temp is a reference variable
{
  return (temp.payRate * temp.hours);
}
```

Program 16.4a produces the same output as Program 16.4, except the `calcNet()` function in Program 16.4a receives direct access to the `emp` structure instead of a copy of it. This means the variable name `temp` in `calcNet()` is an alternative name for the variable `emp` in `main()`, and any changes to `temp` are direct changes to `emp`. Although the same function call, `calcNet(emp)`, is made in both programs, the call in Program 16.4a passes a reference, and the call in Program 16.4 passes values.

Passing a Pointer

Instead of passing a reference, a pointer can be used. Using a pointer requires modifying the function's prototype and header and modifying the call to `calcNet()` in Program 16.4 to the following:

```
calcNet(&emp);
```

This function call clearly indicates that an address is being passed (which isn't the case in Program 16.4a). The disadvantage is the dereferencing notation required inside the function. However, as pointers are widely used in practice, becoming familiar with this notation is worthwhile.

To store the passed address, `calcNet()` must declare its parameter as a pointer. The following function definition for `calcNet()` is suitable:

```
calcNet(Employee *pt)
```

This definition declares the `pt` parameter as a pointer to a structure of type `Employee`. The `pt` pointer receives the starting address of a structure when `calcNet()` is called. In `calcNet()`, this pointer is used to access any member in the structure. For example, `(*pt).idNum` refers to the `idNum` structure member, `(*pt).payRate` refers to the `payRate` structure member, and `(*pt).hours` refers to the `hours` structure member. These relationships are illustrated in Figure 16.3.

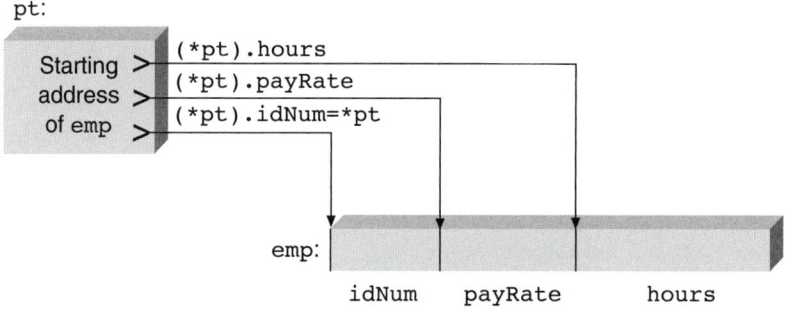

Figure 16.3   A pointer can be used to access structure members

The parentheses around the expression `*pt` in Figure 16.3 are necessary to access "the structure whose address is in `pt`." The `(*pt)` is followed by an identifier to access the structure member. In the absence of parentheses, the structure member operator, `.`, takes precedence over the indirection operator, `*`. Therefore, the expression `*pt.hours` is another way of writing `*(pt.hours)`, which would mean "the variable whose address is in the `pt.hours` variable." This expression makes no sense because there's no structure named `pt` and `hours` doesn't contain an address.

As shown in Figure 16.3, the starting address of the `emp` structure is also the address of the first structure member. Using pointers in this manner is so common that a special notation exists for it. The general expression `(*pointer).member` can always be replaced with the notation `pointer->member`. The `->` operator is a hyphen followed by a greater-than symbol.

Either expression can be used to locate the member. For example, the following expressions are equivalent:

```
(*pt).idNum      can be replaced by pt->idNum
(*pt).payRate    can be replaced by pt->payRate
(*pt).hours      can be replaced by pt->hours
```

Program 16.5 shows passing a structure's address and using a pointer with the new notation to reference the structure directly. The name of the pointer parameter declared in Program 16.5 is, of course, selected by the programmer. When calcNet() is called, emp's starting address is passed to the function. Using this address as a starting point, structure members are accessed by including their names with the pointer.

Program 16.5

```cpp
#include <iostream>
#include <iomanip>
using namespace std;

struct Employee  // declare a global data type
{
  int idNum;
  double payRate;
  double hours;
};

double calcNet(Employee *);    //function prototype

int main()
{
  Employee emp = {6782, 8.93, 40.5};
  double netPay;

  netPay = calcNet(&emp);    // pass an address

    // set output formats
  cout << setw(10)
       << setiosflags(ios::fixed)
       << setiosflags(ios::showpoint)
       << setprecision(2);

  cout << "The net pay for employee " << emp.idNum
       << " is $" << netPay << endl;
```

```
   return 0;
}

double calcNet(Employee *pt)   // pt is a pointer to a
{                              // structure of Employee type
   return (pt->payRate * pt->hours);
}
```

As with all C++ expressions that access a variable, the increment (++) and decrement (--) operators can also be applied to them. For example, the expression

```
++pt->hours
```

adds 1 to the hours member of the emp structure. Because the -> operator has a higher priority than the increment operator, the hours member is accessed first, and then the increment is applied. Alternatively, the expression (++pt)->hours uses the prefix increment operator to increment the address in pt before the hours member is accessed. Similarly, the expression (pt++)->hours uses the postfix increment operator to increment the address in pt after the hours member is accessed. In both cases, however, there must be enough defined structures to ensure that the incremented pointers actually point to legitimate structures.

As an example, Figure 16.4 shows an array of three structures of type Employee. Assuming the address of emp[1] is stored in the pointer variable pt, the expression ++pt changes the address in pt to the starting address of emp[2], and the expression --pt changes the address to point to emp[0].

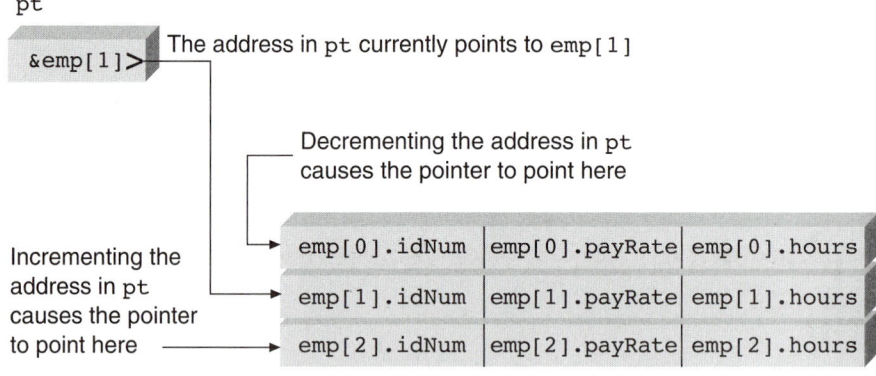

Figure 16.4   Changing pointer addresses

Returning Structures

In practice, most structure-handling functions get direct access to a structure by receiving a structure reference or address. Then any changes to the structure can be made directly from inside the function. If you want to have a function return a separate structure, however, you must follow the same procedures for returning data structures as for returning scalar values.

These procedures include declaring the function appropriately and alerting any calling function to the type of data structure being returned. For example, the getValues() function in Program 16.6 returns a data structure to main().

Program 16.6

```
#include <iostream>
#include <iomanip>
using namespace std;

struct Employee     // declare a global data type
{
  int idNum;
  double payRate;
  double hours;
};

Employee getValues();     // function prototype

int main()
{
  Employee emp;

  emp = getValues();
  cout << "\nThe employee ID number is " << emp.idNum
       << "\nThe employee pay rate is $" << emp.payRate
       << "\nThe employee hours are " << emp.hours << endl;

  return 0;
}

Employee getValues() // return an employee structure
{
  Employee next;

  next.idNum = 6789;
  next.payRate = 16.25;
  next.hours = 38.0;

  return(next);
}
```

The following output is displayed when Program 16.6 runs:

```
The employee ID number is 6789
The employee pay rate is $16.25
The employee hours are 38
```

The `getValues()` function returns a structure, so the function header for `getValues()` must specify the type of structure being returned. Because `getValues()` doesn't receive any arguments, the function header has no parameter declarations and consists of this line:

```
Employee getValues();
```

In `getValues()`, the variable `next` is defined as a structure of the type to be returned. After values have been assigned to the `next` structure, the structure values are returned by including the structure name in the parentheses of the `return` statement.

On the receiving side, `main()` must be alerted that the `getValues()` function will be returning a structure. This alert is handled by including a function declaration for `getValues()` in `main()`. Notice that these steps for returning a structure from a function are identical to the procedures for returning scalar data types, described in Chapter 6.

EXERCISES 16.3

1. **(Program)** Write a C++ function named `days()` that determines the number of days since January 1, 1900 for any date passed as a structure. Use the `Date` structure:

```
struct Date
{
  int month;
  int day;
  int year;
};
```

In writing the `days()` function, follow the convention that all years have 360 days and each month consists of 30 days. The function should return the number of days for any `Date` structure passed to it.

2. **(Program)** Write a C++ function named `difDays()` that calculates and returns the difference between two dates. Each date is passed to the function as a structure by using the following global data type:

```
struct Date
{
  int month;
  int day;
  int year;
};
```

The `difDays()` function should make two calls to the `days()` function written for Exercise 1.

3. (Modify) a. Rewrite the `days()` function written for Exercise 1 to receive a reference to a `Date` structure rather than a copy of the structure.

b. Redo Exercise 3a, using a pointer rather than a reference.

4. (Program) a. Write a C++ function named `larger()` that returns the later date of any two dates passed to it. For example, if the dates 10/9/2010 and 11/3/2012 are passed to `larger()`, the second date is returned.

b. Include the `larger()` function written for Exercise 4a in a complete program. Store the `Date` structure returned by `larger()` in a separate `Date` structure and display the member values of the returned `Date`.

5. (Modify) a. Modify the `days()` function written for Exercise 1 to account for the actual number of days in each month. Assume, however, that each year contains 365 days (that is, don't account for leap years).

b. Modify the function written for Exercise 5a to account for leap years.

16.4 Dynamic Structure Allocation

You have already learned about allocating and deallocating memory space with the `new` and `delete` operators (see Section 8.2). For convenience, Table 16.1 repeats the description of these operators.

Table 16.1 Operators for Dynamic Allocation and Deallocation

Operator Name	Description
`new`	Reserves the number of bytes requested by the declaration. Returns the address of the first reserved location or `NULL` if not enough memory is available.
`delete`	Releases a block of bytes reserved previously. The address of the first reserved location is required by the operator.

Dynamic allocation of memory is especially useful when dealing with a list of structures because it permits expanding the list as new records are added and contracting the list as records are deleted. In requesting additional storage space, the user must provide the `new` operator with an indication of the amount of storage needed for a particular data type. For example, the expression `new(int)` or `new int` (the two forms can be used interchangeably) requests enough storage to store an integer number. A request for enough storage for a data structure is made in the same fashion. For example, by using the declaration

```
struct TeleType
{
  string name;
  string phoneNo;
};
```

both the expressions new TeleType and new(TeleType) reserve enough storage for one TeleType data structure.

   In allocating storage dynamically, you have no advance indication where the computer will physically reserve the requested number of bytes, and you have no explicit name to access the newly created storage locations. To provide access to these locations, new returns the address of the first location that has been reserved. This address must, of course, be assigned to a pointer. The return of an address by new is especially useful for creating a linked list of data structures. As each new structure is created, the address that new returns to the structure can be assigned to a member of the previous structure in the list. Program 16.7 shows using new to create a structure dynamically in response to a user-entered request.

Program 16.7

```cpp
// a program illustrating dynamic structure allocation
#include <iostream>
#include <string>
using namespace std;

struct TeleType
{
  string name;
  string phoneNo;
};

void populate(TeleType *); // function prototype needed by main()
void dispOne(TeleType *);  // function prototype needed by main()

int main()
{
  char key;
  TeleType *recPoint;   // recPoint is a pointer to a
                        // structure of type TeleType

  cout << "Do you want to create a new record (respond y or n): ";
  key = cin.get();
  if (key == 'y')
  {
    key = cin.get();    // get the Enter key in buffered input
    recPoint = new TeleType;
    populate(recPoint);
    dispOne(recPoint);
  }
```

```
    else
      cout << "\nNo record has been created.";

    return 0;
}
    // input a name and phone number
void populate(TeleType *record)  // record is a pointer to a
{                                // structure of type TeleType
    cout << "Enter a name: ";
    getline(cin, record->name);
    cout << "Enter the phone number: ";
    getline(cin, record->phoneNo);

    return;
}
    // display the contents of one record
void dispOne(TeleType *contents)  // contents is a pointer to a
{                                 // structure of type TeleType
      cout << "\nThe contents of the record just created are:"
           << "\nName: " << contents->name
           << "\nPhone Number: " << contents->phoneNo << endl;

      return;
}
```

A sample run of Program 16.7 is as follows:

```
Do you want to create a new record (respond y or n): y
Enter a name: Monroe, James
Enter the phone number: (555) 617-1817
The contents of the record just created are:
Name: Monroe, James
Phone Number: (555) 617-1817
```

In reviewing Program 16.7, notice that only two variable declarations are made in main(). The variable key is declared as a character variable, and the variable recPoint is declared as a pointer to a structure of the TeleType type. Because the declaration for the TeleType type is global, TeleType can be used in main() to define recPoint as a pointer to a structure of the TeleType type.

If a user enters y in response to the first prompt in main(), a call to new is made for the required memory to store the designated structure. After recPoint has been loaded with the correct address, this address can be used to access the newly created structure.

The populate() function is used to prompt the user for data needed in filling the structure and to store the user-entered data in the correct structure members. The argument passed to populate() in main() is the pointer recPoint. Like all passed arguments, the value in recPoint is passed to the function. The value in recPoint is an address, so populate() receives the address of the newly created structure and can access the structure members directly.

In populate(), the value it receives is stored in the argument record. Because the value to be stored in record is the address of a structure, record must be declared as a pointer to a structure. This declaration is provided by the statement TeleType *record;. The statements in populate() use the address in record to locate the structure members.

The dispOne() function displays the contents of the newly created and populated structure. The address passed to dispOne() is the same address that was passed to populate(). Because this passed value is the address of a structure, the parameter name used to store the address is declared as a pointer to the correct structure type.

EXERCISES 16.4

1. **(Modify)** As described in Table 16.1, the new operator returns the address of the first new storage area allocated or NULL if not enough storage is available. Modify Program 16.7 to check that a valid address has been returned before a call to populate() is made. Display an appropriate message if not enough storage is available.

2. **(Program)** Write a C++ function named modify() that modifies an existing structure in a list of structures consisting of names and phone numbers. The argument passed to modify() should be the address of the structure to be modified. The modify() function should display the existing name and phone number in the selected structure, request a new name and phone number, and then display the final structure.

3. **(Program)** Write a function named insert() that inserts a structure in a linked list of structures consisting of names and phone numbers. The argument passed to insert() should be the address of the structure preceding the structure to be inserted. The inserted structure should follow this current structure. The insert() function should create a new structure dynamically, call the populate() function used in Program 16.7, and adjust all pointer values accordingly.

16.5 Unions[4]

A **union** is a data type that reserves the same area in memory for two or more variables that can be different data types. A variable declared as a union data type can be used to hold a character variable, an integer variable, a double-precision variable, or any other valid C++ data type. Each of these types, but only one at a time, can be assigned to the union variable.

---

[4]This topic can be omitted on first reading with no loss of subject continuity.

The definition of a union has the same form as a structure definition, with the keyword union used in place of the keyword `struct`. For example, the following declaration creates a union variable named `val`:

```
union
{
  char key;
  int num;
  double price;
} val;
```

If `val` were a structure, it would consist of three members. As a union, however, `val` contains a single member that can be a character variable named `key`, an integer variable named `num`, or a double-precision variable named `price`. In effect, a union reserves enough memory locations to accommodate its largest member's data type. This same set of locations is then referenced by different variable names, depending on the data type of the value currently stored in the reserved locations. Each value stored overwrites the previous value, using as many bytes of the reserved memory area as necessary.

Union members are referenced by using the same notation as structure members. For example, if the `val` union is currently being used to store a character, the correct variable name to access the stored character is `val.key`. Similarly, if the union is used to store an integer, the value is accessed by the name `val.num`, and a double-precision value is accessed by the name `val.price`. In using union members, it's the programmer's responsibility to make sure the correct member name is used for the data type currently stored in the union.

Typically, a second variable is used to keep track of the current data type stored in the union. For example, the following code could be used to select the appropriate member of `val` for display. The value in the `uType` variable determines the currently stored data type in the `val` union:

```
switch(uType)
{
  case 'c': cout << val.key;
            break;
  case 'i': cout << val.num;
            break;
  case 'd': cout << val.price;
            break;
  default : cout << "Invalid type in uType : " << uType;
}
```

As in structures, a data type can be associated with a union. For example, the declaration

```
union DateTime
{
  int days;
  double time;
};
```

provides a union data type without actually reserving any storage locations. This data type can then be used to define any number of variables. For example, the definition

```
DateTime first, second, *pt;
```

creates a union variable named `first`, a union variable named `second`, and a pointer that can be used to store the address of any union having the form `DateTime`. After a pointer to a union has been declared, the same notation for accessing structure members can be used to access union members. For example, if the assignment `pt = &first;` is made, `pt->date` references the `date` member of the union named `first`.

Unions can be members of structures or arrays, and structures, arrays, and pointers can be members of unions. In each case, the notation used to access a member must be consistent with the nesting used. For example, in the structure defined by

```
struct
{
  char uType;
  union
  {
    char *text;
    float rate;
  } uTax;
}  flag;
```

the variable `rate` is referenced as

```
flag.uTax.rate
```

Similarly, the first character of the string whose address is stored in the pointer `text` is referenced as follows:

```
*flag.uTax.text
```

EXERCISES 16.5

1. **(Practice)** Assume the following definition has been made:

```
union
{
  double rate;
  double taxes;
  int num;
} flag;
```

For this union, write `cout` statements to display the members of the union.

2. **(Practice)** Define a union variable named `car` containing an integer named `year`, an array of 10 characters named `name`, and an array of 10 characters named `model`.

3. **(Practice)** Define a union variable named `factors` that allows referencing a double-precision number by the variable names `watts` and `power`.

4. **(Practice)** Define a union data type named `Amt` containing an integer variable named `intAmt`, a double-precision variable named `dblAmt`, and a pointer to a character variable named `ptKey`.

5. **(Desk check) a.** What do you think the following section of code will display?

```
union
{
  char ch;
  double btype;
} alt;
alt.ch = 'y';
cout << alt.btype;
```

b. Include the code in Exercise 5a in a program, and run the program to verify your answer to Exercise 5a.

16.6 Common Programming Errors

Three common errors are often made when using structures or unions:

1. Structures and unions, as complete entities, can't be used in relational expressions. For example, even if `TeleType` and `PhonType` are two structures of the same type, the expression `TeleType == PhonType` is invalid. Members of a structure or union can, of course, be compared if they're of the same data type, using any of C++'s relational operators.

2. When a pointer is used to "point to" a structure or a union or is a member of a structure or a union, take care to use the address in the pointer to access the correct data type. If you're confused about exactly what's being pointed to, remember: "If in doubt, print it out."

3. Because a union can store only one of its members at a time, you must be careful to keep track of the currently stored variable. Storing one data type in a union and accessing it by the wrong variable name can result in an error that's particularly troublesome to locate.

16.7 Chapter Summary

1. A structure allows grouping variables under a common variable name. Each variable in a structure is accessed by its structure variable name, followed by a period and then its variable name. Another term for a data structure is a record. One form for declaring a structure variable is as follows:

   ```
   struct
   {
     // member declarations in here
   } structureName;
   ```

2. A named data type can be created from a structure by using this declaration form:

   ```
   struct DataType
   {
     // member declarations in here
   };
   ```

   Structure variables can then be defined as this `DataType`. By convention, the first letter of the `DataType` name is always capitalized.

3. Structures are particularly useful as elements of arrays. Used in this manner, each structure becomes one record in a list of records.

4. Complete structures can be used as function arguments, in which case the called function receives a copy of each element in the structure. A structure's address can also be passed as a reference or a pointer, which gives the called function direct access to the structure.

5. Structure members can be any valid C++ data type, including other structures, unions, arrays, and pointers. When a pointer is included as a structure member, a linked list can be created. This list uses the pointer in one structure to "point to" (contain the address of) the next logical structure in the list.

6. Unions are declared in the same manner as structures. The definition of a union creates a memory overlay area, with each union member using the same memory storage locations. Therefore, only one member of a union can be active at a time.

Appendix A

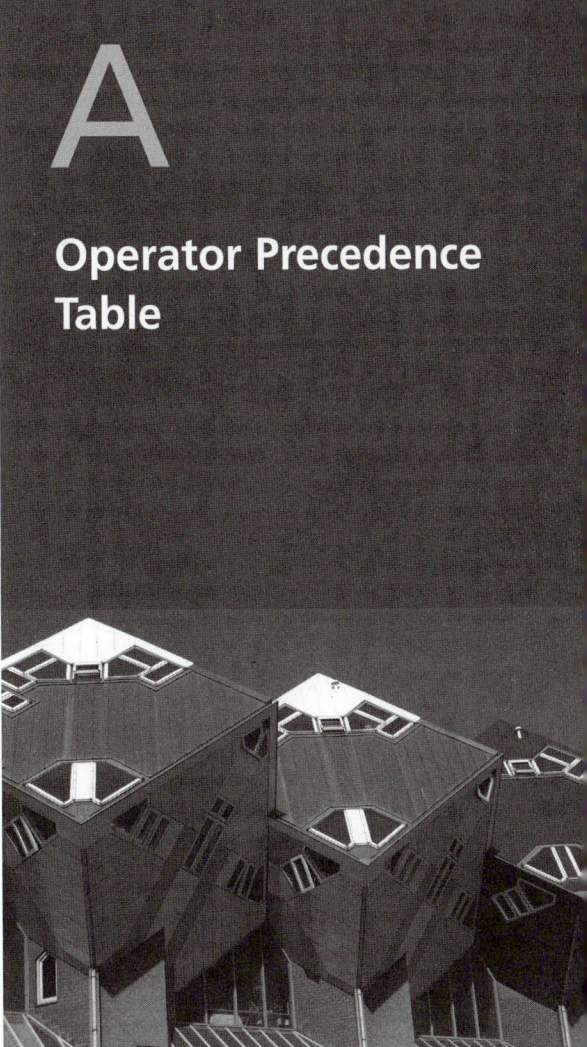

Operator Precedence Table

Table A.1 lists the symbols, precedence, descriptions, and associativity of C++'s operators. Operators toward the top of the table have a higher precedence than those toward the bottom. Operators in each section of the table have the same precedence and associativity.

Table A.1 Summary of C++ Operators

Operator	Description	Associativity
()	Function call	Left to right
[]	Array element	
–>	Structure member pointer reference	
.	Structure member reference	

Table A.1   Summary of C++ Operators (*continued*)

Operator	Description	Associativity
++	Increment	Right to left
--	Decrement	
−	Unary minus	
!	Logical negation	
~	One's complement	
(type)	Type conversion (cast)	
sizeof	Storage size	
&	Address of	
*	Indirection	
*	Multiplication	Left to right
/	Division	
%	Modulus (remainder)	
+	Addition	Left to right
−	Subtraction	
<<	Left shift	Left to right
>>	Right shift	
<	Less than	Left to right
<=	Less than or equal to	
>	Greater than	
>=	Greater than or equal to	
==	Equal to	Left to right
!=	Not equal to	
&	Bitwise AND	Left to right
^	Bitwise exclusive OR	Left to right
|	Bitwise inclusive OR	Left to right
&&	Logical AND	Left to right
||	Logical OR	Left to right
?:	Conditional expression	Right to left
=	Assignment	Right to left
+= −= *=	Assignment	
/= %= &=	Assignment	
^= |=	Assignment	
<<= >>=	Assignment	
,	Comma	Left to right

Appendix

B

ASCII Character Codes

Key(s)	Dec	Oct	Hex	Key(s)	Dec	Oct	Hex	Key(s)	Dec	Oct	Hex
Ctrl 1	0	0	0	Ctrl K	11	13	B	Ctrl V	22	26	16
Ctrl A	1	1	1	Ctrl L	12	14	C	Ctrl W	23	27	17
Ctrl B	2	2	2	Ctrl M (Ret)	13	15	D	Ctrl X	24	30	18
Ctrl C	3	3	3	Ctrl N	14	16	E	Ctrl Y	25	31	19
Ctrl D	4	4	4	Ctrl O	15	17	F	Ctrl Z	26	32	1A
Ctrl E	5	5	5	Ctrl P	16	20	10	Esc	27	33	1B
Ctrl F	6	6	6	Ctrl Q	17	21	11	Ctrl <	28	34	1C
Ctrl G	7	7	7	Ctrl R	18	22	12	Ctrl /	29	35	1D
Ctrl H	8	10	8	Ctrl S	19	23	13	Ctrl =	30	36	1E
Ctrl I	9	11	9	Ctrl T	20	24	14	Ctrl -	31	37	1F
Ctrl J (line feed)	10	12	A	Ctrl U	21	25	15	Space	32	40	20

Key(s)	Dec	Oct	Hex	Key(s)	Dec	Oct	Hex	Key(s)	Dec	Oct	Hex
!	33	41	21	A	65	101	41	a	97	141	61
"	34	42	22	B	66	102	42	b	98	142	62
#	35	43	23	C	67	103	43	c	99	143	63
$	36	44	24	D	68	104	44	d	100	144	64
%	37	45	25	E	69	105	45	e	101	145	65
&	38	46	26	F	70	106	46	f	102	146	66
'	39	47	27	G	71	107	47	g	103	147	67
(	40	50	28	H	72	110	48	h	104	150	68
)	41	51	29	I	73	111	49	i	105	151	69
*	42	52	2A	J	74	112	4A	j	106	152	6A
+	43	53	2B	K	75	113	4B	k	107	153	6B
,	44	54	2C	L	76	114	4C	l	108	154	6C
-	45	55	2D	M	77	115	4D	m	109	155	6D
.	46	56	2E	N	78	116	4E	n	110	156	6E
/	47	57	2F	O	79	117	4F	o	111	157	6F
0	48	60	30	P	80	120	50	p	112	160	70
1	49	61	31	Q	81	121	51	q	113	161	71
2	50	62	32	R	82	122	52	r	114	162	72
3	51	63	33	S	83	123	53	s	115	163	73
4	52	64	34	T	84	124	54	t	116	164	74
5	53	65	35	U	85	125	55	u	117	165	75
6	54	66	36	V	86	126	56	v	118	166	76
7	55	67	37	W	87	127	57	w	119	167	77
8	56	70	38	X	88	130	58	x	120	170	78
9	57	71	39	Y	89	131	59	y	121	171	79
:	58	72	3A	Z	90	132	5A	z	122	172	7A
;	59	73	3B	[	91	133	5B	{	123	173	7B
<	60	74	3C	\	92	134	5C	|	124	174	7C
=	61	75	3D	]	93	135	5D	}	125	175	7D
>	62	76	3E	^	94	136	5E	~	126	176	7E
?	63	77	3F	-	95	137	5F	del	127	177	7F
@	64	100	40	`	96	140	60				

Appendix C: Bit Operations

This appendix is available online at *www.cengagebrain.com*.

Appendix D: Floating-Point Number Storage

This appendix is available online at *www.cengagebrain.com*.

Appendix

E

Solutions to Selected Exercises

Chapter 1

EXERCISES 1.1

1. Define the following terms:

   a. computer program: A structured combination of data and instructions used to operate a computer; another term for software.

   b. programming language: The set of instructions, data, and rules used to construct a program.

   c. programming: The process of writing a computer program in a language that the computer can respond to and other programmers can understand.

   d. algorithm: A step-by-step sequence of instructions describing how to perform a computation.

   e. pseudocode: A means of describing an algorithm with English-like phrases.

   f. flowchart: A diagram that uses symbols to depict an algorithm.

   g. procedure: A logically consistent set of instructions that produce a specific result.

   h. object: A specific case, or instance, of a class. An object consists of data and methods.

i. method: An operation or a procedure that can be applied to the data in a class; a member function.

j. message: The means of activating a particular method in an object.

k. response: The predictable result of sending a message.

l. class: A broad category that defines the characteristics of the data an object can contain and the methods that can be applied to the data; also a programmer-defined data type.

m. source program: A file consisting of a program's statements in C++ or another programming language.

n. compiler: The program that translates source code into machine language all at once, before any code is executed.

o. object program: The result of compiling a source program. It's created by the compiler and is assigned the extension .obj.

p. executable program: A program that's ready to be run.

q. interpreter: The program that translates source code into machine language, one line at a time, as the source code is executed.

2. a. Fix a flat tire:

Stop vehicle in a safe, level location
Set the parking brake
Get jack, lug wrench, and spare tire
Check air pressure in spare tire
Use jack to raise vehicle so that damaged tire is clear of ground
Remove hubcap
Use lug wrench to loosen each lug nut
Use lug wrench to remove each lug nut
Place lug nuts into hubcap
Remove tire from axle
Place spare tire on axle
Restore each lug nut, and tighten by hand
Tighten all lug nuts securely with lug wrench
Replace hubcap
Release jack
Return jack, lug wrench, and damaged tire to trunk of vehicle

b. Make a phone call:

Lift phone receiver
Dial a number
Wait for answer
Speak to person, or respond to electronic instructions

c. Go to the store and purchase a loaf of bread:

       Transport yourself to the store
       Find bakery department
       Select a loaf of bread
       Proceed to checkout area
       Exchange money for the loaf of bread

3. Label cups #1, #2, and #3, with #3 being the empty cup
Rinse #3
Pour contents of #1 into #3
Rinse #1
Pour contents of #2 into #1
Rinse #2
Pour contents of #3 into #2
Rinse #3

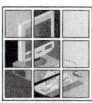

EXERCISES 1.2

1.

`1m1234`	Invalid; begins with a number
`power`	Valid; mnemonic
`add_5`	Valid; mnemonic
`newBalance`	Valid; mnemonic
`newBal`	Valid; mnemonic
`absVal`	Valid; mnemonic
`taxes`	Valid; mnemonic
`a2b3c4d5`	Valid; not mnemonic
`abcd`	Valid; not mnemonic
`invoices`	Valid; mnemonic
`netPay`	Valid; mnemonic
`salesTax`	Valid; mnemonic
`A12345`	Valid; not mnemonic
`do`	Invalid; C++ keyword
`123435`	Invalid; begins with a number
`amount`	Valid; mnemonic
`1A2345`	Invalid; begins with a number
`while`	Invalid; C++ keyword
`int`	Invalid; C++ keyword
`$taxes`	Invalid; begins with a special character

2. a. getLength()   get a length measurement
     getWidth()   get a width measurement
     calcArea()   calculate an area
     displayArea()   display or print the area
  b. getLength(), getWidth(), calcArea(), and displayArea()

3. a. inputPrice()   input an amount of a sale
     calcSalestax()   determine sales tax on the purchase
     calcBalance()   calculate sum of the sale and the tax
  b. inputPrice(), calcSalestax(), and calcBalance()

EXERCISES 1.3

4. a. 5 (not including the lines under the column headings)
  b. 1

5. Carriage return and line feed

EXERCISES 1.4

1. a. Yes
  b. It doesn't represent good programming style, and it's not easy to read.

2. a.
```cpp
#include <iostream>
using namespace std;

int main()
{
  cout << "The time has come.";
  return 0;
}
```
  b.
```cpp
#include <iostream>
using namespace std;

int main()
{
  cout << "Newark is a city\n";
  cout << "in New Jersey.\n";
  cout << "It is also a city\n";
  cout << "in Delaware\n";
  return 0;
}
```

3. a. a backslash

    b. \\ (two backslashes with no space between them)

EXERCISES 1.7

1. a. One output is required: the dollar amount in the piggybank

    b. Five: the number of half-dollars, quarters, dimes, nickels, and pennies

    c. `dollars = .50 * no. of half dollars + .25 * no. of quarters`
        `+ .10 * no. of dimes + .05 * no. of nickels +.01 * no. of pennies`

    or

        `dollars = (50 * no. of half dollars + 25 * no. of quarters`
         `+ 10 * no. of dimes + 5 * no. of nickels + no. of pennies) / 100`

    d. dollars = .5(0) + .25(17) + .10(24) + .05(16) + .01(12) = 7.57

2. a. One output is required: distance

    b. Two inputs are required: rate and (elapsed) time

    c. distance = rate × time

    d. distance = 55 mi/hr × 2.5 hr = 55(2.5) mi = 137.5 miles

    e. Convert minutes to hours by dividing the minutes by 60.

3. a. One output is required: number of Ergies

    b. Two inputs are required: number of Fergies and number of Lergies

    c. Ergies = Fergies × Lergies

    d. Ergies = 14.65 × 4 = 58.60

Chapter 2

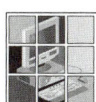

EXERCISES 2.1

1. a. `float` or `double`

    b. `int`

    c. `float` or `double`

    d. `int`

    e. `float` or `double`

    f. `char`

4. Students should create a figure similar to Figure 2.3 that includes the following:

```
8 bytes of storage
01001011 01001001 01001110 01000111 01010011 01001100 01000101 01011001
-------- -------- -------- -------- -------- -------- -------- --------
   K        I        N        G        S        L        E        Y
```

EXERCISES 2.2

1. a. `(2 * 3) + (4 * 5)`
  b. `(6 + 18) / 2`
  c. `4.5 / (12.2 - 3.1)`
  d. `4.6 * (3.0 + 14.9)`
  e. `(12.1 + 18.9) * (15.3 - 3.8)`

2. a. 27   **f.** 20
  b. 8   **g.** 6
  c. 1   **h.** 2
  d. 220   **i.** 10
  e. 23   **j.** 1

3. a. 27.0   **e.** 23.0
  b. 8.0   **f.** 20.0
  c. 1.0   **g.** 6.0
  d. 220.0   **h.** 2.0

EXERCISES 2.3

1.

`prod_a`	valid
`newbal`	valid
`9ab6`	invalid (begins with a number)
`c1234`	valid
`while`	invalid (C++ keyword)
`sum.of`	invalid (decimal point not allowed)
`abcd`	valid
`$total`	invalid (begins with special character)
`average`	valid
`_c3`	invalid (begins with special character)
`new bal`	invalid (contains a space)
`grade1`	valid
`12345`	invalid (begins with a number)
`a1b2c3d4`	valid
`finGrad`	valid

2. salestax   valid
   harry   valid (not meaningful)
   maximum   valid
   3sum   invalid (begins with a number)
   a243   valid (not meaningful)
   sue   valid (not meaningful)
   okay   valid
   for   invalid (C++ keyword)
   r2d2   valid (not meaningful)
   c3p0   valid (not meaningful)
   a   valid (not meaningful)
   tot.al   invalid (contains decimal point)
   firstNum   valid
   average   valid
   awesome   valid (not meaningful)
   c$five   invalid (contains a special character)
   cc_al   valid (not meaningful)
   sum   valid
   goforit   valid (not meaningful)
   netpay   valid

3. a. int count;
   b. float grade;
   c. double yield;
   d. char initial;

Chapter 3

 **EXERCISES 3.1**

1. c = 2 * 3.1416 * 3.3;

2. a = 3.1416 * r * r;

3. celsius = (5 / 9) * (fahrenheit - 32);

EXERCISES 3.2

1. The corrections are as follows:
   a. `cout << "\n" << 15;` `// Quotes misplaced, substitute`
   `// semicolon for parenthesis`
   b. `cout << setw(4) <<  33;` `// No quotes`
   c. `cout << setprecision(5) <<  526.768;` `// No quotes`
   d. `cout << "Hello World!";` `// Statement reversed`
   e. `cout << setw(6) << 47;` `// Statement out of order`
   f. `cout << setw(10) << setprecision(2) << 526.768;`
   `// set should be setw, statement out of order`

2. a. `|5|`   e. `|  5.27|`
   b. `|    5|`   f. `|53.26|`
   c. `|56829|`   g. `|534.26|`
   d. `|  5.26|`   h. `|534.00|`

3. a. `The number is 26.27`
   `   The number is 682.30`
   `   The number is   1.97`
   b. `  26.27`
   `  682.30`
   `    1.97`
   `  ------`
   `  710.54`
   c. `  26.27`
   `  682.30`
   `    1.97`
   `  -----`
   `  710.54`
   d. `36.16`
   `10.00`
   `-----`

EXERCISES 3.3

1. a. `sqrt(6.37)`
   b. `sqrt(x - y)`
   c. `sin(30 * (3.1416/180))`
   d. `sin(60 * (3.1416/180))`
   e. `abs(a * a - b * b)` or `abs(pow(a,2) - pow(b,2))`
   f. `exp(3)`

2. a. 10   **g.** 21
   b. 13   **h.** 23.9
   c. -3   **i.** 24
   d. 24   **j.** 24.5
   e. 20.48   **k.** 1.81659
   f. 20.58

3. a. `area = (c * b * sin(a)) / 2;`
   b. `c = sqrt(pow(a,2) + pow(b,2));`
   c. `p = sqrt(abs(m - n));`
   d. `sum = (a * (pow(r,n) - 1)) / (r - 1);`
   e. `b = pow(sin(x),2) + pow(cos(x),2);`

EXERCISES 3.4

1. a. `cin >> firstnum;`
   b. `cin >> grade;`
   c. `cin >> secnum;`
   d. `cin >> keyval;`
   e. `cin >> month >> years >> average;`
   f. `cin >> ch >> num1 >> num2 >> grade1 >> grade2;`
   g. `cin >> interest >> principal >> capital >> price >> yield;`
   h. `cin >> ch >> letter1 >> letter2 >> num1 >> num2 >> num3;`
   i. `cin >> temp1 >> temp2 >> temp3 >> volts1 >> volts2;`

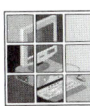

EXERCISES 3.5

4. See solution file pgm3-5ex4.cpp. Answers are shown in italics:

Planet (emissivity = 1)	Average Surface Temperature (° Celsius)	Heat Radiated (watts/m²)
Mercury	270	*301.311*
Venus	462	*2583.020*
Earth	14	*0.002*

5. See solution file pgm3-5ex5.cpp. Answers are shown in italics:

Substance	Average Surface Temperature (° Celsius)	Emissivity	Heat Radiated (watts/m²)
Automobile	47	.3	*.082999*
Brick	45	.9	*.209244*
Commercial roof	48	.05	*.0150486*

Chapter 4

EXERCISES 4.1

1. **a.** True. Value is 1.
   b. True. Value is 1.
   c. True. Value is 1.
   d. True. Value is 1.
   e. True. Value is 1.
   f. False. Value is 10.
   g. False. Value is 4.
   h. False. Value is 0.
   i. False. Value is 10.

2. *Note*: In any relational expression, a non-zero value is considered true and a zero value is considered false.

   a. `((a % b) * c) && ((c % b) * a)`
   ```
   = ((5 % 2) * 4) && ((4 % 2) * 5)
   = (1 * 4) && (0 * 5)
   = 4 && 0    // same as True AND False
   = 0
   ```
   b. `((a % b) * c) || ((c % b) * a)`
   ```
   = ((5 % 2) * 4) || ((4 % 2) * 5)
   = (1 * 4) || (0 * 5)
   = 4 || 0    // same as True OR False
   = 1
   ```
   c. `((b % c) * a) && ((a % c) * b)`
   ```
   = ((2 % 4) * 5) && ((5 % 4) * 2)
   = (2 * 5) && (1 * 2)
   = 10 && 2    // same as True AND True
   = 1
   ```
   d. `((b % c) * a) || ((a % c) * b)`
   ```
   = ((2 % 4) * 5) || ((5 % 4) * 2)
   = (2 * 5) || (1 * 2)
   = 10 || 2    // same as True OR True
   = 1
   ```

3. a. `age == 30`
   b. `temp > 98.6`
   c. `height < 6`
   d. `month == 12`
   e. `letterIn == 'm'`
   f. `(age == 30) && (height > 6)`
   g. `(day == 15) && (month == 1)`
   h. `(age > 50) && (employed >= 5)`
   i. `(id < 500) && (age > 55)`
   j. `(length > 2) && (length < 3)`

EXERCISES 4.2

1. a.
```
if (angle == 90)
    cout << "The angle is a right angle";
else
    cout << "The angle is not a right angle";
```
   b.
```
if (temp > 100)
    cout << "above the boiling point of water";
else
    cout << "below the boiling point of water";
```
   c.
```
if (number > 0)
    number += positivesum;
else
    number += negativesum;
```
   d.
```
if (slope < 0.5 )
    flag = 0;
else
    flag = 1;
```
   e.
```
if (slope1 - slope2 < .001 )
    approx = 0;
else
    approx = (slope1 - slope2) / 2.0;
```

2. a.
```
if (ace < 25)
    sum = sum + a;
else
    count = count + 1;
```

b.
```
if(c == 15)
  {
    credit = 10;
    limit = 1200;
  }
else
  {
    credit = 8;
    limit = 800;
  }
```
c.
```
if (id > 22)
   factor = 0.7;
```
d.
```
if (count == 10)
  {
    average = sum / count;
    cout << average;
  }
```

3. If the two numbers are equal, the `else` statement is executed, which produces an incorrect display.

EXERCISES 4.3

7. b. Typically, a runtime error message, such as "Floating-point error: Divide by zero," is displayed.

11. a. Both programs produce the same output.

  b. Program 4.5 is better because it requires less processing. In Program 4.5, when the correct monthly sales figure is evaluated, the income value is calculated and the `if-else` statement is exited without further processing. In the program in Exercise 11a, the system must evaluate every `if` statement, even if the first one is the statement that evaluates to true. Consequently, Program 4.5 is better because it potentially requires less processing.

12. a. The program runs but calculates incorrect results, except for the case in which monthly sales are less $20,000.

  b. If monthly sales are less than 20000, the program produces correct results because either the first `if` or first `else-if` is executed. For any and all amounts >= 20000, the income for the first `else-if` statement is obtained, and the other `else-if` statements aren't evaluated.

EXERCISES 4.4

1. ```
switch (letterGrade)
  {
    case 'A':
      cout << "The numerical grade is between 90 and 100";
      break;
    case 'B':
      cout << "The numerical grade is between 80 and 89.9";
      break;
    case 'C':
      cout << "The numerical grade is between 70 and 79.9";
      break;
    case 'D':
      cout << "How are you going to explain this one?";
      break;
    default:
      cout << "Of course I had nothing to do with the grade.";
      cout << "\nIt must have been the professor's fault.";
  }
```

7. The expression in the `switch` statement must evaluate to an integer quantity and be tested for equality. The `if-else` chain in Program 4.5 compares double-precision values, violating the `switch` statement's requirements for integer relational expressions.

# Chapter 5

## EXERCISES 5.1

3. **a.** 21 numbers are displayed, with 1 being the first and 21 being the last.
   **b.** See solution file pgm5-1ex3.cpp.
   **c.** 21 numbers would still be printed, but the first number would be 0 and the last would be 20.

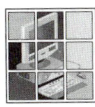

## EXERCISES 5.2

5. **a.** Yes, the program yields the correct results because the last time through the loop, it takes the average of the final total.
   **b.** Having the average calculate outside the loop is better because the program does the calculation once instead of each time the loop executes.
```

EXERCISES 5.3

1. a. `for(i = 1; i <= 20; i++)`
   b. `for(icount = 1; icount <= 20; icount = icount + 2)`
   c. `for(j = 1; j <= 100; j = j + 5)`
   d. `for(icount = 20; icount >= 1; icount--)`
   e. `for(icount = 20; icount >=1; icount = icount - 2)`
   f. `for(count = 1.0; count <= 16.2; count = count + 0.2)`
   g. `for(xcnt = 20.0; xcnt >= 10.0; xcnt = xcnt - 0.5)`

2. a. 20   e. 10
   b. 10   f. 77
   c. 20   g. 21
   d. 20

3. a. 10   d. -5
   b. 1024   e. 40320
   c. 75   f. 0.03125

Chapter 6

EXERCISES 6.1

1. a. requires one int value
   b. requires three values in this order: an int and two doubles
   c. requires three values in this order: an int and two doubles
   d. requires three values in this order: a char and two floats
   e. requires two doubles
   f. requires six values in this order: two ints, two chars and two doubles
   g. requires four values in this order: two ints and two chars

2. a.
```
void check(int num1, double num2, double num3)
{
  cout << "In check()\n";
  cout << "The value of num1 is " << num1 << endl;
  cout << "The value of num2 is " << num2 << endl;
  cout << "The value of num3 is " << num3 << endl;
  return;
}
```

3. a.
```cpp
void findAbs(double number)
{
  cout << "The absolute value of " << number << " is: ";
  if(number < 0)
    number = -number;
  cout  << number << endl;

  return;
}
```

EXERCISES 6.2

2. a. `void check(int num1, float num2, double num3)`
   b. `double findAbs(double x)`
   c. `float mult(float first, float second)`
   d. `int square(int number)`
   e. `int powfun(int num, int exponent)`
   f. `void table(void)` or `void table()`

3. a.
```cpp
double rightTriangle(double a, double b)
{
   return sqrt((a * a) + (b * b));
}
```
   b. See solution file pgm6-2ex3b.cpp.

4. a.
```cpp
double findAbs(double number)
{
   if(number < 0)
     number = -number;
   return number;
}
```
   b. See solution file pgm6-2ex4b.cpp.

EXERCISES 6.3

1. a. `double& amount`
   b. `double& price`
   c. `int& minutes`
   d. `char& key`
   e. `double& yield`

2. `void time(int& sec, int& min, int& hours)`

3. a.
```
void findMax(int x, int y, int& max)
{                        // start of function body
  int maxnum;            // variable declaration

  if (x >= y)            // find the maximum number
    maxnum = x;
  else
    maxnum = y;
    max = maxnum;

  return;                // return statement
}
```

EXERCISES 6.4

1. a.

Variable or Constant Name	Data Type	Scope
PRICE	int	global to `main()`, `roi()`, and `step()`
YEARS	long int	global to `main()`, `roi()`, and `step()`
YIELD	double	global to `main()`, `roi()`, and `step()`
bondtype	int	local to `main()`
interest	double	local to `main()`
coupon	double	local to `main()`
mat1	int	local to `roi()`
mat2	int	local to `roi()`
count	int	local to `roi()`
effectiveRate	double	local to `roi()`
first	double	local to `step()`
last	double	local to `step()`
numofyrs	int	local to `step()`
fracpart	double	local to `step()`

2. a.

Variable or Constant Name	Data Type	Scope
KEY	char	global to main(), func1(), and func2()
NUMBER	long int	global to main(), func1(), and func2()
a, b, c	int	local to main()
x, y	double	local to main()
secnum	double	global to func1() and func2()
num1, num2	int	local to func1()
o, p	int	local to func1()
q	float	local to func1()
first, last	double	local to func2()
a, b, c, o, p	int	local to func2()
r	double	local to func2()
s, t, x	double	local to func2()

3. All function parameters have local scope in their defined function. Note that although function parameters assume a value that depends on the calling function, these parameters can change values in their functions. This makes them behave as though they were local variables in the called function.

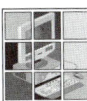

EXERCISES 6.5

1. a. The storage categories available to local variables are auto, static, and register.

   b. The storage categories available to global variables are extern and static. A local auto variable is unique to the function in which it's declared. Every time the function is called, the auto variable is re-created, as though it never existed. A local static variable is also unique to the function where it's declared. However, a static variable retains its last value and isn't re-created when its function is called again.

2. The first function declares yrs to be a static variable and assigns a value of 1 to it only once, when the function is compiled. Each time the function is called thereafter, the value in yrs is increased by 2. The second function also declares yrs to be static but assigns it the value 1 every time it's called, and the value of yrs after the function is finished will always be 3. By resetting the value of yrs to 1 each time it's called, the second function defeats the purpose of declaring the variable to be static.

Chapter 7

EXERCISES 7.1

1. **a.** `const int SIZE = 100;`
   `int grades[SIZE];`
   b. `const int SIZE = 50;`
   `double temp[SIZE];`
   c. `const int SIZE = 30;`
   `char code[SIZE];`
   d. `const int SIZE = 100;`
   `int year[SIZE];`

2. **a.** `grades[0]` refers to the first item stored in the array, `grades[2]` refers to the third item, and `grades[6]` refers to the seventh item.
   b. `prices[0]` refers to the first item stored in the array, `prices[2]` refers to the third item, and `prices[6]` refers to the seventh item.
   c. `amounts[0]` refers to the first item stored in the array, `amounts[2]` refers to the third item, and `amounts[6]` refers to the seventh item.

3. **a.** `cin >> grades[0];`
   `cin >> grades[2];`
   `cin >> grades[6];`
   b. `cin >> prices[0];`
   `cin >> prices[2];`
   `cin >> prices[6];`
   c. `cin >> amounts[0];`
   `cin >> amounts[2];`
   `cin >> amounts[6];`

EXERCISES 7.2

1. **a.** `const int SIZE = 10;`
   `int grades[SIZE] = {89, 75, 82, 93, 78, 95, 81, 88, 77, 82};`
   b. `const int SIZE = 5;`
   `double amounts[SIZE] = {10.62, 13.98, 18.45, 12.68, 14.76};`
   c. `const int SIZE = 100;`
   `double rates[SIZE] = {6.29, 6.95, 7.25, 7.35, 7.40, 7.42};`
   d. `const int SIZE = 64;`
   `double temps[SIZE]`
   `   = {78.2, 69.6, 68.5, 83.9, 55.4, 67.0, 49.8, 58.3, 62.5, 71.6};`
   e. `const int SIZE = 15;`
   `char codes[SIZE] = { 'f', 'j', 'm', 'q', 't', 'w', 'z' };`

6. ```
char goodstr1[] = "Good Morning";
char goodstr1[] = {'G', 'o', 'o', 'd', ' ', 'M', 'o', 'r', 'n', 'i', 'n',
 'g'};
char goodstr1[12] = {'G', 'o', 'o', 'd', ' ', 'M', 'o', 'r', 'n', 'i', 'n
','g'};
```

7. a. ```
char message1[] = "Input the Following Data";
char message2[] = "-----------------------";
char message3[] = "Enter the Date: ";
char message4[] = "Enter the Account Number: ";
```
   b. See solution file pgm7-2ex7b.cpp.

EXERCISES 7.3

1. ```
void sortArray(double inArray [500])
void sortArray(double inArray [])
```

2. ```
char findKey(char select [256])
char findKey(char select [])
```

3. ```
double prime (double [256])
double prime (double [])
```

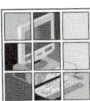

## EXERCISES 7.4

1. a. ```
const int NUMROWS = 6;
const int NUMCOLS = 10;
    int val[NUMROWS][NUMCOLS];
```
   b. ```
const int NUMROWS = 2;
const int NUMCOLS = 5;
    int val[NUMROWS][NUMCOLS];
```
   c. ```
const int NUMROWS = 7;
const int NUMCOLS = 12;
    char val[NUMROWS][NUMCOLS];
```

2. The output is as follows:

```
8    16   9    52   3    15   27   6    14   25   2    10
```

Index